SWIFT

THE MAN, HIS WORKS, AND THE AGE

VOLUME TWO
Dr Swift

Irvin Ehrenpreis

METHUEN

First published in 1967
Reprinted with corrections in 1983 by
Methuen & Co. Ltd
11 New Fetter Lane, London EC4P 4EE

© 1967, 1983 Irvin Ehrenpreis

Printed in the United States of America

British Library Cataloguing in Publication Data

Ehrenpreis, Irvin
Swift.
Vol. 2: Dr Swift
1. Swift, Jonathan—Criticism and interpretation
I. Title
828'.509   PR3727
ISBN 0–416–27730–6

An index to the complete work appears
at the end of the last volume

SWIFT

The Man, his Works, and the Age

VOLUME II

To Marion and Rudolf Gottfried

CONTENTS

[vii]

CONTENTS

A*   [ix]

CONTENTS

[xi]

CONTENTS

[xii]

[xv]

CONTENTS

PREFACE

This volume—though comprehending the shortest span of years—deals with the most interesting chapters of Swift's life. Not even the brilliant quadrennium 1723–7 can be said to shine with the intensity of the epoch Swift passed beside Oxford and Bolingbroke; and no other period is so minutely and accurately documented. I have tried to dwell upon his expectations and the degree to which he felt they were fulfilled. Inevitably, the search for preferment became the boldest line of this pattern. By showing how he sacrificed some of his hopes to certain political and religious principles, I have tried to modify the old story of his ambitions. Not all my changes tend to the enhancement of Swift's reputation for integrity; and in the end I mean to indicate that his rewards were greater than his bitterness let him admit. In following Swift's political development, I have used the distinction between 'old' and 'new' Whig to weaken the common belief that he stood on one side before 1710 and on another afterwards. I do not think he ever published a political essay in support of the leadership that he attacked as a Tory journalist, though I describe him as keeping silent in the face of policies he disliked and as playing up to men he distrusted. If I have been more severe when judging his conduct toward Stella and Vanessa, it is partly through the influence of new evidence found in his account books and elsewhere; and again I mitigate the blame, by arguing that the first person he deceived was himself. Although my analyses of Swift's prose and verse may appear unusually detailed, I hope a number of the interpretations offered will be unfamiliar without seeming strained; and I think much of the bibliographical information is new. His literary achievement has too often been defined in terms of a 'Swiftian' style that some of his most powerful essays fail to exemplify; I have tried to recognize the true merits not only of works like *An*

Argument against Abolishing Christianity but also of those like *The Conduct of the Allies*, which have suffered from the preoccupation of critics with Swift's talen for irony and impersonation.

While working on this volume, I have enjoyed peculiar advantages and incurred great obligations. For grants of money in support of the research I am deeply grateful to the John Simon Guggenheim Foundation, Indiana University, and the University of Virginia. The staffs of several great research libraries have been characteristically helpful: Indiana University, Harvard University, the University of Virginia, Trinity College, Dublin, and the Bodleian Library, Oxford. Lord Rothschild has very kindly allowed me to quote from the account book of Swift in his collection. I am grateful to Sir Basil Blackwell for permission to quote from the *Prose Works* of Swift edited by Professor Herbert Davis; to the Delegates of the Clarendon Press for permission to quote from Sir Harold Williams's editions of Swift's *Correspondence, Poems*, and the *Journal to Stella*; to the Trustees of the British Museum for permission to publish extracts from the papers of the Earl of Egmont; and to the Librarian of the John Rylands Library for permission to publish Rylands English MS. 659, no. 13. Professor Maurice Quinlan generously allowed me to make use of an important paper before he published it. Mr M. R. Ridley has again given me the benefit of his authoritative judgment on general questions of scholarly style.

I. E.

Chapter One

SWIFT IN 1699

When Swift was thirty-two, his prospects looked very different from what his fate was going to be during the fifteen years immediately ahead of him. Since these years before the decisive, but not final, withdrawal from England were also to seem the period of his most dramatic history, the contrast between outlook and hindsight might be described as the sharpest of his life. Privately, he remained a gentleman fearful of the deprivations of matrimony, yet elaborately involved with the affections of a very young lady. In temperament he could grow quickly overheated—'[When] you are angry . . . there is something in your look so awful, that it strikes me dumb', said Vanessa[1] —but could mask his anger when he desired to; and his face was often only ironically stern. On his own evidence Swift's character should be defined as naturally cheerful,[2] and George Berkeley called him 'one of the best-natured and agreeable men in the world'.[3] But while he loved society, he also suffered from an upside-down pride which would not let him make advances to people who appeared either too much sought after or too accessible. As a talker Swift sounded fluent and crisp, floating his conversation on witty allusions, on complimentary mock-insults and pitiless puns. Any tendency to bawdry or blasphemy, however, he neither allowed to himself nor tolerated in others.[4] His voice was not sonorous but sharp.[5] By the standard of mid-twentieth-century physiques he would look short (probably five and a half feet tall), though neither heavy nor thin. His large blue eyes protruded slightly[6]; his forehead rose as his hair withdrew; his chin inclined

---

[1] Williams II. 150.   [2] *Journal*, 18 Sept. 1712.
[3] Letter of 27 Mar. 1713 to Sir John Percival.   4 Delany, p. 83.
[5] *Ibid.*, p. 42.   [6] *Ibid.*, p. 146. Cf. below, p. 4, n. 1.

[1]

to double. Partly because his health seemed unreliable, Swift looked upon himself as moving rapidly through middle age. Unforeseeable dizzy spells continued to frighten him away from the fruits which he yearned to eat but which he regarded as causing vertigo. Deafness continued to occur in fits. To keep himself well, he exercised in many ways: during suitable weather, by walking, running, riding, and swimming; when he could not go out, by climbing stairs.

As Swift in 1699 saw it, his supreme purpose had to be to establish himself with dignity in a safe, sufficient, lifetime economy. While he was at Moor Park, remittances had still reached him from his father's relatives.[1] Now he must find a way of looking after all his own requirements. Though he would have to realize this scheme through some favour in the power of the civil or ecclesiastical authorities, Swift did not look upon himself as confined to the church for a career. As an old man, he told a young relative that King William had once offered to make him a cavalry captain. The cousinly listener teased him for refusing and noticed that Swift seemed far from displeased by the insinuation that he should have accepted the commission.[2] Similarly, if Swift did reject Temple's provision of a deputy mastership of the rolls in Ireland,[3] he nevertheless kept in prospect the possibility of a civil employment; and this was probably among the hopes he had placed in the fallen Sunderland. Now that Temple was dead, Swift might in actual fact take the post of chaplain to a newly appointed Lord Justice of Ireland; but he was careful—in old age—to describe the post as that of Lord Berkeley's 'chaplain and private secretary'. Not that chaplains did not often act as part-time private secretaries; but such adjunct responsibilities belonged under a different heading from the true place of a secretary to a Lord Justice as such.

Whatever Swift's career or living might come to, it would not absorb the literary ambitions which still possessed him. Among such desires, however, the order of value for Swift differed from

[1] Lyon, p. 27.
[2] MS. note, crossed out, in transcript of Swift's fragment of autobiography in the Pierpont Morgan Library (MS. 455, fol. 14).
[3] Lyon, p. 25.

what it would be for us. Since financial returns were the last thing he expected from publication, Swift never identified literary merit with popular success. Still, he yearned for a reputation, to a degree that impelled him to screen the ardour even from himself. His passion for anonymity of authorship therefore represents a mixture of elements: not merely an attachment to the aristocratic tradition of writing exclusively for recreation, nor a self-protective impulse when the material he employed seemed inflammatory, but also what Freudians might call a reaction-formation against the hunger for reputation; for he needed fame so badly that while he could expose the need to certain friends, he liked to act indifferent before the world. Not unfairly, then, it transpires that some genres to which he devoted his most serious energies were not what he would be known for to posterity. History, for instance, now seemed to Swift perhaps the noblest form of prose composition; the 'pindaric' or heroic epistolary ode, the highest verse form which he himself could attempt. Comical verses and political satires, I believe, Swift at this time regarded either as frivolities or as occasional productions—though the satires claimed a functional merit through the fact that they might draw upon him the benevolence of those who supplied the world with preferments and pensions.

Admitting such calculation, it would still be misleading for one to imply that to Swift the church meant merely a stepping-stone. At no point does his *hypocrite-renversé* character appear more startling than in his distaste for exhibited piety. All his life he appreciated the challenge which Tartuffe offered to religion; and it was only in his priestly function or in his least observable actions that he showed the reverence which he thought proper to the doctrine and liturgy of his church. Before all men's eyes he might parade his charities or his decencies, but it was to his own conscience that he reserved the privilege of witnessing his devotions. How deep Swift's conviction ran that the Established Church deserved his unqualified allegiance, we may estimate from the number of worldly chances which he sacrificed to this loyalty.

Where Mammon did menace the Christian in Swift's life, we usually enter a political arena. Before the death of King William,

[3]

Swift regarded himself as detached from political issues. The Revolution had been the great crisis of his youth; and no Protestant Irishman could possibly have desired an association with Jacobite Tories. Coming to England, Swift lived among the King's personal friends: in the young newcomer's view, the nation, the crown, and the principles of justice must have seemed in at least fundamental harmony during the last decade of the seventeenth century. When all right-thinking persons see alike, no man in their tribe understands the value of organized dissent. Whether in Dublin or at Moor Park, the young Mr Swift would have discovered little evidence that a good churchman ought to distrust the line of thought which was soon to be called 'old Whig'.[1]

[1] On Swift's appearance I can add details to the description given above, pp. 1–2. According to Edward Young, Swift around 1710 described himself as 'a plump man, just five feet five inches high, not very neatly dressed' (recorded by Joseph Spence in 1757; see Spence I. 340–1). According to Pope, the well-known portrait by Jervas was 'very like him'. Pope said Swift's face had 'a look of dullness in it', but his eyes were 'very particular'; 'they are quite as azure as the heavens, and there's a very uncommon archness in them' (recorded by Spence in 1735; see *ibid.*, p. 52). Swift, in 'Lady Acheson Weary of the Dean', describes himself, probably in 1728, as having a 'tallow face and wainscot paws, . . . beetle-brows and eyes of wall' (*Poems* III. 861).

Chapter Two

PREFERMENTS

The story of Swift's growth from the death of Temple in 1699 to the fall of the Junto in 1710 can be summarized as the emergence, development, and expansion of his political pursuits until they became the determining frame for the other aspects of his life. How many days he might spend with his beloved, which friends he would make and lose, how far his income would rise, what topics he would treat as an author, where he would place himself in the church—these questions, which originally seemed independent of opinions as yet unformulated, were metamorphosed into corollaries of Swift's propositions in political philosophy.

To begin with, Swift looked at his advancement in any career as hinging rather upon private merit and personal relationships than upon the obligations—or, better still, immediate needs—felt by executive administrators. (Although this, by the way, seems a simple attitude, it may reflect Temple's view of the dependence of government upon intrigue.) While Swift was cultivating the Earl of Berkeley, however, he could not know that a rival near his own level was before him in the field; and the same disappointment which at last made this fact clear also dimmed his mind to its meaning. The titled object of these double attentions happened to be a fifty-year-old plain man who not only still wore mourning for the death of his eldest son but was soon to be stricken again by the loss of a young daughter. In these grim distresses he could no doubt exercise his genuine piety and lean upon his chaplain; but the chaplain's judging eye remained unsoftened, and Swift in later life was to recall his patron as 'intolerably lazy and indolent, and somewhat covetous'.[1]

---

[1] Davis v. 259.

Berkeley had received sudden and brusque instructions from court. He quickly began the preparations for the journey and paid a brief visit to his great castle in Gloucestershire. Swift meanwhile had probably taken leave of his friends at Moor Park, gone to see his mother at Leicester, and joined the new Lord Justice at an early point in the expedition. (Exactly where, is unknown; but Swift was never the man to pay his own travel expenses when he did not have to, and so he would have met the official party as soon as he could.) Earl and entourage reached Wales only in early August; but even then they had to endure two weeks of delay, and move on to Bristol, their port of embarkation. Finally, and with Swift certainly included, they sailed from Bristol, landed at Waterford (17 August 1699), and began to travel toward Dublin.

Though Swift says he acted as secretary during 'the whole journy' to Dublin,[1] Berkeley did not intend to keep him in the job. When the Earl—then Lord Dursley—had lived at The Hague as an English diplomatic representative, his secretary had been the rakish Matthew Prior, hardly a clerical precedent. After disembarking at the south coast port of Waterford, the Earl travelled north to Kilkenny, where he met an elaborate reception managed with all ceremony. Then the party set out again, for the capital itself. Meanwhile, the competitor against the ambitious chaplain was emerging in the shape of a friend of Swift's old schoolmaster, Ryder.[2] This rival schemer, Arthur Bushe, already held an office in the Irish customs; and he had once hoped to be granted so great a post as a Commissionership of the Revenue, at a salary of £800 a year, with allowances and perquisites. With this in mind he had spent much of the preceding spring in England, ingratiating himself with whoever he thought might give him a hand up. But eventually he found out that this lucrative promotion was going to another aspirant. When he also learned about Berkeley's appointment, Bushe suddenly and efficiently altered all plans. He scrambled back to Dublin just before his

---

[1] Davis v. 195. Lyon, p. 29, emends this to 'some little time during' the journey to Dublin.

[2] B.M. MS. Ad. 28,877, fols. 113–16ᵛ.

lordship arrived. Outside the city Bushe met the travellers; and when Berkeley made his entry into the capital, the Lord Justice's coach held not only some of the Privy Councillors of Ireland but also Arthur Bushe.

Besides being older and more experienced than Swift, Bushe was furnished with an itch for tireless, if futile, scheming. Though there is no sign that he measured himself against the young chaplain, he certainly won the coveted place. Yet it is worth noticing how little Swift lost and to what sort of person. For if Bushe thought this was the lowest tread on an easy stairway, he was wrong. While he did gain the satisfaction and moderate profit of acting as Berkeley's private secretary during the year and a half which the Earl spent in Ireland, the only lasting advantage which he obtained through this *entrée* was the trifling place of Judge-Advocate, at 6s. 8d. a day, with no perquisites.[1] As a taste of Bushe's character, I quote one of his remarks upon his emotions when he first returned to Dublin under the Earl's patronage: 'My own reception here was very agreeable to me, for between the true love of some and the aparent fear of others I have spent these two days much to my mind . . .'[2]

As it finally turned out, Swift profited much more from Berkeley's good will than Bushe did. In the summer of 1699, however, when he appeared only to have been warming somebody else's pillow, he misunderstood the events. In recalling them, half a lifetime later, I am afraid Swift attributed uncharacteristic finesse to his rival:

Another person had so far insinuated himself into the Earls favor, by telling him, that the post of ⌈private⌉ secretary was not proper for a clergyman, nor would be of any advantage to one who aimed

---

[1] B.M. MS. Ad. 28,884, fol. 291ᵛ; *SPD. 1699–1700*, p. 311. In 1714, when Swift was earning about £1,000 a year, Bushe, then secretary to the Commissioners of the Revenue, petitioned to have his own salary raised from £300 to £500 a year (*Cal. Tr. P. 1708–14*, p. 615). In 1699 the office of Secretary of State in the Irish government was held by Sir Robert Southwell, who in 1702 was succeeded in the same office by his son Edward. But the job of first secretary to the Lords Justices belonged in 1699 to Matthew Prior, who farmed out the duties to a deputy, Henry May (Eves, pp. 140–6). Bushe and Swift were competing to be Berkeley's personal secretary, though Bushe also hoped to become first secretary.

[2] B.M. MS. Ad. 28,884, fol. 197.

onely at church-preferments, that his lordship after a poor apology gave that office to the other.[1]

The two reasons with which Berkeley apparently tried to mollify his chaplain sound neither over-subtle nor unconvincing. A clergyman would indeed be expected to seek advancement within the church; and a political administrator, especially in a kingdom where religious differences formed the basis of government, would not wish his secretary to be a priest. It hardly seems necessary to attribute to the froth and venom of an Arthur Bushe such reflections as might easily occur to the unaided understanding of even the second Earl of Berkeley. That Swift could still smoulder over such a disappointment thirty-five or forty years afterwards may betoken the violence and bitterness of an old autocrat's temper; for he may have seen this humiliation of his youth against the eminence of his great years. But it is also a lifelong trait of Swift's that he enjoyed reviving, exaggerating, and contemplating the injustices which he thought he had suffered.

A grosser opportunity to indulge such feelings came at the beginning of the new year, when a new post and a new rival appeared. Although Swift was 'domestic chaplain' to Berkeley, the Lord Justice had as well one or more official chaplains, among them a Dr John Bolton. While Swift attended to the needs of the Berkeley household and lived intimately with the Earl and his family, the other—a well-established clergyman with good livings of his own—served at public and state functions. If each appointment carried with it the implication that something better would be found for the incumbent, the domestic chaplain had claims upon the individual—i.e., Charles, Second Earl of Berkeley—while the other had claims upon the officer—i.e., one of His Majesty's Lords Justices in Ireland.[2] Swift's duties were hardly onerous. Family prayers and perhaps an occasional sermon in Dublin Castle—little more was expected. Outside the household, he had no parochial duties. For his stipend,

[1] Davis v. 195.
[2] Cf. Galway's English secretary, Stanley, telling the Dean of St Patrick's, Edward Smith, why all of those recommended by Smith could not be made chaplains to the Lord Lieutenant: 'his grace has not in all above a dozen, being unwilling to entertain more than he has a prospect of providing for' (20 Nov. 1697, Froude I. 251–2, n. 1).

he endured no vexatious dependence upon tithes. He was left free, consequently, to enjoy several of his favourite recreations, such as social talk, lengthy hours of reading, and the composition of prose essays and occasional light verses. As a means of making himself known to the great of the land, a residence in Dublin Castle had clear advantages even over Moor Park. But Swift would never have undertaken the office of chaplain if he had not supposed it would lead him to a more valuable place; and the necessity of being always on call, always congenial, could not have pleased him. Ten years after his easy service with Berkeley was ended, Swift said, 'I will be no man's chaplain alive.'[1]

At the end of January 1700 died the incumbent of one of the best-endowed deanships in Ireland, leaving Swift to suppose that a way lay open for him. The deceased, Coote Ormsby, Dean of Derry, had won his great promotion while acting as chaplain to a Lord Deputy (i.e., sole governor) of Ireland, Swift's one-time nominal patron, Henry, Lord Capel. But when the splendour had fallen upon Ormsby, he had already been at least thirty years older than Swift was in 1700, and he had correspondingly stored up thirty years of meritorious service to the Establishment. If we turn to the new case, Swift should be judged against John Bolton, the man soon chosen for the deanship: Bolton was about eleven years Swift's senior; he had been a doctor of divinity for eight years; and he had been in holy orders for twenty-two.

Berkeley no doubt kept a number of preferments as it were in his simple gift. Nevertheless, he was only one of three Lords Justices, and there is nothing to suggest that the deanery of Derry was his own to bestow. When Ormsby died, it was another Lord Justice who mentioned the vacancy to Bolton. Meanwhile, the man most directly concerned would of course be neither a candidate nor an elector but rather the new dean's superior, i.e., the Bishop of Derry; and this was William King, an early member of the Dublin Philosophical Society, and soon to become Swift's diocesan as Archbishop of Dublin. Not only would Swift have remembered William King's history as the very active

[1] *Journal*, 25 May 1711.

[9]

rector of St Werburgh's, Dublin; he would also recall that during the Troubles—when Swift and his cousin had fled to England—King had been elected dean of St Patrick's Cathedral and had undergone months of imprisonment in Dublin Castle on account of his opposition to James II. Swift would know of King's record as the aggressive Bishop of Derry since 1690, and he would be familiar with his character: 'passionate, tenacious and vindicative, but firm to the interest of his country'.[1]

As soon as Dean Ormsby died, Bishop King wrote letters not only to Berkeley and another Lord Justice but also to the then Archbishop of Dublin, the scrupulous Narcissus Marsh, who had governed Trinity College while Swift was an undergraduate there, and had demanded a testimonial from Temple when Swift was a candidate for ordination. However confident the chaplain's hopes for the deanship may have been, Bishop King in no way shared them. So far from supporting Swift's intention, the bishop never observed it. Writing to Marsh, King said he supposed that one of the 'state chaplains' would be made dean, and he mentioned five who would suit him.[2] Although the list (obviously meant to be seen by the Lords Justices) passes entirely over Swift's name, it includes three men with whom he was to have dealings in the years ahead: Dr John Stearne, then rector of Trim; Dr Edward Synge, vicar of Christ Church, Cork; and Dr John Bolton of Ratoath and Laracor. Out of these the serious contenders, in the eyes of the Lords Justices, were two: Synge and Bolton.

Berkeley indicated to Bolton that the deanship would be conferred upon him 'with an encouraging advantage'[3]—i.e., with a financial advantage over his present circumstances; and according to Bolton, the Earl told Marsh about this intention. Nevertheless, in spite of these promises and Marsh's persuasions, Dr Bolton could not look upon a translation to the difficult northern eminence as a sufficient recompense for giving up his easy livings near Dublin. In the face of the doctor's refusal, the Lords Justices gave him up and turned their benevolence upon Edward

---

[1] John Percival, 1711, in B.M. MS. Ad. 47,087, fol. [15].   [2] Landa, p. 30.
[3] *Ibid.*, p. 31.

Synge of Cork, son of one bishop and nephew of another. But whatever Synge himself may have desired, he had a settled and widowed mother who objected to his emigrating from Cork; so he too rejected the appeal. If anybody had ever remotely thought of Mr Swift for the deanship, this was the time to produce his name. But nobody did. Instead, Archbishop Marsh decided to put up the value of the offer to Dr Bolton. He said he would ask the Lords Justices to let Bolton keep the valuable living of Ratoath along with the deanship. This concession would mean an extreme sort of pluralism, since the two places were very far apart. Yet the arrangement was designed and promoted not only by a remarkably conscientious archbishop but also at a time when the trend of government was at least momentarily to reform just such abuses. Swift's hopes clearly belonged to the realm of self-deluding fantasy. When Bolton did at last stoop to accept the enlarged conditions, Bishop King wrote to each of the two Lords Justices involved and acknowledged their excellencies' 'kindness and goodness' in accommodating themselves to his episcopal desires.[1]

Swift's fury at the imagined insult to his capacities rebounds and resounds down the decades of his life; for his account of the affair (as composed in the late 1730s) has no visible connection with fact:

> In some months, the deanry of Derry fell vacant; and it was the Earl of Berkeley's turn to dispose of it. Yet things were so ordered that the secretary [i.e., Bushe] having received a bribe, the deanry was disposed of to another,[2] and Mr Swift was put off with some other church-livings not worth above a third part of that rich deanry, and at this present time, not a sixth. The excuse pretended was his being too young, although he were then thirty years old.[3]

While Swift's suspicions in this case were unfounded, they

---

[1] *Ibid.*, pp. 29–32. The negotiations had lasted from 29 Jan. to 15 Feb. 1700.

[2] Lyon emends the passage to read that the secretary 'knew best how to please his patron and gave a hint to Mr. John Bolton's friends of a step fit for them to take, which advice being followed the said deanery was given to Mr. Bolton' (p. 29); but if Lyon means that a bribe went rather to the Earl than the secretary, the evidence for this allegation seems no stronger than for the original claim, since Bolton would hardly have rejected a deanship which he was bribing the Earl to offer him.

[3] Davis v. 195.

imply no remarkable depth of cynicism. 'The clergy here seem mighty dependent and very great courtiers', said an officer of the Irish government about the same time, 'for the livings are pretty good and there is a constant expectation of preferment and a very great greediness to obtain. Nay, they hardly scruple offering what they hope will be the most prevailing argument' (i.e., a bribe).[1] But if the generalization was not perverse, the application was wrong.

Granted that Swift's poor memory undermines his own argument—for he was not thirty but thirty-two in January 1700—it remains true that he looked absurdly young, inexperienced, and by ordinary standards undeserving at the time. Ormsby had suffered a long illness while waiting to die, and his consequent neglect of duties had left the business of the deanery in confusion. A conscientious archbishop like Marsh would obviously prefer a tried and sober churchman to a place-seeker who had resigned his first benefice after at most a bare year's residence. To give Swift the appointment would have demanded an unusual divergence from custom; and that even the disappointed chaplain understood this reasoning, we may suspect both from the lack of virulence in his later allusion to Berkeley and from the length of time he stayed on good terms with the Earl.

One reason those good terms lasted is that when all the Derry negotiations were over, Swift did have his turn and was not left gaping. What he got instead of a deanship was the remainder of Bolton's vacated livings (after Ratoath was detached) and Bolton's cathedral stall of Dunlavin, in St Patrick's Cathedral. With these preferments we reach at last one of the two solid supports on which Swift's lifetime economy would stand. For ten years he had been picking and losing: when he left Moor Park in 1690, Temple's recommendation failed to get him a Trinity College fellowship. When he returned to his patron, he chose not to accept a military commission or a post in Ireland under the Master of the Rolls. Instead, he went to Kilroot and regretted it. Returning once more to Moor Park, he thought Sunderland would look after him, but Sunderland fell too soon. When

[1] Southwell to Nottingham, 23 July 1703, in Froude I. 245, n. I.

Temple died, Romney omitted to place Swift in a prebend of Canterbury or Westminster. As a chaplain, he came to Ireland with Berkeley and found Bushe dislodging him from a secretary-ship. Ormsby died, but Bolton succeeded. Now finally he received a nourishing cup of honey, however little it might be and however mingled with gall.

Swift not only took Bolton's livings: he cherished them till death. For over a dozen years they supplied the bulk of his income; and the prebend of Dunlavin was his first entry into a province (the deanery of St Patrick's) which he would eventually rule. To appreciate the complicated nature of the whole gift, we can briefly go through its elements; for they will remain fixed, visible guideposts of his long career.

Fundamental was a union of three parishes collectively known by the name of their largest constituent, Laracor. This union included the small rectory of Agher and the somewhat larger vicarage of Rathbeggan, as well as the really substantial vicarage of Laracor (over half again the size of the other two combined). The parishes covered a total area of more than ten square miles, mainly farmland, and brought Swift about £230 a year—though in his first year he had to pay out £117 on fees and curates.[1] It is true that when Swift described his financial condition (admittedly to a woman whose connection with him he was trying to break), the statement was presented as a 'dismal account'.[2] But his advancement to livings of this description hardly appears a mark of failure—not only Bolton but Synge as well had once been vicar of Laracor. In the diocese of Dublin, if we count only the rural parishes and except the city parsons residing in the capital, there were only six or seven clergymen with incomes over a hundred pounds a year. In some dioceses two hundred pounds amounted to nearly a fifth of the combined incomes of all the lower clergy.[3]

While Agher and Laracor adjoined one another, the parish of Rathbeggan lay some miles away from both of them; but they were all located less than half a day's journey from Dublin, and Laracor church was only a mile and a half south of the town of

[1] Lyon, p. 29.   [2] Williams I. 34.   [3] Lecky I. 203–4, n. 4.

Trim. Since Bolton's place of residence had belonged to Ratoath, Swift was expected to use another house within a mile of Trim.[1] There was no manse on the glebe itself, which consisted, alas, of a single acre.[2] In spite of Bolton's precedent, Swift had to petition the Primate for a dispensation to let him hold Rathbeggan with Laracor and Agher, on the grounds that the income of all together would be 'but a comfortable support' and would 'encourage his residence, and due performance of his duty'. The petition was referred to the Bishop of Meath, Tenison, who reported favourably; and the dispensation was granted (for a composition of twenty pounds).[3]

Presented to Laracor in February 1700, and instituted in March, Swift nevertheless stuck close to the Castle; for he put off till June the essential formalities of reading assent and consent on the spot.[4] As for the cathedral appointment, not until autumn was he collated to Bolton's vacated prebend of St Patrick's.[5] But this prebend, without demanding many duties of him, meant far more than a source of a mere fifteen or twenty pounds a year. For the actual parish of Dunlavin, the prebendary had no responsibility at all. Even in the cathedral itself his chief duty was only to preach in his turn; and since this obligation was shared out among some twenty-odd canons, it could not be called heavy—least of all by Swift, whose absences stand out for their frequency and length. According to generally careful records, Swift, over the decade from 1702 to 1712, attended the annual visitation of his dean no more than five times and the common meetings of the cathedral chapter only thirteen times.[6]

Nevertheless, as a means of enlarging and consolidating his own social world (as distinguished from the Castle's array of useful but elevated greatnesses), the cathedral takes an obvious precedence over Moor Park, and belongs rather with Trinity College. On the public stage of castle or court Swift would meet the peers and ministers whom he must thank for his promotions. Within the cathedral precincts or liberties he would discover the

[1] Ball I. 32–3, n. 1.   [2] Landa, pp. 37, 40.   [3] Craik I. 100, n. 1.
[4] Landa, pp. 35–6.   [5] Collated 28 Sept., installed 22 Oct. 1700.
[6] Lyon in Forster, pp. 16–17.

daily comfort of routine acquaintance. Already attached to the chapter of St Patrick's were two men early to be counted among his best-trusted, if least illustrious, friends: Thomas Walls, master of the cathedral school, and John Worrall, the humble master of the song[1] (who would be very remarkable in St Patrick's history for his sixty years' tenure as a canon).

Several canons had been undergraduates with Swift and were familiar to him even before he was installed. The once notorious John Jones, hero of the *terrae filius* scandal at college—and one of those who had taken their A.B. degree *speciali gratia* at the same time as Swift—held a minor canonry.[2] Among the older prebendaries who knew Swift already was Enoch Reader, now Archdeacon of Dublin but once a fellow prebendary in the Cathedral of Connor.

Besides supplying him with a ready-made society to choose from, a prebend also meant the privilege—which a merely parochial clergyman could not enjoy—of regular contact with the episcopal hierarchy. Through the bishop, Swift had access to a high level of political influence; and since the bishop of Swift's diocese was also the Archbishop of Dublin, second in ecclesiastical authority only to the Primate of all Ireland, this access meant an advantage which could transform glittering possibilities into powerful facts.

[1] Delany, p. 91.
[2] Lawlor, p. 203. Other fellow students among the prebendaries were John Hinton, son of Swift's schoolmaster; John Travers; and Jeremiah Marsh.

Chapter Three

VARINA DISMISSED

A s I have said, the society which Swift cultivated on the grand stage of the great world yielded him two main satisfactions. People like the Berkeleys were exciting to live with because their hereditary glory and their splendid associations could not help throwing a flicker of reflection upon even the cassock of a domestic chaplain. At the same time, by belonging to their household, Swift could cultivate persons otherwise too remote, who controlled the avenues of patronage. For a more casual, less demanding set of acquaintances, he employed men of his own or a humbler level in the church, the lower clergy of Dublin; and these sometimes produced the warmest kind of masculine comradeship. Yet for the most profound human intimacy outside sexual passion or marriage, Swift needed women of no higher than the middle class—young ladies whom he could scold and teach and love; and this deep feminine comfort was what Ireland did not now afford.

Meanwhile, the family life of Dublin Castle had its charms and rewards. Accompanying the Earl and Countess of Berkeley were two daughters, Mary and Elizabeth, as well as a large staff. Three sons had apparently stayed behind, and a girl about twelve years old had died soon after they arrived in Ireland.[1] Of the entire establishment the one whom Swift was to remain in touch with longest was the fifteen-year-old Lady Betty. Upon her receptive character the chaplain's puns, jingles, and vivacity worked an enduring spell; and she never lost her fondness for him. In addition, Swift's functions introduced him to the whole span of Castle population, from footmen's wives to visiting peers. So

[1] Penelope died 3 Sept. 1699; in 1733 Swift put up a monument to her in St Patrick's Cathedral, at her sister's expense, bearing an inscription by himself (Ball IV. 377, n. 1).

many chances for odd and bright observation were veins of gold to an inventive mind, and their value appears in Swift's poems of this period.

If he looked about him for a less light-hearted sort of female sympathy than Dublin Castle supplied, Swift was not going to find it in his own immediate family. On the contrary, so far from comforting him, the behaviour of his elder sister Jane was to darken his suspicions of all her sex. While the first-hand evidence on this subject does not seem conclusive, the testimony of men close to Swift in his later years agrees that Jane offended her brother deeply enough for him to keep her at some distance as long as she lived.[1] There is no doubt that in December 1699 she was married in Dublin to a man named Joseph Fenton—as his second wife.[2] She had been living with their uncle William Swift in Bride Street—the street where Fenton too seems to have lived[3]; and since this district belonged to the 'liberties' of the cathedral, it was the dean of the very chapter which Swift would soon join, who granted the licence for the marriage.[4]

Our safest authority says that Swift had developed a dislike for Fenton purely on account of his character—'a particular and personal dislike'.[5] But others, who knew Swift less closely, blame the resentment upon the new brother-in-law's connection with trade, for Fenton was a tanner or currier.[6] That he was unprepossessing we may silently assume: since Jane Swift had already passed her thirty-third birthday, and could offer small provision in the way of a dowry, her expectations must have been rationally moderate. Yet the match does seem to have proved unsatisfactory. Swift himself called Fenton 'a dunce',[7] and Swift's mother

---

[1] Orrery, p. 33; Delany, pp. 71–2; D. Swift, pp. 101–5, 347–9.

[2] Joseph 'Penton', *coriarius*, is named by Burtschaell and Sadleir as father of Peter, entered 1693. He had at least two other children by his first wife: Alice and Richard. See Le Brocquy, pp. 150–1.

[3] Mason, p. 241.

[4] Licence dated 13 Dec. 1699; see Lyon, preliminaries, p. 7; Mason, p. 217, says Fenton is described as 'coriacus' in the licence.

[5] Delany, p. 72.

[6] Orrery, p. 33; D. Swift, pp. 101–5, 347–8. According to documents in the Registry of Deeds, Dublin, Joseph Fenton was a tanner. Other references describe him as a currier.

[7] *Journal*, 25 Sept. 1711.

[17]

left money for his sister in his trust with the stipulation that it was
'not to come to her husband'.[1] While there is no ground for thinking that Jane ever separated herself formally from Fenton, she
did, about twelve years after the marriage, go to work for Lady
Giffard at Sheen[2]; and whether or not she stayed uninterruptedly
with her ladyship, she did witness her will,[3] and she did remain in
Surrey after Lady Giffard's death, dying herself in 1736 in Guild-
ford.[4]

It is wrong to suggest, as several early biographers did, that
Swift simply dropped his sister after her marriage. He saw her in
England during the last years of Queen Anne, and doubtless
earlier in Dublin (where it is certain that Esther Johnson knew
her). Not only did she repeatedly look to him for advice and
assistance, but he certainly corresponded with her and used his
influence on her behalf.[5] From at least the time of Fenton's death,
he paid her a regular allowance.[6] On the other hand, it is clear
that Jane always felt more eager to see Jonathan than he to see
her[7]; and on a day of bad temper when he was an old man, Swift
said he did not care a straw what became of a sister who had
'during her whole life disobliged me in the most [om.?] circumstances of her conduct'.[8]

Supreme among these disobliging circumstances one must
place Jane Swift's marriage. If it is true that she had seemed a disappointment to him during his childhood, when long separations
would have led him to demand impossible compensations from

---

[1] Journal, 1 Jan. 1710–11.

[2] Ibid., p. 357, n. 2; Longe, p. 352. Her salary was ten pounds a year (Longe,
p. 355).

[3] Longe, p. 350. Lady Giffard left her a legacy of money, clothes, and furniture
(Longe, p. 348).

[4] Journal, p. 101, n. 38, corrected by Le Brocquy, pp. 149–50. According to docu-
ments in the Registry of Deeds, Dublin, Joseph Fenton, a tanner, was dead by 1720.
By Jane Swift he had two children, Swift and Anne, both baptized in St Michan's,
Dublin. Anne also seems to have worked for Lady Giffard (Journal, p. 357, n. 2). Cf.
Williams IV. 401.

[5] Journal, 23 Nov. 1710.

[6] Delany, p. 72. The amount was probably fifteen pounds a year (Williams III.
380 and n. 2). An intestacy grant of Fenton's goods was made to his wife in 1720
(Ball VI. 216).

[7] Journal, 24 Sept. 1711, 10 May 1712.

[8] Williams IV. 411. A word like 'material' seems omitted before 'circumstances'.

her presence; if it is true that he felt jealous of her for enjoying an unfair share of their mother's company; and if he transferred to Jane, rather than their mother, the blame for this injustice—then the marriage revived many bitter emotions. Returning to Ireland after a long stay in England, suffering the failure of two hopes for advancement, and even at this instant withdrawing himself (as we shall see) from the vertiginous cliff-edge of matrimony, he found his only sister insulting his judgment and defying his wishes, repeating his parents' blunder of an imprudent marriage, deserting her lost brother just when he was restored to her. 'I did not know . . . nor will ever believe such a breed had either worth or honor', he wrote in 1735.[1]

Yet the spring of 1700 was, of all the times in the world, precisely the season which Varina, Swift's once-courted lady of Belfast, chose to resurrect the pledges he had so liberally buried around her feet a few years before. From the manner in which he now addressed himself to Jane Waring, we may retrospectively imagine how he harangued Jane Swift. Uncle Adam, who owned property in the north near the Warings, had kept Swift informed of his erstwhile mistress's condition, and even intimated that Swift's vacillations hindered her from encouraging other suitors. Varina had also taken it upon herself to send Swift an inquisitory letter after receiving several messages from him that sounded evasive. If their correspondence had not lapsed,[2] the bloom of his rhetoric had visibly faded. To the 'household thoughts' which commonly drove matrimony out of his head, Swift could now of course add those ideas of Hetty Johnson which had found a permanent repository there.

On this ground Varina possessed wisdom enough both to suspect a motive and to defer alluding to it. Her first challenge derived rather from the strong and general fact that the tone of Swift's letters had altered since his return to Ireland. Next she did indeed wonder whether he now had thoughts of a new mistress.

[1] *Ibid.*

[2] Besides the letters from Swift to Varina noted above (vol. i, p. 168, n. 2), there were at least two between July 1699 and May 1700, since Swift's expression is plural: 'my letters since I last came over'. He also mentions 'abundance' of letters from her (Williams i. 33).

From this question she advanced, with the logic of the heart, to a corollary doubt imputing (I think) dissimulation to Swift—viz., why was he curious about Varina's finances? Finally she presented a concrete and ineluctable demand: when was he coming to see her?

In courtship as in other contests Swift made it a rule to put the opposite side as much in the wrong as he could.[1] Two of her vulnerable places Varina had already marked out to him; for she had originally withheld her hand with the rather brittle arguments that her frail physique made marriage a risk for her health, and that Swift's low income made it a threat to her comfort. He could now return these upon her head and add inventions of his own; for it is clear that Swift, having lost interest in the lady, had already tried to let her down with a minimum of distress. If a decorous vagueness had not detached her, however, he felt well enough fortified to deliver charges as concrete as her own.

To begin with, Swift wrote, his alteration—such as it was—had been occasioned by her indifference to his prayers for her amendment. In a speech which convention would assign rather to a divorced husband than an anxious suitor, he said, 'All I had in answer from you, was nothing but a great deal of arguing, and sometimes in a style so very imperious as I thought might have been spared, when I reflected how much you had been in the wrong.'[2] She had, he said, neglected her health and manners as much as ever, clinging to the foul neighbourhood of her remarried mother. As to a rival sweetheart—here his wording grows casuistical. Without explicitly denying that one exists, he swears it is not thoughts of one that have changed his attitude: 'Neither had I ever thoughts of being married to any other person but yourself.' Her fortune nevertheless was indeed a relevant fact, because she expected to live in a handsomer style than he could afford even with the addition of almost a hundred pounds a year from Varina's property. No, he said, he would not yet visit Belfast, since his duties confined him to Dublin.

Swift's letter ends in a frothing cascade of challenges which, so far as is known, effectively stifled the relationship:

[1] Davis VIII. 96.   [2] Williams I. 33.

I desire, therefore, you will let me know if your health be otherwise than it was when you told me the doctors advised you against
marriage, as what would certainly hazard your life. Are they or you
grown of another opinion in this particular? Are you in a condition
to manage domestic affairs, with an income of less (perhaps) than
three hundred pounds a year? Have you such an inclination to my
person and humour, as to comply with my desires and way of
living, and endeavour to make us both as happy as you can? Will
you be ready to engage in those methods I shall direct for the
improvement of your mind, so as to make us entertaining company
for each other, without being miserable when we are neither visiting
nor visited? Can you bend your love and esteem and indifference to
others the same way as I do mine? Shall I have so much power in
your heart, or you so much government of your passions, as to grow
in good humour upon my approach, though provoked by a —?
Have you so much good-nature as to endeavour by soft words to
smooth any rugged humour occasioned by the cross accidents of
life? Shall the place wherever your husband is thrown be more welcome than courts or cities without him? In short, these are some of
the necessary methods to please men, who, like me, are deep-read in
the world; and to a person thus made, I should be proud in giving
all due returns towards making her happy. These are the questions
I have always resolved to propose to her with whom I meant to pass
my life; and whenever you can heartily answer them in the affirmative, I shall be blessed to have you in my arms, without regarding
whether your person be beautiful, or your fortune large. Cleanliness in the first, and competency in the other, is all I look for.[1]

As it happens, Varina's doubts of her own good health seem
not ill-founded, since, although Swift was the elder of the two, she
died many years before him.[2] But if she expected to find another
bridegroom her hopes were visionary; for she remained a spinster. To a man afraid as much to marry the woman he loves as to
be abandoned by her, the charm of chronic illness is that it takes
events out of his hands. A wedding can be endlessly postponed, a
separation occasioned by death will not be his fault, the pains of
disease may even punish the beloved for the flight which he fears
she meditates. If the symptoms of illness are grave, they may in
prospect relieve him of the worrisome suspense which a long
period of waiting to be deserted would mean.

Since Swift's raptures seem to have risen as he left his beloved

---

[1] *Ibid.*, pp. 35–6.   [2] *Ibid.*, p. 36, n. 1.

and sunk as he returned, she might be described as repeating the disappointments which childhood had accustomed him to anticipate. In the demands which he imposed upon Varina, Swift also echoes those experiences. Not a wooer but a father speaks when he either scolds her for ignoring his recommendations for her health, or else insists that she improve her mind under his instruction. Has any other suitor required only cleanliness in his lady's 'person'? Swift also reiterates that to live with him she must give up her own family and risk captive poverty. If to us such conditions suggest utter dependence, Swift goes further yet and wants his bride to join Dekker's Grissel with Wordsworth's Margaret.

The submissiveness which Swift defines would surely be less correct in a wife than a daughter. A few years earlier he had assumed the posture of cringing obedience, and solemnly offered to forgo all else 'for your sake'.[1] Now he breathes the arrogance of a poorhouse warden to an orphan waif. Either attitude is hardly that of a partner in marriage. On the contrary, in his bold replies to the fatherless Varina, Swift seems to betray a remarkable degree of autonomy. Apparently, her defects provided a foil to another woman's virtues; and Swift could now be so short with the one because he knew how willingly the other would desert her mother and accept his tutelage, live in his way and cheer his despair, abide with him but never require what Varina did—marriage.

<hr/>

[1] Williams I. 21.

Chapter Four

VERSE AND PROSE

―――――――――――

I

Until now we have found the best embodiment of Swift's literary gifts to be either his letters or his early prose satires. Of verse we have seen only the odes, which reveal more Swift than poetry. Political essays, serious or satirical, he has not yet attempted. About the year 1700, however, there were two great turns in Swift's literary development: he found the verse style which would give him fame as a poet, and he composed his earliest essays on politics.

Today it is still uncommon, if no longer eccentric, for critics to praise Swift's poetry; and when it is praised, the terms are never those of Hazlitt, who set him 'in the first rank of agreeable moralists in verse'.[1] Long before Hazlitt's day, however, the prose was already receiving a far higher eulogy than the verse; and even Hazlitt's commendation of the poetry was narrowly bounded by complaints against 'slip-shod, tedious, trifling, foolish' elements. Johnson's praise sounds moderate but positive. To him, Swift's poems

> are often humorous, almost always light, and have the qualities which recommend such compositions, easiness and gaiety. They are, for the most part, what their author intended. The diction is correct, the numbers are smooth, and the rhymes exact. There seldom occurs a hard-laboured expression or a redundant epithet; all his verses exemplify his own definition of a good style, they consist of 'proper words in proper places'.[2]

The attitude here is neither defensive nor pugnacious; the observations are those of a specialist assigning qualities to a recognized object. While no reader today would divide the world of early

―――――――――――

[1] *English Poets*, lecture vi (*Works*, ed. P. P. Howe, v. 109).   [2] *Life of Swift.*

eighteenth-century verse equally between Pope and Swift, this judgment was not rare in the lifetime of the two writers. Since the bulk of literary lights of their generation had reason to be strongly prejudiced either for or against them both, such contemporary opinions must be produced with caution. Yet I think one can appreciate the note of spontaneous pleasure which the very best of Swift's poems evoked in an original reader from what Steele had to say about two of them: 'My ingenious kinsman, Mr. Humphrey Wagstaff [*alias* Swift] ... treats of every subject after a manner that no other author has done, and better than any other can do.'[1]

The characteristic aspects of Swift's settled reputation make themselves clear in these four opinions. His father is Butler; his brother (or half-brother) is Pope. His purpose is explicitly moral; his tone is humorous; his versification, skilful. The language is humble; the meaning, plain; the appeal, immediate—above all, the appeal is immediate. If Swift had not been immensely popular in his own era, Goldsmith would not have selected three of his long poems for inclusion in an anthology of forty-odd *Beauties of English Poesy* (1767); and he would not have named one of them among 'the best-versified poems in our language'.[2]

The reason for Swift's popularity is probably the same as for both the fading of his reputation as a poet and the very recent brightening. Clarity of sense and ingenuity of versification, didactic purpose and humorous tone—all together—are hardly sufficient to support the kind of minute and repeated study which has become identified with the uses of poetry. Even adding to these the peculiar irony—in Cowper's encomium, the 'droll sobriety'[3]—which looks to us like the hallmark of the author, Swift can rarely supply the intense lyric pathos that makes the modern standard of 'poetry', as distinct from 'mere verse'. Out of the four hierarchical classes into which Joseph Warton divided

---

[1] *Tatler*, no. 238.

[2] Goldsmith, *Works*, ed. Gibbs, 1886, v. 153–61. The poem praised for its versification is *On Poetry*, which Warton, 1756, plaintively described as 'far more popular, than Akenside's noble ode to Lord Huntingdon' (*Essay on Pope* 1, p. vi). The two other poems chosen by Goldsmith are *Baucis and Philemon* and *Cadenus and Vanessa*.

[3] *Table Talk*, l. 658.

English poets, he placed Swift in the third from the top, with 'men of wit, of elegant taste, and some fancy in describing familiar life'.[1] Of 'pure poetry' Warton said Swift left not a trace, for he (like Donne!) lacked a 'creative and glowing *imagination*'.[2]

Of course, Swift was in revolt against the genres and moods which might have produced the lyric intensities dear both to Warton and to most of us today. If one does seek a pathetic sublime—that Longinian excellence possessed by Gray, and in the face of which Warton says 'no man of a true poetical spirit is *master of himself*'[3]—he will miss it in Swift precisely because Swift repudiated it. Epics, odes, love-songs, and pastorals were just what he wished to avoid. The veins seemed exhausted; the feelings, false. In disgust with Cowley's pindarics and Cowley's conceits, he turned to Butler. He turned to the didactic, moral, satirical kinds upon which Warton was to paste the label that stuck for almost two centuries, viz., 'not of the most *poetic* species of *poetry*'.[4]

If at the same time Warton praises Pope as 'adapted to all ages and stations',[5] he grants him a title which Swift desired as well. When Warton stops to characterize Swift's verse directly, he mistakenly says it represents things 'as they really exist in life, without heightening or enlarging them, and without adding any imaginary circumstances'.[6] But though the characterization is mistaken, Swift would have read it as a compliment. Tickell abandoned the possibility of criticism when he said (1711), 'Unless poetry is taken in at the first glance, it immediately loses its force and point',[7] and I think even Swift would have boggled at the vulgarity of that principle. Nevertheless, Tickell stands beside Swift and opposed to Warton. If the effect of such tendencies is often to leave Swift, in Johnson's phrase, clear but shallow,[8] he might rejoin that to be dark is not always to be deep. It does seem true, however, that when Swift accepted all these demands at

---

[1] *Essay on Pope* I, p. xi. In this class are Prior, Waller, Parnell, and Fenton.

[2] *Ibid.*, pp. iv, v.   [3] *Ibid.* II (1782), p. 478.   [4] *Ibid.* II. 477.

[5] *Ibid.*, p. 477.

[6] *Ibid.*, p. 114. Warton picks out for special praise *A Description of the Morning, A City Shower, Baucis and Philemon,* and *Verses on the Death of Dr. Swift.*

[7] Quoted by James Sutherland, *A Preface to Eighteenth-Century Poetry,* 1948, p. 103.

[8] Boswell, *Johnson,* ed. Hill-Powell, v. 44.

once, he wrapped himself in a strait-jacket. How can a poet escape triviality while trying to seem at once amusingly easy and true to ordinary life?

The superficial and the trivial are indeed what glare at us from the lines of the two earliest performances in Swift's new style. Other than marking the start of a very long division in his work, they have small importance. So it is their method, rather than their meaning, that calls for comment. To begin with, both poems use the octosyllabic couplet, the form which came to be Swift's own and which was regarded at the time as improper for solemn themes.[1] For although this couplet had of course been employed in many moods by many poets, it was then connected less with *Il Penseroso* or *The Garden* than with *Hudibras*; and it is Butler's form that Swift adopted. But whereas Butler had made it the vehicle for direct ridicule—with thin strands of burlesque or mock-heroic—Swift imbued it with epic or pastoral echoes and other ironical tones. In vocabulary too there are dissimilarities between the two satirists: for whereas Butler went after freaks of diction, gathering and exhibiting a museum of strange words, Swift limited himself to what he considered proper English speech, wishing less to exploit than to refine the possibilities of his language.[2]

Apart from these divergences the two men shared important leanings. Both of them use a slight framework of fable or analogy as support for a miscellaneous structure of ridicule, moral reflection, and expository argument.[3] Both also like to strew or even smother their lines with odd similes, normally humble in tone and often drawn from parallels between beasts and men. Feeling perhaps too much at home among the inventions of their witty forebears, they apply their own metaphysical imaginations to parody rather than sublimity. Both men also seem fascinated by the problem of rhyme, and strain to manufacture double and other surprise endings in order to mock their victim and titillate

---

[1] Goldsmith complains that the great fault of Parnell's *Night Piece* is its being in eight-syllable lines, 'very improper for the solemnity of the subject' (*Works*, 1886, v. 158–9).

[2] Seriously, of course, Butler shared Swift's dislike of jargon and cant; and even in *Hudibras* when purity is called for, the language is pure: see Jack, pp. 27–30, 36.

[3] Jack, pp. 25, 70–1.

their reader. Finally, they both possess enough skill in handling the four-beat couplet to modulate freely from the clumsiest doggerel into a polished tetrapody.

The faults they share are as solid as the virtues, and seem related to them. By deserting the dignified genres or by inverting them through parody, Butler and Swift may admit themselves to regions crying for cultivation; but the scope thus allowed them opens the way for unpleasant temptations which they seldom resist. Digression lures them to digression, amplification sinks into loquacity, climax becomes bathos. The reader often has no sense of direction; he is tired out by the diffuse variations on an obvious theme; he feels let down by the lack of fulfilment at the end of a poem.

Since these sins are gross, they need no illustration. But the elegance which *Hudibras* can offer for emulation is not often recognized. So I quote a passage to show the high as well as humble trend of what Swift found in Butler:

> Love in your heart as idly burns,
> As fire in antique Roman-urns,
> To warm the dead, and vainly light
> Those only, that see nothing by't.
> Have you not pow'r to entertain,
> And render love for love again?[1]

This ridicule of sexual passion (the words are those of an ageing fortune-hunter to a rich widow) is also the theme of many poems by Swift, including the two earliest in his *amaro stile nuovo*.[2] Like

[1] Part II, Canto I, p. 113.

[2] The chronology of Swift's first poems in his mature style has been a little unclear, though largely settled by Sir Harold Williams. Like Sir Harold, I assign 'A Ballad on . . . Traffick' to 1702, partly—as he does—because of the reference to the election of July 1702, but also because of the reference to Swift as 'Doctor', a title which he received only in February 1702. Sir Harold has shown that 'The Problem' probably alludes to Romney and therefore belongs to 1699. Since 'The Discovery' deals with the first week of Berkeley's lord justiceship and the 'new state-airs' of Bushe, his secretary, it can be assigned to the autumn of 1699. This date is confirmed by an allusion to rumours of the Great Northern War, rumours which became current toward the end of that year. 'Verses Wrote in a . . . Table-Book' was dated 1698 in the 1711 *Miscellanies*. This evidence is not strong, but there is no other. 'Mrs. Harris's Petition' certainly belongs to the beginning of 1701. Here is the resulting chronology: 1698, 'Verses Wrote in a . . . Table-Book'; 1699, 'The Problem'; late 1699, 'The Discovery'; early 1701, 'Mrs. Harris's Petition'; 1702, 'A Ballad on . . . Traffick'.

Butler, Swift also delivers his satire in a wrapping of parody. The first poem, 'Verses Wrote in a Lady's Ivory Table-Book', is based on the device of ironical bathos: a list of incongruous phrases presented in a series of incongruous rhymes, so that a moral chaos is suggested by the verbal discords. Taking clichés from the idealization of courtship in contemporary love lyrics, he rhymes them with coarse phrases taken from the low but real preoccupations of empty-headed women; and he pretends to find both classes of banality side by side on the ivory, erasable pages of a lady's table book (kept out where its owner could make quick notes, or admirers could enter sentiments):

> Here you may read, 'Dear charming saint',
> Beneath 'A new receit for paint'.
> Here in beau-spelling, 'Tru tel deth',
> There in her own, 'For an el breth'.
> Here, 'Lovely nymph pronounce my doom'.
> There, 'A safe way to use perfume'.

The device has no claim to originality. Among the earlier instances of it is an often-quoted passage in Canto One of the Third Part of *Hudibras*, where a pretended demon carries on a dialogue with a Puritan hypocrite. (Since the bathetic rhymes occur at spaces among several others, I shall omit the verses between and extract those which exemplify the device.)

> What makes a knave a child of God,
> And one of us? 'A livelihood.'
> What renders beating out of brains
> And murther godliness? 'Great gains.'
> What's orthodox and true believing
> Against a conscience? 'A good living.'
> What makes all doctrines plain and clear?
> 'About two hundred pounds a year.'
> And that which was prov'd true before,
> Prove false again? 'Two hundred more.'[1]

Unlike Butler, Swift cannot remain a cool reporter but lets his disgust break loose. To express his disproportionately violent feeling, he employs the imagery of filth. In the last lines of the

[1] Pp. 229–30.

poem Swift tries to make a thundering epigram, but he cannot; and the final couplet sounds weak after the violence of the lines preceding it:

> Who that had wit would place it here,
> For every peeping fop to jear.
> To think that your brains issue is
> Expos'd to th' excrement of his . . .
> Whoe're expects to hold his part
> In such a book and such a heart,
> If he be wealthy and a fool
> Is in all points the fittest tool,
> Of whom it may be justly said,
> He's a gold pencil tipt with lead.

Here we have a group of traits constantly reappearing in Swift's poems: imagery of filth associated with imagery of passion; violent disgust, out of proportion to its source; an unintentionally anti-climactic ending. Here, as in many of Swift's prose pieces, the reader feels attracted by the irrelevant or indecorous strength of the poet's emotions, and is thereby distracted from the meaning of the lines. The object of Swift's satire here is also typical of his poetry; for it is not women or the female body but the convention of simultaneously praising women for their bodies and pretending they are ethereal. In other words, Swift attacks the hypocrisy of sexual passion as Butler attacks the hypocrisy of religious enthusiasm. If we now recall that at the time when Swift wrote these lines, he was in the process of throwing over Varina and opposing his sister's marriage, we may assume that his shift from the idealizations of the early odes to the cynicism of his later poems is connected with the parallel changes in his dealings with these women.

Similar ingredients meet us in the other poem. But while this too is in octosyllabics, it deals not with Swift's but with the Earl of Romney's ladies. Swift probably wrote 'The Problem' in order to avenge himself for the Earl's failure to recommend him to the King; and although the poem was circulated in manuscript, it was printed only after Swift's death. Both facts are revealing. When Swift felt furious with men too powerful to be attacked openly, he would often fall back on a pasquinade. In 1710 after the Earl of Godolphin gave him a chilly reception, he was to say, 'I am almost vowing revenge,' and would proceed to write the poisonous 'Virtues of Sid Hamet's Rod'.[1] He believed it was only fair that a private gentleman might compose anonymous invectives against evil-doers in great office, whether the subject was alive or dead, since the alternative was not merely silence but the unopposed triumph of lying praise published by any paid flatterer. 'Such creatures are not to be reformed; neither is it prudence, or safety to attempt a reformation. Yet, although their memories will *rot*, there may be some benefit for their survivors, to smell it while it is *rotting*.'[2]

'The Problem' deals with Romney as a rake, tracing a parallel between his erotic and flatulent proclivities: three lady admirers try to decide which of them he really loves, through observing which one, by flirting with him, can make his lordship break wind: 'None but the fav'rite nymph can smell it.' The joining of filth and passion is Swiftian; so is the use of a conceit as the formula of the poem—for a systematic analogy is drawn between the effects of lust and the effects of wind. One of the coarsest details of the analogy may reflect Swift's rage over the failure of his schemes for preferment; nothing else in the poem seems to refer to him:

> Besides all this, deep scholars know
> That the main string of Cupid's bow,
> Once on a time, was an arse gut,
> Now to a nobler office put,
> By favour, or desert preferr'd
> From giving passage to a turd.

Other Swiftian points will be familiar by now: viz., the use of bathetic rhymes—

> But still, tho' fixt among the stars,
> Does sympathize with human arse—

and the attempt, not unsuccessful here, at an epigrammatic close.

But there are other features still, which have not been noticed.

---

[1] *Journal*, 9 Sept. 1710.   [2] Davis XII. 25 (*An Answer to a Paper Called A Memorial*).

Among poets of the period the use of mythological allusion
('Jove', 'Cupid's bow') is ubiquitous; in Swift, however, it commonly takes the special form of burlesque, the classical deities
manifesting themselves in very inelegant surroundings. His colloquial rhythm also seems peculiar, for he carries over the patterns of common speech without making them sound empty
('None but the fav'rite nymph can smell it'). Finally, there is his
preoccupation with rhyme as such, his pushing for tricky and far-
fetched jingles, sometimes regardless of their effect in the poem.
Hudibras is notorious—more notorious than it should be—for
such marvels as *whiskers–discourse* and *sparkles–charcoals*.[1] Swift
was eventually to match Butler, and his talent appears here in
ferment–vermin.[2]

I am sorry that most readers feel disturbed and distracted by
the foulness of imagery in many of Swift's lampoons, because I
think filthy material often excites him to produce highly imaginative diversions; and I quote the following couplets as a sample of
what squeamish critics may be missing:

> And now the ladys all are bent,
> To try the great experiment;
> Ambitious of a regent's heart
> Spread all their charms to catch a f - - -;
> Watching the first unsav'ry wind,
> Some ply before and some behind.
> My lord, on fire amidst the dames,
> F - - - s like a laurel in the flames.
> The fair approach the speaking part,
> To try the back-way to his heart;
> For, as when we a gun discharge,
> Altho' the bore be ne'er so large,
> Before the flame from muzzle burst,
> Just at the breech it flashes first:
> So from my lord his passion broke,
> He f - - - ted first, and then he spoke.

Weaker than either of the two poems in couplets is one in tetrameter quatrains rhyming *abab*. This is 'The Discovery', an ineffectual satire upon Berkeley and Bushe. If the lines have any
interest, it must be due to the verse form, as this is the earliest

---

[1] Pp. 109, middle; 116, top.   [2] Both pronounced to rhyme with *garment*.

instance of what was to be a common stanza for Swift's poems—though nothing like so common as the four-beat couplet. The point of the poem is simply that the Lord Justice and his secretary acted, at the court in Dublin Castle, as though they were conferring about highly important business when really they were going over the price of hay and oats. Aimed more at the secretary than the Lord Justice, it gives a not over-coloured portrait of him as a pretentious toady mixing 'new state-airs' with a 'congee circumflex'. The twelve quatrains open and close with Swift's usual effort to work up and then resolve a tension. But neither the language nor the metre has much distinction; and the dull anecdote is too weak to carry the sting which the author intended.

At the opposite limit of Swift's abilities stands his 'Petition of Frances Harris'. Perhaps no poem by him has been more often reprinted, and yet the form is one which he is known to have used on only one other occasion[1]—and then with less success. The 'Petition' is in four-beat, doggerel couplets, from twelve to twenty-four syllables a line. For its story the poem recites in the first person the petition of a waiting-woman employed by Lady Betty, Berkeley's daughter. Through several accidents, Mrs Harris has lost not only her savings but also the hope of marrying his lordship's chaplain (i.e., Swift). So she prays the Lords Justices to help her both replenish her purse and recapture the parson. In line after line Swift draws a good-natured, comical bathos from the speaker's language, using exact, appropriate, but unpredictable rhymes (*bed–maidenhead, Shrewsbury's–gooseberries*). A feature, henceforth characteristic of him, is the proverbial turn of phrase and the idiomatic exclamation: 'just about the time of gooseberries', 'three skips of a louse'. In a scramble of saws and colloquialisms, Swift hits off a dozen personalities below and above stairs, including himself. Of all the beauties in the poem the supreme is Swift's use of vulgar speech patterns, the coarse sententiousness of the semi-literate, for effects which are funny and decorous at once:

> 'Tis not that I value the money three skips of a louse;
> But the thing I stand upon, is the credit of the house.

[1] 'Mary the Cook-Maid's Letter'.

The 'Petition' has a breathless dog-trot motion, suited to the speaker of the monologue. Conversely, the poet has managed to put on the mask of a garrulous female. This use of a mask may account for the poem's good nature and charm. Speaking in his own voice, Swift tends to grow denunciatory. Disguised as a woman, he can sound tolerant and humorous. Swift did not often adopt a true dramatic mask of this sort, whether in verse or in prose. When not saying ironically the exact opposite of what he honestly means, Swift may fill out a pseudonym with a few appropriate traits and then go on to argue as he would without a screen. But for him to create or to mimic a person from within is rare. The 'Petition of Frances Harris' represents one of his best productions in this line.

Under the theme of the poem, nevertheless, we may speculate that there lies an autobiographical allusion. In the spring of 1701, after all, Swift had reached a position to sympathize humorously with the pangs of a woman who had lost a bridegroom. By now he had himself evaded Varina's embrace and was free to arrive at an extra-matrimonial understanding with another young lady, not a waiting woman in the household of Lord Berkeley but one in that of Lady Giffard at Sheen.

II

When Swift had last lingered among the ladies of Sheen and Moor Park, he had been concerned with literary affairs too, though they were neither poetic nor his own. Yet these works supply the first of the few occasions when he willingly set his name upon a title-page; and they conceal a cache of his prose which has never been examined. Even before going over to Ireland from England, Swift had begun to execute Temple's literary trust. Taking himself rather seriously in the face of such a début, he wrote,

> Not knowing how soon I may cross the seas into Ireland, where some concerns are like suddenly to call me; and remembering how near I have been [to] perishing more than once in that passage, I am more unwilling to venture those papers than my self . . .

He added, with somewhat less dignity, that the profit of the publication also attracted him.[1] These remarks, not printed at the time, suggest that the need for haste was thrust on Swift by his acceptance of the chaplainship, although he would naturally have wished to capitalize on the letters' news value by releasing them as soon as possible after Temple's death. But he might still have delayed if another agent had not threatened to undercut his sales with another manuscript. An officer in the English army who claimed to have been involved in negotiations with the great general Louvois suddenly brought out a collection of Temple's letters to Arlington and Trevor. His name was David Jones; his edition appeared before the end of May 1699; and it was advertised as printed from originals in Temple's own handwriting.[2]

Swift had hardly agreed to go to Dublin; but almost at once, in the *Post Boy* and the *Flying Post* for 3 June, his bookseller, Tonson, announced, 'I am directed by the Reverend Mr. Jonathan Swift (to whom Sir William Temple, Baronet, left the care of his writings) to give notice, that with all convenient speed he will publish a collection of letters . . .'[3] Following what became his common procedure, Swift arranged for the two volumes to come out after he would have left the country. Though dated 1700, they were announced for sale on 30 November 1699.[4] The editor took care to identify himself above the imprint as 'Jonathan Swift Domestick Chaplain to his Excellency the Earl of Berkeley, one of the Lords Justices of Ireland'. But the dedication, alas, was directly to his most sacred majesty, with no humbler person named who might have intervened for the King's friend's employee's benefit: 'These letters of Sir W. Temple having been left to my care, they are most humbly presented to Your Majesty

[1] Davis i. xix.

[2] Advertisements of Jones's edition appear in the *Flying Post* and the *Post Man*, 20 May 1699, 'yesterday was published'; later advertisements appear in these newspapers on 3 June. Jones is in the *DNB*. See Alfred F. Robbins, 'Swift and Temple's Letters', *N. & Q.*, 13 Jul. 1907, pp. 21–2.

[3] A similar advertisement appeared in the *London Gazette*, 8 Jun. 1699.

[4] In the *London Gazette*. In the December 1699 number of the *History of the Works of the Learned* there is a full notice of the two volumes. It includes some quotations from Swift's 'Epistle to the Reader' but is otherwise merely a sketch of the contents with extracts.

by Your Majesty's most dutiful and obedient subject.' Even Mr
Jones had the shrewdness to dedicate to Sir Thomas Littleton,
a medium-weight Whig politician.

For obvious reasons Swift was at pains to represent the letters
as authentic and himself as the authorized editor; he reprinted
these facts in the newspaper advertisements, on the title-page, in
the dedication, and in the preface or 'Publisher's Epistle to the
Reader'.[1] In his preface Swift also wrote,

> I found the book among Sir William Temple's papers, with many
> others, wherewith I had the opportunity of being long conversant,
> having passed several years in his family. . . I had begun to fit them
> for the press during the author's life; but never could prevail for
> leave to publish them: Tho' he was pleased to be at the pains of
> reviewing, and to give me his directions for digesting them into
> order. . . He having done me the honour, to leave and recommend
> to me the care of his writings; I thought, I could not at present do a
> greater service to my countrey, or to the author's memory, than
> by making these papers publick . . . I beg the readers pardon for
> any *errata's* which may be in the printing, occasioned by my ab-
> sence.[2]

Besides thus intimating several facts which we have already
gathered, the preface also reveals the most important and hitherto neglected aspect of the two volumes; for Swift makes himself
largely responsible for the translations from Latin and French.[3]

Dozens of such exercises are in the two volumes, and the great
bulk of them being Swift's versions deserve thoughtful appreciation. Not only are they far from literal, but the prose style of
the English ranks in idiomatic refinement with the elegance of
Swift's original letters. Briefly we can say the main tendencies will
startle few readers who are familiar with his works. In general,
and especially where the French or Latin is formally expansive,
Swift leans toward an interpretative précis: thus 'une addresse
recherchée, et des manieres trop etudiées pour etre sincere' becomes 'a great deal of affectation and disguise'.[4] Often whole

---

[1] 'Publisher' here means 'editor'.
[2] Temple, *Letters* I, sigg. A2ᵛ–4; Davis I. 257–9.
[3] 'The few Spanish translations, I believe, need no apology'—a compliment, I
suppose, to Lady Giffard (sig. A2ᵛ; Davis I. 258).
[4] *Ibid.* I. 336.

phrases will drop out.[1] At the same time Swift likes to substitute the force of a verb for an expression which was originally substantive, e.g.,

que le moment de la premiere desunion entre quelqu'un de nos voisins, ou de la plus legere mesintelligence . . .	till we are engaged in a quarrel with our neighbours, or till some misunderstanding happen . . .[2]

Finally, he gives epigrammatic design and power to a sentence which Temple has built around a subdued parallelism or antithesis, e.g.,

dans un siecle comme le nôtre, il y a trop peu de gloire á etre homme de bien, pour s'attirer le soupçon d'avoir tourner ses veues á ce coté lá, et borné sa vanité á si peu de chose.	in this age there is so little honour in being a good man, that none are suspected to employ their vanity about it, any more than their pursuits.[3]

By these means he arrives at a freshness of speech which Temple rarely affords; and in doing so, he keeps to a conception of letter-writing which most men of taste would still recommend, a conception made explicit by Swift in his preface. For there, after some praise of Temple's epistolary style, he indicates what he takes to be the peculiar excellence of letters as judged against other forms of literature: 'Nothing is so capable, of giving a true account of story [i.e., history], as letters are; which describe actions, while they are alive and breathing.'[4] In this view, which exalts the value of letters for the historian, Swift reflects his own practice in the useful, brilliant series of his correspondences with Archbishop King, Charles Ford, and Esther Johnson. Through all of them his effort is to describe actions while they are alive and breathing.

[1] E.g., 'je me garde bien de supposer comme les autres, une feinte en V.E. et de lui attribuer de nous avoir tendu un piege' becomes 'I will not, as others do, impute to your excellency such a *feinte*' (*ibid*. I. 363).

[2] *Ibid*. I. 350.   [3] *Ibid*. II. 300.

[4] Sig. A3; Davis I. 258. A detailed study of these translations has recently appeared: Archibald Irwin, 'Swift as Translator of the French of Sir William Temple', *Studies in English Literature* VI (Rice University, 1966), 483–98.

Chapter Five

THE POLITICS OF TRAVEL

S wift was about to be shipped back to Hetty Johnson by the same piece of machinery that had carried him away from her. If we look once more at the months following Temple's death, we can easily fit both Berkeley and his chaplain into the operations of this machinery. In those days, when Swift crossed St George's Channel in either direction, his movements meant that the vast, clumsy equilibrium of English politics had shifted so as to nudge his small affairs. For fifteen years he would continually have to reckon with the governors of Ireland, regardless of how their notions sat with him. But the parade of these excellencies into and out of Dublin Castle depended on contingencies so remote that the dissatisfied parson could hardly hear of them before he felt their effect. All of what Sir William Temple liked to call the transactions which passed in Christendom had to combine in order that the Reverend Jonathan Swift might be induced to travel from Dublin to London by way of Bristol.

To say this about Swift has further implications than to say it about the hundreds of other ambitious men to whom the remark would seem to apply with equal justice. Not only had he lived next door to the great world. He was going to enter it eventually and to influence it to the point where viceroys would be remembered for having been rebuked by Swift. The rulers of Ireland, the politics of England, and the wars of Europe would become figures in his domestic carpet.

What makes the story ironical is that Swift looked for eminence without foreseeing how it would alter him. In a bitter competition for public money and fame, no contestant can win with only half his emotions. Swift was never to abandon the image of himself as a cool observer of softer men's passions. But until Swift could identify his private feelings with partisan or national issues, he failed to reach the recognition he wanted.

European and national issues became both near to him and tangible in the process by which Lords Justices were named. The admirers of William III wished to help the King use England as the strongest part of an opposition to Louis XIV. If William was to feel unhampered in his schemes to control the French, he needed men he could perfectly rely on in Ireland. But by the time Berkeley's appointment was in view, though the King might trust all of his Lords Justices there, he could rely on only one.

Usually, of course, the crown gave the government of Ireland to a single executive, whether his title was 'Lord Lieutenant', 'Viceroy', or 'Lord Deputy'. Either during the absence of this eminence or during a space when the post was vacant, at least two lesser figures, the 'Lords Justices', would be named. After the blundering term of Henry Sidney (before he became Earl of Romney) and the energetic work of Capel (who died in office), the King left Ireland under a commission of three such officers; so when the court was planning to replace one of these by Swift's patron, there had been no Lord Lieutenant or Deputy since the country parson's farewell to Varina in 1696.

At the new juncture, in the spring of 1699, the effective member of the commission was a French expatriate, Henri de Massue, born to be Marquis de Ruvigny. He belonged to a Huguenot family well known for military and diplomatic honours. Driven into an English exile by the renunciation of the Edict of Nantes, Ruvigny joined his new country's military campaigns and served as a very brave, very modest soldier in both Ireland and Europe; William rewarded him with the title of Earl of Galway and gave him 40,000 acres of Irish land. Yet however visibly his talents had shone in the field, the new Earl made too candid a statesman and too clumsy a speaker (of English) to manage his civilian subordinates. Irish politics called for nimble partisanship while he persisted in straightforward moderation. After two years as a Lord Justice, therefore, Galway found himself still floundering in the undulations of William's policy and Ireland's interest. Swift's notes on the émigré Earl have no validity as portraiture. They

[38]

work rather to demonstrate how savagely the divisions of politics and religion could undermine his judgment. Writing in the margins of another man's description of Galway, Swift—in middle or old age—put down the comments bracketed here, after underlining the words italicized:

Lord Galway, Lieutenant General: is very modest, vigilant, and *sincere*; a man of *honour* and *honesty* . . .   [In all directly otherwise]

[A deceitfull hypocritical factious knave a damnable hypocrite of no religion][1]

Galway was a steady Whig, loyal to his King and sympathetic with the Dissenters. During a war in which Tories both favoured the navy and clamoured for peace, he was to remain an eminent, if often unvictorious, soldier; and one of Swift's heroes, the Earl of Peterborough, was to quarrel cantankerously with him. In his later years he was to be honoured by George I. Swift, who measured out his detestation of the Dissenters, the Whigs, and King George with equal freedom, could see Galway only as an egregious member of an evil tribe.

Another Lord Justice was Edward Villiers, Earl of Jersey, who had little to do with administration beyond meticulously collecting his stipend or fees. Since he was a favourite courtier of the King and an aggressive secular pluralist, Jersey felt no qualms about adding Irish responsibilities to functions which required him to live in England or Holland. The supreme service which he had rendered in return for many pensions was to be born the brother of Elizabeth Villiers, Countess of Orkney. Jersey was handsome, Tory, and not incompetent; but his course would have been less brilliant if Lady Orkney had not spent six years as the King's mistress. (Jesse pays a rather specialized compliment in calling her the only Englishwoman ever selected by William III to be his mistress.[2]) Jersey's protégé, Matthew Prior, enjoyed

---

[1] Davis v. 261.

[2] Cf. Froude's curious analysis: 'This lady's sole claim to consideration lay in her being the daughter of Sir Edward Villiers, Knight Marshal of Charles the Second's

the post of first secretary to the Lords Justices. But he paid a deputy to do the work and never saw Ireland himself.

It was the remaining Lord Justice whom Berkeley replaced: Charles Paulet, Marquis of Winchester. Paulet had exhibited great providence in 1688 by joining the Prince of Orange in Holland. Returning to England with the Prince, he had carried the orb at the coronation. One observer said he made no figure at court—to which Swift added, 'nor anywhere else'.[1] For once a character looks the same to Tory and Whig. Lady Cowper noticed Paulet's habit of lolling his tongue; Thomas Hearne said he was lewd, lying, and bibulous; Swift called him 'a great booby'.[2] Paulet's third marriage gave Irish gossips something to tell England about. According to rumour, while he was journeying to Ireland in order to take office as a Lord Justice, he met 'the blazing star of that kingdom' in the shape of a bastard daughter of the Duke of Monmouth, travelling in the same direction.[3] He fell so far in love with the lady that, to his father's disgust, he felt it necessary to marry her in Dublin.[4] Galway thought he had 'a sound judgment in matters of business',[5] but in the spring of 1699, Paulet's father died; and as the son now became Duke of Bolton, he wished to go home and look after his property.

Of course, by substituting a Berkeley for a Bolton, the King was once more indulging the inborn preference of statesmen for loyalty over brains. A compliant Whig whose reports could be trusted would be more help to an overworked monarch than a self-reliant administrator who might intrigue with the Tories. What the King tried to encourage as policy in Ireland included a toleration of the Roman Catholics, a rapprochement between the Dissenters and the Church of Ireland, and a readiness of the Parliament to fall in with his own plans. It is not odd that he considered any one of these policies reasonable, but it is odd that he thought they could work together; or, rather, it is a sign of his Dutch education. True, events since 1685 had so terrified the

household, and of Lady Villiers, who had been governess to the Princesses Mary and Anne' (I. 223).

[1] Davis v. 258.   [2] *Ibid.*   [3] *SPD. 1697*, p. 293.   [4] *Ibid.*, p. 419.
[5] *SPD. 1699–1700*, p. 225.

Anglican minority in Ireland that they were willing to bow completely under English control sooner than relax their own grip
upon the native Irish. So in exchange for the freedom to inflict a
hideous penal code upon the mass of Papists, the Irish Parliament
—now exclusively Protestant—had given up its fundamental
power, the right to originate money bills. At the same time and
on the same grounds it should have seemed obvious that Protestants of all sects must unite to stand strong against the Papists.
But the English government's control of the Irish Parliament
depended upon the Anglican bishops in the House of Lords; and
naturally the bishops were in no hurry to pull down the wall between Presbyterianism and the Established Church. By tolerat-
ing the Roman Catholics, therefore, his majesty would infuriate
the Protestants; yet by conniving at Dissent, he would alienate
the very episcopacy upon which rested the management of the
country. Furthermore, however enlightened the King might
feel, a harmony of the three Christian sects would scarcely have
eased the manipulation of politicians in Dublin by a minority in
Whitehall. Only by preventing them from acting in unison
could the English impose their will.

That the King should have planted Whigs everywhere is
understandable. They shared his tolerant sympathies and backed
his campaigns. But after the Treaty of Ryswick was signed, their
strength decayed. In common opinion the end of a war meant the
end of an army. Tory leaders made a slogan of this doctrine,
pressing the King so hard that for a time they could dictate to
him. Tired and exasperated, William threatened to retire to
Holland, but at last he met their terms; and among these was a
violent change in Irish affairs, as well as a reduction in all armed
forces. The estates in Ireland which had been forfeited to the
crown during the Williamite wars had amounted to hundreds
of thousands of acres. The King had promised to let Parliament
dispose of these, but Parliament took no action; and at last
the King, using a wholly traditional prerogative, made colossal
grants to such favourites as Galway and Lady Orkney. When the
Tories became mighty, they forced a reconsideration of these
grants to be brought before the House of Commons in England;

but the commissioners of investigation complained that his majesty's officers in Ireland blocked their researches. The Tories supported their commissioners; and soon William underwent the shame of seeing his munificence nullified by a vote to 'resume' the grants. In due time, trustees would be named to arrange the sale of the 'resumed' lands; and these trustees, selected in order to embarrass his majesty, would naturally find themselves at odds with the existing Lords Justices, who now included Berkeley. Of course, the Tory leaders would hardly wish the King's own men to preside over the redistribution of his majesty's own grants; and of course William would have to knuckle under to his belligerent antagonists. 'It will be impossible', he told Galway, 'to continue the commission of the Lords Justices in Ireland, as it is at present.'[1] Berkeley had hardly taken over from Bolton before his own dismissal was in sight. Even now one great Whig minister still held power in England, Lord Somers; but he went out in May 1700. During the autumn new cabinets were planned, and by December it was known that the Lord Lieutenant of Ireland would be Lord Rochester.

Laurence Hyde, Earl of Rochester, was the Queen's uncle and director of the high-church Tories in Parliament; for a while the King was trying the effect of putting him at the head of affairs. As a statesman his peculiar talent was simply to voice unchanging principles, a sort of indolence which often passes for integrity. True, he could also be both a hard worker—'at the Treasury an hour before the rest'—and a cunning manager of other men. But he possessed some tiresome drawbacks: arrogance, habitual explosions of bad temper ('in which he would swear like a cutter'), and an addiction to wine in large quantities.[2] To satisfy his immense vanity, Rochester planned to surround his state entrance into Dublin with regal splendour. Accordingly, he was in no hurry to start out, but prolonged his activities as chief minister in London. Berkeley was recalled; but for caretakers to follow him and Galway, and to precede Rochester, the King had to name other Lords Justices again, a process complicated by one

[1] 11 May 1700 (*Parliamentary History* v. 1222).
[2] Feiling, *The Tory Party*, 1950, p. 191.

nominee's illness. Delay produced delay, keeping Berkeley hanging about in Ireland until April 1701. Consequently, Swift, whose plans turned upon those of his master, had to hover with him for more than three months after Rochester was commissioned.[1] At last, early in April, the retiring officers were free to move. Sailing on 9 April, they took Swift along.[2]

[1] 28 Dec. 1700.
[2] According to the London *Flying Post* of 22 Apr. 1701, Berkeley and Galway sailed on 9 Apr. Swift himself says he accompanied Berkeley (Davis VIII. 119).

Chapter Six

THE *CONTESTS AND DISSENSIONS*

Whenhen the vicar of Laracor reached London, he found
that the new Parliament, sitting since February, was
occupied with a furious pursuit of the beaten King
and the destruction of the King's friends. Since the immediate
course of English politics was now to guide not only Swift's
travels but his writings, it becomes part of his private history;
and in watching him, we watch some of the high dramas of
European diplomacy.

In the late 1690s the main strength of the resistance to Louis
XIV came from the Austrian or 'Imperial' court, the Dutch, and
the English. Although the Treaty of Ryswick had halted a general war, the enemies of France did not expect a megalomaniac
like Louis to lie still, satisfied with what he possessed. What made
their worries especially bitter was the situation in Spain. There
it looked as though the idiot Charles II, dying without an heir,
was going to leave not merely the Spanish possessions in America,
Italy, and the Netherlands, but the throne of Spain as well, to be
snarled over by a pack of hungry claimants. In order to keep such
an uproar from breaking loose, the powers mainly concerned—
the French, the English, and the Dutch—had arrived at a careful
disposition of the various territories; for they agreed to divide up
the Spanish empire by a secret instrument which historians now
call the First Partition Treaty. But this fabrication fell apart
when one of the beneficiaries happened to die. The same powers
were compelled, therefore, to piece together another compact,
also secret, now known as the Second Partition Treaty. They
awarded the crown of Spain, with the Netherlands and the
American colonies, to the Archduke Charles, second son of the
Austrian emperor; and they assigned the Italian possessions

mainly to the King of France, except that the Duke of Lorraine would get the Milanese and would in exchange turn his own duchy of Lorraine over to the French. The fulfilment of this diplomats' daydream was never likely; and anyhow the Archduke's father refused to put his name to it, hoping, with simple Habsburg greed, that the whole of Spain and her empire would fall to his own family. The court of Madrid, however, felt inclined to participate in the destiny of their own nation. So while their disintegrating King—who had sometimes laid himself in his own coffin—was finally consenting to die in fact, his ministers worked upon his superstition until he made a will designed to send all of western Europe to war; for it not only kept the whole empire intact but, taking it all away from the candidate of the Second Partition Treaty, laid it undiminished in the lap of the French King's second grandson, Philip, Duke of Anjou. Europe was thus presented with two new kings of Spain, a Habsburg 'Charles III' and a Bourbon 'Philip V'.

To the inflamed House of Commons no provision of the Partition treaties—since neither of the schemes ever came into effect—meant so much as the manner of their conception. True, international treaties came under the King's acknowledged prerogative. Nevertheless, in both these agreements the secrecy preserved had been so radical as to look like treason. Or, putting subtlety aside, we may say that the King had trusted none of his English ministers but had negotiated through those foreign confidants who were his old friends. Even when the articles were settled, he had shared them only with the innermost circle of his Whig supporters, and then only to demand their acquiescence, so that the ministers necessarily involved had acted without the knowledge of the King's Tory enemies. Not only Parliament but the Privy Council had remained outside the circle of light. Somers, the canniest of the Whigs, had not approved of the second treaty; but acting as Lord Chancellor, he had rashly attached the great seal to it. In drawing up the first treaty, Somers had behaved with even less care, for he had set the seal to a commission in which the names of the negotiators were not yet specified.

[45]

While Swift was on his way to England, the high-churchmen in Parliament were pushing hard with these facts in order to upset the court faction. Led by Sir Edward Seymour in all his arrogance, and by the virulent John Grubham Howe, they insisted on impeaching Somers and three other lords whom they accused of arranging the Partition treaties without keeping Parliament informed. 'Jack' Howe himself had begun William's reign by working with the loyal courtier Whigs, but he had soon found it expedient to become a lead horse for the opposition Tories. This opposition, however, was diverse, and included a troop of 'country' Tories who showed rather less fury than their high-church comrades. Led by a sometime Presbyterian, Robert Harley, and his young lieutenant, Henry St John, these quieter men really tried to hold off the impeachment proceedings. Even though Harley was Speaker of the House, however, his following had to give way as Seymour and Howe, waved on by Rochester and Nottingham in the Lords, refused to silence their baying hounds.

When Swift at last ended his journey in London, he found the frenzied atmosphere startling. As an Irish Protestant of English extraction, an Anglican priest, and a sufferer from the Troubles caused by the Jacobites, he could only align himself with 'old Whig' principles: the conservative defence of the constitution as laid down in 1688 and elaborated since by the Act of Settlement. Jacobitism seemed absurd to him, and he was coming to regard it as more absurd than dangerous. But mob rule really frightened him, as it would have frightened anyone nursed on anecdotes of the 1641 rebellion. The turncoat Howe's appeals to an inflammable rabble outside Parliament must have reminded Swift of Tyrconnel's lying opportunism in 1688. After many years' service with Temple, the King's own friend, and a short term of service with Berkeley—to whom a knave of any suit looked like Jack Howe—Swift could not approve of the Commons' reckless violence. He put aside some historical researches he had been working on, and turned his indignation into an anonymous pamphlet.[1] If he opposed the impeachments, however, it was less for

[1] For Swift's account of the composition of the book, see Davis VIII. 119; V. 11–12.

the sake of either side than in the name of national unity behind the King. With this as his cardinal doctrine Swift worked through the summer of 1701 to compose a defence of the four lords, in a book published that autumn under the title *A Discourse of the Contests and Dissensions between the Nobles and the Commons in Athens and Rome*.[1]

There is some evidence that Swift wrote the *Discourse* in two instalments. Although it consists of five chapters, the fourth reads like a terminus, and I suspect that he originally stopped here, adding the last chapter later. If this is so, the change in tone between the first four and the last makes sense; for those sound as if the crisis were still impending, while the last explicitly remarks that the proceedings have been interrupted. The main topics of the earlier chapters are the impeachments and the separate but simultaneous constitutional struggle between the Commons and the Lords. The main topic of the last chapter is the menace of political parties as such.

The opening chapter of the book is on the balance of power within a state; the next gives illustrations of unhappy impeachments from Athenian history; the third offers more examples, from Roman history, of power struggles between nobles and commoners; the fourth returns to the balance of power, draws conclusions from the Greek and Roman examples, and ends with an elegiac figure of speech. Here the author evidently felt he was done. In the fifth chapter, therefore, he seems to treat the earlier parts as a finished discourse and the new one as an addendum. He consciously recalls propositions already stated but introduces a fresh theme as well, the danger to the national constitution from political parties. Similarly, he fulminates against two heretofore unmentioned political leaders, Clodius and Curio, who are probably Seymour and either Howe or Charles Davenant.

If Swift did write the *Discourse* in two instalments, the reason must be that the original conception was left behind by the train

[1] Published around mid-October 1701. The earliest advertisement I have seen is in the *Post Boy*, 21 Oct.; the price when mentioned in the newspapers is 1s. The book is listed in the *Term Catalogues* for Nov. 1701 (III. 276); here the price is 4s., the format 4to. Advertisements can be found at least as late as Jan. 1702.

of events. He afterwards intimated that he composed his arguments 'in a few weeks', while the squall was at its gustiest.[1] But
near the end of the whole he refers to a 'present lucid interval'[2]
which from its context must mean the period between the close of
the session (24 June) and the news that Parliament was not to be
prorogued but altogether dissolved. I think we may assume that
Swift tried to make his pamphlet ready while the impeachments
hung fire. The finish of the session, however, meant the collapse
of the proceedings. It was not in Swift's character to waste a piece
of writing once he had composed it. So he tacked on Chapter
Five and gave the entire work a current significance.

II

In rhetorical genre the *Discourse* seems an example of 'parallel
history', a common method of evading censorship or of teaching
by indirection. The principle goes back to the dawn of historio-
graphy and flourished during the Renaissance. In its subtle
form it meant the deliberate cooking of a biography or history so
as to imply doctrines subversive of established beliefs; this is the
method of Bayle's *Dictionary*. For Swift's *Discourse*, however, the
model was less likely to be Bayle than a not so daring effort by
Temple, whose life of William I, in his *Introduction to the History of
England*, was obviously designed to reconcile the English to the
rule of William III.

In its humblest form 'parallel history' was merely the reprinting of a historical work in circumstances which made the affairs
related seem parallel to recent events, as, for example, the re-
appearance of Sir John Temple's *Irish Rebellion* at the time of the
Popish Plot. This device Swift also imitated in 1701, by bringing
out as the first piece in a volume of Sir William Temple's works an
old unpublished essay by Sir William which had clear relevance
to the parliamentary crisis. The essay, *Of Popular Discontents*,
though never printed before, had been conceived during the
Exclusion controversy with Shaftesbury as a central figure. Now

---

[1] Davis VIII. 119.   [2] *Ibid.* I. 234-5.

of course it bore upon the impeachments crisis, with Howe and Seymour in Achitophel's seat.

Swift's opinions were thus under not the remote but the direct influence of Temple's; for it is while he was actually writing his own book that he also sent to the press the new volume by his late patron, *Miscellanea. The Third Part*.[1] In this we should expect the opening essay, dealing as it does with the very material of Swift's study, to affect his fundamental arguments[2]; and we do discover that *Of Popular Discontents* grows out of the same preoccupations which dominate not only the *Discourse* but also the *Tale of a Tub*. These preoccupations, an expression of the deepest sympathy between the two men, appear in Temple's analysis of the ultimate cause of uprisings of any sort within a state. Such 'popular discontents', whether riot, rebellion, or civil war, Temple finally traces, as Swift does, to an essential ingredient of human nature, described by Temple as 'a certain restlessness of mind and thought'. It leaves us dissatisfied with what we can at any time possess and enjoy; it makes us rave constantly after what is not at hand. Such restless ambition, says Temple, is the origin of faction, sedition, and 'fatal revolutions'.

To Swift, like Temple, the final source of dissension within a state is not a social pattern or a multiple cause but a single constituent of individual human nature. For Temple's vaguer formulation, however, Swift substitutes the irrational 'spirit of opposition' which in *A Tale of a Tub* he identifies with enthusiasm. That the same general principle is in both men's minds seems borne out by the imagery in which they express it and the conclusions to which they carry it. From this *fountain* and *spring*, says Temple, issue those *streams* of faction which at last overflow governments and laws.[3] It is from the *fountains* and *spring* of enthusiasm, says Swift, that those *streams* proceed which break forth at last in military conquests and fanatical sects.[4]

[1] Entered in the *Stationers' Register*, 28 July 1701. I have seen only two advertisements, in broken runs of newspapers: *London Gazette*, 16 Oct., and *Post Man*, 21 Oct. Both advertisements are based on the title-page of the book.

[2] See Robert J. Allen, 'Swift's Earliest Political Tract and Sir William Temple's Essays', in *Harvard Studies and Notes in Philology and Literature* xix (1937), 3–12.

[3] *Miscellanea* iii. 10, 36.   [4] Davis i. 107.

At the climax of the 'Digression on Madness' Swift had said that the brain, in its natural condition, disposes its owner to pass his life in 'common forms'; and the more he shapes his understanding by the pattern of human learning, the less he is inclined to 'form parties, after his particular notions'.[1] 'Parties' here can mean either alliances for military conquest, schools of metaphysical thought, or sects of religious belief (so long as these are schismatic); for what is rational is the common inheritance of mankind, and the adherent of established truth has no need to make or to follow a party. In politics the same rule holds: if a man's arguments are sound and *pro bono publico*, they will convince all responsible listeners. To form a party or to appeal to party loyalty, therefore, is to expose oneself as irrational.

At the same time, we must recollect, an irrational restlessness, or spirit of opposition,[2] or 'enthusiasm', seems to Swift as to Temple a distinguishing trait of human nature. In *The Mechanical Operation of the Spirit* the author says he remembers no other temper of body or quality of mind in which all nations have 'so unanimously agreed'.[3] In *An Argument against Abolishing Christianity* Swift calls it 'one darling inclination of mankind'.[4] In *Gulliver* he calls it 'the same disease, to which the whole race of mankind is subject'.[5] It is such a germ that the party leader must cultivate.

If this is the great axiom of Swift's political philosophy, it cannot be said to reveal a deep understanding of how institutions evolve. By identifying the right course of action only as the obvious, established course, Swift gives us no clue for recognizing it ahead of time; and people differ bitterly as to what is either obvious or customary. By stigmatizing the wrong course as eccentric or irrational, he supplies us not with a logical analysis but with a means of ridicule. Furthermore, to limit oneself to the advocacy of self-evident truths, the common consent of mankind, is to isolate oneself—as Swift regularly did—from the most profound intellectual transactions of one's time; and these are the forces ultimately responsible for self-evident truths.

[1] *Tale*, p. 171.   [2] Davis II. 34.   [3] *Tale*, p. 266.   [4] Davis II. 34.
[5] *Ibid*. XI. 122.

Nevertheless, what would mean loss for the philosopher is gain for the polemicist. Any pamphleteer who holds privately to the view that the science of government is a simple matter of 'nothing but common sense'[1] will find himself powerfully driven and powerfully equipped to destroy the logic of his political antagonists. Not only the young priest but the elderly dean believed that 'God has given the bulk of mankind a capacity to understand reason when it is fairly offered; and by reason they would easily be governed, if it were left to their choice.'[2] In *A Discourse of the Contests and Dissensions* he uses the doctrine to scold the Tories. A few years afterwards he will be using it to undermine the Whigs. Never, alas, can it tell one which of two alternatives should be taken, since the decision must be made before the doctrine can be invoked. Yet by employing it as his invariable slogan, Swift forced himself always to treat the phenomenon of parties as unreal: 'The species of folly and vice', he says, 'are infinite, and so different in every individual, that they could never procure a majority, if other corruptions did not enter to pervert men's understandings, and misguide their wills.'[3] When Swift supported what we might call a side, he had to assert that it was the whole. With no exception his political essays ground themselves on the proposition that whereas he speaks for the nation, his opponents speak for negligible, contentious, tiny factions that refuse to control what Temple would describe as their 'restlessness of mind and thought'. By not only tracing this 'spirit of opposition' to essential human nature but also defining it as irrational, Swift justifies himself for not trying to see his enemy's point of view: it would after all be absurd for a wise man to look for sense in a fool's case.

Unfortunately, if one follows such postulates a short distance farther, one sinks into an apparent self-contradiction. Irrational,

---

[1] *Ibid.* viii. 77. Cf. *Gulliver's Travels*, Pt iv, Ch. viii; also Davis viii. 138: 'sufficiently obvious to common capacities'; also *ibid.*, p. 139: 'diligence, honesty, and a moderate share of plain naturall sense'.

[2] *Some Free Thoughts*, in Davis viii. 77. Cf. *Gulliver's Travels*, Pt iv, Ch. viii. Cf. also, in the *Discourse of the Contests and Dissensions*: 'This must be said in behalf of human kind; that common sense, and plain reason, while men are disengaged from acquired opinions, will ever have some influence upon their minds' (Davis i. 232).

[3] Davis i. 232.

restless, petty factionalism seems rooted in our kind; so also seems
the desire to be governed by reason. Is it simply caprice that
determines which of the two instincts shall prevail? No, says
Swift. The central tendency, the harmonious striving of the various bodies which make up the community, is the essential and
rightful direction: 'the universal bent and current of a people;
not the bare majority of a few representatives'.[1] If he is right,
however, the universal current contradicts the 'one darling
inclination of mankind'; and how both can operate inexorably
without annihilating one another, he never explains. Of course,
it is the sober reformer who dwells upon our 'capacity to understand reason' and the bitter satirist who laments the disease 'to
which the whole race of mankind is subject'.[2] So long as Swift
prevents the two from meeting, he need not reconcile them.

III

Trying to bring out the absolute, real nature of the equilibrium
underlying the English constitution, Swift occasionally resorts to
metaphors from mechanics. In Chapter One there is an elaborate picture of Commons, Lords, and King as a pair of scales with
their fulcrum. In Chapter Five there is a picture of the Commons
as an over-extended pair of compasses. Such images, however,
are either unconvincing or peripheral; and they rarely occur
in the *Discourse*. Like his own contemporaries and like Temple,
Swift draws his common, effective imagery from animal nature
and from landscape. When Sir William speaks of the state as a
carriage with four wheels, or as a ship in a mechanical sense, he
appears self-conscious and forced. When he treats the state as a
stream, a plant, a man, or a ship's crew, he is at ease. Restless
ambition is a weed, says Temple; factious parties are rats; a public registry is a fruit.[3] To Swift a deceived populace is like mind-
less silkworms; Louis XIV is a vulture; party followers are sheep.[4]
The beast figures are notably more common in Swift's work than
in his master's, and his imagery always seems more incisive,

---

[1] Davis I. 225.   [2] *Ibid.* XI. 122.   [3] *Miscellanea* III. 10, 36, 58.
[4] Davis I. 227, 229, 232–3.

less commonplace, applied in wittier turns of mind or language.

Yet the fundamental image used by both men is precisely the same. It reflects old, impotent thinking; it implies a complacent acceptance of dubious assumptions. This is the image of the state as a man, civil dissension as illness, the political theorist as a physician. Cliché invites cliché while the microcosm–macrocosm releases its inevitable association of ideas: the fever of rebellion, the death of the constitution, purges, humours, symptoms, and the rest. Swift even lowers himself to invoking the fable of the belly and the members. That Davenant, a high-church propagandist widely read by Tories, should serve up this bowl of chestnuts seems proper; for he is writing as a hack, paid to echo the voice of his owners. But when Swift, a free agent, resorts to obvious figures in obvious ways, we must presume that he has little power of original thought on the science of government. In this conclusion we are justified. Although he conceived of himself as a man of steady, rational principles in politics, his integrity was not on the level of ideas. He felt loyal to specific men or to institutions like his own church, but he voiced his loyalties in the words of recognized, conventional propositions.

Here, however, is one of those places where the thinker's loss is the writer's advantage. To treat kings as fathers and nations as families, war loans as butchers' bills, and cabinets as household staff brings political economy right down to the fender and allows every fireside orator to imagine himself a Grotius. Yet when Swift makes his unique power felt, it is not in these terms but in the manipulation or reversal of such ordinary devices. On the conceptual level he does this when he associates not the Whigs but the Tories with mob rule, or when he uses 'balance of power' for an internal rather than external equilibrium. In his use of parallel history he does so when he suddenly breaks through the indirect allusiveness of his remote, general parallels and employs not a historic Greek leader but a classicized pseudonym to point directly at a recognizable Englishman: i.e., not when he treats the ancient Aristides as Somers because their careers were alike,[1] but when, having accustomed us to such

---

[1] 'Aristides' for Somers may have been commonplace.

indirect analogies, he suddenly calls Seymour Clodius merely because of a phrase in Plutarch (*Pompey*, 46). By suddenly giving a
new turn to a figure which he had himself been using conventionally, he lends life to his rhetoric. Thus 'Athens' appears repeatedly
as equivalent to all England; but suddenly Swift introduces a
quotation from Polybius which has meaning in context only if
'Athens' is the House of Commons and 'Greece' is England. This
bold shift occurs dramatically at the end of a chapter; and the
effect is of the author narrowing the direction of his appeal from
the country at large to the Commons in particular.[1]

IV

The positive argument of Swift's pamphlet is based on the idea of
a balance of power within the state. This is probably his answer
to arguments from the other side based on the idea of a balance of
power among various states. Thus Charles Davenant (an uncle
of Swift's cousin Thomas, and a spokesman for the Seymour–
Howe gang) published an anonymous volume of *Essays* (1701) in
which the first section was devoted to 'the balance of power',
here interpreted to mean a traditional policy by which England
prevented any European nation—above all, the French or the
Spanish—from growing supreme. Davenant followed the history
of this policy with particular praise for Elizabeth, whose holding
of the balance between Spain and France made England 'safe
and happy during her time'[2]; and he argued that the Second
Partition Treaty threatened to upset the balance by strengthening Louis XIV.[3]

In opposing Davenant, Swift treats of an internal equilibrium
which corresponds to the external relationship; he surveys the
history of that equilibrium in Davenant's manner, with special
praise again for Elizabeth; and he draws an elaborate parallel

[1] Davis I. 210.   [2] Davenant, p. 9.

[3] He revealed a violently high-church orientation, asking whether many churchmen had not risen to places of the highest trust thanks to 'the open enmity which they
have, almost from their cradles, professed to the divinity of Christ?' A complaint
was lodged against this book in the Upper House of Convocation, countering the
heresy hunt of the Lower House, aimed against Burnet and other Latitudinarians
(Every, p. 96). See further F. H. Ellis's edition of Swift's *Discourse* (Oxford, 1967).

between the two concepts.[1] But while Swift may call his idea a balance of power,[2] it is in fact the notion of 'mixed government', derived from antiquity, though particularly attached by him to 'Gothic' institutions. This is the doctrine that the constitution which allows the most freedom consistent with a rule of law is one in which sovereignty resides in the whole people but administration is tripartite, or divided among the King, the Lords, and the Commons.

As recently as 1683 the doctrine that the three estates rule together in King, Lords, and Commons had been condemned as damnable by the Convocation of Oxford University. During the trial of the seven bishops five years later, however, the desirability of tripartite government was assumed by the defence counsel, which included both Somers and Heneage Finch (Daniel's brother). In the Convention Parliament the next year it was common to hear the constitution of England praised as a mixed form; and by the time of the trial of Sacheverell, 1709–10, the doctrine was to be expounded by Harcourt, whom both Tories and Whigs were eventually to honour with peerages but who was identified with the Tories from 1709 to 1714. In other words, Swift, writing in 1701, might remember that before the accession of James II the high-church royalist Tories had denounced this doctrine, and he might himself link it to Somers and the 'old' Whigs. Ten years afterwards, however, it would also belong to Harley's 'Tory' coalition of country and church parties.[3]

The remaining postulates of the *Discourse* Swift would have met in Temple's writings, however easily he might also have picked them up elsewhere. Like Sir William, he distrusted all innovation, wishing as far as possible to cling to the constitution established in 1688 to 1690. Like him he feared the common people, regarding an appeal to them as an appeal to chaos. Like him he loathed factionalism and the operation of political parties. Like him he regarded the naval (rather than land) forces as the 'true and constant interest' of England.[4]

Unlike his master, however, Swift owes his anxieties to the

---

[1] Davis i. 202–3.
[2] For a direct allusion to Davenant on this subject, see *ibid.*, p. 200.
[3] Cf. Clark, pp. 246–7. [4] Davis i. 207.

House of Commons. Where Temple had argued against the Lords' extending their power of judicature and had prophesied a collision of the two houses if this proceeded, Swift thought the Commons, overreaching themselves with impeachments and 'tacks', were creating the crisis of 1701. Yet behind this divergence there lay again a still deeper sympathy. It was not the Commons as such that Swift meant to chastise but those leaders who, instead of swaying the other members through appeals to reason, were coercing them either by emotional outbursts or by beating up the excitable mass of people outside Parliament.

In Chapter Three he is not against the populace for liking Tories but against the Tories' hunger for popularity. As he goes over the successive Roman constitutions, he measures their decay by the level of plebeian authority. He makes a show of studying impartially the contests for power between the patricians and the many. In fact, his examples are all of the commons turning greedy and destroying liberty. In Chapter Four, when he finds fault with the whole concept of impeachment, it is not for its injustice but for its unvarying effect of handing sovereignty to the mob.

But if Swift, like Temple, poured vitriol upon the face of *mobile vulgus*, it is no paradox that he none the less believed in 'the body of the people' as the vessel of a nation's sovereignty.[1] He first meant, like Temple, that a government needs effectual support in order to exist at all. He also meant that the three orders of the nation must operate together—Commons, Lords, and King—for the government to be just. A hegemony of Commons over Lords, even though the former represented the vast majority in the nation, would mean tyranny in the form of a *dominatio plebis*. Furthermore, by Swift's reasoning, the ideal electorate must be far more exclusive than the whole body of subjects; for in it ought to be counted only those men who through the very nature of their estates had strong motives to keep the country flourishing.

What obsessed Swift was not the strength but the fragility of the tripartite equilibrium. Like most political theorists of the time, he overlooked the feasibility of a shifting but healthy state, always in evolution. Great changes, he admitted, might indeed be made in a government without overthrowing the balance of

[1] Davis I. 196.

[56]

power; but 'large intervals of time' must pass after any innovation, 'enough to melt down, and make it of a piece with the constitution'.[1] And anyhow the perils of innovation troubled him so that the admission of its possibility is only a faint squeak among the trumpet tones of more direful warnings. Swift took it for granted that if political power were properly reduced to system, the outcome would be an engine steady as a clock, that wanted correction, repair, and fuelling but never a new design. The Revolution had perfected England's engine; later generations were committed to preserve it.

He now saw little threat to this constitution from the crown or the nobility. But a Dissenting rabble had butchered Charles I, vandalized the Church, and destroyed the monarchy. An Irish Catholic mob had exiled its own landlords, brought back James II, established popery, and driven Swift to England. These forces were as ready as ever for upheaval. 'The people are much more dextrous at pulling down, and setting up', said Swift, 'than at preserving what is fixed.'[2] Here he is neither anti-Tory nor pro-Whig but aboveeither. His fifth chapter he closes with a slashing condemnation of all parties, claiming that to keep good, landed men of family in high places, even bribery is safer than popularity.[3]

To condemn all parties might ring to a modern ear like high-minded patriotism; it might in any age be interpreted as neutrality. Of course, if non-partisanship were indeed the mark of a specific faction, the plea might tie the pleader to its members. But such a motto could never mean support for a political body which actively worked as a party and had the reputation of putting its own success ahead of the nation's welfare.

Yet this was the case of the Junto. Sunderland, Wharton, Somers, Halifax, and Orford indisputably formed a mutual aid society. 'They lost no opportunity of pressing each other's claims to office, and one by one they gained it.'[4] The 'country' party,

---

[1] *Ibid.*, p. 202.   [2] *Ibid.*, p. 219.

[3] This is probably in answer to Davenant's accusation that the Whigs had undermined liberty by their use of bribery in the election of 1700 (Davenant, pp. 45–8). Swift deleted his defence of bribery from the text of the *Discourse* included in his 1711 *Miscellanies* (Davis I. 301–2).

[4] Clark, p. 215.

ancestor of Harley's Tories, was congenitally unstable. The Tories by tradition possessed little in the way of political theory. The Jacobites, who could openly participate in government only as Tories, had of course a distinct philosophy, but this was hardly for public display. 'Down with parties' in 1701 could not mean 'up the Whigs', but it could mean 'down with new Whig practices'. During the election of that year it was not the Tories but the Whigs whose constituencies bound their members to vote with a Junto, and it was the Tories who resisted the radical view of Parliament as subordinate to the electorate.[1] In denouncing Seymour, Davenant, and Howe, therefore, Swift was in a sense scolding the Tories for behaving like 'new' Whigs.[2]

Unlike most critics of the impeachments, therefore, Swift did not attack Tory principles, praise the opposition, eulogize the Whigs, or prostrate himself before the King. He showed that the men under fire were eminent for their statesmanship and that William deserved some concessions as well as much gratitude. In tone his *Discourse* sounds dignified, almost condescending; for a novice, unwarped by years of wasted zeal, can more easily afford the grace of unambiguous serenity than the practised, embittered master. Oppression makes a wise man mad; so middle age was to colour Swift's language with a fury barely adumbrated in this *Discourse*.

It is hard to suppose that Swift did not intend his book as a service to the party of the impeached lords. So I assume that he expected it to strengthen his claim to preferment. A glance at the work either of other men who succeeded in such aims or of Swift himself when spokesmen for a ministry, will reveal how improbable it was that the Junto should feel indebted to the author of his *Discourse*. What they wanted was an unambiguous assertion that they were right and their enemies all wrong. What they got was a statement of general laws according to which they might be on the right side in this case but would very likely be wrong in the next.

[1] Clark, p. 191.
[2] William King, then Bishop of Derry, said, 'I perceive the Whigs go down, but it's by the Tories' outdoing them in Whiggery' (letter of 25 Apr. 1701, to Thomas Lindsay; my spelling, etc.).

Chapter Seven

HISTORICAL SKETCHES

W hen Swift moves from dignity to intensity, from ancient to current, and from parallels to pseudonyms, he
is changing roles; for it is the historian who has the
mild voice and the satirist who has the sharp. The *Discourse*,
though a pamphlet with a thesis, also embodies generalizations
which its author drew from a systematic study of the English past.
It represents in a transitional form his abiding wish to be an
historian; and it bears traces of those attempts at a great work
on the evolution of England which the *Discourse* itself had interrupted.

The strength and endurance of this wish in a man whose
genius operated against it suggests that the appeal of the goal to
Swift was deeply emotional. There is evidence enough that he
would have liked to belong to England rather than to Ireland. By
a minute knowledge of his adopted land's past, he could attach
himself to the nation of his forebears. By placing an unusually
high value on such knowledge, he could make himself out to be
more native than the aborigines. In producing a history of the
country, he would establish his racial genealogy. Perhaps there
is significance in the fact that after his patron's death, while Swift
was in Ireland, and during the wait before a return to the kingdom of his choice, he busied himself with such researches.[1]

Yet there were impersonal reasons that Swift should have
offered large tribute to Clio. During his life the prestige of historical scholarship reached a height which had an inverse relationship to the reputation of English historians. Never had the
subject seemed more estimable or the writers less worthy. During
the seventeenth century the appreciation of such studies rose

[1] Davis v. 11; viii. 119.

abruptly while statesmen, lawyers, and priests looked for data to strengthen them in dynastic contests or religious disputes. If the medieval polemicist grounded himself on principle, his successor appealed to history.[1] The span of Swift's life was almost co-terminous with the 'most prolific movement of historical scholarship' ever seen in England.[2]

Meanwhile, however, Bacon's lament on the unworthiness of English historians[3] was repeated by Savile, Selden, and others[4]: the English translator of Lemoyne said (1695), 'We neither know how to write nor to judge of history'[5]; Sir William Temple said he had often complained that his nation, 'so adorned by excellent writers in other kinds, should not yet have produced one good or approved general history of England'.[6] Into the next century the cry went on. 'Our histories are gazettes', says Bolingbroke (1723), 'ill digested, and worse writ.'[7] The young Voltaire, moderating his anglophilia, says, 'Pour de bons historiens [sc. anglais] je ne leur en connois pas encore. Il a fallu qu'un français ait écrit leur histoire.'[8] Hume, in mid-eighteenth century still despairs: 'There is no post of honour in the English Parnassus more vacant than that of history.'[9] And when at last we arrive at Gibbon, we find him inspired not by a compatriot but by Montesquieu.[10]

If we assume that Swift had unconscious reasons for wishing to be an historian and Temple encouraged this desire, if men of taste set history near the top of the hierarchy of genres but regarded English letters as peculiarly defective in this article, we shall not

[1] G. P. Gooch, *History and Historians*, 1952, p. 3.

[2] D. C. Douglas, *English Scholars*, 1939, p. 13.

[3] *Advancement of Learning*, Bk II (ed. Aldis Wright, pp. 92–5).

[4] See D. Nichol Smith, introduction to *Characters . . . of the Seventeenth Century* (1920), pp. x–xviii.

[5] 'To the Reader', by the translator of Pierre Lemoyne, *Of the Art Both of Writing and Judging of History*, 1695, sig. A2ᵛ.

[6] *Introduction to the History of England*, 1695, sig. A2. Temple gives a detailed outline of a collaborative history of England in a letter of February 1694/5, dictated to Thomas Swift; but while the contents reveal the strength of his desire to see a comprehensive work produced, they include little in the way of theory: see *Letters by Several Eminent Persons Deceased. Including . . . John Hughes*, 1772, I. 1–8.

[7] Sherburn II. 220. Cf. Addison, *Freeholder* 35; Johnson, *Rambler* 122.

[8] *Lettres . . . sur les anglois*, Basle, 1734, pp. 200–1. (Rapin de Thoyras is presumably the French historian of England.)

[9] *Letters*, ed. Greig, 1932, I. 179.   [10] *Memoirs*, ed. G. B. Hill, 1900, p. 96.

be surprised that Swift undertook to supply the want. Exactly how he thought one should go about the work, we may begin to infer from his *ex post facto* statement of intention: he had meant, Swift said, to write 'an exact relation of the most important affairs and events, without any regard to the rest'.[1] Now which, according to Swift, were the most important affairs?

Two separate fragments suggest the answer. The shorter one he called 'An Abstract of the History of England, from the Invasion of It by Julius Caesar to William the Conqueror'. This occupies only four or five pages in a modern edition of his prose. In composing it, Swift did little more than condense drastically the pre-Norman section of Temple's *Introduction*, emending the précis from Temple's own chief source, the *Collection of the History of England* by Samuel Daniel.[2] The other fragment of an English history by Swift is much bulkier, making more than twice the length of the *Battle of the Books*. He had been composing it when the business of the impeachments had driven him to write *The Contests and Dissensions*.[3] As far as he got, the material of the large fragment gives accounts of the reigns of William II, Henry I, Stephen, and Henry II. For these accounts Swift relied mainly upon Holinshed, Daniel, and Baker's *Chronicle*. But he also drew upon an impressive range of medieval or later texts. For instance, his derivation of the term 'War of the Standard' belongs to the *Historia Ricardi Hagustaldensis*; and his character of Henry II is largely out of Polydore Vergil.

The connection of both fragments with Temple's *Introduction* has a special meaning; for although that work ends with the death of William I, only a quarter of it is spent on the centuries before the Conquest. Swift brings his 'Abstract' up to 1066 and starts his 'Reigns' with William II. Evidently he meant to depend upon Temple for the era of the Conqueror. In selecting his materials, moreover, or judging which were 'the most important

---

[1] Davis v. 11.

[2] Both books were in Swift's library, and Swift was the amanuensis for the *Introduction*. See my 'Swift's History of England', in *JEGP*. LI (1952), 177–85, for these and other facts relating to the two fragments of a history.

[3] Davis v. 11. Swift says he wrote the 'Reigns' 'about sixteen years' before 1719. Since his dating is rarely trustworthy, I assume that he erred by two or three years.

affairs', Swift displays a bias somewhat similar to his master's. Thus he plays down church affairs and seems generally more dubious than his monkish sources in regard to the motives or ambitions of worldly clerics. I attribute these leanings to his disrespect for popery and his distrust of monastic annalists. Toward kings Swift tends to feel kindly, extenuating their faults, enhancing their physical appearance, and magnifying their virtues. Military actions clearly bored him: he either telescopes or eliminates the many battles which one finds painstakingly recounted by the chroniclers. Gallantry, amours, meant less to Swift than to Temple. Erotic episodes in royal or aristocratic careers he tends to avoid, though he never fails to censure lust or other vices in general terms, wherever the facts appear.

But one subject seems endlessly fascinating to him: this is the growth of the English constitution. In the 'Reigns' he announces that the progress of representative councils will be his peculiar concern; and he tries, within each reign, to review systematically the advance of parliamentary government. Indeed, a lengthy paragraph on the subject is to be seen, with large changes, taken from one of these fragments and distributed through the discussion of mixed government in *The Contests and Dissensions*.[1]

Such tastes reflect a philosophy of history. If a medieval chronicler had purposes, these were mainly to show God as first cause acting on the sublunary stage of mortal life and to expose the odiousness of sin or felicity of virtue as shown in human fate. They also tried to strengthen the authority of rulers through examples which discouraged rebellion; and they would often display typologically in early events the foreshadows of things to come later. Renaissance scholars invoked another doctrine, and this Swift inherited. For them the great value of history was to instruct the prince. Philosophy, teaching by example, had rulers as her pupils. In Swift's day these had dwindled to the level of gentlemen likely to enter Parliament or to become magistrates and army officers. But Henry Dodwell, in the 1690s, still treats history as a study for lawmakers, 'more useful for *gentlemen* than *scholars*'; and he extends himself to show its use in politics and

[1] Cf. Davis v. 36–8 and i. 195–7, 199–200.

war.[1] God as first cause has grown too remote for sublunary study; men as second causes take his place. The miracles and disasters—comets, plagues, and fires—which, as God's judgments, had delighted the monks, Sir William Temple utterly excludes from his *Introduction,* as mere 'accidents of time or chance' and therefore of no service for that example and instruction to posterity which constitute the 'great ends of history'.[2] With Machiavelli, Bodin, and Bacon, the searchable motives of kings had come to replace the will of God. Yet the strengthening of authority remained supremely important. Consequently, the use of an absolute moral judgment has now to be suspended; for we study not the good or bad in princes but the how and why of their deeds. In place of the prophetic 'typology' of persons and actions, we now see almost the reverse, viz., parallel history.

All great turns in public affairs may be derived, said Temple, from the nature of the men who 'conduct and govern them'.[3] With this Swift firmly agreed. Therefore, he looked upon history as a study of individual men. In handling Norman times, he shows the deepest concern with the characters and conduct of the monarchs and the chief nobles or churchmen. At the end of each reign he mounts a full portrait of the deceased king: his appearance, his ambitions, his defects and vices, his talents and virtues. Through the course of the narrative as well, Swift posts psychological and ethical guides. To explain, for example, why William Rufus failed to keep promises made during illness, Swift writes, 'It is the disposition of men who derive their vices from their complexions, that their passions usually beat strong and weak with their pulses.'[4]

If so much weight falls upon the character of rulers, a tiny change in their heart must bring enormous consequences to the world: hence the deep significance which Swift, like his contemporaries, attached to the power of hidden intrigue upon poli-

[1] Dodwell, introduction to Degory Wheare, *The Method and Order of Reading . . . Histories,* tr. Edmund Bohun, 3rd ed. (1698), sig. A4.

[2] *Introduction,* pp. 300–1.

[3] *Ibid.,* p. 301. In his letter on a collaborative survey of English history, Temple assumes that the lives of the kings will provide the substance of the work: see *Letters by Several Eminent Persons . . . John Hughes* i. 5–6.

[4] Davis v. 16–17.

tical history. Among those requirements which Machiavelli and
Guicciardini had taught Bacon and Hobbes to recommend in
an historian, was a gift for unravelling intrigues. Even if Swift,
though endowed by nature with little skill in this art, had not
profoundly enjoyed it, he would have found himself urged to the
practice both by his patron and by the times. From 1658 to 1688
private intrigue lay behind a succession of high national crises.
The Restoration, the Treaty of Dover, the Popish Plot, the Revolution, all hinged on a glittering assortment of whims and passions; open proceedings repeatedly seemed a cloak for hidden
tiptoes; and Temple boasts of his own familiarity with such 'true
springs and motions'.[1]

A taste for interpretations of this sort often leads men toward
the reflection that, as Bacon says, God loves to hang 'the greatest
weight upon the smallest wires'.[2] In both Temple and Swift we
find a bias favouring such *maxima e minimis* patterns,[3] a bias which
Swift repeatedly indulges as he takes us across Norman England.
For example, when Prince William, godson of the Conqueror,
receives a slight wound, Swift sounds eager echoes of 'For-want-
of-a-nail':

> . . . a wound in his wrist, which, by the unskilfulness of a surgeon,
> cost him his life. This one slight inconsiderable accident did, in all
> probability, put a stop to very great events; for if that young prince
> had survived his victory, it is hardly to be doubted but through the
> justness of his cause, the reputation of his valour, and the assistance
> of the King of France, he would in a little time have recovered
> Normandy, and perhaps his father's liberty . . . nor could he well
> have missed the crown of England after the king's death.[4]

(No wonder Swift blamed his own failures on accidents like
Romney's laziness or Bolton's bribe.)

In the way of parallel history Swift found abundant resources
among the Normans. Writing on King Stephen, for example,
Swift keeps in mind the events leading up to and flowing from the
Glorious Revolution. In summarizing the early part of Stephen's
reign, he elaborates the parallels with William III: the succession
problem, the contractual element in the royal election, the new

[1] *Memoirs* II, sigg. A3–3ᵛ.   [2] *Works*, ed. Spedding and Micklem, III. 334.
[3] *Supra*, vol. I, pp. 123–4.   [4] Davis v. 44.

king's preoccupation with wars, his advancing of newcomers and granting them lands and honours, his difficulties with a pretender (the Empress Maud), and his placing a foreigner (cf. William's Bentinck) at the head of his councils and army. In handling the later part of the reign, Swift draws covert analogies with James II: he treats Henry Fitz-Empress as the Prince of Orange; he describes the co-operation of the French king and the English king against Henry; he relates Stephen's useless effort to guarantee his own son's succession; and he bears down on the bishops' refusal to comply with Stephen. Swift represents Duke William, Stephen's son, in terms of the Duke of Monmouth, and he sketches William's conspiracy in terms of the Rye House Plot.[1] Even Swift's self-conscious research into constitutional history must be directed toward the constitutional crises of 1685–1701.

It seems appropriate therefore that when Swift broke off his work on the Normans, it was to embark on the *Contests and Dissensions*. 'I was diverted from pursuing this history', he said many years later, 'partly by the extreme difficulty, but chiefly by the indignation I conceived at the proceedings of a faction, which then prevailed.'[2] Yet if he never completed the task, the energy intended to be so employed did not fly off unused. It supported an imposing line of political arguments drawn from historical analogies, and only extinguished itself in the allegory of Swift's masterpiece. There was, after all, one common purpose in writing history which we have not yet mentioned: the celebration of heroes, the dispraise of villains. Not alone did the historian sit in the place of judgment, labelling crimes and good deeds. He was also equipped either to execute sentence or to award honours. An evil reputation with posterity was a punishment to an evil king; a good name meant a reward to the father of his people. It is when Swift assumes the role of executioner that he points the way his career will go. In his reigns of the early Normans, he finds very little scope for this bent. In the *Contests and Dissensions* he finds more. As he lashes Clodius, Curio, and Bibulus, we hear the voice of a negligible historian drown in that of a great satirist.

---

[1] See Myrddin Jones, *Swift's View of History* (unpublished B.Litt. thesis), Oxford, 1953. [2] Davis v. 11.

Chapter Eight

PPT AND DD

I

While Swift was arranging for both his own book and Temple's to appear after his departure for Ireland, he was also making an arrangement of another sort. Judging from the outcome of this, I suppose that he had been keeping in touch with Esther Johnson while he was resisting the logic of Jane Waring. I also suppose that he saw Mrs Johnson often during May, June, and July 1701. The reason for these inferences is that he actually succeeded in persuading her to leave England at this time and come to live near him in Dublin. Swift had been attached to Hetty for years, and I think he knew she returned his feeling. Otherwise he would not have found it so easy to discard Varina. On his side at least I think the scheme had been laid in detail even before his arrival in England, although he preferred to represent it as arising during talks between them.[1]

In the spring of 1701 Hetty still held her old place with Lady Giffard, but the household had been moved; for an affectionate nephew of her ladyship's had inherited Moor Park with the baronetcy, and Hetty's mistress now divided most of the year between the cold seasons in her Dover Street house and the warm

[1] In his own version of the affair Swift implies the opposite of my analysis: 'going to visit my friends in England, I found she was a little uneasy upon the death of [Sir William Temple]. . . I prevailed with her and [Mrs. Dingley] . . . to draw what money they had into Ireland . . .' (Davis v. 227–8). But it is hard for me to believe that the loss of Temple in 1699 sent Esther Johnson to Dublin in 1701. She and Swift were both at Moor Park at least until the time of the funeral; he must have known of her reactions to Temple's death (including the money worries) immediately, and not had to wait almost two years to discover them; and he must have corresponded with his beloved Hetty between the summer of 1699 and the spring of 1701. Swift, I think, felt properly embarrassed at his role in the affair and tried to screen it in his memoir.

seasons at Sheen. Hetty's sister Anne was no longer with the family, having married a man named Filby the summer before[1]; but their mother remained, and so did gossipy Rebecca Dingley, Hetty's spinster friend.

From Swift's point of view the situation was reminiscent of earlier groupings. His own mother had been in a sense deserted when his father suddenly died and left her with two infants. In the persons of the bereaved Lady Giffard, her ladyship's waiting woman, and Mrs Dingley, the young chaplain could discern shadows of Abigail Swift, her daughter Jane, and the nurse of the infant Jonathan. In a separate but parallel way, for Swift to leave Moor Park and go to Dublin in 1699 would have reminded him of leaving his widowed mother and his sister for Kilkenny School when he was a child. According to Swift, it was a 'mortification' for him to be settled in Ireland, and he had in 1701 'few friends or acquaintance' there.[2] As a boy he had found the remedy for loneliness in the comradeship of cousin Thomas, another half-orphan, also isolated from his family. The remedy for the young chaplain was to be the same. What he proposed to a twenty-year-old girl who was fourteen years his junior was that she should sacrifice her home for the benefit of his comradeship.

This is the proposal he had made five years earlier to Varina—that before marrying him she should renounce her mother for his sake. We have solid grounds for believing that Swift respected Bridget Johnson. Nevertheless, he had no very high opinion of Hetty's ancestry. Her father he described as a 'younger brother of a good family in Nottinghamshire'; her mother, as 'of a lower degree'. This is close to the analysis Swift made of his own parentage, although the conclusion is different: 'Indeed she had little to boast of her birth.'[3] By excluding the true mother from the

[1] In a letter of 14 July 1700 Lady Giffard says Bridget Johnson returned 'yesterday week' from London, 'where she has married her other [i.e., younger] Daughter'. Although the year is not given, it is evident from several allusions, such as one to the recent death of the Lord Privy Seal, Lonsdale, which occurred 10 July 1700. The letter is in B.M. MS. Egerton 1705 A, fol. 25. It is printed from an unreliable transcript in Longe, p. 215.

[2] Davis v. 227–8. When he wrote this (1728), he must have been using a very special definition of 'friends' and 'acquaintance'. I think he liked to make England the locus of friendship and Ireland the locus of isolation.

[3] Ibid., p. 227.

scheme as he envisaged it, he could free the daughter for an imagined connection with a preferable, ideal family.

Against Varina's mother the charge had been not humble extraction but moral defect. It was to preserve Miss Waring's health and character that Swift had wished to play Perseus to her parent's dragonhood. In Hetty's case, though Madame might be respectable, her forebears were not; and a separation would only elevate the daughter. With either young lady, however, Swift seems to have felt that the test of love was willingness to put friend before family.

This exacting test Esther Johnson was prepared to meet. Swift had known her from his coming to Temple's house. He had taken 'some share' in educating the child and had watched her grow from sickliness into plump adolescent health. When he departed in 1699, she appeared to him 'one of the most beautiful, graceful, and agreeable young women in London'.[1] Whether sound or in-accurate, his impression could only have endeared him to a quiet girl who lived generally in the country. With her own father dead she must have found the attentive priest an excellent substitute, even in competition with Sir William Temple. But after Sir William followed Edward Johnson, Swift's authority would have touched its zenith. He found himself in the comfortable pos-ture of being chief adviser to the person he wished most to in-fluence.

Not only would her removal to Dublin raise Hetty's rank in society and relieve Swift's solitude: it carried financial benefits as well. Temple had left the girl a lease of lands in Ireland worth a thousand pounds; she had four hundred more held at interest for her by Lady Giffard, and another hundred in exchequer funds also under her ladyship's care. From all this accumulated capital she could draw only a modest income, especially if she chose to remain where she was. In Ireland, however, not only were some living expenses as low as half the cost in England, but the interest rates stayed high. 'Money was then at ten *per cent.* in Ireland', says Swift, 'besides the advantage of turning it, and all the neces-saries of life at half the price.'[2] Land was cheap, money dear.

---

[1] Davis v. 227.   [2] *Ibid.*, p. 228.

Such conditions were the effect of the government's tampering with the land settlement until few titles seemed quite secure, of rewarding absenteeism and imposing the abominable penal laws, of methodically sacrificing the greatest economic welfare of Ireland to the meanest benefit of England. Furthermore, Swift himself would contribute fifty pounds a year to her support.[1]

All these inducements together might not have drawn Hetty across the Irish Sea if a last refinement could not have been applied. This was the fact, according to Swift, that she had 'contracted an intimate friendship'[2] with an older woman, Mrs Dingley, who felt willing to accompany her. This co-operative, anxious creature was Temple's dependent relation on his mother's side, and sometimes took up Hetty's role as waiting woman to Lady Giffard. Although both her parents were first cousins to Temple, she possessed little money, but had just received an annuity of fourteen pounds on her father's death. Since neither intelligence nor youth (she was thirty-five or forty in 1701) was available to supply other deficiencies, the prospect of living as second in command of an independent household should have appealed to Mrs Dingley. If she already possessed the traits which Swift later attributed to her, she was a poor listener, a great worrier, and on these very accounts perhaps a prudent choice for duenna.[3]

By accepting in this manner a remarkably full responsibility for both his young pupil and her older companion, Swift was doing more than establishing for himself a fantasy family in which he might act father, brother, lover, or husband as he chose. He was also reversing the old relationship which once made him dependent upon two women. To guide him, he saw the example of his patron; for Sir William had not only lived with his sister and his wife interchangeably: he had travelled between England

---

[1] Since it is evident from his account books that he did so, I assume that he promised to do so.

[2] Davis v. 227.

[3] My information about Mrs Dingley comes from Margaret Toynbee, 'The Two Sir John Dingleys', *N. & Q.*, vol. 198, pp. 417–20, 478–83. Since her parents were married in 1659, and she was the eldest of nine surviving children, I suggest that she was more than thirty-five in 1701. Her father is said to have been married on an income of £80 a year to a lady with only £500. He died 28 Sept. 1700.

and Holland, shifting the women to suit his convenience; and when Lady Temple died, he had found Lady Giffard remaining to preside over his household.

When Swift in his turn was not benignly controlling the lives of Hetty and her motherly companion, he could identify himself with his beloved charge herself. His habit of admiring fatherless girls much younger than he was, and in poor health, can be linked to his own posthumous birth, his early lack of an immediate family, and his constant wrestling with illness. The role of parent thus gave him a double pleasure. Not only could he provide his beloved with that guidance and warmth which he himself had missed and therefore treasured. He could also make up to himself for the shortcomings of his childhood, since the women he chose had wants like his own. Without realizing it, he might imagine he was reaching back into the 1670s and in an odd but powerful way treat the other person as a deputy for his boyhood self. This was one reason (though far from the only reason) that he praised in women traits often classified as masculine; for these facilitated his identification with them.

That the girls should also have been eldest children seems to strengthen the connection with his infancy. While Swift's mother first lost and then left Jonathan, she kept with her the only other child in the family, Jane, his elder sister (by two years) and the namesake of Miss Waring. When he was not supplying his women friends with the father he would have liked to possess, Swift was regaining in them the sister whom he had missed and who had disappointed him.

II

While the two ladies at Sheen prepared for their emigration, Swift wrote his *Discourse* and settled the publication of Temple's third *Miscellanea*. In Westminster the last Parliament but one of William III held its final meetings, and fixed the succession of the English throne upon the House of Hanover. Abroad, the armies of France, which had already occupied the 'Dutch Barrier' fortresses of the southern Netherlands, swept on to take towns in southern Germany and northern Italy; for Louis assumed that war was inevitable and wished to forestall his enemies. Frightened by these events, the magistrates and gentlemen of the county of Kent petitioned the Commons to give over bickering and vote his majesty supplies for the military crisis.

In Dublin, meanwhile, anticipations of the arrival of Lord Lieutenant Rochester turned from springtide hope to fevers of suspense. 'Everything stays in expectation of him', said the Lord Chancellor of Ireland.[1] Unhappily, the arrogant Earl, procrastinating but imperious, delayed from day to day. Since Swift was travelling back in the viceregal train, he must have been alerted for duty from almost the moment he came to town.[2] But as packet followed urgent packet from the Continent, Rochester kept putting off his going; and Swift had time to give the last touches to the book attacking the Earl's domestic politics. By July the King was in Holland with Marlborough, negotiating an alliance with the Austrians and the Dutch. His majesty no longer trusted the Lord Lieutenant, whose term of standing at the head of affairs had only created an uproar in Parliament. Inevitable though a new war might seem to others, Rochester continued to work against the involvement of England. Between fits of illness and intrigues against the coming of autumn, he found deskfuls of business to block his exit from London. Consequently, although Mrs Dingley and Mrs Johnson did not reach Dublin till August, they had to wait longer for their protector than Swift had planned.

Midsummer passed. In Lombardy, the Austrians' great general, Eugene of Savoy, led a magnificent campaign of Imperial troops against the French. At the Hague, the Grand Pensionary of Holland, the King of England, and the Imperial Austrian diplomats moved quickly toward agreement. But in the Irish capital, Swift tells us, the two new maiden residents felt let

[1] *SPD. 1700–2*, p. 403 (Methuen to Vernon, 29 Jul. 1701).
[2] It is barely possible that Swift joined Rochester at the port of Chester, or even that he made the entire journey at his own expense. But this is most improbable; for if he had done so, he would have accompanied the ladies; it would be an unexplained break with his custom at a time when he particularly wished to save money; and it would deprive us of the obvious reason for the ladies' suffering an unexpectedly long wait for him in Ireland.

[71]

down, 'much discouraged to live in Dublin, where they were wholly strangers'.[1]

At last even Rochester's standard of dignity for a Lord Lieutenant's equipage was approximated. Servants went ahead with his horses and coaches in order to mount the state entry of the Queen's uncle into the second capital. During the closing week of August he paraded forth from London himself, and Swift went in his entourage. When they reached Chester, however, the winds failed to respect his excellency; and the great assemblage had to pause two and a half weeks for a favourable gale. So it was 17 September before they sailed from Holyhead, anchoring in Dublin Bay the next morning. But once arrived, they did not want for greetings. All the social and military resources of the anxious city were drained for a waterside reception at ten o'clock. Cannons erupted, troops drilled, and civic eminences bowed for their governor. Swift was home.

III

The lonely women welcomed their friend with as much relief as the city fathers did Rochester, and with rather more sincerity. Apart from a trip to England in 1708, neither Mrs Johnson nor Mrs Dingley ever left Ireland again.[2] They lived together until the younger woman died. During the autumn and winter of 1701–2 Swift's chief occupations included not merely attendance on the Lord Lieutenant and the care of Laracor, but also duties at the cathedral. However, his most absorbing work was probably to introduce the ladies into that Dublin clerical society in which Swift ordinarily spent his leisure. At first there were awkward explanations—or rather, an awkward lack of explanations. Mrs Johnson attracted the notice which naturally falls on a good-looking girl setting up house under the sponsorship of an eligible bachelor. 'Her person was soon distinguished', says Swift.[3]

In Ireland, the ladies' movements usually depended upon his. He kept shifting between Laracor and Dublin; and his two

---

[1] Davis v. 228.   [2] There is a tradition of a 1705 visit, but no evidence.
[3] Davis v. 228.

friends often contrived to lodge themselves near him. When he was not in one or the other of his homes, and it was inconvenient for the ladies to move to his neighbourhood, they often occupied Swift's vacated quarters, especially during his long visits to England. Disapproval of several sorts could hardly be avoided in the circumstances, and so we meet yet another case of Swift's 'nettle-grasping'. The very consciousness of his rectitude led him now as before to slight the normal tokens of rectitude. At the same time, however, with the perverse subtlety of his instinct for decorum, he hung out his own flags of virtue; and he imposed corresponding signs upon the behaviour of Mrs Johnson. 'The adventure looked so like a frolic', he said later, 'the censure held, for some time, as if there were a secret history in such a removal; which, however, soon blew off by her excellent conduct.'[1] No one has disproved the tradition that a third person invariably witnessed any meeting between Mrs Johnson and Swift; and that person was, whenever possible, Rebecca Dingley. The rigour of their ceremony was baroque: to see Mrs Johnson in the morning, Swift said in 1726, was what 'I her oldest acquaintance have not done these dozen years, except once or twice in a journy'.[2]

Supported by the fiction that his concern extended no more to one maiden lady than to the other, these friends could dispel the threat of scandal. While Swift's open attachment to either alone would have burned them all with slander, a respectful service to both could smother any rumour before it grew. Even in private memoranda Swift felt it prudent to maintain the disguise. By 1701 he had already formed the habit of writing 'Ppt' (poppet?) for Mrs Johnson, 'Dd' (dear Dingley?) for Mrs Dingley, and 'Md' (my dears?), crushed—symbolically?—into a digraph, for the two together. With all his precautions, however, he probably underestimated the persistence of gossip; and six years after the ladies' arrival in Dublin his cousin Thomas could still wonder whether Jonathan 'has been able to resist the charms of both those gentlewomen that marched quite from Moore-Park to Dublin (as they would have marched to the *north* or anywhere else), with full resolution to engage him?'[3]

[1] *Ibid.*   [2] Williams III. 138.   [3] *Ibid.* I. 56.

Chapter Nine

CAST COURTIERS

If Swift hoped to discover repose in the new order of his life, he found himself mistaken. Once again it was external events that were to set the direction for his feet. Among those events the decisive turn was the coming of war; for this brought the issues which were to supply him with materials for his best-known essays on English affairs. Swift's private ambitions, his political philosophy, and his clerical loyalties—those fundamental aspects of the very career which their mutual conflict would obstruct for a decade—would by the outcome of this war be brought into a productive harmony. Swift would enjoy four years of specious glory in rooms where the lines of development were drawn for unexplored continents and unborn generations. The greatest literary work and the noblest public deeds of his entire life would be overshadowed in Swift's own view by the second-hand splendours of that busy term.

It was in order to give energy to the management of the war that the King came to some decisions which were to touch Swift eventually. During the summer of 1701 his majesty had concluded in Holland a treaty of Grand Alliance with the Dutch and the Austrians. The members of this alliance thereby agreed that the crowns of France and Spain should never be united. They also guaranteed to Holland and England the liberty of trading with both the Spanish possessions in the Old World and the Negro-worked colonies in the New: the blessings of freedom at home maintained by the profits of slavery abroad.[1] To speed up proceedings, William appointed as his ambassador and chief agent in these negotiations that same Earl of Marlborough whom

[1] Ogg II. 470.

he had already made head of the English forces in Holland. If this brilliant general and negotiator was to be effective, however, he needed, as partner and first minister at home, the highly competent public servant whose son had married Marlborough's daughter, i.e., the Earl of Godolphin. Yet this all-important appointment remained unthinkable so long as peacock Rochester held a commanding position in the government.

So even before King William returned from Holland, he began to arrange for a dissolution of Parliament. Louis XIV had already undermined the peace parties in England by a series of bad miscalculations. Instead of letting his grandson's new kingdom of Spain appear to follow a policy of its own, Louis had compelled the Spanish to deliver the highly lucrative Asiento—or contract for supplying slaves to their colonies—into French hands. Louis had also begun to block English and Dutch trade in the Belgian and Italian territories of Spain. At this point, even with Harley as Speaker, Parliament had to sound bellicose and encourage the King to prepare for war (May 1701). A stronger shove came after the summer, when the exiled James II died (September 1701); for Louis could not resist playing God: he recognized James's son —later to be called the 'Old Pretender'—as King of England, and thereby outraged every respectable party in the country. Soon English and Dutch merchants in Spanish ports were being forced by the French-controlled authorities to sell their goods at half price.[1] By now no public figure in London could openly oppose a mobilization against France. Swift could regard his recent book as a true prophecy. From being a triumphant and patriotic party, the anti-military Tories now found themselves blamed as a faction and tainted with treason. This was the outcome of their 'dissensions'.[2] William naturally assumed that a new election would give him a more docile House of Commons, and he went on accordingly.

Still, the dissolution caught the Rochester–Seymour clique by surprise. Though they had at last come around to abetting the military preparations during the spring and autumn, the leaders of the 1700–1 Parliament had nevertheless failed to keep pace

[1] Trevelyan I. 140.　　[2] Craik I. 111.

with his majesty's impetuousness; and they did not love him for gaining on them. On the other hand, the parties in the new Commons were distributed so evenly that the court could enforce its will—though yet again the members elected Harley as their Speaker (December–January 1701–2). Only during the election campaigns did William (recently arrived in England himself) give Rochester permission to return from Dublin.[1] The Earl landed about a week after the new Parliament met, and just before the Commons voted the King forces of 80,000 men, on land and at sea, to support the Grand Alliance. In such an atmosphere it was natural that Rochester should quickly but alas prematurely be reported dismissed from 'any farther service'.[2]

Throughout this season of somersaults and turnabouts there is no sign that Swift thought of leaving Ireland or visiting England. However darkly he may have sneered at Rochester's politics, he could presumably have accompanied the Lord Lieutenant in January 1702. But he preferred to remain near the ladies. Perhaps this reluctance to attend his excellency is illuminated by an observation Swift once let fall upon the 'insolence and haughtiness' with which 'some lords of the high-church party' used to treat their own chaplains.[3] In February, at any rate, Swift took the degree of Doctor of Divinity at Trinity College, paying a fifth of his annual income on fees and treats.[4] In mid-April he attended the chapter meeting of the cathedral.[5] During some leisure hours he occupied himself with editing a fresh batch of Temple's manuscripts. Even before the advent of spring, however, he had found himself suddenly faced with the need to start on a new set of travels. Putting his editorial labours aside, he made rushed preparations for departure. The reason for hurrying was single, public, and urgent. The King of England, celebrated by Swift as 'our happy prince', had ended his

[1] *SPD.*, 9 Dec. 1701.

[2] Luttrell, 6 Jan. 1702, says Rochester has 'landed from Ireland'; under 27 Jan. he says that Rochester was dismissed on 25 Jan. but that his successor was not yet known. In fact, Rochester's term of office ran from 28 Dec. 1700 to 4 Feb. 1703.

[3] Davis VIII. 120.

[4] The 'fees and treat' came to £44 (Mason, p. 245, n. w). The degree was granted 11 Feb. 1701/2. (I am indebted to Carl P. Daw for the correct date.)

[5] Forster, p. 17.

reign. On 21 February the ailing, exhausted hero was thrown from his horse; on 8 March he died.

II

From the immediate effects of a king's death there could be no security for a man in any public service, still less for one trying to get preferment. So exalted a churchman as Gilbert Burnet, Bishop of Salisbury, Ecclesiastical Commissioner, Privy Councillor, and Chancellor of the Garter, rushed from the royal deathbed to prostrate himself before Queen Anne. The Earl of Marlborough, whose family stood closest to the new ruler, now found himself the most important person in England. At the opposite limit, far from the scene, was Joseph Addison, still touring the Continent. He had received welcome news, during what became the last days of the King, that he would be made royal secretary to Prince Eugene in the field. Under the new reign, however, the appointment lapsed before it could take effect; and Addison found himself left with no immediate prospects apart from the remainder of his travels. Perhaps he belonged too openly to the party of Halifax and Somers, whom the new court circle distrusted.

Matthew Prior, on the other hand, had been granted a profitable commissionership on the Board of Trade in the summer of 1700. The next year, as M.P. for a pocket borough of Lord Dorset's, Prior had voted in favour of the impeachment of the four lords of the Junto; and with the supreme mistake of this vote, he threw away the support of his early patrons, including Dorset himself. Nevertheless, Prior had by this time entwined his own plans so closely with the desires of the Earl of Jersey that even as the Tory Earl retained the Lord Chamberlainship after the King's death, so also Prior found his commissionership renewed.

Meanwhile, Addison's friend Steele had won goodwill at the old court by dedicating his first staged play to Lady Albemarle, bride of King William's favourite. The playwright was named 'to be provided for' among the King's last memoranda.[1] Since

[1] Blanchard, p. 442.

the army was now expanding fast and since Marlborough had no cause to disapprove Steele's name, his majesty's death meant no obstruction. So the *Funeral*'s author was commissioned captain before his royal master was buried.

Contrariwise and unfortunately, Swift's friend Congreve was finding his fame for a while more solid than his preferments. The accession of William III had marked the opening of an era, now almost three centuries old, in which card-games and horse-flesh would outrank belles-lettres in the amusements of English crowned heads. In 1700 Congreve's half-salaried tenure as a commissioner for hackney coaches had been augmented by an office in the customs, at £48 a year. But this new income he had to share with a resident deputy; and if both appointments were happily renewed on the King's death, the 'customership' was taken from Congreve by the end of the following year. It was not only that his connection with the Kit-Cat circle would not have endeared him to Queen Anne's earliest ministers. But with competition so strenuous, his momentary failure to accumulate jobs seems inevitable: 'Ease and quiet', said Congreve, 'is what I hunt after.'[1]

Such delicacy was what Swift could not afford. To Queen Anne, a princess of celebrated piety, the Church of England counted for more than it had to her unlamented brother-in-law. She rescinded the dismissal of her high-church uncle Rochester; and though the Lord Lieutenant stayed on in England, his appointment lasted another eleven months—during which he bolstered his shaken position by publishing his father's great *History of the Rebellion*. The Queen also displayed her feelings by encouraging a six-year-old project of Burnet's to employ certain ecclesiastical fees in a fund to improve poor benefices.[2] The final fruit of this scheme is still known as Queen Anne's Bounty. She took church preferments to be her special province; and distrusting the latitudinarian Tenison, Archbishop of Canterbury, she confided in the high-churchman Sharp, Archbishop of York. The accession of such a princess was momentous for her clergy.

[1] Hodges, p. 83.   [2] Foxcroft, p. 345.

Swift needed no advice to appreciate the opportunities. He came to England during the second half of April,[1] carrying the manuscript of a final volume of Temple's letters. Swift claimed that he would have delayed publishing the volume if he had not felt threatened by rivals owning copies of the correspondence which they were smuggling into print. Thus from his own text he omits a number of letters authorized by Temple for inclusion, since these had already appeared under other imprints. Swift does not explain what the advantage of delay would have been, but one assumes that he would have had the leisure to edit the manuscript more carefully than he did. His preface sounds hastily written and reverberates with insinuations against competitors. The one letter not in English remains untranslated. In a book of five hundred and fifty pages Swift supplies only five notes, of which four are trifling.[2]

Nevertheless, the work contains one long, highly significant note which reflects the editor's views on the year's events. Through this gloss Swift apparently wishes to direct readers to the letter itself, as revealing an instructive parallel to the crisis of 1702. Writing in the summer of 1678, Sir William Temple had quoted an opinion which he himself shared, viz., that France aimed at a 'universal monarchy', and no one but England could stop it.[3] The fact has been proved, Temple says, by the refusal of the French to restore Dutch towns. Temple also reports that the King (i.e., Charles II) is so strictly resolved to oppose Louis XIV that nothing can shake him except the fear of being weakly supported at home or in Holland. Peace is impossible, Temple continues, since no longing for peace can establish it if Louis desires war.

The parallels of 1678 with 1701–2 are sufficiently obvious. But

[1] Lyon says that Swift went to England in April 1702, first visited his mother at Leicester, proceeded to London in May, visited Moor Park in July, and returned to Ireland in October (p. 36). Since Swift attended the chapter meeting in Dublin on 15 April, he must have left Ireland during the second half of the month.

[2] The untranslated letter is in French, pp. 415–16. Two of Swift's notes (all marginal) are brief identifications, pp. 81, 216. One seems intended to be an identification but has no apparent connection with the text beside it, p. 524. Another note was apparently intended to be a translation of a French sentence in the text but instead merely reprints the sentence, p. 234.

[3] *Letters* III. 355.

D

[79]

Swift reinforces them by his extraordinary note.[1] Here he claims that Temple told him the reason behind Charles II's change to an anti-French policy. Although Louis had offered Charles a vast bribe[2] to support the French in the negotiations at Nimeguen, the English king had boggled at an unexpected article in the agreement. Louis, according to what Swift retails from Temple, had required Charles to promise that he would never keep more than 'eight thousand men of standing troops' in all his armies. This demand stunned Charles and ended the Anglo-French *entente*.

In warning us that he 'may be a little mistaken' as to the number of men, Swift seems to be emphasizing the parallel between his anecdote and the vote of the Commons in 1697 that the number of men under arms in England should be reduced below seven thousand.[3] Even in 1698 Parliament had voted for a force no larger than seven thousand in England and twelve thousand in Ireland. During the struggles over these policies the leaders of the anti-military parties had included Rochester, Nottingham, Harley, and St John. We may therefore infer that Swift was moving with the swell of national sentiment. He distrusted those who gave only qualified support to England's belligerence, and he insinuated that their principles were bent by the weight of French gold. He thought the war to be just and inevitable.

So far, so good. If these are his views, should Swift attach himself to the men who had initiated such policies, or to the ministers now in power? He was unhappily seldom one to let expedience get in the way of quixotic principle. Marlborough, Godolphin, and Harley were managing the nation. Swift approached a set of men doomed for a decade—all but one of them—to have little power to help their friends—and that one possessed of opinions on church and society which Swift found repellent.

After seeing his mother in Leicester, he moved on to London, arriving there in May 1702.[4] If we are to credit him, the *Contests and Dissensions* had enjoyed so favourable a reception as to be

[1] For the complete text of Swift's note, see above, vol. I, pp. 98–9. In Temple's *Letters* III it will be found on pp. 355–6.

[2] Swift's figure £400,000 or £500,000 is correct: see Clark, p. 90.

[3] *Ibid.*, p. 188.   [4] Lyon, p. 36.

fathered alternately upon Lord Somers and Bishop Burnet.[1] While this claim seems exaggerated, we know the book went through at least two editions.[2] Lord Weymouth called it a work of 'much reading and great sincerity'.[3] Swift tells us it was 'greedily bought and read'. Since, however, he had sent it 'very privately to the press, with the strictest injunctions to conceal the author', few men knew he had written it.[4] What happened next, we know from Swift himself:

> Returning next year [i.e., 1702] for England, and hearing the great approbation this piece had received, (which was the first [*sc.* original book] I ever printed) I must confess, the vanity of a young man prevailed with me, to let myself be known for the author: Upon which my Lords Sommers and Hallifax, as well as the Bishop above mentioned [i.e., Burnet], desired my acquaintance, with great marks of esteem and professions of kindness: Not to mention the Earl of Sunderland, who had been of my old acquaintance. They lamented that they were not able to serve me since the death of the King, and were very liberal in promising me the greatest preferments I could hope for, if it ever came in their power. I soon grew domestic with Lord Hallifax, and was as often with Lord Sommers, as the formality of his nature (the only unconversable fault he has) made it agreeable to me.[5]

This reminiscence belongs to a period of composition twelve years later than the events retailed. It comes out of an apology designed by Swift to expose the flaws of the statesmen he names. When he wrote it, he intended these men to appear as false friends and false promisers. With a pride barely suppressed but wholly characteristic of him, Swift wished the reader to believe that the first advances in his acquaintance with such great figures were from their side; yet he also wished to shine a light upon the chasm which divided their principles from his, as though no change had affected these during the years between the event and the memory.

[1] Swift says that Burnet told him 'he was forced to disown it in a very public manner, for fear of an impeachment, wherewith he was threatened'; but the assertion is improbable, and no evidence for it appears (Davis VIII. 119). There may be some confusion with the arguments of Burnet's first *Pastoral Letter*, for which the bishop was indeed threatened with impeachment (Foxcroft, pp. 317, 374).

[2] R. H. Griffith, in *N. & Q.*, 22 Mar. 1947, pp. 114–17. Fresh advertisements appear in the *London Gazette*, 1 and 27 Nov. 1701, possibly a sign of the new edition.

[3] H.M.C. *Portland* IV. 25.   [4] Davis VIII. 119.   [5] *Ibid.*

Allowing for so many distortions, we can still understand why their lordships were glad to know Swift and why he felt delighted to meet them. Those out of office welcome new friends as those in office avoid them. In all the explosions of partisan politics Swift's dignified pamphlet reproaching Seymour's extremists must have made him *persona grata* to the Junto—however much they might have expected bolder service before considering him ready for reward. But while Swift found in the constitution of 1689 the terminus of his own political speculations, he was recommending himself to leaders who made that the jumping-off point for theirs. After the *Contests and Dissensions*, seven years were to pass before Swift would again commit to print his opinions on government.[1] Although he did write essays as well as letters which expressed his convictions, he had excellent reasons for delaying publication. During those years the administration of England came under a higher and higher proportion of zealous believers in a continental war and of tolerant sympathizers with Dissent, of spokesmen who championed the mercantile classes, of ministers trusted by neither parson nor squire. As Marlborough and Godolphin operated with a growing concentration of such ingredients, they lost the support of high-churchmen, the 'new country party', the gentry who paid those land taxes which accounted for much of the expense of campaigning.

If Dr Swift discovered with time that his fundamental doctrines were opposed to the policies of the chiefs of state, he was not called upon to say so. No duty obliged him as a priest to shout aloud what lay in his heart. While he hoped for advancement to a bishopric, a deanery, or a prosperous canonry, he could only apply to the ministerial springs of promotion. So long as silence or connivance met their standard, he was apparently ready to shut up in public, speak out in discreet privacy, and use his chances. After 1703, moreover, Swift had an assigned duty to urge upon the government a scheme for the financial relief of the Church of Ireland; and as such an agent he was bound to discretion for religion's sake if not his own. He felt unwilling, he

---

[1] *A Letter ... on the Sacramental Test*, published December 1708, though with a 1709 imprint.

once said, to ruin himself in 'any man's favor', when he could do the public no good.[1]

By a doubled irony, not only was Swift compelled to deal with a party he would some day denounce, but his great friends there remained out of the highest places just when their views were growing influential. The exception was Charles Spencer, Earl of Sunderland, son of Temple's treacherous friend. Newest and narrowest Whig lord of the Junto, Sunderland was also to be the first to push himself into high office under Queen Anne. As a young man he had visited Moor Park with his tutor; so Swift could describe him as 'old acquaintance'. Since he had also assembled a virtuoso's library, Swift could call him a 'most learned' lord.[2] Having no love for the church, however, and no debt to Swift, the Earl[3] would hardly have wasted patronage on the as yet unpolitical parson. Anyhow, for all his king-baiting insolence, Sunderland would only handle public power when he became Secretary of State in 1706.

Older but less impudent than the Earl was Charles Montagu, Lord Halifax, the schoolmate, patron, and literary collaborator of Matthew Prior. But Halifax had already known a quick and dazzling rise to power. At the peak of his career in the House of Commons (according to Lady Giffard) another member said, 'He could persuade them to vote a man a horse if he had a mind to it.'[4] To such genius in debate and to an astonishing inventiveness as a financier, Halifax owed his unfaltering climb to the post of First Lord of the Treasury. He was 'successful in all things', said Lady Giffard. But the turn had come with the Peace of Ryswick. Not only had Halifax soon lost his place: he had met the impeachment from which Swift defended him, and he was to remain out of office during the lifetime of the Queen. Furthermore, though Swift in 1701 had given him distinguished praise as a minister, speaker, and scholar, Halifax already faced deeper obligations than this to other creditors whom he was powerless to reward.

Somers, the confidant of King William, and a man from whom

---

[1] Williams I. 94.   [2] Preface to Temple, *Memoirs* III.
[3] His father died in 1702.   [4] Longe, p. 198 (29 Jul. 1697).

even Sunderland took advice, was the son of a Puritan lawyer. His well-regulated journey to high office had a secure base in his legal erudition. Although he had certainly proved his forensic abilities when he defended the seven bishops in 1688, Somers's peculiar service to William III had been a talent for discovering precedent and argument to support the policies of the crown. As a result, many schemers thought he was the hidden generator of royal motion; and this notoriety in turn brought nemesis down: for Somers was hounded out of the Lord Chancellorship in 1700 during the political recoil of the post-war years. In 1702 he had seemed about to return, but the King's death destroyed such prospects; and though Somers was old enough to be Sunderland's father, he was compelled to wait for the accession of George I to make him once more a cabinet minister.[1]

All three of these men had connections distasteful to Swift and out of keeping with his moral or intellectual bias. The Royal Society, ridiculed in *A Tale of a Tub*, had elected Somers and Halifax not merely as members but as presidents in turn. Sunderland could not only talk like a republican; he had lived and fed his religious tolerance in Holland. Halifax had befriended Newton. Somers's father had fought for Parliament in the Civil War.

III

But none of the three could have struck such ambivalent vibrations in Swift as Bishop Burnet, a man who had spent more years avoiding preferment than Swift spent in pursuit of it. Burnet's aims and opinions were so close to Swift's, his character so unlike; his pretensions so outran performance, yet his achievement seemed so daunting; he knew so much and talked so loosely, that he must have imbued his visitor with the most reluctant admiration. As an author the tall old busybody was to influence or annoy Swift over a stretch of forty-odd years; for the *History of the Reformation* appears on a reading list of 1697, and a copy of the *History of His Own Time* carries marginalia written in 1737. As a

---

[1] In 1708 he became Lord President of the Privy Council, but this was not a post of real power.

churchman Burnet, till his death in 1715, was to stand a monument of what ambition could do to good intentions. If one sets him off against Swift, one can observe in detail the positions which the younger man held on the issues of church and state. By comparing the priest with the bishop, we shall not only see the lines of Swift's idea of the British constitution; we shall also be able to mark the shifts in those lines at a time when he would have been glad to represent them as steady.

This desire to seem consistent was an ideal common to both men. But it embarrassed Burnet the more because at sixty he was defending principles directly opposed to what he had preached at forty. Swift, on the contrary, had declared his politics only so far as to support those axioms which all respectable men took for granted. Both he and Burnet were always monarchists and Erastians. They utterly adhered to the Revolution Settlement and the Hanoverian Succession. They utterly repudiated the Pretender. But throughout the reign of Charles II Burnet had made passive obedience the mainstay of his theory of government. Only toward the end of the reign had he begun to explain that concept as directed not at the King but at the legislative power embodied in King and Parliament together. Similarly, it took the blunders of James II to persuade Burnet that *salus populi* was the supreme law. To Swift of course these doctrines appeared self-evident.

Both men formed their political philosophies around the assumption that attaching oneself to a party meant abandoning one's conscience. During the crisis of the Rye House Plot, Burnet was delighted to be counted neither a Whig nor a Tory. In the years of the Revolution he would have resented either label as an aspersion. For a while after this time he still preserved friendly relations with men of almost all colours. If he then felt a bias, his vocation inclined him toward the so-called church party, and Nottingham was the statesman in whom he confided. By 1693, however, we detect hints of the hatred which the 'rigid' clerical majority would soon bestow on him as one of the 'moderate' ecclesiastics who were monopolizing preferment; and even Burnet then said he was disliked by Whig and Tory both.[1] Under the

[1] Foxcroft, p. 318.

pressure of Jacobite insults and high-church sneers he turned increasingly partisan; a paranoid fear of France and popery drove him into the Whig enclave; and when Swift met him, the bishop wore the uniform of the Junto.

While Swift blandly supposed himself to be impartial, he realized that 'Whig' would have been the usual epithet for his rules of government. To him, however, no other rules seemed feasible. Though disdainful of taking sides, he had in fact walked on to the political stage when objectivity did look like Whiggism; and the common ground under himself and Burnet must have felt very firm in this sector. Anyhow, at the start of the War of the Spanish Succession the open issues of parliamentary politics lay more in persons than in ideologies. Though the spokesmen of the various cliques might smear one another with the pernicious doctrines of their past or their parents, there was little in Swift's analysis of the constitution that anyone took public exception to. For Jacobite as for republican, silence was the open alternative to exile or execution.

In his manners Burnet could never have agreed with a delicate sensibility. Although he could claim excellent birth and breeding, he had as little of taste as of tact. Like Swift he possessed a facetious flow of speech that made him a shining conversationalist. But he was essentially humourless; and like many inquisitive people he was unable to control his garrulity. While it is true that Swift seldom rose above an ordinary human power to keep secrets, the bishop's volubility of indiscretion was something he never approached. Charles II said Burnet would be willing to be hanged so as to have the pleasure of making a speech on the scaffold.[1] Dryden called him 'invulnerable in his impudence':

> So fond of loud report, that not to miss
> Of being known (his last and utmost bliss)
> He rather would be known for what he is.[2]

Even if Burnet had behaved himself with less choler or more deliberation, Swift would have found his ecclesiastical policies unsavoury. Sancroft, the archbishop whom Swift had apotheo-

[1] Foxcroft, p. 197.   [2] *Hind and Panther* III. 1189–91.

sized in a pindaric ode, had refused to consecrate Burnet. This gesture had of course been ineffectual; and in any case it was essentially a reaction to the Erastianism which the Bishop of Salisbury shared with the vicar of Laracor. The two also shared a lifelong belief in episcopacy and a certitude that the Sacramental Test was the palladium of the constitution. Being convinced Church of England men, they both condemned Presbyterianism as well. In matters of doctrine, consequently, they tended to support the peculiar tenets which then seemed to distinguish their established church—neither of them showed any genius as a theologian. They rejected Calvinistic notions on predestination and refused to allow that the leadings of the 'divine spirit' could supersede the promptings of our reason, provided that 'reason' meant not formal logic but 'the clear conviction of our faculties'.[1] Neither were they allured by speculation, since, like most men of a practical temperament, they seldom questioned their own fundamental beliefs. When nice disputes about mysteries were laid aside—they both thought—the right interest of the Christian faith would be best advanced.[2]

Yet the bishop loved to trace the immediate hand of Providence in human affairs; and he allowed himself a warmth or effusiveness, in describing the consolations of Christianity, which the vicar could not adopt and which seemed to him the mark of either fanaticism or hypocrisy. For Swift, intensity of belief went with restraint in expression. What Burnet desired to sound deeply sincere rang in Swift's ear like a tinkling cymbal. He could never have brought himself to stomach—much less to use—Burnet's epithet for religion: 'the earnest of that supreme joy [for] which I pant'.[3]

Such enthusiasm, however, did betoken a whole congeries of Anglican attitudes which were beginning to offend Swift. According to these 'Latitudinarian' lights the maintenance of peace

---

[1] Foxcroft, p. 149: the quotation is from Burnet in 1677; there is no evidence that he ever moved from this position or that Swift ever held another. Cf. Burnet in 1680: Reason is 'nothing but a communication of divine light to make me understand those propositions, of which some hints were born with my soul, and the rest are offered to me in sacred writings' (Foxcroft, p. 162).

[2] *Ibid.*, p. 452.   [3] *Ibid.*, p. 437.

and unity in the church was incumbent upon all Christians. Burnet opposed any persecution for the sake of religious opinions; he tried to conciliate the Dissenters' prejudices; he pleaded for the support of Protestants abroad; he supported occasional conformity. Although a period of study in Holland had fortified his distrust of Calvinism, it had also deepened his bias toward toleration.

In 1702 if Swift did not sympathize with these 'Broad Church' principles, he was still able to respect them. Even a year later he would take advice from the bishop as to the wisdom of occasional conformity[1]; and he would always regard Burnet as generous, good-natured, and 'very communicative'.[2] Nevertheless, the two men's intellectual paths met at this moment only because they were headed in intersecting directions. Both agreed, for example, that if a religious sect regularly made disturbances in the government, it should be excluded from all places of trust or power; but the sect which frightened Burnet was Papist and the sect which frightened Swift was Presbyterian. What Burnet called toleration Swift would soon call madness; and since the evolution of English politics would depend very much upon ecclesiastical policy, they would soon find themselves facing one another across barricades.

If it seems curious that persons planted so similarly should grow so far apart, we may by connecting them with social circumstance account for some of the anomaly. Though neither Swift nor Burnet was born in England, both looked for preferment there; so in a sense they brought a comparable possibility of detachment to their view of the Established Church, even if, being newcomers, they saw political and religious issues in starker, simpler terms than the English themselves could. But though each came from a land where Episcopalians formed a minority, Swift's aboriginal countrymen were mostly broken Irish Papists; Burnet's were vigorous Scottish Dissenters. It is true that Swift's paternal grandfather and, in the same generation, Burnet's father, had both been persecuted by Presbyterians; it is also true that Swift's mother's father, like Burnet's mother and her rela-

[1] Williams I. 39.   [2] Davis v. 184.

tives, had suffered for Nonconformity. But Burnet, after his father's early death, was the single Episcopalian in his whole family, and his own uncle had been seized in France and hanged in Scotland by ministers of Charles II. In Swift's Ireland no officer of state could dare show the least concern for Roman Catholicism, the least respect for France, or the least distaste for monarchy, since the Anglican hegemony depended on the support of a Protestant English king. Yet in Burnet's Scotland the Presbyterians had been practically an established church since 1690, having maintained their strength earlier in the teeth of royal opposition. After migrating to London, moreover, Burnet had found himself repeatedly menaced by Roman Catholics at court. It was natural therefore that the bishop should feel panic at what the vicar thought contemptible, that the Scot should tolerate what the Irishman feared, and that Burnet should come finally to stand to Swift for the bugbears which Tory convention identified with radical Whiggery: Scotland, regicide, the Presbyterians. Nevertheless, when the two men had their first meetings, the threat of France, Popery, and the Pretender not only united the nation but created the issues of a great new war. One decade later the danger would be gone in fact for ever, and Burnet's obsessive anxiety would deserve the label 'thirty years behind the times'.[1] In 1702, however, the Scottish bishop and the Irish parson could still understand one another.

Consequently, there seems to be a particular significance in the degree to which their philosophical outlooks already failed to coincide. To a certain extent this divergence was inevitable; for some of it can be blamed on an older generation's loyalty to ideas which for them had kept the freshness of first discovery but which to Swift's coevals appeared as error long exploded. Yet the two men show so much agreement both with one another and with the usual tendency of their time that some of the divergence must be traceable to the bents of their separate minds. Beneath the impressive parallels in political and moral sympathies, for example, may be discerned a common and indeed commonplace distrust of the speculative reason, especially as that seemed embodied in

[1] Foxcroft, p. 448.

the logic of the schools. Nevertheless, such pursuits as algebra, chemistry, and metaphysics attracted the bishop as much as they repelled Swift. Burnet turned to them for recreation and refreshment. He had felt delighted to be elected a fellow of the Royal Society. He thought the mathematical arts and sciences to be a 'fit and almost necessary' prelude to theological study![1] Although no love was lost between him and Locke, Burnet preached a celebrated funeral sermon on his own 'close and entire' friend, Robert Boyle[2] (whom Swift called 'a very silly writer'[3]). He invited William Wotton to London, and afterwards gave him a prebend of Salisbury. He sat on the commission which chose Richard Bentley as master of Trinity College, Cambridge. From the idea which Swift formed of Burnet during their early conversations, he could draw lifelong support for his belief that an unsteady judgment in practical affairs went naturally with a taste for the new experimental philosophy.

IV

The death of William III meant the dissolution of the Ecclesiastical Commission and therefore a sudden decline in Burnet's resources as a patron. Like Wharton and the rest of the Junto, he did not belong to the small circle on which the new Queen most relied. Of course, a Somers or a Halifax would always have means to satisfy his most meritorious clients. But as Swift indicates in a wry admission of the following year, he could make no such claim for himself: 'I have here the best friends in nature, only want[ing] that little circumstance of favour and power; but nothing is so civil as a cast courtier.'[4]

During July, Swift visited Moor Park while the first new Parliament of Queen Anne was being chosen.[5] Burnet says her majesty now appeared so plainly inclined to the Tories that they elected at least twice as many members as the Whigs could.[6] Certainly the strength of the Junto fell sharply in the House of Commons: the 'New Country Party' was the prop which the Marl-

[1] Foxcroft, p. 136.   [2] *Ibid.*, p. 39.   [3] Davis v. 271.
[4] Williams I. 39.   [5] Lyon, p. 36.   [6] Burnet v. 45.

borough–Godolphin ministry preferred to lean on; and the representation of Robert Harley and his allies in Parliament suddenly rose.[1]

In August Swift stayed with the Berkeleys at their celebrated castle in Gloucestershire, the county where Jack Howe had shamelessly won an election on the sheriff's scrutiny after losing it at the polls.[2] While the Earl bemoaned the successes of Harley, St John, and Howe, Swift played 'traffic', teased Lady Betty, and acted as comic laureate to the family. One unfinished poem not only shows us the Berkeley household through Swift's eyes but also shows us him through theirs; for the final stanza was added by Lady Betty when she came upon the manuscript in his room. She was about the same age as Esther Johnson, whom Swift would be rejoining only after several months; and he had evidently renewed with the Earl's daughter the parental, pedagogical teasing which he always enjoyed with the young and fair. 'My Lady' is the Countess; 'Dame Floyd' is probably the mother of Lady Betty's companion; the other gentlewomen named also waited on or acted as companions to the female Berkeleys.

> My Lady though she is no player
>   Some bungling partner takes,
> And wedg'd in corner of a chair.
>   Takes snuff, and holds the stakes.
>
> Dame Floyd looks out in grave suspence
>   For pair-royals and sequents;
> But wisely cautious of her pence,
>   The castle seldom frequents.
>
> Quoth Herries,[3] fairly putting cases,
>   I'd won it on my word,
> If I had but a pair of aces,
>   And could pick up a third.

[1] Robert Walcott, *English Party Politics in the Early Eighteenth Century*, 1956, pp. 97–109.

[2] The date of the visit to Berkeley Castle is established by the reference to Howe in the 'Ballad on the Game of Traffick': see Williams I. 74–7 and notes; Burnet v. 46–7. Possibly 'A Meditation on a Broomstick', traditionally supposed to be a joke at the expense of the Countess of Berkeley, was also composed during this visit. (It was dated August 1704 in Swift's 1711 *Miscellanies*, and 1703 in the 1735 edition of his *Works*.)

[3] The famous Frances Harris, of the *Petition*.

But Weston has a new-cast gown
On Sundays to be fine in,
And if she can but win a crown,
'Twill just new dye the lining.[1]

'With these is Parson Swift,
Not knowing how to spend his time,
Does make a wretched shift,
To deafen 'em with puns and rhyme.'[2]

Before going back to Ireland, Swift gave Benjamin Tooke the copy and instructions for the third, concluding volume of Temple's *Letters*; and in return the publisher paid him fifty pounds.[3] While the anonymous *Contests and Dissensions* (and, in 1704, *A Tale of a Tub*) carry the imprint of John Nutt, the acknowledged editions of Temple's writings were handled by Tooke and Jacob Tonson, who were eminent, respectable booksellers; and I suspect that Tooke was also the real agent for those books which were ostensibly marketed by Nutt.[4] Like the run of Swift's productions, the *Letters* III came out after he was gone; for though he left the country in October 1702, the book was not put on sale till January 1703.[5]

[1] 'A Ballad on the Game of Traffick' is the earliest of Swift's extant poems in ballad measure. Its immediate sequel ballad 'To the Tune of the Cutpurse' is in a difficult form copied from Nightingale's song in *Bartholomew Fair* III. v.

[2] Lady Betty's stanza.

[3] Receipt by Swift signed and dated 3 Sept. 1702: Rothschild no. 2256.

[4] Cf. Nichol Smith in *Tale*, pp. xiii–xiv.

[5] The earliest advertisement I know of is in the *London Gazette*, 14 Jan. 1703: 'This day is published'.

Chapter Ten

LARACOR AND DUBLIN

I

For a period of more than twelve months now Swift withstood the lure of London. It is not easy for us to throw off the impression which he himself encourages, that Swift felt awake in England and asleep in Ireland. Yet I think there is always a first-handedness in his experience of his native country which the life in England lacked. Even on the political level, what happened in an Irish Parliament not only altered Swift's immediate plans but became a long-term preoccupation. Toward the end of this stay at home, for example, Ireland received its Test Act, to which Swift devoted one of his earliest and several of his latest polemical tracts. On the social level the men he confronted in Ireland were those he had known early and deeply, whose characters he could judge directly, thanks to an abundance of common memories and desires. In the labours of his vocation, if the great challenges were indeed such as to evoke despair, and if that response was indeed justified by the true conditions of the church, yet within those conditions he found continual opportunity for personal if limited achievements, based upon his independent resources. On the bench of bishops if he found many enemies, he also possessed some old and serviceable friends. In his domestic routines Swift could never feel so unstrained abroad as he felt at home, where expenses were low and the human instruments familiar. Throughout his activities in Ireland one notices a zestfulness, a contact with reality, a depth of insight, which Swift often fails to exhibit in England where, living so often the suspended life of a spider, a waiter-about in ante-rooms, he had to act a part which deceived not only others but himself.

[93]

Much of these months in Ireland Swift passed at Laracor, which he loved to visit and improve. Although in correspondence regarding this rural parish Swift does mention parochial matters, these show themselves less commonly than the willows and fruit trees, the canal and the river walk of his glebeland. There is no doubt that he went to work on the amenities of landscape as soon as he returned from England. Over the following year he was at a total charge of more than two and a half pounds to have a walk put down, trenches and a ditch dug, and willows planted.[1] How he transformed the ruined church and unkempt glebe may be seen outlined in an official report made decades after his arrival; for the description is given there of a handsome, well-built church, properly ceiled and flagged, 'furnished with all conveniences except a surplice and carpet'. The churchyard was enclosed in part with a stone wall, in part with a ditch. The glebe was 'exceedingly well inclosed'; and there was a good garden as well as a 'neat cabbin made by the present incumbent', valued at sixty pounds.[2]

From the beginning of Swift's incumbency it was clear of course that he would not serve the cure of Laracor himself. Any suggestion that he made himself the residing minister should be heavily discounted. If he did preach there from time to time, he otherwise treated his priestly duties as casual and incidental; for a curate was normally in charge. However, he chose and supervised the man with unusual care, and paid him unusually well.

Like his curate—at this time, a Mr Smith, who actually performed the many labours of a country parson—Swift at first put up in Trim (the county seat, about a mile from Laracor) with a landlady named Malaly, who looked like the celebrated Lady Masham.[3] Swift's personal servant, John Kemp, went with him to the country but was generally boarded out.[4] Joe Beaumont of Trim, a linen draper and general merchant, became a useful,

---

[1] *Accounts 1702–3*, fol. 14ᵛ.   [2] Landa, p. 39.
[3] Williams I. 34. I assume that the 'Malaly' of the *Accounts 1702–3*, fol. 15, 14ᵛ, is the husband of the Mrs 'Malolly' of the *Journal*, 17 Aug. 1711.
[4] *Accounts 1702–3*, fol. 2. He was, according to the *Accounts*, regularly paid board wages.

humble friend—when not indisposed by spasms of insanity—and a financial factotum. For the collection of tithes and some transfers of funds Swift employed Isaiah Parvisol, the great length of whose service is cheerfully at odds with the sins his patron laid to his account. Trim itself kept some vestiges of its early importance, in the form of a castle, a fifteenth-century church, and the yellow steeple of its ruined abbey. The town was now the commercial centre of a busy and important Protestant island in a sea of Roman Catholicism.[1]

The rector of Trim, John Stearne, was short, dark, unmarried, and endowed with a 'good face'.[2] What his hospitality lacked in elegance it made up in quantity[3]; and he had a good conversational wit. In Dublin as well as the country Swift saw him regularly, for Stearne held a prebend in St Patrick's Cathedral, where he had just been made chancellor. Although their friendship suffered several exposures to chills and strains, it was to endure until Stearne became a bishop.

As vicar of Laracor, Swift came under the visitation of the Bishop of Meath, Richard Tenison. There is no record of his bearing any crosses from this man, and there should be none, since they had common enough ground for understanding one another. Having grown up at Carrickfergus and gone to school there, the bishop was familiar with the neighbourhood of Swift's first parish, Kilroot; and he had himself once served as vicar of Laracor. His own son had been a friend of Swift's at Trinity College. Tenison was a protégé of the Ormondes; and before accepting Meath (the ranking bishopric of Ireland, after the four archbishoprics), he had made sure that the bishopric of Clogher, which he was vacating, would go rather to Swift's old tutor, St George Ashe, than to the rival candidate.[4] If he seemed well disposed, however, he was also undistinguished. Although related to the Archbishop of Canterbury, Tenison had no influence on great affairs and exerted himself for little beyond the conventional steps to put down popery, oppose Presbyterianism, and rebuild churches.

[1] Craik I. 118. [2] *Journal*, 6 Jan. 1711. [3] Delany, p. 182.
[4] *SPD. 1697*, p. 198.

Not that these steps were less urgent in the vicinity of Laracor than in the rest of Ireland. If Swift soon made his own triple parish an exception to the rule, the general wretchedness of Meath diocese must have reminded him continually of the blight upon Down and Connor, to which Kilroot belonged. In Meath only a quarter of the churches were in good repair, and over a quarter of the clergy did not reside on their livings. Though Swift in the course of time built a sturdy parsonage for his benefice, yet glebes as well as manses were scarce throughout the diocese, and lay impropriations were common.[1] In his own Rathbeggan parish there were no Protestants; in Agher, there were few or none. Wherever Swift turned, he saw the decay and ruin which were to blacken his picture of the work to which he consecrated his life.

Even in Laracor itself, where the houses around the church belonged to gentlemen of property,[2] the Protestant families numbered only sixteen, though some of them were very rich.[3] The gentry lived on their own good estates and seldom inclined to absenteeism; but for a while in the preceding generation the lack of an Episcopal minister had compelled them to worship in a Nonconformist chapel at nearby Summerhill.[4] Among those still inclined to Nonconformity the least affable and most recalcitrant was certainly Sir Arthur Langford, a wealthy bachelor. Afflicted with a lamentable devotion to his errors, the baronet squire sponsored the Presbyterian meeting-house at Summerhill in spite of Swift's exhortation to him 'to shut up the doors of that conventicle'.[5]

Sir Arthur's neighbours seemed less troublesome. Garret Wesley, M.P. for Trim, who also lived under Swift's vicarial eye, not only showed himself more amenable than Langford, but so far ingratiated himself that Swift once, in all sincerity, expressed 'entire love' for him.[6] On the recorded story, none the less, Wesley impinges merely as an important landowner whom Swift visited, wrote to, played cards with, and obliged. The premier parishioner, John Percival, another member of the Irish House of

---

[1] Landa, p. 35.　　[2] Craik I. 118.　　[3] Landa, p. 44, n. 1.　　[4] Ibid., p. 37.
[5] Williams II. 141.　　[6] Journal, 4 Mar. 1712.

Commons, was to Laracor what Mr Dobbs had been to Kilroot. Swift played piquet at his home in Knightsbrook and distinguished him as a man of 'very good understanding and humor'.[1] While Percival at first tasted too sourly Tory for Swift's stomach, they eventually established a comfortable political rapport. But he never became a real favourite, and his land-hunger made Swift complain that Percival 'would not lessen his rent-roll to save all the churches in Christendom'.[2]

II

Percival's obsession with land was no greater than Swift's preoccupation with money. Whether for Laracor or for Dublin, the doctor's annual budget is full of surprises. It seems an impressive paradox that he could watch his cash so closely without giving up his travels both to England and within Ireland. He saved, and accounted, and invested; but he also devoted himself to charity on a scale to parallel the beneficence of an Archbishop King or a Primate Marsh. Swift kept track of current expenses in small, thin account books which display his love of making lists, his interest in money, his orderliness, and his astonishing attention to detail. Certain payments—cash advanced to Esther Johnson, servant's requirements, clothes, and so forth—he entered under special labels. The small miscellaneous items he jotted down continuously by date, line after line, cumulated at the end of each line. Tithes being due at harvest time, his financial year began 1 November.

Swift's funds went in many ways. Mr Smith, as the curate of Laracor, received a base pay of fifty-seven pounds and supplementary fees for extra work[3]; this was more than twice as much as many curates were paid. Swift reckoned his own expenses amounted to about a hundred and sixty pounds, but this included the regular allowance of fifty to Esther Johnson. The servant cost him four pounds a year in cash, about ten pounds in room and

---

[1] Williams I. 55.   [2] *Ibid.* II. 236.
[3] *Accounts 1702-3,* fols. 13–16. I assume that the item of £14 5s. 0d. 'in full' to Mr Smith represents his regular quarterly salary.

board, and a few pounds for clothes and travel. When he bought
horses—twice this year—he paid about four pounds apiece for
them; and their upkeep cost almost ten pounds a year. His own
housing (apart from meals) took less than sixteen. On clothing
(with shoes and wig) he spent about eleven.

Ordinary meals hardly amounted to nine shillings a week;
wine, a shilling or so more; coal, two shillings or less; candles,
another shilling; laundry, one or two shillings. For household
articles Swift gave unpredictable sums such as nine shillings for
dishes, three for a coffee roaster,[1] or three for a saucepan.[2] He
might spend up to three shillings in a tavern, or five at an inn.
Then there were incalculables like letters, paper, books, card
games (where he won more than he lost), hired coaches, fruit in
season, treats for friends (26 February: Treat MD 3^s-9^d), old
debts, gingerbread, and a silver pencil.

Perhaps the most appealing items of all are his little charities,
which Swift entered as distinct from his much larger and more
regular benefactions. Many of these meant tips, to coachmen,
messengers, and servants. Others were handouts to beggars, as
two shillings eightpence halfpenny, to a 'poor woman'.[3] A few
were bestowed on friends like Beaumont or Mrs Dingley. Swift
also put down 2s. 8½d. to 'Sac^{rmt}' at least three times—two Sundays and Christmas Day—this year (i.e., between 1 November
1702 and 31 October 1703): perhaps these mean offerings given
when he communicated in churches other than his own. All such
small 'gifts' he normally reckoned in units of thirteen pence
Irish, then worth one shilling English. So he gave away 6½d.,
1s. 1d., and 2s. 8½d., instead of sixpence, a shilling, or half a
crown. On these impromptu presents of money, he laid out an
average of ten shillings a month, or more than half what he did
on all his clothes. The equivalent in the reign of Elizabeth II
would run into several pounds a week.

When special sums, like three pounds, seven shillings, for
lawyer's fees,[4] are added to the rest of Swift's accounts, it grows
obvious that he had resources, business dealings, and responsibilities which are not comprehended in the statements of the

[1] *Accounts 1702-3*, fol. 5.　[2] *Ibid.*, fol. 5^v.　[3] *Ibid.*, fol. 7.　[4] *Ibid.*, fol. 1^v.

little notebooks. But what these were will only appear from later records.

III

The public works beginning at this time to engage the benevolence of Swift's archbishop and the Primate were not financial charities. But they clearly illustrate the aggressive practicality of King, the reclusive studiousness of Marsh, the tenacity of both, and the difficulties Swift would face in dealing with either. While Lord Lieutenant Rochester was away, these were the most important people for Swift to please. Though both of them may have known him since his college days, neither had marked him out for particular favour. They were stately, rigid men, sooner to be impressed by compliance than by brilliance. Swift, who considered the soundness of his principles the least of his merits, never stooped to flourish it in the eyes of his superiors. If correct opinion in fundamentals was all they looked for, he had so much confidence in his own that to admit they might doubt it was to admit his life might be a sham; for if they required proof of that, how could they trust him in anything? The unctuosity by which Swift sometimes polished his relations with statesmen is sometimes unexpectedly absent from his dealings with the Anglican hierarchy. Consequently, however, we find a record of friction between him and many Irish bishops, and we observe the slow pace of his promotion.

William King was certainly not to be satisfied with lip-service, though with him Swift could be oily enough. When King became Archbishop of Dublin (March 1703), he showed his character in a dramatic gesture which prolonged itself for twenty years. His purpose was to enforce the authority of the archbishop throughout the province, in order to reform what he regarded as disastrous corruptions in the management of ecclesiastical affairs. Though often indiscreet and impetuous, and though upon some points quick to lose 'both his temper and his reason',[1] King seldom misdirected his energies. When Swift (at the end of 1708) published an elaborate, not wholly sincere, commendation of the

---

[1] Letter from the Duke of Grafton, in Coxe, *Walpole* II. 357.

archbishop, he underlined his devotion to the church, thereby implying that this was the reputation which King desired most: the archbishop, said Swift,

> does not busy himself by entering deep into any party; but rather spends his time in acts of hospitality and charity, in building of churches, repairing his palace; in introducing and preferring the worthiest persons he can find, without other regards: in short, in the practice of all virtues that can become a publick or private life. This and more, if possible, is due to so excellent a person, who may be justly reckoned among the greatest and most learned prelates of his age . . .[1]

A token of the support which his stubbornness gave to his ecclesiastical integrity is the notorious train of litigation which King set in motion as soon as he knew of his own promotion to the archbishopric; for he determined at once to set Christ Church Cathedral, Dublin, in the upright way of the just; and his style of undertaking this project will explain a good deal of the awkwardness in his connection with Swift.

By King's lights the dean and chapter of Christ Church had been conducting themselves less like devoted shepherds than like careless wolves. As he saw it, the resources of the institution were being scandalously exploited for the material profit of the canons. So vile were their offences that even twenty years after he started legal proceedings, the archbishop was still trumpeting his accusations: the canons were squandering their 'oeconomy', letting out their chapter-house for a toy-shop, employing their vaults as wine-cellars, hiring out rooms in the building for money. 'Their cathedral is in a pitiful condition, and though St Patrick's has not half the oeconomy that Christ Church has, yet it is much better beautified, and great sums of money laid out on it.'[2] During the final period in his immense litigations he mentioned other unsavoury details to the Archbishop of Canterbury: 'They have appropriated to their church about twenty-seven parishes, many of which are not supplied at all, and most of them very indifferently. They will not concur to rebuild churches where

---

[1] Davis II. xxi–xxii, 282.
[2] Letter of 4 Feb. 1724, to F. Annesley, in C. S. King, *A Great Archbishop*.

they are necessary, for fear they should be obliged to supply them with curates.'[1]

The moment he took office, one of his immediate acts was to demand that the dean and chapter of Christ Church enthrone him, and not those of St Patrick's Cathedral, where the ceremony was traditional. His chosen opponents refused to associate themselves with so flagrant a confession of his authority, on the grounds that as a royal foundation, their discipline was independent of any power but the crown's. Christ Church, they said, was where the State went to church; it was the chapel royal; and as such it stood exempt from the archbishop's visitation.

After due warning, King at last marched in form to the cathedral (May 1704), where he 'was pleased, in the time of divine service, to come into the church in his robes, to take possession of the dean's seat; and, prayers being ended, to call his visitation'—from which the local rebels of course conscientiously absented themselves—'to pronounce the dean and members of the chapter contumacious, and to order the sexton to break open doors, and to command Dr Burridge, his vicar-general, to enthrone him'.[2] This one attempt hardly satisfied him. Soon the Dean of Christ Church, who was also Bishop of Kildare, was bursting with exasperation, and wrote to the Lord Lieutenant, 'The Archbishop goes on in great fury still, insomuch that if I had not kept both the church doors and the doors of the precincts locked against him both upon Wednesday and Saturday last, for which I have precedents as well as the reason of the thing, he had most certainly pronounced the sentence of excommunication against me.'[3]

The lawsuit which ensued fell little short of Jarndyce v. Jarndyce in dilation. 'It is a very unhappy thing', the baffled chapter protested, 'to be dean in any place, where the Archbishop of Dublin has been, or is concern'd.'[4] When the Court of Common Pleas in Ireland upheld the archbishop with three separate judgments, Christ Church appealed to the Court of King's

[1] Letter of 23 May 1724, *ibid.*
[2] *Account of the Innovations Made by the Archbishop of Dublin* ... (London, 1704), p. 6.
[3] Letter of 29 Aug. 1704, in H.M.C. *Ormonde*, n.s., VIII. 110.
[4] *Account of the Innovations*, p. 21.

Bench. When that court affirmed the original decision in four additional judgments, the appeal went to the Court of King's Bench in England. When that court reaffirmed King's plea in four more judgments, the appeal went to the House of Lords in England. After a thumping set of judgments by this last authority in the archbishop's favour, Christ Church did give in; Queen Anne had died meanwhile; even King George was ending his reign; and the world could remark the uselessness of opposing so tenacious a character. Such was the confident, heavy-handed prelate under whose immediate rule Swift was to labour for more than twenty-five years.

IV

King's inroads on Christ Church were just beginning when Narcissus Marsh, with another sort of public spirit, undertook a very different project. Even before he became Primate, Marsh had had to assume many of the Primate's duties, since Michael Boyle, who was then lingering in that great office, was 'almost deprived of his sight and hearing'.[1] Yet apart from these heavy responsibilities and his own metropolitan duties, Marsh had cherished an old favourite scheme of his, to found a public library in Dublin along the lines of the Bodleian Library at Oxford. The buildings and books he was prepared to endow from his own sufficient wealth. A salary for the 'keeper', however, would have to come from the generosity of the state. Unfortunately, Erastianism had spread such wide roots in the projector's character that he failed to reckon with the controversy then exploding over the dependence of the Anglican church upon the civil government. Without taking warning from the arguments hurled about in the Convocation of the province of Canterbury, Marsh looked for funds in sources just on the border between laity and clergy. As a result, his quiet plan for public service was to provoke a chain of crises almost as unpleasant as the case between King and Christ Church.

Swift had no reason to feel involved yet himself, but he would be eventually; and he could already notice the involvement of the

---

[1] Letter from Marsh to Thomas Smith, 13 Oct. 1697, in Mant II. 72.

person who had been secretary to Galway when Swift had wished to be secretary to Berkeley.[1] This person was Elie Bouhéreau, a Huguenot refugee with a scholarly mind, an advanced age, and a fine collection of books: it was he whom Marsh wished to put in charge of the proposed library. If we pause to contrast Bouhéreau's fate with Swift's, we must again conclude, in spite of Swift's dissatisfaction, that Berkeley's chaplain had done well. Bouhéreau had come to Ireland with the Earl of Galway, whom he served for a total of eight years. Now, at fifty-eight, he was being offered a librarianship to be worth two hundred pounds a year, on condition that he donate his own books, easily worth five hundred pounds, to Marsh's institution. The vicar of Laracor need feel no jealousy.

Originally, Marsh had begged an allowance for his purpose out of the first fruits and twentieth parts, fees which the Irish clergy paid to the crown.[2] Then he had asked King William to grant the librarian two hundred pounds a year until the chancellorship or treasurership of St Patrick's could be given him. Marsh overlooked the fact that he was mixing civil and ecclesiastical offices together, and he put forward Bouhéreau not as a deserving priest but as a 'very learned gentleman' who corresponded widely with continental scholars.[3] As for adding the librarian's job to the chancellorship, Marsh saw no impediment to one's doing so since no other duty belonged to the cathedral office 'besides preaching three or four times in a year'.[4] Although the direct pension was soon forthcoming,[5] however, Bouhéreau succeeded to his canonry only after the Irish Convocation held some bitter sessions in which Swift participated. But in 1703 these struggles were not even adumbrated, and the work of the new Primate (Marsh accepted the elevation in February 1703) offered a pacific contrast to the violence of Archbishop King.

[1] Bouhéreau, who had been naturalized in 1687, had become secretary to Galway (then Ruvigny) in Piedmont, 1693; see D. C. A. Agnew, *Protestant Exiles from France*, 3rd ed. (1886), II. 260–2, also H.M.C. *VII Report*, p. 215a, where the name is misread as 'Bobereau', also Newport White, *Four Good Men*. In Dublin the Earl of Galway also had his English secretary, Stanley.
[2] *Cal. Tr. P.*, 26 June 1699. [3] *Ibid.*, 6 May 1701. [4] *Ibid.*, 22 Jan. 1709.
[5] His granddaughter says the stipend was later raised to £400 (Newport White, in *P.R.I.A.* XXVII. 151).

With neither of these superiors could Swift feel very comfortable. What all three men shared was a loyalty to the Established Church which seems to have been strengthened by their common choice of the celibate life. But Marsh, who lacked the others' up-and-doing practicality, loved study more than administrative chores. Smothered in the vapour of his glory, he complained, 'Worldly business is that which above all things I do hate.'[1] Neither he nor King possessed Swift's literary gifts or Swift's taste for frivolous recreations. But King, while no stylist, wrote a number of influential tracts for political and ecclesiastical occasions; and he displayed a fund of genuine learning (he was famous for bad latinity) in polemical support of his churchmanship. *De origine mali*, his ponderous synthesis of theodicean argument, achieved a European reputation and became one of the main sources of the *Essay on Man*. In both him and Marsh could be observed what Swift knew to be the obvious requisites of sure advancement: stolid industry, intelligence without idiosyncrasy, an elephantine regularity in their public habits. Swift, with less erudition than either and more eccentricity than both, lived too far from their beaten path and simplicity of ambition to escape maddening frustration.

Yet cultivate them he must, and this was one more excuse for passing long seasons in town. Though he could hope for preferment from England, Swift had to give some of his days in Dublin to appearances before these unconvivial powers. There is a hint in one such appearance, outside Dublin, that Swift's effort to ingratiate himself with the archbishop met with early success. His grace, while just entering on the litigation with Christ Church, wished as well to enforce his authority over the sister cathedral, and therefore claimed the right of 'Visitor' over the 'petit' canons of St Patrick's, a station which would give him a quasi-judicial authority. The dean and chapter made some polite claim, like that of their colleagues in Christ Church, to be exempt from the archbishop's visitation. But unlike Moreton's proceedings it was hardly more than a formal protest. Thus when Arch-

---

[1] Letter of 4 May 1700, to Thomas Smith (Bodl. MS. Smith 52, p. 85, spelling modernized).

bishop King commanded the 'petit' canons to appear before him at Leixlip (a few hours from Dublin) in July 1703, the men of St Patrick's resolved that their dean, Jerome Ryves, and one or two others should wait upon his grace and ask him to withdraw the summons. Swift went with the dean, and I infer that the chapter picked on him as a person particularly agreeable to King.[1] As it happens, the archbishop seems to have won this dispute effortlessly.[2]

Travels and visits elsewhere Swift also indulged in freely. During warm weather, or when the Irish Parliament was not in session and the Lord Lieutenant was not in residence, he lived a great deal at Trim, and he went there for Christmas 1702. Elsewhere as well he saw his friends: at the Pace, a village in Meath; or Ringsend, at the mouth of the Liffey.[3] But Dublin must have meant more than any place except London. Besides the heads of the church and state, there were Swift's relatives and the bulk of his purely social acquaintances, most of whom usually spent as much of the year as they could in the capital.

At the same time, a return to London could never be far from his meditations. Although the Irish Parliament was to meet in September 1703,[4] the English Parliament was to meet in November, and a natural migration flowed from the lesser capital to swell the crowd in the greater. Swift joined the stream on 11 November, two days after the sittings began in London. Sailing for England by way of Chester, he found the other passengers included the Bishop of Cloyne and Lord Mountjoy, both in the Irish House of Lords, and several Irish M.P.s.[5] As it happens, this was some weeks after there opened in Dublin what Froude

---

[1] I assume that Swift was chosen because King summoned the canons to meet him originally on 7 July (Mason, p. 217), and Swift went to Leixlip on 14 July (*Accounts 1702–3*, fol. 8v).

[2] Mant I. 173.   [3] These visits are recorded in the *Accounts 1702–3, passim*.

[4] The session actually opened on 21 September.

[5] According to *SPD. 1703–4*, p. 197, the following persons left Dublin for England on the same day as Swift and, I assume, therefore in the same boat: Thomas, Lord Coningsby, and his family; William Stewart, Viscount Mountjoy; Dr Charles Crow, Bishop of Cloyne; Francis Annesley, the friend of Archbishop King; Brigadier John Tidcomb, a friend of Addison's; and several Irish M.P.s. Since Mountjoy in 1710 paid Swift's travel expenses from Chester to London (*Journal* I. 5, n. 1), he may have been responsible for Swift's travelling at this time too.

has called 'the most eventful session' of Parliament in Irish history.[1]

V

To mark the significance of this memorable Parliament, the Duke of Ormonde had come over in June; for he was now Lord Lieutenant, and would manage the session.[2] This glittering figure had not yet revealed how small was the ratio of his performance to his potentialities: good nature and great courage were insufficient to qualify him for the rôle into which he was being pressed. Two years older than the vicar of Laracor, the Duke belonged to the most magnificent family in Ireland; patrons of Swift's school, university, and church, the Butlers had a history which was part of the doctor's memory. Ormonde's grandfather, the first Duke and the most splendid courtier of his generation, had lost a promising eldest son and a grandson; but in James, his namesake, flowered a garland of apparent virtues. The second Duke, and now Lord Lieutenant, had received a good education; he seemed intelligent, and was charming; he looked healthy and handsome; he was a brave soldier and possessed unlimited wealth. His first wife had been Queen Anne's cousin; his second, Lady Mary, daughter to the princely Duke of Beaufort. Ormonde had chosen a military career, and Marlborough's enemies loved to celebrate his deeds. At the Battle of Landen, 1693, his heroism had lost him his horse and almost his life. At Vigo, in 1702, he and Sir George Rooke had destroyed the enemy fleet and captured a million pounds' worth of Spanish treasure. When he came over as Lord Lieutenant, the Irish gentry treated him like an angel dropped from the clouds; and Swift succumbed with the rest. Years later, looking back over Ormonde's career, Swift wrote that apart from youthful sins and a chronic willingness to suffer fools gladly, the Duke was about as unblemished as mortal man could be.[3] This was in a defensive eulogy, written for publication; but Swift

---

[1] Froude I. 293.   [2] He reached Dublin, 4 June (*Life of Ormonde*, 1747, p. 292).
[3] Davis VIII. 133, written around 1715–17; Swift's first impressions may have been different.

genuinely admired the Duke, blaming his mistakes on those around him: 'He is governed by fools; and usually has much more sense than his advisers, but never proceeds by it.'[1]

During the preparation for the Parliament and during the sittings, Ormonde's charm, such as it was, met many tests: 'were it not that my Lord Duke has a great personal interest, and many are ashamed to deny him whom they have talked themselves into, nothing at all would be done.'[2] Little secrecy was feasible with the intended business of an Irish Parliament. In Dublin the members of the Privy Council of Ireland sketched the heads of the bills desired by the government. These were then sent to England for approval or alteration, and afterwards returned to the Council in Dublin before Parliament met. The feeling of the country could be found out through conversation or by direct inquiries; and for weeks before the sittings began, the state correspondence was generally crowded with discussions of the legislation being planned. Once a bill was submitted to the Irish Parliament, it could be accepted or thrown out, but it could not be changed. If the Commons or Lords wished to propose alterations, they might do so; but these had to be approved in Westminster before the redesigned bill came to a vote.

During the months of investigating opinion in Ireland and asking for approval in England, Ormonde and his council formulated a programme drawn out of one enormous principle, the economic destruction of the native Roman Catholics. To these measures the Privy Council in London added another, for the political destruction of the Dissenters in Ireland. For both these policies the energy came from the fear of new threats to the English establishment in that kingdom. Alternatively, a legislative union of Ireland and England, such as was being planned between the Scots and the English, might have eliminated the threats without being oppressive; and many leaders in Ireland desired this. But a union would have appeared dangerous to the financial interests of English merchants. Instead, therefore, a

---

[1] *Journal*, 20 Sept. 1711.
[2] Edward Southwell to Nottingham, 25 Sept. 1703 (in Froude 1. 295, n. 1). Parliament met in Dublin, 21 Sept. 1703.

scheme was proposed which would end the Papists' remaining hold on Irish landed property.

At the same time, this very scheme could not be carried through without allowing the Dissenters to take advantage of it and thereby granting them much of the power the Papists would lose. To weaken the Roman Catholics while strengthening the Dissenters seemed a quixotic procedure to the bishops of the Anglican church. Consequently, in order to safeguard their establishment they had for years been hoping to see the Sacramental Test extended to Ireland as it had already flourished for almost a generation in the mother kingdom. Yet the bishops at this time did not first propose the Test; for it appeared quite mysteriously, added in England to the long bill sent there for approval.[1]

Before the spring of 1704 the bills passed into legislation, with the new restrictions on Roman Catholics pouring a concrete foundation for the whole jail-house system of penal laws. The nearest thing to a moral occasion for these enactments has been expressed by their denouncer, Lecky: 'They were largely modelled after the French legislation against the Huguenots, but persecution in Ireland never approached in severity that of Lewis XIV, and it was absolutely insignificant compared with that which had extirpated Protestantism and Judaism from Spain.'[2] But any quick comfort which might be found in this comparison is easily exhausted by a glance at merely the anti-popery acts of the 1703–4 Parliament. Under these, and especially the general Act 'to prevent the further growth of popery', crippling limits were imposed on the freedom of Roman Catholics to practise their religion, to educate their children, or to bear arms. They were also restricted as to residence and disabled from voting. But

[1] Beckett, pp. 43–5. I suspect that Nottingham added it as a uniformitarian support for his fight against occasional conformity in England, knowing that it would be welcome to Anglican clergy and laymen in Ireland. Burnet says the English ministers, not liking the bill as a whole but knowing the Irish House of Commons would be furious if it were not approved, tacked the Sacramental Test to it in the belief that some of the promoters would dislike this provision so deeply that they would withdraw their support from the whole. I am willing to believe that Nottingham gave this account to Burnet, and that the bishop was taken in by it.

[2] Lecky I. 137. But cf. J. G. Simms, 'The Making of a Penal Law', *Irish Historical Studies* XII. 105–18.

the most ferocious clause was that intended to detach them from
their own soil, to make the landlord class almost exclusively
Protestant, the tenant class almost exclusively native Catholic.[1]
This was the prohibition against the purchase of any real estate
by a Roman Catholic at all: he might not even lease land for a
period longer than thirty-one years. If he had an estate, it might
descend to his sons, but only by being broken up into equal parts
among them. Yet if his eldest son declared himself a convert to the
Church of Ireland, he became heir at law to the entire property,
and the father was reduced at once to being tenant for life.
According to one computation the value of land fell about ten
per cent the year after the act was passed.[2] By this law and later
elaborations, titles to land in Ireland were once more tampered
with and shaken; and if we shift our eyes from the plight of the
victims who fell under it, to look at Swift, we may reflect that
here was one more source for his anxiety about his own accumulation of an estate. With most of the soil of the country held by
titles based on recent confiscations, with many of the old possessors or their children 'still living, still remembered, still honoured
by the people', a dread of a fresh and cataclysmic transfer of
property underlay all the politics of the landlords.[3]

About the Sacramental Test, however, which was tacked on to
the same bill, anxiety contributed much less than triumph to the
emotion which Swift felt. As a fortress of the church in England,
the Test had stood since his earliest years. Introduced now into a
kingdom where half the Protestants were Dissenters, it guaranteed the exclusion of all but Anglicans (and 'occasional conformists') from the making of public policy. To Swift it seemed
essential for the survival of the Church of Ireland. The Presbyterians had established themselves in Scotland and were in a
position there to persecute Episcopalians. They were rapidly
increasing in Ireland, and refused to accept a mere act of toleration as proper for their merits. Unless all holders of public office
were compelled at least to appear to be Anglicans, Swift feared
the true faith could not live. His doctrine had practical flaws
apart from the injustice of the Test. After King George came in,

[1] Lecky I. 151–2.   [2] *Ibid.*, p. 189, n. 2.   [3] *Ibid.*, p. 278.

a series of indemnity acts undermined the essential provision that anyone occupying a civil or military office under the crown must prove that he had taken communion in the Established Church. But the Test did keep non-conforming Dissenters out of Parliament, and it profoundly weakened their strength in municipal government. Swift's belief in it possessed him. He was to publish his first essay on Irish politics in defence of the Test; and twenty-five years later he would still be flinging a barrage of polemics against its enemies.

Chapter Eleven

ENGLAND: NOVEMBER 1703
TO MAY 1704

I

Although the Test Act became law in Ireland months after
Swift left, he reached England only to find the same
subject obsessing the Parliament there. While he shows
little consciousness of being caught up in it himself, his observations are ripe with emotion, and his presence in London during
these episodes drew him further along the stages of a logical journey. In the course of a visit which lasted over six months, Swift
now renewed the second-hand life of suspense and unreality
which England still gave him. Socially, he managed without that
easy level of casual acquaintanceship which supported his routines at home. He also did without Hetty Johnson, though his
correspondence with her flourished. To keep his vocational prospects hopeful, he waited on politicians in London as he had to
wait upon bishops in Dublin. For the actual service of his vocation, however, he could exercise himself only to support general
projects of value to the church. As a writer, at this point, he
moved away from imaginative freedom, and confined himself to
the needs of ambition or of partisan argument. As a public figure
he barely existed in England, but that embryo existence began
already to evolve toward commitments which could be labelled
in ways he did not like to recognize. As a private person the
sharpest feelings he would suffer in this familiar exile would be
provoked by the conduct of his dearest friend at home.

Yet, pervading all these aspects of his experience, the heated
atmosphere which steadily enveloped Swift from November to
May was still that of church politics; for the English Test was
touching off explosions in the House of Commons. While it took

him less than two weeks to arrive at the scene of the uproar, Swift almost coincidentally witnessed a performance by nature herself which seemed designed to illustrate the character of political passion. Wishing to have all the time he could in London, he had travelled from Chester to Leicester and then quickly up to the capital. Landing in England on 13 November, he was able to visit his mother and complete the subsequent journey south by the twenty-fourth.[1] This speed was fortunate, since the wildest storm in recorded English history struck the country the night of the twenty-sixth.[2] Ships, trees, chimneys, and men lay blasted after it. Besides the numbers killed by houses, walls, and stacks caving in, hundreds of seamen of the Royal Navy drowned.[3] A part of the new buildings, not quite finished, of St James's Palace, fell down; in the middle of the night, the Queen stood at her windows and watched the gale rip up ancient elms in the park.[4] No one could remember such a hurricane: '5200 weight of lead was blown down from the Old Mathematical School in Christs Hospital, and 4000 from the new, which is wrapt round a stack of chimneys.'[5] Admiral Beaumont perished in the Downs; Bishop Kidder was crushed to death in Wells. The seas flooded Bristol, rushing into cellars and underground warehouses. Plymouth, Portsmouth, Deal, Harwich, and Yarmouth harbours were among the worst hit. From the south-west the wind dashed across southern England on the twenty-seventh and hurled itself at the Low Countries and Germany.

The tempest was emblematic of the weather in both Parliament and Convocation; for the war against France, which had been openly declared in the spring of 1702, had meant great changes for each. To see these changes as Swift could, one must recall that just as the years of peace had given strength to the combination of Rochester, Nottingham, and Seymour, so the

[1] *Accounts 1703–4*, fol. 2ᵛ. He put to sea 11 Nov. and landed at Chester 13 Nov. His expenses from Dublin to Leicester (including a stay there) to London came to £6 7s. 8d.

[2] Years later, Swift said he had arrived in London just in time to have his share of this storm (Ball 1. 66).

[3] *Daily Courant*, 7 Dec. 1703, says 1,326; Trevelyan 1. 308 says 1,500.

[4] Trevelyan 1. 310; *The Storm* (attributed to Defoe, 1704), pp. 77, 81.

[5] *Post Man*, 30 Nov. 1703.

return of war undermined them. Since their combination drew its energy not only from the country gentlemen but also from the clergy, the fields of action open to it included both the House of Commons and the Lower House of Convocation. Francis Atterbury in Convocation, Seymour and Howe in the Commons, Nottingham and Rochester in the Lords, all worked for similar ends.

To Swift, at this time, there seemed no contradiction between a concern for the Established Church and an acceptance of the need for war. He could censure the anti-military machinations of the leaders of the Tory–church alliance without feeling that he was deserting the sacred institution which employed him. As it happens, a new political grouping was coming forward that would suit him better than either the Junto or the so-called high-flying Tories; and this was Harley's 'new country party', co-operating at a preliminary stage with Rochester and Nottingham.

Behind all these relationships lay the war. In order to direct his campaigns successfully, Marlborough as commander-in-chief required Godolphin, his daughter's father-in-law, to be Lord Treasurer and head of the government. If they meant to maintain the administrative staff essential to their plans, Marlborough and Godolphin could not turn out of office all the Whigs whose places the Tory leaders needed to stable their draft horses.

Meanwhile, within the church the old division between lower clergy and bishops was running parallel to the difference between the balanced House of Lords and the Tory-driven Commons. When William III became King, those bishops who stood by their oaths to James II not only left places vacant for the new King to fill; they also made it unthinkable for many honest men to step into those vacancies. Inevitably, the additions which William could make to the episcopal bench consisted of persons not embarrassed to wear a disputed mitre and willing to accommodate their opinions to the new regime. Meanwhile, the mass of the lower clergy had remained both out of sympathy with the Dutch Calvinist King and suspicious of the weakening effect his tolerant views and bishops would have on their own hegemony over Dissenters. Thus the parish priests of the Establishment felt as a rule bitterly distrustful of that very episcopacy which distinguished their own body from that of their schismatic rivals. At the same time, the furore over unitarianism and deism had not declined in temperature, and Convocation still seemed the authority equipped to deal with these dangers. Nor had Atterbury failed to follow up his *Letter to a Convocation Man* with further demands that the Convocation of Canterbury Province be revived in a form which would make the Lower House independent of either the bishops or the King. Naturally, Rochester took advantage of these crises; and when he enjoyed his term of power, he wangled permission for the province of Canterbury to sit in Convocation for the first time since the Revolution. This was precisely when the Junto was under attack in the House of Commons and the four lords were impeached. Throughout the spring of 1701, therefore, the minority of episcopal sympathizers in the Lower House of Convocation had to work with the bishops in the Upper House to prevent Atterbury's gang from creating precedents which could then be used to strengthen his shaky arguments. But his forces not only mastered the English Lower House. Soon as well they reached out for parallel and supporting action in Ireland. Furthermore, during the spring of 1702, with the accession of a Queen 'entirely English', and a devoted daughter of the Established Church, Atterbury's men were able to add royal authority to their armaments. As the movement of the war made it awkward for Tories in Parliament to attack the administration without appearing traitorous, the utility of Convocation as an offensive weapon increased. So the 'rights of Convocation' joined the other Tory hunting cries.

It was at this point that the practice of occasional conformity emerged as one more issue, seemingly independent of the war, which could be safely exploited in Parliament against the ministry and the Junto. Among Anglicans in England there was naturally the same feeling of exasperation as in Ireland against those Dissenters who evaded the meaning of the Test Act through occasionally attending the Established Church instead of sticking to their own meeting-houses or chapels. Even before King William died, there had been a push to amend the Abjuration Bill so as to penalize office-holders who practised such occasional conformity. In Parliament as in Convocation, however, the Upper House was less excitably intolerant than the Lower; and bishops like Burnet were at hand in both assemblies to help defeat such measures even while exacerbating the indignation of their clergy.

Swift had no doubt about the value of the Test; and toward those Dissenters who evaded its purpose he felt only hostility; the *Tale of a Tub* has a quick stab at an occasionally conforming lord mayor of London.[1] But as to the wisdom of punishing the culprits, he was at this time still undecided. In the winter of 1702–3 a bill against occasional conformity was passed in the Commons, where Harley's associate, St John, stood one of its godfathers. With the Queen promoting the bill, the Lords could not easily throw it out. However, with Burnet's assistance, amendments were introduced which not only made the bill unacceptable to the Commons but raised a constitutional impasse between them and the Lords. The bill was finally lost about the same time that Rochester, who had refused to leave the front lines in Westminster for the remoteness of Dublin Castle, was forced to give up his Lord Lieutenancy (February 1703).[2]

Yet Nottingham held on as Secretary of State, and it was under his management that the Test had found its way to Ireland. So it is not surprising that when the English and Irish parliaments reassembled in the autumn of 1703, not only did the Convocation of the province of Canterbury meet as before, but in addition the Convocation of the Church of Ireland met for the first time since 1666.[3] From Swift's comments and related circumstances, we can fairly infer that while he rejoiced in the new birth of this organ of ecclesiastical authority,[4] he disapproved of the schemes of those who revived it. That the Convocation would fight deism, Dissent,

---

[1] Davis I. 131.   [2] *J.H.L.* XVII. 306–18 (24–26 Feb. 1702/3).
[3] Summoned with the Irish Parliament for 1 Sept. 1703 (Mant I. 163), though not meeting till much later.
[4] This sentiment was practically unanimous among the Irish clergy. The petition for a Convocation was signed by all but one of the bishops of Ireland (Mant I. x–xi), in express agreement with the lower clergy's desire for such a meeting. But the form of summons requested was obviously designed to assist Atterbury's intrigues: e.g., in the principle that each house acted and adjourned by itself (Mant I. 163).

and immorality, he certainly wished. That it might serve as the vehicle of Atterbury's ambitions or as an engine in political warfare, he simultaneously regretted.[1] Nevertheless, at this time as earlier, in his last years at Moor Park, he was called upon neither to judge the doctrinal disputes connected with the convocations nor to take sides in the ecclesiastical parties built around them. Although the polemical torrent which had streamed since the middle of William's reign did not flag, Swift kept his feet out of it. He neither attacked Sherlock nor defended Atterbury, nor challenged Kennett.

Not so with the controversy about the bill against occasional conformity. As soon as the Commons gathered in 1703, they flung themselves into a renewed pandemonium over this, while the English clergy imitated them with their own hubbubs in Convocation. Through Swift's reactions to the parliamentary turmoil, we can see him reluctantly driven to formulate positions and unwillingly lured to express judgments. We can see his private ambitions struggling against his unadmitted principles, his loyalty to the church tried by his desire to please statesmen.

II

The Rochesters and Seymours were still furious with the Queen because she refused to weaken either Marlborough's control of the army or Godolphin's control of the government; and without doing so, she could not give them the patronage they needed to reward their supporters. Consequently, in the autumn of 1703 the subscribers to the Nottingham–Rochester high-church combination again withdrew their backing from the ministry. But the milder faction opposed to the Junto was meanwhile developing quietly under Harley's care. Dominated by him and Henry St John—who possessed youthful energy and the oratorical gift which his master lacked—this 'new country party' had little

---

[1] Williams I. 121 has a good clue to Swift's view of Atterbury before 1710. Another is Swift's description of himself, in the *Sentiments of a Church-of-England Man*, as one who does not 'reckon every schism of that damnable nature, which some would represent' (Davis II. 11); for Atterbury, following the leads of Dodwell and Leslie, exaggerated the sinfulness of the Dissenters' schism with the Church of England.

eagerness to revive the intrigues that Rochester had connived at under Charles II. Harley got much of his strength from great merchants and landholders enriched by speculative investments during the years between the Restoration and the death of William III. Happy in their gains, these magnates had reached their balance with the Revolution Settlement, and wished to keep what they owned. The far more numerous class of small squires who had lost out through commercial timidity distrusted the central government and stood faithful to that symbol of their golden days, the Established Church, exalting her mitred front in courts and parliaments. If Harley and St John could draw enough of these landed gentlemen into their own train, they might, with the Queen's help, hope to dominate the Commons. Actually, to do this, they needed as well the promise of a peace which alone could undercut the entrenchments of the Whigs; and peace was not to be approachable for five years.

Swift had no love for Rochester and only contempt for factions. He did not object to 'interests', or what we might call 'lobbies'; for Parliament to him was properly an arena where miscellaneous local and economic rivals met to settle their secondary differences. This is where Burke was to disagree with him. Swift assumed that the elements of the English constitution could be rationally accepted by all members of the classes responsible for government; the rubs that remained under this acceptance, their representatives could discuss not through cliques but as individuals, each adhering to his own highest principles. Burke believed that a loyalty to the state—including the constitution—indeed came first, but that the superstructure of compromise must grow out of each man's participation in an organized group with responsible leadership. The polarization that horrified Swift was what would become the mark of democratic government a century later; for he wished to avoid conflicts based on ideology, and he condemned the idea of a team of men pledging themselves to capture the vehicle of government and drive it as they liked. The Whig and Tory clusters, which in both these tendencies were unlike older groupings, had by the same token a continuity of life that enabled them at length to absorb the rest.

[117]

While particular crises, issues, or personalities must have a stop, political philosophies—however superficial, inconsistent, and hypocritical—can prolong their identity, achieve a history, and animate a popular movement.

Swift therefore censured the followers of Harley as well as Seymour, so long as those factions seemed to be spoiling what were otherwise good chances for a fundamental unity of purpose in the elements of government. Since the constitutional dilemma at this time offered two broad alternatives in the shape of large party groupings, he implicitly joined the 'old' Whigs. But how deeply he resented the intrusion of the whole political schism into public behaviour generally, one can measure by the disgust with which (in 1706) he blamed Rochester for promoting it in Ireland:

> I am sorry we begin to resemble England onely in its defects; about seven years ago, frogs were imported here,[1] and thrive very well; and three years after a certain great man [i.e. Rochester] brought over Whig and Tory which suit the soyl admirably.[2]

III

In the autumn of 1703, English party strife throve at least as well as Irish frogs. Queen Anne had grasped that she could not openly back both the war and the revived bill against occasional conformity. Dropping her aggressiveness of the preceding winter, she closed her speech from the throne on the note of 'perfect peace and union'. Advising her heavy-breathing parliament to 'avoid any heats and divisions', she now left any new launching of the bill to Nottingham and Rochester; and without her aegis over them, they easily foundered. At the very first reading, the Lords —this time sure of their strength—rejected it.[3] Swift, freshly

---

[1] Not true, but a common story.

[2] Williams I. 55. Burnet also says that before Rochester's government, 'the only division in Ireland was, that of English and Irish, protestants and papists: but of late an animosity came to be raised there, like that we labour under in England, between whig and tory.' With this, Dartmouth's note disagrees: 'There is nobody in Ireland that does not know, that these distinctions were first begun by that very wise, but over-zealous whig, the lord Capel' (Burnet v. 100 and note).

[3] *J.H.L.* xvii. 348 (14 Dec. 1703). Yet it is often said to have been the second reading.

arrived in London, imagined himself to be observing the wrestling in perfect sang-froid. When he wrote home two days after the defeat of the bill, he exercised his free wit on the spectacle just past, and achieved enough success for his words to be regularly quoted:

> I wish you had been here for ten days, during the highest and warmest reign of party and faction, that I ever knew or read of, upon the Bill against Occasional Conformity, which, two days ago, was, upon the first reading, rejected by the Lords. It was so universal, that I observed the dogs in the streets much more contumelious and quarrelsome than usual; and the very night before the bill went up, a committee of Whig and Tory cats, had a very warm and loud debate upon the roof of our house.[1]

This is indeed the tone of disengagement. But Swift misunderstood himself. During his half-year's visit he came to a turn not intimated by the style of his gossip. If the abyss between parties had yawned since his schooldays, yet his own Irish upbringing, retirement among the Temples, and absorption with clerical and emotional demands had successively clouded the direct view of its depth. Now at last he saw it directly exposed; and now he began to take sides.

Known as a controversialist, Swift was asked to have a fling at the target. But he felt too many doubts to wish to publish any opinion. How one could love the church and oppose this bill, it was not easy for Swift to perceive; and he sounded out his highest-placed acquaintances. To those figures whom he had been used to approach before, he could now add the unpredictable but very conversable Earl of Peterborough, a spendthrift roué in his mid-forties, who had taken an early and giant step in the right direction when, during the Revolution crisis, he contributed all his influence toward bringing William III over to England. Peterborough possessed Burnet's talkativeness and impetuosity, but his temper flickered like a bird's wing. While he had plenty of courage and energy, he could neither sit still nor tell the truth for very long. At the present juncture, Peterborough was interested in diplomatic or military opportunities and he was

[1] Williams I. 38–9.

co-operating with Marlborough; so he could have delivered only one sentiment on the much-discussed bill. The high-churchmen, of course, held the perfectly opposite opinion: 'The whole body of the clergy', said Swift,

> with a great majority of the House of Commons, were violent for this bill. As great a majority of the Lords, amongst whom all the bishops, but four, were against it. The court and the rabble (as extremes often agree) were trimmers.

Peterborough, Burnet, Somers, all assured him that rejection would aid the church and do no kindness to the Dissenters. 'I know not what to think', he said, 'and therefore shall think no more.'[1] But he did think more, and at last wrote on the Whig side, probably during the first half of December 1703.

What he wrote is perhaps less significant than that he never printed it. The reason he gives is, 'It came too late by a day'— i.e., he only finished it after the bill's defeat was conceded. His *Discourse of the Contests and Dissensions* had come 'too late' by months, but he had committed that to the press. It was not chagrin but relief that prompted his reversal. Our detailed knowledge of his mind at this turning depends on his letters to William Tisdall, a fanatical Tory whom he confided in but did not respect. Swift teased and insulted him to a degree that would have made an enemy of some men; and Tisdall's extremism tempted Swift to colour his own views out of deviltry:

> Pox on the Dissenters and Independents! I would as soon trouble my head to write against a louse or a flea. I tell you what; I wrote against the bill that was against occasional conformity; but it came too late by a day, so I would not print it. But you may answer it if you please.[2]

This is how he wrote in order to provoke his high-flying correspondent. The real story seems to be that with a harsh strain on his sympathies Swift performed an uncongenial task. For his own sake he would not alienate his powerful friends; but if he did not purposely procrastinate, he certainly fell into an agreeable mischance: the outcome might possibly keep him in with the Junto

---

[1] Williams I. 38-9. [2] *Ibid.*, pp. 43-4.

and yet leave him his principles. Perhaps he was exemplifying a rule he elsewhere made explicit: 'A wise and a good man may indeed be sometimes induced to comply with a number, whose opinion he generally approves, although it be perhaps against his own. But this liberty should be made use of... only with a view of bringing over his own side another time to something of greater and more publick moment.'[1] If the church could aspire to convert the Irish, Swift may possibly be forgiven for boring the Whigs from within.

It also looks as though Swift, having made his original acquaintance at court under William III, was clinging to the traditions of Moor Park. From Marlborough, Godolphin, Nottingham, Rochester, or Seymour, he expected no help. Harley and St John, who were still rising to power, he does not mention. Yet none of his would-be patrons—Somers, Burnet, Peterborough, Halifax, or possibly Sunderland—now held a ministerial post. It is fair to say he knew the right people at the wrong time. What preferments these benefactors might distribute, they could hardly afford to throw away on a hesitant Irish parson.

IV

If he had to choose a single player to lay his money on, he picked Lord Somers, a sincere churchman though of tolerant views, and (in these years) the most widely respected chief of the Junto. To Swift he appeared the head of his party and, I think, perhaps the one who required the least distortion of Swift's own inclinations. Even in the course of maligning Somers, near the end of Queen Anne's reign, he granted him 'an excellent understanding adorned by all the polite parts of learning'.[2]

Swift had brought over a copy of *A Tale of a Tub*, to be published at last; for he evidently believed that this demonstration of his gifts would establish his reputation as an extraordinary writer

[1] Davis II. 1.
[2] *Ibid.* VII. 6. Cf. the 'great influence' attributed by Swift to Somers in 1707 (Williams I. 57). The 'great man' whom Swift in 1704 described as having 'as much influence in England as any subject can well have' was probably Somers (Williams I. 48).

and thus recommend him and his useful talent to the men whom the court must soon employ. As a radical bid for Somers's immediate patronage, he decided to give the book an additional dedication, pretended to be from the bookseller (or, as we should say, publisher) and addressed in the boldest language of panegyric to his lordship. The result is a remarkable achievement in prose elegance; but apart from its literary qualities, the dedication tells something about Swift's views when he wrote it.

For the praise of Somers does have a visible tendency. Swift could have dwelt on his work as Lord Chancellor or mentioned his desire for all Protestants to stand united against popery. Instead, he chooses unconventional traits: wit, learning, wisdom, eloquence, etc., with 'evenness of temper in all scenes of life'. Only two concrete allusions appear. One, to the attempt of Somers's enemies to impeach him, is of course a means of reminding his lordship of a service already rendered by the *Discourse of the Contests and Dissensions*. The other allusion is to Somers's defence of the seven bishops during the 'late reign' of James II; and this naturally associates the senior member of the Junto with the very church which his enemies claimed was in danger from his party. Thus in dedicating his masterpiece to John, Lord Somers, Swift was refraining from an appeal to the Whig partisan. Whether this was the most effective way for a vicar to recommend himself for a bishopric, the reader may easily judge.

How Swift was to receive credit from Somers for his authorship of either the anonymous book or the pseudonymous dedication is a question not easily answered. Writing another work for publication under another disguise about this time, Swift said, 'I am not under the necessity of declaring my self by the prospect of an employment', and 'I industriously conceal my name; which wholly exempts me from any hopes and fears in delivering my opinion.'[1] Yet though he conscientiously suppressed all the external evidence of the *Tale*'s paternity, he undoubtedly thought its publication would help him get access to the men of power.[2] If Somers recognized the author, the job was done. Through familiarity with Swift's ironical compliments in conversation, his

[1] Davis II. 2.   [2] Cf. *Journal*, 7 Oct. 1710.

lordship might simply be depended upon to know the man behind the faces presented. The allusion to the impeachment proceedings might have given him a further clue; and Swift might
also have conveyed the truth by more direct means, such as an
inscribed copy, or a word in a letter after he knew the success of
the book was assured. I suspect, however, that with his love of
practical jokes he hid in the dedication itself an allusion which
Somers would be certain to notice but which we can no longer
detect.

As a piece of rhetoric, the 'bookseller's' dedication to Somers
easily substantiates the case against those who assume that denigration alone brought out the highest powers of Swift. Actually,
in the genre of eulogy his productions have not often been surpassed, and an appreciative study of these subtle compliments
would repay the scholar's labour. In dealing with Somers, as it
happens, Swift does not employ his most characteristic device,
the mock-insult. Instead, he rather daringly creates the parody
of a trite dedication. Thus the effect of this tribute depends upon
the conceit that what is normally a lie becomes the truth when
applied to his lordship, that the banalities of mercenary hacks
will seem fresh and alive if Somers is their subject.

To frame this conceit, Swift adopts another, familiar to his
admirers: the mask (transparently meant to be seen through) of
a naïve speaker. Here this is the supposed publisher of the *Tale*,
represented as ignorant of the author, incapable of reading the
book itself, and therefore all the more effective as a witness to the
universality of Somers's reputation. Besides this mask and the
form of a parody, Swift employs, in a double degree, another of
his usual devices, the dramatization of a commonplace. Starting
from a motto supposedly found on the manuscript—*detur dignis-
simo* ('let it be given to the worthiest', said to be Alexander's disposition of his crown on his death-bed)—Swift has the bookseller
discover that while every expert whom he consults chooses himself as the obviously *dignissimus* person, the second choice is invariably Somers. In other words, as the old saying goes, 'those,
to whom every body allows the second place, have an undoubted
title to the first.' By the time the bookseller has done relating the

history of his Socratic search, both the ancient motto and the overworked aphorism seem to have been acted out and infused with genuine significance.

But following his customary unwillingness to limit the direction of his irony to a single topic, Swift also takes the opportunity to ridicule the 'wits' responsible for the run of either stale dedications or stale works to be dedicated. Such ridicule was itself conventional at this time. Yet Swift makes it new by turning the satire back on itself; for the naïve bookseller expresses disappointment not with the triteness of the materials his hacks have given him but with the triteness of their application to Somers:

> I expected, indeed, to have heard of your lordship's bravery, at the head of an army; of your undaunted courage, in mounting a breach, or scaling a wall; or, to have had your pedigree trac'd in a lineal descent from the house of Austria; or, of your wonderful talent at dress and dancing; or, your profound knowledge in algebra, metaphysicks, and the Oriental tongues. But to ply the world with an old beaten story of your wit, and eloquence, and learning, and wisdom . . . with forty other common topicks: I confess, I have neither the conscience, nor countenance to do it.[1]

V

The vanished pamphlet on the bill against occasional conformity and the vague tendency of the dedication to Somers seem to mark the extreme limit of Swift's power to stretch his own opinions to fit those of the Junto. But while we have lost what he wrote on their side, we have not lost what he later described as opposed to the measures taken by their party.[2] This essay, not published till 1711, is *The Sentiments of a Church-of-England Man, with Respect to Religion and Government*.[3] Although Swift in writing the *Sentiments* and most other people in reading it have taken the piece to be a balanced exposition of the author's plain views, his ostentatious disinterestedness seems misleading. As a guide to his inclinations at this important moment, the *Sentiments* deserves a fair amount of brooding over. But to digest either the shell of systematic generalization or the bulk of digressive filling without analysing

[1] Davis I. 15.　　[2] *Ibid.* VIII. 122.　　[3] See Appendix A.

the contrasts in tone would be to ignore the best hint of Swift's meaning. For the essay seems ultimately a disguised attack on policies normally attached to the Whigs, and an exposition of the doctrines which the anti-Jacobite 'church party' shared with the 'new country party'. If we look for Swift's views on the conduct of the war or foreign relations, on the needs of merchant traders or problems of finance, we shall find blanks. Instead, he reduces all political questions to constitutional principles, and he handles the constitution as comprising a state church and a limited monarchy. These assumptions underlie the real structure of the piece. Thus for its rhetoric, the *Sentiments* depends on the premise that the church and the civil government are of equivalent weight in the constitution—an opinion which hardly seems un-prejudiced now, though common enough in Swift's day; and from this dubious starting-point he can go on to treat the Whigs as responsible for profound errors in church policy, the Tories for venial errors in political theory. By examining either the logical framework or the detailed contents of such an essay, one learns less about Swift's deliberations than by following the shifts in its tone.

In Section One of the *Sentiments*, devoted to church matters, Swift's thin outline of logic is plain enough. He pretends to argue that there are faults on both sides, Tory and Whig, and that party spirit as such is the great evil. Next he seems to admit that the censures laid against each party by the other are all extravagant and unfair. Then he presents the supposedly impartial views of an unbiased middle-of-the road Anglican. Thus a member of the Church of England, Swift says, should believe in God, Provi-dence, revelation, and the divinity of Christ. He should prefer episcopacy to other forms of church government but should be willing to tolerate non-episcopal sects while discouraging their proliferation. So he considers the Test Act necessary as a defence of the constitution but may doubt the expediency of an act to end occasional conformity.

If we look closer at the details of Section One, we find Swift here taking the Church of England as the proper system of a nation's faith, and allowing for change only in peripherals. He is willing to tolerate the Nonconforming sects already in being but not by any means to broaden their liberties. He scolds men of all politics but particularly the Whigs, for failing to respect the priestly order. The remission of the First Fruits[1] in England he interprets as an acknowledgement that the state had in the past executed more than justice on any excessive growth of ecclesiastical property. Disapproving of the freedom of the press allowed to immoral and impious books, he asks for a stronger censorship.

The head and front of his wrath is bent against the Protestant Dissenters. Here his speech has two personal accents: he deplores schism, and he does so on secular grounds. For him the outermost boundary of toleration must be the Test Act. Nonconformity is an evil, to be endured in so far as it is ineradicable, yet to be contained, not freed. The reason is that it creates a body of men prepared to overthrow the state if rebellion can further what they fancy as the true religion. In a sense this stand seems near the middle. Unlike the most fanatical of the nonjurors, Swift seeks no shortest way with Dissenters. Unlike his friend Tisdall, he does not call for a rooting out of all Presbyterian or Independent worship, schooling, and seminaries.

When he mentions the uproar over the bill to abolish occasional conformity, however, Swift insinuates that the critics of the bill had hoped as a next move to repeal the Test altogether. To him that step meant the undoing of his church; and the allegation shows that he has pulled out of the uneasy position into which he had just been manœuvred by the decision to write against the bill himself. It is instructive therefore to compare the *Sentiments* with the speech which Burnet published attacking the bill,[2] for Swift may in part have been answering that. The bishop, as the world knew, had learned his points from Edmund Calamy, a mannerly apologist for Dissent; and perhaps Swift would have recoiled less abruptly from Burnet's speech if he had not heard the meeting-house voice over the episcopal hands. Where Burnet, in his plea, sounds afraid of the Papists, Swift in the *Sentiments* is

---

[1] See below, p. 131.
[2] *The Bishop of Salisbury's Speech ... against Occasional Conformity*, 1704.

worried about the Dissenters. Where the bishop thinks the bill may mean the beginning of the end of toleration, the vicar thinks its defeat threatens the Test. Where one seriously attacks the non-juror Leslie as a spokesman for the high-church Jacobites, the other tosses aside Leslie's fulminations as absurd and harmless. Where one boasts of his 'moderation', the other picks up that word—the subject of many recent pamphlets[1]—and shows it has sinister ambiguity.

Still, moderation seems spread like a film across the logical surface of Swift's Section Two, which deals with the civil government. Here, after opening again with a complaint against all party spirit, Swift argues that absolute monarchy is intolerable, but that law as established by King, Lords, and Commons is not to be resisted on any ground. He defends the Revolution against the objections of nonjurors and closes the whole essay with yet a fresh denunciation of party rule. Whoever puts a proper value on the 'constitution in church and state' will, says Swift, 'avoid the extreams of Whig for the sake of the former, and the extreams of Tory on account of the latter'.[2]

When we come closer to the details of Section Two, we find them less consistent or coherent than the skeleton of logic which barely supports them. Swift ostensibly maintains that the Whigs and Tories avow the same fundamentals though each party accuses the other of opinions denied by both; and in presenting these fundamentals, he does, very sketchily, describe and defend the English constitution as settled in 1689 and explained by Locke. Even on a casual reading, however, he seems at more pains to conciliate the Tories than to apologize for the Whigs. By liberty, for instance, he means the rule of law in a bicameral constitutional monarchy. Yet the gnat at which he strains is the right of the Convention Parliament, in 1688–9, to depose James II and enthrone William of Orange. His solution—neither

[1] Cf. James Owen, *Moderation a Virtue*, 1703; Daniel Defoe, *The Sincerity of the Dissenter . . . with Some Reflections on . . . Moderation a Virtue*, 1703; Charles Leslie, *The Wolf Stript . . . in Answer to Moderation a Virtue*, 1704; James Owen, *Moderation Still a Virtue*, 1704.

[2] Davis II. 25. This formulation, of an honest man's being part Tory and part Whig, seems to have been a commonplace: Boyer applied it to Temple; Tickell to Addison; Burnet to himself. Cf. also George Savile, Marquess of Halifax's *Character of a Trimmer*.

original, consistent, nor convincing—is, first, that sovereignty rests in the King, Nobles, and Commons acting together, and not in the crown alone; secondly, that force is the only possible answer to tyranny; and, thirdly, that since free government exists by consent, the people naturally resume power after they overthrow a king. More informing than such reasons is the space, amounting to a quarter of the section on government, which he devotes to 'this digression'. One infers that Swift is appealing to those Tories who boggled at the Hanoverian succession, since for them alone were these scruples serious.

While the *Sentiments* is a dull essay, the source of its dullness may be interesting. Apparently Swift was trying to combine two aims, only one of which was the honest exposition of his principles. A second aim was polemical; and the drift of the polemic worked against not only his career ambitions but also the fundamental design of the tract. So the main value of the work seems biographical: there is a split in his rhetoric which reflects the division in his mind. It is by considering the tones of the *Sentiments*, therefore, that we can get a glimpse of his prejudices.

Although much of the essay may consist of digressions from the ostensible topics, the harangues in both sections against party spirit do seem as sincere and unbiased as their speaker claims. Besides indicating his honest belief, they are commonplaces in the mouths of men on both sides, and they echo the theme of his recent *Discourse of the Contests and Dissensions*. For temperateness of judgment and steadiness of standpoint, moreover, these harangues are matched by the long paragraphs in Section Two devoted to those objections which were brought against the Revolution by the nonjurors, by many old-fashioned country gentlemen, and by most of the lower clergy. At the same time, while Swift dismisses the Jacobite dogmas of absolutism and divine right with a self-important severity, as though he were concerned to enlighten the nation regarding errors which had in fact been elaborately exposed during the Exclusion Bill crisis of his infancy, he shows an un-Swiftian patience in undermining the high-churchmen's reservations concerning the Act of Succession. Three solemn, long paragraphs, with careful transitions, are given up to the statement and disproof of these reservations; and nothing is more significant in them than the respect with which Swift goes over the ground. He does so with unbroken sobriety and in contrast to the biting manner used at other points.

Thus distinctly less tact is to be found in the digressions of Section One, where Swift disposes of the Whigs' attitude toward religion. If the prevalent timbre of this section is gentlemanly good temper, the insinuations against 'moderation' are a diversion into acerbity. When Swift sideswipes the Dutch, an audible sharpness penetrates his note of velvet impartiality. Elsewhere not only irony but scarcasm breaks through, whether he is denouncing Whiggish pamphlets written against the clergy, or echoing the Convocation's fury over the propagation of heresies, or else identifying the Dissenters with a mob of republican, regicide, Puritan forebears. It is at such points that his heat rises and his language grows absorbing. The historian loses himself in the pamphleteer.

When Swift about ten years later reviewed the evolution of his political ideas, he attributed to the period 1702–5 a set of principles so close to several he had expounded in this essay that I think we may regard the inner substance of the *Sentiments* as a not unfair approximation of his conscious opinions; for these views follow a drift we should not have looked for in a man openly associated with the Whigs; and unless they were sincere, he would hardly have troubled himself to expound them:

> I found myself much inclined to be what they called a Whig in politics; and that, besides, I thought it impossible, upon any other principle, to defend or submit to the Revolution: but, as to religion, I confessed myself to be an high-churchman, and that I did not conceive how any one, who wore the habit of a clergyman, could be otherwise: that I had observed very well with what insolence and haughtiness some lords of the high-church party treated not only their own chaplains, but all other clergymen whatsoever, and thought this was sufficiently recompensed by their professions of zeal to the church: that I had likewise observed how the Whig lords took a directly contrary measure, treated the persons of particular clergymen with great curtesy, but shewed much ill-will and contempt for the order in general: that I knew it was necessary for their party, to make their bottom as wide as they could, by taking all

denominations of Protestants to be members of their body: that I
would not enter into the mutual reproaches made by the violent
men on either side; but, that the connivance, or encouragement,
given by the Whigs to those writers of pamphlets, who reflected
upon the whole body of the clergy, without any exception, would
unite the church, as one man, to oppose them.[1]

Swift's resolution to think such thoughts in private is not so surprising as his willingness to communicate them—for he said he
did—to Somers, Halifax, and others of that colour. After the
Earl of Nottingham fell (May 1704), only one person in the
ministry quite shared these convictions, and that was Robert
Harley, who had replaced the Earl as Secretary of State. The
two giants who were carrying all before them, i.e., Godolphin
and Marlborough, acted as courtiers working through the Queen
and for the nation, feeling prepared to take on the colleagues
whom they needed to back up their policies in the war. Since the
Whigs were committed to support the war, it was they whose
power was to grow; and their hunger was far too intense for
Swift's mild meat to satisfy them. We may therefore describe
his ambition as tempered with a fair degree of integrity if not
naïveté. Connivance, not assent, was as far as he could move toward belying himself. He ought to have known better. Perhaps
he did.

In keeping with my analysis, I think Swift was not speaking
simply but was having Tisdall on when he used a different tone
from that of the *Sentiments* while addressing his high-flying friend
on the same issue: 'You know you and I are Whig and Tory.
And, to cool your insolence a little, know that the Queen and
Court, and House of Lords, and half the Commons almost, are
Whigs; and the number daily increases.'[2] In the spring before
Blenheim, Swift was indeed a Whig like Queen Anne. It was now
a dozen years since he had apotheosized a nonjuring and deprived Archbishop of Canterbury, in a poem that described
'the state' as a weathercock 'hung loosely on the church's pin-
nacle'.[3] It was seven years since he had composed the bulk of a
satire ripping up those very Dissenters who became generally

---

[1] Davis VIII. 120.   [2] Williams I. 44.   [3] *Poems* I. 37.

attached to the Whig party. It was in 1704 that he sent this satire to the press; and I think his principles had by now relaxed only sufficiently for him to repudiate the dogmas of nonjurors but not so far that he could accept the creed of the Junto. He was an 'old Whig' after all, dressed mainly in the cut of Sir William Temple and 1689. He was not and never would be a 'new Whig' after the fashion of Wharton, Sunderland, and Walpole.

VI

After his first three weeks in London, at the end of 1703, Swift had put on an air of cynical aloofness for Tisdall's benefit. 'I have here the best friends in nature', he said, 'only want[ing] that little circumstance of favour and power; but nothing is so civil as a cast courtier.'[1] He had no hopes left, and said he expected to be home after two months more. In fact, Swift was to remain another six months in England, living the life of a spider. In April, still stuck to London, he had less wit to spare and an over-supply of acid: 'I find nothing but the good words and wishes of a decayed ministry, whose lives and mine will probably wear out before they can serve either my little hopes, or their own ambition.'[2]

Yet an event had already occurred at court which would supply a new handle for Swift's hopes, a new opportunity for him to serve his church, a new excuse for the vicar of Laracor to linger out months in Westminster. This was the consummation of Burnet's old scheme to turn back those ancient fees paid to the crown by the clergymen under the title of First Fruits and Twentieth Parts, and to use the resulting income as a fund for the augmentation of poor livings in the Church of England. At the instance partly of Burnet, who had originally recommended the plan to King William, and partly of the Archbishop of York, Queen Anne had announced her consent on her birthday in February 1704; and later that year an act was passed to make her will effective. In the Convocation of the Church of Ireland this auspicious event had not been unforeseen; and during the session of 1703–4

[1] Williams I. 39.   [2] *Ibid.* I. 46.

the Lower House petitioned the Upper to obtain the same relief for the weaker kingdom.[1] Some time after[2] her majesty's announcement, therefore, the Bishop of Cloyne, Charles Crow, who had left Ireland with Swift and who saw him in London,[3] gave the Queen a petition begging her to grant the favour to the sister church. Although her majesty made him a 'gracious answer', Crow had to travel back to Dublin before he could follow up the encouragement.

To Swift, who evidently heard about the interview from the bishop, this hint suggested two further possibilities. Double the burden of the First Fruits and Twentieth Parts were some additional fees called the crown rents. The remission of these, as well as of the others, in Ireland would cost her majesty altogether only half the value of the original grant alone in England. So Swift thought of proposing that the petition be extended to include the heavier charges.[4] Although he did not make it explicit at the time, we may deduce from his later conduct Swift's simultaneous reflection that a particular agent devoted to the advancement of the proposal would bring it to accomplishment more certainly and speedily than the spare-time dabbling of transient bishops. Who that agent might best be, Swift very easily resolved; and before the end of 1704 he was at work identifying himself with the project. The advantage of such an agency to Swift was that it would give him a respectable occupation requiring him to call upon ministers of state and thereby familiarizing them with the countenance and qualities of a man who could serve them. So far, any entrée Swift had been granted to the levees of the great he had won through informal and unstable connections, through the effect of his person and his writings. But as the solicitor for the Church of Ireland in the matter of the First Fruits and Twentieth Parts, he could obtrude himself on a Lord Lieutenant, a Secretary of State, or a Lord Treasurer.

[1] Landa, p. 52; Phillips III. 179.   [2] *Journal* II. 679.

[3] Williams I. 48. Swift lost 4s. 6d. playing ombre at Crow's lodgings in London, 29 Nov. 1703 (*Accounts 1702–3*, fol. 1ᵛ).

[4] It did not apparently occur to Swift that a remission of the crown rents in Ireland would be a precedent for the same motion in England, and that the consequent loss of income would be greater than even Queen Anne could contemplate.

Yet above the self-seeking aspect of the affair there always sparkled the aspect of duty. From his earliest remarks on the First Fruits to his last, whether in diary letters, in private correspondence, in memorials, or in published writings, Swift transparently prided himself on the benefit which he hoped to bring about for the sickly mother institution that had nursed him. No one knew better than he that hardly one Irish parish in ten possessed any glebe; and the rest, very small, scattered pieces of land, seldom with a house on them; that thanks to impropriations and national poverty the livings were worth so little that five or six united would often hardly amount to fifty pounds a year; that even such a half-dozen distinct parishes would rarely provide more than a single church fit to be used. All this he knew, resented, and wished to remedy. If, in attempting to do so, he could as well remind Lord Somers, Lord Halifax, or the Earl of Godolphin that Dr Swift was waiting his turn, he may be excused for availing himself of such opportunities.

VII

With all his eagerness to be named to a bishopric, Swift could not spend every moment in London, if only because of the expense. Though delaying his home-coming from month to month as new false lights beckoned, he nevertheless found time to visit the household at Sheen, to see Lady Giffard, and to discuss Hetty's finances with the elder Mrs Johnson. During May 1704 he visited the Berkeley family at their now-vanished seat, Cranford, near Hounslow. Still later, he went to see his mother, just before starting on the journey to Ireland.

On 19 April, coming back to town from a country visit, he found a letter he had been expecting, which related to Hetty and signalized the greatest emotional discomfort he had met since persuading her to join him. She and Mrs Dingley were living in William Street, a newish neighbourhood on the edge of Dublin. Swift had probably encouraged several of his friends to look in on them while he was away; and at this time William Tisdall stood high in the rank of Swift's friends. As early as Kilroot days, Swift may have known Tisdall, who was about two years his junior and whose father was a sufficiently prominent citizen of Carrick-fergus to be twice made sheriff.

As a friend Tisdall belongs to the tradition of Thomas Swift—more intimate than honoured. Something of a name-dropper and something of a climber, he was what Swift called a 'puppy', one of those men who accommodate themselves to the manners of superiors without losing either self-assurance or loquacity. He had entered Trinity College after Swift left and in 1696 had won a fellowship there. His slovenliness and lack of discretion bothered Swift, who also took exception to Tisdall's absent-mindedness, halitosis, and smelly feet. But what teased Swift more was his indulgence in literary exercises. Although Tisdall made a fine preacher, he set peculiar and unwarranted value on a habit of producing not only occasional verse but also angry essays about controversial questions: as an entertainment to the ladies in William Street, he used to review the arguments raised in the Convocation of the Church of Ireland.[1]

Swift's good-humoured condescension toward this friend was not wholly shared by Hetty. She heard him with enough sympathy and welcomed his visits with enough warmth for Tisdall to feel their relationship might well grow into something deeper: he began to move toward a proposal of marriage. Although circumstances would have made it conveniently easy for her to discourage his advances, we have no hint that she did so.

Tisdall must have felt genuinely drawn to Hetty if he was willing to overlook the inconsequence of her family. Though she possessed a substantial property, he already held a good position and had better things awaiting him. Archbishop King had formed high expectations of Tisdall's future in the church.[2] On the suitor's side every step in the affair seems to have been taken soberly and managed with the utmost propriety.

On Hetty's side there emerge a number of possible motivations. Most probably she felt unsure of her course and turned for advice to her best friend, who, alas, happened as well to be the rival for her attentions. Certainly in her eyes Tisdall appeared

[1] *Journal* i. xxxiv–xxxv and *passim*.   [2] Ball i. 44, n. i.

perfectly eligible as a suitor. Equally certainly she did not respond to his gestures with anything like his degree of confidence. That she suspected Swift might be intending to marry her himself seems unlikely. But that she thought the information of Tisdall's proposal might alter Swift's intentions is surely possible.

To Swift belonged the most awkward corner of the triangle. His opinion of Hetty at this time we have in his clearest, unambiguous language: 'I never saw that person whose conversation I entirely valued but hers', he said, and 'Though it hath come in my way to converse with persons of the first rank, and of that sex, more than is usual to men of my level, and of our function; yet I have nowhere met with a humour, a wit or conversation so agreeable, a better portion of good sense, or a truer judgment of men and things.'

According to Swift only a single obstruction stood in the way of his own offer to marry Mrs Johnson, and that was a determination never to marry at all. 'If my fortunes and humour served me to think of that state', he told Tisdall, 'I should certainly, among all persons on earth, make your choice.'[1] This was undoubtedly true, and he must already have made Hetty understand as much.

Before mid-November 1703, when Swift left Ireland, Tisdall displayed no matrimonial inclination toward Mrs Johnson. It was probably February when he opened the vista to her. Hetty, with a prudence that would do credit to Miss Price of Mansfield Park, referred him to her mother and her oldest male counsellor. Thereupon, the gentleman wrote to their common friend, asking him to make overtures to the elder Mrs Johnson on behalf of Mr Tisdall.

As Swift did not mean to propose marriage to Hetty himself, and as he knew Tisdall to have no drawbacks which she could not judge at least as well as her absent mentor, there was no more than one straight road for him to follow, and that was to keep out of the case, allowing mother, daughter, and suitor to settle things among themselves. Almost certainly, Hetty appealed to him for distinct guidance; but Swift knew perfectly well how to sound

[1] Williams I. 45–6.

reassuringly non-committal when he wished to. During the early eighteenth century, English maidens even at the age of twenty-three were not supposed to judge matrimonial prospects without assistance from friends and relatives. Nevertheless, Swift, by his own attachment to Hetty had put it out of his power to seem disinterested; and she had fallen under too many obligations to him for her to ignore his preferences in such a decision, however subtly they might be communicated to her: one does not accept fifty pounds a year from a man without submitting to his authority. If he wished to act honourably, he was bound to warn Hetty that such considerations must not affect her judgment, and to warn her in such a style that she would feel free from guilt if she were inclined to accept Tisdall.

What in fact Swift did, we may infer from his language to her suitor:

> Nor shall any consideration of my own misfortune of losing so good a friend and companion as her, prevail on me, against her interest and settlement in the world, since it is held so necessary and convenient a thing for ladies to marry; and that time takes off from the lustre of virgins in all other eyes but mine. I appeal to my letters to herself, whether I was your friend or no in the whole concern; though the part I designed to act in it was purely passive, which is the utmost I will ever do in things of this nature, to avoid all reproach of any ill consequence, that may ensue in the variety of worldly accidents.[1]

In this kind of situation, pure passivity toward a conscience-ridden dependent, and the admission that her marriage to another would afflict Swift as a misfortune, were hardly the best means to allow her freedom of choice. Certainly Swift did nothing to speed the 'whole concern'. When Tisdall broached the subject, Swift said he could not bring it up with Hetty's mother until he had Hetty's permission to do so, 'under her own or her friend's [i.e., Mrs Dingley's] hand'. Since Swift himself had encouraged Tisdall's friendship with the ladies, this seems to me a curious formality to impose on the girl. Unless Tisdall were the sort of dishonourable person whom one never presents to decent

---

[1] Williams I. 45–6.

women, how could Swift refuse so simple a request as that he should ask the elder Mrs Johnson to give Mr Tisdall permission to make advances to her daughter?

If Hetty had wished to end the proceedings, she could have done so with the utmost ease at this turn, merely by a private message to Swift. But she did not. So he was compelled to report Tisdall's petition to Hetty's mother. Obviously, that lady in turn could rely for counsel on nobody except her old friend, for he alone among her acquaintance could give her a reliable, first-hand account of the daughter's suitor. Again Swift made delays. On the one hand, he thought marriage at such a time might 'be a clog' to Tisdall's rising in the world; on the other hand, he did not think Tisdall was rich enough to make himself and Hetty 'happy and easy'. But surely, we may reflect, Tisdall at thirty-five was quite well placed to judge what would help or hinder his own ambitions; and as for happiness and ease, surely Swift was familiar enough with the condition of Tisdall's estate to know, before he was told, that this issue was not serious: for in the end it was Tisdall's word that he was willing to take as to the state of Tisdall's finances.

Inevitably, the lover grew suspicious, wondered whether Swift was not blocking his wishes in order to forward his own, and assumed that what had appeared to be a well-disposed comrade was in fact a jealous rival. In order to placate him, Swift wrote a careful, reassuring reply, calculated to meet Tisdall's charges without forfeiting his respect and friendship.

After all the correspondence demanded by these exchanges of views, Hetty must have realized that Swift intensely desired no alteration in her state. I think one of the most damaging admissions he made to Tisdall was, 'Nay, I went so far both to her mother, herself, and I think to you, as to think it [i.e., the engagement] could not be decently broken; since I suppose the town had got it in their tongues, and therefore I thought it could not miscarry without some disadvantage to the lady's credit.' To tell Hetty that she should hesitate before breaking her engagement on the grounds that doing so might expose her to unkind gossip was surely a way of saying that apart from the danger of unkind gossip there was no strong reason for her not to break the engagement.

Of course, this is exactly what happened. Hetty obeyed her master, refused to accept Tisdall, and saw him in a couple of years married instead to Miss Eleanor Morgan of county Sligo.[1] The springtide crisis of romance did not destroy Tisdall's acquaintanceship with either Mrs Johnson or Dr Swift, although we are not surprised, as years elapse, to see condescension turning to contempt in Swift's allusions to him.

To press my own speculations on the episode still further, I may describe Swift's immediate, unthinking response to the news of Tisdall's designs on Hetty as elementary panic. With more pains than most men devote to choosing a spouse, Swift had re-created the domestic pattern which gave him the deepest comfort. As a dependent, compliant confidant, part daughter, part pupil, part mistress, Hetty was a miraculous prize. Every assistance he gave her made her more his own. He could be uniformly benevolent because she must be uniformly docile. It was not conceivable that he should find yet another fatherless young beauty, equipped with intelligence and polite breeding; that he should isolate her too from her family and obligate her to the point where she would indulge his unspoken wishes.

For a man of Swift's morality, however, it was not possible to admit the selfishness of his motives. He had to seem to be acting disinterestedly; he had to seem to feel concern only for the good of Tisdall and Hetty. Luckily for his own composure, he had the shrewdness to manage this while keeping safe and handy the spring of the fullest emotional pleasure in his life. Tisdall was surely right to divine that while a negative came from Hetty, the omens came from Swift. Yet this is not to say that the doctor failed to trick himself into believing that the initiative had been the lady's, and that his own performance had been at least as impartial as duty demanded. Paternalism and possessive need are easily masked as the kindly advice of an experienced senior, ostensibly delivered only after particular pressure from the recipient.

[1] *Journal* i. xxxv.

At the same time, without in any way excusing Swift, we may reflect that Hetty gained as well as lost by her submission. Whoever feels like mourning over the wraiths of her unconceived children might apply his imagination to Queen Anne's fate of at least fifteen pregnancies and no survivors, or the burden that marriage imposed on Dorothy Osborne, Charlotte Fielding, and Margaret Boswell. We hear no laments in the eighteenth century over the wretchedness of independent gentlewomen living comfortably alone on decent incomes. Far ahead lay the age of asepsis and anesthesia; all around stood drunken, imperious husbands, satisfying themselves, during their ladies' breeding periods, on rented companions who supplied diseases to both man and wife. If Hetty had married Tisdall, she would have had no less rigour to endure from her wedded master than from Swift; she would have enjoyed the amenity of physical passion as far as respectable husbands at this time seem to have produced it; but her health was not so strong that the consequent treadmill of motherhood would have meant unalloyed delight. Her circle of acquaintance, without Swift, would have been dull and narrow. Her knowledge of the great world would have been negligible. She would have missed the excitement of his intellectual range; she would have missed the homage of a genius; she would have drifted into the obscurity out of which Eleanor Morgan emerges only as the woman who married a man who once knew Dean Swift.

By the time Tisdall received Swift's epistle, its writer was preparing to abandon his siege of the gilded gates in Whitehall. But I suspect that some unlooked-for obstacle still rose up to detain him, because he now broke his custom of having books published in England only after he was out of the kingdom. It was almost three weeks before his going that the first edition of *A Tale of a Tub* came on sale (10 May 1704[1]). Nothing he was ever to write would seem more daring, and he certainly wished to hide his connection with it; so I suppose this is why he had Tooke, Swift's usual printer and sometime publisher, screen his own responsibility by omitting the printer's name from the title-page and re-

[1] In the *Post Man*, 9 May, it is advertised to be published the next day; in the *Daily Courant*, 10 May, it is advertised as published that day.

presenting the book as distributed by John Nutt, who had also put out the anonymous *Contests and Dissensions*. About the same time that the *Tale* appeared, Swift made what was probably a farewell visit to the Berkeleys. Next, to sweeten his time in Ireland, he bought a miscellany of articles, some, I assume, as gifts for the ladies in William Street: several kinds of tea, including a pound of bohea for sixteen shillings; twenty-three pounds of chocolate for £4, and two pounds of coffee for 6s. 2d.; sugar and snuff; pills, cards, and pins. Then he went to see his mother before he sailed. At last, leaving Leicester on 29 May, he reached Neston the following day and landed at Dublin on Thursday morning, 1 June.[1]

[1] The details of Swift's travels and purchases are from his *Accounts 1703–4*, fols. 2ᵛ, 4ʳ.

Chapter Twelve

IRELAND FOR THREE AND A HALF YEARS, 1704-7

I. CHURCH PREFERMENTS

Coming back empty-handed, Swift found more than one reason to think now of cultivating his opportunities on the western side of the Irish Sea. If we reckon his expenses for the year ending 31 October 1704, we shall discover that he was not managing to keep them within his income. From the livings united in Laracor and from his prebend of Dunlavin, Swift estimated he was due to receive this year a sum of money totalling just under two hundred pounds. But he found that his simple personal expenses, including lodging, food, clothing, travel, servants, and so forth, drained off all but about ninety of the sum. From the remainder he had to pay fifty pounds to Esther Johnson; £37 10s. od. to his curate at Laracor, Mr Smith; and over fifteen pounds in crown rent. Besides such ordinary items there were many demands which are hard to survey. No doubt, Swift had by now other sources of money to add to his livings; but those investments he wished to accumulate and not spend.

The variety of his disbursements will surprise anyone who imagines that conditions of life have grown peculiarly complicated in the twentieth century. Besides paying his servant wages, Swift had to supply him with clothes; and we find entries in the parson's accounts for shoes, stockings, buttons, cravat, hat, etc., for John Campbell or John Bunting. Horses, whether hired or owned, involved him in stable rent at four pounds a year; in feeding expenses for hay, oats, or grazing; and in any number of odd essentials like straw, currycomb, brush, bridle, and saddle. At Laracor the vicar not only paid to have his half-acre of glebe planted with willows and fruit trees, or cleared of weeds; he also spent ten pounds on the church chancel.

Swift's own clothing cost him more than one might expect so thrifty an economist to devote to external vanities: a periwig for £2 7s. 6d.; gown and cassock for £6 os. 6d.; crepe scarf for fifteen shillings; not to mention shirts, cravats, handkerchief; breeches and gloves; shoes, stockings, and hat. There were workmen to be hired, candles and coals to be bought. Besides barrels and barrels of beer, he had cider, ale, and wine; coffee, tea, and chocolate. There were inns' bills and agents' bills, housekeeping bills, and laundry; there were tips to constables and fares for chairs and coaches; postage fees and customs-house fees; books bought and bound. Even for changing money as it passed between Ireland and England, the fee was a heavy expense. And finally there were the continual, innumerable, untraceable charities of every sort, many not listed, and some appearing under screens, such as 'G. Mrs D—s – – – – 0–10–0': i.e., gave ten shillings to Mrs Peter Davys,[1] widow of a Dublin schoolmaster, who had been at college with Swift.

In England years after this and under somewhat improved circumstances, the vicar of Laracor was to win the sympathy of a noble lord for having to undergo a 'necessity of leaving the town [i.e., London] for want of money to live in it'.[2] We may imagine therefore what sort of economies he used to practise during an extended visit when his earnings could not keep up with his spendings. If we wonder too what induced him to stay so long on so narrow a budget, I think we must assume that possibilities kept emerging which seemed to demand only a few weeks' rapid pursuit to turn into realized rewards. Since, after his long-deferred return to Ireland, Swift remained in his native country for three and a half years, we may further surmise that he now wished to repair his finances so as to lighten the weight of the next trip. 'My little revenue is sunk two parts in three', he said in 1706, 'and

---

[1] These expenses are taken from Swift's *Accounts 1703–4*, *passim*. The gift to Mrs D—s appears on fol. 3 and again on fol. 8. I have assumed that she is the Mrs Davis of the *Journal* II. 625 and n. 21; Ball I. 382–3 and n. 10; Williams IV. 83 and n. 5; 106–7.

[2] Williams I. 275.

the third in arrear.'[1] He must simultaneously have planned that the next trip should be long enough to let him follow through and conclude any project of advantage to himself which might come to birth while he lived in London.

As an inducement to stay put for a while, Swift had also his archbishop's well-known dislike for non-residence. King worked hard to supply usable churches to parishes which lacked them. If no sufficient glebe existed, he either assigned some property at a low rent from the episcopal lands (when these were convenient); or else found the means to buy a glebe for the living. But having made residence possible, he tried to make it obligatory. When Swift wrote 'Trim' at the head of an early letter to the archbishop, it was probably not without some attention to the happy impression that this parochial address would make upon his lordship. The vicar had gone almost straight to Laracor from the boat, arriving there on 3 June,[2] and he was there again at the end of the year, when he sent King a long message, mainly about his grace's lawsuit with Christ Church. But if the purport of the letter dealt with the archbishop's affairs, the effect must have been intended to keep him favourably aware of Swift's powers and interests. After retailing some dangerous symptoms in the state of King's case, and characteristically playing up the importance of facts he happened to have direct knowledge of, Swift made it glaringly plain that he had himself been employed so far otherwise in London as to spread those favourable truths which would conduce to the success of his lordship's litigation. Having thus indicated his utility and goodwill with regard to the archbishop's personal aims, he went on to suggest his own value to the church, by begging his lordship, who was about to sail for England, to think of adding the crown rents to the First Fruits as fees which her majesty might be urged to remit to the clergy. The letter bears the inevitable shimmer of unctuosity demanded by any unsolicited communication from inferior to superior in an authoritarian hierarchy.[3] But one cannot help regretting that even a man of Swift's temperament should have submitted himself to

---

[1] *Ibid.*, p. 54. 'Sunk' does not mean 'reduced' but 'spent in advance'.
[2] *Accounts 1703-4*, fol. 4ᵛ.   [3] Williams I. 47-9.

such a discipline. As he once observed, 'Climbing is performed in the same posture as creeping.'[1]

Within a few weeks, Swift had another opportunity of strengthening his right to preferment, this time through a job of work done directly for the church. One of his friends, Jerome Ryves, had become seriously ill after almost six years in the deanship of St Patrick's Cathedral. Early in the new year Dean Ryves held his last visitation, and on 1 February 1705 he died.[2] For the members of the chapter this event produced a quadruple crisis out of which Swift emerges as a person highly respected, though perhaps of less importance than he was later willing to allow.

Primarily, the canons wished to assert their right to elect Ryves's successor for themselves, rather than surrender this privilege by allowing the crown to name a new dean. True, the power of election belonged to them under the constitution of the cathedral church. However, it had for a long time been a mere form, and the genuine style of a free election had only come back at the Revolution, when the researches of William King (then chancellor of the cathedral) uncovered the old rule and enabled the chapter to defeat an attempt to give James II the patronage of the deanery. King's virtuous scholarship had been rewarded at once, inasmuch as the canons chose him for the office—out of which he had soon risen through promotion to be Bishop of Derry; and since he was now the Archbishop of Dublin, they could expect him to support their assertion of the ancient right.

But in the relationship of the chapter to the archbishop was to be seen a difficulty of another sort. Before the canons could proceed to an election, they had to secure a licence from his grace. Naturally, King's willingness to grant one depended to some extent on the likelihood that the chapter's selection would be agreeable to him; so it was essential that they should be informed of his leanings. In February 1705, however, the archbishop was newly arrived in London, where he had gone to fight his lawsuit against Christ Church. For the chapter meanwhile to support a candidate whom he disapproved would be to invite his opposition

[1] Davis I. 245.   [2] Mason, p. 217.

and, with it, the probable failure of their choice. Yet King's distance from the field of the contest made it hard for them to keep in touch with his opinions.

To aggravate such anxieties, there were the legitimate and historic roles of the crown. If the government, the chapter, and the archbishop had happened to be in agreement as to the name of the new dean, the distress of the canons might have been weaker. On the contrary, however, an additional uneasiness stabbed them when it became known that Edward Synge, one-time vicar of Laracor and now a prebendary of the cathedrals of Cork and Cloyne, had won support in Westminster. (This was the very Dr Synge who had refused the deanery of Derry when Swift panted for it.) Naturally, the English ministry wished to impose a dean of the government's choice upon St Patrick's. Whenever the deanship became vacant not through a death but through a dean's advancement to a bishopric, the crown, as source of this promotion, had regularly the privilege of appointing a successor; and the right of election was then waived. Similarly, if the archbishopric of Dublin was vacant at the same time as the deanship, the crown as head of the church assumed the archbishop's powers. With such precedents to encourage them, his majesty's officers were always inclined to press further and force their own candidate on the chapter even when they had no legal ground for doing so. Something therefore depended on yet another element, the nature of the Lord Lieutenant, whose sympathy with the Established Church might be judged by his degree of co-operation in such an emergency. Something also depended upon speed; for if the chapter should delay too long, the government's patent might gain too much legal recognition to be recalled.

Several of these difficulties were smoothly resolved, and Swift acted prominently in the negotiations. We cannot doubt from the line of events that he had reached a place of authority in the chapter. While it will appear that his good standing with the archbishop was a factor in the case, yet Swift could perform few solid favours for his friends. He must therefore have secured their respect mainly by the strength of his character, an accomplishment which deserves its portion of admiration against the background I have sketched.

Nobody on either side seems to have thrown away many moments. At two o'clock in the morning, only twelve hours after Ryves died, the members of the chapter raced to assemble in the room of Dr John Stearne, Swift's good friend and the chancellor of the cathedral.[1] In keeping with convention, they made the precentor, Samuel Synge, their president *pro tem*. Through his office in the chapter Synge stood next in precedence to the dean. He was also the son of a late Bishop of Cork, son-in-law to the late Primate Boyle, nephew of a late Bishop of Cloyne, and brother of the government's candidate for the deanship of St Patrick's. But a youthful scandal had distinguished Synge as a man of 'ill fame'; and in spite of pressure from the Earl of Romney (who was then still Lord Sidney), even the Church of Ireland had not submitted to having him as a bishop.[2] To Swift, Synge was a loyal and appreciative senior who would have liked to see him ascend the scale of pluralities.[3]

Now the canons turned at once to their critical business, and noted that a petition should be delivered to the Lord Lieutenant, the Duke of Ormonde, setting forth their established right to elect a dean. In order to present this petition, they enlisted three men: Samuel Synge as president, a prebendary named Ralph Rule, and Dr Jonathan Swift. I assume that Swift was picked as an emissary who would seem *persona grata* to Ormonde. At three o'clock that afternoon, or twenty-five hours after Ryves's death, the deputation appeared before the Duke, whereupon their immediate success rose so high as to procure them the answer they had hoped for, intimating that his excellency wished to preserve the chapter's privilege.

Yet this action, welcome thought it might be, carried them over only a very low stile; for the case had now to be argued before the Attorney-General and the Solicitor-General of Ireland. To meet this foreseen jump in their steeple-chase, the chapter

[1] Mason, pp. 218–19 and 220, note *b*, gives details of the proceedings.
[2] Mant II. 31–3.
[3] Ball I. 71–2 and n. 5; II. 76 and n. 2 (n. 1 is mistaken; the reference is to Synge's death).

took the precaution of retaining not only the Recorder of the City of Dublin but also the Speaker of the Irish House of Commons as their counsel. Still it was seven days before they could be heard. But at last, at six o'clock in the morning, on 9 February, the pleadings were entertained; and again the chapter landed satisfactorily.[1] Next they ran to send Archbishop King an account of their transactions and to ask respectfully for his advice. Less than three weeks after the old dean's death, they had a letter of instruction from the archbishop which led at once to their formal requisition of a licence from him for the election.

Nevertheless, with all their dispatch, the chapter found themselves outraced by the patrons of Edward Synge. It was 14 March before the president could produce the archbishop's licence at a meeting of the chapter; and five days earlier a patent for Edward Synge's presentation to the deanship had already been passed by the crown. In spite of this, 20 March was fixed on as the polling date; and Swift was appointed to look through the records so as to ensure that all the proper forms were observed.

When the election took place, it did not proceed by simple ballot. Instead, the method of 'compromise' was followed. In this the electors delegated their power to a small number, usually odd, of 'compromisers', who were supposed to sound out the separate canons in private and then choose the dean in conformity with the wishes of the 'greater and sounder part' (*maior et sanior pars*) of the chapter.[2] Since it is obvious by now that Swift was a chief mover in the Trollopian operation of the chapter's schemes, it will hardly seem a surprise that he was chosen as head of the three compromisers.[3]

United though they might be on the need to preserve their freedom of election, yet the decanal preferences of the chapter at this time turned to a limited extent on internal politics. Some support for the government's candidate existed; so the remaining

[1] Mason, p. 220, note *b*.   [2] Lawlor, pp. 22-8.

[3] Mason, pp. 218-19. I assume that Swift was the chief compromiser because it was he who formally announced the election, and according to the established rule this was done by one of the compromisers 'in the place and name of all the canons' (Lawlor, p. 25). One of the other compromisers was probably Enoch Reader, Archdeacon of Dublin, since the compromisers were deputed to present the decree of election to the archbishop. and it was Reader who co-signed the decree with Swift.

influences naturally concentrated on a single alternative. Like the majority, Swift backed his country neighbour, John Stearne, rector of Trim and chancellor of the cathedral, whom Addison was to describe as 'a man of great learning and modesty'.[1] While other prebendaries also canvassed for this candidate, Swift considered himself to plump the hardest; and he was in a commanding position to strengthen Stearne's chances.

Without denying Swift's character either the virtue of friendship or a will to support the best qualifications, we must admit that the vigour of his advocacy was in part derived from a principle of self-interest. Certain livings lay in the gift of the dean and chapter of the cathedral; and since the dean's voice was powerful if not determining in such business, Stearne could give his friend the impression that he would name Swift to one of the livings if he himself should be chosen dean. From later allusions it seems clear that Stearne delivered explicit though possibly conditional promises, even if he did not, as Swift once insisted, 'absolutely and frequently promise' to give him the curacy of a particular church.[2]

'I was the most busy of all your solicitors', Swift reminded Stearne some decades afterwards,[3] and his word may be trusted. On 20 March there was a full meeting of the chapter. After 'taking the suffrages', it was Swift who pronounced that Stearne was elected. The happy candidate, being present, at once declared his 'assent and consent'; and the chapter deputed the compromisers to send the Archbishop of Dublin the decree of election accompanied by the usual request that he ratify their choice.[4] It was again Swift and an old acquaintance, Enoch Reader, who now had to communicate with his absent lordship. Reader, though belonging to this chapter as Archdeacon of Dublin, was also Chancellor of Connor, where Swift would have met him in his Kilroot days. He had been planning a trip to England,[5] which was apparently postponed in view of the crisis in the chapter. Besides drafting the formal message, Swift appended a note warning the archbishop not even to accept the 'subscription' of

[1] Graham, p. 147 (13 June 1709).
[2] Williams IV. 182; cf. I. 66–7 and p. 67, n. I.   [3] *Ibid.* IV. 182.
[4] Mason, pp. 218–19.   [5] Williams I. 50–I.

Edward Synge's party, for fear (I think) that such a gesture might be treated by the government's lawyers as a signal that the last item of protocol had been complied with, and that the crown's patent was valid.[1]

Stearne's obligations to Swift increased at every stage of the race. And yet in spite of these deeds of industry and sagacity, the chancellor would probably have lost out if another force had not been employed on his side, a force in itself superior to all the vicar's labours together and sufficient perhaps to carry the contestant to first place with no extra thrust. This was the friendship of the archbishop. Five years earlier when he was still Bishop of Derry, King had listed Stearne among those whom he would be glad to have as his dean.[2] He had not lost any confidence in Stearne, whom he later described as a 'bosom friend'[3]; and the chapter were no doubt aware of his attitude. In 1713 Ormonde complained that Stearne was too deeply influenced by King.[4] With both the archbishop and most of the chapter pushing him, the chancellor could not attribute the decisive shove to Swift.

This balance of stresses became more visible when the government refused to dismiss Edward Synge's claim. Although King's confirmation is dated 21 March, the day after the election[5]— whether because he sent it beforehand or because he predated it from London—not until 11 April could Stearne be instituted. This length of delay cannot be blamed on King's absence, since the ceremony was finally carried out not by him but by his vicar-general; rather, it followed from the need to produce a consolation prize for the runner-up. The need was at last met through the promise of the chancellorship which Stearne was vacating. 'The compromise was made', Swift later reminded Stearne, 'between the government and you to make you easy and Dr. Synge chancellor.'[6] If the office of chancellor as such was not alluring,

---

[1] *Ibid.*, pp. 51-2.

[2] Landa, p. 30. He also listed Edward Synge of Cork, but Ball, *passim*, makes it clear that the tie between King and Stearne was particularly strong.

[3] Williams I. 349.   [4] *Journal*, 19 Apr. 1713.

[5] It was also the day *before* Swift drafted the letter to the archbishop announcing the election and requesting the confirmation (Williams I. 51-2).

[6] *Ibid.* IV. 182. It is barely possible that Swift had entertained some hope of winning the chancellorship for himself.

it carried with it the rectorship of St Werburgh's, the fashionable Dublin church with a state seat for the Lord Lieutenant, in the parish of Swift's birth. An Irish clergyman would hanker after this almost as an English clergyman after St James's, Piccadilly. To change Cork for the capital under these circumstances satisfied Dr Synge at least temporarily: it was not for nothing that he had delivered a sermon in Ormonde's presence, the year before, on 'The Wisdom of Being Religious'. With distributive justice now accommodated, the canons were free to watch their chosen dean occupy his new stall in the choir and to hear him take the oaths.

But for Swift the outcome of these inter-urban machinations was to light up his place among the canons and to set an obliged friend of his at their head; or, as he hoped, to widen and smooth the way to preferment. A couple of months later he could observe, as an edifying sub-plot, the movement of a parallel intrigue which altered the framework of his responsibilities at Laracor. In his quality as vicar of the country parish he came under the authority of Richard Tenison, the conscientious Bishop of Meath, who was the father of Swift's college friend, Henry.[1] When Tenison died (July 1705), it seemed to Primate Marsh as though this timely act might provide a convenient wedge for opening the impasse between King and his Christ Church antagonist. The scheme was to elevate Moreton, who only held the deanship of Christ Church *in commendam* through being the Bishop of Kildare, to the superior eminence of Meath. In the episcopal hierarchy of Ireland, Kildare ranked second only to Meath; so no other promotion, apart from an archbishopric, could lure him. Marsh therefore proposed that the Duke of Ormonde should recommend Moreton's removal from King's jurisdiction to the newly vacated see. As Swift once said of Marsh, 'He hath found out the secret of preferring men without deserving their thanks; and where he dispenses his favours to persons of merit, they are less obliged to him than to fortune.'[2]

By consenting to the Primate's scheme, the Duke disobliged a number of other willing candidates—the Bishop of Down, the

---

[1] *Supra*, vol. I, pp. 71–2.   [2] Davis v. 211.

Bishop of Ossory, a Prolocutor of Convocation, and a chaplain of the House of Commons—but he also made sure of the Primate's connivance in locating an 'honourable' berth for Ormonde's domestic chaplain, Dr Welbore Ellis.[1] The unimpugnable merits of an English origin and a Lord Lieutenant's patronage speedily put Ellis in possession of the bishopric of Kildare, just as the virtue of opposing his own metropolitan had established Moreton as Bishop of Meath: it's the squeaky hinge that gets the oil. Soon Swift could begin to enjoy the finest irony of the whole episode: that the original purpose of Marsh's scheme was foiled, since Ellis, picking up the cudgels Moreton had dropped, fought Archbishop King almost twenty years longer. But such amusement did not lack a tinge of wryness; for there is no sign that Tenison had ever quarrelled with his subordinate at Laracor, and since it was Moreton who had originally consented to ordain Swift (in Christ Church) as both deacon and priest,[2] the new Bishop of Meath had the basis for a comfortable relationship with the protégé of a decade earlier. But Welbore Ellis and Swift were to act upper and nether millstone over many years, in several connections, to the repeated grinding-down of both.

At the same time, the removal of Stearne from Trim meant the arrival of Anthony Raymond to replace him. On accepting the rectory, Raymond—who was nine years Swift's junior—had to resign from a fellowship in Trinity College; but he continued to pursue with enthusiasm his antiquarian researches into early Irish history. Although his distinguished neighbour at Laracor was more than once to be of service to him, the utilitarian balance of their connection was probably tilted the other way, since Raymond and his wife made themselves peculiarly gracious to Esther Johnson and helped to smooth several of her and Swift's financial arrangements. Swift seems to have appreciated Raymond's friendship in proportion as he realized that living among one's inferiors can be the key to a sort of happiness.

Apart from the acquisition of Raymond, Swift found few alterations in Laracor. Smith was still his curate, Parvisol his chief tithe-collector, and Joe Beaumont his man of business. The

---

[1] H.M.C. *Ormonde*, n.s., VIII. 167, 180, 181.   [2] *Supra*, vol. I, p. 153.

Percivals and Wesleys remained his weightiest parishioners; Sir Arthur Langford remained Presbyterian. And when Swift faced the congregation, he was still likely to find them—in this densely Catholic region—'an audience of at least fifteen people, most of them gentle, and all simple'.[1]

II. CONVOCATION AND PARLIAMENT

Even when the Convocation of the Church of Ireland had assembled in 1703 after thirty-seven years' intermission, Swift's later comment on such gatherings was tediously verified; and during the spring of 1705 it was even more bleakly pertinent. 'They meet but seldom, have no power, and for want of those advantages, cannot make any figure when they are suffered to assemble. You fetter a man seven years, then let him loose to shew his skill in dancing, and because he does it awkwardly, you say he ought to be fettered for life.'[2] Between the Upper and the Lower houses extended only a narrow isthmus of co-operation. Since the bishops had been originally chosen in part for their subservience to the government, most of them desired only such changes as would secure them in power or improve their stipends: few of them had grown up in Ireland; the majority had come over from England to make their fortunes by obliging their masters. Meanwhile, the lower clergy, educated in the Irish interest, felt anxious about the ineffectualness of the evangelical church, the parochial difficulties of priests, the number of untended cures, or the burdens of overworked vicars. With the difference so deep between the two houses, nobody could expect them to undertake a serious programme of reform.

In September 1703 Convocation had no sooner sat down than the Lower House pointed out that the manner of their summoning was incorrect. The true reason for such complaints was that one incentive for the revival of the whole body had been to manufacture evidence for Atterbury to employ in his arguments con-

---

[1] Williams I. 163. 'A parish with an audience of half a score', he calls it in Jan. 1709, writing to Archbishop King (*ibid.*, p. 119).

[2] *Ibid.* II. 342.

cerning the rights of Convocation in England. Through not harmonizing with Atterbury's theses, the Irish writs had failed to accomplish this aim. So all machinery was stalled while the 'correct' forms were fulfilled. Not till January 1704 did a perfect and entire Convocation hold its first meeting, in the chapter-room of St Patrick's, with Daniel Jackson attending as the proctor (or delegate) for the canons of the cathedral.[1] But by then the concurrent Irish parliamentary session had moved so far along that the clergy could do little besides making recommendations to be followed up in later convocations.

Even these recommendations imply the futility of the proceedings. Many of them were designed to improve public morality and the respect shown to religion. There was a proposal for the censorship of the stage, looking forward, I am afraid, to the English Licensing Act of 1737. Other reforms were to be of internal church discipline: for instance, the Lower House urged the bishops to maintain strict standards in admitting candidates for ordination. Besides the large range of particular suggestions, the members of the Lower House took up some questions of general policy, such as the remission of the First Fruits and the treatment of French Protestant refugees.[2]

Yet to realize how thin was the ground for such busy optimism, we have only to observe that hardly any of these numerous proposals were acted upon either by the bishops or by Parliament. Apart from the lack of men, money, and resources to carry them out, there were desperate and essential difficulties. Even if the bishops had not been toiling overtime in the House of Lords, they could not really strengthen the church because the government did not wish them to. Many admirable ecclesiastical programmes ran counter to the ambitions of the Members of Parliament. Thus the church wished to intimidate the Dissenters, but the crown wished to protect them. The Lower House wished unqualified persons to be refused institution to any living, but many M.P.s wanted their younger brothers placed in good benefices regardless of their blazing stupidity. The clergy thought that families who refused to pay vestry assessments ought to be cor-

---

[1] Mason, p. 217.   [2] The recommendations are surveyed in Phillips III. 178-81.

rected, but no parson could flourish if he lived on ill terms with his wealthiest parishioners.

One detailed account will represent the general sterility. It was at this time that the Irish Parliament was conscientiously designing the clauses of the act 'to prevent the further growth of popery'. If any moral justification could exist for these frigid incitements to inhumanity, it must be the faith that Irish souls were redeemed from a damnable superstition when they were by any means at all persuaded to join the true, Anglican communion. As the absolutely essential counterpart of the act, there had to be a great missionary campaign to turn native Roman Catholics into decent members of the Church of Ireland. Otherwise the penal laws amounted to the most bestial sort of calculated avarice.

We are relieved therefore to learn that the Lower House of Convocation did indeed raise the question of the conversion of the Irish Papists. Arguing that the wisest procedure would be to employ special preachers using the Irish language, the lower clergy begged the bishops to consider how many of these each diocese would require and how the Established Church could find the means to support them. Swift's old tutor and friend, St George Ashe, now Bishop of Clogher, had already encouraged a parson in his diocese to follow this high aim. The man selected not only knew the Irish language but performed works of charity, preached industriously, endeared himself to the people, and brought many natives into the Anglican church. In the diocese of Cloyne, Swift's acquaintance Bishop Crow had got a clergyman to perfect his own knowledge of Gaelic and to labour among the Irish until many of them brought him children to be baptized, young couples to be married, and the dead to be buried.[1] Archbishop King, when Bishop of Derry, had made similar efforts to prevent Gaelic-speaking Scottish immigrants from drifting into popery. Swift's college friend, the pious, scholarly John Richardson,[2] was devoting his life to the cause of converting the natives.

Yet when, in March 1704, the Lower House of Convocation

---

[1] Mant II. 165–8.   [2] *Supra*, vol. I, p. 73.

courteously asked the Upper House for guidance, the bishops responded with frosty brevity: 'We think, that endeavouring the conversion of the papists is very commendable; and, as to preaching in the Irish tongue, we think it useful, where it is practicable.'[1] Of course, the notorious fact was that the conversion of the natives could not be allowed to succeed; for if it did, it would annihilate those lucrative advantages on which the Anglo-colonial families built their solid comforts. From Whitehall's point of view, a divided Ireland was easier to rule than a united kingdom.[2] Should the whole population turn Anglican, or even Protestant, the strongest principle of division would be lost. As an aid to administration, the religious split had the virtue of holding the political unit together while keeping its inhabitants apart. Wherever colonists and their descendants lived, they needed protection against the alien Irish and had therefore to co-operate with the policies dictated in Westminster. For the 'English in Ireland', it was an endless felicity to have broken-backed sub-sub-tenants on their lands, stripped of civil rights, and condemned to suffer under laws which might be enforced more or less harshly as the caprice of the conqueror inclined. The larger the ratio of Papist to Protestant, the easier the supply of domestic servants, manual labourers, and farmhands. Forbidding the Roman Catholics to buy or sell real estate meant opening a new frontier to property for the rulers. Converting the Roman Catholics would have meant a sharing of goods with them. Inside the Church of Ireland the prospect of enlarged congregations could hardly appear joyful. With so many livings impropriated, so few stipends adequate, with pluralities spread over exhausting distances and honest parsons already overworked, with Anglican landlords coldly resentful of tithes and Presbyterian landlords detesting the whole Established Church, the means to support an increased number of beneficed clergymen simply could not be found.

Just as the proposal to speed up the conversion of the Irish

[1] Mant II. 165.
[2] Cf. Archbishop King's honest remarks on the whole issue in Ball I. 273-4 and p. 274, n. 1.

could only remain a fraudulent insult to the name of charity, so most of the other plans recommended by the Lower House of Convocation had to be abortive. Contrary to the conclusion of a modern historian of the Church of Ireland, the close alliance of the church with the state did not put her 'in a most favourable position to attain her aims or amend her defects so far as this could be done by administrative action or by parliamentary statute'.[1] Precisely the opposite was true. It is the voluntary instincts that a living religion is designed to satisfy in mankind, and no church can flourish when its organs of voluntary belief have decayed. A few dozen John Richardsons would have accomplished more toward strengthening the Established Church than the appointment of Primate Marsh as Lord Lieutenant. It is precisely because the bishops played an essential part in government that they could obtain so few administrative decrees or parliamentary laws to amend the defects of their church. They had a terrifying case of responsibility without power, and were forced to compromise with their destroyers.

To most of the landlords, religion signified above all a card of admission to an exclusive class. Few appeals to the moral and spiritual needs of the church could move them; for beyond its value as a label, a kind of yellow-star-in-reverse, the church seemed only a needless expense, a reduction through tithes of the income divinely deserved from their estates. If a law could improve the church as a religious institution, the Irish gentry were scarcely the persons most likely to pass it. Yet these landlords were the men who sat in the Irish House of Commons. It was they whose co-operation the bishops had necessarily to win as political agents. For the landlords felt no need to accommodate the bishops; it was the bishops who had to please them.

Thus where the higher and lower clergy did try to work together, they were often defeated by the government. Especially in the treatment of Dissenters, this relation held. When Anglican churchmen tried to invalidate marriages performed by Presbyterians, or else to convert the government's annual grant (*regium donum*) to Dissenting ministers into a device for managing and

---

[1] D. A. Chart, in Phillips III. 175.

restraining them, they failed. The cases fought in Ireland were regularly quashed in London:

> The Bishop of Kildare had excommunicated one Mr. Person for preaching, and was proceeding against him to have him taken. But some sent a representation of it to England, and there came a letter discharging him [i.e., the bishop] to trouble any upon the account of nonconformity.[1]

What lay behind the government's inaction was nothing like a high-minded principle of religious toleration, as we know from the coarse opportunism of Lord Treasurer Godolphin, discussing with Ormonde the possibility (which remained unrealized) of an act of toleration for Nonconformists by the Irish Parliament:

> On the one hand a toleration by law may probably prove an encouragement for the sects to augment their number in Ireland, and make them still more dangerous to the English interest there, so on the other hand a distinction amongst Protestants in Ireland, where the Papists are so numerous, seems much more inconvenient than it is in England, and therefore my humble opinion is, that the matter ought to be governed wholly according to the natural inclinations of the Parliament of Ireland, without affecting or endeavouring to influence them one way or other.[2]

Supposing the Convocation of 1703-4 had failed to impress these axioms on an observer, the Convocation of 1705 must have done so. On 10 February, at the same time as Parliament, they assembled, again in St Patrick's chapter-room, and again with Daniel Jackson as proctor for the cathedral. But this time the clergy's soft skins were soon torn on the bristles of parliamentary arrogance. Overshadowing events in Ireland now were the reactions in England to the recent passage of the Scottish Act of Security; for under this the Scots were menacing their southern neighbours with a possible refusal to receive the Hanoverian succession. Since Irish leaders felt envious of the Scots for being offered a union which was denied to themselves, they went out of their way to advertise their own contrasting loyalty. The Irish House of Lords in an address proclaimed: 'We are resolved to oppose all attempts that may be made by Scotland, or any other

---

[1] Reid II. 523, n. 1 (letter of Oct. 1704).
[2] H.M.C. *VII Report*, p. 776: letter of 20 Jan. 1704/5.

nation whatsoever, to divide us from [England], or defeat the succession of the Protestant Line.' In an attempt further to distinguish themselves as sharing the culture of their overlords where the Scottish Presbyterians rejected it, they praised Queen Anne as the 'support and ornament of our Established Church'. It does not seem accidental that the House of Commons' allusions to the differences between Scotland and England were palpably milder: there were no bishops in the Commons.

Soon the Commons began to consider a bill 'for the improvement of the hempen and flaxen manufactures'. This may have looked like a harmless scheme to assist the linen industry. One of the chief clauses, however, was a provision to reduce the tithe on land sown in flax or hemp. In other words, the clergy's income was to be reduced as a means of benefiting one type of landlord— although obviously, if the industry expanded, the income of churchmen would correspondingly grow. Not only immediately but as a precedent for other tithes, the clause endangered clerical finances.

This bill became for a while the main and miserable business of the Lower House of Convocation, displacing several possibilities of useful transactions. The troubles flowed from a sufficiently humble source. On 12 March the Lower House petitioned the Commons, begging that they might be heard against the clause 'to ascertain the tithes of hemp and flax'; this provision, said their memorial, amounted to an invasion of freehold and was prejudicial to 'the civil rights and properties of the clergy'.[1] In its boldness of tone the memorial reflected the Atterbury faction's excessive claims for Convocation.

No roaming alley cat likes to be admonished by a caged canary. The Commons voted that the person who brought this message from Convocation was guilty of a breach of privilege, and ordered the serjeant-at-arms to take him into custody. The clergy's allusion to civil rights drew an especially angry growl; and the Commons voted that in pretending to look after the 'civil rights of the clergy', Convocation stood guilty of 'a contempt and breach of privilege' of Parliament. Therefore, the Commons

[1] Landa, p. 126.

expected the clergy to submit and acknowledge that they had nothing to do with civil rights, indeed that their meddling with those rights was an act of contempt.

Instead of ignoring these loud noises, the Lower House of Convocation sent the Commons a letter in which they not only justified their memorial—as no encroachment on the privileges of the Commons—but also and apologetically disclaimed any desire to question Parliament's right to represent both clergy and laity in civil rights. As a return for these conciliatory gestures, the Commons belligerently demanded that all matters relating to the memorial should be 'razed out' of the journals and records of Convocation. What might have happened next, we cannot tell. It looks as if Ormonde was not a very strong manager of Irish politics; but he had no wish to preside over a battle of the frogs and the mice. To stop 'greater heats' from rising, therefore, he followed a common practice of stalemated executives and adjourned Parliament (as well as Convocation) on 21 March.

Then his excellency travelled north to inspect the island's defences against another kind of belligerence. Presumably, his progress was made with an eye to the co-operation of Scottish Jacobites with the invasion schemes of the French; for Irish affairs at this time seem almost entirely limited to problems produced by the war. As a possible base for the enemy's military preparations, the island needed protection, since the Pretender might make a descent upon it either directly or through a Scotland which appeared dangerously unreliable under the Act of Security. For shipments of personnel and equipment, the Irish ports were valuable. As a source of manpower, Ireland was essential to England and alluring to France. Roman Catholic and Jacobite agents never stopped their recruiting and transporting of Irish volunteers for Louis XIV.

While the Lord Lieutenant in Ulster was touring fortified places and accepting Presbyterian panegyrics, Archbishop King in London was choking with exasperation over his brethren's lack of accomplishment. 'For God's sake', he exploded to St George Ashe, 'endeavour to procure a few canons for the regulation of things amiss in our discipline; if we do so, all other things

[159]

will come in course. We have our Saviour's promise, "Seek first the kingdom of God, and all these things shall be added to you." But if the Convocation only mind the secular profit of the church, or such things as the Parliament must do for them, the world will look on all this as priestcraft and carnal interest, and we shall get nothing.'[1] He had heard that the lower clergy sent up excellent proposals to the Upper House of Convocation but that the bishops never gave them any answer.

But when Parliament and Convocation reassembled, their absurd quarrel shifted in a more spiteful direction; for the Commons passed resolutions insinuating that the clergy possessed leanings toward Jacobitism. These malicious motions reflected in part the English parliamentary hubbub over the revived bill against occasional conformity, as well as Irish Protestant doubts concerning the intentions of Atterbury's propaganda. However, they also betoken the sympathy with Dissent felt by those M.P.s who would have liked to repeal the Sacramental Test. So the Commons resolved, among other and similar fatuities, that to 'promote misunderstandings' among the Protestants of the kingdom (i.e., for Anglican priests to oppose Nonconformity) tended to aid Papists, encourage seditions, and endanger the Protestant Succession.

Though silence might have rescued some fraction of clerical dignity, the Lower House of Convocation could not sit still; and they struck back with a resolution, self-incriminating by implication, in which they asserted their loyalty to King William, Queen Anne, and the Protestant Succession.

> And after this publick and solemn declaration, we hope no person whatever will be so unjust and uncharitable as to declare, or insinuate, that the clergy of the Church of Ireland, as by law establish'd, were not intire in their affections for the late King William, of glorious memory; or are not in the true interest of the present government; or that they are any way disaffected to the succession in the Protestant line, as by law establish'd.[2]

On hearing of this ignominy, Archbishop King erupted, 'I

---

[1] Mant II. 176 (letter of 15 Mar. 1704/5).
[2] Boyer, *History of the Reign of Queen Anne* IV. 26.

confess I wondered at those resolutions, or what could occasion them.' He pointed out that enemies of Ireland were always ready to condemn the inhabitants as showing less gratitude to King William than they ought to; 'and why you should declare it at this time, except it be to make yourselves suspected that you are not so, I can't tell.'[1] The sittings of Parliament and Convocation ended in the middle of June; but it is hardly necessary to report that although many laws were passed—including the amended act for the improvement of hempen and linen manufactures—no single measure was taken that could produce any good for the church. 'Some men are very dexterous at doing nothing', said Archbishop King; 'I wish those of that temper would keep out of places that require something to be done.'[2] Lest this lack of accomplishment should seem the effect of mere chance, the animus of the Commons appeared undeniably in the speech delivered by the Speaker of the House when he presented the money bill; for after a formal assertion of devotion to the Established Church, he went out of his way to compliment the Dissenters and include them among the body of Irish Protestants, with an allusion to their conduct during the Williamite wars: 'the same unanimity against the enemies of our religion, laws and liberties, still continues in the breasts of Protestants, (though of different perswasions in other matters) that eminently shewed it self in their joint and brave defence of London-Derry and Inniskillin.'

What Swift's judgment was of the 1705 Convocation, we can easily infer. With the meetings being held in his own cathedral's chapter-room, with Daniel Jackson as the chapter's proxy in the Lower House, and St George Ashe sitting in the Upper House, we may be sure that the active and curious Dr Swift knew minutely what language was used and what motives were revealed in the futile discussions. Regarding the need to convert the Irish, he felt as tepid as any bishop, and much more so than Ashe or King.[3] But on the general unproductivity of the recent session, he must have agreed with the archbishop's sentiments. In the offensive disrespect of the Commons for the clergy he would have seen

[1] Mant II. 180 (letter of 4 Jul. 1705).   [2] *Ibid.*, p. 178 (26 June).
[3] Cf. *Journal*, 2 Mar. 1711.

his ancient opinion of the Irish gentry confirmed. The clause to reduce the tithe of flax and hemp must have driven him to outbursts as vibrant as King's; and even many years later he argued, as the memorial of the Lower House had contended, that this kind of legislation was an invasion of property.[1] Insinuations such as those of the Commons against the patriotism of the clergy, Swift always handled with scornful contempt; and the Speaker's display of fellow-feeling with the Dissenters, he was soon to attack in print.[2] 'We have just religion enough to make us *hate*, but not enough to make us *love* one another' is an aphorism Swift made up around this time.[3]

When the rising of Parliament freed Ormonde for his return to England, he left two Lords Justices behind: Richard Cox, who was Lord Chancellor of Ireland, and John, Lord Cutts, an Irish peer who arrived in Dublin a few days before the Duke sailed.[4] It is clear that Cutts's views on church and state were closer to those of the Speaker than to Archbishop King's. It is also clear that of the two Lords Justices this brave but vicious soldier was the one who counted.

As a young man at the taking of Buda, Cutts had been the first to plant the Imperial Austrian standard on the city walls. At Namur in 1695, his disregard of enemy fire had got him the traditional *nom de guerre* of rash fighters, *Salamander*. When Venloo was stormed in 1702, he had his troops discard traditional strategy and pursue the besieged defenders from post to post, to capture the outer works. At the miraculous victory of Blenheim, ten months before coming to Ireland, Cutts had brilliantly commanded the operation of blockading the masses of French infantry caught in the village which gave the battle its name. He was a poet, a wit, an easy conversationalist, with a tall and well-built figure. Cutts had acted as an early patron of Richard Steele[5]; he had sat repeatedly in the English House of Commons; and he had been governor of the Isle of Wight. To Ireland he came not

---

[1] Landa, pp. 123–35 and *passim*.
[2] Ferguson, p. 33 and *passim*; Davis II. 112, 130.   [3] Davis I. 241.
[4] Cutts landed 13 June at 6 p.m.; Ormonde sailed 16 June, the last day of Parliament.
[5] *Supra*, vol. I, pp. 249–50.

merely as Lord Justice but as lieutenant-general in charge of her majesty's forces there.

But his lordship managed affairs of state—if his own letters do not misrepresent him—with a lack of scruple and an eye to the main chance, that earned him a varied catalogue of enemies. It looks as though Cutts dared not give up his post in Ireland partly because he could not face the consequent loss of income and partly because his unsavoury record would then lie wide open to exposure by the many who hated him.[1] In a letter to his sister (July 1706) he writes,

> I swear to you, and give you my honour, that if any one should, without my knowledge or consent (which would be barbarous) if they should get me leave to come over [i.e., get him recalled to England], and if another Lord Justice were named in my place (which would be a step to my ruin) I would not stir out of this kingdom till I saw the Duke of Ormonde here, cost what it will.[2]

On his death, some months later, a clergyman writes that though Cutts's income had risen 'above £6,000 per annum, [he] is yet dead vastly in debt, insomuch that the poor butchers, bakers, and all others that dealt with him are half ruined. His two aides-de-camp clubbed their 10*l.* a piece to pay for the embalming his corpse, which is deposited in a vault in St. Patrick's till it be known whether his friends will send for it over to bury it in England.'[3]

With his record as a placeman and 'government member' in King William's parliaments,[4] and as a trusted army officer under Marlborough, Cutts had inevitably preferred the success of the war to the security of the church; and I assume that he sided with the Junto. I also assume that one of his lordship's aims, while in the government of Ireland, was to prepare the way for the removal of the Sacramental Test. In the English House of Commons, November 1704, he had made a well-known speech against the attempt of Seymour and others to force passage of the bill against occasional conformity by 'tacking' it to the absolutely essential land tax. In Ireland his haughtiness and his strenu-

---

[1] This is my own inference from the scattered evidence available.
[2] H.M.C. *Astley*, pp. 194-5.   [3] H.M.C. *Egmont* II. 215.   [4] Walcott, *passim.*

ous pursuit of women must have added a particularly distasteful flavour to his views on religion and politics.

Even Cutts's admirers said he showed too much 'vanity and self-conceit'.[1] Upon Swift his boastful, lecherous temperament made an unusually disgusting impact. Even if the princely and affable Ormonde had not just left behind his own record of sympathy with the Irish people and consideration for the Established Church, the manners and measures of Cutts would, I think, have enraged Swift.

So we have a poem by Swift attacking Cutts with virulent bitterness but through a style we already know.[2] As usual, the metrical form employed is octosyllabic couplets; and as too often happens, the closing couplets leave the reader with a sense of flatted notes. The structure depends on an explicit analogy, with an expository introduction followed by alternate passages of description and application; and in a characteristic line of imagery Swift ties filth, lust, and sickness together. By these means the *Salamander* of Namur is compared, in seventy verses, with Pliny's description of a salamander in the *Natural History*. As paraphrase of source alternates with parallel in human subject, the Roman naturalist's terms undergo ripples of sinister interpretation, and Cutts's allegedly undeserved fame is opposed to his alleged dunghill origin. The body of the poem sustains an impressive degree of nausea, but the best lines are comparatively restrained in vocabulary: Swift's finest effects are derived from innuendo, from placement and restraint; it is the contrast between meaning and tone that produces the shock:

> So have I seen a batter'd beau
> By age and claps grown cold as snow,
> Whose breath or touch, where e'er he came,
> Blew out love's torch or chill'd the flame.

[1] Trevelyan I. 242.

[2] 'The Description of a Salamander' reads like a characterization of a living person, and I assume that Swift's knowledge of Cutts was due to his lordship's term as Lord Justice. Therefore, since Cutts arrived in Ireland in June 1705 and died in Jan. 1707, the poem was probably written within those nineteen months: rather near the beginning, I suspect, than the end, since Swift inclined to respond quickly to his early impressions of people. When the poem was first published, in Swift's *Miscellanies* of 1711, it was dated 1705. In Faulkner's edition of Swift's *Works*, 1735, it is dated 1706.

The drift of the poem is to picture Cutts as an impotent rake trying to practise fornication in Ireland. Through this conceit it recalls Swift's lampoon on Romney. But in several other works Swift alludes to Ireland as a woman who has been ravished by England.[1] Under the narrowly personal satire, therefore, the poet may be using Cutts as the emblem of what Albion has done to Hibernia. By the same token, if these implications are present, Swift is also giving Ireland the character of a woman who connives (if no more) at her own undoing. Surely the behaviour of Convocation and Parliament would have seemed to support this view.

III. BRITAIN

In Dublin's policies could generally be seen the advance shadow of English events. When Alan Brodrick, as Speaker of the Irish Commons, rang changes on the chord of Protestant unity, he anticipated the effects which Blenheim and the discipline of the Junto would have upon the decisions of the ministry in Whitehall. A few days before Stearne was installed as Dean of St Patrick's, the Queen dissolved the Parliament of England. It was necessary for Godolphin and Harley to collect a new House of Commons that would follow up the triumphs of their general in the field. By refusing assistance to the clients of Rochester, Nottingham, and Seymour, by dismissing several of the clique's lieutenants from office and giving posts to some non-Junto backers of the war—by these and similar manœuvres—the chiefs of state hoped to manage the election so that the government might remain independent of either the church extremists or the Junto.

Instead of producing an equilibrium, however, the election of 1705 not only cut down the strength of Rochester and his allies, but added sharply to the numbers of the Junto connection even while increasing as well the size of the 'government interest'—

---

[1] Cf. *The Story of the Injured Lady* and 'An Excellent New Ballad: or, The True English Dean to Be Hang'd for a Rape'. Swift's allegory seems peculiarly significant when we recognize that in many political allegories of the seventeenth and eighteenth centuries Ireland appears as England's younger brother or sister (Ferguson, p. 6).

i.e., those members who depended directly on the court.[1] Against this new alignment Godolphin could hardly resist the claims of the Junto to high office except by alluding to the insistence of her majesty and the Secretary of State upon a government above party; and even these allusions had no more than a short-term power. The chief target of Whig suspicions now was bound to be Harley.

But in the greatest task which Godolphin faced apart from the war, the Junto continued to co-operate assiduously with him, viz., in negotiating a treaty of union between Scotland and England. The supporters of the war who felt least sympathetic with the discomforts of Ireland showed the highest zeal to speed this transformation of the constitution. On the large English commission named to draw up the treaty sat all five lords of the Junto. Really, the desire for a parliamentary union was dictated by profound economic and political requirements on both sides of the Tweed—requirements which were now aggravated by the urgencies of the war. Yet Swift, like many clergymen and xenophobes, liked to reduce the origin of the union to anxieties provoked by the Act of Security. Repeatedly denied such a union themselves, Irish leaders could not help giving distorted expression to their jealousy of the Scots.

When the Act of Security had emerged from the Parliament of Scotland in 1703, it stood as the most dramatic in a series of defiances which were nevertheless to lead, tortuously and surprisingly, to the result Godolphin sought. The contrast with Irish docility was blatant. Instead of agreeing to a toleration act for the Episcopal Church in Scotland, the Edinburgh Parliament had earlier passed a law for securing the true Protestant religion and Presbyterian government. On top of this they had piled an act depriving Queen Anne's successors of the power to declare war for Scotland without the consent of that nation's Parliament. Amid a debate freer than Dublin ever heard, they had then constructed the notorious act, under which, when her majesty died, the Edinburgh Parliament would choose a successor for Scotland who need not be the same as for England unless a complete free-

[1] Walcott, p. 132.

dom of trade were part of the bargain. Irish onlookers, conditioned by their own frustrations, might have expected this act to be denied royal assent. But just before the Battle of Blenheim, the war seemed to be going so badly in Europe, and the English were finding it so hard to control the unrest of Scotland, that Godolphin had to advise the Queen to sign.

Fortunately, the negotiations for a union of the two kingdoms had begun soon after Anne's accession, though suspended within a few months. Thanks to a change of ministers in Edinburgh, however, and the effect of Blenheim—with some sensible legislation and a number of facilitating factors—it was possible to reopen the negotiations at the end of 1705. Meanwhile, the relation between the Act of Security and the whole issue of the succession was so close that the same influences which were heading toward a union also led in England to the Regency Act, assuring the peaceful installation of the Hanover line. From the well-reported discussions of these events Swift, it seems, got so much stimulus that he thought briefly of writing about them. At least, that is my inference from his making notes, in December 1705, on an old book dealing with the succession to Queen Elizabeth.[1] But when he did decide to write, he chose another theme.

By this time the English election of 1705 had forced a deep change upon court policy. Although even beforehand the Queen had allowed the Jacobite Duke of Buckingham to be dismissed as Privy Seal, and the Whiggish but extra-Junto Duke of Newcastle to be brought in, neither this nor several other small replacements could satisfy the Junto. Yet Godolphin had now to lean harder than ever upon their skill, what with the new supplies required for the war and the endless manœuvring demanded by the Anglo-Scottish crisis. The Queen still refused to admit Sunderland as one of the two Secretaries of State; but in October 1705 she consented to endure the even-tempered, well-spoken William Cowper as Lord Keeper. Though Cowper was Whiggish, he belonged with Newcastle rather than the Junto[2]; yet his attitude toward Ireland remained the opposite of Swift's.

Godolphin and Marlborough were coming to understand that

[1] Davis v. 241–3.   [2] Walcott, p. 132.

Harley, with his proclaimed ideal of a non-partisan government, would have to be sacrificed to the Junto's conception of rewards for services rendered. Not till the end of 1706, however, did they take the next big step away from him. Meanwhile, Marlborough's defeat of the French at Ramillies occurred, surpassing the wonders of Blenheim and opening the Spanish Netherlands to the Allies. And scarcely had England heard of the occupation of Brussels when the fall of Turin followed, driving the French out of Italy. By the autumn of 1706, the war party in Westminster could not be resisted. It was now therefore that the great lords —Somers, Wharton, Halifax, Sunderland, and Orford—absolutely compelled the crown to admit one of their number to cabinet rank. Though the Earl of Sunderland might be the youngest among them, he was son-in-law to Marlborough, whose Duchess still seemed the Queen's dearest friend. So they chose him to be first. At the prospect of forcing this stubborn, rude, angry man on her majesty, Godolphin felt less uncomfortable than the young Earl's own father-in-law, but Marlborough felt easier than Harley. For to Harley the establishment of Sunderland as the second Secretary of State could mean nothing but the effective displacement of his own power by his lordship's. Not till December, when Parliament gathered, did Sunderland receive the seals of office; and even if the Queen did thus bow to Godolphin in public, she felt so much the closer to Harley in private.

But now when the English Parliament met, Lord Treasurer Godolphin had no qualms to trouble him for either the future of Scotland or the fate of Marlborough's armies. As it happened, he need not have worried about the Scots in any case. Thanks to the most delicate management, they had come around to sending a commission, selected by the Queen, to London to draw up the terms of the union; and for two months in the spring of 1706 the separate nations' delegates met in separate rooms in Whitehall, exchanging information only by written minutes. Near the end of July it was possible for the Queen at a state ceremony in St James's Palace, to receive their signed and completed articles.

Not that the danger signs had all blown away. During the

early months of 1705 Scottish militia men had drilled themselves in the menacing gesture against England which had sent Ormonde up to survey the defences of northern Ireland. And again while the Treaty of Union made its way through the last Scottish Parliament, mobs rioted in Edinburgh or seized the town in Glasgow; Presbyterian zealots marched in Dumfries; and Jacobites conspired in eastern or northern Scotland. Yet as 1706 closed, it was obvious that the treaty was passing in a form the English would accept. Week after week, the *Dublin Gazette* reported to its envious readers, in the most minute detail, the treatment of the articles by the Estates. The full terms of the treaty were printed and sold as a pamphlet in Dublin. And today, as one sees column upon column of the small, four-page, semi-weekly newspaper concerned with the progress abroad of the blessing denied to its readers at home, one imagines the cowed, baffled Irish as a band of starveling waifs nosing a window which reveals the feasting, rebellious Scots.

IV. SWIFT AND THE INJURED LADY

Something like this was Swift's reaction. We know, because he heaped up his bitterness in a clever short poem and a dull prose tract. Though both appeared posthumously, the prose piece *The Story of the Injured Lady* is probably the earlier, composed after the Scots ratified the Act of Union (16 January 1707) but before it took effect (1 May 1707).[1] However unexcitingly it may read now, the *Injured Lady* suggests a good deal about not only Swift's political opinions but also his methods as a pamphleteer; and it exhibits several features worth scrutinizing. For one thing the essay is allegorical in form, though with a vehicle too ponderous for its tenor. Using the hint of the *Salamander*, Swift makes Ireland into a woman seduced and England into her seducer. But to triangulate the affair, he also turns Scotland into the fallen woman's successful rival. Even while suffering mistreatment from her betrayer, the injured lady sees this one-time suitor marrying the beggarly adventuress who has displaced her. Most of Swift's

[1] Ferguson, pp. 28–32. It was not published until 1746.

[169]

essay comprises the cast-off's statement of her case in a letter to a confidant who must give her some overdue instructions. In a brief answer, filling a third the length of the letter, the confidant tells her what actions to take.

As a set of arguments, the implications of the story cannot be mistaken. Its most comprehensive thesis not only underlies all Swift's writings about Ireland; it supports an ethical tendency which commonly contradicts and, in his greatest political essays, sometimes overpowers, his ordinary assumptions as a member of the hired gang administering Ireland. To persuade men of good will that slaveholding is respectable, one must confuse power with justice and presume that not all men are truly human. To persuade them that the comfort of the few does not violate charity in a land where the many are debased, one must admire renunciation only as it spiritualizes social rank. English land-lords employed such presuppositions to distinguish their labour-ing poor from themselves, and the English generally employed them to account for their treatment of Ireland. In political cant, descendants were identified with ancestors and God was made responsible for conquests but not rebellions: so the beaten natives owed allegiance to their imported rulers. Thus by human and divine law both, the inferior Irish possessed no civil rights not donated to them by England, and colonists who educated them-selves out of this faith were as sinful and seditious as the natives. 'You would hardly believe there should be such a creature as an Irish Protestant Jacobite', a newly-arrived English official wrote to Sunderland from Ireland, 'and yet 'tis most certain there are a great many such monsters.'[1]

Swift's most comprehensive theses, on the contrary, are that one's impotence to relieve the agonies of another does not grant one the right to connive at them, that the sufferings of the humble, however irremediable, are as painful as those of the great, that the less chance the wretched have to throw off their misery, the louder they ought to speak to reveal the shame. In attacking the weakeners of the Established Church, Swift often forgot his com-mon humanity, but in defending the whole of Ireland against her

[1] George Dodington to Sunderland, 14 Aug. 1707 (Froude I. 321, n. 1).

foes, he always proclaimed it. Political justice, he then insisted, had the same meaning in Dublin as in London.

This was a view that the settlers could often not afford to maintain, least of all when they needed English troops to protect them from the natives; for it was then undeniable that their government relied upon England's support. By 1698, however, the utter pacification of the country had become so obvious that the deeper principles could be expounded by a writer less brilliant than Swift but in a fresh and admired form in which Swift perhaps first studied some of them. This was *The Case of Ireland's Being Bound by Acts of Parliament in England*, a book written by the father of the Dublin Philosophical Society, William Molyneux.[1] Although Molyneux's argument can be found in earlier authors, his statement of it is the *locus classicus*, based on the distinction between a colony and a sister kingdom.[2] He argued that Ireland was never conquered but willingly accepted the English king. The two nations, he said, were united solely through the crown, and Ireland's Parliament had all the authority in the one kingdom that England's had in the other. According to Molyneux, the settlers, whether as descendants of free English citizens or as recent migrants, possessed the same rights as their forefathers in either country. Modelled on the political theories of Molyneux's friend Locke, the *Case of Ireland* forms a kind of specialized appendix to the great *Second Treatise*, and applies to Ireland some of the doctrines used to justify the Glorious Revolution in England. While the argument against conquest sounds less persuasive today than ever, the slogan of a union through the crown still vibrates with a faintly appealing constitutionalism; and the concept of an Englishman's rights quickly enlarges itself into the idea of human or natural rights. In a letter to Locke, Molyneux stated the issue as Americans were to learn it, stripped of narrow legalism: 'How justly England can bind us without our *consent* and *representatives*, I leave to the author of the two treatises of government to consider.'[3] Ireland, it appeared, endured all the limitations of a colony with all the responsibilities of a sister kingdom.

The *Injured Lady's* case is to some extent an allegory of Moly-

---

[1] *Supra*, vol. I, p. 80.   [2] Ferguson, pp. 20–2 and *passim*.   [3] *Ibid.*, pp. 21–2.

neux's book,[1] and rests therefore on the postulate that Ireland put herself under English protection at least partly of her own will. In doing so, she committed herself no further than agreeing to share the same executive head. For the rest of her constitution, since Ireland owned a competent House of Lords and House of Commons, the English Parliament had no authority to dictate laws to her. Within this fundamental scheme Swift reviews some terrible if incidental grievances. Of those the most staggering, for the Protestants, were the restrictions placed by England upon industry and trade. While such edicts might be admitted as proper for a colony, they were unbearable for a constitutional entity. Even if commerce were free, however, the economy of the nation would still be undermined by the non-residence of its high officers and great landlords, who lived most of the time in England and spent Ireland's wealth there. And supposing the officers stayed home? Unfortunately, most of them had originally been sent over from England and therefore deprived the native-born of both income and power.

All these elements Swift complicates with the doings of recent Irish parliaments; and in the framework thus produced, he turns to reflect upon the Treaty of Union. In this polemical aspect of the allegory he declares that Ireland, not Scotland, deserves such a treaty. Her natural resources are abundant; her people are loyal; her established church is episcopal; her political traditions are monarchical. Scotland is a poor, mountainous land; its people invaded England and helped kill Charles I; its church is Presbyterian; politically it would like to be republican. In the last paragraph of the Lady's letter she reports the steps toward a marriage between her master and her rival. Here Swift implies, rather fatuously, that it was Ireland who made the Treaty possible. During the Scottish uprisings of 1705, when the cause of union seemed failing, he says the loyal declarations of Ireland scared the Scots into compliance.

Next, the 'Friend's' answer to the Lady appears, interesting mainly as reiterating the familiar themes: Ireland's independence, her right to freedom of trade, her need to halt the absentee-

[1] Ferguson, p. 32.

ism of statesman and landlord. Again Swift brings in recent history. Thus he says, very curiously, that sooner than promise her loyalty, Ireland should have collaborated with Scotland during the 1705 crisis: to frighten England into offering 'reasonable terms', silence would have served Ireland better than addresses of allegiance. Presumably, Swift's 'terms' would have meant an increased degree of constitutional freedom. He also says that several of the Irish leaders are 'rascals', probably with a stare at the Speaker, Brodrick, and his relations. Finally, he urges the Irish Parliament to declare itself to be constitutionally on a par with the English, under the crown; to insist on freedom of trade; and to require state officers to live in the country of their employment.

If the explicit themes of the 'Answer' sound familiar, one of its tendencies seems peculiar to Swift, and it reappears in all his discourses on Irish problems. This is the insistence that Ireland is in part to blame for her own miseries and therefore that she is capable of alleviating some of them by herself. There are rogues among the nation's leaders, Swift warns, who have given bad advice. But there are still resolutions the Irish Parliament can easily and single-handedly make, which would repair some of England's injuries. To act together for the welfare of Ireland, Swift says, is the high duty of all the country's inhabitants.

If the *Injured Lady* establishes a more admirable doctrine than Swift's famous essays on English politics, it hardly matches them in rhetorical skill. The allegory itself was imprudently chosen. True, it has for Swift's purpose one strong advantage: that it discards the portrayal of Ireland (conventional in political allegories of the time) as England's younger brother or sister,[1] and substitutes for this the role of fiancée; for by doing so it implicitly fixes her status as a separate kingdom which needs to be won, rather than a colony lacking the rights of a first-born heir. But with his gingerly attitude to sexual encounters of all sorts, Swift seems hardly the man to handle the details of a fantasy in which one lover is deceiving two mistresses. Possibly, his own recent dealings with Hetty Johnson both encouraged and impeded his approach to this theme. Anyhow, in its very starting point the

[1] *Ibid.*, p. 6.

fable seems awkward, since the Lady's resistance to seduction is necessary for the reader's sympathy, but her willingness to yield is requisite to the legal argument. Still worse, with material so risqué, Swift dare not indulge either his humour or his irony. The Lady's account and her Friend's answer must be sober, or innuendoes of the most indelicate nature will creep out. So the prose has a bare, colourless surface, quite unlike the style of Swift's earlier allegories. As a metaphor of the affairs of three nations the theme of double courtship works only roughly. It is easy to treat whole families as kingdoms, with mothers as queens, stewards as prime ministers, estates as provinces, and so forth. Fielding's *Grub Street Opera*, Arbuthnot's *John Bull* show how amusingly the details can be adjusted. But the relation of lady to suitor does not go far to embody a dependent people's desperation when their trade is restricted.

Possibly the feebleness of *The Story of the Injured Lady* accounts for Swift's decision not to publish it. Strong or weak, however, it could not stop the union of England and Scotland, while if it should be traced to its author, the *Story* could block Swift's way to promotion. Archbishop King certainly sympathized with the tone of the allegory: nearly ten years earlier, as Bishop of Derry, he had lost a great lawsuit when his opponents appealed to the House of Lords in England over the House of Lords in Ireland. This very appeal, in fact, belonged among the occasions for Molyneux's writing his book. But King had doubted that the *Case of Ireland* would do more than exasperate the mischief falling on Ireland,[1] and he probably would have felt the same about the *Injured Lady*.

Swift's own caution seems the likeliest reason for the *Story*'s remaining in manuscript, since some well-turned couplets on the same topic also lay unpublished till after his death. These *Verses Said to Be Written on the Union* represent not an Irish but an English protest against the event; and it seems remarkable that with all his virtuosity in shifting viewpoints it is in this pose, and not the other, that Swift can permit himself to employ irony. The lines open with an allusion to Queen Anne's description of her heart

[1] Ferguson, p. 27, n. 4.

as 'entirely English',[1] and contrast this royal expression of devotion to Anglicanism with the loss of the Episcopal cause in Scotland through the Act of Security and its accompaniments:

> The Queen has lately lost a part
> Of her entirely-English heart,
> For want of which by way of botch,
> She pieced it up again with Scotch.
> Blest revolution which creates
> Divided hearts, united states.

Swift is obviously refurbishing the false logic by which the Treaty of Union was alleged to follow from the Act of Security. He objects that the Scots differ from the English in their church, their laws (Scotland kept her separate system of jurisprudence under the Union), and their wealth.

Though designed around Swift's old skill with elaborated similes, the rest of the brief poem sinks below its opening. Part of the trouble seems that he deserts those analogies with plants and animals that he can sustain with steady force, and takes up the mechanical image of a two-keeled ship, a vessel familiar to Dubliners through Sir William Petty's repeated but unsuccessful experiments.[2] By drawing out the parallels between this and the new-fangled 'ship of state', Swift brings his complaint to an unimpressive close.

A pathetic side of the poem is the author's identification of himself with 'our commonweal' of England. Just as victims of long persecution tend to adopt the standards of their persecutors, so Swift, whose failure to win the posts he desired was partly due to his Irish birth and education, clung to the picture of himself as entirely English. It is for the sake of 'our crazy double-bottom'd realm' and not for Ireland that in this poem (though not in the *Injured Lady*) he resents the Union.

V. PEMBROKE IN IRELAND

Ormonde's position as Lord Lieutenant could not remain easy. He had the great virtue of popularity; and during the period of

[1] Trevelyan I. 175. [2] *DNB.*; also *supra*, vol. I, pp. 81-4.

fears concerning Scottish restlessness, his presence strengthened Irish loyalty while his military science found direct employment in improving the defences of the island. Although Ormonde was Rochester's son-in-law and politics normally threw him in with the Earl's associates, he did not side with them over the Union question. While Seymour, Rochester, and Nottingham were inflaming the high-church partisans to oppose the Treaty, Ormonde helped its progress either by his conduct in attending the English House of Lords or by goodwill during his residence in Dublin. Though sympathetic with the clergy of the Established Church, he did not feel driven against the Dissenters. He may even have tried to broaden the degree of toleration allowed them[1]; and he was quickly dissuaded from prosecuting Presbyterian ministers who refused to take the oath of abjuration.[2]

Yet after the 1705 election the deepest currents were running the other way. Harley might believe that an ideal administration should be independent of organized cliques, and the Queen might parrot his lessons. But Godolphin was realizing that he could simplify the whole engine of government by leaning on the ready-made Junto apparatus that suited his policies. This trend, however, was not the whole source of Ormonde's decline in authority. Early in 1706 there appeared a clear sign that if his tenure was growing less secure, the reason was partly his hereditary respect for the 'Irish interest'.[3] At this time an important judgeship, the post of Lord Chief Baron of the Irish Exchequer, had to be filled; and the incompatibility of English desires with native aspirations glared forth. The Lord Lieutenant had assumed that it would be his prerogative to fill the vacancy. In England, however, the new Lord Keeper, Cowper, was warning Queen Anne that if a person born and educated in Ireland should take the post, he would add to the difficulties Whitehall already faced in managing the Dublin Parliament. Since Ormonde nominated Robert Rochfort, the Attorney-General, who belonged to an ancient Kildare family, the Queen put off her judgment. After four months, Ormonde and Rochfort lost, and Richard Freeman, a friend of Somers, was sent over from Eng-

---

[1] H.M.C. *VII Report*, pp. 776–7.   [2] Reid II. 499.   [3] *Supra*, vol. I, p. 9.

land.[1] Ormonde's loyalty to Anne through all the flickerings of the Scottish crisis saved his authority for a while. In February 1707 Dublin heard the Duke was ill of a fever in England; but he soon recovered and in the middle of March came the false prophecy that he would set out for Ireland the following month.[2] By now, however, the Union had found its happy consummation; and in the wake of Sunderland's appointment the Junto lords, released from their commissionerships, were pressing on again, demanding payment on the line for work done to order.

Instead of returning as Lord Lieutenant, the Duke found himself replaced by another English peer, who stood independent of the Junto on the one side and the Rochester–Nottingham combination on the other. This was the Earl of Pembroke, who had a large family, an ancient name, vast outlays, experience of high office, and much property in Ireland. In political action Pembroke seems to have been a steady servant of the throne rather than of any party. Although scholars tend to classify him as tied more to Tories than Whigs, he was repeatedly praised by Burnet, and he opposed such important 'Tory' motions as the resuming of King William's grants and the impeaching of those who had connived at the Partition Treaties. Like several lords of the Junto, he was a past president of the Royal Society. King William had trusted him; Queen Anne liked him; he had carried the sword at both their coronations. On the whole he seems a patriotic aristocrat who wanted the great pensions which went with employment and who normally did what he was told in return for them; yet who, for all his allegiance to the throne, would not support measures he thought dangerous to the constitution.

Thus Pembroke was less a statesman than a great courtier. Though he had been a diplomat at the Hague—Matthew Prior remained an old friend from those days—he really liked the Admiralty. There, however, it was now the royal consort, the

---

[1] H.M.C. *Ormonde*, n.s., VIII. xlv. N.B. that in June 1707 when Cox was forced out and Freeman became Lord Chancellor, Rochfort could be allowed to move up to Lord Chief Baron, but Brodrick then rose from Solicitor-General to Attorney-General (*Dublin Gazette*, 24 June 1707, from Whitehall, 17 June). Cox had been made a baronet in November 1706.

[2] *Dublin Gazette*, 22 Feb., 22 Mar. 1706/7.

Prince of Denmark, who by his Queen's determination held the highest rank: so the Earl had to look elsewhere. Since 1702 he had been acting as Lord President of the Privy Council, an employment of more income than weight. His appointment as Lord Lieutenant seems a makeshift to avoid or delay a stronger choice. By moving Pembroke out of the Lord Presidency, the Junto intended to make it available for Somers. But Queen Anne could not yet stomach Somers, and another course had temporarily to be taken. Meanwhile, not only did Pembroke retain the Lord Presidency, but the announcement of his additional post came rather late and suddenly. If it was Junto pressure that eliminated Ormonde, it looks as if Pembroke was slipped in by the Queen on Harley's advice as an apparent neutral whom the Junto could not resent. Early in April 1707 the decision to appoint him was made at court, and by 10 April Ormonde had notice that the Earl would succeed him.

Pembroke, who was a little over fifty, had many tastes to endear him to Swift. His reputation for 'humour and oddness' was 'remarkable and indeed most extraordinary'.[1] Liking conversation, puns, and *la bagatelle*, he enjoyed just the sort of social entertainment in which Swift was proficient. Moreover, Pembroke preserved some traces of the Renaissance fashion of aristocratic scholarship and connoisseurship. Not only books and sculpture but curiosa and antiquities were among the objects he collected. In his acquaintanceship with Swift we shall see an example of how the vicar could enjoy the company of a good-natured and powerful lord even when their political principles were in disagreement.

Setting out in the middle of June, the new Lord Lieutenant reached Dublin on the morning of the twenty-fourth and was treated to a splendid reception, with a state dinner at which Primate Marsh distinguished himself by getting sick.[2] The immediate impression Pembroke made on Archbishop King suggests that the reputation he finally left as a successful governor was not misleading:

My Lord Lieutenant acts the same obliging prudent part he did in

[1] *Complete Peerage.*   [2] Mant II. 181.

England, talks with great reserve of business and with great freedom of other affairs. I observe that his learning and general knowledge make conversation easy to him and enable him to divert any [who] would penetrate his thoughts or engage him in subjects wherein he is not willing to discover himself.[1]

Addison said, 'The Parliament of Ireland seems very much pleased with their new Lord Lieutenant.'[2] Soon the Privy Council were sitting as much as eight or ten hours almost every day while they prepared bills to be sent to the Council in England for approval before the Irish Parliament acted on them.[3]

To serve as his court officer of the 'black rod', or usher between the Lord Lieutenant and Parliament, Pembroke had brought along a protégé who was even more likely to seem charming to Swift than the Earl himself.[4] This was a handsome young courtier-scholar, Sir Andrew Fountaine of Narford Hall, Norfolk. Though Swift's junior by nine years, Sir Andrew had already a remarkable history. As an undergraduate at Christ Church, the Oxford college with perhaps the highest social and intellectual prestige, he had performed well enough to receive a 'student's place', or fellowship. He had studied Anglo-Saxon, travelled extensively, collected objets d'art, and established himself as an exquisite virtuoso. Visiting Rome in 1698, he assembled a collection of drawings which reflect admirable discrimination in an amateur of twenty-two; for it contained works by Dürer, Raphael, Titian, Poussin, Rubens, and Tintoretto.[5] The following year, he was knighted by King William. From Venice in 1702 he wrote, 'I buy nothing but silver imperiall medalls, and prints after Rafaell . . . I shall, if it please God I return safe, have one of the best collections of silver coins in England after that of my Lord Pembroke.'[6] In 1705 appeared his monograph on Danish

---

[1] Ball I. 60, n. 3 (letter of 1 July 1707).
[2] Graham, p. 75 (letter of 29 Aug. 1707).   [3] Mant II. 181.
[4] Fountaine was much younger than Pembroke and seems to have been in some ways dependent on him. He often stayed with the Earl, accepted favours from his lordship, sold part of his collections to him, and in a letter of 16 Dec. 1711 apparently acted as social secretary, arranging an appointment for Hans Sloane with Pembroke (B.M. MS. Sloane 4043, fol. 14).
[5] *Catalogue of a Collection . . . formed by Sir Andrew Fountaine* (Sotheby sale 21 June 1902), pp. 7-10.
[6] Bodl. MS. Rawl. D. 377, fol. 61ᵛ (23 Feb. 1701/2 to E. Thwaites).

and Saxon coins, *Numismata Anglo-Saxonica et Anglo-Danica*, dedicated to Pembroke.[1] By this time he had a generous collection of manuscripts—originals and copies—going back to medieval times and concerning coinage, ecclesiastical foundations, Tudor history, and a rather Gimcracky mélange of other topics.[2]

Fountaine made the new experimental science one of his hobbies and cultivated literary and learned acquaintances. He visited or corresponded with a number of persons whom Swift came to know: William Stratford, canon of Christ Church, Oxford, and a family friend of the Harleys; Humphrey Wanley, who became Harley's librarian; William Nicolson, a painstaking historical scholar who was to become Bishop of Derry; Hans Sloane, whose collections formed the basis of the British Museum.

However, Fountaine suffered few illusions concerning the life of the mind or the blessings of piety. The shrewdness and geniality which he mingled in his advice to an Oxford classicist were true to his permanent character, and they give us the tone he used in talking to Swift:

> Methinks Dr soe wise a man as you are shd not take soe much pains for soe little profit, but rather like some of your neighbours come to London, turn whig and get preferment; you may like Dr Stratford, as soon as your business is done, return to the side you left; pray advise with him upon this affair, and Ime sure hee'll tell you that getting a good benefice is a more effectuall way to gain reputation among the Dutch Literati than publishing Greek Authors... I have since I saw you laid out almost 220^{li} in Medalls, and almost as much more in books and prints soe that I'me very near being a Bankrupt.[3]

In Ireland, Pembroke gave him the court appointment of Gentleman-Usher of the Black Rod, and Trinity College made him LL.D. *honoris causa*.

With both Pembroke and Fountaine Swift hit it off better than with any of their predecessors in Dublin Castle. Yet the special

---

[1] It is the last section of George Hickes's *Antiquae literaturae septentrionalis libri duo*, vol. I.

[2] See Thomas Hearne's list of MSS. in Fountaine's Christ Church study, Dec. 1705 (Bodl. MS. Smith 24, pp. 21–32).

[3] Letter of 5 Aug. 1706 to Dr Hudson of University College, Oxford, from Narford (Bodl. MS. Rawl. D. 316, fols. 139^v–40).

goal of the Earl as governor could only have disturbed him, since Pembroke had received instructions that the Sacramental Test must be removed; and Alan Brodrick, the Speaker, whom Swift hated, was eager to hurry this work. Opponents of the Test had spread reports in England that the Protestants of Ireland, whether Anglican or Nonconformist, felt 'wonderfully fond'—as Archbishop King sarcastically noted—of repealing the clause. The same propagandists told political leaders in Ireland that the ministry held this as their main design.[1] When Sir Richard Cox was ousted as Lord Chancellor of Ireland in June 1707, he blamed his dismissal on his notorious unwillingness to repeal the Test[2]; and it was indeed the Englishman, Freeman, backed by Cowper, who took his place, while Alan Brodrick moved up from Solicitor-General to Attorney-General.

Throughout the parliamentary session, a war of allusions was waged, as grotesque as it was conventional; the weapons were addresses which aligned Pembroke, Brodrick, and many M.P.s in one camp against the Lords, dominated by the bishops, in another. Thus when the Lord Lieutenant opened Parliament on 7 July, he began at once to fulfil his orders with a direct hint in his speech: the Queen, he said, recommended unanimity to them, and would be glad to consider any expedient for the strengthening of the Protestant interest against the Papists. In other words, he would have liked to see the main division between Protestants, the Test clause, disappear.

The Commons, under Brodrick, responded by addressing extraordinary and emphatic congratulations to her majesty on the union of England and Scotland, and praying that a 'yet more comprehensive union' might be designed—i.e. to include Ireland. Addressing Pembroke, they not only dwelled on their gratitude for the Queen's wish to unite 'her Protestant subjects of this kingdom', but specifically challenged those who tried to create 'misunderstandings amongst Protestants'. Thus two objects of Swift's least tender feelings were cordially joined in the Commons' recommendations.

The Lords, on the contrary, delivered less emphatic felicita-

[1] Mant II. 186.   [2] *Autobiography of Sir Richard Cox*, p. 21.

tions on the Union, describing it merely as one of all Britain under 'the same Protestant succession'; but the Queen's love of the Established Church they singled out for peculiar mention; and when praying for a union to include Ireland, they slipped in an ambiguous reference to 'such as by their own forwardness or disaffection to the publick good' debarred themselves from her majesty's favour—a reference which could mean Roman Catholics or Dissenters and was (with puerile cunning) aimed at the latter. Addressing the Lord Lieutenant, they exhibited the same level of shrewdness by picking up the watchword of 'unanimity' and reducing it to 'unanimity amongst our selves', which of course could mean against repealing the Test.

Again near the end of the session, Brodrick, presenting the money bill, delivered a speech with a warm eulogy of 'unanimity and unity'. Then the Commons, addressing Pembroke, went so far as to attach the service of the Queen to the 'common safety' of the Protestant interest—two elements, they said, which were so interwoven that 'what strikes at the one, necessarily proves prejudicial to the other'. And Pembroke once more sang his part in the opera with variations on the same themes.[1]

A number of bills desired by the government did pass successfully through both houses, especially the invaluable act for the public registration of deeds, which was a really sound move toward a legal security for land titles. But the possibility of altering the Sacramental Test barely came to an open issue: the Presbyterians were fought and defeated behind scenes; and when Swift said the odds went four to one against them,[2] he hardly exaggerated. For Archbishop King wrote at the time,

> Upon trial it proved that nothing was more averse to the universal inclination of the parliament here. I believe some few might be for it; but it was their interest to make things go smoothly in parliament, and they found this was the way to obtain it; and, therefore, they came in with the rest, and have really gained great reputation by being so. You can hardly imagine what a healing measure this has proved, and how far it has prevailed to oblige those that were in

[1] For the whole series of addresses and speeches, see Boyer VI. 237(Q)–237(R). N.B. that the two gatherings Q–R are numbered alike.
[2] Davis II. 118.

great animosities against one another, to comply in all reasonable proposals; whereas, if the repeal of the test had been insisted on, it would have broken all in pieces, and made them form parties on principles which before were founded only on personal quarrels.[1]

An observer on the other side had the same impression. Pembroke had brought George Dodington over as his secretary; and when Dodington wrote to Sunderland, who felt fanatical about repealing the Test, he assured the Secretary of State that the prospect was hopeless, blaming the resistance upon Jacobites and bishops:

> I entirely agree with you, that nothing less than the taking off the Sacramental Test can remedy the growing evils this country labours under; but unless the government will call a new parliament, and sincerely espouse taking it off, it will not be done. Two-thirds of the members of the present House of Commons are high flyers. In the other house the bishops, every man of them, are as high as Laud was, and have so great an influence over the temporal lords, most of whom have as little sense as Lord Abercorn, that they are at least six to one against the honest lords. Believe me this country is priest-rid, very near as much as the Portuguese and Spaniards are.[2]

Even without actually precipitating the Test issue on the floor of the House, Pembroke forced it too far; and Addison later reported that the 'jealousy' which the pressure aroused had made this whole session of Parliament 'very uneasie to this government'.[3]

Instead of a row over the Test, the parliamentary session treated itself to a satisfying attack on a pamphlet relating to the Rev. Francis Higgins, who was sometimes called the Irish Sacheverell. Higgins loved to make inflammatory denunciations of the Godolphin ministry, insinuating that those in power meant to destroy religion. To Swift, Higgins seemed an embarrassing grotesque on the outworks of the Established Church, a figure that would have been more useful in silent stone than in noisy life.[4] The Irish House of Lords, with a cheerful display of indignation, agreed that *A Postscript to Mr. Higgins's Sermon* was

---

[1] Mant II. 186 (letter of 16 Aug. 1707).
[2] Froude I. 321-2, n. 1 (letter of 28 Aug. 1707).   [3] Graham, p. 137.
[4] *Journal*, 9 Nov. 1711 and *passim*.

a false and seditious libel, and ordered it to be burned by the common hangman. The following year, Higgins was had up in England for a scandalous sermon.[1]

Convocation, this year, was more imaginative, and diverted itself with an exhilarating debate on a topic equally remote from the advancement of the church and the improvement of morality, but well calculated to disgust laymen. Even if Swift had not been drawn indirectly into the quarrel, he would have found it absorbing. At the centre stood the now Rev. Elie Bouhéreau, formerly Galway's secretary. Behind Bouhéreau stood the Primate, who hoped to give him an official stipend as keeper of the public library which Marsh was trying to found. Alongside Marsh stood King, who wished to join with the Primate in sponsoring an act of Parliament that would establish the library. Against the whole scheme were ranked four of the Upper House and most of the Lower House of Convocation. This opposition, capricious though it seems today, did spring from honest fears and hopes.

Marsh wished to annex the lay office of keeper to the ecclesiastical office of treasurer or precentor of St Patrick's Cathedral. Yet the trustees of the library were to include four laymen *ex officio*; and a vote of five trustees, if the Primate were among them, had the power to remove the keeper. Furthermore, not only did the bill name Bouhéreau as first keeper, but it stated that one reason for the appointment was his gift of five hundred pounds' worth of books. Thus, since ecclesiastical tithes and ancient benefices were attached to the cathedral offices, the enemies of the proposal could claim that it alienated church property from the Establishment and gave laymen authority over a priest. Inasmuch as Bouhéreau's gift was a ground of his appointment, it could be charged that the proposal involved simony, through the sale of an ecclesiastical office. Because the office in question belonged to the cathedral, the bill could be described as infringing on the power of the dean and chapter to use their ancient prerogatives.[2]

Naturally enough, the two bishops who spirited the opposition

[1] Boyer vi. 230(Q), 367.   [2] Landa, p. 51.

to Marsh's bill were John Pooley of Raphoe and Thomas Lindsay of Killaloe, for it was they who in 1705 had opposed the giving-in of the lower clergy to the Commons over the Flax and Hemp Bill; and they were both in sympathy with Atterbury's schemes for the Convocation of Canterbury. Two other bishops, including Swift's friend, Lloyd of Killala, backed them up. The complaints made a far more indecent noise than the occasion warranted. Some of the most fiery denouncers were hoping to assist Atterbury's clique in England by asserting the rights of the lower clergy. Other outcries seemed expressions of personal dislike for Marsh and King. A powerful undertone suggests the general frustration of the clergy over their helplessness to control their own fates. But these accountings do not eliminate other facts: that the bill did set dangerous precedents, that the Primate had consulted too narrow a circle in planning it, and that it was rammed through with an insolent disregard of valid anxieties. Swift said of Marsh, 'Doing good is his pleasure; and as no man consults another in his pleasures, neither does he in this; by his aukwardness and unadvisedness disappointing his own good designs.'[1]

Since the bill was pending not in Convocation but in Parliament, no clerical histrionics could do much to block it. And even while the froth accumulated, the bill was passing the House of Lords. When Archbishop King was informed of the attitude the Lower House was taking, he not only refused to let the bill drop, as requested, but raised his voice in heat and passion to add, 'Convocation has meddled with matters that do not belong to them, and they shall soon know it and tell them so from me.'[2] It is not surprising that many in the Lower House, 'particularly such whose preferments lie in and about Dublin',[3] quickly decided the bill was harmless; and the House sent a delegate to thank the Primate for his philanthropic deed. Nevertheless, several of the censures were voted as reported, and discussion of the other resolutions continued until the bill was finally enacted on the last day of the session for Parliament and Convocation.

[1] Davis v. 211. Mant ii. 111–18 gives many details of the controversy over Marsh's library.
[2] Bodl. MS. Ballard 36, fol. 47.   [3] *Ibid.*, fol. 47ᵛ.

Supporters of the bill in the Lower House now moved that the resolutions already accepted be stricken from the records. To affirm their indignation, however, a majority of the Lower House of Convocation voted to keep the resolutions in their journal as a form of permanent protest. It was precisely such a record that the Irish Parliament had attempted to make Convocation expunge in the spring of 1705. At this turn Swift enters as prebendary of Dunlavin, in a sadly ineffectual rôle.

The prolocutor chosen by the Lower House for the session of 1707 was Swift's friend Samuel Synge, precentor of St Patrick's. But Daniel Jackson, who had attended two earlier convocations as the chapter's proctor, had died. At Synge's instigation, therefore, the chapter had recognized Swift's importance by electing him to succeed Jackson (21 July 1707).[1] Only once during the session do we know that Swift asserted himself independently of the other members of Convocation, and this was over the vote on the resolutions. Although he shared the fears of the majority concerning the dangerous precedents set by Marsh's bill, he argued that the motion to keep the record of the resolutions was superfluous: since the effort to expunge the original resolutions had failed, they remained on the books and were in themselves 'sufficient to inform posterity of the sense of the said house relating to the said bill'.[2]

If this gesture hardly makes Swift appear heroic, it does raise him above contempt. When he stood by his colleagues in Convocation, Swift was exposing his fate to the anger of his most powerful superiors. Then by entering a protest against a fatuous motion, he risked isolating himself from those very colleagues. Yet in these turnabouts he honoured two commissions he was to uphold steadily in later years: the guarding of ecclesiastical rights against the encroachment of laymen and the defence of the lower clergy against the ambition of bishops. Meanwhile, however else Swift might hope to rise beyond a vicarage, it would not be by the manipulation of committees or synods. And however

---

[1] Landa, p. 50; Mason, p. 221.

[2] Bodl. MS. Ballard 36, fol. 51^v (30 Oct. 1707, the last day of this session of Convocation).

subtly he might recommend himself to the archbishop, he would not do so by betraying his simplest loyalties. Surely King had the perceptiveness to measure Swift's rigidity, and surely his awareness that this man could not be, as King would say, 'trusted', was the reason that in Irish churchmanship, as in Whig politics, there appeared no hand willing and strong enough to raise Dr Swift. If the beneficent transformation was to touch him, the magic wand would take the shape of a power Swift could control alone, the talent England was discovering in *A Tale of a Tub*.

In Dublin, meanwhile, King's annoyance at being resisted by Convocation found a match in the pharisaical satisfaction of Marsh upon his own ultimate triumph; for he wrote a remarkably self-indulgent account of the affair to a sympathetic correspondent:

The opposition continued to the last (not levell'd against me directly, or my design in it; but that the bill conteind in it simonie, sacrilege and perjury; though not one of them prov'd. Notwithstanding after all the exclamations made against it by two turbulent men[1] on the above mentiond accounts all other the lords both temporal and spiritual appear'd very zealous for it and it pass'd the Hous of Lords, and was sent down to the Hous of Commons, where it was very kindly and favourably received. In the meantime the dissenting lords enter'd their protestation against it, with such reasons as the House of Lords thought to be very reflective on them and therefore at the next session immediately voted those dissenting lords should be sent prisoners to the Castle unless they would withdraw their reasons, which accordingly they did, and all was quiet. In the meantime the Hous of Commons pass'd my bill without any mans opposing it, or as they say, nemine contradicente, and presently voted that a comittee of eight of their members should be appointed to give me the thanks of that hous for the benefaction, which was done out of hand. The Lords knowing this, presently voted the same, and pitch'd upon the dissenting lords to do it (for their mortification) but only one of them being at that time in the Hous, a temporal lord was join'd with him; and that likewise was done openly in the Hous of Lords. Next the Lower Hous of Convocation, which had been influenc'd by some others to declare themselvs against the bill (which they had nothing to do with) voted

[1] Lindsay and Pooley.

likewise that thanks should be given me in the name of all the inferiour clergy for the benefaction; which accordingly was done by the prolocutor accompanyd with six or seven of his assessors. And now you will think all rubs are over. I wish they were.[1]

During all these commotions which were so unlikely to join Swift and King together, there occurred one transaction not only tending to do just this but also promoting the project Swift hoped would carry him back to England with enhanced respectability. More than three years of activity in Ireland had supplied little that was palpable toward his advancement. He had the promise of a small city living from Stearne; he was representing his cathedral chapter in Convocation. Now he felt ready to enter a new campaign. In preparation for the move, he would cultivate Pembroke and the viceregal circle, ingratiating himself with them through his wit in speech and writing. But he wanted an additional, solider footing for his approaches to the great; and the Convocation managed to supply it. For the Lower House urged the Upper to make a fresh effort at having the crown grant in Ireland the same remission of First Fruits that England had received. To this prodding the bishops replied that a speedy application would indeed be made to the government.[2] Swift therefore could now assume the role he had sought, as agent to solicit the favour; and in doing so, he could serve himself, work for his church, and please the archbishop.

Pleasing the Lord Lieutenant meant a different manœuvre. Swift enjoyed Fountaine's society more than Pembroke's, but he enjoyed conversing with both Earl and usher. Since it would have been most uncommon for a Lord Lieutenant to remain in Dublin many days after Parliament rose, Swift had no more than a few months in which to establish connections. The end of October brought the royal assent to all legislation, including the act for the library. Having settled these and other signal deeds, such as granting Fountaine two hundred pounds for his services as Black Rod,[3] the Irish Parliament rose simultaneously with Con-

---

[1] Letter of 13 Dec. 1707 to Thomas Smith (Bodl. MS. Smith 52, p. 149), printed with some errors in Mant II. 115–17. I have expanded contractions, lowered superior letters, and altered capitals and punctuation.
[2] Landa, pp. 54–5.   [3] *J.H.L.I.* II. 235–6. This was fifty pounds more than usual.

vocation; and Pembroke prepared for a return to England. Dr Thomas Milles, his chaplain, said the Lord Lieutenant had been very popular among all levels of people, and their regret at his departure was darkened by the fear 'without any manner of ground', that he would not remain in office.[1] Rumour held that Pembroke was to be Lord High Admiral, and that his success in managing Parliament had been due to the friends of Ormonde, who was expected over again as Lord Lieutenant.[2]

Whether or not Pembroke was popular with all levels of people, his company had evidently agreed with the vicar of Laracor. Just as Swift could stand out against an archbishop whose principles he normally approved, so he could enjoy friendly visits to an Earl whose politics he was soon to attack in print. At Dublin Castle during Pembroke's few months of residence Swift found an easy welcome. Although he was not a court chaplain, his old friend St George Ashe, now Bishop of Clogher, saw much of the Lord Lieutenant, and brought his own brothers along: Dillon Ashe, Swift's contemporary at college, and Thomas Ashe, the bishop's older brother, who lived on the family estate near Trim. The bishop was sitting in both the House of Lords and the Upper House of Convocation; Thomas Ashe came to town as a Member of Parliament. Two physicians often met them at the Castle: Thomas Molyneux, son of the late author of *The Case of Ireland*, and Ralph Howard, Molyneux's father-in-law, whom Pembroke had heard about before coming over. The Lord Lieutenant's chaplain, Dr Thomas Milles, and Sir Andrew Fountaine regularly kept his excellency company. When Swift joined them, the conversation was likely to break out in word-games. Even if the bishop and his brothers had not encouraged the trifling, Swift's addiction to puns would have shown itself. Fortunately, both Pembroke and Fountaine had enough wit and linguistic learning to delight in such nonsense.

---

[1] Bodl. MS. Ballard 8, fol. 125ᵛ.
[2] Letter to Sir John Perceval from William Perceval, Dublin, 7 Nov. 1707 (H.M.C. *Egmont* II. 217).

VI. LITERARY EXERCISES

The connection between word-play and character ran very deep in Swift.[1] His love of secrets and practical jokes, his list-making and orderliness, his habit of withdrawing from mundane disappointments into ludicrous fantasy, all found expression in this typically English toying with speech. A strong tradition traces Swift's language whimsies as far back as his Kilkenny school days.[2] Yet the earliest written examples of any substance belong to this time, about his fortieth birthday.

The inevitable parallel in our own day is Joyce; and it is of course much more than an accident that allusions to Swift tinge *Ulysses* and permeate *Finnegans Wake*.[3] In both men the obsession with the sound and form of words apart from meaning seems linked to the authors' concern with the imagery of filth; in both, however, the same obsession seems bound up with their search for elegance of style. It is as though they felt that if their diction, syntax, rhythm, and euphony were pure enough, these elements would cleanse the dung they wished to handle. Orderly accumulation is another way to deodorize foul materials; so we find Swift, like Joyce, gathering linguistic oddities of several descriptions and arranging them in classes. Puns make the largest group of categories. Swift collected common words that sounded like proper names, Latin words that sounded like English, and English that sounded like Latin. He was a connoisseur of short words which when stuck together produced a number of quite different longer words. He heaped up puns ending with the same syllable or relating to the same subject. There is a punning speech to Pembroke[4] (occasioned by the rumour, premature by a year, of the Earl's becoming Lord High Admiral), stuffed with puns on river names and naval terms; it loudly anticipates the similar section of *Ulysses* and the endless playing with the Liffey in *Finnegans Wake*. There is a punning death-bed speech pretended

---

[1] Professor George P. Mayhew has published a series of valuable studies of Swift's word play.

[2] *Supra*, vol. I, p. 41.

[3] Mackie L. Jarrell, 'Swiftiana in *Finnegans Wake*', *ELH*. xxvi (1959), 271–94.

[4] Davis iv. 261–2.

to be delivered by an expiring Thomas Ashe, in which the reference of the puns changes to suit the person addressed at different points: medical for Dr Howard, watery for Sir Andrew. On the critical hearing of a remote student of letters these effects fall with a chilling cacophony. But I venture to quote a passage addressed to Fountaine as a sample of the frenetic ingenuity with which Swift could mingle echoes of two distinct themes: death and water:

> Tell Sir Andrew *Fountain* I *ran* clear to the *bottom*, and wish he may be a late *a-river* where I am going. He used to *brook* my compliments. May his *sand* be long a *running*; not *quicksand*, like mine. Bid him avoid *poring* upon monuments and books, which is in reality but *running* among *rocks* and *shelves*, to *stop* his *course*. May his *waters* never be troubled with *mud* or *gravel*, nor *stopt* by any *grinding stone*. May his friends be all true *trouts*, and his enemies laid flat as *flounders*. I look upon him as the most *fluent* of his *race*; therefore let him not des*pond*. I foresee his black *rod* will *advance* to a *pike*, and destroy all our *ills*.[1]

Stimulated by the enthusiasm of his friends, old and new, Swift drove himself to such excesses as recording a whole conversation, foggy with puns, which Pembroke and the rest supposedly enjoyed at Dublin Castle and which Swift therefore called a 'Dialogue in the Castilian Language'.[2] The allusive virtuosity of this piece is stifling; and with all his fondness for his own compositions Swift never saw fit to publish it.

But there is still another pastiche, of genuine interest because it carries us beyond mere word-games and clarifies some intentions of Swift's finest imaginative works. This is *A Tritical Essay upon the Faculties of the Mind*, dated 6 August 1707 and addressed to 'a lover of antiquities' whom I take to be Sir Andrew Fountaine. Here, instead of heaping up puns, Swift stitches together platitudes and hackneyed quotations, to manufacture a hardly readable pseudo-essay on moral philosophy. Nowadays the intended effect of stereotype is utterly dissipated because few modern readers can be familiar with either the concepts or the allusions. But if we glance over the essay, keeping in mind that every phrase is cliché, we shall appreciate one of the deepest causes of

[1] *Ibid.*, p. 265.   [2] *Ibid.*, pp. 257-9.

Swift's obscurity in works like *A Tale of a Tub*. Again and again, as in the *Tritical Essay*, Swift ridicules doctrines not because he rejects them but because they seem commonplace to the point of nausea. When Swift says here, 'How can the Epicureans opinion be true, that the universe was formed by a fortuitous concourse of atoms; which I will no more believe, than that the accidental jumbling of the letters in the alphabet, could fall by chance into a most ingenious and learned treatise of philosophy', he means to reject neither the logic of the question nor the analogy in which that logic is embodied. Rather, he is recalling a serious motif from the 'Digression on Madness', as well as anticipating an experiment in the Academy of Lagado. The intention is far less critical than Flaubert's in the *Dictionnaire des idées reçues*; for the sole object of Swift's satire is the triteness of the materials in their unvarnished condition. He is not saying, 'This argument is nonsense', but 'I wish people were subtler in their employment of this argument.' Tone can be the essence of Swift's art; it is dangerously easy to take his parody of a manner as a satire against the matter. In the *Tritical Essay* will be found hints applicable from this point of view not only to *A Tale of a Tub* but also to *The Mechanical Operation of the Spirit*, *The Battle of the Books*, *Gulliver's Travels*, and many of Swift's poems.

Like Swift's other exercises of this period the *Tritical Essay* seems worth attention solely for the light it throws on the author's more readable productions or on his character. If we still ask for genuine literary accomplishment, we shall have to be satisfied with a different work, in a form new to Swift as an independent genre but already settled as an essential feature of all his prose. This is the aphorism. Swift's *Various Thoughts, Moral and Diverting*[1] were certainly intended to stand as finished articles for a general audience. Unlike the word-games they are almost devoid of private allusions; and they carry no internal evidence by which one

---

[1] These *Thoughts* were first published in Swift's 1711 *Miscellanies*, but they are there headed 'Written October the 1st. 1706'. An exact date at the head of a work by Swift is normally trustworthy and normally indicates the time when he began to compose. I assume that he first wrote down many of these *Thoughts* on the day stated but that he continued to add new aphorisms up to the time of printing. In later volumes of his works still others were added: see Davis IV. xxxix–xl, 300.

might date them. In English the aphorism has remained an unpopular form of art. We have few deliberately formulated maxims which did not originally depend for their force upon a narrative or expository context. Proverbs, folk sayings, extracted quotations scatter themselves over our speech. But the unit of thought consciously, artfully designed to stand free and distinct seems rare beside the itemized abundance of La Bruyère, La Rochefoucauld, Saint-Evremond, and the other French moralists.

I think that Swift was guided by French example. Yet in the *maximes* of his presumed models there are few close parallels to his 'thoughts'. In emphasis too Swift does not always remind us of the French. Religion, love-making, the court, may be touched on two or three times; but they do not overwhelm the other subjects. On history, a theme which hardly magnetizes the French moralists, he has half a dozen reflections. But the fields which he shares with his predecessors are the inevitable ones: self-love, moral philosophy, the inconstancy of human character. The essential property of the successful aphorist is his tone: he must sound experienced, detached, intelligent, and well bred. These traits Swift amply exhibits, though it is in a few sentiments which might have sprung directly from his own fate that he is most effective; it is like Swift to achieve a special degree of lapidary impersonality when characterizing himself:

> When a true genius appears in the world, you may know him by this infallible sign; that the dunces are all in confederacy against him.[1]

* * *

From the thinness of the literary harvest it must be apparent that Swift at this period was not finding a prolonged residence in Ireland the happiest provocative of imaginative creation. But he did not need a search for poetic materials or the aspiration for a bishopric to revive the wish to see again a country he loved. Some of his nostalgia for English places and discomfort among Irish scenes colour the answer he gave a nephew of Sir William Temple's, inviting Swift to visit Moor Park (June 1706):

[1] Davis I. 242.

I am extremely obliged by your kind invitation to More-Park, which no time will make me forget or love less. If I love Ireland better than I did, it is because we are nearer related, for I am deeply allyed to its poverty. My little revenue is sunk two parts in three, and the third in arrear. Therefore if I come to More-Park it must be on foot; but then comes another difficulty; that I carry double the flesh you saw about me at London; to which I have no manner of title, having neither purchased it by luxury nor good humor.[1]

Fifteen months after writing this, Swift thought his revenue sufficiently restored to allow him to travel again. He had won the friendship of Lord Pembroke and Sir Andrew, and planned to go with them. The archbishop gratified him both by asking that he act as solicitor for the First Fruits and by telling the Earl of his responsibility. Besides its other advantages this arrangement would ease Swift from attending visitations and meeting similar obligations in Ireland while he wished to be away; and he eagerly awaited a signed representation of the clergy to carry as proof of his status. This, however, could not be got ready before his excellency chose to depart. So on Friday, 28 November 1707, Swift, lacking the representation, formed a part of the Lord Lieutenant's entourage sailing for Parkgate under a wartime convoy of three ships.[2]

[1] Williams I. 54–5.   [2] Ball I. 61, n. 3.

Chapter Thirteen

ENGLAND: WINTER AND SPRING 1707–8

I. ARRIVAL

Though coming to England, Swift could not leave Ireland wholly behind; for some of the friends, cares, and pastimes of Dublin came with him. It was on the eve of his fortieth birthday that he arrived at the port of Parkgate, near Chester, with the Lord Lieutenant and his Black Rod.[1] While Pembroke waited for the viceregal equipage to land, and Sir Andrew started on the route to London, Swift travelled by way of Derby on the usual trip to visit his mother in Leicester. Full of Irish cares and English impressions, he then went up to the capital in December, staying for a while with Fountaine in Leicester Fields.[2] Besides thinking about the First Fruits, he now had company to remind him of the land he had just come from, because Hetty and Mrs Dingley, supported by their dog Pug, came over about the same time as Swift, for what was to be their last sight of England. I suppose they spent time at Sheen with the elder Mrs Johnson and with Lady Giffard; they certainly enjoyed some of the spectacles of London, including an expedition to Greenwich with Swift; but they returned to Ireland before the summer.[3]

Their friend, meanwhile, was responding to the attractions of another Dublin family, the Vanhomrighs, newly arrived like himself. Again a widow and her daughter constituted the poles of a loadstone. Exhilarated by the effect of London in highest

[1] *London Gazette*, 11 Dec. 1707, reports that Pembroke came to Chester 3 Dec., dined, and went to Wrexham, planning to be at Shrewsbury the next day.
[2] Williams I. 56–8, 62.
[3] *Ibid.*, pp. 66 and nn. 2–3, 76 and n. 4. No further details are known of their visit. Certainly the ladies were back in Ireland again long before November 1708, when Swift (who wrote to them about once a fortnight) sent his tenth letter to them since their departure from England (*ibid.* v. 217).

season, Swift's social temper had remained playful in spite of some let-downs. Avoiding Child's and Truby's—the coffee-house and tavern beloved by most clergymen—he patronized establishments like St James's coffee-house, a centre for news, politics, Irish visitors, and Whigs.[1] He also visited and punned with the Berkeleys, collected political gossip, pursued Lord Pembroke, and concocted practical jokes. Mrs Vanhomrigh, herself the daughter of a one-time commissioner of the Irish revenue, and the widow of a prosperous citizen, had just moved to London with her four children. Even if Swift had never known the lady in Dublin, he would surely have heard of her late husband, an émigré Dutch merchant, who had made his fortune as commissary-general for the army in Ireland during the Williamite war. When she reached England, Mrs Vanhomrigh set herself up in an elegant location near St James's Square,[2] at a convenient distance for anyone walking from Leicester Fields. Here she began entertaining a kind of fringe-of-court society which included Sir Andrew and Swift. And it was she who provided the setting for a spoof that perfectly illustrates the ease and boldness of Swift's new plunge into London society.

This lightest of Swift's *jeux d'esprit* was a mock-edict involving himself, the Vanhomrighs, and a beautiful young woman named Anne Long, whom the Kit-Cat Club had elected as one of their toasts. Although Mrs Long was a baronet's sister—and apparently related by cousinhood to the Vanhomrighs—Swift liked the lady not for her family but for what he described as 'all sorts of amiable qualities' and no faults except carelessness in managing her money.[3] He once publicly complimented her as being famous for 'beauty, virtue, and good sense'.[4] But instead of simply letting Mrs Vanhomrigh or her firstborn daughter Esther introduce him to the beauty, Swift claimed a privilege which he also asserted on other occasions, of requiring the charmer to make the first advances. Since Mrs Long, in the same spirit, pretended she could not betray the privileges of a Toast, Swift drew up a bur-

---

[1] *Poems* I. 194 and n.; *Tatler*, no. 1; *Spectator* I. 4, n. 2; Williams I. 91 and n. 3.
[2] Ball I. 390. [3] Williams I. 280; *Journal*, 25 Dec. 1711.
[4] *Journal*, p. 446, n. 21.

lesque decree supposed to be issued by the youngest Vanhomrigh, Ginkel, a fourteen-year-old[1] named after Lord Athlone. In form, this odd 'Treaty of Acquaintance' could seem, ironically enough, to be an unconscious, remote echo of the sober Irish preoccupations of Swift's sad 'Injured Lady' and her betrayer's 'treaty of marriage'. But in tone, of course, the trifling divertisement only suggested how well the pleasures of London relaxed Swift's Irish anxieties and sustained the 'bagatelle' mood of his word-games with Pembroke and Fountaine. Concluded about New Year's Day 1708,[2] the 'decree' naturally granted Swift all the prerogative he had looked for:

> We, out of our tender regard to truth and justice, having heard and duly considered the allegations of both parties, do declare, adjudge, decree, and determine, that the said Mrs. Long, notwithstanding any privileges she may claim as aforesaid, as a Lady of the Toast, shall, without essoin or demurr, in two hours after the publishing of this our decree, make all advances to the said Doctor, that he shall demand; and that the said advances shall not be made to the said Doctor, as *un homme sans consequence*; but purely upon account of his great merit.[3]

II. THE BICKERSTAFF PAPERS

The same mood of hoax and play belonged supremely, for Swift, to the First of April, which he loved to celebrate by ingenious inventions. This year the most brilliantly executed of all his jokes marked the approach of the great anniversary. In origin, his new practical joke went back to Swift's loathing for any saboteur of true religion, whether atheist, Dissenter, or quack. The main target of the wonderful scheme was not, however, pseudo-faith but pseudo-science—the art of astrology. In Swift's day no less than now, fortune-tellers competed with the church when they were not taking business away from the stockbrokers. And as the *Petition of Frances Harris* records, when the waiting-woman asked the chaplain to 'cast a nativity', he writhed in fury to hear himself muddled with conjurors. In Dublin, near St Patrick's Cathedral, a charlatan named John Whalley, said to be a Dis-

---

[1] Ball III. 456.   [2] *Ibid.*, p. 457.
[3] Davis v. 198. On 'sans consequence' see *Cadenus and Vanessa*, l. 659.

senter by inheritance and a shoemaker by training, had been supporting himself through astrology.[1] With almanacs, prescriptions, and prophecies, he attracted the trade of the low and the abuse of respectable Dubliners. As the war with France grew, the general provision of such counsellors expanded to meet a growing hunger. For example, by placing bets on battles still to be fought, Londoners used to try to win easy gains; even Marlborough's officers were not backward to employ their special knowledge in such traffic.[2] In fact, Parliament went so far as to pass a ridiculous law 'to prevent the laying of wagers relating to the publick'.[3] Besides all this, at the end of 1706 a small sect of French Protestant refugees who called themselves 'Prophets' had started a number of scandals by claiming to foretell dire events and by attacking the Established Church. Teaching Pentecostal doctrines, they suffered ecstasies in Soho and won over some of their own exiled countrymen. Although their claims to the gift of prophecy were anathematized by the authorities, the Prophets went on to print their forecasts. Finally, being suspected of Socinianism and accused of rioting, three of them were condemned to the pillory, just before Swift came to London.[4] Even as reported by others, the Prophets sound like an extract from *The Mechanical Operation of the Spirit*; and Tom Durfey produced a farce ridiculing them.[5]

Far falser prophets than these cloven-tongued émigrés were the almanac-makers who pretended to see the future, to guide the lovelorn, and to heal the sick. Among those in England one of the best known was John Partridge, who published annually a *Merlinus Liberatus*.[6] Like Whalley of Dublin, he was supposed to be a shoemaker *manqué*. For decades, Partridge had been bring-

[1] *DNB*.

[2] See Godfrey Davies, 'The Seamy Side of Marlborough's War', *HLQ*. xv (1951), 21–44.

[3] Boyer vii. 266 and *passim*.

[4] *Ibid*. vi. 368–71; see also James Sutherland, *Background for Queen Anne*, London, 1939.

[5] *The Modern Prophets*, Drury Lane, May 1709; comment in *Tatler*, 5 May.

[6] George Mayhew shows that Partridge was never named Hewson, and that he was born in 1644, in East Sheen; see his essay, 'The Early Life of John Partridge', in *SEL*. i (1961), 31–42. Swift's familiarity with East Sheen, from his years in Temple's family, may have brought Partridge to his attention very early.

ing out in various forms his clumsily written books and leaflets, violently Protestant in tone. He had succeeded in acquiring the peculiar displeasure of the clergy for his frantic attacks on the church party:

> *High-Church*! the common Curse, the Nation's Shame.
> 'Tis only *Pop'ry* by another Name.[1]

In 1707 he denigrated the revived bill against occasional conformity:

> 'Twas such a Bill, it's like was never seen,
> To *Squeeze* the *Subjects*, and Embroil the *Queen*.[2]

Besides defending Nonconformity, Partridge made many aggressive claims for his prognostic power and challenged competitors to match his skill. One year he boasted he had exactly foretold a particular death. Such egregious arrogance in so great a cheat could hardly escape some degree of punitive attention. Time after time, beginning in the 1680s, journalists like Tom Brown or Ned Ward burlesqued the nonsense of Partridge and his species.[3] One rival quack, George Parker, went so far, on occasion, as to predict the astrologer's own illness[4]; and in 1707 Parker called for 'some able polite pen of the Church of England' to chastise Partridge for his scandals.[5]

Hardly had Swift arrived at Sir Andrew's residence than he decided to join in the sport of Partridge-shooting. For not only did this faker undermine the church by his occupation and teachings; he also wrote like an illiterate babbler and corrupted the idea of good prose. To destroy the vermin with its own poison, Swift wrote a little burlesque almanac which came out early in the year and was signed, 'Isaac Bickerstaff'.[6] The thing presented

---

[1] Davis II. x.   [2] *Ibid.*, p. xi.

[3] See Benjamin Boyce, *Tom Brown* (Cambridge, Mass., 1939), pp. 129–33 and *passim*; H. W. Troyer, *Ned Ward* (Cambridge, Mass., 1946), pp. 51–3 and *passim*.

[4] *A Further Proof Demonstrating the Verity of Heliocentrick Directions*, ca. 1706.

[5] W. A. Eddy, 'The Wits *vs.* John Partridge, Astrologer', *SP.* XXIX (1932), 29–40.

[6] In the absence of other evidence the time of publication may be deduced from allusions in the original pamphlet and related works. In the original *Predictions* the author says he has read several almanacs 'for the year we are now entered', thus implying that the pamphlet appeared after 1 January. He also says Partridge will

itself as a set of fascinating, exact, earnest predictions for the approaching spring and summer, sandwiched between an introductory and a concluding section of sober argument concerning astrology. As the truly explosive thrust of Swift's satire, Bickerstaff not only condemns Partridge as an unworthy practitioner of a genuine but maligned science, but he also predicts his death.

Swift's burlesque looks like, and is probably modelled upon, the *Infallible Astrologer*, a series of anti-Partridgean mock-almanacs by Tom Brown.[1] In these earlier spoofs the author had pretended to be redeeming a noble field of learning which ignorant make-believers had defiled; but the attempt is transparent mockery, not an effort to deceive anyone; thus Brown admits to negligible errors in his own work but accounts for these on deliberately absurd grounds; and his forecasts do not even attempt to sound serious but are open caricatures of Partridge's formulae.[2]

Swift, on the contrary, in 'Bickerstaff's' *Predictions*, uses one of his 'simple' masks. In the manner of Brown (and indeed most

---

die on the '29th of March next', thus implying (though not necessarily) that the month is not yet March. In Swift's sequel, the *Accomplishment*, which, according to internal evidence, went on sale after 29 March but before 4 April, the author says the *Predictions* were published 'about a month ago', i.e., about 29 February (Davis II. 153). One of the contributions not by Swift, but necessarily published after the *Predictions*, is *Mr. Partridge's Answer*; in this the author speaks of the *Predictions* as to be disproved 'next month', implying that his own pamphlet, and therefore the *Predictions*, were published before March (*ibid.*, p. 203). Another follow-up is called *An Answer to Bickerstaff*. I think that this was written by Swift: it has small and large marks of his style; it echoes other works by him; and it was published from a collection of manuscripts which has great authority (printed in a volume edited by Deane Swift: vol. VIII, pt I [London 1765] of the large quarto edition of Swift's *Works*). But since it was not published at the time of the original hoax, it can be evidence of no more than Swift's intentions (Davis II. xii, 290). In this *Answer* the author mentions 'seven weeks' still remaining before the first prophecy can be tested, and he remarks that there were two months between the time of publication of the *Predictions* and that date (*ibid.*, pp. 196, 198). This would set the *Predictions* at the end of January. The Dublin edition was advertised as 'Published Yesterday' in *Dickson's Dublin Intelligence*, 14 Feb. 1708, and the London edition had to be earlier. Teerink (item 483) and Davis say the *Predictions* appeared at the end of January; I assume they are relying on *An Answer*. Although Davis (II. x) tries to narrow the probability further by referring to a visit of Swift to Cranford the same month, that visit did not occur, as he assumes, in January 1708 but in January 1709 (*Accounts 1708 9*, fol. 3ᵛ).

[1] See W. A. Eddy, 'Tom Brown and Partridge the Astrologer', *MP.* XXVIII (1930-1), 163-8.
[2] *Ibid.*

charlatans), he makes believe he is laying down the true principles of an art which Partridge has never learned. But instead of exaggerating his pose so as to be seen through and identified as a satirist, he keeps up a judicious tone and sounds consistently like the public-spirited student of a fundamental science, determined to establish its validity in the face of an imposter's blunders. As usual with Swift, this 'mask' embodies several of the doctor's genuine traits and tastes—his conception of himself as essentially reasonable, his impulse to write for the benefit of society. So Bickerstaff boasts, as the doctor might, 'My fortune has placed me above the little regard of writing for a few pence, which I neither value nor want'—an echo of Swift's own pride in not writing for pay. Both man and mask similarly find the style of the almanacs and hack journalists sickening; both of them loathe quacks of all species and honour Socrates among 'the wisest of uninspired mortals'. Such attitudes appear emphatically in Bickerstaff's introductory and closing paragraphs of exposition, but they hardly emerge from the body of his predictions. These, on the contrary—like the run of almanac forecasts at the time— relate mostly to deaths in the French royal family and happy events of the war; and though stated with unparalleled exactness, they bear few further implications. When, however, Bickerstaff anticipates the 'utter dispersing of those ridiculous deluded enthusiasts, commonly called the Prophets', he uses Dr Swift's serious language.

It is in the first and most important of the predictions that one can observe how very carefully Swift worshipped at the shrine of Stultitia. For he opens with the offhand, cool announcement that 'Partrige the almanack-maker' will 'infallibly die upon the 29th of March next'. This calm remark, presented as a throwaway line, in Swift's usual play-act of dismissing what he is really stressing, is of course the centre of the entire hoax. Partridge himself is only one of its objects; for if the trick succeeded, it would do more than humiliate the almanac-maker: it would also arouse the curiosity of the vulgar in the season when they might most appropriately exhibit their silliness; it would expose the gullible by the same method that punished their deceiver.

To build up his scheme ahead of time, Swift wrote and meant to publish a mock-analysis of the *Predictions*, called *An Answer to Bickerstaff*.[1] The first pamphlet had sold endlessly: though John Morphew had published it for Swift at the price of a penny a copy, pirates had sent out careless versions at half the price; reprints, translations, and take-offs had proved the success of the hoax.[2] Now Swift thought he would come in, through the *Answer*, as a 'man of quality' who doubted the honesty of Bickerstaff and pointed out the signs of a cheat. For its complex brilliance of impersonation, this *Answer* has never been suitably praised. Here is Swift pretending to be a man who sees through a man whom Swift is pretending to be. Some passages come so close to autobiography that to read them gives one a dizzy, happy sense of infinite regress:

> I believe it is no small mortification to this gentleman astrologer, as well as his bookseller, to find their piece, which they sent out in a tolerable print and paper, immediately seized on by three or four interloping printers of Grub-street, the title stuffed with an abstract of the whole matter, together with the standard epithets of *strange* and *wonderful*, the price brought down a full half, which was but a penny in its prime, and bawled about by hawkers of the inferior class, with the concluding cadence of *A halfpenny apiece*. But *sic cecidit Phaeton*; and, to comfort him a little, this production of mine will have the same fate: Tomorrow will my ears be grated by the *little boys* and *wenches in straw-hats*, and I must an hundred times undergo the mortification to have my own work offered me to sale at an under-value. Then, which is a great deal worse, my acquaintance in the coffeehouse will ask me, whether I have seen the Answer to 'Squire Bickerstaff's predictions, and whether I know the puppy that wrote it? And how to keep a man's countenance in such a juncture, is no easy point of conduct. When, in this case, you see a man shy either in praising or condemning, ready to turn off the discourse to another subject, standing as little in the light as he can to hide his blushing, pretending to sneeze or take snuff, or go off as if sudden business called him; then ply him close, observe his looks narrowly, see whether his speech be constrained or affected, then charge him suddenly, or whisper and smile, and you will soon dis-

[1] See above, pp. 199–200, n. 6.
[2] See Teerink, items 483 and following; Davis II, *passim*; Eddy, 'The Wits *vs.* John Partridge'.

cover whether he be guilty. Although this seem not to the purpose I am discoursing on, yet I think it to be so; for I am much deceived if I do not know the true author of Bickerstaff's Predictions, and did not meet with him some days ago in a coffee-house at Covent-garden.[1]

Obviously, whoever writes with such flutters between self-concealment and self-revelation yearns for the credit of his pseudonymity. At the end of the *Answer*, Swift moves still closer to unmasking, through a direct allusion to *A Tale of a Tub*. Although the wit here shows an unpleasant touch of arrogance, the effect of Swift's publicly mimicking a figure who publicly looks at Bicker-staff and suspects he is privately Dr Swift does produce a dense-ness of dramatic irony which is rare even in his work:

> He [i.e., Bickerstaff, in the *Predictions*] concludes with resuming his promise, of publishing entire predictions for the next year; of which the other astrologers need not be in very much pain. I suppose we shall have them much about the same time with *The General History of Ears*. I believe we have done with him for ever in this kind; and, although I am no astrologer, may venture to prophesy that Isaac Bickerstaff, Esq; is now dead, and died just at the time his Predic-tions were ready for the press: That he dropt out of the clouds about nine days ago, and, in about four hours after, mounted up thither again like a vapour; and will, one day or other, perhaps descend a second time, when he hath some new, agreeable, or amusing whimsy to pass upon the town; wherein, it is very probable he will succeed as often as he is disposed to try the experiment, that is, as long as he can preserve a thorough contempt for his own time and other people's understandings, and is resolved not to laugh cheaper than at the expense of a million of people.[2]

The real purpose of the *Answer* is to illuminate the beauties of the *Predictions*: Narcissus on Narcissus. But some spasm of discretion or modesty pulled back Swift's hand before he gave the copy to the press; and the piece came out only after his death. That he

[1] Davis II. 197.

[2] *Ibid.*, p. 199. In par. 1 of the *Answer* Swift says seven weeks still remain before Partridge's death; in par. 6 he says two months lay between the publication of the *Predictions* and Partridge's death; in the last paragraph, as quoted, he says the *Predic-tions* were published nine days before the *Answer*. It appears therefore that he meant the *Predictions* to appear 29 January and the *Answer* 7 February. Teerink (item 494) apparently took him at his word, not realizing that the 1765 printing was the *Answer*'s first appearance and that consequently it is weak evidence for the date of the *Predictions*; Scouten, in the revised edition of Teerink, does not alter this impression.

should even have contemplated linking the vicar of Laracor to *A Tale of a Tub* when he believed the Queen's favourite archbishop detested the book demonstrates yet again the bitterness with which Swift's pride fought against his prudence.

To allow the hoax an extra stretch of days until it collapsed, Swift made Paris the scene of his second prediction, the death of Cardinal de Noailles, 4 April. Since a week might easily pass between the moment of an event in the French capital and the arrival of the news in London, Bickerstaff had a fortnight's breathing space, not to mention the possible confusions of Old Style and New Style. During this critical wait, Swift showed how skilfully he had formed the grand design. As part of his original scheme he must have planned what was a most startling sequel to the *Predictions*, and he must have sent this fresh publication to the printer beforehand; its purport appears in the title: *The Accomplishment of the First of Mr. Bickerstaff's Predictions. Being an Account of the Death of Mr. Partrige, the Almanack-maker, upon the 29th Instant. In a Letter to a Person of Honour.* This pamphlet supplies the true climax of the entertainment; and as an act of impersonation it almost outdoes the *Answer*. Rarely did Swift hide more verve and humour under a straight-faced façade of solemnity. In less than four small quarto pages he gives the details of Partridge's supposed death. At no point does the mask crack. Swift pretends to be a gentleman in employment, like Congreve or Prior, writing to a titled friend, such as Halifax, to whom he seems obligated. The pretended writer is a cautious, well-bred person, formerly a commissioner of revenue but now in another sinecure. Quickly, unaffectedly, but exhibiting some uneasiness over the event, he tells how he wished to check the first of Bickerstaff's predictions against the facts and therefore looked into the condition of Mr Partridge: rather to the writer's surprise, the astrologer did sicken and die as foretold.

Besides imitating the gravity and polite manner of a man of fashion engaged in such a distasteful task, Swift introduces his own special concerns. To denigrate all fortune-tellers, he has the dying man admit his ignorance and quackery. Then, so as to turn the attack against a more dangerous enemy, he has Partridge exposed as a Dissenter: 'On his death-bed he declared himself a Nonconformist, and had a fanatic preacher to be his spiritual guide.' Here, therefore, as in *A Tale of a Tub*, pseudo-learning and religious Dissent are treated as different forms of a single human tendency: the same vicious irrationality produces the cheats, the false scientists, and the Puritans. Swift never seems to have realized how simple it was for sceptics to turn this sort of allegation—which is peculiarly treacherous because it can be neither proved nor disproved—against everything he himself believed in.

As the cap of his enterprise Swift had to bring the *Accomplishment* out for sale just before 1 April.[1] By doing so, he could be sure of drawing a crowd of inquisitors to Partridge's house on a perfect fool's errand. While we have no count of the exact number of such sheep, we do possess a poem Swift used to bell them on. This is 'An Elegy on Mr. Patrige', published about the same time as the *Accomplishment*,[2] and pretending to be an ordinary Grub Street ballad on a current topic. Except as part of the snow-balling funny business, most of the *Elegy* has little interest, only repeating devices which Swift used earlier and better. But the 'Epitaph' at the end represents his compact, forceful style. Here, in neat rhymes, strong rhythms, and unstrained phrases, Swift

[1] Since the 'death' occurred the evening of 29 March, the *Accomplishment* could not appear before 30 March. Because the 'author' of the *Accomplishment* explicitly looks forward to the second prediction, dated 4 April, the paper could not appear after about 11 April, when the news would have arrived from Paris. I assume the *Accomplishment* went on sale the day before All Fools' Day. Teerink (item 495) gives the date of 30 March, which is retained by Scouten in the revised edition of the bibliography, but he supplies no reason; I assume he bases this date on the fact that 'yesterday' is specified in the pamphlet as the time of Partridge's death; and I assume the same reasoning lies behind Sir Harold Williams's accepting the same date (*Poems* 1. 97). On the April Fool element see George P. Mayhew, 'Swift's Bickerstaff Hoax as an April Fools' Joke', *MP*. LXI (1964), 270–80. On the general background of the Bickerstaff papers see Richmond P. Bond, 'Isaac Bickerstaff, Esq.', in *Restoration and Eighteenth Century Literature: Essays in Honor of A. D. McKillop* (Chicago, 1963), pp.103–13.
[2] W. A. Eddy says the *Elegy* went on sale 30 March, but gives no reason (ed. Swift's *Satires and Personal Writings*, Oxford Standard Authors, p. 160). Teerink and Scouten (item 496) give the same date, also with no reason. I think one can only suppose it was published soon after 29 March. Internal evidence suggests a later date than 30 March, because Partridge's body is represented in the poem as already buried. Defoe said the *Elegy* appeared 'the very day' of the death (*Review*, 20 Apr. 1708).

gives an impersonal view of a corpse which symbolizes a fraud exposed; for the end of a lie means the end of the liar's life. By contrasting the steadiness of these verses—especially the first three couplets—with the faker's vacuity, Swift suggests truth staring at falsehood. But instead of throwing all his weight on the vanished Partridge, he blames the customers who paid to be victimized. As a satiric method, the argument carries the whole Bickerstaff affair out of the realm of jokes into reality; for Swift is treating his readers just as the astrologer had treated his own. The difference is that when the priest's hoax is revealed, the victims will be left with something better than they asked for. The priest, unlike the quack, tricks men to teach them, asks no pay, and wants his game to be seen through:

> Here five foot deep lyes on his back
> A cobler, starmonger, and quack . . .
> Who to the stars in pure good-will,
> Does to his best look upward still.
> Weep all you customers that use
> His pills, his almanacks or shoes.

The joke was too good for Swift to keep it to himself. Imitators sprang up; extensions followed sequels; hacks and journalists joined the mêlée. Of all these Partridgiana not due to Swift, the best is *Squire Bickerstaff Detected*, which Addison attributed to Congreve.[1] Here Partridge is made to tell how one trouble after another has ruined his days while men who think him dead bother him at home or tease him in the street. An undertaker arrives to drape rooms for mourning; the sexton asks about arrangements for the burial; an elegy is printed; a gravestone is carved. Mrs Partridge is cited to take out letters of administration of her late husband's estate. The repartee between the sexton and Partridge makes finer humour (as distinct from satiric ridicule) than Swift could manage:

> 'I am Ned, the sexton', replies he, 'and come to know whether the doctor left any orders for a funeral sermon; and where he is to be laid, and whether his grave is to be plain or bricked?'

[1] Davis II. xiv, n. 2. Davis dates the piece April, although from internal evidence it seems to have come out after June; it is listed as 'new' in the *Stationers' Register*, 16 Aug. 1710.

'Why, sirrah', says I, 'you know me well enough; you know I am not dead, and how dare you affront me after this manner?'

'Alack-a-day, Sir', replies the fellow, 'why it is in print, and the whole town knows you are dead.'[1]

Truth outdid even this fantasy when Partridge tried to get back at his persecutor. We know from a letter that he sent a cry of distress to an acquaintance early in April 1708. In this account he had enough penetration to assert that there was no such man as Bickerstaff. 'It is a sham name, but, his true name is Pettie; he is allways either in a cellar, a garret, or a gaile.' The villain was mercenary, said Partridge: 'In a word, he is a poor scandalous necessitous creature, and would do as much by his own father, if living, to get a crown.'[2] Whether the style of this letter is sincere or not, we also know that in an almanac for 1709 Partridge behaved so weakly as to attack the 'impudent lying fellow' who had predicted his end. Swift naturally felt delighted at the chance to kill him again. So he wrote *A Vindication of Isaac Bickerstaff*,[3] which, without dropping the sober, thoughtful tone of a judicious philosopher, abandons any real attempt to maintain the hoax; for the first words reveal that the author is joking. Swift's mask here is not simple but ironic; his pose is meant to be seen through; the device has turned wholly literary. Of the various effects in the squib the finest is the author's prolonging the puzzlement of the reader while slowly coarsening the game. Ostensibly, the matter of the pamphlet is a demonstration that Partridge is dead. Instead of treating the astrologer as a corpse, however, Swift from the start alludes to him as alive, and yet continues to insist on the proofs of his decease. Between the absurdity of this situation and the reasonableness with which Swift expounds it, runs the contradiction that produces comedy. Gradually, the

---

[1] *Ibid.*, p. 220. I have modernized the punctuation.

[2] *Gentleman's Magazine* LV (1785), 166; MS. in collection of Mr Robert H. Taylor.

[3] It seems to have been published in 1709 as dated on the title-page, for the author mentions 'the present year' of 1709 and 'the end of the year' of 1708. It was advertised in the *Daily Courant*, 7 Apr. 1709 and in *Tatler*, no. 5, 21 Apr. 1709, in which Steele recommended Swift's *Project*. These dates do not mean it first appeared in April, but they set an outer limit to the time of publication. The 'paper by it self' mentioned in the first *Tatler's* paragraph 'From my own apartment' (12 Apr.) probably is the published *Vindication*.

dignified disinterestedness of the opening, wittiest sentences slips into a parody of pedantry and then a farcical mock-logic. Only in the last paragraph does Swift recover the elegance of his start, and then it is through the ineffable assurance of Bickerstaff's comment on Partridge's resentment over being called dead: 'To call a man *fool* and *villain*, and *impudent fellow*, only for differing from him in a point meerly speculative, is, in my humble opinion, a very improper stile for a person of his education.'[1] In the *Vindication* there remains no trace of any edifying purpose. The work is unmitigated entertainment.

Still, imagination fell behind fact. Apparently, the Company of Stationers struck Partridge's name from their rolls and applied to Lord Chancellor Cowper for exclusive rights to issue a *Merlinus Liberatus* of their own. Certainly, the *London Gazette* in October 1709 advertised an injunction of the Lord Chancellor's, prohibiting the printing or sale of Partridge's almanac except by allowance of the Company.[2] Eight weeks later, the *Post Boy* closed the story with a report that the Lord Chancellor had heard Partridge plead against the Stationers but had decided in their favour.[3] So the almanac lived on though its author was buried.

Although the whole saga of Bickerstaff, from the *Predictions* to the *Vindication*, has perhaps more significance as social history than as literary achievement, it does suggest some elementary truths about Swift's art and the general nature of literary irony. In the Bickerstaff papers a number of separate devices seem to grow from the same impulse. Hoax, impersonation, irony, and satire all start from the satirist's wish to humiliate his victims without being punished by them. In the nature of the wish a paradox is concealed; for though the humiliation remains imperfect till the true author is known, he cannot disclose himself without risking disgrace. To transcend the paradox, he may com-

---

[1] Davis II. 159.   [2] 13 Oct. 1709.
[3] *Post Boy*, 8 Dec. 1709. The *Tatler*, no. 105, 10 Dec. 1709, carried an advertisement by the Stationers' Company against Benjamin Harris's attempt to publish a *Merlinus Liberatus* by 'John Partridge' in competition with their own, and stated that there would not be any almanac published by John Partridge for the year 1710, 'the injunction granted by the Lord High Chancellor against printing the same being still in force'. For 1714 Partridge nevertheless brought out a *Merlinus Redivivus* with an attack on his would-be assassin.

pensate his victims for their shame by providing them with some pleasure due to the same cause, and thus ease their anger. In a true hoax the pleasure would be the satisfaction of watching others taken in after one has seen through the deceit. In a fantasy hoax, or the literary telling of a hoax, the pleasure would be putting oneself in the author's place and safely executing the dangerous trick along with him. Swift provided the first variety in the *Predictions* and the *Accomplishment*, because anybody who pursued the scheme far enough to discover Partridge alive could then reveal the fact to others not in the know and expose them as dupes. He provides the second variety in the *Answer* and the *Vindication*, at least for modern readers, inasmuch as the finest wit in these depends on our knowing the truth. Of course, the earlier squibs, read over after the event by one who has learned the whole history, have the same effect as the fantasy.

Impersonation belongs to the nature of these practical jokes, but it performs a double function. Concealment of identity is one part; irony is the other. Not only does Swift make believe he is someone else; he also attributes to that person a character which he really detests: Swift hates astrologers; yet Bickerstaff is one. For an author to mimic a man he disagrees with is the essential operation in irony. As we shall soon see from one of Swift's masterpieces, the *Argument against Abolishing Christianity*, the true identity or real views of the author need not be clear or welcome to the reader. But the fact that the work is mimicry must be perceptible. As soon as we realize that Bickerstaff 'is' the Anglican vicar, his views on Partridge become irony.

III. ASPIRATIONS

Between the pyrotechnic farce of the Bickerstaff project and the emotions Swift felt about his own career at this time, the degree of contrast is less comic than pathetic. Yet again it makes one question his motives and wonder at his paradoxes. Why should a man of Swift's powers, experience, and wisdom have secured so little where weaker men received so much? If his essential traits deserve the final blame, his circumstances must share it. Even men who are in flight from caution, discretion, and convention- ality can end their travels in comfort if rashness is what the age demands. In Swift's history, character had to work with politics; talents had to appear under patronage; and manners could recommend a man sooner than genius.

Swift felt ambitious in a more complicated way than most office-hunters. He yearned for eminence, knew how it was nor- mally reached, and possessed the intellectual ability to meet all the requirements. For any particular post, however, he was in competition with others who could satisfy the demands as well as he, though lacking his higher talents. What Swift wanted was to be recognized as most worthy on the double basis of generally superior merit and an adequacy to the particular assignment. But what the dispensers of jobs desired was above all a third quality which Swift refused to admit: i.e., some clear advantage or satisfaction to themselves in granting the appointment, an advantage distinct from the general or particular merits of the candidate.

If a Lord Lieutenant could reward a useful servant, earn a substantial bribe, please a powerful ally, or appease a dangerous enemy by seating a vicar on a bishop's throne, he would cheer- fully do so. An aspirant with limited abilities, a weak conscience, but immense charm could ingratiate himself with mighty lords until the fruit fell from the tree without his even shaking it. But Swift would not deliberately attach his mind to a party or his will to a patron's. What was worse, he might do so uncon- sciously but would not appear to. He flattered the great or amused them; he made sure they knew who Swift was; he pur- sued them at their levees and tables. But he wanted them to appreciate him for what he really had: wit and a conscience.

When he finally met a statesman whose policies matched Swift's conscience and whose needs required his wit, the doctor would reach the longed-for eminence. Until then, however, we must wonder why he could not contain either his hopes or his frustrations. Consistently, Swift put his trust in particular men who he thought would recommend him for a bishopric or some other exalted station. From all his dealings with the heads of the world, Swift knew they required devout obedience. When they asked for advice, they wanted not arguments or facts but a mirror of their desires. When they spoke of integrity, they meant loyalty. In bestowing offices or influence, a man in power tended to look among those he could trust and from them to choose one who had something like the abilities needed. Other, superfluous gifts might ornament the successful candidate; but they would affect the governor or archbishop only if they somehow served him.

Yet I think Swift tended to parade what a minister of state must have regarded as unreliability. Commonplace though his views tended to be, he had to display them as his very own, the independent outcome of Dr Swift's reflections. In ordinary social conversation, he liked to sound publicly witty, daringly unconventional, even if his moral principles were the most hidebound. Actually, it is just because his substance was orthodox that his style grew iconoclastic. If this was so, he should have expected his superiors to distrust him. As the price of his free-soaring style, he should have planned to face dark suspicions.

The puzzle is that he did not. When Lord Somers asked for his honest opinion, Swift gave it, though he knew it would clash with his lordship's. Then he expected Somers to make him a bishop. If asked why the ordinary rules of life should not apply to him, I think Swift would have said he was not an ordinary man ('one law for the lion and the ox is oppression'), to which I suspect Somers would have replied, that was precisely why the ordinary rules must be observed. ('C'est avoir fait un grand pas dans la finesse, que de faire penser de soi que l'on n'est que médiocrement fin.'[1]) To delegate power to a person of both independent judgment and unusual genius is hardly the way for a politician to stay on top of his government.

Under all Swift's difficulties, I think, lay a kind of admirable naïveté. Like a small boy playing with bigger boys, he would wonder why he got hurt and yet refuse to leave the game. Unconsciously, he seems to have felt that failure was the best sign of good intentions: services and sufferings were joined in Swift's praise of his own grandfather and of Sir William Temple.[2] I think

[1] La Bruyère, *De la Cour*, no. 85.   [2] *Supra*, vol. I, p. 24.

he underestimated the strength of his deep aspirations. Morally, he believed that naked ambition led to many vices. Personally, he felt he should be above such temptations. In his own life an easy success would perhaps have meant shame and disgrace.

In a satirist, of course, such assumptions are scarcely a defect. By the increasing despair with which Swift received bad news, he supported the indignation that fed his creative energies. If he had not felt so bitter over a fate which he really should have expected, he would have felt less profoundly driven to correct the circumstances that produced his bitterness. At the same time one might diagnose his disorder as one not unknown among members of the intellectual class today—an insistence on the privileges of a martyr without the willingness to suffer a martyr's fate.

IV. DR SWIFT AND ARCHBISHOP KING

Among Swift's relations with various patrons no equilibrium was so delicate as the balance between him and Archbishop King. In one way or another it was necessary for Swift to rely upon King as he had earlier relied upon Sir William Temple. It was not necessary for Swift to confide in a man who had never tangibly helped him. Yet the two had some broad ground in common, and on each side there were reasons for confidence. Like the vicar of Laracor, the archbishop had been born in Ireland, felt profoundly attached to the country, and wished the people to prosper. Like Swift, he wanted Ireland to enjoy more legislative autonomy than she possessed, and he instinctively believed that offices and benefices there should be given to native Anglicans.

Like Swift, the archbishop was unmarried. In his life no passion interfered with a boundless loyalty to the Established Church. On the improvement of her condition he spent his intellectual and moral powers. Where church buildings were decayed, he rebuilt them; where they were wanting, he tried to supply them. The sees which he governed he subjected to an equable and careful discipline. He confirmed thousands, distri-

buted noble charity, gave much of his own income to ecclesiastical purposes. Although he was no less an Erastian than the
bulk of his contemporaries, he wished Convocation to be summoned and to act with independent powers.

With Burnet and Swift the archbishop shared a faith that
episcopacy was a mark of the true church and that the Sacramental Test was essential to the nation's constitution. Inevitably,
therefore, he condemned Presbyterianism. More like Swift than
Burnet, he had no wish to compromise with Dissent, nor did he
think it a better friend to his own church than Roman Catholicism. On every front he resisted Nonconformity. About the time
Swift went to Kilroot in 1694, King published a sarcastic assault
upon Calvinist worship which may have been a source for *A Tale
of a Tub*.[1] Fifteen years later, before a Lord Lieutenant who
favoured Dissent, he delivered a gigantic sermon attacking the
doctrine of predestination.[2]

As a person, the archbishop had Burnet's outspokenness without his bluster; he was stubborn but not capricious. By his steady
principles and surprising degree of candour, he encouraged many
to trust him. He had Burnet's early and continued experience of
political leadership, which the vicar of Laracor lacked and to
which the vicar must have felt drawn. As Addison said,

> The arch bishop is lookt upon as the oracle of the church party in
> this kingdom, and is a great speaker both in the House of Lords, and
> at the Council table. He seems to have joined a good knowledge of
> the world to a great deal of learning and bears a very high figure
> among the laity as well as the clergy for his hospitable way of living
> and exact care of his diocese.[3]

When at this time Swift himself wished to praise the archbishop
in print, and I suppose to please him with what Swift wrote, he
gave King the principles and character which his own behaviour
was meant to exemplify: accomplishments and sufferings recalling Swift's grandfather at Goodrich; Revolution principles,
devotion to the Protestant Succession, loathing for the Pretender.

---

[1] *A Discourse concerning the Inventions of Men in the Worship of God.*
[2] *Divine Predestination and Fore-knowledge Consistent with the Freedom of Man's Will.*
[3] Addison to Godolphin, 26 May 1709 (Graham, p. 144).

Swift praised King's love for the Established Church, his charity, and (not unobtrusively) his practice of patronage: 'introducing and preferring the worthiest persons he can find, without other regards'.[1]

If the archbishop looked for the 'worthiest persons', he also wanted men he might lean on. When he found them, his affection could run as deeply as the expressions he used with John Stearne: 'It would be a comfort to me, if I were dying, to think that you would be my successor, because I am persuaded that you would prosecute right methods for the good of the church.'[2] In many ways Swift prosecuted methods that King considered right. He informed the archbishop of doings that might concern him, and consulted his grace before releasing a controversial pamphlet. At statesmen's tables he defended King's character and supported his lawsuit. In the affairs of St Patrick's Cathedral he seems to have worked intimately with his grace.

Yet eight years had gone since Swift's presentation to Laracor and Dunlavin. Through the archbishop's hands had passed recommendations and appointments that would have made Swift happy. When the valuable prebend of Swords fell vacant in 1704, King did not promote Swift to it but gave it to a nephew, Thomas King[3]; and when that deserving relative died (1709), the archbishop gave the prebend to another meritorious nephew, Robert Dougatt. If King was essentially ingenuous, his frankness does not always shine in his dealings with Swift. It could not, partly because of the differences between them. In temperament, the archbishop has analysed himself:

> I am often alarmed with the fears of some good men, who would persuade me, that religion is in danger of being rooted out of the hearts of men; and they wondered to see me so sanguine in the cause. But I tell them, that I believe it is with religion, as with paternal affection; some profligate wretches may forget it, and some may dose themselves so long with perverse thinking, as not to see any reason for it: but in spite of all the ill-natured and false philosophy of these two sorts of people, the bulk of mankind will

---

[1] Davis II. 282. I assume that the stress in this passage on King's sympathy with the Dissenters was intended merely to appease the Junto.
[2] Mant II. 247–8.   [3] So described in *Liber munerum*, pt v, p. 257, col. 1.

love their children. And so it is, and will be with the fear of God and religion: whatever is general hath a powerful cause, though every one cannot find it out.[1]

No depth of psychological insight is required for one to imagine the recoil with which a man of Swift's moodiness would have greeted such apparent complacency. Over this hopeful character of the archbishop lay an orderly routine of life: he divided his day among regular pursuits, and followed them through with truly episcopal assurance: 'eating, sleeping, praying, studying [i.e., reading], business, and trifling'. Of these, he said, comfortably, only the last two were exceptional, and yet both of them seemed necessary: 'I should be good for nothing without business, and unfit for it without relaxation.'[2]

Upon such methodical heartiness could be founded the optimism that made King, like Burnet and St George Ashe, sympathetic with intellectual movements which left Swift less than indifferent. Besides associating himself with the Dublin Philosophical Society and the new natural philosophy, King had Burnet's readiness to leap into metaphysical speculations that climbed too high for his reach; and in *De origine mali* he wrote a Lockean account of the origin of evil, which exalted the rightness of the world's design at the expense of the misery of human life. In forming his political opinions, King had undergone too many pains at Jacobite hands to view the threat of popery and the Pretender quite so lightly as Swift did. During the reign of James II, he had shown enough boldness to issue some fiery pamphlets against Roman Catholicism. At the height of the Troubles he had been twice jailed on suspicion of aiding King William. Soon afterwards he wrote a powerful and popular defence of the Revolution.[3]

On the other side, the congenitally 'unhappy restless thoughts'[4] of Swift could not have delighted a mind like King's. An archbishop who later complained that the Queen was 'too forward to gratify the importunity of such as leave their cures and

---

[1] Williams I. 111-12.   [2] *Ibid.*, p. 61.
[3] *The State of the Protestants in Ireland under the Late King James's Government*, 1692.
[4] *Poems* I. 55 (on Temple's illness, l. 132).

charges to solicit preferments at court'[1] would hardly have admired the pattern of Swift's travels. Where the vicar offered polite flattery or sincere advice, the archbishop wanted John Stearne's variety of sympathetic, instinctive obedience. That Swift understood as much seems likely from his reply to King's self-characterization:

> I very much applaud your grace's sanguine temper, as you call it, and your comparison of religion to paternal affection; but the world is divided into two sects, those that hope the best, and those that fear the worst; your grace is of the former, which is the wiser, the nobler, and most pious principle; and although I endeavour to avoid being of the other, yet upon this article I have sometimes strange weaknesses. I compare true religion to learning and civility which have ever been in the world, but very often shifted their scenes; sometimes entirely leaving whole countries where they have long flourished, and removing to others that were before barbarous; which hath been the case of Christianity itself, particularly in many parts of Africa, and how far the wickedness of a nation may provoke God almighty to inflict so great a judgement, is terrible to think.[2]

To press honesty so close to insolence and still to expect rewards from the hearer, is surely a quixotic form of heroism.

V. PREFERMENT

Swift came to London anxious, determined, half-confident, half-desperate, to realize the substance of that bountiful vision which for eight years had eluded him. He was familiar with Peterborough, the captor of Barcelona; with Bishop Burnet and the Duke of Ormonde; with the lords of the Junto. Fountaine was his intimate. Berkeley and Pembroke seemed like patrons. *A Tale of a Tub* was exhausting its fourth edition. If interest, merit, genius, charm, and the social graces could raise a man above men, he had modest hopes. For nineteen months he was to watch the dazzle grow and the glory shrink.

A month after Swift left Ireland, Nathanael Foy, the Bishop of Waterford, died.[3] From Pembroke or Fountaine, Swift somehow

---

[1] Mant ii. 265 (letter of 15 Dec. 1713).   [2] Williams i. 117.
[3] 31 Dec. 1707.

picked up the impression that both of them would support him for the see; and he came to believe that they seriously pressed his name upon the court and the Archbishop of Canterbury.[1] But the learned Dr Thomas Milles had prior claims. Though English-born and a few years younger than Swift, he had given up the regius professorship of Greek at Oxford to go as Pembroke's chap-lain to Ireland; and it is hard to believe he did not consciously expect to receive a bishopric. To Swift went the grim satisfaction of finding out the bad news early, after a week or two of suspense. It seems obvious that Pembroke had demanded Waterford for Milles and that Fountaine must have agreed with his patron. Yet Swift showed enough innocence to imagine that if Sir Andrew had not been out of town when the appointment was settled, 'perhaps things would not have gone as they did'.[2]

Adrift in the frustrations of London, Swift thought of saving what he could. In Dublin, as the population grew and the sub-urbs filled, Archbishop King was dividing parishes and spon-soring acts of Parliament to build churches for the west, south, and east sides of town.[3] To accommodate the pressure toward the south, King cut up the old parish of St Nicholas Without and laid out a new one of St Luke. It was precisely the curacy of St Nicholas Without that Swift understood Stearne to have pro-mised him at the time of the deanship contest.

Already, however, Swift suspected that the promise stank. Not only did he therefore try to obtain the living; he also tried to put it out of the power of his friend the dean or his patron the arch-bishop to keep him on tenterhooks. At least, that is how I inter-pret the bitter and complicated postscript he added to a letter for the humble schoolmaster Thomas Walls: Swift tells Walls to have a second friend, the physician William Smith,[4] approach a third friend, Samuel Synge, and 'as from himself' to ask Synge to inquire which parish Dean Stearne really meant to give Swift,

[1] I assume this is what Swift means when he says the court and the archbishop 'were strongly engaged for another person', but I may be finding the wrong sense between the lines (Williams 1. 68 and n. 2). In November 1709 Swift said, 'Lord Somers thought of me last year for the bishoprick of Waterford' (*ibid.*, p. 159).

[2] *Ibid.*, p. 65.   [3] G. T. Stokes, *Some Worthies of the Irish Church*, 1900, pp. 242-3.

[4] I accept Ball's identification, 1. 71, n. 4. Cf. *Journal* 11. 539, n. 1.

St Nicholas Without, or St Luke, the latter having still no church. Swift writes, 'If he means that which has the church to build, I would not accept it, nor come for Ireland to be deceived.'[1]

The reason for this remark is probably that he had heard how the cost of the church would be provided. King and Stearne had been discovering that there was no money to supply a church for the new parish. Although the dean and chapter of the cathedral were rectors of St Nicholas Without, and therefore had the power to name a curate, Stearne would of course take no step without King's order. But instead of appointing Swift or anyone else to either the new parish or the old, the archbishop decided on a scheme which was not unheard of but which did infuriate the vicar of Laracor. This was for the dean to hold both livings himself but to put the stipends aside until enough money had been accumulated for the construction of St Luke's church.[2]

Knowing that King had heard very quickly about Milles's success, Swift mentioned his own disappointment in the same letter in which he reminded his grace of the promised curacy: Swift had scarcely been eight weeks in London when he proposed returning to Dublin, in a manœuvre meant, I think, to sound King out: 'If I have no directions from your grace by the end of this month, I shall think of my return to Ireland against the 25th of March, to endeavour to be chosen to the living of St Nicholas, as I have been encouraged to hope.'[3]

Since the archbishop possessed all the power, as well as all the facts, he could brush the vicar off without even a promise:

> As to your own business I have discoursed the Dean [i.e., Stearne] about it and I doubt the thing can't possibly be done so soon as you expect. We have not yet bin able to pay for the act of parlement much less purchase ground for a church and least of all to lay a scheme for the building it. And some progress must be made in these before we can think of separating the parishes. But it will be time enough to concert these matters, when you come over.[4]

If this statement gave Swift any serious shock, he must have been infatuated. Yet he registered some kind of uneasiness in his answer, hinting that the expectation of reversions was a cold sub-

---

[1] Williams I. 67. [2] *Ibid.*, p. 67, n. 1. [3] *Ibid.*, pp. 67–8. [4] *Ibid.*, p. 73.

sistence and that there were legal objections to Stearne's procedure[1]; whereupon the archbishop took some iced comfort out
of the episcopal larder and served it to him:

> I hope however that this may turn to your advantage, for to deal
> ingenuously with you I do conceive that you would have no pros-
> pect of temporall interest if you were to morrow put into one of
> those parishes. And therefore that you lose no profit and secure
> your ease whilst you are out of it. But this is soe far from being an
> argument against you with others that on the contrary every good
> man will be uneasy till you be settled in that or a better. If a new
> lord lieutenant should be thought on with which we are threatned,
> pray be early to come in his family, for you see that is the only
> merit.[2]

Swift hid his fury from Stearne, well aware, I suppose, that the
dean had to be the archbishop's instrument in these operations.
With King, he tried to ingratiate himself by a façade of ob-
sequious compliment:

> I must caution your grace once for all, that you must either resolve
> never to write to me, or be content that I answer immediately, tho
> I have nothing material to say, which I allow to be hard usage, and
> just the reverse of what all my other correspondents meet with. But
> the fault is in your grace, who gives the provocation, and whose
> letters are full of everything that can inspire the meanest pen with
> generous and publick thoughts.[3]

It's not easy to say which moved more vigorously in the speaker
of such remarks, his squirming or sneering. But at the end of the
same letter, when Swift handles his lordship's advice on the
vicar's ambitions, the sneer rises so close to audibility that only a
patron could miss it:

> I most humbly thank your grace for your favorable thoughts in
> my own particular, and I cannot but observe that you conclude
> them with a compliment in such a turn as betrays more skill in that
> part of eloquence than you will please to own [i.e., 'every good
> man', etc.], and such as we whose necessityes put us upon practising
> it all our lives, can never arrive to.[4]

---

[1] This letter, dated 9 March 1708, is now missing (cf. Ball I. 80), but some of its
contents can be gathered from King's reply (Williams I. 74-6).
[2] Williams I. 76. [3] *Ibid.*, pp. 78-9. [4] *Ibid.*, p. 81.

Praise undeserved is scandal in disguise, and no friend of Swift's can avoid wincing at the pressure of such flattery. Certain compliments should be delivered only to a man of whom one has no favour to ask.

With all his courtship of Archbishop King, Swift had still some resources left over for Dean Stearne. Writing to him in the same post, he says nothing about a curacy, but offers repeated services, gives entertaining news, and sounds confidently cordial. One can only infer that Swift had decided to let no merely personal compunction weaken his chance of even a token preferment at this time. One must therefore assume that his gloom upon failure was all the darker. A quarter-century later, reviving his feelings at this juncture, Swift wrote to Stearne, 'Upon the affair of St Nicholas, I had told you frankly, that I would always respect you, but never hope for the least friendship from you.'[1]

VI. POLITICS

What fell in the way of Swift's hopes was as usual not only his personal character but also the politics of those he had to lean on. As the country grew tired of the war, and Godolphin turned to a wider use of the Junto, a series of 'church' men had to be put out of office. But the 'church' or 'country' followers of Rochester and Nottingham lost patience as they lost employment, and naturally stepped up their opposition to Godolphin's policies. In reaction, the government required increasingly single-minded backing from its own side. Thus the pressure spiralled upward; the ministry began losing touch with the bulk of Englishmen; and anyone wanting preferment might be expected to follow a line set by Somers and Sunderland. Compromise with Dissent was necessarily in the air; so the Test came under attack; and soon Swift had to choose between a change of heart and a loss of hope. It was long before he realized that the figures falling from power were the men he would finally have to join. In 1708 he could not possibly have foreseen that Robert Harley, Henry St John, and

---

[1] Williams IV. 182. Cf. Swift's assumption, in November 1711, that he might yet receive the living (*Journal*, 30 Nov. 1711, his birthday).

Abigail Masham were to become themes for compliments higher though less affected than the epithets he fed to the archbishop.

To the manœuvres of the parties Pembroke contributed an essential line of strategy. Throughout Anne's reign he had held great offices. At the moment, he occupied two. But Pembroke seems to have felt he had served enough for one lifetime, and now wanted a pension he could retire on.[1] The Junto peers had every wish to help him. His Lord Lieutenancy they meant to give to Wharton, his Lord Presidency, to Somers; and after allowing him a short term as Lord Admiral, they hoped to deliver that place to the Earl of Orford. Against this scheme stood the Queen and her adviser Harley, leader of a broadening 'Country–Church–Tory' group in the Commons, who still kept his office as Secretary of State. Her majesty loved to see the royal consort, Prince George of Denmark, carry the title of Lord High Admiral; nor had familiarity dulled her distaste for the Junto. She was pleased therefore to speak of government above faction and prayed God to keep her out of the hands of either the Whigs or the Tories.[2] Meanwhile, Mrs Masham, whom the Duchess of Marlborough had originally brought to court as one of her majesty's waiting-women, had employed a compliant humility to displace the domineering Duchess in the Queen's confidence, and was now acting as sympathetic intermediary between Harley and the crown. Under his coaching, Mrs Masham transmitted to Queen Anne those arguments which might help her majesty to stand off the Junto. Among the Queen's warmest, recurrent anxieties were appointments to ecclesiastical posts; and for these she still leaned not on her low-church Archbishop of Canterbury, Tenison, who co-operated with the Whigs, but on Sharp, Archbishop of York, whose views were as high as her own. Harley encouraged her majesty to follow Sharp's advice at points where it collided with Godolphin's, making the Lord Treasurer look ineffectual. The Secretary was hoping that by a palace revolution he might take over Godolphin's position and thus prevent his own dismissal; but he did not expect Marlborough to resign with the Earl if this wish should be consummated.

[1] Williams I. 115 and n. I.   [2] Trevelyan II. 385.

Swift took Marlborough's leadership for granted and received the usual stories about Harley and Mrs Masham without objecting to them. If he felt increasingly furious with the government's policies on Ireland, Scotland, or the church, he did not therefore suppose that a change in the direction of Harley and St John would benefit the country. In letter after letter he reported to Archbishop King the political gossip which he collected in St James's coffee-house or among Whig bureaucrats. While his tone in general is deliberately non-committal or even—for King's benefit, I assume—prissy, one still feels that he finds the political situation essentially acceptable. Just after arriving in England, Swift told the archbishop that around the city of Leicester there was 'a universall love' for the government.[1] When Parliament tediously scrutinizes the war in Spain and Peterborough's rôle there, Swift writes, 'It is a perfect jest to see my Lord Peterborough, reputed as great a Whig as any in England, abhorred by his own party, and caressed by the Tories'[2]; he does not mention what he must have known, that the Tories wished to exalt Peterborough and the value of Spain in order to depreciate Marlborough and the value of Flanders.[3] On the Commons' vote concerning the Battle of Almanza, when the Junto's men showed their strength in opposition but then came to the rescue of Godolphin,[4] Swift reveals little understanding of the issues, but merely says, 'It seems to have been no party question, there being many of both [viz., Whig and Tory] glad and sorry for it.'[5]

In all these letters the most significant anecdote is the account of Harley's collapse. If Swift suspects that he and the Secretary have more in common than either of them has with Sunderland, he does not hint at the suspicion. Behind the original account lie two facts: that Harley foresaw Godolphin's decision to sacrifice him to the Junto, and that Harley's method of defending himself involved his own replacement of the Lord Treasurer by methods which Godolphin understood. Soon the Treasurer saw the danger of working longer with Harley; for after a certain point, any government which included a man so deeply in the Queen's con-

---

[1] Williams I. 58. [2] Ibid., p. 68. [3] Ibid.; Trevelyan II. 324.
[4] Walcott, pp. 138–45. [5] Williams I. 68–9.

fidence was likely to become Harley's government. The desire for a peace was spreading so far, the Tories and the lower clergy were so furious, and Harley had moved so quietly that it was not easy to resist them. But besides the vast entrenched power of Godolphin and Marlborough, a fortunate accident weakened their rival outside Parliament and the court.

Some weeks after Swift came to London, one of Harley's clerks, William Greg, was arrested for spying for the French. Although Greg pleaded guilty at the trial, the House of Lords decided to make an elaborate investigation, and seven peers sat on a committee which repeatedly examined him. This committee included three of the Junto lords: Wharton, Somers, and Halifax. The four others were the Duke of Somerset, a friend of the Queen's but a sympathizer with the Whigs; Lord Townshend, one of the Whigs connected with the Duke of Newcastle; and the dukes of Devonshire and Bolton, who also worked with Newcastle. Since all seven would have liked to see Harley implicated in Greg's treason, the rumours which floated out of the hearings undermined the Secretary's reputation. Yet at the same time as the committee sat, her majesty was trying to dismiss Godolphin and keep Harley without losing Marlborough. St John, an admirer of the general and a partner to the Secretary, tried to reconcile them to one another. But at the crisis of the episode, both Godolphin and Marlborough resigned. When Harley tried to form a ministry and direct the cabinet, he failed, because Somerset and Pembroke refused to connive at his leadership. Although the Queen, like a true Stuart, would not back down, Harley had to give up the attempt. Here is how Swift told the story:

Mr. Harley had been some time, with the greatest art imaginable, carrying on an intrigue to alter the ministry, and began with no less an enterprise than that of removing the Lord Treasurer, and had nearly effected it, by the help of Mrs. Masham, one of the Queen's dressers, who was a great and growing favourite, of much industry and insinuation. It went so far, that the Queen told Mr. St. John a week ago, that she was resolved to part with Lord Treasurer; and sent him with a letter to the Duke of Marlborough, which she read to him, to that purpose; and she gave St. John leave to tell it about the town, which he did without any reserve; and Harley told a friend of mine a week ago, that he was never safer in favour or employment. On Sunday evening last, the Lord Treasurer and Duke of Marlborough went out of the Council; and Harley delivered a memorial to the Queen, relating to the Emperor and the war. Upon which the Duke of Somerset rose, and said, if her majesty suffered that fellow (pointing to Harley) to treat affairs of the war without advice of the general, he could not serve her; and so left the Council. The Earl of Pembroke, though in milder words, spoke to the same purpose: so did most of the lords: and the next day the Queen was prevailed upon to turn him out, though the seals were not delivered till yesterday. It was likewise said, that Mrs. Masham is forbid the court; but this I have no assurance of. Seven lords of the Whig party are appointed to examine Gregg, who lies condemned in Newgate; and a certain lord of the Council told me yesterday, that there are endeavours to bring in Harley as a party in that business, and to carry it as far as an impeachment. All this business has been much fomented by a lord whom Harley had been chiefly instrumental in impeaching some years ago. The Secretary always dreaded him, and made all imaginable advances to be reconciled, but could never prevail; which made him say yesterday to some who told it to me, that he had laid his neck under their feet, and they trod upon it.[1]

Writing to the archbishop, Swift had not only to avoid any risk of offending the reader by observations on the facts; he had also to say nothing that might embarrass his grace if the letter should happen to come under a third pair of eyes; and for discretion's sake he wrote to him in care of Dean Stearne. Nevertheless, the description of Harley's methods as constituting an intrigue carried on with 'the greatest art imaginable'; the character of Mrs Masham as 'of much industry and insinuation'; the phrase 'all imaginable advances' for Harley's attempts to reconcile the lord he had once helped to impeach—these hints, and the casual tone of the reflections on party strategies, all suggest that Swift felt partly unmoved and partly pleased but not particularly touched by the Secretary's defeat. Though addressing an Irish archbishop, he does not relate the event to the welfare of the church or to the affairs of Ireland.

[1] Williams I. 69–70. This account must be compared with the one given by Swift six years later, when he makes Harley the victim of Godolphin's treachery (Davis VIII. 113). The lord who would not be reconciled is probably Halifax.

King received Swift's news as a proper reflection on Harley, especially because the Pretender, backed by Louis XIV, was at last trying to carry out a long-awaited invasion of Britain. The great cry in Ireland, said King, 'is, that this was H[arle]y's plott, and if he had continued 3 days longer in his place, the French wou'd have landed at Greenwich'.[1] In fact, the French landed nowhere, but sailed up the east coast of Scotland with Admiral Byng behind them, then rounded Cape Wrath, and sailed down the west coast of Ireland, home to Dunkirk. As a result, the Irish Protestants, whether Anglican or Dissenting, underwent interesting palpitations, and the Test Act came under attack as weakening the militia. The abortive invasion was also a blessing to Godolphin and the Junto, inasmuch as a general election was due in May, and most Englishmen were inclined to rally behind the government in power. For Swift, however, these effects of the would-be invasion only threatened his mission in London.

VII. FIRST FRUITS

If the failure of his private hopes had not shaken Swift's respect for the ministry and soured his mood of good humour, the failure of his public errand would have done so. To induce her majesty's government to remit the First Fruits of the Irish clergy, Swift's simplest plan involved reminding the Lord Lieutenant of the need for action. While tactfully jogging Lord Pembroke's elbow, Dr Swift could also feel out the men of influence whom he knew, and quietly encourage them to support the project. If protocol permitted, he might rise so high as to approach Godolphin himself; but this gesture would hardly be practicable unless some great personage agreed to present the vicar to the Lord Treasurer. In all these manœuvres, Dr Swift's eloquence could use the advantage of an official paper or 'representation' fixing his status as the emissary of the Established Church of Ireland and providing authentic data on the finances of its clergy.

But each element of the project transformed itself from a plain case into a Machiavellian coil as soon as Swift grasped it. The

[1] Williams I. 73.

representation took months to arrive, either because Irish parsons were shy about confessing their poverty, or because Irish bishops were hesitant to sign his commission, or again because King decided the postage would be too dear, and waited therefore till he could send the papers under cover with a franked letter.[1] Meanwhile, Swift waited to prod Pembroke into nudging the court. Even for so quiet a purpose he would have to be sure that the Lord Lieutenant would recognize him as a proper agent. So Archbishop King told the Earl of Pembroke that Dr Swift would put him in mind of the First Fruits of the Church of Ireland.[2] At the same time, however, if Swift was going to operate through his excellency, he could not feel free to go either over his head or around him without Pembroke's consent. Supposing, moreover, that he did manage to sound out Somers and Godolphin in a way that did not offend the Lord Lieutenant, he would then have to report to him nothing that they might wish Swift to keep quiet, and yet to give his excellency the impression that he was keeping nothing back.

As he was revolving these strategies, Swift heard a rumour that transcended them all in importance. According to this, the government intended to use the promise of the First Fruits as a bribe to obtain a repeal of the Test in Ireland. The stronger the Junto grew, the more the Dissenters could make themselves felt; and in the wake of the French invasion fleet, the arguments in favour of Protestant unity sounded peculiarly strong. By removing the Test in Ireland, the ministry could produce an example to support the same policy in England. Moreover, the granting of the First Fruits to the English clergy, so far from softening their distrust of the administration, had become an argument on Atterbury's side: for if the state had not (mainly under Henry VIII) taken too much from the church to begin with, this return of ancient property would have had no reason; so the act was allegedly a confession of guilt and indebtedness. The ministry felt disinclined to grant the boon again without an assurance of better 'acknowledgements'.

In April Dr Swift had a conversation with Lord Somers, who

---

[1] Williams I. 60–1 and n. 2, 71–3.   [2] *Ibid.*, p. 60.

was still waiting to be made Lord President of the Privy Council. Several friends familiar with Irish affairs had advised the worried vicar that he should go to Godolphin directly; so he now asked whether Somers might persuade Sunderland, the principal Secretary of State, to introduce Swift to the Lord Treasurer. Although the answer came back that Sunderland would gladly oblige him, this success at once precipitated the foreseen embarrassment over what Pembroke might say if he discovered that Swift was not proceeding by way of the normal channels. The humble parson found himself reduced to sharing this secret anxiety with three great men, none of whom, I suspect, would have hesitated to bellow it in Pembroke's ear: 'I told Lord Sommers, the nicety of proceeding in a matter where the Lord Lieutenant was engaged, and design to tell it Lord Sunderland and Lord Treasurer.'[1]

When Dr Swift did finally get in to see the Earl of Godolphin, weeks had passed, and the Secretary of State did not after all go with him. But the Lord Treasurer took the vicar of Laracor into a private room and then heard his story out. When he was done, Swift found himself treated to a marvellous carousel ride, complete with trick mirrors. The wider his eyes opened, the dizzier he felt:

He [i.e., Godolphin] said, in answer, he was passive in this business: That he supposed my Lord-Lieutenant would engage in it, to whom, if I pleased, he would repeat what I had said. I replied, I had the honour of being well known to his excellency, that I intended to ask his leave to sollicit this matter with his lordship, but had not mentioned it yet, because I did not know whether I had credit enough to gain that access he was now pleased to honour me with: That upon his lordship's leave to attend him, signified to me by the Earl of Sunderland, I went to inform his excellency, not doubting his consent; but did not find him at home, and therefore ventured to come; but, not knowing how his excellency might understand it, I begged his lordship to say nothing to my Lord-Lieutenant, until I had the honour to wait on him again. This my Lord Treasurer agreed to, and entering on the subject, told me, that since the Queen's grant of the first fruits here, he was confident, not one clergyman in England was a shilling the better. I told him, I

[1] *Ibid.*, p. 80.

thought it lay under some incumbrances. He said, it was true; but besides that, it was wholly abused in the distribution, that as to those in Ireland, they were an inconsiderable thing, not above 1000 *l.* or 1200 *l.* a year, which was almost nothing for the Queen to grant, upon two conditions: first, that it should be well disposed of. And, secondly, that it should be well received with due acknowledgments; in which cases he would give his consent, otherwise, to deal freely with me, he never would. I said, as to the first, that I was confident the bishops would leave the methods of disposing it entirely to her majesty's breast; as to the second, her majesty, and his lordship might count upon all the acknowledgments that the most grateful and dutiful subjects could pay to a prince. That I had the misfortune to be altogether unknown to his lordship, else I should presume to ask him, whether he understood any particular acknowledgments. He replied, by acknowledgments, I do not mean any thing under their hands, but I will so far explain my self to tell you, I mean better acknowledgments than those of the clergy of England. I then begged his lordship, to give me his advice, what sort of acknowledgments he thought fittest for the clergy to make, which I was sure would be of mighty weight with them. He answered, I can only say again, such acknowledgments as they ought. We had some other discourse of less moment; and after licence to attend him on occasion, I took my leave.[1]

What Godolphin meant, of course, was what Swift had been afraid to discover, that the rumour he had heard was correct and that the English government would not advise her majesty to remit the First Fruits unless the Irish clergy let the Test be repealed. Quivering with edification, he went on to absorb another shock. In order to complete his little intrigue, Swift planned *ex post facto* to request Pembroke's permission to approach Godolphin. He would then of course pretend that he had not seen the Treasurer before receiving the Lord Lieutenant's consent. But alas when he did speak with Pembroke, nothing went right, as he quickly told the archbishop:

At evening, the same day, I attended my Lord Lieutenant, and desired to know what progress he had made; and at the same time proposed that he would give me leave to attend Lord Treasurer only as a common sollicitor, to refresh his memory. I was very much surprised at his answer, that the matter was not before the Treasurer, but entirely with the Queen, and therefore it was needless;

[1] Williams I. 84–5.

upon which I said nothing of having been there. He said, he had writ lately to your grace an account of what was done; that some progress was made, that they put it off because it was a time of war, but that he had some hopes it would be done: but this is only such an account as his excellency thinks fit to give, although I send it your grace by his orders. I hope that in his letters he is fuller. My Lord Treasurer on the other hand assured me, he had the papers (which his excellency denied) and talked of it as a matter that had long lain before him, which several persons in great employments assure me is and must be true. . . . I design to tell my Lord Treasurer, that this being a matter my Lord-Lieutenant hath undertaken, he doth not think proper I should trouble his lordship; after which, recommending it to his goodness, I shall forebear any further mention.[1]

It was a miserably bathetic close to a painful melodrama, and the approaching summer must have seemed a season of futility to Swift. Half a year's energy and scheming had produced nothing for him in any of the categories of hope which had brought him to England. He might easily have thought that his expedition had shut more gates than it opened. For someone who wished to be influential and famous, the scene could only have been nauseating —the picture of himself at forty-one, unable to aid his church or win any personal advancement, a favour-hunter identified to doorkeepers and politicians as nothing more respectable than the vicar of Laracor in Ireland. And yet, more important than any of the rebuffs or blank walls he had met, more distinguishing than a bishopric or the honour of improving the state of the Irish clergy, was the series of eager appreciations which came to Swift that same spring from men whom the world would finally value above Godolphins and Pembrokes, men for whom no Anglican primate could be ranked with Dr Swift: these were the essayists and poets of England's Augustan age.

---

[1] *Ibid.*, p. 86. Swift gradually discovered that Archbishop King in the summer of 1708 appealed to George Dodington (secretary to Pembroke as Lord Lieutenant) and asked him to remind Pembroke of the First Fruits. The Archbishop tried, during the summer and autumn, to work through Dodington as well as Swift and others. See Andrew P. Isdell-Carpenter, *Archbishop King* and *Dean Swift* (unpublished Ph.D. dissertation, National University of Ireland, 1970), pp. 312–15. See also Archbishop King's letters to Addison, 12 Mar. 1709, and to Pembroke, 3 Apr. 1709, on the First Fruits. For Swift's efforts from Jun. 1708 to Mar. 1709, see below, pp. 323–6.

Chapter Fourteen

ADDISON AND POETRY

I. ADDISON AND SWIFT

If Dr Swift could not claim preferment as a parson, he could claim social attention as a wit; and the bleakness he faced in his prospects found relief in the value set on his talents. Within a few months of Swift's coming to England, he had been introduced to a circle of Whig authors with Addison at the centre, Steele close beside him, Ambrose Philips arriving and departing, and Philip Frowde (an ex-pupil of Addison's at Magdalen) hanging on. Perhaps because of the popularity of his writings, Swift was approaching the status of an insider. No longer did Irish connections, church superiors, or former patrons have to provide him with bases of operation. After so much loitering in the antechamber, he found himself in the salon. After a career of seeking, Dr Swift began to be sought. This intoxicating, uncertain pleasure, he struggled to prolong.

As he came to know the literary sinecure-hunters of London, Swift, who had once contemplated a career like theirs, drew inevitable comparisons. Government secretaryships remained among his aspirations. He must have measured his own progress by the status of his contemporaries. To judge the validity of Swift's feelings of disappointment, one may employ his own kind of yardstick. One may also try to make out the qualities or opportunities the other men possessed, that Swift wanted.

Certainly the doctor himself could observe, both from the fate of the authors he now met and from his own career, how unpredictably private character and state politics might be mixed either to block or to advance men's wishes. With the pamphlet press showing its usefulness to party leaders, and with gifted essayists moving in on the territory of hack journalists, the style of patronage had altered; and the older sponsorship by courts or aristocrats was taking on the less personal form we have repeatedly noticed, in which government posts became the measured payment for services classified today as propaganda or 'public relations'. Unlike ecclesiastical benefices, most jobs given to laymen were terminable when a shift of policy made a shake-up of staff convenient. So a modest stipend for a clergyman meant more than the same income to a board member who might lose it in a few years. Yet the difference in degree of security did not make the relation between 'merit' (in any sense) and compensation much more precise for state than for church offices. In Whitehall as in Lambeth no set of rules could insure success. Looking over the range of plum-seekers, Swift could observe how a pliable nature and delightful conversation might keep a negligent man in employment when a few rash somersaults and hasty indiscretions stripped a veteran bureaucrat of his little gains. He could watch luck, talent, hard work, and complaisance lift a modest scholar to the limit of his hopes while a restless friend with more stubborn emotions mishandled the few jobs he got.

Among the literary servants of the state, Matthew Prior, for example, whom Swift still knew only by name, was in 1708 facing a season of dearth and humiliation *entre deux paix*. As the pressures of the Junto rose, Prior's outlook darkened. Although he had clung to his place on the Board of Trade after King William's death, his patron Lord Jersey had worked too closely with Seymour and Nottingham for the war ministry to tolerate the Earl as Lord Chamberlain; and Jersey was dismissed long before Prior. If the poet felt insufficiently menaced by this turn, he did quail to discover that Marlborough's lioness wife thought he had lampooned the Duke or herself. For years Prior tried to appease her grace, offering congratulations to Marlborough on his victories and producing the best of the poems on Blenheim to come out before Addison's *Campaign*. But not even an ode celebrating Ramillies could dissolve the Duchess's pique, and at the end of 1706 Prior's place had looked noticeably shaky.[1]

Soon he felt driven to write a humble appeal to Halifax, whose

[1] Graham, p. 66.

impeachment he had once voted for; but the great Whig remained as tough as the Duchess. Foreseeing disaster, Prior told
Godolphin his troubles. Instead of reassurance, however, the
Lord Treasurer gave him warning that the Board of Trade
might be reconstituted. Dismissed from the Board at last in the
spring of 1707, the poet rashly took shelter as secretary to a
bishop; alas, the job involved work which could be done only in
person and not by a deputy; a small experience of this, and Prior
resigned. Now in desperate pursuit of sinecure chances, he called
upon both Halifax and Marlborough. Handed a plain snub from
the one and polite lies from the other, he withdrew for a while
to arrange a collection of his works. When this book, *Poems on
Several Occasions*, came out (December 1708), Swift, who was still
in London, called it the only publication 'of any value' to have
appeared in recent months.[1] To Prior, however, at the age of
forty-three, the success of his volume was no consolation for the
loss of his jobs. After sixteen years on public payrolls, he had
nothing left but the slight Linacre lectureship at his old college.

To Swift's old friend Congreve, who was both a generous judge
of Prior's verse and a fellow member of the Whigs' fashionable
Kit-Cat Club, these years brought similar anxieties but fewer discomforts. Though he felt more at home with the Junto than Prior
could, Congreve by 1704 had advanced no further in preferments than his condition nine years before. Since he was publishing little besides some odd poems and essays, he might not have
expected much. But he did glorify Marlborough and Godolphin
in poetry; he was charming company; and he cultivated friends
like Halifax; so he secured enough 'interest' to be allowed to
stick as half-salaried commissioner for hackney coaches with a
hundred pounds a year. When Congreve's mild requests for
something additional met with courtly negatives, he said, 'I must
have patience.'[2] Notwithstanding many fair promises from great
men, he thought the changing political front seemed to lour upon
even his modest office. But in 1705 he had the pleasure of abandoning the hackney coaches in order to turn a commissioner of
wine licences (rather closer to his own pastimes) and find his

[1] Williams I. 122.   [2] Hodges, p. 83.

salary doubled; for the lucrative improvement the credit was supposed to belong to the same Halifax who was snubbing the disconsolate Prior. At this modest but comfortable point, on a rough par, financially, with Swift, Congreve was to hover for some years, while he floated out of the literary life and into his attachment to the Duke of Marlborough's daughter.

Already, Congreve had drifted apart from his old friend Addison, whose stately progress gives more disgust to a later historian than it did at this time to the vicar of Laracor. Starting from a position essentially weaker than Swift's, Addison had pumped himself up to the nearly continuous success which carried him till he died. When he returned to England in 1704, after the years of travel abroad, Addison had only the Magdalen College fellowship to support him. For a steady patron, however, he too possessed the loyal Lord Halifax, who brought him into the Kit-Cat Club and named him to Godolphin as a poet qualified to immortalize the Battle of Blenheim. After seeing a rough draft of Addison's *The Campaign*, Godolphin made him a Commissioner of Appeal in Excise, where he filled the late John Locke's chair in an office said to be worth two hundred pounds a year. Thanks to the great elegance of Addison's verses, as well as to some clever advance notice, *The Campaign*, when published, became one of the best-known poems of the age, bequeathing to imitators and parodists the climactic image of Marlborough like an archangel managing a hurricane:

> Calm and serene he drives the furious blast;
> And, pleas'd th'Almighty's orders to perform,
> Rides in the whirlwind, and directs the storm.

If the image points at the actual wind which had stricken England on Swift's previous visit, late in 1703, the eulogist's reward was less rarefied than his analogies; and in the summer of 1705, seven months after *The Campaign* came out, he found himself employed as an undersecretary in the office of Sir Charles Hedges, the second Secretary of State. Just as Harley outranked Hedges, so, within Hedges's office, there was a more experienced undersecretary who outranked Addison. Yet the fees Addison received came to something like £550 a year. Of course, besides pushing tact to the edge of obsequiousness, Addison did work hard and was an efficient administrator. That autumn, when his *Travels* appeared, they were dedicated to Somers, a patron almost as faithful as Halifax; and two seasons later, when Halifax himself went on an embassy to Hanover, he took Addison along as secretary, giving him the opportunity to meet the future rulers of Britain. Even from the crisis following Hedges's replacement by Sunderland as Secretary of State, Addison drew nothing but gain; for not only did Harley now sink to second place, but in the undersecretaryships, Addison's superior partner lost his post, sending the poet to a fresh elevation. On the side of poetry, what might have seemed an irredeemable loss, the failure of his opera *Rosamund* (1707), Addison was able to turn to advantage by dedicating the printed text to the Duchess of Marlborough. Toward the end of the same year, he wrote a pamphlet which was published about the time he met Swift, and which suggests not only the distance separating the two men politically but also some reasons the Junto felt pleased with the undersecretary.

Readers today will hardly find this pamphlet, *The Present State of the War*, an impressive model of argumentative prose, but they may still value the piece for defining the differences between Swift and its author, and it serves at least as well to illustrate the ways in which Addison could outshine men like Prior, Congreve, or Swift. As a semi-official statement of party policy, the pamphlet sets forth those doctrines on which Somers could agree with Sunderland and which they intended to press upon Marlborough and Godolphin. That the war absolutely must go forward, Addison does not think of questioning. At this time even some soldiers close to Marlborough were beginning to feel that the strain and bloodshed should not be permitted to last much longer; but Addison makes the continuing war the whole ground of his argument. In order to do so, he dramatizes the necessity of placing the Austrian candidate, the Archduke Charles, at the head of the Spanish empire.

Incidentally, Addison does not care to observe that the makers of the Grand Alliance in 1701 had distinctly not included the succession of a Habsburg prince to the crown of Spain among their great purposes (though by 1707 this had admittedly become widely accepted as a war aim). In Parliament, both the Junto and the Rochester–Nottingham faction played up the importance of Spain: the Junto, because expanded trade with Spanish America would provide fresh outlets for British merchants; the church and Tory leaders, because the demand for a strong Peninsular campaign promised to dim Marlborough's glory in the Netherlands. So it is easy for Addison to produce the bait that his patrons wished Godolphin and Marlborough to swallow; and this emerges when he says that only after the Spanish empire has been 'entirely torn' from France, can England feel safe enough to make peace.

Addison could not yet foresee that the slogan of 'no peace without Spain' would become an article of national policy when the House of Lords debated the course of the fighting in Spain. For though Louis XIV's grandson was now rooted more firmly than ever upon the Spanish throne, nevertheless the whole trend of the arguments during this debate ran toward the essential importance of unseating him. Yet Marlborough, in a famous speech, refused to diminish the forces in Flanders so as to free a larger army for Spain. Instead, he called for such an augmentation of troops as would crush the French on their own borders while Prince Eugene led an expedition to Spain. With the government, the Junto, and the Rochester–Nottingham faction all facing the same way, Somers easily carried a motion that no peace would be safe or honourable if 'Spain, and the Spanish West-Indies be suffer'd to continue in the power of the House of Bourbon'. Thus the Junto's creed became Britain's programme.

Writing a month before this debate was held,[1] Addison prepares the reader to agree with all the claims put forward by the Junto: 'Let us suppose that the French King would grant us the most advantageous terms we can desire; without the separation of the two monarchies they must infallibly end in our destruction.' This is his reiterated ground bass. On it he calmly imposes a second principle, that the way to defeat the French in the field is to overwhelm them with superior force:

[1] His preface is signed November 1707; the date of the debate was 19 December.

The only means, therefore, for bringing the French to our conditions, and what appears to me, in all human probability, a sure and infallible expedient, is to throw in multitudes upon them, and overpower them with numbers.

Finally, he takes up the Tories' objections: that Britain's allies are not carrying their proportion of the war burden, and that Britain herself cannot afford the expense of further campaigns. To defend the allies, he claims that they have less concern in the war than his own country, and insists that they are exerting themselves according to their respective strengths. In discussing the financial strain, he says Britain is the richest nation in Europe:

She had never more ships at sea, greater quantities of merchandise in her warehouses, larger receipts of customs, or more numerous commodities arising out of her manufactures than she has at present. In short, she sits in the midst of a mighty affluence of all the necessaries and conveniences of life.

After thus dimly anticipating the glowing picture that closes *Windsor Forest*, Addison finishes his own pamphlet with an appeal for larger war supplies.

On hardly an issue raised in *The Present State of the War* had Dr Swift yet committed himself. In dealing with public affairs, Swift had gone over constitutional problems, public morality, and the relations of church and state. Never had he mentioned the war except as an item of news. Foreign policy he had barely alluded to. Trade and finance he had almost ignored. In four years he would be handling precisely these matters; and like Addison he would be delivering a party programme on the eve of a session of Parliament. But point by point he would then oppose each of Addison's arguments; for the pamphlet would be Swift's brilliant, most effective work on English politics, *The Conduct of the Allies*.

Meanwhile, on the very eve of the two men's introduction, we can see advance signs of the future rift. In Swift's political theory the basic form of wealth was land, and the possessors of the soil were the proper rulers of the state; what was good for agriculture was good for mankind. To Addison, trade and finance seemed the foundation of Britain's prosperity, and whatever improved com-

[236]

merce improved the country. For Swift one way to test a good policy would be to observe its effect on morals and religion; the prominence given to military men by the war, for example, corrupted manners (he thought) and weakened the influence of the clergy. Among the Whigs he detected too many leanings toward a toleration of the Dissenters and a disrespect for the church. Addison, in his pamphlet, does not remotely glance at the effect of the war on religion except to say hurriedly that if France should succeed, she will force popery on Britain.

Even the tone and style of Addison's pamphlet suggest a contrast with Swift. Little of his space goes to polemic. He neither ridicules nor slanders those whom he opposes. Instead, he briefly presents their arguments as weak-minded and his own as more hopeful. England's happiness, honour, justice are themes he loves to play upon. Swift's rhetoric has another kind of urgency, derived from gloomy possibilities, dangers to be shunned. Addison tries to capture this effect at the opening of his pamphlet, but the mild language contradicts the strong sentiments: 'At present, if we make a drawn game of it, we are in a condition which every British heart must tremble at the thought of.'

Addison's style remains steady and forbearing throughout; he always sounds rationally in control of himself. Rather than thunder his logic, he tranquillizes the reader by the undulating rhythm of his sentences. Using low-keyed turns of phrase, he implies respect for the reader's intelligence, a certainty that his own doctrines will appear self-evidently sound. Even when beating the drums in his last paragraph, he cannot raise much noise: 'Let us, therefore, exert the united strength of our whole island, and by that means put a new life and spirit into the confederates, who have their eyes fixed upon us . . .' This is not a battle-cry but a modest proposal. Swift, who seldom felt much respect for his audience, would have aroused the reader with sarcasms, innuendoes, violent accusations.

As a political pamphlet, *The Present State of the War* could hardly be made weaker or duller. At best it preaches to the converted; and as Blake has said, 'damn' braces, but 'bless' relaxes. Yet if Addison's elementary views clash with Swift's, they agree exactly with those of his masters. Nowhere in *The Present State of the War* does he take an independent line or imply that he speaks for himself. As an author he is directly and wholeheartedly serving a specific group by complying with the desires of its leaders. This kind of devotion a statesman appreciates, however faint the prose which reveals it.

Implicit in Addison's tone is a distinct ethical attitude which Swift could not accept, a benevolism appearing in the cheerful undercurrent of his reasoning: 'we have already done a great part of our work, and are come within view of the end that we have been so long driving at . . . One vigorous push on all sides, one general assault, will force the enemy to cry out for quarter. . .' Within this frame Addison hints that freedom, rather than constraint, will best move mankind to high action: 'there is a kind of sluggish resignation, as well as poorness and degeneracy of spirit, in a state of slavery.' Of course, it is in other writings that Addison really establishes his moral outlook, for *The Present State of the War* catches up whatever doctrines fit the propaganda. But from those other works we do learn that Addison inclines to dwell on the natural dignity of rational man, as against Swift's obsession with the stumbling passions of crippled humanity. Addison gives to natural benevolence the credit for conduct that Swift would attribute to egoism or 'self-love'.

Intellectually too, we find the undersecretary opposed to the doctor. Le Clerc, Bayle, and Leibniz are names Addison honoured and Swift neglected. The new natural philosophy, which Archbishop King supported with contributions to the *Philosophical Transactions* of the Royal Society, made a current that Addison wished to deepen but Swift to diminish. Whiston, a heterodox theologian who pursued experimental researches, was satirized by Swift but patronized by Addison.[1]

It was by opposite routes that they came to public affairs: Swift with an eye on 'little England' and the welfare of common, country people, Addison with an eye to splendour abroad and far-flung commerce; Swift being a xenophobe who distrusted foreign alliances and standing armies, Addison being the brother

[1] Bertrand A. Goldgar, *The Curse of Party* (Lincoln, Nebraska, 1961), pp. 7–27.

of a rich India merchant, the brother-in-law of a French refugee, and the nephew of an American colonist. Swift's father
had left his native country to die young and unmarked in his new
home. Addison's father spent years as a chaplain in Dunkirk and
Tangier, wrote books on northern Africa, and became Dean of
Lichfield. We need not feel puzzled if Swift yearned for boundaries and Addison for expanses.

Yet they became friends as soon as they met. Whoever
prepared the way—Congreve, Halifax, or some other common
friend—it looks as though Swift sought the meeting and therefore
felt determined to please.[1] That he succeeded, we cannot doubt.
On Addison's side it must have been a gratification to know the
author of *The Contests and Dissensions* and the sensational *Tale of a
Tub*. That he soon set 'a very great value' upon Swift's conversation, we discover from his own words.[2] I think Swift's five-year
seniority in age helped persuade Addison to associate his new
friend with the late Dean of Lichfield, his beloved father, who
had anticipated Swift's struggle for preferment and shared not
only his ebullient temper but also his views on church and state.

Both Swift and Addison had the habit of keeping politics separate from social ties, of keeping business apart from literary
leisure. Addison's combination of outward reserve and intimate
charm must have delighted the protégé of Sir William Temple.
The elegant manners and decent piety of Addison, his distinction
in politics and in literature, his easy scholarship and general cultivation of arts such as music and painting, re-create the image of
the highest-grade dilettante, first shown to Swift by Sir William.
To his shyness, modesty, and courtliness, Swift must have responded eagerly. Though Addison was the younger, his habitual
reserve enhanced his value for those whom he accepted. As Pope
once said, 'Addison was perfect good company with intimates;
and had something more charming in his conversation than I
ever knew in any other man; but with any mixture of strangers,
and sometimes only with one, he seemed to preserve his dignity

---

[1] He preserved Addison's invitation to dinner, a sign that he valued the acquaintanceship deeply (Williams I. 74 and n. 1).

[2] *Ibid.*

much; with a stiffer sort of silence.'[1] Since Swift found an extra relish in good company when he felt it to be exclusive, Addison's courtliness probably heightened his powers of charming the reverend doctor. Nor did the dignity of the undersecretary's bearing weaken his taste for good wine, an indulgence in which Swift was at least his peer. Even their religious leanings had something in common; for Addison had nearly entered holy orders himself, and his father had wished him to do so. Tickell says, 'His remarkable seriousness and modesty, which might have been urged as powerful reasons for his choosing that life, proved the chief obstacles to it. These qualities, by which the priesthood is so much adorned, represented the duties of it as too weighty for him.'[2] Wherever there is evidence, there is support for the remark attributed to Swift, that as often as he and Addison spent an evening together, 'they neither of them ever wished for a third person'.[3]

Their earliest meeting that we can date took place about the time Swift was carrying out the Bickerstaff hoax and while Mrs Johnson and Mrs Dingley were visiting England. But the two men had met before, and they soon met again. Since their common acquaintances included a string of Whig wits, it was easy for the two to see each other in familiar company. By the end of May, Addison was sending his 'hearty service' to Swift in a message to another poet.[4] By July, Swift felt himself so much at home in the Addison–Steele–Philips neighbourhood that he complained about the increase of government business having cut down the frequency of Addison's meetings with him.[5] Two months later, Addison tells a friend of drinking his health in a threesome with Swift.[6]

II. STEELE AND THE *TATLER*

When Addison asked Swift to dine with him on 1 March 1708, he also invited Richard Steele. By now the undersecretary's old school friend had given up the captaincy of foot bestowed on him at King William's death. Thriftless, quick-spirited, self-con-

---

[1] Spence, p. 114.   [2] *Preface* to Addison's *Works*, par. 4.   [3] Delany, p. 32.
[4] Graham, p. 115.   [5] Williams I. 90–2.   [6] Graham, p. 121.

scious, he had formed many connections besides the supreme tie with Addison. To Congreve, who shared his Irish background, Steele had written a complimentary poem as early as 1701, praising the dramatist's many talents and ingenuous character. Following his own first success in the theatre, Steele had composed two more comedies, one of them with Addison's help. When he was thirty-four, he had married a widow named Margaret Stretch, with a heavily encumbered estate in Barbados. Her death, soon after, seems to have done more to help his shaky finances than to lower his spirits or reduce his appetite for casual companionship. About the same time, an appointment as gentleman usher to Prince George gave him a hundred pounds of annual income. Steele's next step up followed Addison's rise upon Sunderland's becoming Secretary of State; for in May 1707 the post of Gazetteer, or editor of the government newspaper, came to him, with a stipend newly improved to £300 a year. I assume that Addison was responsible for this windfall.[1] In Steele's domestic life the decisive turn came only a few months before he met Swift; for it was then he married his beloved second wife, Mary Scurlock, a spinster nearing thirty but heiress to over £300 a year.[2] From the scrambling ups and downs of Steele's existence one can perhaps surmise something about his character as well as the vicissitudes of fortune. He spent money too quickly to emerge from debt; he wrote too easily to produce work of a generally high standard; he spoke too freely to be discreet. Yet he preserved the friendship of a cautious civil servant who liked to lend him cash and name him for jobs. He stuck consistently to the Junto side in politics, supporting Marlborough and the war in his published writings. And he kept after preferment in every possible form, offering himself for any post that might remotely seem to suit him.

Swift liked Steele at first. Their relatives must have known one another in Dublin; and Steele's unfailing lip-service to morality would have pleased the Cato in the vicar. Certainly Swift delighted to feel inside the government's confidential news service at the office of the *London Gazette*, and he welcomed the oppor-

---

[1] Smithers, pp. 123–4.   [2] Graham, pp. 201–2 and n. 3.

tunity of saving postage by the use of covers addressed to Steele. When in the spring of 1709 the scheme for the *Tatler* was being laid, Swift gave Steele aid and advice. The Bickerstaff amusements had made Swift's pseudonym so popular, Steele later said, that they 'created an inclination in the town towards any thing that could appear in the same disguise'; and he therefore determined to use it for the author of what was to become the first periodical essay of high literary distinction. But Swift's help went deeper than supplying a *nom de plume*: as Steele said, with that generosity which belongs among his most attractive traits,

> I must acknowledge also, that at my first entring upon this work, a certain uncommon way of thinking, and a turn in conversation peculiar to that agreeable gentleman [i.e., Swift], rendered his company very advantageous to one whose imagination was to be continually employed upon obvious and common subjects, though at the same time obliged to treat of them in a new and unbeaten method.[1]

Several of the early *Tatlers* contain passages worked up from hints which Steele talked over with Swift.[2] The very first number ends with a paragraph based on the *Vindication of Isaac Bickerstaff*. In no. 4, the sketch of a treatise against operas, with a digression on London cries, sounds exactly like Swift. The next number has a paragraph in praise of Swift's *Project for the Advancement of Religion*. In no. 9, his *Description of the Morning* appeared. No. 11 makes use of the anecdote of a dying farmer, told to Swift by a friend.[3] The longest contribution Swift made to the *Tatler* during this visit to England was a two-paragraph letter in no. 31, ridiculing London wit for being unintelligible to the provinces and provincial wit for being fatuous anywhere. In mood this suggests an ambiguous farewell to London by an urbane clergyman forced to forsake bright society.

The social pleasures which Swift missed when in Ireland were not, however, the appeal of the capital to another Whig poet—come up from a middle-class, county-town family—whom he met with Addison and Steele. Among the most meditative, abstracted

---

[1] Preface to the first collected edition of the *Tatler*.
[2] Davis discusses the *Tatler* attributions in detail (II. xxv–xxxii).
[3] Williams I. 103; Davis IV. 244; *N. & Q.*, 16 May 1931, p. 350.

companions of the pair was Ambrose Philips, a draper's son from Shrewsbury, and a former fellow of St John's, Cambridge. After a brief stay in Holland, probably as an aide in some small diplomatic mission, Philips had attached his pastoral-poetic talent to a military career; for he had got himself made a lieutenant in the army during the patriotic enthusiasm which followed the Battle of Blenheim. Unlike Steele, Philips saw active duty. Sent to Spain, he had served at both the well-timed relief of Barcelona in 1706 and the disastrous Battle of Almanza a year later. Though captured by the French, he had escaped and eventually returned to England, where he entered the regiment of Lord Mark Kerr.[1] About this time, Swift met him, liked him at once, and praised the pastorals which Philips had been irregularly writing and publishing.

Philips, like Prior, was on the lookout for a job in diplomatic affairs. His gifts as a poet, too little appreciated today, received from Swift an order of praise like that he gave to Prior's book. But Swift, in writing his brilliant letters to the pastoralist, never foreshadows the motions that were to carry him at last entirely out of the group of Philips and all the Whig poets into the coterie which he and Prior would form with Pope, Arbuthnot, and the rest.

III. *BAUCIS AND PHILEMON* AND OTHER POEMS

The advice which Swift gave Steele for the *Tatler* worked rather better than the advice he took, for his own writing, from Addison. An unlucky outcome of the vicar's respect for the undersecretary was the transformation wrought in one of his best-known poems, *Baucis and Philemon*. The tale is a free burlesque of the story told by Ovid about Jupiter and Apollo coming to earth incognito and testing the hospitality of mortals. In the valley the two gods visit, no family welcomes the disguised Olympians except a peasant couple, who share their humble food unstintingly with the sudden guests. To punish the uncharitable neighbours, the gods drown them in a flood. But to reward the generous couple, they create a temple for them to officiate over; and when the pair

[1] Segar, 'Introduction', *passim*; Graham, pp. 49–50, n. 4.

grow old, they do not die but are metamorphosed into trees.

Ovid uses the episode as proof that, contrary to the Epicureans' argument, the gods do intervene purposefully in the affairs of men. When Dryden translated this part of the *Metamorphoses*, he subtly and mockingly insinuated that the anecdote was very slim evidence in favour of a special providence. Prior wrote a comic poem called *The Ladle*,[1] combining the theme of *Baucis and Philemon* with the folk tale of the three wishes. He too treats the story as showing that providence directly appears in human affairs; and with some witty, though not very lighthanded, reasoning, he supports that thesis.

As a priest, Swift naturally retains the moral implications of the legend. In his telling, Jupiter and Apollo become two Christian, pre-Reformation saints making the rounds of an English village. As in Ovid, they promise to drown the selfish villagers; but in place of a pagan temple, they build a church for Baucis and Philemon, by transforming the old couple's cottage. Philemon becomes a parson and continues to live happily with his wife.[2] Instead of dying at last, they are, as in Ovid's original story, changed into trees. However, Swift, departing from his Roman model, does not allow the trees to endure. Like the medieval saints' legends, the events of *Baucis and Philemon* carry the marks of Popish superstition; therefore, I think, Swift ends the poem by rejecting the history while keeping the morals: for in the closing couplets a parson of recent, presumably Protestant, times cuts 'Baucis' down for lumber to mend his barn:

> At which, 'tis hard to be believ'd
> How much the other tree was griev'd,
> Grew scrubby, dy'd a-top, was stunted:
> So, the next parson stub'd and burnt it.

No proof of the legend remains; it has been sublimated into a didactic fable whose value becomes independent of its veracity.

The tone and style of Swift's poem have the humorous charm of *Mrs. Harris's Petition*, though in this case Swift opposes common life to the regularity of normal metrics. As the familiar, humble

---

[1] Composed 1703, published 1704.
[2] Suddenly we are in post-Reformation England.

sights and gestures break across the restraints of conventional feet or rhymes, one feels that human nature is poking its way through the forms of mere politeness. In a parallel movement, the simple, unaffected kindness of the cottagers stands against the surly but conventional prudence of their neighbours.

Both the humour and the meaning of the poem hang therefore on Swift's skill in making his phrases sound fresh but idiomatically right while his liberties with prosody rattle the form of the tetrameter couplet. There are two states of the bulk of the poem, one the draft before Swift showed it to Addison, the other the text printed after Addison's criticism. The first version, in the manuscript that has come down, is 180 lines long, unfinished.[1] According to the report of a friend of Swift's (fifty years later), 'Mr. Addison made him blot out fourscore [lines], add fourscore, and alter fourscore.'[2] In the earlier version, besides his freedom of phrasing, Swift allows himself a piling-up of dialogue and description which threatens the narrative structure. Yet it is through this Chaucerian excess, as in the strain he imposes upon the tetrameters, that one feels the humorous conflict between reality and literary form. This fundamental virtue is what Addison attacked; for his great impulse was to lop Swift's exuberance and to slice away the coarse life of passages like the following succulent speech of the pretended beggars:

> They call'd at ev'ry dore, Good people,
> My comrade's blind, and I'm a creeple.[3]
> Here we ly starving in the street,
> 'Twould grieve a body's heart to see't:
> No Christian would turn out a beast
> In such a dreadfull night at least;
> Give us but straw, and let us ly
> In yonder barn to keep us dry.[4]

Addison's thinning of details, which Swift had laid on in concrete

---

[1] Sir Harold Williams suggests that the 'etc.' at the end means the poem was to continue substantially as it does after line 129 of the printed text (*Poems* I. 89); I think so too.

[2] Delany, p. 19.

[3] This rhyme occurs in Cotton's *Virgil Travesty*, p. 136, sect. IV, about line 1800.

[4] *Poems* I. 90. I have altered the capitals and punctuation.

excess, was similarly misguided; so 'a small kilderkin of beer' vanished, as did the method of frying bacon 'tosst up in a pan with batter'. At some points Swift's vocabulary and syntax were refined to an elegance without individuality: thus 'full up' became 'replenished'. Elsewhere the metrical jig was slackened sometimes to an inoffensive monotony; so instead of 'went clamb'ring after', we hear 'climb'd slowly after'.

In the use of colloquial rhythms and comical rhymes, *Baucis and Philemon* keeps to a high standard, but these trademarks Swift has shown before. The new technical development in the poem is an extension of analogy into metamorphosis. Throughout his career as a poet, Swift liked to design his works, as in the *Salamander*, around systematic analogies between a situation immediately presented and a remote parallel drawn from mythology or nature. The bridge between the real and figurative aspects of the analogy is usually a play on words; so Swift's peculiar structure tends to be a set of parallels, each illustrating a pun and all based on a far-fetched simile; if the simile happens to be a commonplace, Swift will often, as in the *Salamander*, reverse its ordinary implications.

In *Baucis and Philemon* he brings the two aspects of the analogy together as though answering a riddle—'How is a cottage like a church?' The most entertaining part of the poem is the central episode describing the transformations; through these, Swift sets his static analogical structure in motion. The treatment of the jack's turning into a clock is a good example. Here the chimney has already become the church steeple, and now Swift seems to be solving the riddle, 'How is a jack like a clock?'

> The wooden jack which had almost
> Lost by disuse the art to roast
> A sudden alteration feels,
> Encreas't by new intestin wheels,
> But what adds to the wonder more,
> The number made the motion slower.
> The fly'r, altho't had leaden feet,
> Would turn so quick you scarce could see't,
> But now stopt by some hidden pow'rs
> Moves round but twice in twice twelve hours.

> While in the station of a jack
> 'Twas never known to turn its back—
> A friend in turns and windings try'd—
> Nor ever left the chimney side.
> The chimney to a steeple grown,
> The jack would not be left alone
> But up against the steeple rear'd,
> Became a clock, and still adher'd,
> And still it's love to houshold cares
> By a shrill voice at noon declares,
> Warning the cook-maid not to burn
> That roast-meat which it cannot turn.[1]

While Swift's most characteristic poetry incorporates col-loquial rhythms and low language with a quick eye for the humorously homely, Addison's talent is to refine and trim his verses until their texture sounds uniformly decorous. Yet not all his influence was bad. One big shift was sensible—moving the transformation of the jack near that of the chimney, with which it is linked in the action. Besides, several of Addison's improve-ments within the lines sound less unfortunate than the effect of his surgical knife. Although these improvements may tend to regularity, Swift's bumptiousness is not so weak that a few polish-ings can suppress it. The following lines, for example, gain force but lose no humour in their Addisonian state; and the implicit social or political satire, of the chimney's tie to its humble friend, seems clearer:

> The flyer, tho't had leaden feet,
> Turn'd round so quick, you scarce could see't;
> But slacken'd by some secret power,
> Now hardly moves an inch an hour.
> The jack and chimney near ally'd,
> Had never left each other's side;
> The chimney to a steeple grown,
> The jack would not be left alone . . .[2]

---

[1] *Poems* I. 93–4. This is the early version. I have altered the capitals and punctua-tion.

[2] The date of composition of *Baucis and Philemon* is uncertain. I do not trust the 'Written, 1706' in the text given in Swift's 1711 *Miscellanies*; but this poem was among the works Swift listed for a projected volume in the autumn of 1708 (see Ap-pendix B); and since the manuscript was given to Sir Andrew Fountaine, I suspect

In its relation both to literary convention and to the great body of Swift's verse, *Baucis and Philemon* seems unusual. I think Swift, more than Addison realized, knew how to fit his style to the form he used. In Pindarics he followed Cowley; in eulogies and epistles, the Horatian manner of Dryden. For a burlesque like *Baucis and Philemon* he went to the uneven rhythms and the coarse concreteness of Butler or Cotton. Unlike *Hudibras* or the *Virgil Travesty*, however, Swift's poem has little ridicule and few sneers. It is an example of humour which is neither sentimental nor mocking, but deeply sympathetic. Whenever Swift writes about decent, humble people, this tone tends to appear, though never more benignly than in *Baucis and Philemon*. This quality is uncommon in Swift's work, and so is the genuinely narrative form. One reason for his remarkable success here, in telling a story without obtruding himself through either violence of tone or lengthy digressions, is, I think, the natural identity Swift felt with his subject. The vicar of Laracor's familiarity with church construction and parochial duties was balanced by Dr Swift's eagerness to be metamorphosed; and while he accepted more hospitality than he gave to Somers or Halifax, he would have been glad to see them both descend from their Whitehall Olympus and miraculously transform the poet into a bishop.

Compared with *Baucis and Philemon*, Swift's later, short *Description of the Morning*[1] has a simple relation to conventions. In the first poem, there are what might be called mock-pastoral elements, just as there are pastoral elements in most epics. One could even treat *Baucis and Philemon* as a dig at the traditional picture of the farmer presented by the imitators of the *Georgics*. And if we think of Boileau's *Lutrin* or Garth's *Dispensary*, we shall remember lines in those mock-epics which anticipate the method Swift uses for the *Morning*.[2] Here, however, the whole poem is

---

the poem was written after they met; my guess places it between the summer of 1707 and the autumn of 1708. The opening lines sound like lines 21–2 of *Apollo Outwitted*, which was written around January 1709 (*Poems* I. 119).

[1] The date of composition is unknown. It was first published 30 April 1709, in *Tatler* no. 9.

[2] *Lutrin* II. 125 ff., IV. 1–6; *Dispensary* III. 51–6, V. 110 ff. Cf. Tassoni, *La Secchia Rapita*.

formed to reflect upon the serious pastoral; and the essential quality which gives the little work its large vitality is just this reference to a common genre.

So it seems more than coincidence that the *Morning* was published almost the same day as Tonson's sixth *Poetical Miscellanies*, which Steele called 'a collection of the best pastorals that have hitherto appeared in England'.[1] Without ridiculing these authors, Swift makes a plaything of their formula. It is the landscape, rather than the dialogue, of the pastoral that he mimics; and the aspect of landscape he dwells on is the fashionable particularity of such descriptions: i.e., the choice of images to indicate the exact season and the exact hour of the day represented. However, in seizing the established diction and attitudes, Swift reverses their usual direction and applies them not to the countryside at all but to London. Through this characteristic reversal of ordinary connotations but preservation of formal elements, he produces the humour and the special success of the poem.

If we compare the *Morning* not only with pastoral generally but also with the great line of *aubades* which includes the lovers' argument in *Romeo and Juliet*, the distinguishing features of Swift's poem will appear. In his couplets, not an imaginary Arcadia but a real city becomes the scene. Love becomes not a first passion or an innocent courtship but a facile and practised adultery. 'Maidens' take the form not of unspoiled shepherdesses but of experienced housemaids; songs become street-cries; and sheep become jailbirds. There is particularity as to locale— Steele said the lines represented the morning 'at this [i.e., the west] end of the town, where my kinsman [i.e., Swift] at present lodges'[2]—and time of day, but not as to time of year, climate being in general less noticeable to townspeople than to countryfolk. After the first couplet, therefore, all imagery of sky or light vanishes. Not only is the weather indifferent; even the season is unspecified; for every day in town begins alike.

As a result, the main structural device is bathos. Swift employs the usual poetic diction to arouse hopes which his coarse imagery foils. The 'ruddy morn', for example, is heralded not by a lark

<hr>

[1] *Tatler*, no. 10 (3 May 1709).   [2] *Ibid.*, no. 9 (30 Apr. 1709).

but by a 'hackney-coach'. A series of deliberately incongruous observations replace the sights and sounds one normally connects with the freshness of morning. Though all of these may at first seem original, some of them have surprising antecedents. Thus, 'Duns at his lordships gate began to meet' is an echo of Horace, and suggests, behind the contrast of false rustic with genuine town, that of Roman realism with modern affectation. The last line, 'And school-boys lag with satchels in their hands', is quite traditional, with analogues to be found in Horace, Juvenal, and Shakespeare.[1] Contrary to Swift's frequent ineptness in closings, it provides a graceful conclusion. Following so much particularity, it gives the London setting an urban generality, through a detail it shares with all cities and which was noted by the poet's ancient, Augustan precursors. After the vice and squalor of the preceding lines, there enters the innocence appropriate to dawn, lingering like Swift himself over the engrossing spectacle.

The poem should not be categorized as merely an attack on the pastoral or on London, because what comes out of it is, as with *Baucis and Philemon*, not satire but a charming, 'un-Swiftian' humour. For all the impartiality of the tone, an affection for London infuses the language. Through Swift's parody of the Virgilian clichés which epigones were copying from Dryden, his fondness for the city shimmers. While each of the nine heroic couplets does have at least one bathetic image, the total effect is far from anti-climax because, although pastoral expectations are regularly provoked and disappointed, the observations themselves are witty and full of life, implying a loving attentiveness. This is London as Gay and Pope saw it.

Judging Swift's several verse triumphs of this era all together, one has to feel some surprise at the pervading comfortableness, the general lack of satire or violence. Addison's influence may be a factor; and in *Biddy Floyd* particularly the polish of the language, the tidiness of rhyme and rhythm, the lack of grotesque conceits, are possibly signs of his restraining hand. But I think a deeper explanation lies in the reasons for Swift's writing these poems.

[1] Horace, *Sat.* I. vi. 73–5, *Juvenal* x. 117, *As You Like It* II. vii. 145–7.

They tended to be occasional works, meant for a known audience and celebrating agreeable people or moments. They reflect the number of real social pleasures he enjoyed during the period, in spite of all the disappointments. Swift was producing a good deal of prose at this time, and into it he fed his anger or censure. Verse, he seems to have reserved, momentarily, for the things he liked.

Chapter Fifteen

CHURCH AND STATE

I. A PREACHER'S POLITICS

To Swift himself belongs the first credit for encouraging people to believe that his political ideas developed from Whig to Tory in the decade before 1710. He told Tisdall in 1704, 'You and I are Whig and Tory' (i.e., Tisdall a Tory and Swift a Whig).[1] Five years later, teasing the Tory Mrs Finch—Nottingham's sister-in-law—he said that in receiving his compliments she would have to endure being praised by 'a Whig and one that wears a gown'.[2] He expected advancement from the Junto lords, describing them as 'those I have credit with'[3]; and he dedicated his most brilliant book to their chief counsellor, Somers. In the course of the year 1708 Swift saw all he could of Addison and his fellow Whig civil servants, with whom he joined in literary projects as late as 1709 and 1710.

If I still refuse to classify Swift among the Whigs during those years, my reason is that he showed no sympathy with the tenets peculiar to their cluster of factions and made no gesture to support them. In the rare instances when he openly adopted the label, he was making fun of radically 'Tory' friends and implying that they displayed immoderate zeal. Naturally, he wanted preferment from a powerful party, and spent many tedious hours pursuing their leaders. Certainly he admired Addison, whose company seems to have delighted Swift more than any other man's at the time. Certainly Swift did not regard himself as Tory.

Yet it was by no means automatic that a man should belong to any 'party' so long as the conventional assumption flourished, that organized parties were an evil. Even within the House of Commons the primary allegiance of most members was not to a

[1] Williams I. 44.   [2] *Poems* I. 121.   [3] Williams I. 108.

programme identified with a set of group leaders. Many M.P.s either felt pledged to distrust the government regardless of the ministers and principles it might from time to time comprise, or else were so chosen that they nearly always supported the programme of the government that happened to be in power. In the 1701 House of Commons all the organized 'Whig' cliques together amounted to about eighty, if we exclude men normally attached to the court; while the Nottingham–Seymour–Harley connections totalled less than a hundred. Yet the members who did not belong to an organized group (apart from the government interest) numbered something like 250.[1] Among those outside Parliament the tendency to feel unaffiliated was even stronger. Though a Whig or Tory position might exist on the great public issues, it was the expression of social and political traditions rather than the declared platform of a specific coterie; and a citizen might be a 'Whig' in his acceptance of Whiggish doctrines without supporting either the Junto or the Newcastle Whigs.

As far as public declarations went, Swift never identified himself as a follower of the Junto. Before 1710 he published only a single partisan argument, and this was an onslaught upon a policy recommended by all those from whom he expected advancement. I do not regard the *Contests and Dissensions* as partisan or as 'ideologically' Whiggish, though it was conceived as a defence of Junto leaders then under attack; for the writer's whole case hinges on his independence of all parties. After the book appeared, Swift wrote several poems and essays on distinctly political subjects; but while none came out in print—except for *A Letter from a Member of the House of Commons*—all expressed opposition to some notion or doctrine for which the Junto felt responsible: toleration of Nonconformity, repeal of the Sacramental Test, Ireland's dependence on England, the Act of Union.

In his sympathies Swift, unlike Addison, agreed with the bulk of the House of Commons as it was constituted in 1701; for the majority were either exclusively or primarily country gentlemen, landed proprietors, whose occupation (in so far as they attended

[1] Walcott, pp. 68–9.

to it) was the management of hereditary estates.[1] Swift hankered for a government dominated by such agricultural interests in a nation sanctified by the true, Established Church. To assure justice in the state, he believed the great political institutions of crown, peers, and commons had to work harmoniously for the good of the whole people. But to locate the welfare of Britain, as Addison did, in ships at sea, merchandise in warehouses, customs receipts, and manufactures[2] (without even mentioning agriculture) was to defy Swift's deepest beliefs. The Revolution of 1688 Swift honoured for having safeguarded the English constitution, rescued the kingdom from despotism, and made the church secure. He did not regard it as a sudden advance in a direction to be further pursued. When we discover Swift, as late as the middle of 1713, reminding Steele, 'I have in print professed myself in politics, to be what we formerly called a Whig', the word we should italicize is *formerly*.[3]

II. THE LIMITS OF SELF-RESTRAINT

Swift's problem was to survive, without bursting, under a regime which demanded more and more wholehearted allegiance as it drifted further and further from his convictions. He was like a tiger being exhorted to live on grass and behave like a lamb. The question is whether he pushed the fodder aside only when someone offered him flesh, or whether he began to tire of both diet and pose before that offer was made. Although the best evidence for Swift's autonomous fatigue appears in the *Letter concerning the Test*, there were earlier signs as well. In the way of provocations to the vicar's explosiveness, the government imposed what he judged to be unfair curbs on some legitimate, benign forces, and allowed an unnecessary freedom to certain evils. As Swift saw it, a number of quite proper complaints against existing corruptions were being suppressed, Ireland was being abused, and the Established Church was being weakened. At the same time, he thought many immoralities were being practised openly, deism

---

[1] Walcott, pp. 24–5.   [2] *The Present State of the War*, par. 4 from the end.
[3] Williams I. 359.

was thriving unhindered, and a pernicious race of journalists was being in effect encouraged.

After the general election of May 1708 it was easy for a parson to feel that the church lived under cruel restraints, if only because the sittings of Canterbury Convocation were suspended. Since neither Godolphin nor Sunderland wished to encourage Atterbury's high jinks, and since the clergy grew more militantly antagonistic as the government ignored their desires, a convenient solution was simply to prevent Convocation from assembling. The Queen herself wrote a letter to Archbishop Tenison for him to use as a warning against those members of the Lower House who wished to adjourn themselves or to hold 'intermediate sessions' without the concurrence of either the archbishop or their brethren in the Upper House. In November 1708 Tenison prorogued his Convocation, and they did not meet again for two years. By any definition this was muzzling if not gagging.

While Rochester and Nottingham were declaring the church in danger, the Scots in Parliament were busy strengthening the Presbyterian interest. Over the same period, many Lutheran and Huguenot refugees received naturalization without being required to conform to the Established Church. Some parsons felt the centrifugal pressure would soon force upon the nation a complete toleration of all 'Protestant' religionists, including Unitarians and even Deists.

In Ireland, an example of the power of Nonconformity became notorious. Two Presbyterian ministers who preached in the town of Drogheda found themselves prosecuted. The leaders of the Established Church alleged that no Dissenting congregation existed in Drogheda, and that not content with *de facto* toleration, the Presbyterians were trying to proselytize. Primate Marsh himself, although he was a Lord Justice, took part in the prosecution behind scenes; and one of the preachers did land in jail. Nevertheless, thanks to persistent intervention by Wharton (then Lord Lieutenant), the prosecution finally had to be dropped, the prisoner went free, and the Presbyterian conventicle stood unharmed in Drogheda. The Kirk had defeated the Church.[1]

[1] *Ibid.*, p. 114 and n. 5.

[255]

Even the powers supposed to be at work putting down public immorality and irreligion seemed unnaturally lax. To Swift's inquisitorial eyes the stage, the press, and manners generally appeared licentious. When Steele wrote his dedication of *The Tender Husband* to Addison, he indicated what the Irish vicar found distastefully common in the theatre, for Steele claimed to avoid anything that might seem 'ill-natur'd, immoral, or pre-judicial to what the better part of mankind hold sacred and honourable'.[1] The *Tatler*'s campaigns against duelling and swearing suggest that such complaints were not limited to the mouths of captious parsons. England under Queen Anne showed nothing like the tolerance of immorality that her uncle's court had enjoyed. Yet it was inevitable that the free flow of money produced by wartime speculations should supply the occasion for glaring examples of loose living. What bothered Swift was that so many of these examples displayed their blossoms and fruits in Whitehall or the Royal Exchange. The capture of Barcelona was not merely a national triumph for Britain; it meant five-to-one odds for wagers in the City, just as the weakening of the Toulon expedition meant 'our wagers on Toulon are sunk'.[2] While the same country gentry who objected to continental wars and foreign entanglements had to pay for the campaigns through the land tax, Marlborough's quartermaster and paymaster (not to mention the great Duke himself) were receiving a cut on prompt remittances to foreign mercenaries, or else they were buying and selling stocks at home according to the prospects of the war, or they were buying up various European coinages at cheap rates and paying the army in the field with them at high rates.[3] Yet during all this, the law which required Englishmen to attend some church was never enforced. Blasphemous and scurrilous publications circulated freely. Doubts concerning the Trinity and arguments for deism flowed smoothly from the press; and disguised attacks on the clergy remained commonplace.

[1] Blanchard, p. 448.   [2] Graham, pp. 53, 74.
[3] Godfrey Davies, 'The Seamy Side of Marlborough's War', *HLQ.* xv (1951–2), 21–44.

III. *REMARKS* ON TINDAL'S *RIGHTS OF THE CHRISTIAN CHURCH*

Among the sharpest incitements to Swift's indignation had been the success of Matthew Tindal's misleadingly titled *The Rights of the Christian Church Asserted*. Tindal's argument, published in 1706, united all divisions of the Church of England against it. Swift's old enemy Wotton, a Latitudinarian and a protégé of Burnet, preached a sermon denouncing the book. John Potter, a Whig but a high-churchman, published a detailed refutation of Tindal's proofs. (It was Potter, a friend of Marlborough, whom Godolphin forced upon the Queen as Regius Professor of Divinity at Oxford, in spite of the antipathy of both her majesty and the university; but under George II, Potter was to be made Archbishop of Canterbury.) George Hickes, who had tutored Tindal at Lincoln College but was now secretly a nonjuring bishop, produced a savage attack on his pupil. Charles Leslie, one of the ablest controversialists among the nonjurors, added another. A fleet of miscellaneous parsons and polemicists swam along with the current. As late as 1711 the Upper and Lower Houses of Convocation were able to act with rare and uncharacteristic harmony in deploring the *Rights of the Christian Church*, and labelling it an attempt to destroy 'all notion of a church, as a society instituted by Christ, with peculiar powers and privileges, and proper officers to administer the word and sacraments'.[1]

After labouring long and hard to write a satirical answer to Tindal, Swift finally gave up, leaving the production unfinished and unpublished.[2] I think he had originally conceived the bold ambition of destroying the arch-deist's influence through ridi-

[1] Every, p. 136.

[2] The date of composition is uncertain. In the course of his attack, Swift makes several allusions which can be dated: to three editions of Tindal's book, the third having appeared in 1707; and to the Battle of Almanza, which occurred in late April 1707, though the news did not reach England for some weeks. In January 1708 Tindal seems to be on Swift's mind, for the name occurs in one of his puns (Williams I. 65). In March 1708 Swift told Ford his scheme of answering Tindal was 'long layd aside' (Williams I. 126 and n. 2); but he must have mentioned the project to Ford after arriving in England at the end of 1707. So we may assume that Swift began to write his *Remarks* in the latter half of 1707 and stopped writing early the next year.

cule, because he regarded as misguided those learned authors who by their very earnestness conferred dignity on a book which deserved contempt. If Swift soon withdrew from the rather crowded field, it was in part because he resented the censure which his own *Tale of a Tub* had met from clergymen; for he immodestly, if not fatuously, intimated that they were unworthy of the assistance he might have given them by an exposure of the 'errors, ignorance, dullness and villany' of a Tindal.[1]

But I think he also came to realize that Tindal's book was invulnerable to his peculiar methods. Apart from vituperation, the main lines of Swift's satire are connected with impersonation and analogy. His pseudonyms, parodies, and even his irony can be viewed as kinds of impersonation. His allegories, conceits, and word-play can be viewed as kinds of analogy. Again and again Swift's vituperative style depends on his taking a familiar figure and giving it the opposite of its normal connotations. In order to show up Tindal, he tries continually, by surprising or grotesque analogies, to produce a *reductio ad absurdum* of the arguments of the book. He mimics the author and in doing so exaggerates the faults of Tindal's style. He turns on the man directly and covers him with excellent abuse. Always, however, in spite of many minor successes, Swift is trapped here between his purpose and his method. He wishes to sound flippant or at least contemptuous, and to avoid the stiff solemnity of Potter, Hickes, and Wotton. Yet he dare not go too far with a parody for fear of being misunderstood, as he was misunderstood in *A Tale of a Tub*. When he resorts to vituperation, he feels impelled to justify his sneers, and the result is heavy, logical refutation. The reversed conceits typical of Swift find some part-time employment; however, he must not risk sounding ludicrous on a sacred subject.

The ultimate cause of the impasse is the nature of the philosophical differences between Swift and his victim. Bishop Burnet understood the risks any clergyman faced who tried to defend the church systematically against Tindal, and he warned Tenison not to sponsor an official reply.[2] Tindal argues that a state church can assert no authority separate from the government which

---

[1] Davis I. 3.   [2] Every, p. 170.

supports it; Swift tries to answer by distinguishing between lawful human power and divine truth or authority, which he identifies with natural law. He tries to make a distinction but no opposition between a divinely lawful right and a humanly lawful power to block the exercise of that right. But in good logic he cannot do this: if a right is lawful, it cannot lawfully be blocked; a right which cannot be rightfully exercised is a self-contradiction. To put it concretely, a church cannot claim to be both part of the constitution and above the constitution. The true alternative to either Erastianism or theocracy seems just what Swift rejected: i.e., the nonjuror Dodwell's principle that the catholic church must be conceived as a society distinct from and independent of the state.[1] For if the state has an obligation to enforce the sanctions of the church (as Swift insists), then either the church is a department of the state or the state is a department of the church. There are sophistical expedients for evading these consequences, but they are neither so simple nor so easy to grasp as Swift pretends, and they therefore make a very risky topic for irony. When he tries to present them briskly and concisely, he finds himself compelled, like anyone else, to invoke historical, philosophical, and theological arguments in a normal, mind-taxing way. Even so, his instinct for clarity and his congenital ineptness at abstract ratiocination make him a poor crux-hider; and the sophisms and question-beggings of his case glower upon the reader.[2]

Because Swift cannot disprove Tindal's central thesis, he cannot make his own style support his own programme. Repeatedly and emphatically, he calls Tindal's book a failure, a poor jejune production, a bulky, spiritless volume, an insipid, worthless tract, a treatise wholly devoid of wit or learning.[3] Yet he is forced to acknowledge its immense success, the number of editions it has already passed through, the weight of learned replies it has provoked, and of course the care with which even the sneering Swift must go about dealing with assertions which he says explode themselves. Thus, to indicate how consistently ineffectual the

---

[1] *Ibid.*, p. 66.

[2] The paragraph in Davis ii. 77–8 is a good example of an argument riddled with gaps of this sort.

[3] Davis ii. 69, 72.

book is, Swift employs a brilliant figure, 'the same rapid venom sprinkled over the whole; which, like the dying impotent bite of a trodden benumbed snake, may be nauseous and offensive, but cannot be very dangerous'.[1] This is superb, of course; but the reader is bound to find the simile at odds with the general impression created by Swift's lengthy, elaborate argument, and wonder why it should take so much water to drown a dead viper. That underlying disdain for his audience which Swift's hoaxes bring out might have been usefully applied here, for the true object of his ridicule is those Englishmen who have taken seriously a work which does not deserve to be noticed. But if Swift did release his scorn upon them, he would of course alienate the very public he wishes to influence.

However weak Swift's main argument and exposition may sound, the *Remarks upon . . . the Rights of the Christian Church Asserted* contain a number of satirical thrusts which only a literary genius could have produced. The more closely Swift sticks to the real issues here, the less vigorously his imagination operates. But when he allows himself a free fantasy, he remains dazzling. Particularly in ridiculing the style of Tindal's expression (which in fact has unusual clarity, force, and character), Swift can be highly, if not profoundly, diverting. In such places we meet that irrepressible playfulness which seems the reverse side of his violence. Thus, in order to jeer at Tindal's defining of 'government' by telling 'what is contained in the idea', which for Tindal involves the imposition of punishments not naturally consequent upon a punishable deed, Swift says,

> Suppose he had thought it necessary . . . to shew us what is contained in the idea of a mouse-trap, he must have proceeded in these terms. It would be vain for an intelligent being, to set rules for hindering a mouse from eating his cheese, unless he could inflict upon that mouse some punishment, which is not the natural consequence of eating the cheese. For, to tell her, it may lie heavy on her stomach; that she will grow too big to get back into her hole, and the like, could be no more than advice: Therefore, we must find out some way of punishing her, which hath more inconveniences than she will ever suffer by the mere eating of cheese. After this, who is so

[1] Davis II. 68.

slow of understanding, not to have in his mind a full and compleat idea of a mouse-trap?[1]

Here impersonation is hardly separable from irony and parody; the analogy between government and mousetrap is itself a splendidly satirical conceit; and the common association of 'mousetrap' with political intrigue gives this passage the connotative fullness toward which the word-play in Swift's writing always tends.

IV. *A LETTER FROM A MEMBER OF THE HOUSE OF COMMONS IN IRELAND*

Although the immediate purpose of Tindal's book was to undermine Atterbury's case for the rights of Convocation, its general purpose was to apply more broadly those principles of religious liberty which Locke had taught in the *Letters on Toleration.* Inevitably, therefore, Tindal employed some of his energies to condemn the bill against occasional conformity. Inevitably, he gathered together some solid arguments for the repeal of the Sacramental Test. If Swift felt hesitant to use either mockery or systematic logic upon the general themes of Tindal's book, he was not slow to use both in defence of the Test.

Just as Nottingham had extended the Test to Ireland[2] as a method of strengthening his party's programme in England, so the Junto wished to repeal it there as a precedent for doing so at home. Among the inducements to this change, their followers seem to have tried tampering with the 'loyal addresses' which showered upon Whitehall after the attempted invasion. From every sort of public body these bombastic messages arrived. In Ireland as in England the various city corporations, county grand juries, diocesan clergies, mayors, sheriffs, commonalties, and citizenries bellowed their immaculate devotion to the Queen. And in some of them, to Swift's fury, means were found to insert reflections upon the Test. The Protestant Dissenting ministers of the South of Ireland, amid pledges of unconquerable attachment to her majesty, managed to remark that since the

---

[1] *Ibid.,* p. 80.   [2] Trevelyan III. 173.

government of their kingdom appeared apprehensive of 'our common danger from the vast numbers of Irish Papists', it was deplorable that the Dissenters found their hands 'unhappily ty'd up' from serving as fully as possible (i.e., from accepting commissions in the army and the militia), and they urged that the Test be repealed.[1] The Protestant Dissenting gentlemen in Ireland, in a similar submission, called the Test new and unjust, as putting Dissenters on the same foot as the Roman Catholics.[2] The Presbyterian ministers in the North of Ireland said, 'We can't in conscience, neglect this opportunity of expressing our deep regret that the gentlemen and people of our persuasion are depriv'd of serving your majesty and their country'; and they reminded the Queen of their heroism in the Williamite wars.[3] Perhaps no one should have felt astonished to hear the Dissenters speak in such appreciative terms of themselves. But by some clever ruse even the City of Dublin's address contained a clause glancing at the Test: 'The hearts of all your Protestant subjects of this city are intirely devoted to your majesty's service, though the hands of some be restrain'd from serving in commission.'[4] It seemed suspicious to Archbishop King that these addresses were printed at large in the government newspaper, the *Gazette* (already edited by Steele, under the ultimate supervision of Sunderland).[5] Many other addresses came in from Ireland without being so advertised, although some few of them too appeared in full. One which could hardly have been passed over even by a Secretary of State was sent up by the diocesan clergy of Archbishop Marsh in Armagh, with a tribute to Queen Anne's championship of the Established Church: here, after asserting their loyalty to the state and their devotion to the Revolution, the signers prayed God to preserve their royal mistress, 'the true defender and ornament of his church, which enjoys so many advantages under your majesty's protection, and when both church and state shall be so unhappy as to lose the best of queens, to transmit these blessings to our posterity in the Protestant Succession'.[6] In this puerile

---

[1] *London Gazette*, 1 Apr. 1708.   [2] *Ibid.*   [3] *Ibid.*, 12 Apr.

[4] *Ibid.*, 8 Apr. 1708: address of the mayor, sheriff, commons, and citizens of Dublin.

[5] Williams I. 88.   [6] *Gazette*, 21 Jun. 1708.

battle of addresses, one hopeful sally seems never to have got so far as either the *Gazette* or the court. This was an invention of John Pooley, Bishop of Raphoe, one of Atterbury's most aggressive allies in the Upper House of the Convocation of Ireland. Addison described him as 'a man of ungovernable passions enflamed with the most furious zeale and generally passes for mad tho' I think nobody imputes it to too much learning'.[1] Swift called him 'an old, doating, perverse coxcomb'.[2] Pooley and his clergy drew up an address to her majesty, invidiously contrasting the professions of the Dissenters with the true loyalty of the Church of Ireland: "'Tis to be feared that subjects who will not be for you, but on such conditions as repeal those laws which are framed as the bulwark against Popery and all its adherents, may be against you.' They also saw fit to describe their affection to the Queen as admitting 'no rival alive or dead', a stupid form of words which could only allude to William III as less pious than his sister-in-law, and which could only offer evidence that the clergy of Ireland were, as their English accusers claimed, wanting in gratitude to the victor of the Boyne. Unfortunately for the episcopal strategist, his address had to be forwarded by way of the Privy Council in Dublin, where Pooley anxiously feared that Archbishop King or Bishop Ashe (Swift's friend but a government sympathizer), if chosen to read it publicly, might 'give it [i.e., the phrase 'alive or dead'] a turn of madness, or make it look as if it were words tending to sedition'.[3] Whoever happened to read the address publicly, all the Councillors must have realized that it would necessarily harm the cause of their church at court; but they did not succeed in burying it in Dublin Castle, for the London *Post Boy* printed it complete,[4] whereupon the Whig *Observator* pounced on the silly phrase and expounded it as an innuendo against not merely William III but also the House of Hanover, and therefore undeniably Jacobite.[5]

Both Swift and Archbishop King felt resentfully bitter over the Dublin address, and gave no credit to the claim that the Test

---

[1] Graham, p. 162.   [2] *Journal*, 8 Sept. 1711.   [3] Froude I. 328, n. 1.
[4] Tuesday, 23 Nov. 1708, according to the *Observator* of 24 Nov.
[5] *Ibid.*, 24, 27 Nov.

weakened either the will or the power of the Dissenters to fight any invasion. Swift urged both his grace and Dean Stearne to obtain an address 'from the uncorrupted part of the city'; and he further—rather officiously—advised the archbishop, 'I should hope from a person of your grace's vigilance, that counter addresses should be sent from the clergy and conforming gentry of Ireland, to sett the queen right in this matter.' He hoped the clergy of the province of Dublin would comply with this request, and he wished to be the one to present the address when it was ready.[1]

After a long and immensely prudent silence King answered Swift's not particularly sagacious letter, warning him that mail was often opened at the post office. As for addresses, he remarked, 'I cannot have so mean a soul as to stoop to such artifices.' With a sanguine shrewdness which the impolitic vicar was incapable of emulating, the archbishop said, 'I am of opinion that the great men you mention lay little weight on them, and make their computation not from such, but from the real affection and bent of the people. I believe that all schemes not built on these foundations will fall of themselves.'[2] Swift was more than middle-aged before he understood this lesson.

Meanwhile, the Irish opponents of the Sacramental Test did not put all their reliance on devices so refined as hints dropped and suppressed in a *Gazette*. During the spring of 1708 Alan Brodrick and his brother Thomas were in England, spreading rumours and reasonings against the Test. They even agitated for a law to be passed in the British Parliament that would end the act for Ireland—evidently not realizing that this would vitiate the usefulness of the repeal as a precedent for England. Swift, who would have loved to see Brodrick impeached, wrote from London to Dean Stearne, 'I have reason to fear it will be repealed here next session, which will be of terrible consequence, both as to the thing and the manner, by the Parliament here interfering in things purely of Ireland, that have no relation to any interest of theirs.'[3] To Archbishop King, Swift wrote, 'If such a project should be resumed next session, and I in England; unless your grace would

[1] Williams I. 75–9.   [2] *Ibid.*, p. 88.   [3] *Ibid.*, p. 78.

send me your absolute commands to the contrary, which I should be sorry to receive, I should hardly forbear publishing some paper of opposition to it, or leaving one behind me, if there should be occasion.'[1]

King did not forbid Swift to publish a 'paper', but neither did he give him any encouragement: 'I profess I find myself in a wood, and do not know but in such a case it is best to stand still till the mist clear.'[2] If Swift needed an incentive to push on anyhow, he found it in a sermon delivered during October 1708 by an ambitious Irish parson, Dr Ralph Lambert, whom Swift had known at college and who had also come to London with the hope of advancing himself.[3] Preaching on Isaiah lix. 7, 8, and addressing a congregation of Irish Protestants in London, Lambert recommended his own merits to the Junto by the direction of his sentiments. Although he was known as a supporter of the Test, he now performed a graceful somersault. Mainly he devoted the occasion to trumpeting the dangers of popery. The old enemy had not changed, Lambert said (in words that had changed even less, since his many models had uttered them): the leopard kept its spots. Even the Puritans' rebellion against Charles I, he said, was largely traceable to the 'intrigues and cabals, and emissaries of the church of Rome'. He announced that divisions among Protestants were incompatible with a true acceptance of the Revolution, or with loyalty to the Queen, or with adherence to the Hanoverian succession.

From other propagandists or journalists came reinforcements of the time-honoured rhetoric. The Whig *Observator* picked up the Drogheda story in November,[4] and indignantly represented it as a case of persecution for conscience. In the *Review* and elsewhere, Defoe wrote defences of his co-believers. Abel Boyer used his several periodicals to teach parallel lessons. And Dr Swift predictably responded by feeling that truth was being stifled while falsehood shouted freely.

One of these productions finally won the distinction of being

---

[1] *Ibid.*, p. 81.   [2] *Ibid.*, p. 87.
[3] *A Sermon Preach'd to the Protestants of Ireland . . . October XXIII.* 1708.
[4] Issues of 27 Nov. and following; Tutchin, the founder of the *Observator*, had died in September.

censured by the House of Commons as a scandalous, seditious libel, ordered to be burned by the common hangman. This had a title, as well as text, which probably caught Swift's eye: *Of the Sacramental Test: To a Member of This Parliament, Who Was for the Occasional-Bill in the Former.*[1] The author addressed himself to a high-churchman; and, adopting the arguments usually advanced for the bill to prohibit occasional conformity, he transformed those into a brief against the Test. He claimed that no prejudice had befallen either the Established Church or the civil constitution from the Dissenters admitted to office since the Revolution. He said, 'To make the sacred ordinance of Christ a qualification to civil office, is profaning it.' So he advised his readers to press for a repeal and thus to prevent men from 'eating and drinking their own damnation' when they accepted the sacrament to secure a job.

In order to offset the effect of either Dr Lambert's sermon or the 'cooked' addresses, to expose the false representations of the Brodrick brothers and the journalists, and above all to block any movement for a repeal of the Irish Test through an act in England, Swift composed a pamphlet which he evidently meant to bring out at the beginning of the British Parliamentary session of 1708–9. Though of course anonymous, this piece took the form of a letter, signed from Dublin, 4 December 1708; and it was published just before Christmas 1708.[2] The censured pamphlet and another epistolary diatribe against the Test[3] seem to have suggested the title and form Swift chose for his defence: *A Letter from a Member of the House of Commons in Ireland, to a Member of the House of Commons in England, concerning the Sacramental Test.* But I think the internal organization may be traceable to a talk with the

[1] Censured 12 Jan. 1708/9; see Boyer VII. 275. The text is reprinted by Boyer in an appendix.
[2] Davis II. 284. Advertised as 'just published' in the *Daily Courant*, 24 Dec. 1708, it was probably written not long before. The allusion to the *Observator* (Davis II. 113) may be to the numbers on Drogheda, 27 Nov. and following; Swift's letter of 30 Nov. goes over several points which are raised again in his pamphlet (Williams I. 114–16). But the germ of the pamphlet may have been his conversation with Somers in April (Williams I. 79–80).
[3] *A Letter from a Gentleman in Scotland to His Friend in England against the Sacramental Test*, published 17 Nov. Since Boyer particularly mentions it under that date in his *Annals*, he may have been responsible for it.

'head and oracle'[1] of the Junto, which Swift had reported in April: 'Some days ago my Lord Somers entered with me into discourse about the Test clause,[2] and desired my opinion upon it, which I gave him truly, though with all the gentleness I could.'[3] The restraint which Swift had imposed on himself when speaking to Somers added a deeper intensity to the tone he used in his anonymous exposition of the same subject. For the organization of the pamphlet within the epistolary form, he seems to have started from the sort of questions that his lordship must have put to the vicar: What was his opinion about repealing the Test? Would an attempt to repeal it in the Irish Parliament be likely to succeed? Would not the repeal benefit Ireland?[4] To all these topics Swift prefixes a long paragraph denouncing what he calls the lies of the venal press. Then he discusses each of the three queries with so much clarity, force, and wit that nobody who knew him well could have mistaken the true authorship.

Although the essay is not a satire, the rhetoric throughout depends upon a line of thought that underlies much of Swift's satirical writing: the difference between an absolute or static condition or category, and a dynamic or changing tendency; between the fixed good and the transforming evil; between an equilibrium barely arrived at, and a restless motion to disturb it. For Swift, the world contains a few noble achievements painfully secured, and a swarm of corruptions trying to destroy them: religion, good government, and civilization facing a landslide of heathens, anarchists, and barbarians.

Not only Thomas Brodrick or Lord Somers but Bishop Burnet and Archbishop King thought of Christianity as a firmly established institution, subject to many variations but permanently rooted in human nature. Swift, perhaps because he had suffered so many uprootings himself, thinks of Christianity as an almost miraculous phenomenon, subsisting among men by a Providential blessing, and always on the edge of decay. From Somers's standpoint, to make an alteration in the doctrine or discipline of

---

[1] Davis VII. 5.   [2] That is, the Irish, not the English, Test.
[3] Williams I. 79–80.   [4] Davis II. 113, 118, 120.

a Protestant Christian church might either strengthen or weaken the church but would be unlikely to work it an essential injury. From Swift's standpoint, any change was likely to form the ground of a further change which would ultimately lead to the collapse of the whole structure.

For these reasons, where Burnet might see the Episcopal and Presbyterian churches as superior and inferior bodies, existing side by side in mutual toleration, Swift sees them as established right menaced by innovating wrong and in danger of being consumed. Where Addison might treat the repeal of the Test as a simple deed, bearing limited effects, Swift, with his Platonic cast of mind, foresees a terrifying spiral of consequences, such that the end of the Test means, in strict order, the end of the church establishment, of the Anglican Church itself, of Protestantism, of Christianity, and at last of religion. To admit the Dissenters to offices under the crown is therefore to condemn mankind to an atheist's damnation; and whoever would allow the one act would welcome the other. So it appears that the *Letter . . . concerning the Sacramental Test* was a counterpart to the great *Argument against Abolishing Christianity*.

All this is perhaps less admirable as morality than as rhetoric; for on the relationship of state to church Swift's anxieties shrivelled his sympathies to a range deplorably less generous than Sir William Temple's. But beneath Swift's narrow sectarianism there stirred a deeper tide of humanity, an impulse fed by his patriotic fears for Ireland. In this direction, he recalls, near the start of the *Letter*, a doctrine which had pervaded his *Story of the Injured Lady*, the assertion that Ireland's Parliament was independent of England's. Through the *Letter concerning the Test* he not only employs the theme of the earlier pamphlet but turns it furiously against the supposititious counter-principle. For the legislative authority sometimes claimed by the English over the government of Ireland went back to two statutes of Henry VIII. According to one of these the Irish houses of Parliament might not convene without the consent of the crown; according to the other, they might pass no laws not approved by his majesty and the Privy Council of England. It was in keeping with the second act, known as Poyning's Law, that the government of Ireland had been accustomed to send bills to England for approval before a Parliament entertained them in Dublin. But such a custom was far from equivalent to letting a Parliament in Westminster originate and pass laws for Ireland. Nevertheless, the English House of Lords had asserted its own power as final appellate court for Irish legal issues even when these did not bear on English national interests; and both houses of the English Parliament were inclined to view Ireland as no more than a 'depending kingdom', for which England might indeed make laws at will. Yet on the enraged Irish side, as Addison reported in a deceptively mild understatement, there was 'a great reluctancy in all sorts of people . . . to the having it thought that they are a conquer'd and dependent kingdome, and thatt even acts of parliament in England may not be superseded in Ireland as to what relates purely to the affairs of their own country'.[1]

Against the unjust applications of Poyning's Law, Swift's prose rises to a peak so splendid that readers of his works remember this when they forget all the rest of the *Letter concerning the Test*. It sounds a yell like the heroic outburst against imperialism in the closing pages of *Gulliver's Travels*. It gives the anticipatory trembling of the earthquake that produced the *Drapier's Letters*. The occasion for so much eloquence is Swift's answer to the first of his three questions, explaining his own attitude to repeal. In the *Remarks* upon Tindal, Swift had laid down a rule which he constantly followed for polemical writing, that in one's judgment of a controversial work a main ingredient ought to be one's opinion of the author's motives. So here he applies the rule to the advocates of repeal; and instead of considering the case abstractly, he looks into their intentions. These, he concludes, are simply to prepare the ground for a repeal of the Test in England, and to give rewards in the form of high offices to Dissenters now barred from them. In other words, the good of Ireland had no slightest part in the calculations of the English advocates of repeal. When Swift pounces on this fact, he speaks not merely for a party among the Anglicans in the Protestant minority of Ire-

[1] Graham, p. 161.

[269]

land but for all those nations where justice is sacrificed to the greed or vanity of an irresistible conqueror:

> I do not frequently quote poets, especially English, but I remember there is in some of Mr. Cowley's love verses, a strain that I thought extraordinary at fifteen, and have often since imagined it to be spoken by Ireland.
> > Forbid it Heaven my life should be
> > Weigh'd with her least conveniency.
>
> In short, whatever advantage you propose to your selves by repealing the Sacramental Test, speak it out plainly, it is the best argument you can use, for we value your interest much more than our own. If your little finger be sore, and you think a poultice made of our *vitals* will give it any ease, speak the word, and it shall be done; the interest of our whole kingdom is, at any time, ready to strike to that of your poorest *fishing town*; it is hard you will not accept our services, unless we believe, at the same time, that you are only consulting our profit, and giving us marks of your love. If there be a fire at some distance, and I immediately blow up my house before there be occasion, because you are a man of quality, and apprehend some danger to a *corner of your stable*; yet why should you require me to attend next morning at your levee, with my humble thanks for the favour you have done me?[1]

After this climax, Swift deals ingeniously with the issue of liberty of conscience, on the rough *ad hominem* basis which was among his favourite logical suits. Reversing the Lockean arguments advanced for toleration, he shows very fairly that the Dissenters were unwilling to enlarge liberty of conscience beyond the limits of their own freedom. He also insists that the Test seemed essential to the preservation of the Established Church of Ireland; for without that bulwark, he claimed, the Dissenters would find enough strength and cunning to alter the whole constitution of religion in the kingdom. Next, he answers his second question, about the success of any attempt to repeal the Test within the Irish Parliament, and declares that it would be impossible. Finally, he takes up his third question, and refutes the claim that a repeal would help Ireland. Here Swift puts forward familiar arguments. The weakest assertion on the side of his opponents he seems to have thought the plea which had been maintained in the

[1] Davis II. 114.

censured pamphlet *Of the Sacramental Test*, viz., that the law pro-
faned the sacrament of the eucharist. Swift points out that the
Dissenters themselves would not agree to replace the Test by an
oath which would serve the original purpose of the act. Several
other claims he disposes of with similar cogency. But in handling
one of them he climbs to a pitch almost as piercing as the attack
on English greed. This passage is the flowering corona of Swift's
response to the best-known, oldest argument of the Whigs: that
the Roman Catholics were too dangerous for any distinction
within Protestantism to matter in the common cause against
them. Here Swift broadcasts his certainty (history of course
proved him wrong) that the immediate peril to the true church
from the Dissenters was radically more menacing than the threat
from the Papists. In a famous, brilliant set of images he rejects
Lambert's warning that the Roman leopard never lost its spots:

> It is agreed, among naturalists, that a *lyon* is a larger, a stronger,
> and more dangerous enemy than a *cat*; yet if a man were to have his
> choice, either a *lyon* at his foot, bound fast with three or four chains,
> his teeth drawn out, and his claws pared to the quick, or an angry
> *cat* in full liberty at his throat; he would take no long time to deter-
> mine.[1]

Besides considering problems directly related to the Test,
Swift reveals once and for all the casuistry with which he called
himself a 'Whig'; for he gives a definition of the two political
parties which have satisfied neither Addison nor Wharton.
Or rather, while pretending to make definitions, Swift really
shifts the entire political spectrum to the right, but keeping the
labels fixed, so that the nonjurors, Jacobites, and high-churchmen disappear, while the Dissenters, the Junto, and the anti-
monarchists are all lumped together. He then proceeds to give
the title of 'Whigs' to the Hanoverian, Tory church party (whose
views, we know, were close to Harley's); and against these he
aligns the most aggressive of what other men would have called
'Whigs':

> Whoever bears a true veneration for the glorious memory of
> King William, as our great deliverer from *popery* and *slavery*; who-

[1] *Ibid.*, p. 122.

ever is firmly loyal to our present queen, with an utter abhorrence and detestation of the *Pretender*; whoever approves the succession to the crown in the House of Hanover, and is for preserving the doctrine and discipline of the Church of England, with an *indulgence* for scrupulous consciences; such a man, we think, acts upon right principles, and may be justly allowed a *Whig*. . . So that the parties among us [i.e., in the House of Commons of Ireland] are made up, on one side, of *moderate Whigs*, and, on the other, of *Presbyterians* and their *Abettors*; by which last I mean, such who can equally go to a *church*, or a *conventicle*; or such who are indifferent to all religion in general; or, lastly, such who affect to bear a personal rancor towards the clergy.[1]

Swift's criteria for *Whig* might possibly have suited the Ireland of his youth; for of course no member of the minority that governed that country could possibly be a Tory as defined in the 1680s, or wish to see the Stuarts restored. But Swift wholly omits from his definition the Junto's tests of loyalty: support for the war effort, especially on land and in Flanders; removal of the Test; devotion to the party leaders. It is highly significant that he refuses to employ the term *Tory* at all.

This remarkable manœuvre thus represents one more instance of the rhetorical device we have met before, and which Swift was to manage with even finer skill in the *Argument against Abolishing Christianity*, viz., the reversal of connotations of crucial terms, the employment of 'loaded' expressions not with their usual overtones but with a tendency directly opposed. Thus what Swift calls 'Whig' is what Sunderland would have called either 'Tory' or 'Jacobite'. Elsewhere in the *Letter*, Swift uses 'common enemy', a term normally reserved for Roman Catholics, to designate Dissenters[2]; and instead of 'passive obedience', a phrase associated with high-churchmen, he speaks of the 'passive Presbyterian principle'[3] of refusing to resist an invasion unless they held commissions in the army.

These reversals of implication had been abundantly anticipated in *A Tale of a Tub*, where, as later, they seem an aspect of Swift's talent for mimicry and impersonation. For by assuming the vocabulary of his opponents but turning the connotations

[1] Davis II. 118.   [2] *Ibid.*, p. 121.   [3] *Ibid.*, p. 123.

upside down, Swift creates a momentary parody, an ironical disguise which is meant to be penetrated so that the reader will see the author's true principles. In the *Letter concerning the Test*, however, the effect depends on the simpler disguise (not in itself ironical) which Swift wore in the rôle of author, because, as the title declares, he issued the pamphlet as if it were the work of a member of the Irish House of Commons. The chief aim of this pretence was, I think, simply to increase the persuasiveness of the essay. To those whom the deceit took in, the *Letter* of a Member of Parliament would appear more authoritative and disinterested than the biased complaint of a priest. In addition, Swift was also displaying a commendable caution by shielding himself from the anger which the Junto would surely feel against the writer of the piece. To push the trickery all the way, he allowed his playfulness enough scope for a passage alluding to himself as one suspected of favouring repeal:

> However that be, he will find it a difficult matter, with his skill in politicks, or talent at ridicule, backed by all the wit he is said to be master of, to reason or laugh us out of the *Sacramental Test*; and will find by the event that my PREDICTIONS are truer than *his*.[1]

Here is a powerful hint of the sort of self-satire that was to become a dominating feature of *Gulliver's Travels*. If Swift could allow himself this rash frolic with his own character, he could do as much with other men's. Besides seeming to malign Dr Swift, therefore, he also pretended to 'defend' Dr Lambert, but in terms which could only mortify that adaptable preacher; for Swift describes him as one who always declared himself *against* repealing the Test—'He is reckoned a worthy person, and I know not how it can be consistent with that character to employ his pen either in a publick or private manner against his opinion, neither do I think he designs it.'[2] In this sideswipe there is as much prankishness as satire. Under the anonymity of the *Letter* Swift seems to have felt a magical and reckless freedom from the restraints he had so long suffered; and he used his liberty to execute yet one more prank, this time with no satiric design at all. In a careful and elaborate passage he produced a character of Arch-

[1] *Ibid.*, p. 284.   [2] *Ibid.*

bishop King as one 'justly reckoned among the greatest and most learned prelates of his age'.[1] The emphasis in this eulogy falls on traits which would recommend a man to the Whigs, but the facts and judgments are sound. If Swift hoped the compliment would ingratiate himself with his master, he did not try to do so by falsifying his real sentiments.

But no aspect of the disguises and impersonations running through the *Letter concerning the Test* seems so impressive as the light they throw on Swift's motivation. In publishing the pamphlet, he knew he could win only the antagonism of the Junto. Yet the month before the *Letter* appeared, the death of Prince George had opened the way to new advancements for the Whig leaders. Somers at last became Lord President of the Privy Council; Wharton became Lord Lieutenant of Ireland. If these were the men Swift wanted favours from, they had never been in a more comfortable position to grant them. Furthermore, Swift at this time was under the impression that the First Fruits had already been remitted to the Church of Ireland; so he could suppose that he would not endanger his mission by circulating this paper.[2] If he did succeed in hiding his authorship, he could be neither praised nor blamed for the piece. If he failed to hide it, he would lose the chance of securing patronage from the most powerful persons in England. It is possible that he thought nobody would identify him at least for a while; and in general, of course, he preferred to publish all his things in such a way that nobody could prove he had written them. Yet even by now he had enjoyed enough experience of political journalism to realize the secret could not be kept very long. Of course, Swift also liked having his fatherhood recognized, and he often left precise clues for the purpose. In this *Letter*, therefore, a desire to make Archbishop King see him as defender of the Test may have come up against an unwillingness to stand forth as openly defying the Junto. But he knew how little he could expect from King; and I suspect all Swift wished to accomplish on that side was to justify himself. Lord Somers, on the other hand, was exactly informed of Swift's position and would certainly have advised Wharton if

[1] Davis II. 282.   [2] Ferguson, p. 34.

advice was wanting. It is true that Swift may have delayed publication until he was sure Wharton would not choose him as chaplain. Even after that fact was settled, however, Swift still had hopes to lose. This pamphlet, therefore, can be considered nothing but a pure case of moral protest. Swift made the gesture solely because he thought it would help the church and in spite of the probability that it would harm him. In his first partisan pamphlet since *The Contests and Dissensions*, the job-hungry vicar had broken through the restraints of prudent self-interest in what amounted to a public declaration of war against the Whigs.[1]

[1] Archbishop King's comment on the pamphlet does not suggest that it altered his cautious, paternalistic attitude toward Swift. Writing to a friend, the Archbishop said, 'We have a letter here said to be writ by a Parliament man in Ireland to a Parliament man in England concerning the Sacramental Test. . . . It has a very fine turn of expression and the arguments well concluded. I wish he had forbore some matters of fact that I believe will prove false and likewise some characters [i.e., of King and of Lambert] that do not belong to persons on whom they seemed fixed, and this may give it a warm entertainment in the House of Commons this session. . . . I should wonder he that wrote that paper should have so little sense as to put in it anything false, since he might be sure it would be laid hold on and spoil perhaps the whole; and yet to my knowledge the gentleman [i.e., Lambert] that [he] pointed out to write for the repeal of the Test Act has done more to support it than most of station, of which I think I could give demonstration' (27 Jan. 1709, to Annesley).

Chapter Sixteen

MORALITY AND RELIGION

I

Out of the same circumstances that gave rise to the *Letter concerning the Test* came both the finest and the flattest of Swift's essays on religion and morality. *An Argument against Abolishing Christianity* belongs among the masterpieces of comic satire in English. *A Project for the Advancement of Religion and the Reformation of Manners* reflects so shallow and banal an intellect that some acute scholars have thought it a parody. Yet both were written about the same time.[1] To reconcile the two as dropped from the same noble tree, one must, I think, distinguish between the public moralist in Swift and the anonymous, playful satirist.

The questions started by this distinction lead to consequences of the most fundamental kind not only for a judgment of Swift's entire achievement as a writer but for the understanding of comic satire as a literary genre. It will appear that psychologically the hidebound moralist is the necessary origin of the prankster, yet that as a literary accomplishment the prankster's work must be read in isolation from the moralist's. For the whole art of works like the *Argument against Abolishing Christianity* and *A Modest Pro-*

---

[1] Probably mid-1708. Although the *Argument* was not published until 1711, it was included in the list made in October or November 1708 (see Appendix B); it alludes to Tindal, whose book had appeared in 1706, and to the active career of Mrs Tofts, who retired in 1709; to the Act of Union (1707), and to Asgill, whose book was condemned in December 1707. The *Project* alludes to a pastoral *Letter* of Bishop Burnet's (dated April 1708) and was also included in the list made in the autumn of 1708. I think the praise of Queen Anne's 'conjugal love' suggests a date before the death of Prince George, 28 Oct. 1708; and the immediate occasion of Swift's writing may possibly have been the royal proclamation of 18 Aug. 1708 against vice and to encourage piety and virtue. The *Project* was published in April 1709, advertised as published 'this day' in the *Daily Courant*, 9 Apr., and recommended by Steele in the *Tatler*, 21 Apr.

posal depends upon the most exquisite of Swift's acts of impersonation, the case in which he parodies himself, or rather, in which the
hidden comedian mimics the official priest; and his entire career
can be described as the partnership of a clown and a preacher.

In the *Letter concerning the Test* the playful impersonator had to
break through a double restraint: first, the caution, largely irrelevant to his rhetoric, which Swift was compelled to exercise with
regard to statesmen whom his thesis would antagonize; secondly,
the sobriety appropriate to his rhetoric, with which the author of
A Tale of a Tub had at last learned to represent himself in handling matters ecclesiastical. Comic impersonation does burst out
in the game with King's, Lambert's, and Swift's own reputations.
From the rest of the *Letter*, however, the ghost of Bickerstaff seems
absent. Instead, we hear the doctor of divinity addressing an
audience in either bitter or straightforward language, using a
simple disguise, but delivering his genuine sentiments about as
freely as one ever does in a piece of persuasion. He keeps the dignity which a counsellor of the public must assume when trying to
move serious minds by serious reasons. With all its vigour and
intensity the *Letter* does not lose a solemn tone; the sarcasms do
not disrupt the single-voiced body of the work.

With the *Argument* and the *Project* the separation becomes more
pure. Although Swift signed neither, he acknowledged the *Project* at once, and the restraint he shows in it has no source but the
severity of his rôle as censor. The *Argument*, on the other hand, he
suppressed for three years, bringing it out when the views he
expounded were in no way distasteful to the new government.
Neither piece was written as a compromise, therefore. Together,
they represent the two rôles in which Swift voluntarily cast himself, both of them morally instructive, but one by way of explosive satirical comedy and the other through direct, earnest
exhortation.

Anyone who tries to combine the *Project* with the *Argument* as
existing on the same level of discourse will plunge himself into
unnecessary contradictions. The elaborate form of Swift's comic
satire allows readers to participate in it who share none of the
author's religious views, even though he wrote it in order to pro-

pagate those views. The simple form of his exhortation can only repel modern readers, since the author allows his rhetoric no greater employment than the direct strengthening of his doctrine: the reader has nothing to do here but accept or reject the goods on the counter. As the point of a direct exhortation, for example, what could a religious man possibly mean by saying that to establish true religion in the world would be to destroy civilization, to 'break the entire frame and constitution of things'?[1] If he is sincere, how can he claim as a possible vocation for himself the establishment of true religion? Suppose he doubles the paradox and insists that hardly one in a hundred among people of consequence seems to act in accord with decent religious principles; but suppose he also claims that faith and morality could, 'in a short time and with no very great trouble', be raised to as high a perfection as ordinary humanity is capable of enduring?

What can such a man mean, is one question. Another is, assuming his arguments make coherent sense, why should his meaning matter to an agnostic or at least to a non-Christian today? Surely it ought to appear wonderful that one of the most brilliant satirical essays in the English language, admired perhaps even more in our time than when it was published two and a half centuries ago, should be constructed from attitudes so violently at variance with one another and with those of its modern audience. In attempting to resolve these difficulties, I assume not only that few modern readers are religious in the same sense as the long-dead, high-church Anglican priest, but also that nearly all of them feel highly satisfied with *An Argument against Abolishing Christianity*. And I further assume that all literary works, whether by Swift or anyone else, depend for their life on a relationship between author and audience. What the reader may see does not exist in the work unless it can be imputed to the author (known or unknown) in his capacity as artist. Conversely, what the author may intend has no literary reality unless it can be discovered in his work by a proper reader. Each man exists in art only as an object for the other's contemplation, de-

[1] Davis II. 27.

fined by those aspects of himself which can be interested or embodied in the public, literary terms of the work as read or heard.

While comic satire has become increasingly a topic for serious critical discussion, satirical works are rarely criticized as structures which involve author and reader at once. By far the most common approach starts from the axiom that the purpose of satire is to reform abuses through the ridicule of those who practise them. Upon this supposition the critic often looks into the author's objectives as such. We are presented with a survey of the abuses condemned and with probable reasons for the author's effort to correct them. When, on the other hand, the focus shifts to the reader, one's judgment becomes coloured by the problems of effectiveness and rhetoric. Some critics, adopting this approach, will consider how influential the *Dunciad* was in defining an ideal of culture. Some will analyse the use of particular devices, like parody and mock-epic. What should discourage the explorer of these detached avenues to satire is their limited relevance to the literary status of a work. After all, the heaviest-handed appeal to mob-prejudice is more likely to alter the course of events than the fables of La Fontaine. And while the discrete study of rhetorical devices may seem revealing, it in fact tells one no more than what a genius like Pope shares with an epigone like Charles Churchill.

Perhaps the important demand to make is neither why one man composed the work nor how another man altered his behaviour upon reading it but why the reader enjoys watching the author in the business of acting it out. After all, is not the lasting appeal of even serious hortatory literature so far from the incitement of action that it rather takes the place of action? Does not one read *Areopagitica* in order to relieve oneself of an urge to alter the laws of censorship? And is not the case of comic satire the same, at least in so far as it claims to be imaginative literature? Does not a reading of Dryden's attack upon Shaftesbury reconcile one to the prosperity of people like Achitophel?

Treating satires not as documents but as poetry, drama, or narrative prose, we may therefore try to deal with this provocative situation: that one man, the reader, is listening with pleasure to the abuse or ridicule which a second man, the author, is dropping upon a third man, the object of satire. At the same time we may remember what gives the situation enigmatic properties: this is that the reader will often not only feel no dislike for the object of satire but will positively admire him or indeed feel at one with him.

II

Swift's *Argument* raises the issue in its extreme form. The principle which the author is defending is not merely religion in general, nor Christianity as true religion, nor even Protestantism as the purest form of Christianity. It is the Episcopal Protestant faith as distinguished from Presbyterianism, Roman Catholicism, all non-Christian creeds, and any form of irreligiosity. To agree with Swift, one would have to believe that the nearest available approach to a church which in discipline and doctrine embodies God's own ordinances is the Church of England. If one denies the divinity of Christ, rejects the doctrine of the Trinity, or insists that a true church need not possess bishops, one belongs among the objects of Swift's satire. There may of course be modern admirers of the essay who can station themselves outside the range of his missiles; but their number is negligible.

To proceed further, we may define Swift's immediate object still more narrowly. The historical occasion for his essay was the agitation for the repeal of the Test Act. As a strong-minded Anglican priest, Swift considered the Test essential to the prosperity of his church. In attacking its opponents, moreover, he hoped to make them appear subversive not of a single piece of legislation but of the foundations of virtuous behaviour. So he treats repeal as leading inevitably to the collapse of morality. 'There are too many', he once said, 'who would talk at the same rate if the question were, not only about abolishing the Sacramental Test, but the sacrament itself.'[1]

Following his common practice, however, Swift barely remarks the principle which he hoped to uphold, and he does even

---

[1] Davis II. 132. Cf. his remark twenty-five years later, on a new attempt to repeal the Test in Ireland: Swift says £50,000 has been collected, 'sufficient among us—to abolish Christianity itself' (letter to Ford, 20 Nov. 1733).

so much with only a sidelong glance, not far from the end of his satire. Five paragraphs before closing he says, in a monumental bathos, that if men abolish the Christian faith, they may weaken the Established Church. The reason for this likelihood, he continues, is that atheists, deists, Socinians, anti-Trinitarians, 'and other sub-divisions of free-thinkers' have no love for the Church of England and would be glad to repeal the Test. While to a modern reader this list of sub-divisions of free-thinkers may look haphazard, it is in fact decidedly not. There is in the list a subtle and graduated progression from the obviously criminal to the merely Nonconformist; and Swift is implying that the last class is as dangerous potentially as the first is immediately. For he took the sects to be a psychological or biological tendency, representing not the devout conscience of a variant revelation but an instinct for perverseness of every sort. To yield the Test, consequently, would be to yield government, morality, faith.

In order to demonstrate his thesis, Swift must assume that the natural and rational inclination of the great bulk of Englishmen is toward, rather than against, the Anglican church. *A priori*, therefore, the opposers of the church must be irrational monsters. Secondly, the objections which these opposers raise are either to mysteries, i.e., matters beyond proof and disproof, or else to forms, i.e., matters of indifference. So their ostensible objections cannot be sincere but are a blind of respectability, a show of logic, to conceal their true resentments. Finally, Swift implies that what they in fact desire is a release from moral restraint, a liberty to give way to vice; he represents their goal as the embodiment of the unnatural, irrational tendencies in all men; and he touches the motifs of the 'Digression on Madness'. But if this is so, there is no point at which compromise might be useful. Those who deny the divine ordination of bishops are on their way to denying the Trinity. Anti-Trinitarians can only wish to reject the godhead of Christ. Socinians privately believe that Christianity is not essential to morality. And deists are really atheists. Anybody who would abolish the Test would abolish virtue.

Rather than refute his enemies heading by heading, therefore,

Swift pretends to argue *a fortiori*. He will prove the value of Christianity and thus, by necessary implication, prove the value of the act; for if Christianity is utterly good, anything which advances it must be good. Of course, however, none of his readers would offer to deny the proposition which Swift pretends to advance as his conclusion; and so the essay is a systematic parody of a demonstration. It falls into logical partitions; it opens with a statement of the thesis; it continues in a set of objections to the thesis, with a refutation of each objection; and it concludes with a set of evil consequences which would follow from the defeat of his thesis, i.e., from the abolition of Christianity. All the arguments on either part are, to be sure, wildly ridiculous—both the separate points and the disproof of each. Yet the examples employed, the asides, the turns of phrase and their connotations invariably disparage those whom Swift immediately aims at, the opponents of the Test.

III

Swift's essay would be clever enough if he had left it in this shape. Rather than do so, alas, he chose to stand the entire construction upon its head by distinguishing between two forms of Christianity, one being *real* and the other *nominal*. Of these two forms he wishes, he says, to defend only one; and the meaning of his decision is profound. The first form of Christianity, the *real*, is the pure, aboriginal faith as taught by the gospels and practised by the earliest converts. The second, the *nominal*, is modern hypocrisy, preserving the name of Christian without either the faith or the charity. It is easy to follow Swift's irony when he says he has no intention of defending real Christianity, which is, he acknowledges, utterly inconsistent with his contemporaries' schemes of wealth and power. The enigma is what he means by ironically proposing to support the hypocritical retention of the name and title of Christians.

If we tried to interpret this proposal as an ironical repudiation of hypocrisy, we should be brought at once to a stand. Swift cannot mean simply that it is absurd for men to keep the name when the thing it designates is gone; for in his scheme, nominal

Christianity is parallel to the nominal communion demanded of office-holders by the Test Act; and we can be certain that the author wishes to defend the act. On the other hand, not only do we not like to suppose that he is counselling hypocrisy, but also we can hardly interpret the bitterly ironical style of the pseudo-defence, throughout the essay, as expressing anything but a ferocious derogation of *nominal* Christianity as contrasted with *real*.

By looking once more into history, we can find a solution. Not only were there those who supported the Test and those who opposed it. There were also many who felt indignant at the perversion of the sacrament which resulted from the use of it as a prerequisite to power. In the devout eyes of these men the Nonconformist office-seekers who felt unwilling to accept Anglican doctrine and ritual as full members of the church, but who were ready to undergo a yearly charade so they might qualify as officers in the army or as aldermen in corporations, seemed traitors to two creeds, the Anglican and their own. For if they suffered qualms of conscience about the Established way of worship, how could they bring themselves ever to receive the host according to that rule? And if they could endure the nauseating ordeal once a year for the sake of wealth and power, why could they not submit regularly? Surely such 'occasional conformists' were double-dyed hypocrites. To men of the Church of England who purpled with righteous resentment against the shifty Presbyterian and the split-tongued Congregationalist, it seemed that an equitable law would have prevented anybody from holding an office under the crown if he ever took communion outside the Established Church. It was these men of course who agitated for passage of the bill against occasional conformity. So far from wishing to repeal the Test, they wished to strengthen it by shutting every wicket against the masked and wily volpones.

While they awaited this consummation, nevertheless, they felt no impulse to relax the law already in operation. True, it admitted many, but it excluded some. And they perfectly well knew that critics of the law from the other side wished to replace active hypocrisy not by dutiful conformity but by a libertine indiffer-

ence to all rational restraint. What emerges seems a quite understandable series of attitudes: that members of the Church of
England are the truest Christians; that Nonconformists have
their feet set on the road to atheism; that occasional conformists
are hypocrites; but that the true church will be stronger if men
are forced into hypocrisy than if they are released into unlimited
freedom of worship. Thus without ever softening their contempt
for those who underwent occasional conformity, men with such
views could insist upon the enforcement of its practice.

Putting the historical terms in the language of Swift's essay, we
may say that real Christians may have no respect for nominal
Christianity but they do not see how its mere abolition, unmitigated by some form of coercive invigilation, can do other
than weaken the real institution.

IV

We may now examine the early passage in which Swift ironically
repudiates real Christianity and says that to restore this would be
'to break the entire frame and constitution of things'. Passing
over the synecdoche by which Christianity means Anglicanism,
let us consider the ultimate significance of the paragraph and the
essay. To begin with, the statement must be more than irony,
since it is in fact true. By restoring the primitive church, by living
perfectly Christian lives, we should most certainly annihilate
civilization; and to propose this would indeed be absurd. Yet by
all evidence Swift was a devout priest; and in this essay he is defending his religion against what he considers to be an onslaught.
Seriously, therefore, he cannot think of real Christianity as anything but the most important aspect of earthly existence. The
'entire frame and constitution of things' has no value at all when
judged against this supreme good. Furthermore, if he is a conscientious priest, his very vocation must be to stand up for real
Christianity.

To resolve the contradiction, I think we shall have to cut our
author in two. Of these twins the one is a hopeful pastor endlessly
attempting to pen his erring lambs into the secure fold of their

[284]

proper hillside. He preaches and preaches the gospel, and shows the path to salvation. But the other twin walks behind and studies him with pitying amusement. He sees that the lambs are possessed by evil spirits and cannot keep from straying, that the walls of the fold are too much decayed either to hold in the flock or to shut out the wolf, and that the pastor is exhausting his body without preserving his wards. Swift is both twins; and like every good pastor he says, 'I know these things are so, but I must act as if they were not.' The satirist is satirizing himself.

The passage is therefore one of his bitterest outbursts, and reflects his conviction that the noblest of all causes was a lost cause. On this conviction the whole structure of his irony rests. If the disease were not incurable, the doctor would not look ridiculous. It is by laughing finally at himself that Swift wins the privilege of laughing at others.

The tone of the *Argument* carries the dichotomy into the corners of Swift's sentences, through an irony which depends on his habit of impersonation. In its air of ease and worldliness the style of the essay captures the manner of a libertine gentleman in a Restoration play, freed from the blinkers of common decency. For the experienced reader this manner has associations opposed to preachments and piety. It recalls a licentious court and an intellectual milieu receptive to dangerous ideas. Above all, it connotes a loathing of the hypocrisy which Swift feels willing to tolerate. By adopting this tone, Swift does more than ingratiate himself with an audience likely to associate good breeding with dissolute manners. He inverts the normal employment of the style; and he subtly, continuously titillates the reader by devoting the bold phrases and daring images to the promotion of just those unexciting doctrines which one least expects them to support: so the voice of King Charles speaks the views of Queen Anne. The charge of hypocrisy which Restoration courtiers flung at their middle-class censurers, Swift hurls back at their descendants; for he accuses them of falsely pretending to the title of Christian.

V

For there is a still larger context in which the *Argument* can be set. During the decade that preceded its composition, a controversy had been aflame which concerned the status of the mysteries in Anglican doctrine, above all, the mystery of the Trinity. Whether there were three real and distinct persons who constituted a single God, or merely a symbolic and therefore nominal distinction of three aspects of the one God, became the main subject of a quarrel which burned about the heresies of Sabellianism, Tritheism, and Socinianism.[1] When, at the opening of his essay, Swift derives his distinction between nominal and real Christianity from the difference between 'nominal and real Trinitarians', he invites us to call up this larger setting.

Surely among Swift's deepest preoccupations here is the meaning of the noun *Christian*. Out of all the ways in which the word could be employed, the most common designation and the least controversial sense is of a member of a Christian church, regardless of behaviour or belief. To this notion Swift opposes the strict sense of a man who lives and worships in sincere conformity with the teachings of Christ. The first man is a *nominal* Christian if he bears the label but interprets it as connoting no attributes except those which he is inclined to accept for himself. The second man is a *real* Christian: he assumes that there is an essential Christianity exemplified by the primitive church; and that the name of Christian correctly denotes none but the man who possesses the essence of the thing. If the Church of England is identical with the primitive church, Anglicans alone can be endowed with the real essence; all others must content themselves with a nominal essence the constitution of which they cannot even agree upon.

The literary value of these distinctions is important. For to explain Swift's purpose as the scolding of his readers for living un-Christian lives would be to reduce him to the condition of a tedious pedagogue. Although that is of course his implication, his immediate plan, it seems to me, is much more ingenious. He is ironically advising his readers precisely not to change their lives.

[1] Every, pp. 75–83.

On the contrary, he impersonates them, pretending to identify his own disposition with theirs and to urge them to persist in the ambition and lust which consume them. Even the absurd arguments which he ironically puts forth are appeals not to faith and charity but to sloth and vice. Stay as you are, he seems to say.

One change alone, he does seriously and bitterly desire, however; and this is in his readers' conception of what they are doing when they delight to call themselves Christians. Manifestly, if there were no honour in the name, men would not stick to it. At the same time, however, an open hypocrisy is repugnant to everyone and useful to none; so no man would willingly admit to claiming the title of Christian without minding what the title signified. Hence the claim to be a Christian must always mean publicly an assertion that one is living the Christian life in what Swift would describe as the real sense. Unless the word represented the *real essence* of Christianity, there would be no profit in endorsing oneself with it.

Swift is thus transforming a local quarrel over occasional conformity into a dramatic symbol of the human situation from the Christian point of view, a symbol drawn from those elements of the situation which the reader can share with the author. For are not all human beings occasional conformists as Christians? Is not the man who never communes with anti-Christ as rare as a saint? Is there a person who at some moment is not un-Christian? This is a familiar analysis of our plight; and Swift is hardly so commonplace as simply to retail it. Rather he says there can be decency even in hypocrisy. Sin as you please, he therefore says, and name yourself as you wish; but understand what you are about. Don't flatter *yourself* that the correspondence in nomenclature makes your nominal religion—the list of traits which happen to suit your private depravities—equivalent to the real essence, which may indeed be hidden from the eye of man but lies open to the eye of God. By all means, name yourself after Christ; model yourself upon Mammon; and hide your duplicity from men. But do recognize in your soul what you are, do contemplate the abyss dividing the righteous from the damned.

The flaw in such a resolution of Swift's two attitudes is that it leaves us utterly without a practicable, serious definition, such as he must have invoked from his pulpit. Agreeing that saints alone can unfailingly embody the real essence and that the great bulk of mankind conceive of a variety of nominal faiths, what would he like us to mean when we are thinking of neither sainthood nor hypocrisy? Or in Swift's rôle as a preacher, since it was impossible to make men saints and undesirable to leave them hypocrites, how could he implore them to be Christians?

With such an inquiry, we move outside the *Argument*, outside the relation between author and reader, and into Swift's biography. The answer, unfortunately, is both obvious and dull. Dr Swift believed that human nature had room for a moderate striving toward moral integrity, though sin and ignorance constantly drove this tendency back. To sustain even a mediocre degree of virtue, therefore, meant a constant skirmishing between aggressive vice and the aspiration toward goodness. I think the tone of the *Whole Duty of Man* applies to the doctor's ethical ideas in adulthood as it did to the conditions of his schooling. Unlike Addison and Steele, Swift distrusted the psychology of natural benevolence taught by Latitudinarian preachers, and he hastened to disown Shaftesbury's 'free Whiggish' *Letter concerning Enthusiasm*.[1] Like the author of the *Whole Duty*, he regarded the passions as 'disordered and rebellious, even against the voice of reason'.[2] So any timbers were welcome that might shore up man's weak shelter: example, punishment, reward, exhortation.

Therefore, it is not in terms of being but in terms of becoming that Swift expected his parishioners to follow their saviour. Since humanity is fallible and virtue is unrelenting, the Christian, as described to a congregation, is one who would like to practise the pure faith, who sincerely strives to, and who regrets those lapses which are genuinely beyond his control. That this positive, practicable definition is neither powerful nor interesting, I freely confess; and this reflection was probably Swift's reason for keeping it out of his *Argument*.

---

[1] Williams I. 100.   [2] *Supra*, vol. I, pp. 39–40.

VI

To admirers of the greatest prose satirist in English, it may appear that I have abandoned him to an awkward posture. For however hot the scorn I may have allowed him to drop upon hypocrisy, I have still represented him as encouraging it in preference to a naked career of vice. No other implication can be drawn from the logic of the *Argument*. Whether nominal Christianity stands for occasional conformity or signifies saving the name of religion while defying the essence, Swift's ironical defence cannot mean that it should be simply abolished. That absolute conformity is the only proper conduct, that real Christianity is the highest good—and the destruction of a corrupt 'civilization' a trifling price to pay for its establishment—these propositions never weaken the inference that where either is not to be had, the pretence of it is to be substituted.

Despite the aversion which such reasoning will probably provoke in modern candour and integrity, it patently belongs to Swift. For if the *Argument* is the shining face of his genius, another essay is the lustreless reverse. This is *A Project for the Advancement of Religion and the Reformation of Manners*, a serious, didactic exposition of a method to discourage sin.[1] Between this essay and the *Argument* the connection is that it supplies, in pedestrian detail, the positive recommendations with which a man converted by the comical satire of the *Argument* might be expected soberly to agree. Here Swift's example suggests that the great Augustans speak best by indirection, that when they are most affirmative they are least splendid. Like Martin in *A Tale of a Tub*, like the Houyhnhnms in *Gulliver's Travels*, like the commonplaces of the *Essay on Man*, the lights which the author of the *Project* holds

---

[1] See Maurice J. Quinlan, 'Swift's *Project for the Advancement of Religion and the Reformation of Manners*', *PMLA*. LXXI (Mar. 1956), 210–12. Professor Quinlan suggests that Swift may be speaking ironically when he says, at the start of his essay, that in his age there have as yet been no 'schemes' for the improvement of religion and morals; Professor Quinlan points out that Swift later does mention 'other projects' for these ends (Davis II. 57). I do not think the opening remark is ironical; the sort of 'schemes' Swift has in mind there appear to be simple, immediately efficacious devices as distinct from the ineffectual laws, proclamations, and societies which he intends later by 'other projects'.

before us are not such as either to cheer or to lift high the spiritual gaze. Nevertheless, if these were not his lights, his masterpieces could never have been his works. Only by mocking his own 'projecting' optimism does the satirist create his comedy.

The *Project* fits decorously into the squads of reform programmes which had been marching across England since the Revolution. As the kingdom suffered a turn against the easy manners of the Restoration court, a whole breed of institutions arose to purify men's conduct and thought. Societies for the 'reformation of manners' began to appear when Swift was twenty-five. Within a decade the S.P.C.K. and S.P.G. were established, and Jeremy Collier delivered the complaints which infuriated Congreve while delighting Blackmore. Soon the *Tale of a Tub* became a victim of the crusade which its author was to join. Meanwhile, if Swift had formed no intimacy with Collier himself, he did become the friend of another nonjuring reformer, Robert Nelson, who had married the Earl of Berkeley's sister. So his dedicating of the *Project* to the pious Countess of Berkeley was a way of drawing public attention to a specimen of the mode of life which he desired to recommend.

Following this dedication, Swift opens his *Project* with the claim that the author has a prescription by which a decaying faith and morality might 'in a short time, and with no very great trouble', be raised to an unprecedented zenith of health. Next he avers that crime and vice in England have never before been committed so generally and so openly: hardly one in a hundred among persons of consequence appears to guide himself by any religious principle. Indeed, his displeasure seems at least as great at the publicity as at the performance. Instead of hiding or palliating their sins, men 'expose them freely to view, like any other common occurrences of life, without the least reproach from the world, or themselves'.[1]

Biographically, the most revealing aspect of this complaint is not so much the items themselves as the visible link made by Swift between the abuses he attacks and several themes peculiarly associated with the most aggressive Whigs. One is reminded

[1] Davis II. 45.

that he censured the 'free Whiggish thinking' of Shaftesbury's *Letter concerning Enthusiasm* and described his own writings at this time as 'quite of another sort'.[1] In the *Project* Swift jeers at the sanctimoniousness of Gilbert Burnet[2]; he demands the suppression of deist literature[3]; and he condemns the one-sidedness of the Junto in distributing patronage:

> Every man thinks he has laid in a sufficient stock of merit, and may pretend to any employment, provided he has been loud and frequent in declaring himself hearty for the government. 'Tis true, he is a *man of pleasure*, and a *free thinker*, that is, in other words, he is profligate in his morals, and a despiser of religion; but in point of party, he is one to be *confided* in; he is an asserter of liberty and property; he rattles it out against *popery* and *arbitrary power*, and *priestcraft*, and *high-church*. 'Tis enough: he is a person fully qualified for any employment in the court or the navy, the law, or the revenue; where he will be sure to leave no arts untried of bribery, fraud, injustice, oppression, that he can practice with any hope of impunity. No wonder such men are true to a government, where liberty runs high, where property *however attained*, is so well secured, and where the administration is at least so gentle: 'tis impossible they could chuse any other constitution without changing to their loss.[4]

The language here sounds so palpably and furiously anti-Whig that one feels amazed at Swift's publishing the *Project* while he still hoped for something from the Junto. I find it hard to disagree with Swift's godson, Thomas Sheridan, who called the *Project* a 'strong, though covert attack, upon the power of the Whigs'.[5]

But how does Swift, then, propose to cure these ailments? The reply is staggeringly simple. He would merely have the Queen make it one's interest and honour to pursue religion and morality. And how should she accomplish this end? She would make vice an insurmountable obstacle to preferment. Among her majesty's domestic servants, among her courtiers, among her ministers of state and her officers of the army, among bishops, magistrates, and commissioners, wherever her prerogative gave

---

[1] Williams I. 100.   [2] Davis II. 54; see above, p. 276, n. 1.   [3] Davis II. 58.
[4] *Ibid.*, p. 62; I have taken my text from Swift's *Miscellanies*, 1711, pp. 227–8.
[5] *Life of Swift*, 1785, p. 51.

her authority to appoint, promote, and dismiss, the Queen would insist upon religion and virtue—so far as these could be outwardly recognized—as prerequisites to office. Once this system was established, said Swift, a pious, moral life would grow fashionable. (He does not seem to have contemplated the possibility that the court might grow unfashionable.) 'The empire of vice and irreligion would soon be destroyed in [London] and receive a terrible blow through the whole island'—this is his promise. If Parliament felt inclined to join the zealous enterprise, the members could pass laws to control taverns, to punish quackery and fraud, to censor the press, and to increase the number of churches in London.

This is not so much an original design as a nightmare expansion of the Test Act. To any thoughtful reader, the colossal amount of bribery and blackmail which such a proceeding would necessarily engender, the desperate inefficiency with which it would clog the mechanism of government, the appalling opportunities it would make available to malice, scandal, and gossip, will be at once so evident that he will suspect Swift of some new depth of irony. Unhappily, he will be mistaken. Not only is the *Project* straightforward; but the Earl of Berkeley besought Swift to deliver a copy of it to the Queen[1]; the *Tatler* praised the author for going to heaven like a gentleman[2]; and Samuel Johnson regretted that the scheme assigned too great a share of concord and perseverance to human nature.[3] Swift himself was to boast that a subsidiary recommendation of the *Project* had indeed been carried out.[4] He meant seriously everything he said in it.[5]

There are hints for Swift's scheme in the works of his master Sir William Temple.[6] But what immediately set him writing was

---

[1] Williams I. 139. [2] No. 5 (21 Apr. 1709). [3] *Life of Swift.*

[4] Davis II. 61, n. *; cf. *Examiner*, 24 May 1711 (no. 42). Actually, this was an old recommendation, going back at least to 1688, though Swift claimed it as original with him: see Every, p. 42.

[5] There is an incredibly earnest parallel to Swift's scheme in the *New Statesman*, London, 26 May 1956, pp. 588–9, a proposal that the members of the royal family should encourage an attitude of 'social responsibility' among the 'upper classes' by reforming their own social pattern.

[6] See especially 'Of Popular Discontents', *Miscellanea* III. 25–30.

more likely a royal proclamation 'for the encouragement of piety and virtue, and for the preventing and punishing vice'. Besides issuing many strenuous commands to persons of all levels and conditions for the avoidance of profanity and debauchery and so forth, her majesty in one passage came close to the central recommendation of Swift's dreary advice, as she declared that

> for the greater incouragement of religion and morality, we will, upon all occasions, distinguish persons of piety and virtue by marks of our royal favour. And we do expect and require, that all persons of honour, or in place of authority, will give good example by their own virtue and piety, and to their utmost contribute to the discountenancing of persons of dissolute and debauch'd lives.[1]

It is even possible that among the other incentives for concocting his simple-minded proposals, Swift hoped to recommend himself at court.[2]

Though he hardly appreciated the crippling extent of his programme's drawbacks, Swift did deal with the obvious criticism that would occur to even the sympathetic reader, that the plan might encourage hypocrisy. But instead of refuting the indictment, he hugged it to his side, saying,

> And I readily believe it would. But if one in twenty, should be brought over to true piety by this or the like methods, and the other nineteen be only hypocrites; the advantage would still be great. Besides, hypocrisy is much more eligible than open infidelity and vice; it wears the livery of religion, it acknowledges her authority, and is cautious of giving scandal. Nay a long continued disguise, is too great a constraint upon human nature, especially an English disposition; men would leave off their vices out of meer weariness, rather than undergo the toil and hazard, and perhaps expence, of practising them perpetually in private. And I believe it is often with religion as with love; which by much dissembling, at last grows real.[3]

While this statement would be hard to phrase more felicitously, its meaning is bound to appear unfortunate. As threadbare

---

[1] Dated 18 Aug. 1708, published in the *London Gazette*, 23 Aug. Swift seems to echo the essential phrase, 'distinguish persons of piety and virtue by marks of our royal favour', in his own focal sentence in Davis II. 47, ll. 14–16; cf. p. 48, ll. 26–33; p. 50, ll. 27–9.

[2] Especially if he thought, as seems likely, that Archbishop Sharp, her majesty's chief adviser for ecclesiastical patronage, was responsible for the *Proclamation*.

[3] Davis II. 56–7; my text is from Swift's *Miscellanies*, 1711, pp. 214–15.

cynicism or as muddled psychology, it is equally deplorable and naïve. But rather than explore the branches of Swift's fallacies, I should like to comment upon the relation between author and audience. Supporting the bitter or playful comedy of a great satirist, one intuitively, though illogically, expects to find some variety of radical idealism. If in place of exhilarating adherence to principle one stumbles over a makeshift compromise with self-interest, one begins to doubt the validity of the censure implicit in satire. It is one thing for Swift in the *Argument* barely to admit Tartufe as a despicable *pis aller*; it is another thing for him in the *Project* to hold up false godliness as second only to true.

From this blind alley there is no exit. So long as we read the *Argument* with our attention upon the complete author, we are bound to limit its value and smother its glow. For all his desire to appear consistent, Swift did exercise a prudence in his sober, acknowledged works which he abandoned in pseudonymous, comic satire. It is not the proposer of an academy to reform the English language who is immortal, but the author of the 'Digression on Madness'. In reading *An Argument against Abolishing Christianity*, the only aspect of the writer which we should attend to is that embodied in his willingness to sacrifice 'the entire frame and constitution of things' in order to restore true religion. Although biographically the *Project* may indeed answer the questions we ask about the person of whom the author is an aspect, in the way of literary judgment it is more likely to baffle than to help us. There is of course a discernible and fundamental bridge between the projector and the satirist; however, it leads not toward but away from genius.

VII

Our boldest paradox now stands higher than before. What is the reader to make of an *Argument* in support of a faith that is not his own? Among admirers of the essay today there can be few indeed who are not objects of Swift's gunfire. Using the conventional analysis of satire, we meet one closed gate after another. If the author's purpose is to defend the Sacramental Test, the essay is futile. If his purpose is to recommend Christianity, the essay is a set of copy-book commonplaces. If we work out the rhetorical devices, we discover mock-syllogisms which creak as they unfold. And if we were ever to be asked to estimate the influence the essay might exert upon the moral behaviour of a modern reader, we should have to treat the inquiry itself as a kind of satire.

As R. C. Elliott intimates (in *The Power of Satire*), the element of satire which belongs to imaginative literature is the element that invites not action but contemplation. The audience must be able to consider the author as a spokesman for themselves; they must regard the work as in some sense their own expression. No matter how furiously a writer may intend his poem to scold them, they must feel themselves speaking through it.

Offhand it may be difficult for us to see how the *Argument* can be the concrete expression of a relationship between Swift and us unless we treat it as a sermon. However, if we resolutely exclude the hortatory principle which to Swift of course was the excuse for writing, we can perhaps interpret the act of reading the essay as a contemplation of the author safely chastising persons other than ourselves. It is true that outside the literary frame we may be identical with those persons. Imaginatively, nevertheless, we may yet be distinct. Such an explanation can be valid only if we agree that each reader has an ambiguous attitude toward moral convention. The upper self respects conventions; the under self loathes them. Freudians make such a division between the ego and the id. If we admit this distinction, it will follow that the more the upper self dominates, the more the under self has to fume, and the strain between them will in most people impose a more or less painful burden upon their moral character, a burden that naturally wants to be eased. But to allow a free hand to the rebellious spirit would usually be to terrify the conservative and ultimately, perhaps, to destroy the whole person. Comic satire, I think, may be a way to satisfy both.

Thus the special charm of the *Argument* is that though the tone is irreverent, the objects of satire are customary ones. For this reason both of the reader's selves could feel placated. He who resents taboos may, if he pleases, listen to the fascinating tone and ignore the basic implications. He who obeys taboos may follow

[295]

the meaning and be deaf to the irreverence. I suspect that these possibilities are the reason a modern reader need never have come across the Test Act, the Trinitarian controversy, or, least of all, the *Project for the Advancement of Religion*. So long as he picks up enough clues to feel that the author has real and not imaginary victims in view, so long as he understands that the doctrine defended is important and conventional, so long as he appreciates the rashness and mockery of the tone, the essay will operate upon him.

That the subject should be a religion is crucial, for the weighty movement of this satire hinges on its dealing with the profoundest of human concerns. It is not, however, the content of the faith but its associations which make the literary work brilliant. Religion normally receives the most cautious, reverent handling. It did so in Swift's day and does so in ours. If this premise could not be shared by author and reader, the essay would now seem ineffectual. When Christianity is treated frivolously in public, the speaker is commonly assumed to be irreligious. This truism too holds for Swift as for us. At the head that mocks Christianity it is normal to fling public insults and legal penalties. This yet again was so in the eighteenth century and remains so today. In every man, finally, there will always have been the opposed parties, one who bows before icons and one who breaks them.

If we now put together these traits which appear in the work and which belong as well to the author as to the audience, we may conclude that the pleasure of reading the *Argument* is the pleasure of listening without risk while another man defies the shibboleths which we resent and fear. He mocks in our place, and we securely but vicariously enjoy the courage he displays. To protect ourselves from punishment, we align our upper selves with the moral righteousness of the speaker. Any remnant of guilt that we still feel, we may easily assign to him, letting the author punish himself, on our behalf, through the self-satire built into the structure of the essay.

If this analysis is sound, the relationship between Swift and us seems that of a double conspiracy; for we join him in mockery and in reverence; he feeds our hunger both for quixotry and for

Sancho-Panzism. Though we repeatedly, if at one remove, violate the taboos, we feel no contraint to punish ourselves; for the
conscious theme of Swift's work and the pseudo-manœuvres of his
attack give our whole person the bliss of safe self-indulgence. The
reader can feel the rash excitement of burning a jail without
losing the serene complacency of wearing a policeman's uniform.
And this is the triumph of comic satire.

Chapter Seventeen

ENGLAND, 1708–9

I. SOCIETY

Along with the frustrations that soured his dealings with statesmen and bishops during this visit to England, Swift submitted to the usual domestic interruptions of his health. Under the impressive display of energy spent on new friends, new writing, and old attempts at self-promotion there ran an opposing and often depressing current of physical discomfort. Though the information Swift preserved about illnesses in this period may seem grotesquely detailed, the humiliations of this sort that bothered him most were neither new nor diminishing. Obscure troubles with his legs seem to have been oddly chronic; and when a lacerated shin kept him indoors for over a week in April, the accident was a token of past and future bruises.[1] Like his recurrent haemorrhoids, however, this type of straightforward ailment gave Swift more embarrassment than anxiety. The bleak spring of 1709, following the terrible winter, brought the respiratory afflictions which seem a defining property of the human species, although in this article the British are allowed a special abundance. 'Head ake frequent', Swift notes in early March; and then, toward the close of the month, 'cough a week but end in a cold.'[2] Writing to Archbishop King, he confides, 'I am extremely afflicted with a cold, and cough attending it.'[3] But the common healer had its therapeutic effect, and in April Swift notes, 'cough turnd to cold, well by the 6th.'[4]

If nothing else had been disturbing Swift's body, he would perhaps never have kept such notes. But besides feeling sick, he often felt desperate, thanks to the mortifying fits of nausea and vertigo

---

[1] Williams I. 76, 80.　　[2] *Accounts 1708–9*, fol. 5ᵛ.　　[3] Williams, p. 138.
[4] *Accounts 1708–9*, fol. 6.

which had pursued and frightened him half his life.[1] These symptoms medicine had not yet recognized as due to labyrinthine vertigo, or Ménière's syndrome; and Swift misguidedly doctored them with the irrelevant treatments of violent exercise and abstinence from fruit. The winter of 1708–9 brought on such debilitating attacks that Swift jotted down a series of pathetic notes which I have arranged in order:[2]

November: 'From 6 to 16 often giddy gd help me. so to 25 less —16 Brandy for Giddiness. 2s.'

December: '—5. Horrible sick. 12 much better. thank Gd & Md's Prayers. —6. Vomit. 11d. —16. bad fit at Mrs Bartons. —16. Chair sick. Mrs Barton. 1s. 24. better, but dread a Fitt. better still to the 2nd'

January: '—21. an ill fitt but not to excess. 29. out of order. 31. not well at times'

February: '—7. Small fitt abroad Pretty well to th end & better Still'

In January he complained to Archbishop King of 'a cruel distemper, a giddiness in my head, that would not suffer me to write or think of anything, and of which I am now slowly recovering'.[3] In March he described it as a prolonged incapacity, now quite past: 'a cruel illness, that seized me at fits, and hindered me from meddling in any business'.[4] The fiercely cold weather of this winter he does not connect with his symptoms.

Swift's rational acceptance of disease in general seems different from the horror and panic with which he responded to his dizzy spells. Of course, the danger of disgracing himself in company was constantly unnerving to a man who put as high a value as Swift did upon a public appearance of self-composed dignity. Nevertheless, although medical authorities seem to make no connection between Ménière's syndrome and emotional crises, I am inclined to wonder whether the near-shame Swift felt over his nausea or vertigo may not have been symptoms of uneasiness originating in difficulties which were not exclusively physical.

[1] *Supra*, vol. I, p. 106.

[2] For the following list I have combined, in chronological order, separate entries to be found in several places. See *Accounts 1708–9*, fols. 2ᵛ, 3, 3ᵛ, 5. I have not altered the spelling etc., except to bring superior letters down to the line.

[3] Williams I. 116.　　[4] *Ibid.*, p. 136.

Certainly the various great persons on whom his career depended were delivering enough shocks to his self-respect to humiliate him, and certainly Swift would have hated to admit that such shocks could be the cause of any feelings of wounded pride. Perhaps he sometimes preferred to associate the signs of acute embarrassment with an apparently physical debility.

Unlike Swift's health, his finances, which also tended to embarrass him fairly often, seemed well under control. He was spending money at the rate of something like a hundred and fifty pounds a year, but £44 of this went to Hetty and Dingley. From his parishes, even after the costs of proxies, other fees, and curate's stipend (£30 a year) were deducted, he drew enough to cover living expenses, though he exercised many economies to do so. A desire to live, at least on the surface, as a gentleman among gentlemen collided endlessly with Swift's stinginess. For lodgings in London he paid five and a half shillings a week, sometimes less. Dinner 'at home' cost him normally eightpence. He would walk to save the price of a coach (one to two shillings) or a chair (usually a shilling) except when rain prevented him.[1]

While he economized on food and shelter, coals and candles, he did allow himself some luxuries. Coffee at fourpence a time was a common indulgence which of course gave him access to the company and amenities of a coffee-house. For supplies of tea he paid as much as twenty-five shillings (green tea) or thirty shillings (bohea),[2] not to mention three shillings for a canister and four shillings and sixpence for six cups. For a waistcoat he gave as much as thirty shillings, and for a beaver hat thirty-three.[3] Above all, he was willing to risk his cash on sociable card-games, though he was careful to tote up the amounts won or lost: his worst loss came to £1 1s. 6d., and he reckoned himself sixteen shillings ahead at the year's end.[4] If one remembers that besides receiving sizeable lump sums from the sale of Temple's papers, Swift had made investments which he did not touch, it will not seem strange that he could continue to hand out his many varie-

---

[1] *Accounts 1708–9*, fols. 2ᵛ, 3, 3ᵛ, 5.
[2] I assume the quantity is a pound, though Swift does not say so.
[3] *Accounts 1708–9*, fol. 4ᵛ.   [4] *Ibid.*, fol. 1ᵛ.

ties of charity. Yet the customary tips, or vails, to the servants in a house where a gentleman was entertained must have gnawed painfully at his budgetary conscience. Ten shillings to the Earl of Berkeley's servants was about twice as much as a week's rent.[1]

If Swift had not insisted on living in the court end of London and had not passed leisure hours with persons of high fashion, he would have lowered his expenses and felt less edgy about illness. But he wished to make a figure in the polite world, and he did not wish his figure to be spoiled by shabby clothes or spasms of groping dizziness. In elegant, friendly talk or repartee Swift found one of the deepest pleasures of his life. By exchanging Dublin for London, he intended not only to advance his career but also to gorge himself on this pleasure. Reading and writing were of course his usual amusements; but when he gave up time to ombre, picquet, taverns, and coffee-houses, he expected the games or conviviality to make avenues to conversation. More vulgar entertainments too Swift gladly enjoyed, without troubling himself about their intellectuality. He loved the common physical exercises of walking, riding, and swimming. Gardening was almost a vocation, and of course he liked most forms of travel though deploring the expense.

But Swift had no ear for music, no eye for painting or sculpture, little understanding of architecture, not the faintest interest in dancing. That he was never an amateur of the arts is one of the essential differences between his genius and the modern ideal of the creative imagination. It is not simply an apparent difference in the vocabulary of awareness, but an essential difference in taste and values. Literature for Swift amounted to the intersection of two principles: craftsmanship and morality. Artists entered his life as portrait painters, musicians as assistants in holy offices, architects as builders. In Temple, Fountaine, and Addison, Swift encountered the start of a tradition of varied esthetic experience, of authors whose sensibility is versatile and who genuinely appreciate other arts than those they practise—for whom the experiencing of art is itself a literary subject. Of this class, Gray and Walpole make perfect specimens, uniting rôles

[1] *Ibid.*, fol. 2.

Swift had sometimes opposed to one another, of writer and virtuoso. But Swift himself belongs to another class, that of Bunyan
and Johnson, for whom the moral order is all-engrossing, and
literature—which can deal with ethics more directly than any
other art—the only creative, symbolic activity that impinges
truly and without radical distortion (whether they know it or
not) upon their sensibility. In judging other arts, they are ill at
ease or beside the point. But the sombre illumination of their
human insights gives a lean, driving, durable quality to their
writing which protects it from the oscillation of fashions; and the
reader values them for the vision they impose not of taste or metaphysics but of man. In this alignment Swift agreed with several
of the literary friends who mattered much to him. It was therefore easy for him, like them, to underrate literature itself. Where
a nineteenth-century writer might complain about the time
wasted in visits and chats, and lost from books, Swift complains
about a night thrown away on a volume of Congreve: 'I looked
into it, and in mere loitering read in it till twelve, like an owl and
a fool.'[1] But he did not give up spending on books more money
than he said he could afford.

Perhaps this difference in point of view between himself and
Fountaine lies behind the bookish hoax with which he celebrated
All Fools' Day in 1709. Here one sees how much money and
attention Swift could give to the humblest source of entertainment. At a cost of three shillings he had an advertisement placed
in the *Post Boy* for 31 March, announcing an auction the following day, at Mr Doily's in the Strand, of an amazingly choice collection of rare books, prints, and antiquities. As the next number
of the paper explained, 'there was no such auction design'd'.[2]
Swift must have gone to Doily's on the First of April and listened
with a not very grown-up hilarity to the queries of the searching
connoisseurs.

To support his visits, tavern talks, and evenings of ombre,
Swift laid in a large provision of friends. His willingness to enjoy
every kind of amusement seems connected with the wide range of

[1] *Journal*, 29 Oct. 1711.
[2] *Accounts 1708–9*, fol. 4ᵛ, under 14 Apr.; Davis iv. 267.

his acquaintanceships. Some people he visited for the sake of his church or his own advancement. But mostly he chose to see whoever challenged his sympathies or gave him pleasure. In Ireland he tended to confine his intimate circle to men of his own profession. In England neither clergymen nor writers supplied more than one cluster of companions.

Although he drew few friends from the number of his relatives, Swift did not lose touch with his family, rarely though he mentions them. He especially liked to visit and give money to an obscure but agreeable cousin named Patty Rolt; he bought her a three-shilling coffee roaster—Swift liked to make his own coffee —to improve the level of her entertainment.[1] Then there were old friends in London from his Irish background. The Berkeleys often received him in town, and had him to stay with them for long visits at Cranford and Epsom.[2] Young gentlemen of Ireland, émigrés from their own estates, made friends with the sociable vicar. Among these was William Domville of Loughlinstown, whom Swift called 'perfectly as fine a gentleman as I know'—a compliment with ironical overtones.[3] Domville owned a beautiful property on the Bay of Killiney which he rarely saw. Although his grandfather was for over a quarter-century the Attorney-General of Ireland, the son liked the occupations of a man of fashion in London or abroad.[4] Swift, for all his high-minded disapproval of absenteeism, willingly cultivated the friendship of those who practised it.

There was another new friend with a history like Domville's, who was to stick to Swift for thirty years and become one of his most intimate, admiring correspondents. Charles Ford was fifteen years younger than Swift, and encouraged the teasing, fatherly sort of treatment which Swift loved to extend to his juniors of either sex. Recently, Ford had inherited his father's estate of Woodpark, half-way between Laracor and Dublin; and with it came an income of about seven hundred pounds a year.

---

[1] Visits to her are noted in the *Accounts 1708-9*, fols. 5, 5ᵛ, 6; for the coffee roaster see fol. 7ᵛ under 26 May. I assume he gave it to her because he liked to drink coffee with her.

[2] *Accounts 1708-9*, fol. 1ᵛ: ombre with Berkeley at Epsom.

[3] *Journal*, 27 Nov. 1711.   [4] Ball I. 145, n. 2; Ball's *Dublin* I. 92.

His mother was English-born, and he had been educated at Eton as well as Trinity College, Dublin; so his attachments to the two kingdoms must have reminded Swift of his own, all the more since at this time the younger man, in his aimless and light-hearted way, reverberated Swift's affection for London. While Ford and Swift could scarcely have helped meeting in Ireland, they did not become good friends until Ford came to London in 1708. There he was taken up with the pleasures of the senses and the imagination: good food, good wine, and good talk; opera, theatre, concerts; taverns and card parties. Swift had an innate fondness for well-bred gentlemen who did not let sound intellectual attainments spoil vivacious manners.[1] A remark which Swift made some years later tells exactly why he grew attached to the lazy young hedonist: 'Ford is as sober as I please; I use him to walk with me as an easy companion, always ready for what I please, when I am weary of business.'[2] The semi-contemptuous tone is like Swift's manner to his cousin Thomas years before, or to Walls, the schoolmaster of St Patrick's, at this time; and it suggests the kind of dependence which an older man does not like to acknowledge, upon a younger confidant whose inconsequence is one of his attractions. Over twenty years later another friend of Swift's described Ford, on a visit to Ireland, in a report that shows the depth this affectionate dependence was finally to reach, with Swift in the rôle of a doting provincial parent and Ford acting the self-centred, cosmopolitan son. The reporter presents Ford (by then about fifty years old) as 'one of the oddest little mortals I ever met with', and complains that 'upon the strength of being an author, and of having travelled, [Ford] took upon him not only to dictate to the company, but to contradict whatever any other person advanced, right or wrong, till he had entirely silenced them all: And then having the whole talk to himself, (for, to my great surprize [Swift] neither interrupted nor shewed any dislike of him) he told us a whole string of improbabilities.'[3]

[1] For an account of Ford, see D. Nichol Smith's introduction to his edition of *Letters of Swift to Ford*. Swift may well have known Ford's father, a good friend of Arthur Bushe; see B.M. MSS. Ad. 28,880, fols. 178, 347; 28,888, fol. 188; 28,889, fol. 215.
[2] *Journal*, 7 Mar. 1711.　[3] Ford, pp. viii–xiii; Pilkington, 1748, 1. 65–6.

But the rate at which Swift's social circle expanded testifies to his personal graces and indicates how little he had to rely on Irish ties or to feel driven by half-concealed motives. As a general charmer he not only kept the loyalty of his old patron Lord Berkeley, but he also remained a welcome guest at Lord Pembroke's house; and of course he grew so close to Sir Andrew Fountaine that many of Swift's literary manuscripts of this period have come down to us by way of Fountaine's collection. Among the ideal human types which fascinated Swift, the most dazzling and disturbing was the successful man of affairs who, like Temple, combined wit and culture with a reputation for gallantry, the gentleman who had passed his incautious youth as Swift, perhaps, would have liked to pass his own. Not till he met the glittering young Henry St John would Swift see the vision embodied with all the apparent brilliance that had illuminated it in the pages of Temple's early letters. Meanwhile, he sharpened his appetite on slighter figures. Robert Hunter, a scholarly brigadier who had just been made Lieutenant-General of Virginia, met Swift shortly before sailing for his new province and being captured on the way by a French privateer. Hunter belonged to Addison's circle and had shown some literary talent; the ladies liked him, and his religious opinions were bold enough for Swift to wonder half-seriously whether he had composed the anonymous *Letter on Enthusiasm* with which Shaftesbury was shocking sober Anglican moralists. In the remarkably witty letters Swift sent to the comfortably imprisoned Hunter we not only see the effect of Swift's contemplating a bishopric in Virginia[1]; we also observe the ebullience excited in his temperament by contact with such a character.

There was little motive of private gain to draw Swift to Anthony Henley, an old friend of Temple and Lady Giffard. Very much a littérateur and man about town, Henley possessed a government pension of £2,000 a year and a rich, aristocratic wife.[2] In the House of Commons he occupied a government seat

---

[1] Thinking his first letter had been lost, Swift reiterates in a second his desire to be made Bishop of Virginia: this is more than a wisecrack, and Hunter took the hint seriously (Williams I. 120 and n. 4, 134, 335, 362-3).

[2] Walcott, p. 194; Williams I. 101, n. 2; *Journal* I. 153, n. 45.

and made himself highly acceptable to the Junto. Naturally, he might have performed some services in aid of Swift's ambitions, but their friendship endured longer than the doctor's hopes from the Whigs. Henley's puns, repartee, and tales kept Swift entertained; and one of his best stories reappeared as both an aphorism of Swift's and an anecdote in the *Tatler*.[1]

Such men as Fountaine, Henley, and Hunter, in the extent of their social 'mobility', suggest the loosening effect of a pair of long wars upon rank and hierarchy. For a genius as cocksure and uncertain as Swift, who wished to mix with the great but not to appear a climber, it must have been exquisitely tantalizing to see so much of those who treated him as one of themselves when his profession, his Irish origin, and his income marked him as not quite belonging to their community. The realm of belles-lettres was perhaps a democracy, but its honours carried no stipend. In the convulsive outburst against profligate office-holders which closes Swift's *Project for the Advancement of Religion* we may hear a necessary antiphony to the compliments he paid a person like Henley.

Females belonged to a different department. Swift could accommodate his charms to almost every rank of womanhood. Normally, his attitudes toward them needed thinner veils than his motives with men. Among his easiest poems, therefore, are the occasional tributes inspired by ladies he liked. When he wasn't advising them, he was teasing them; with the young he acted tutorial, with peeresses he was courtly, with the comforters of statesmen he became a good listener. The Earl of Berkeley's daughter Betty was now the wife of Sir John Germain, a gentleman of doubtful ancestry, unsavoury reputation, but large estate. Marriage did not break off her fondness for Dr Swift or her willingness to argue with him; and he wrote one of his best poems in praise of her companion, Mrs Floyd. A newer acquisition, though much older than Lady Betty, was Anne Finch, whose husband was the Earl of Nottingham's brother. Swift played picquet with Mrs Finch[2] and celebrated her in a clever poem called *Apollo Outwitted*, one stanza of which shows his virtuosity

---

[1] See above, p. 242 and n. 3.   [2] *Accounts 1708-9*, fol. 1[v].

[306]

with comical rhythms and the kind of double or 'doggerel' rhyme attacked by Addison in the *Spectator*:

> Ovid had warn'd her to beware,
> Of stroling god's, whose usual trade is,
> Under pretence of taking air,
> To pick up sublunary ladies.

Swift also played cards with an attractive, gossipy spinster named Catherine Barton,[1] famous in history as the niece of Sir Isaac Newton and in scandal as the reputed mistress of Newton's friend, Lord Halifax. Although she supervised her uncle's domestic arrangements, she seems to have led an independent social career; for Sir Isaac avoided casual company, and of his eating habits Mrs Barton wrote that he would 'let his dinner stand two hours; his gruel, or milk and eggs, that was carried to him warm for supper, he would often eat cold for breakfast'. When Halifax came to die in 1715, he would leave Mrs Barton a great fortune in token of his affection and the pleasure he found in her 'conversation'.[2] Since the Newton household in St Martin's Street lay on the south side of Leicester Fields, it was easy for Swift to visit her often, either to dine or to talk.[3] She was his type of female: twelve years younger than himself, chatty and *spirituelle*, but religious and of good family.

Another partner at cards and another connection of the Earl of Berkeley was Lady Lucy, daughter of the poet Charles Cotton. She had married a baronet who was the Earl's nephew; and Swift's friendship with her seems one more dividend from his investment in Berkeley's family. Though he played ombre with her ladyship,[4] Swift was moving apart from her politically. When he no longer needed buoyant hostesses to keep him socially afloat, Lady Lucy was among those whom he willingly dropped. 'I don't like women so much as I did', he then could afford to say.[5]

The shape Swift's gallantry took seems neither Caroline nor

---

[1] *Ibid.*, fol. 1ᵛ.   [2] L. T. More, *Isaac Newton*, 1934, pp. 133, 472.

[3] During 1707-9 Swift seems to have lived in the area of Leicester Fields and the Haymarket (Williams I. 59, 61, 139).

[4] *Accounts 1708-9*, fol. 1ᵛ.   [5] *Journal*, 10 Nov. 1710.

Augustan. Though the priest as hero was a more familiar fixture
in Parisian boudoirs than in London chambers, Swift avoided the
rôle of *directeur* as deftly as that of *abbé amoureux*. He would certainly have reminded Mme de Sévigné less of Cardinal de Retz
than of her literary confidant Corbinelli, who 'voudroit bien
m'apprendre à gouverner mon cœur',[1] and who 's'est bien
diverti à . . . prouver tous les attributs de la divinité'.[2] Just as
Swift turned the style of the man of fashion against the vices it
commonly embellished, so he used the couplets of a sensualist
like Prior to praise not the body but the soul of good women.
Swift wrote many lines eulogizing ladies, marriage, and tenderness, although these verses are now seldom quoted. Among the
most charming and most widely copied are those produced about
this time on Lady Betty Germain's friend Mrs Floyd.[3] Here
humour and affection take over so far that no element of ridicule
appears. Rather, the style picks up the complimentary tone of
Swift's prose dedication of *A Tale of a Tub* to Somers, carrying it
into verse. In addition to the form of this elegant, wholly successful poem, what seems significant in it is the exemplification of
Swift's praise of women.

The structure itself seems connected with the sort of discussion
that appeared in the *Tatler* no. 3, concerning recipes for making a
poem. Here the essayist had ridiculed the 'advice' formula, by
which a poet pretended to be giving directions to a painter for
depicting the scene or action he wished to relate.[4] Instead of presenting his subject directly, the poet could present it through a
medium which automatically provided a design for his work.
From painting to tapestry was the step of a generation, and now
other possibilities were declaring themselves, each one a 'receipt
for a poem'.

Swift transforms the thing from cookery or verse carpentry

[1] Letter of 27 May 1675.　　[2] Letter of 7 June 1675.

[3] The date of composition is unknown, but Swift makes a witty allusion to Mrs
Floyd's beauty in a letter 12 Jan. 1709. The poem was first printed in Tonson's
Poetical Miscellanies: The Sixth Part, which was published 2 May 1709 (advertised in
the *Gazette*, 28 April, praised by the *Tatler*, 3 May).

[4] By way of Marvell and the 'Advice' satires of the Restoration, the scheme goes
back to *Il Trionfo Veneziano* of Businello. Cf. Addison's attack in the *Whig Examiner*
no. 2, on the use of the device in the *Letter to the Examiner*.

into a recipe for a human being. In order to praise Mrs Floyd, he pretends that Jove created her from a set of ingredients new to the life of fashion: truth, innocence, and so forth.

> Jove mix'd up all, and his best clay imploy'd;
> Then call'd the happy composition, Floyd.

It is not odd that the poem found many admirers and was often imitated; for it is one of the most refined and unexceptionable pieces of flattery written during the reign of Queen Anne. Few readers, however, noticed the paradox on which it was based. Cupid begs Jove to 'form some beauty by a new receit', but Jove does not in fact form a beauty. Morals and manners are all that Swift credits to Mrs Floyd. In keeping with his principles, while the language climbs to a strain of panegyric, there is no single reference to the subject's appearance. Although the dozen lines of the poem list well over a dozen good or bad attributes, no one of these is tied to a physical trait. All Mrs Floyd's attractions are moral or intellectual.

Such poetry is a protest against the literary and social tendency to debase women by neglecting their mental powers in compliments to their bodies. Swift implies that the whole fault with the normal attitude toward the sex was an obsession with externalities to the exclusion of mind or character. In his own view the charms of a woman did of course include her beauty. In his writing, however, he saw no reason to add further weight to a force which had already been pressed too far.

II. HESSY

Meanwhile, no other woman and no other society was ever to take possession of Dr Swift's emotions with the strength exerted by the eldest daughter of Mrs Vanhomrigh. At the very beginning of this long, long visit to England, when Swift had met the Vanhomrighs, he had cultivated them with the zest that marked his re-entry into the life of the capital. But the young Esther Vanhomrigh's mother was hardly a lure sufficient to keep him dropping in on the family; nor could the moody girl's dead father, the late lord mayor of Dublin, give any help to the doctor's present ambitions. True, Swift always liked her cousin Anne Long, whom he met for ombre at the Vanhomrighs' and also visited at her own home.[1] But if Mrs Long was an amiable 'toast' whose name Swift could toss at Colonel Hunter,[2] Miss Vanhomrigh was someone far more unsettling, though less handsome. That these girls belonged to the same set pleased Swift as providing a bridge not from the awkward one to the beauty but rather the reverse.

Yet the details of his connection with Esther Vanhomrigh have to be read back into this era from odd hints and later allusions. We do know that Swift played cards at 'Mrs. Van's'[3] and that he sometimes went to her house by coach.[4] We know that in May 1709, on his journey back to Ireland, he exchanged letters with the mother; that in June he wrote to her again but had the reply from the daughter, whom he called 'Mishessy'; and that five months later 'Mishessy' wrote to him in Ireland.[5]

We know that in a poem composed a few years after this era Swift described his first relation with Hessy as tutorial. Though the lines have no authority as an exact record of events, they at least disclose what Swift judged to be a decorous account of the affair:

> His thoughts had wholly been confin'd
> To form and cultivate her mind.
> He hardly knew, 'till he was told,
> Whether the nymph were young or old;
> Had met her in a public place,
> Without distinguishing her face.[6]

What he could not call tutorial, he called paternal:

> His conduct might have made him styl'd
> A father, and the nymph his child.
> That innocent delight he took
> To see the virgin mind her book,
> Was but the master's secret joy
> In school to hear the finest boy.[7]

---

[1] *Accounts 1708–9*, fol. 1ᵛ (20 Jan.), 3ᵛ (chair from Long's, 15 Jan.).
[2] Williams I. 133.
[3] *Accounts 1708–9*, fol. 1ᵛ. [4] *Ibid.*, fol. 5 (19 Feb.). [5] Williams V. 219.
[6] *Cadenus and Vanessa*, ll. 630–5. [7] *Ibid.*, ll. 548–53.

It is entirely possible that Swift had met Hessy's family while they were still Dubliners. Her father had made a figure of consequence in Irish affairs even before the Williamite campaigns. As far back as 1683, the young William Molyneux, about to found the Philosophical Society, had become an intimate of the Dutch merchant Bartholomew Vanhomrigh, then living in Dublin.[1] Years afterward, when Vanhomrigh, by now an alderman, came back from a retreat to England during the Troubles, he held the post of commissary-general to the army in Ireland. After the war he sat both in the Irish Parliament and on the Commission for the Revenue. As alderman and then as lord mayor of Dublin, he continued his worldly progress, and became well known to churchmen like Bishop King.[2] The ministers in Whitehall found Vanhomrigh's services more and more pleasing until in 1703 the Earl of Nottingham as Secretary of State wrote him a formal message of congratulation.[3] At the close of that year, when Dr Swift crossed the Irish Sea with a party which included Lord Coningsby, he must have heard some talk of the illness that was soon to kill Vanhomrigh. The following month, the prominent revenue commissioner died (29 December 1703). Though the end was premature, he left his wife an ample fortune (reckoned at £16,000) which she, unfortunately, did not know how to conserve.

After four more years in Dublin, the vivacious, improvident widow brought her family to London in December 1707. En route from Chester to the capital by coach, they probably ran into Swift at Dunstable, when he was coming up from Leicester by horse; for he and the Vanhomrighs seem to have halted there at the same inn. Although Swift did not at first recognize Esther —the eldest child and her mother's namesake—he always remembered that she had spilled coffee in the fireplace at Dunstable.[4] When the travellers reached London, Mrs Vanhomrigh managed to maintain or improve such connections as she had

---

[1] *D.U.M.*, p. 475.   [2] T.C.D. MS. King correspondence, nos. 428, 2328.
[3] *SPD. 1703-4*, p. 111.
[4] Murry, pp. 501-2; *Cadenus and Vanessa*, ll. 634-5; Freeman, p. 121; Williams 1. 364. From the *Accounts 1708-9*, fol. 7ᵛ, it seems obvious that Dunstable was a normal stop for Swift between Leicester and London.

already formed through her husband's career and through Dublin Castle; for among her guests were Schomberg's granddaughter and Ormonde's daughters.[1]

We know that Swift dated his intimacy with Mishessy from 1708 or earlier, because he started his memory of it with the Dunstable episode.[2] We may assume that he began the friendship as usual, by suggesting books for the young woman to read and acquaintances for her to drop. We may also assume that during those initial conversations, as in later encounters, he used to cover his attachment to her under a show of equal feeling for her younger sister, Mary or 'Moll'. Fairly soon he must have advanced to the practices which became habitual, of drinking coffee with Mishessy, or eating an orange and sugar in a room apart, of urging her to ride and walk, and reproaching her for oversleeping, of in fact succumbing where he thought he was patronizing.

Swift eventually came to praise the girl for so many virtues that one might wonder whether she possessed any at all. But even if she had not been clever, responsive, and withdrawn, he would have found her appealing for the old half-conscious reasons. He began to see Mishessy in London during his preparations for Esther Johnson's last visit to England. The presence of both women in the city at the same time must have forced him to make comparisons. Simply the fact of the same Christian name (reinforced by the mother's having it too) would have transferred enough possibilities from the older friend to the new for Swift to feel inquisitive. It was within a few weeks of Swift's own farewell to Ireland that both women had come over; and when Hetty went home, Mishessy could hardly have escaped the work of supplying some of her attentions to the disappointed doctor. Extraordinary parallels made it natural for Swift to identify this young comrade with her predecessors. If Esther Vanhomrigh stayed late in bed and grew quickly fatigued, if her spirits needed raising and she took (by Swift's austere measure) insufficient exercise, the excuse was a weakness of body which at once recalls Varina's sickly constitution and Hetty's frail health during girl-

hood. Like both those ladies, and like Jane Swift, Mishessy was
the firstborn of her parents' children; and like them, she had lost
her father before she met Swift. In fact, Mr Vanhomrigh's premature passing (an omen of the early deaths of his wife and all his
children) had left Hessy and Moll paired like Hetty and Dingley
after Temple's funeral.

The girls' mother proceeded to live with less thrift than show,
in a rather fast set of stylish ladies, civil servants, and men of
fashion. Their regular social amusements ranged freely from
card parties to sight-seeing trips, but it was talk that seemed to
form their continual recreation; and Swift's attendance as a
brilliant conversationalist meant a blessing to the ambitious hos-
tess. To the daughter of the house he meant a sudden replacement
for a missing father—a father who seems to have been too busy,
during his crowded public career, to give to his offsprings' character the steadiness which their mother lacked. Combining the
functions of moral guide, intellectual instructor, and sympathetic
(if teasing) parent, Swift must have overwhelmed the girl's
emotions.

While one needs no depth of insight to appreciate the reci-
procal charms that the new Héloise and the new Abélard disclosed to one another, the question still remains why Swift at
least did not show more reluctance before abandoning the conventional scruples. Mishessy's youth must have excited and re-
assured him at once, as Varina's and Hetty's had done. But if
Miss Vanhomrigh was seven years younger than Mrs Johnson
and twenty-one years younger than Swift, she was still quite old
enough to be a bride; while he, at forty-one, came well within the
span of eligibility. The reason for Swift's indiscretion seems the
old, naïve slogan he had taught Varina when she was Hessy's
age: viz., to rise above the paltry maxims and empty forms of a
prudence 'calculated for the rabble of humanity', to discard
those 'unhappy incumbrances which we who are distinguished
from the vulgar do fondly create to torment ourselves'.[1] The same
impulse of *hypocrite renversé* that drove him to use a libertine's

[1] *Ibid.* I. 22-3.

manner with a priest's gown also drove him to teach Miss Hessy
his favourite lessons:

> That virtue, pleas'd by being shown,
> Knows nothing which it dare not own;
> Can make us without fear disclose
> Our inmost secrets to our foes:
> That common forms were not design'd
> Directors to a noble mind.[1]

The perilous source of such rashness is the kind of integrity
praised by La Rochefoucauld: 'La parfaite valeur est de faire
sans témoins ce qu'on serait capable de faire devant tout le
monde.'[2] In his desperate flight from the temptations of *gloire*,
however, Swift turns the rule seamy side out, and acts as though
his negligence of appearances should guarantee the purity of his
motives. One might say that he ironically impersonates the style
of profligate for whom he feels the deepest contempt. In the crisis
of love, therefore, as in the pursuit of preferment, Swift exhibits
the same character that he employs as an author.

III. AFTER THE ELECTION

The outcome of the elections held in May 1708 did little to reduce
the strain imposed upon Swift's histrionic powers during his meetings with the great. A reason for the length of his stay in England
was, one assumes, a hope that the new Parliament might improve
the prospects of both the First Fruits mission and Swift's own
advancement. With the would-be invasion just past, however,
Godolphin profited from a patriotic reaction which broadened
popular support for the goverment and the war parties. Although
he had to share this advantage with the Duke of Newcastle's
associates among the Whigs, he easily beat back the peace-
mongers and the church leaders. Men like Henley and Addison
were elected, but Harley's lieutenant, Henry St John, ended up
with no seat at all. If at the same time the lords of the Junto
returned fewer M.P.s than they had controlled in the old House,
they nevertheless gained fresh strength by winning over many of

[1] *Cadenus*, ll. 608–13.   [2] *Maximes*, no. 216.

the Scots newly admitted to the Parliament of Great Britain. Sunderland called this the 'most Wig' parliament since the Revolution.[1]

To resist the aggravated force of the Junto, however, Godolphin even now did not have to fall back upon Harley, who went on coaching the Queen in secret. Still less was Godolphin inclined to turn to Rochester or Nottingham. Instead, he continued to reward co-operative Newcastle Whigs like Robert Walpole, who quickly became Secretary of War. Yet the bargaining power of the Junto had necessarily increased, and their main demands, though unchanged, did not seem outrageous to Newcastle's side. So Godolphin prepared to meet some of the terms. In this undertaking he would have had an easier task if the Queen had not deliberately blocked him. In order to fulfil the old Junto scheme of giving Somers the Lord Presidency and Wharton the Lord Lieutenancy of Ireland, Godolphin still had to compensate Pembroke, who had not, of course, stepped down yet from either of these offices. The graceful method of doing so had not altered either, but remained to make him Lord High Admiral again (for a brief term), as he had been twice under William III. Though the Earl felt naturally hesitant to surrender two incomes in exchange for one, he could be persuaded, with a liberal pension, not far in the offing, beckoning him to the comfort of retirement.

Only, of course, it happened that Prince George, the royal consort, was still enjoying the title of Admiral, having held it since his affectionate wife's accession. And Anne no more than before felt any impulse to deprive her beloved husband of his one dignity merely for the purpose of honouring those whom she most detested. Summer passed, and the opening of Parliament impended while she continued to act like her stubborn father's daughter. At last the Prince, with typical inoffensiveness, suffered a fatal attack of a chronic illness and died three weeks before the session began. Exhausted with bedside vigils, and inarticulate with grief, the childless, ailing widow let the political bargainers agree.

[1] Walcott, pp. 150-1; Trevelyan II. 413.

Rarely does Swift's fundamental optimism appear so boldly as in his judgment of how these agreements would affect him. So receptive did he feel to the possibilities of the situation that he hurried to warn Archbishop King not to fear that his taking a post from the ministry would mean any slackening of his devotion to the church:

> Upon such a revolution, not knowing how far my friends may endeavour to engage me in the service of a new government, I would beg your grace to have favourable thoughts to me on such an occasion, and to assure you, that no prospect of making my fortune, shall ever prevail on me to go against what becomes a man of conscience and truth, and an entire friend to the established church.[1]

In spite of this amazing declaration from the author of *A Letter concerning the Test*, the awkwardness which Dr Swift feared never arose to trouble him. Even if he had masked from Halifax and Somers the depth of the distrust he felt for their policies, he failed to produce any positive display of radical commitment to their régime. Though he might act the part of a sympathizer, his speeches meant less than his silences. Swift showed more discernment, at this moment, in judging the destinies of others; for he wrote to Charles Ford,

> On the Prince's death, the ministry resolved to bring Lord Sommers to the head of the Council, and make Lord Wharton Lieutenant of Ireland, therefore Lord Pembroke must be made Admirall. The thing we all reckon is determined; but Lord Pembroke is unwilling, and would stave it if he could.[2]

These important changes were indeed being ratified even as Swift sent off his letter. But more important, for both him and England, was the easy control that Godolphin, the Junto, and the other Whig cliques could now exercise over Parliament. It was a dangerous case. The efficiency with which they managed affairs together, so far from signifying that the country stood united behind the government, only meant that the government was losing touch with the people. Harley, always guiding the

---

[1] Williams I. 105; I have changed 'becometh' to 'becomes'.
[2] *Ibid.*, pp. 109–10.

Queen through Mrs Masham, knew what Sunderland, for all his ranting, failed to appreciate; and this was that most Englishmen saw little for their nation to gain by carrying on the war. Committed though the Whigs were to the principle that Spain must go to a Habsburg rather than a Bourbon, all the ministers and Marlborough together had no means of realizing this aim. By concentrating his armies in Flanders, Marlborough had hoped to bankrupt Louis at home and compel him to shut down the subsidiary in Spain. This grand strategy had in a sense succeeded; but meanwhile, King Philip had managed to detach himself and his new kingdom from his grandfather's government in France, so that the directors in Versailles no longer set the policy for Madrid.

These facts became clear to Marlborough in the course of the dark, freezing winter that brought famine to France and drove the Sun King to treat for peace. While Swift, between bouts of vertigo, was eating gingerbread in a booth by a fire on the Thames,[1] the Allies were negotiating at the Hague with the French secretary of state. Out of forty preliminary articles presented as an ultimatum by the Allies, Louis was brought at last to concede all except the demand that the whole monarchy of Spain be delivered to the Habsburg 'Charles III' within two months of the cease-fire. This requirement that he, in effect, declare war upon his own grandson was neither practicable nor decent; and Louis rejected it. Since the Allies had no alternative to suggest, the negotiations collapsed in the summer of 1709. By allowing the struggle to be renewed in this way, Marlborough, Godolphin, and the Junto seemed to verify their enemies' accusations of bloodthirsty greed for profit and power. There could hardly be a great patriotic groundswell in England to back such belligerence. Among the French, however, Louis won an immense rebound of national support for his now defensive campaign, because he made public the lengths to which he had been willing to go for peace. In other words, a united English government was now moving ahead with what could be described as an unnecessary war against a rejuvenated foe.

[1] *Ib'd.*, p. 121.

IV. PREFERMENT

During the summer of 1708, while the Prince still lived and the plan of redistributing Pembroke's offices hung fire, Swift found an odd possibility held out to him. Lord Berkeley, after seven years of retirement, might be harnessed again to work as envoy to the Imperial court in Vienna; and if he went, he would like Swift to come along as his secretary. A man whose eyes could rove so far afield as Virginia might easily contemplate the landscape of Austria. A special charm in the prospect was that it would carry Swift (so he thought) beyond the range of party artillery without producing any reflections on his clerical loyalties. The pay would amount to forty shillings a day; he might, if he pleased, find company and economy by living in Berkeley's household; and he could hope eventually to land himself in yet another court.[1] One condition he laid down nevertheless: he would not go as private employee; he insisted on a regular appointment as Queen's Secretary. Still the preliminary motions looked favourable; the customary gossip rustled and fluttered; and by the end of August a report reached Robert Harley that Swift would be sent to Vienna as Queen's Secretary. 'Lord Berkeley will follow in the spring with the character of Envoy Extraordinary.'[2]

By November this glowing expectation had turned tepid. Now Berkeley was not so sure he should go, and the metamorphoses wrought by the Prince's death were leaving the plan only a weak possibility. Anyhow, Swift found fresh chances shining before his face as the old one dimmed. So he now told the same story to the archbishop, to Charles Ford, and, most revealingly, to Archdeacon Walls:

> My journey to Germany [i.e., Vienna] depends on accidents as well as upon the favor of the court; if they will make me Queens Secretary when I am there, as they promise, I will go; unless this new change we expect on the Prince's death should alter my measures for it is thought that most of those I have credit with will come into play; but yet if they carry things too far I shall go to Vienna, or even to Laracor, rather than fall in with them.[3]

[1] Williams I. 119.   [2] H.M.C. *Portland* IV. 502.
[3] Williams I. 108; cf. *ibid.*, pp. 105, 110, 126, 128.

The agreeable fatigue of selecting alternatives among a post in England, a secretaryship in Austria, and retirement to Ireland was an ordeal Swift would have to endure only in fantasy. Over his accounts for the year beginning November 1708 he wrote, 'In suspense'; and it was not long before any newly elevated hopes were blown flat by the breath of events. Swift had confided to Ford a doubt that his 'old friends' now come to power might 'turn courtiers' and abandon him, 'which I shall not wonder at, tho I do not suspect'.[1] There was a more solid foundation to this doubt than to any forecast of benefits issuing from Sunderland or Somers.

Not a thing came of all the talk about Vienna. In January Swift admitted, with a rather strained air of equanimity, what he must have surmised with bitterness several months before: 'My Lord Berkeley begins to drop his thoughts of going to Vienna; and indeed I freely gave my opinion against such a journey for one of his age and infirmities. And, I shall hardly think of going secretary without him, although the Emperor's ministers here think I will, and have writ to Vienna.' Delivering this judgment to Archbishop King, Swift could not resist allowing himself further reflections which might remind his grace that not only the court of St James's but also the Church of Ireland had preferments to bestow; for King, with his customary but officious prudence, had warned Swift that he was a bit old to be interrupting an ecclesiastical career with an adventure in diplomacy. Swift wrote,

> I agree with your grace, that such a design was a little too late at my years; but considering myself wholely useless in Ireland, and in a parish with an audience of half a score, and it being thought necessary that the Queen should have a secretary at that court, my friends telling me it would not be difficult to compass it, I was a little tempted to pass some time abroad, until my friends would make me a little easier in my fortunes at home.[2]

A flickering possibility remained that he might return to Ireland as chaplain to the Earl of Wharton. That Swift should have lost this chance seems less surprising and is perhaps more to

[1] *Ibid.*, p. 110.   [2] *Ibid.*, pp. 118-19.

his credit than that Addison, of all the men in the world, should have thrown the lustre of his virtues over the corruptions of the Earl by accepting the post of secretary to the Irish government under his excellency—thus becoming in effect the secretary of state for Ireland. While the promotion was such that no person with Addison's ambitions could reject it, one cannot help murmuring with La Rochefoucauld, 'Les vertus se perdent dans l'intérêt, comme les fleuves se perdent dans la mer.'[1]

Swift repeatedly spoke of Addison as an intimate, if not as 'my most intimate friend'.[2] Though there was some name-dropping at work here,[3] Swift hardly seemed to exaggerate. The busy public servant, even while wrestling with the weight of duties in Parliament time, received Swift at home or met him in coffeehouses and taverns with impressive frequency. Coffee, coaches, chairs, taverns, and dinners labelled 'Adissn' spangle Swift's accounts: February 19, dinner (5s.); 21, coach (1s.); 24, tavern (2s. 6d.); 27, coach (1s.).[4] It may have been with an allusion to Swift's praise of Somers ('the sublimest genius of the age'[5]) that the secretary inscribed a copy of his *Travels* to the doctor as 'the most agreeable companion, the truest friend, and the greatest genius of his age'.[6] But only the candour of unreserved friendship speaks in the message he sent when Swift, going straight from England to Laracor, failed to call on Addison in Dublin: 'I think it is very hard I shoud be in ye same kingdome with Dr Swift and not have the happinesse of his company once in three days.'[7]

Yet this good and honourable friend found himself utterly deceived when he attributed his own complaisance to Lord Wharton. In May 1709 Addison said his excellency had made

---

[1] *Maximes*, no. 171.

[2] Williams I. 118, 119, 120 ('notre bon ami'), 129; Davis VIII. 122.

[3] Swift habitually dropped remarks to one person which he wished repeated to another. He mentions his intimacy with Addison in a manner ostentatiously casual, not only in his first and supposedly lost letter to Hunter but also in its replacement (Williams I. 119, 129).

[4] *Accounts 1708–9*, fol. 5.

[5] *Tale*, p. 23; if there is an allusion, Addison's praise must be directed to the author of *A Tale of a Tub*.

[6] Forster, p. 160. In the *Spectator* no. 135 Addison calls Swift 'one of the greatest genius's this age has produced'.

[7] Graham, p. 165 (4 Jul. 1709).

Swift one of his chaplains 'and will certainly provide for him',[1] but at the most only a meaningless honorary chaplainship was the issue. Reminiscing years later, Swift said that he had been used to tell both Somers and Halifax of his own high-church sentiments in religion, and of the dangers he thought the Whigs were drawing on themselves by encouraging pamphleteers who attacked 'the whole body of the clergy, without any exception'. In the same reminiscence he tells of calling upon the new Lord Lieutenant Wharton in order to sound him out on the First Fruits:

> It was the first time I was ever in company with the Earl of Wharton; he received me with sufficient coldness, and answered the request I made in behalf of the clergy with very poor and lame excuses, which amounted to a refusal. I complained of this usage to Lord Sommers, who would needs bring us together to his house, and present me to him; where he received me as drily as before.[2]

This meeting took place months after Wharton had picked a chaplain,[3] but the delay on Swift's side and the frigidity on the Earl's are signs that their mutual distrust was of long standing. The would-be colourless report which Archbishop King received shortly after the interview makes Swift sound like a mongoose watching a snake: here too Swift said that when he went to Lord Wharton, it was 'the first attendance I ever paid him'. The Earl was standing in a great crowd: 'I told him my business; he said, he could not then discourse of it with me, but would the next day.' But when Swift did see him again, Wharton brushed him off with careless evasions, declaring 'that he was not yet properly Lord Lieutenant, until he was sworn; that he expected the same application should be made to him, as had been done to other Lord Lieutenants; that he was very well disposed, etc. I took the boldness to begin answering these objections, and designed to offer some reasons; but he rose suddenly, turned off the discourse, and seemed in haste; so I was forced to take my leave.'[4] The recoil of

---

[1] *Ibid.*, p. 136.   [2] Davis VIII. 121.

[3] The first meeting probably took place around 21 Mar. 1709, a day or two after Swift received King's letter of 12 Mar.; cf. Williams I. 130–1, Ball I. 383. The meeting at Lord Somers's is recorded with the cost of a chair to carry Swift there, under 27 Mar. in the *Accounts 1708–9*, fol. 5^v: 'Chair Ld Sommrs Ld Wharton 1s 6d'.

[4] Williams I. 136–7.

this arrogance Wharton would begin to feel later, when his character was analysed for the commonweal by the author of the *Examiner*. But from the hints that Swift lets fall of his own early premonitions, one may perhaps imagine the sardonic expression with which he had looked at the archbishop's advice, in November 1708, that he ought to attend 'the next Lord Lieutenant' as chaplain.[1]

So confident had Swift felt of something being done for him by the Junto that he worried about the blots his reputation might suffer from rumours of his reaching a bargain with the enemies of the church.[2] Yet he had known very far ahead that Wharton was to succeed Pembroke; and if the new governor, having showered England with his silver during the elections, wished next to exhaust Ireland's incomparable opportunities for bribery and patronage, Swift knew that the nearest thing to a policy in his administration would be to encourage the Dissenters and try to repeal the Test. 'I never expected any thing from Lord Wharton', Swift said almost two years later, and 'Lord Wharton knew that I understood it so.'[3] Least of all could he expect to be made chaplain to a hard-driving politician who was assured that Swift would oppose his central aims. In believing otherwise, Addison seems to have succumbed to his excellency's notorious inability 'to refuse or keep a promise'.[4] All this does not mean that Swift would have refused the chaplainship if it had been handed to him with no special commitment demanded. It does mean, however, that he 'made no manner of application for it'.[5] Such bashfulness could not compete against the self-sufficiency of his college classmate, Lambert, who had just preached the sermon urging all Irish Protestants to unite against Roman Catholics. When the news came out that Wharton had chosen Lambert to be his chaplain, Swift went ahead with the *Letter concerning the Test*.

Meanwhile, Swift was finding it a common assumption of those he had 'credit' with that provision would be made for him in Ireland. This was when the most valuable prebend of St

[1] Williams I. 112.   [2] *Ibid.*, pp. 105, 108, 112.   [3] *Journal*, 12 Sept. 1710.
[4] Davis III. 181.   [5] Williams I. 113.

Patrick's Cathedral was held by a dying relative of the arch-bishop's. Swift wrote bitterly to Archdeacon Walls that if the living should indeed become available through the prebendary's death, he would make sure his grace learned that Swift wanted it; 'for I like it, and he told me I should have the first good one that fell, and you know, great mens promises never fail.' The man died in a few months, and as we have seen, the 'golden prebend' went to another relative of the archbishop.[1] Two days after this death, however, King wrote to Swift, urging him to try for the newly vacated deanery of Down, even though another clergyman had already applied to the Lord Lieutenant for it. The early bird happened to be Wharton's own chaplain; and by the time Swift was ready to go back to Ireland, Lambert was inevitably Dean of Down.[2]

The outcome of all Swift's manœuvres was his assured realiza-tion that one could thrive as a church Tory and state Whig only while one desired nothing of value from either party. In March he began to arrange for his retreat to an Ireland that meant exile; and he wrote to Charles Ford, who was there on a long visit,

> I believe by this time you are satisfyed that I am not grown great, nor like to do so very soon: for I am thought to want the art of being thourow paced in my party, as all discreet persons ought to be.[3]

He knew in advance how sour the wine of retirement would taste, for the wisdom achieved was only a reminder of the ambi-tions destroyed; unless he wished to amuse himself with the reflection of his admired Bussy Rabutin: 'Je suis mieux que les gens de la cour les mieux établis, en ce que j'espère et je ne crains rien.'[4]

V. FIRST FRUITS

I return now to the busy summer of 1708, before Prince George's death. Just as the essential policies of the government kept Dr Swift from serving his self-interest, so they also kept him from

[1] *Ibid.*, p. 106 and n. 3.　　[2] *Ibid.*, p. 125 and n. 1.　　[3] *Ibid.*, p. 125.
[4] Letter to Mme de Sévigné, 24 Oct. 1672.

accomplishing any good for his church. After the dispiriting conference with Lord Treasurer Godolphin, Swift let the First Fruits
vegetate. The widower Lord Pembroke was getting married to
the widowed and mature Lady Arundel. His lordship had business enough, and the rumour that he would never return to Ireland as Lord Lieutenant became louder every week. Swift meanwhile could hardly prod anyone else. 'I have not stirred a step
further', he told Archbishop King, about twelve weeks after seeing Godolphin.[1] While the doctor took time out for six weeks of
summer visiting,[2] the Earl had his wedding at St James's church,
near Swift's lodgings, and left town till November. Now the report of Pembroke's giving up Ireland was confirmed; and now
even the archbishop was growing gloomy.

Then the ashes suddenly changed to plums. Back from the
country came the remarried Earl, prepared to accept the office
of Admiral. Swift matched puns with his lordship in the old way
but also reminded him that he still had time to obtain the remission of the First Fruits.[3] Behold, the reminder was needless; for
his excellency, it appeared, had had the thing at heart, and lo,
the deed was already done. So Sir Andrew Fountaine informed
Dr Swift; so Swift wrote cheerfully to Archbishop King; and as
the last touch, Lord Pembroke told King that the Earl of Wharton himself was to bring over her majesty's letter granting the
boon.[4] Allowing himself a courtly passage on the happy event in
a letter to King, Swift could not suppress a tone of 'Look, no
hands':

> I have a fair pretence to merit in this matter, although, in my own
> conscience I have very little (except my good wishes, and frequent
> reminding my Lord Pembroke). But, two great men in office,
> giving me joy of it, very frankly told me, that if I had not smoothed
> the way, by giving them and the rest of the ministry a good opinion
> of the justice of the thing; it would have met with opposition: upon
> which I only remarked what I have always observed in courts, that
> when a favour is done, there is no want of persons to challenge
> obligations.[5]

[1] Williams I. 94–5.
[2] *Ibid.*, pp. 104, 113. In Kent he stayed with a man named Collier; at Epsom he
probably visited the Berkeleys.
[3] *Ibid.*, p. 113.   [4] *Ibid.*, pp. 114, 116–17, 123.   [5] *Ibid.*, p. 117.

And so Swift went off for five days at Cranford with the Berkeleys.[1] But the archbishop, for all his sanguine complexion, chose to let public gratitude for the Queen's benevolence wait for expression until the official order was at last transmitted. The devastating frost of the winter gave way to the miserable spring of 1709. While the peace talks began at the Hague, Swift recovered from his vertigoes. Wharton took over the Lord Lieutenancy, and Addison replaced Dodington as chief secretary. The yacht was ordered to convey the new governor to his government. But still, as the archbishop wrote to Swift, the remission of the First Fruits lay 'on the anvil'. Apprehensively, a number of bishops in Dublin clubbed to address the new Lord Lieutenant for his favour in the affair. King asked Swift to consider recovering and setting before Wharton the elaborate survey which Pembroke had received of the state of the diocese of Dublin. He also sent Swift a letter which might be transmitted to Addison concerning the First Fruits.[2]

Meanwhile, the sagacious vicar had grown doubtful himself. At the end of February he learned that Addison had received no orders relating to the grant; then a Treasury official told him that the Treasury could disclose no record of such a grant. Dr Swift, the intimate of statesmen, the veteran courtier, the expert man of affairs, had a black fit of exasperation, and began to despair of the whole project. Lord Pembroke was hard to find; neither did Swift feel much would emerge from a further talk with him. 'What perplexed me most was, why he should tell me, and write to Ireland, that the business was done (for if the account he sent to Ireland were not as positive as what he gave me, I ought to be told so from thence).' When the vicar finally did get hold of the Lord High Admiral, Pembroke's explanation was 'that he had been promised he should carry over the grant when he returned to Ireland', which he was now of course never to do. It was consequently essential for Swift to march at once to Lord Wharton's, where he underwent the corrosive treatment described already. Of course, Wharton was the last person to

---

[1] *Accounts 1708-9*, fol. 3ᵛ; Forster, p. 213, misdates this as 1708.
[2] Williams I. 130-1. The bishops sent their address on 12 Feb. 1709.

surrender so delicious a carrot to a donkey that refused to carry him. In his own good leisure he might come to the bargaining table, but the mere justice of an action would hardly tempt him to perform it. Suffocating with powerlessness, the vicar exploded to the archbishop, 'It is wonderful a great minister should make no difference between a grant and the promise of a grant.' To which one can only reply what Dr Swift himself would have admitted, that the identifying of a promise with its fulfilment is an axiom of politics.[1] The candour which Temple had used with De Witt was not proper for Swift to employ with the Junto.

Soon Parliament would rise, and there would be no excuse for the doctor to linger in Westminster. If he was to rescue any comfort for himself besides the memory of friendships deepened, he would have to turn his ambitions away from levees and ante-rooms; he would have to look at what he could effect by his unaided strength.

VI. *ETCETERA* REVISED

As usual, if the failure of his public works disposed Swift to gloom, the splendour of his talents brightened his self-esteem. No evidence of the doctor's genius cast a more visible flame than the popularity of *A Tale of a Tub*. England was buying out the fourth edition, and Ireland had supported a separate reprint. Pamphlets were devoted to it; occasional writers alluded to it; and Swift decided the book was destined to live 'at least as long as our language, and our tast admit no great alterations'.[2]

Yet the judgments of the careful critics were uneven. In spite of the welcome given the *Tale* when it was first published in 1704, there were enough cases of misunderstanding or misinformation to keep Swift angry. Some censors accused the nameless author of plagiarism, others of blasphemy; and many attributed the work itself to the wrong man. Even Atterbury, an enthusiastic admirer of the *Tale* from the first, had reflected these muddles when he

[1] Williams I. 136–7. The date of the éclaircissement with Pembroke seems to have been 19 Mar. 1709, the day Swift received King's letter; cf. Ball I. 383 and Williams I. 136–7. Cf. also above, p. 229, n. 1.

[2] *Tale*, pp. lxv–lxvi, 3 and nn. 1–3. On the reception of the first edition see P. S. Waygant in the *Library Chronicle* (Univ. of Pennsylvania), 36 (1970), 48–62.

recommended it to the Bishop of Exeter a month after the book was first published: 'I beg your lordship (if the book is come down to Exon) to read the *Tale of a Tub*. For, bating the profaneness of it in some places, it is a book to be valued, being an original in it's kind, full of wit, humour, good sense, and learning.' Since he had composed most of 'Boyle's' polemical *Examination* of Bentley,[1] Atterbury felt an inevitable delight in those Digressions which ridiculed either the great classical scholar or his colleague Wotton; and by a natural error he supposed that Christ Church, Oxford, which had given birth to the *Examination*, had also produced the *Tale*: 'It comes from Christ Church; and a good part of it is written in defence of Mr. Boyle against Wotton and Bentley. The town [i.e., London] is wonderfully pleased with it.'[2] Two weeks later he sent on a false rumour as to the authorship[3]; but almost at once he had a glimpse of the truth, and wrote, 'The author of *A Tale of a Tub* will not as yet be known; and if it be the man I guess, he hath reason to conceal himself, because of the prophane strokes in that piece, which would do his reputation and interest in the world more harm than the wit can do him good.' Still Atterbury concluded, 'Nothing can please more than that book doth here at London.'[4]

Another Christ Church man, the satirical essayist Dr William King—no relation to the archbishop—shrank so violently from the charge of being the author of the *Tale* that he published a denunciation of the book in the form of a letter dated 10 June 1704.[5] Although Swift later said that King had written this 'against the conviction of his talent',[6] the pamphlet sounds candid enough. After proclaiming that he had no part in the composition, King goes on to condemn its profanity, indecency, coarseness, and obscurity. The author, he says, had searched ancient texts for their 'lewdest images'; he had demonstrated a gift for 'cursing and swearing'; he had loitered on dunghills. Yet King admits the book was 'bought up by all sorts of people, and

---

[1] *Supra*, vol. I, p. 228.

[2] Letter to Bishop Trelawney, 15 Jun. 1704, in Atterbury's *Epistolary Correspondence*, ed. J. Nichols, 1784, III. 203.

[3] *Ibid.*, p. 214 (29 Jun.).   [4] *Ibid.*, p. 218 (1 Jul.).

[5] *Some Remarks on the Tale of a Tub*, 1704.   [6] *Tale*, p. 11.

every one was willing to make sense of that which had none in it originally. It was sold not only at court, but in the city and suburbs.' Following a heavily sarcastic discussion of the author's identity, King, like Atterbury (his contemporary at Christ Church[1]), gives a hint of the scandalous truth: 'What if after all it should be a parson; for who may make more free with their trade? What if I know him, describe him, name him, and how he and his friend talk of it, admire it, are proud of it.'[2]

Months later, Congreve sent an opinion to a correspondent in Ireland who had found the *Tale* disappointing. Writing, I suppose, before he knew the author was Swift, Congreve compares his own views with those of still another friend whom he calls 'Bottom' and who had praised the book without reserve:

> I am of your mind as to the *Tale of a Tub*. I am not alone in the opinion as you are there; but I am pretty near it, having but few on my side; but those few are worth a million. However, I have never spoke my sentiments, not caring to contradict a multitude. Bottom admires it, and cannot bear my saying, I confess I was diverted with several passages when I read it, but I should not care to read it again. That he thinks not commendation enough.[3]

This kind of carefully adjusted disapproval by a man of letters would perhaps have troubled Swift more sharply than the complaints made on other grounds; but the passage also demonstrates how eagerly the *Tale*'s merits were being debated half a year after its publication.

Apart from the admiration expressed for Swift's wit, the most common reaction was some variety of the astonishment felt by Atterbury that a clergyman should have stood behind such a work. The 'lower' the religious principles of the reader, the deeper ran the horror. When the latitudinarian, Whiggish Sir Richard Blackmore published his impressions of the *Tale* much later, in 1716, his tone of scandalization drew support from his political and class sympathies; and the treatment he had suffered in the *Battle of the Books* was hardly calculated to soften his indignation.

---

[1] Johnson says Smalridge, yet another contemporary of Atterbury at Christ Church, also disclaimed authorship of the *Tale* (*Life of Swift*).

[2] King, *Some Remarks*, sig. A4, pp. 9, 10, 12–13, 16, and *passim*.

[3] Letter to J. Keally, 28 Oct. 1704.

By 1716, when Blackmore's *Essay on Wit* appeared, Swift was a dean, Queen Anne was dead, and the Whigs' King George sat on the throne:

> Several in their books have many sarcastical and spiteful strokes at religion in general, while others make themselves pleasant with the principles of the Christian. Of the last kind this age has seen a most audacious example in the book intituled *A Tale of a Tub*. Had this writing been published in a pagan or popish nation, who are justly impatient of all indignity offered to the established religion of their country, no doubt but the author would have received the punishment he deserved. But the fate of this impious buffoon is very different; for in a Protestant kingdom, zealous of their civil and religious immunities, he has not only escaped affronts and the effects of publick resentment, but has been caressed and patronized by persons of great figure, and of all denominations. Violent party-men, who differed in all things besides, agreed in their turn to shew particular respect and friendship to this insolent derider of the worship of his country, till at last the reputed writer is not only gone off with impunity, but triumphs in his dignity and preferment. I do not know that any inquiry or search was ever made after this writing, or that any reward was ever offered for the discovery of the author, or that the infamous book was ever condemned to be burnt in publick: whether this proceeds from the excessive esteem and love that men in power during the late reign had for wit, or their defect of zeal and concern for the Christian Religion, will be determined best by those who are best acquainted with their character.[1]

In this clumsy vituperation one hears, still quivering, the anger which suffused men like Blackmore as they went through the *Tale* in the year of Blenheim. (It is sad to have to observe that the author of *The Campaign* praised Blackmore's *Essays*.[2]) Clergymen especially found the satire profane and obscene. Naturally enough, Swift's victim Wotton, the low-church protégé of Burnet, was among the most furious. In 1705 he brought out a third edition of his *Reflections upon Ancient and Modern Learning*, the book which Swift had shredded with ridicule in both the *Battle of the Books* and the *Tale*. To this new edition Wotton added a 'Defense' of his *Reflections* which included *Observations* upon the *Tale*. Once more Swift found his work condemned as immoral and godless. In the course of the polemic, Wotton expounded Swift's allegory

---

[1] *Essays upon Several Subjects*, 1716, p. 217.   [2] *The Freeholder*, no. 45.

at some length, treating each element as illustrating the author's 'contemptible opinion of every thing which is called Christianity'.[1] For instance, from the passage satirizing predestination Wotton quotes Jack's remark that the post which his nose bumped into had always been meant to be bumped: 'Providence [says Jack] thought fit to send us both into the world in the same age.' Then Wotton comments, 'This is a direct prophanation of the majesty of God.' By disregarding Swift's continual use of irony and parody, Wotton can attribute to the author's simple convictions all the indecencies which really belong to the objects of Swift's attack. So Wotton necessarily finds the *Tale* to be 'one of the prophanest banters upon the religion of Jesus Christ, as such, that ever yet appeared'.[2]

These misreadings would have been enough to send blood to the head of a man endowed with more than Swift's patience. But Wotton went further. He declared that the main ingredients of both the *Tale* and the *Battle* were borrowed by Swift from other authors; and, what was perhaps yet more cutting, he surmised that the *Tale* had been written by Temple and prepared for publication by Swift's cousin Thomas.

The question of authorship bothered Swift a good deal, but never so acutely as with *A Tale of a Tub*. He felt immensely proud of his masterpiece but fully aware of the threat it offered to his advancement in the church. How to claim the recognition due a genius without losing the rewards of a priest was an issue he never comfortably resolved. What he did in effect was to suppress all the evidence of his connection with the book, so that nobody could ever prove he produced it, but at the same time to let it be known indirectly that he alone had created the whole work. By such devices he perhaps enabled his patrons to argue that no proof existed of Swift's responsibility; but he did little more. A confidential agent of Robert Harley's, writing in the summer of 1708, referred to Swift not by name but simply as 'the author of the *Tale of a Tub*'.[3] Yet the following spring Swift was still equi-

---

[1] *Tale*, p. 322.   [2] *Ibid.*, p. 324.

[3] H.M.C. *Portland* IV. 502 (21 Aug. 1708), letter from Erasmus Lewis, who may already have known the Vanhomrighs, inasmuch as he was named in several of their wills.

vocating with his then good friend Ambrose Philips: 'I desire, whoever admires or blames the book, you will not think me to have any concern in the matter, tho since people will in spight of my disarming suspect me for an author, I cannot but be better pleased with those who think me so to my advantage.'[1] To rationalize his inconsistency, Swift once told Esther Johnson, 'They may talk of the *you know what*; but, gad, if it had not been for that, I should never have been able to get the access I have had; and if that helps me to succeed, then the *same thing* will be serviceable to the church.'[2] (I'm afraid the logic here does small credit to Swift.)

The truth, I think, is that as usual he hated to admit in public (though he did in private) how frantically he desired fame. From the time of his earliest preserved letters and poems we see Swift yearning to be widely known as a literary genius. It almost looks as if he sometimes tried to punish himself for this impulse by attaching his finest talents to the most disgraceful materials. By menacing himself with exposure, he would thus, perhaps, have enforced the anonymity which he thought should satisfy a gentleman.

These intentions further suggest how the strictness of his early training collided with Swift's consciousness of his own powers. Brought up to consider his essential character as naturally corrupt and to consider the corruption as rooted in his flesh,[3] Swift used the imagery of bodily filth as the hallmark of his most brilliant creations. By a strenuous effort of self-denial he ensured that few of his contemporaries could appreciate his talent without regretting the way he employed it.

Ultimately, this low opinion of himself (which I assume was implanted in childhood) becomes the source of his love of parody, impersonation, and irony. By assuming a false identity, Swift protects his true, weak self. In imagination, any fault committed by a pseudonym leaves the true author blameless. The impurities of the *Tale* Swift can unconsciously charge to the invented fools who supposedly tell it, just as the oaths of Peter leave no stain on his creator. Thus the satirist, like his reader, can in-

[1] Williams I. 128.   [2] *Journal*, 7 Oct. 1710.   [3] *Supra*, vol. I, pp. 38-40.

dulge tastes which he would rather not admit to possessing, and yet feel no guilt for exhibiting them.

It is thanks to such mutually opposed inclinations that caution keeps alternating with prudence in Swift's handling of his responsibility for the *Tale*. After the author had, in his own words, 'all along concealed himself from most of his nearest friends',[1] he sat down and wrote an 'Apology' for the *Tale* that he thought of publishing in a collection of his miscellaneous works. Among the 'subjects for a volume' in the list Swift drew up about October or November 1708, he included an 'Apology for the &c'.[2] Although he never went through with this scheme, but instead made the 'Apology' part of the prefatory matter for a fifth edition of the *Tale*, one can only feel astonished that he so much as contemplated such a revelation. By issuing an 'Apology' along with acknowledged works like the *Project for the Reformation of Manners*, he would have been openly boasting of what he had sedulously concealed.

The changes which Swift made in the original text of the *Tale* when he revised it for the new edition were slight. The most significant are those he would least have wished to be noticed, viz., certain alterations which met objections raised by the contemptible Wotton. Thus 'a conscience void of offence towards God and towards man' was clipped to 'a conscience void of offence'. 'Genitals' was euphemized to 'pudenda'. '*Cunnus*' disappeared from a Latin quotation. The passage on predestination to which Wotton had taken particularly severe exception, underwent some refining; for 'Providence' became 'Nature' in one place and 'Fortune' in another. An allusion to 'cloven tongues', marked by Wotton as blasphemous in the *Mechanical Operation of the Spirit*, was left standing in that work, which Swift pretended to disown anyhow; but a similar allusion in the *Tale* was cancelled in favour of 'marks of grace'.[3]

As if in revenge for being compelled to retrench these youthful freedoms, Swift proceeded to ridicule Wotton in a brand new

---

[1] *Tale*, p. 6.   [2] See Appendix B.

[3] *Tale*, pp. 71, 147, 165, 193, 202. In all these cases the reading of the first edition ought to be restored, though modern editors have not seen fit to do so. See *ibid.*, p. xxii, n. 1.

way. He took two dozen of the interpretations of the religious allegory which Wotton had provided in his *Observations* and turned them into footnote commentaries printed in the new edition of the *Tale* and signed with Wotton's name, thus making the victim into an apparent editor of the satire. At one point Swift even added a further note correcting Wotton's, and signed this correction with the name of a scholar long deceased.[1]

In the earlier editions of the *Tale*, there had been marginal glosses supplying explanations or sources, and sometimes written as parodies of Bentley's scholarship. To the fifth edition Swift added not only the footnotes drawn from Wotton but also many composed by himself, though purporting to be from an editor's hand. In these, besides serious explanations, he gave a few mock-comments, such as, 'I do not well understand what the author aims at here.'[2] But among the most interesting notes biographically are those which reinforce evidence to be found in earlier editions, that the *Tale* was mainly composed about 1696: e.g., 'This was writ before the Peace of Riswick'; or, 'This shows the time the author writ, it being about fourteen years since those two persons were reckoned the fine gentlemen of the town.'[3] Such remarks deserve unusual attention precisely because many parts of the *Tale* were indubitably written two to six years after that date.[4] In other words, Swift was trying to separate himself as far as possible from responsibility for the *Tale* even while he wished to claim the merit of writing it. Often the ostensibly explanatory notes have the same defensive purpose, with Swift pointing out that various shocking statements are to be read as attacks narrowly focused on the Dissenters—that is, I should say, not as profane allusions to Christianity in general. For example, when Jack in the *Tale* argues that his father's will is the philosopher's stone and the universal medicine, Swift notes, 'The author here lashes those pretenders to purity, who place so much merit in using scripture phrase on all occasions.'[5]

---

[1] *Ibid.*, p. 73, n. †.   [2] *Ibid.*, p. 159.   [3] *Ibid.*, pp. 208, 86.

[4] Harth, pp. 6–11; *Tale*, pp. xliii–xlvii. If my analysis is sound, it is unlikely that Swift composed much of the *Tale* before 1696, since that is the earliest year he indicates, and he wished to set the date as far back as possible.

[5] *Tale*, p. 190. (I do not accept 'phrases', a common emendation.)

The gap between impersonation and identity finally vanished when Swift came to feel that notes of all sorts were too confining a medium for justifying his satirical schemes. It was so as to transform his defensive strategies into an offensive rebuttal that he composed the separate 'Apology'[1]; and in this truculent gesture he at last abandoned the pose of bookseller, editor, annotator, or dedicator. Anonymity still remained, but whoever created the *Tale* was by his own confession also the maker of the 'Apology'.[2]

It is a disjointed harangue, obviously scratched out during bursts of quick-rising anger. Swift insists throughout that men of wit and taste have nearly all approved of his book and that the fault-finders have been animated by malice. He admits that the *Tale* contains a few strokes which deserve reproof; but these he attributes to the youth of the author (twenty-nine at least, by his own reckoning!), or else to the publication of an uncorrected copy without the author's approval, and so forth: none of the excuses carries much weight, and all are misleading. He complains that *The Mechanical Operation of the Spirit* was printed without his knowledge and in an absurd, mangled form. He scolds the clergymen who have attacked his book, and declares that the religious allegory only exposes the follies of Dissenting fanatics or of superstitious Papists. He complains that passages written in irony or parody have been considered as simple discourse; that innocent passages have been wrenched into profane meanings. He insists that the work is entirely original and nowhere plagiarized, and that the true author is quite unsuspected. Above all, he refutes and denounces Wotton, whose similarity to himself must have made his judgments very hard to take. On Wotton's character and work Swift performs the very operations which he accuses the victim of performing on him: for he misinterprets Wotton's motives, arguments, tone, and style.

[1] The date of composition of the 'Apology' is indicated by its appearing on Swift's list of October or November 1708 and its being signed 3 June 1709. One need not suppose, with Guthkelch and Nichol Smith, that the piece was written just before the signature date (*Tale*, p. xx); it might have been substantially completed at the time Swift drew up the list. See below, Appendix B. In the summer of 1710, however, writing for publication, Swift said the 'Apology' was composed 'about a year ago' (*Tale*, p. 20).

[2] Cf. such expressions as 'The author cannot conclude this apology' (p. 18).

The essay has immense biographical value. When Swift prevaricates here, as he frequently does, the intention cannot be to trick or hoax the audience in a humorous way. Neither can it be to mimic a person whom he wishes to ridicule. It can only be to misguide the inimical, censorious critic. Swift is fabricating evidence because he feels afraid of punishment. He wishes to condemn his younger self for writing and his mythical friends for publishing what Swift as a man of mature years feels most proud of. To disown what one admires, to boast of one's shamefullest act, to destroy the conventions by which one willingly lives—these paradoxical longings are the springs of both Swift's character and his art. Harshly disciplined as a child, the person accepts and absorbs the imposed laws that condemn his peculiar being. To preserve the creative self from the conventional self, he then resorts to impersonation, blaming the iconoclastic deeds upon the 'other' person. Yet he wishes to label the achievement of the pseudonymous criminal as his own; and so he breaks through the irony or parody with the violence of expression and foulness of imagery that have come to mean *Swift*.

To even the score with the conventional priest, the comical artist invented the style of self-ridicule which became the highest form of Swiftian humour. Just as the priest chastised the free artist through the strictures of a work like the *Project for the Reformation of Manners*, so the artist kicked back at the priest through the doubly ironical mimicry of the *Argument against Abolishing Christianity*. This act of posing as a man who pretends to be (but in fact is not) what one admires, is a yet subtler irony than posing as a man who is truly what one detests.

In contrast with such pyrotechnic wit, the 'Apology' represents as naked a style as Swift could command; simple sarcasm, simple evasion are here, but nothing more involved. Apart from the use of the 'Apology' in the analysis of Swift's genius, therefore, it supplies a test of his purely literary skill. Of course, he rises to this test with a power that depends on language and syntax, with a few adornments of rhetoric. His arguments may be weak; his propositions, misleading; his tone, uncomplicated. But the prose remains clear and strong; the phrasing sounds fresh but

M   [335]

idiomatic, the words humble but exactly chosen. The proportion of verbs to substantives is high; particles and connectives are numerous but never superfluous. Energy and personality are everywhere. Swift gives to the most direct utterance an articulated individuality which radiates one man's character and yet has no eccentricity. One feels the immediate presence of a gifted writer:

> This apology being chiefly intended for the satisfaction of future readers, it may be thought unnecessary to take any notice of such treatises as have been writ against this ensuing discourse, which are already sunk into waste paper and oblivion; after the usual fate of common answerers to books which are allowed to have any merit. . . . Men would be more cautious of losing their time in such an undertaking, if they did but consider, that to answer a book effectually, requires more pains and skill, more wit, learning, and judgment than were employ'd in the writing it. And the author assures those gentlemen who have given themselves that trouble with him, that his discourse is the product of the study, the observation, and the invention of several years, that he often blotted out much more than he left, and if his papers had not been a long time out of his possession, they must have still undergone more severe corrections; and do they think such a building is to be battered with dirt-pellets however envenom'd the mouths may be that discharge them.[1]

A great prose style is self-sufficient and needs no improvement from oratory or spectacle to make its quality felt. Nevertheless, besides inserting new notes and prefixing the 'Apology', Swift decided to embellish the fifth edition with illustrations. For this purpose he ought to have received some admirable designs, since he took advice from Sir Andrew Fountaine, a connoisseur with a highly developed taste in the plastic arts. As it turned out, the sketches provided through Fountaine's agency were full of life, elegantly composed, and reminiscent of the best tradition of scene-painter's art. The final engravings, however, followed them only at a remote distance; these give no pleasure in themselves, although they do provide one or two informative details.[2]

After settling all such essentials, Swift still faced the arrangements for publication, to be adjusted with his bookseller. If the first edition had appeared under the visible imprint of John Nutt,

---

[1] *Tale*, pp. 9–10.   [2] *Ibid.*, pp. xxv–xxviii.

the responsible person even then had been Benjamin Tooke, whose name stands on the titlepages of all but the earliest of Swift's signed editions of Temple's works and also on the *Project for the Advancement of Religion*.[1] So cautiously had Swift dealt with Tooke in the secretive handling of the original *Tale* that, as we have just observed, the true and single authorship was not at once recognized by people to whom Swift had not disclosed it. From Wotton's and Atterbury's statements we know that rumour gave more or less of the composition to Temple, to Swift's cousin Thomas, and to others still farther off.[2] On Swift, who had indiscreetly lent Thomas a piece of a manuscript copy, the gossip left a scorching mark. Though he had, during his visit to England in 1703-4, managed to see Thomas, this business seems to have ended the acquaintanceship which had once been an intimacy. Writing about an alleged *Key* to the *Tale*, which the piratical Edmund Curll had published, Swift gives us a last, hat-to-shoe sneer at the comrade of his youth. Even here the concealment that always veiled his most scandalous masterpiece does not allow him to identify it except by an *etcetera*:

> I cannot but think that little parson-cousin of mine is at the bottom of this; for, having lent him a copy of some part of, &c. and he shewing it, after I was gone for Ireland, and the thing abroad, he affected to talk suspiciously, as if he had some share in it. If he should happen to be in town, and you light on him, I think you ought to tell him gravely, that, if he be the author, he should set his name to the &c. and rally him a little upon it: And tell him, if he can explain some things, you will, if he pleases, set his name to the next edition. I should be glad to see how far the foolish impudence of a dunce could go.[3]

Keeping to his rule of holding back an English publication until he had left the country, Swift met Tooke in a London tavern during March and April 1709[4] and then cleared up fur-

---

[1] *Ibid.*, pp. xiii–xiv. Although Goodwin's imprint appears with Tooke's on Temple's *Letters* III, it was Tooke who paid for the copy; see Rothschild n. 2256.

[2] *Tale*, pp. xiv–xviii.

[3] Williams I. 165–6. Thomas Swift is mentioned several times in the *Journal to Stella*. See also below, p. 338, n. 6.

[4] 23 Mar., 27 Apr. See *Accounts 1708–9*, fols. 5ᵛ, 6. They must also have discussed Temple's *Memoirs* III and Swift's *Miscellanies*.

ther details by correspondence after departing for Leicester.[1]
From his mother's house he sent Tooke the 'Apology' in June.[2]
But then all proceedings quietly fumbled to a halt. Many months
passed. In Ireland, Swift had second thoughts about the 'Apology' and asked the publisher to return it for alterations. Fountaine felt dissatisfied with the cuts for the illustrations but left
town without changing them. Tooke wanted instructions about
how to place the notes. Swift got sick. It began to look as though
some pirate like Curll might get out an annotated edition before
Swift could stop tampering with the copy for Tooke, who meanwhile grew anxious and impatient when the author failed to
answer a worried message. At last Swift patched the whole
assemblage up; the engravings were got ready; and the fifth
edition went to press late in 1710.[3]

For all this haste and bother, the volume that came on sale
toward the end of the year[4] was a falling away in fundamentals.
Setting aside the pictures, the notes, and the 'Apology', one can
only lament what happened to the text. In several places the compositor dropped whole lines which the proofreader failed to restore. Since the new edition was set up from the fourth, it retained
many typographical corruptions that had invaded the text during
successive printings, and added a few of its own. The most substantial revisions made by Swift amount to a weakening of the
force of his satire for the sake of avoiding dangerous ambiguities.
When he refined the style, he tended to make it less colloquial and
more formal.[5] For a sound text of *A Tale of a Tub* exclusive of the
footnotes and the 'Apology', one cannot do better than to start
from the first edition.[6]

[1] Ball I. 384–5 (to Tooke, 19 May; 6, 13 June; from Tooke, 16 Aug.; to Tooke,
13 Sept. 1709).

[2] *Tale*, p. xx.

[3] Williams I. 165–7. For further details of the preparation of the fifth edition, see
Teerink, no. 222.

[4] No newspaper advertisements have been discovered.

[5] E.g., 'written' for 'wrote', p. 22, l. 4, not noticed by Nichol Smith or Davis.

[6] Professor Robert M. Adams has produced evidence corroborating Swift's suspicion that his cousin Thomas claimed to have a hand in writing *A Tale of a Tub*: see
his 'Jonathan Swift, Thomas Swift, and the Authorship of *A Tale of a Tub*', *MP*. LXIV
(1967), 198–232.

VII. TEMPLE'S *MEMOIRS* III

At the same time as he was furtively reframing the *Tale of a Tub*, Tooke was more openly looking after the printing of the final volume of Sir William Temple's works edited by Swift. In the middle of April 1709 he paid Swift forty pounds for the 'original copy' of the so-called 'Third Part' of Temple's *Memoirs*.[1] Six weeks later, the book went on sale.[2]

For posterity of course the volume has none of the explosive power of Swift's own writings; but for Temple's editor even this publication meant a limited sort of explosion. Nobody had less reason than Swift to believe that the contents of the volume would seem innocent. Otherwise, he would hardly have let so much time pass before releasing it. The dangerous ingredients were not added by Swift. He contributed little besides a preface that was designed to ingratiate him with the government and to defend Temple against censures which had been passed on an earlier (so-called 'second') volume of memoirs printed during the statesman's lifetime. The self-serving portion of Swift's preface is a paragraph of half-hearted compliments to Sunderland, Rochester, and Godolphin, which Swift claims to have deduced from Temple's text. Though little or no basis for them exists there, one feels that Swift is refusing to grant the ministers any excuse for overlooking his ten years' persistence in waiting for a lift. But the bulk of the preface consists of a sturdy and admirably loyal defence of Temple's matter and style. Swift shows that his master had been compelled to push himself forward in the narrative because he had dealt with events in which his was the determining rôle. Swift excuses Temple's Gallicisms of expression as the natural consequence of a long confinement to the language of diplomacy. To those concerned with Swift's character the preface will be an instructive demonstration of his fidelity to his patron. Ten years after Temple's death Swift was still eulogizing him both here and in the 'Apology' for the *Tale*.[3] Since the end of

---

[1] Ball I. 150; Rothschild, no. 2259. Of course, no 'First Part' was ever published.

[2] Advertised as published 'This Day' in the *Daily Courant*, 23 June 1709; also, without comment, in the *Post Man*, 25 Jun.

[3] Swift points out what I think has been ignored, that in the 'Appendix' to

the *Memoirs* meant the end of his two decades' labour on Temple's *œuvre*, the preface is in a sense a disciple's farewell to his mentor. Soon Swift would be publishing his own miscellanies and writing his own memoirs.

In the opening paragraph of the preface Swift tells the reader why he had postponed the publication of the manuscript. Although his reasoning is shady, the central and dangerous truth is clearly exposed, that passages of these memoirs 'might give offence to several who were still alive'. The situation was gingerly all round. Temple told stories about the late Earl of Essex that made his lordship out to be a venal front for the most irresponsible, sinister diplomacy. The Earl's widow, Lady Essex, was not only 'still alive'; she happened to be the friend of Lady Giffard and the aunt of the Duchess of Somerset. Naturally, Temple's sister would not have wished either Lady Essex or certain other persons of honour who were brushed by the revelations to suspect that she had connived at the printing of the *Memoirs*. Yet the original manuscript now belonged to her ladyship, although she did not keep it hidden but let some of her acquaintances borrow it. Swift, who possessed the authoritative copy made under Temple's direction, wished to have the profit of the book and could not feel secure against pirates so long as an alternate version was extant and even in limited circulation. He asked Lady Giffard to surrender her original to him, but she, not surprisingly, preferred to deny his request sooner than give any ground for complaint to her intimates. Understanding the source of her uneasiness, Swift decided to issue his authorized text without sending her any advance notice, because the inevitable effect of such a warning would have been to elicit an expressly negative command which he in turn would have been forced to defy.[1]

Instead of preventing a quarrel, Swift's *savoir-faire* only magnified one. Temple's *Memoirs* III came out at the end of June 1709, while Swift was travelling back to Ireland. Soon afterwards Lady Giffard had an advertisement placed in the *Post Man*, the Lon-

---

Memoirs III the note on Sir William Jones is by Swift, not Temple; so is the note on Temple's speech concerning Tangiers and the Exclusion Bill.

[1] Williams I. 154–7.

don newspaper, declaring that Swift had acted without authority and that his version of the *Memoirs* came from an 'unfaithful copy'. While resting on this prevarication, she did not have to feed her wrath in solitude. Her ladyship's rich, powerful, life-long friend, the Duchess of Somerset,[1] was among those who con-doled with her. In a letter of strenuous sympathy, the Duchess clears Lady Giffard of every unkind imputation and recalls how all their circle had agreed that the manuscript was unfit to be made public so long as Lady Essex survived. She cannot, the Duchess intimates, believe that Swift acted unknowingly; on the contrary, his thorough awareness of the facts 'makes his having done it unpardonable and will confirm me in the opinion I had before of him, that he is a man of no principle either of honour or religion'.[2] This was not to be the last evidence her grace would receive of Swift's lack of principle where she herself was involved.

Swift received full information on the affair. He and Lady Giffard wrote back and forth[3]; and his friends sent him the printed advertisement. (The printer of the *Post Man* happened to be Dryden Leach, a cousin of Swift's.[4]) When he asked the editor of the *Post Man* for an explanation of the defamatory announce-ment, he was told that her ladyship's nephew, Lord Berkeley of Stratton,[5] had inserted it, and that the editor had refused to let it appear more than once, though asked to do so by Berkeley's agent. The effect on Swift was intense. Perhaps his deepest pride lay in the consciousness of his own moral integrity. His apparent and rash indifference to what people thought was of course the outward sign of this inner confidence. Living, moreover, by a pro-fession in which his status depended immediately upon his good name, Swift reacted with a complex fury to any slur upon his character. In this case his indignation was enlarged by one of his fundamental virtues, the anger he felt at seeing great persons take unfair advantage of their place in order to abuse or oppress

---

[1] *Supra*, vol. I, pp. 105-6.

[2] Longe, p. 248, normalized, because Miss Longe's transcriptions are not reliable; some of her words may be complete misreadings.

[3] She wrote a letter received 6 Aug. 1709; he answered 17 Aug.; she replied in a letter received 6 Oct. (Williams v. 219).

[4] *Journal* I. 73.   [5] No relation to the Earl of Berkeley.

humbler beings. One of the main sources of the pleasure he took
in his literary talent was its effectiveness as a weapon enabling a
person like himself, of a middling station, to fight against such
oppressions. Ripe with resentment, therefore, he prepared a
counter-advertisement which he still judged to be 'wholly consistent with religion and good manners'[1]; and his mortification
can be smelled burning through the complaint he delivered to
Lady Giffard:

> Your ladyship says, if ever they were designed to be printed, it must
> have been from the originall. Nothing of his ever printed in my
> time was from the originall; the first Memoirs was from my copy;
> so were the second Miscellanea: so was the Introduction to the
> English History: so was every volume of Letters, they were all
> copied from the originals by Sir William Temples direction, and
> corrected all along by his orders; and it was the same with these last
> Memoirs: so that whatever be printed since I had the honor to
> know him, was an unfaithfull copy if it must be tryed by the
> originall. Madam; I pretend not to have had the least share in Sir
> William Temples confidence above his relations, or his commonest
> friends; (I have but too good reason to think otherwise). But this
> was a thing in my way; and it was no more than to prefer the
> advice of a lawyer or even a tradesman before that of his friends, in
> things that related to their callings. Nobody else had conversed so
> much with his manuscripts as I, and since I was not wholly illiterate,
> I cannot imagine whom else he could leave the care of his writings to.
>
> I do not expect your ladyship or family will ask my leave for what
> you are to say; but all people should ask leave of reason and religion
> rather than of resentment. And will your ladyship think indeed that
> is agreeable to either to reflect in print upon the veracity of an inno-
> cent man. Is it agreeable to prudence or at least to caution, to do
> that which might break all measures with any man who is capable
> of retaliating.[2]

He later swore he would not see Lady Giffard again until she
begged his pardon.[3] Since this consummation was hardly probable, one may suppose that Swift welcomed the opportunity to
end a tiresome connection.

The rarity of this sort of personal quarrel is to be noticed during

---

[1] I have not found the numbers of the *Post Man* that carried either the original
advertisement by Lady Giffard or Swift's answer.
[2] Williams I. 155–6.   [3] *Journal*, 21 Sept. 1710, pt 2.

Swift's nineteen months in England. It was a period of expansive conviviality for him, of many friendships quickly made and easily deepened. If he had older friends awaiting him at home, few of them seemed so fascinating as the brightest of those he would leave.

VIII. RETURN TO IRELAND

With what expectations the adversary of Lord Wharton prepared to withdraw to a rural Irish vicarage with a congregation of ten listeners, one can learn from his own sighs; for he wrote from London to Charles Ford in Dublin, promising to visit him the next summer:

> Whether I am agreeably entertained here or no, I would not tell you for the world, unless I were assured I should never be blesst again with a return to Ireland. I must learn to make my court to that country and people better than I have done, thô to lett you into one secret, (and it is a great one) I doubt at my return I shall pass my time somewhat different from what I formerly did, wherein I will explain my self no further than by telling you of the humor of a gentleman I knew, who having eat grapes in France, never lookt up towards a vine after he came back for England. And if you find I pass for a morose man, find some excuse or other to vindicate me. But the fault will not be Ireland's, at least I will persuade my self so; for I am grown so hard to please, that I am offended with every unexpected face I meet where I visit, and the least tediousness or impertinence gives me a shortness of breath, and a pain in my stomack.[1]

A man does not like to raise himself laboriously to a mountain-top celebrated for its vistas only to learn that the inn is full up, the grounds are closed to non-residents, and he must take the waiting coach back to a grimy dormitory below. Swift's reserves of money were dwindling again. The miserable end of the First Fruits negotiation was not needed to finish any tentative thoughts he might have been supporting of a much longer residence in England. So far back as January, he had remarked that Addison had 'half persuaded me to have some thoughts of returning to Ireland'[2]— I suppose he meant, in order to look for a post there under the guiding hand of the new government's first secretary. If Addison,

1 Williams I. 125-6.   2 *Ibid.*, p. 118.

turned patron, could hope to get for Steele the undersecretary-
ship he had himself just vacated,[1] perhaps he could also help
Swift to secure a preferment suited to the aspirant's abilities. He
might also, unfortunately, fail in both attempts. Before he could
really test such powers, Addison had to get on with his own preparations. By the end of the first week in March, he was ordering
the official yacht to be got ready for Wharton, while Swift was
telling two correspondents that the vicar of Laracor would return in the summer.[2] A month later, Addison left London, seeing
Swift just beforehand and carrying a letter from him to St George
Ashe. Almost at once, Addison attached himself to Wharton's
travelling party; but not till Maundy Thursday did they arrive
in Dublin.[3] Swift sent a letter after him en route—'the only good
entertainment' that Addison found in Chester—and he praised
him in messages to Archbishop King and Bishop Ashe. With
England becoming the desert of Swift's hopes, Addison might
give even Dublin some fleeting verdure. The day after landing,
he wrote back to Swift, 'I long to see you.'[4]

Meanwhile, Swift was engaged in what looks like a succession
of farewells, taking care of last-minute chores, and paying business visits. A number of these miscellaneous affairs appear in his
accounts. The First of April, he saw Halifax, on what he would no
doubt have described as a fool's errand. This was about the time
the *Vindication* of Bickerstaff appeared, with ironic appropriate-
ness. As if to prove that no disappointments could stifle his
instinct for foolery, Swift, shortly before this juncture, had indulged himself in a further extension of the honest astrologer's
occupation, for he published a piece of cryptic doggerel, accompanied by a preface and interpretations, called *A Famous Prediction of Merlin.*[5] Right in the face of his unwanted departure, his
humorous vitality showed its underlying strength. The new half-
sheet of nonsense pretended to be a prophecy made in the reign
of Henry VII. By employing archaistic language and typo-

---

[1] Smithers, p. 144.   [2] Graham, p. 129; Williams I. 125, 128.
[3] Smithers, pp. 150–3; Ball I. 383.
[4] Graham, p. 133; Williams I. 118, 131, 138; Ball I. 383.
[5] The copy in the Harvard College Library is endorsed by Narcissus Luttrell as
bought for a penny, 21 Feb. 1709.

graphy, and by imitating the antiquarian scholarship of a virtuoso like Fountaine, Swift gave the hoax enough verisimilitude to
deceive not only the innocent Samuel Johnson but some historians of printing as well. The *Famous Prediction* is like Tom
Brown's parodies of Partridge; and a similar 'prophecy', set up as
a text of doggerel verse in black letter, with interpretive notes,
had been issued by the almanac-maker Benjamin Harris in a
supplement to *Merlinus* for 1704. But the first seed of Swift's hoax
probably came from a prophecy printed, translated, and expounded by Temple in his *Memoirs*. Such prophecies, Sir William
had said with proleptic irony, are sometimes manufactured by
'great wits' who divert themselves by 'writing things at random,
with the scornful thought of amuzing the world about nothing'.[1]
In order to make his own trick send people on an actual fool's
errand, Swift says he will leave the original work with the
printer, 'to let anybody see it that pleases'. If Halifax heard
about the joke, he had no reason to disapprove of it, since the
force of the anti-Bickerstaffian prophecy is to praise Marlborough
and accept the ministry's plans in Spain.

Late in the month, Dr Swift called on Lord Treasurer Godolphin (21 April, chair, one shilling). He also saw the Berkeleys but
could not accept a kind, warm invitation from the Earl to make a
final visit to Cranford over the Easter weekend. The *Project for the
Advancement of Manners* had just come out, and Berkeley praised it
sincerely. At the end of April, Swift passed a day with Steele, who
was to take care of any letters that came for him after he left;
Steele's *Tatler* had just begun to appear, with contributions by
Swift and a puff for his *Project*. Thursday, 5 May, was to be the
date of his setting out; and on the Tuesday he paid up his last five
weeks of rent.[2]

---

[1] *Memoirs* II, pp. 160-2. Swift was amanuensis for the copy from which the
book was printed. Swift's mock-note on 'toune of stoffe to fattyn londe' (i.e., Marlborough) was probably suggested by Temple's etymology of Betow as 'fat earth'
(p. 163). Although he professed disdain for such prophecies, Temple discusses another one in the same volume (pp. 382-3). The printer to whom Swift assigns the
Famous Prediction was an actual one, at work in London the year Swift pretends the
prediction first came out (Davis II. xxiv, n. 2). Cf. Teerink, note following nos.
499-502.
[2] *Accounts 1708-9*, fols. 6, 7; Williams I. 127-30, 139.

Also on Tuesday a tiny symbolic drama was enacted. Going yet once more to Halifax's house, Swift saw a little French book on a table. He begged it as a gift, and the noble lord surrendered it, whereupon Swift asked him to keep in mind that this was 'the only favour he ever received from him or his party'.[1] Halifax was to hear from the vicar again and most flatteringly before he vanished into Ireland; for Swift angled for preferment in England almost until he boarded the boat. This moment, however, seems like a final clasping of hands to mark a release from a contract. Halifax must have recalled the moment eighteen months later, when he began to read the *Examiner*'s judgments upon his party.

Now Swift set out for Leicester, to stay there for a length of time which suggests that he knew his mother's health was sinking. Travelling by the usual route, he reached her house in two days—from Rose Inn to St Albans, Dunstable, Newport, Northampton, and Harborough. Not till the morning after Whit-Monday did he move again. For almost six weeks he remained, delayed if not by his mother's illness, then by his own complaint of the piles, a disease 'incommodious for riding'.[2] For entertainment during the long visit, he took notes upon an old Roman mosaic floor, to send Fountaine, and haggled for some Saxon coins. He stayed with Sir George Beaumont, M.P. for Leicester, whose home, Stoughton Grange, lay outside the town; and he visited nearby Thurmaston.[3] He also wrote dozens of letters, including some to Steele with material for the *Tatler*. If the 'Apology' for the *Tale of a Tub* carries the right date at its foot, Swift finished it here; certainly he wrote four times from Leicester to the publisher Tooke.[4]

Tuesday, 14 June, he was to take off across country on the westward half of his journey. The day before, he dispatched a whole flurry of letters, among which he so far yielded to the naggings of ambition as to appeal in a painfully unshy manner to both Hali-

[1] Forster, p. 252; Craik i. 206. The book was *Poésies chrétiennes de Monsieur Jollivet*; Swift recorded his remark on the flyleaf.

[2] *Accounts 1708–9*, fol. 7–7ᵛ; Williams i. 139–40.

[3] Ball, followed by Williams, reads Throckmorton and misinterprets a note on 'Walls' or 'Wills' man (i.e., servant) to mean a relative of Archdeacon Walls (Ball i. 153, n. 2; Williams i. 140, n. 5).

[4] Williams v. 219.

fax and Somers. The letter to Halifax is unhappily preserved, and forces one to groan alternately over the indignities imposed on genius by a system of *carrières demi-ouvertes aux talents*, and over the weakness of the reverend vicar's resistance to such promptings. Swift thought that his uncle Thomas's old friend Dr South was dying; and he wanted Halifax to encourage Somers to recommend Swift for the livings held by the invalid. The letter carrying his request is a gateau of forced compliments leavened by allusions to Horace and Maecenas. Praising Halifax for his encouragement of 'deserving men' (like himself), Swift says, 'You are the most injudicious person alive, because, thô you had fifty times more witt than all of us together, you never discover the least value for it, but are perpetually countenancing and encouraging that of others.'[1] At this point one may take note of Swift's comment on Halifax a quarter-century later: 'I never heard him say one good thing or seem to tast what was said by another.'[2] In a postscript to the letter of eulogy Swift delivers his immediate message but employs, with grating impropriety, the pose of a blasé man of fashion: 'Pray, my lord, desire Dr South to dy about the fall of the leaf, for he has a prebend of Westminster which will make me your neighbor, and a sinecure in the country, both in the Queen's gift; which my friends have often told me would fitt me extreamly.' Absolutely nothing was the product of so much cleverness, if only because Dr South lived on for another seven years. But Halifax's answer, I think, does even more damage to his reputation than what Swift's receives from his own style of address; half the short letter will convey the well-hung ripeness of the whole carcass:

> Mr Addison and I are enter'd into a new confederacy, never to give over the pursuit, nor to cease reminding those, who can serve you, till your worth is placed in that light where it ought to shine. Dr South holds out still, but he can not be immortal, the situation of his prebendary would make me doubly concern'd in serving you, and upon all occasions, that shall offer I will be your constant solicitor, your sincere admirer, and your unalterable friend.

On this Swift wrote a suitable endorsement: 'I kept this letter as

[1] *Ibid.*, I. 143.   [2] Davis v. 258.

a true original of courtiers and court promises.'[1] But he also arranged, by another hand, a kind of appendix to his clever post-script, and this rather dilutes the protest of the bitter endorse-ment. The third volume of Temple's *Memoirs* was about to be published, with Swift's preface irrelevantly praising Sunderland and Godolphin. Among the directions that Swift sent the pub-lisher from Leicester was a request to inscribe several copies as from the editor and to present these to some of the chief ministers then in power. Although the letter to Tooke is lost, two of the books are extant, one for Sunderland and one for Somers, each presented 'By his most obedient and most humble servant The Publisher [i.e., editor]'.[2] In among the prefatory praises, never-theless, was planted a subtle anticipation of a change ahead, for with the bouquets to Sunderland and Godolphin, Swift had included a casual mention of Rochester, their enemy, as another minister whose capacities Temple had praised.[3] And although no smallest sign is preserved of Swift's ever yet having poked outside Whig territory in his hunt for favour, he did say later that Harley had already 'made some advances' to him.[4]

Now it was time for Swift to depart once more. June 14 and 15 he spent on the road to Chester, never to see his mother again. This route was as familiar as the way north from London had been. He went through Burton-on-the-Hill, Stone, and Nant-wich. In Chester he was able to visit a once-beautiful cousin and to play picquet with the Earl of Meath; but it was still two weeks before he sailed. Delays in travel never pleased Swift. He bought some books, wrote to Addison, and waited for a passage. On the other side of the Channel, Addison was trying to arrange for him to come over on a government sloop, but Swift left before the message reached him. His boxes were carried to Parkgate on Monday, 27 June. He himself sailed on Wednesday, before dawn, in a ship from Dawpool, on the river Dee. They left at three in the

---

[1] Williams I. 143, 150.

[2] Sunderland's copy is Rothschild no. 2408; Somers's is in the Harvard College Library (Houghton EC 7. Sw 551. A 711m); Halifax's, in the Forster Coll. Of course, 'publisher' means 'editor', and 'bookseller' means 'publisher' in Swift's language.

[3] Davis I. 268. [4] Williams I. 173.

morning, perhaps to avoid privateers; and they disembarked at
Ringsend seven o'clock the next morning, after lying for a night
in the Bay of Dublin.[1]

[1] *Accounts 1708-9*, fols. 1ᵛ, 8; Williams I. 144-5 and notes. The once-beautiful
cousin was presumably Abigail Greenvil or Greenfield; cf. Ball II. 46, III. 363;
Journal, 2 Sept. 1710.

Chapter Eighteen

MORE SUSPENSE
JULY 1709–AUGUST 1710

I. ADDISON AND PPT

There were people Swift did want to see in Dublin and people he didn't. Addison and Hetty were there, but so was Wharton. Already Swift wished to detach himself from a man whom he could only condemn as a moral being and who was far likelier to use Swift than to be used by him. Yet the statesmen allied to Wharton remained the ones Swift relied on, and he could not openly challenge the Lord Lieutenant without seeming to oppose persons he respected. Unfortunately, his own account of what happened is coloured by a later determination to make his original motives quite clear; and while the real drama is that of a country vicar's rejecting the coercive blandishments of the most powerful officer in his kingdom, the actual details are less stark than Swift remembered them.

Thus when Swift crossed over to Ireland, he still carried England with him. As if to defer the realities of Dublin and to prolong the contact with the life behind, he went directly from the dockside to Laracor, remaining from Thursday to Sunday without seeing anybody.[1] But nostalgia was not the sole cause of this weekend of delay. Lord Wharton was also involved. Swift said later that though he had taken care to 'be private' about his authorship of the *Letter concerning the Test*, several persons in England had guessed the truth and told Wharton their suspicions, whereupon Swift saw him no more till he went to Ireland. Somers had still wished the two men to reach a *modus vivendi*; so when the doctor came to take his leave, the Lord President asked him to carry a letter from his lordship to the Earl. Swift says that he

[1] *Accounts 1708–9*, fol. 8.

'absolutely refused', but that Somers then had the letter left at Swift's lodgings in London. So far, Swift's account seems accurate enough. But he goes on to say that on coming to Ireland, when he went into retirement at Laracor 'without seeing the Lieutenant, or any other person', he intended to send Somers's letter to Wharton by post; and this seems improbable. If Swift passed even four days at his country parish, he could easily post a letter while there, and we know he did not. It is also unlikely that he would have cut himself off from his intimates for a very long time. Even supposing that he might have had Esther Johnson come and stay at Trim, he would not have utterly sacrificed the pleasure of Addison's company when he knew the secretary would be leaving Ireland at the end of the summer.[1]

Next, Swift says it was the 'incessant entreaties' of his friends— presumably reaching him in the country—that compelled him to change his mind and come up to town. Once there, he did go to the Castle after all and deliver the letter, following which he 'immediately' withdrew. It seems to me probable that though he would have been glad to ignore the Lord Lieutenant, his conscience as well as his friends assured him that he would help rather than injure Wharton, and accomplish no good for himself, by acting the sulky Achilles; and so he performed the simple formality at the Castle.

But the story goes on. 'During the greatest part of his government', says Swift, 'I lived in the country, saw the Lieutenant very seldom when I came to town, nor ever entered into the least degree of confidence with him or his friends, except his secretary, Mr. Addison, who had been my old and intimate acquaintance.'[2] Now we know a fair amount about the period Swift means, and this information doesn't quite bear him out. The fact is, Swift could dodge Wharton only up to a point, especially since Swift was apparently made an honorary chaplain and preached before his excellency.[3] When Swift arrived in Ireland, Wharton had about twelve weeks remaining of his first residence as Lord Lieutenant. During those summer days Swift made

---

[1] Yet he apparently did just that a year later; see below, p. 373 and n. 2.
[2] Davis VIII. 121–2.   [3] Ball I. 188, n. 1; Graham, p. 136.

many brief visits to the Ashe brothers at Finglas, near Dublin; he saw Charles Ford at Wood Park on the way to Laracor; and he visited the dowager Lady Shelburne.[1] Even at Laracor, however, he seems to have remained no more than a few days on one trip during August.[2] In Dublin he had lodgings with a Mr Curry in Capel Street 'over against the Ram' and near Mrs Johnson. Through the summer he seems to have used his lodgings regularly. In town he renewed his links with a good many persons, ranging in opinion from his excellency's secretary to Lord Abercorn, leader of the opposition in the House of Lords.[3] Thus he was not in the country during the 'greatest part' of Wharton's residence, though he was so during most of Wharton's tenure of office. Yet he indubitably meant to keep out of the Earl's way. Addison remarked, three weeks before Swift's coming to Dublin, that his excellency had not missed prayers in the Castle chapel once over the eight weeks since he had arrived, although that very morning (Whit-Monday) he had happened to start on a short recess of horseracing.[4] Like most sons of Belial, Wharton found as much business at the church as at the track; but even the capital of the kingdom had not so much space that he and Dr Swift could always miss each other. Their formal and casual connections mean only that Swift, whatever his impulses, submitted to protocol, and not that he paid any regular attendance on the Lord Lieutenant.[5]

Although Swift was to spend more than a year now in Ireland, his strongest wishes and his deepest decisions were to be guided still by events in England. From an initial gloom of spirit and sickness of body he would rise in a quickening movement to new hope at the end of the year. Meanwhile, with his characteristic resistance to spiritual malaise, he used all the friends he owned in order to make his days agreeable. Addison was now an eminent personage as well as a private comrade. Besides holding the chief secretaryship, he had become an M.P. in both England and Ireland. His brother on the other side of the world had been chosen

---

[1] Presumably at Slane, co. Meath.   [2] *Accounts 1708–9*, fol. 10.
[3] Williams I. 165; *Accounts 1708–9*, fol. 8ᵛ.   [4] Graham, p. 149.
[5] The Drapier says he saw Lord Midleton in Wharton's presence (Davis x. 10).

President of the East India Company and had died leaving Joseph his heir; and when the estate was settled, the secretary would be a man of wealth. Some who wished to make their interest with him thought of approaching the statesman through his friend the vicar. Thus Edward Southwell in London had praised another Irish official to Swift so as to improve the man's standing with Addison.[1] For his own part, Swift had early told Archbishop King that he planned to influence Addison's judgment, and 'set him right in his notions of persons and things'.[2] On his first day in Dublin, Swift got Addison's charming letter, already quoted, promising to call that morning with Bishop Ashe: 'I think it is very hard I shoud be in the same kingdome with Dr Swift and not have the happinesse of his company once in three days.'[3] Only a fraction of the hours they spent together from July to September are recorded in Swift's accounts, but the number of these is impressive. Dublin gave Addison fewer alternatives to Swift than London could; and we find 'tavern', 'dinner', 'chair', not to mention 'wine and olives' connected with Mr Addison week upon week. Besides their parties in town, they went to Finglas together, and Addison became an intimate of the Ashes.

Swift also introduced his great and good friend to 'Ppt' (for 'poppet', I suppose), which is a cipher he came to use for Mrs Johnson. No recent intimacy could have the deep and complex meanings for him that she embodied, and the return to Ireland was sweetened above all by her companionship. Just as Swift brought out the affability in Addison, she seemed to bring out the mildness in Swift. Though he remembered Hessy Vanhomrigh and wrote to her, it is in his praises of Ppt that he describes what he was trying to make of the girl in England. For in addition to good breeding and a well-turned figure, Mrs Johnson possessed the most durable of charms. For Swift, these gifts amounted to a surprising compound of the pliable and the masculine. Though she had a modest teachableness which he judged proper to her sex, she avoided the 'little disguises' and 'affected contradictions' that some men found agreeable in women.[4] Mrs Johnson lacked

---

[1] Ball I. 178–9, n. 4.   [2] Williams I. 118.   [3] Ibid., p. 145.   [4] Ibid., p. 23.

the petulance which had troubled Swift in Varina. In differences of opinion she was never stubborn; and those who were, she commonly treated not by opposing but by encouraging their misapprehensions, for this 'prevented noise and saved time'.[1]

Besides avoiding romantic affectations, she tried to be independent, well read, and courageous, without losing the gentleness that then suited a lady. Once when she was living in an isolated neighbourhood, a gang of burglars tried to break into the house. There was a boy among the servants but no man. While he, Dingley, and the maids withdrew in a fright, Mrs Johnson tiptoed to the dining-room window, carrying a pistol. To prevent her from being seen in the darkness, she wore a black hood. Quietly raising the sash, she aimed straight at one of the thieves and shot him with so much care that he died the next day.

Mrs Johnson enjoyed conversation and made no display of shyness. But she did not speak much at a time, and refused absolutely to discuss fashions, scandal, or immoral topics. Her visitors were more commonly men than women, particularly clergymen. One reason was that she enjoyed reading and talking about books which women seldom read: history, especially of Greece and Rome, though also that of England and France; also books of travel; and the higher levels of recent or contemporary poetry and essays. According to Swift's interested report, she understood Platonic and Epicurean philosophy, could point out the errors in Hobbes's materialism, and exhibited in general a refined literary taste. Thus, as Swift omits to mention, she accurately reflected the leanings of her instructor.[2]

Although Mrs Johnson and Mrs Dingley always lived in lodgings, they kept three servants: a man (or boy) and two maids. Because their joint income never rose very high, Ppt could not entertain company so often or so handsomely as she would have wished. But what resources they possessed, they managed with enough economy to pass as being more prosperous than they were.[3]

When Swift said his dearest friend charmed Mr Addison, he probably did not exaggerate. She had no absence of mind in

[1] Davis v. 235.   [2] *Ibid.*   [3] *Ibid.*, p. 232.

conversation, Swift reports, nor was she given to interruption, neither did she show an eagerness to put in her word by waiting with perceptible impatience for another speaker to halt. Not only did she speak in a pleasing voice, using plain words, but she did not hesitate when her turn came, except when new faces made her reserved.[1] Such a character ought to have commended itself to the Spectator. Not only does Swift say that the secretary, on being introduced, appreciated her virtues at once. He also hints that Mrs Johnson felt sufficiently impressed by Addison's example to imitate some parts of his behaviour.

II. EVENINGS IN TOWN

Swift did not wait for Addison to leave before picking up the lines of his many attachments in Dublin. Like anyone who has experience of both capitals, he found London less sociable than what he described to Ppt as 'your town'.[2] In his native city there were fewer men who had to be pleased and more who had to please him. As Swift aged, he committed the human mistake of giving the pleasers far too great a proportion of his vacant hours. Thomas Walls, the humble Archdeacon of Achonry, was one of those most eager to serve him. Though Walls could mix with any other company Swift liked, he needed little attention and no respect. Swift had 'hedge' friends who were not worth naming, and Walls belonged to a category just above them. A stratum higher were ranked a number of clergymen with respectable benefices and good educations but submissive manners: Anthony Raymond, the rector of Trim, was rather full of his own scholarship and good breeding; but he felt delighted to see Swift whenever Swift would see him, and in conversation he seldom crossed his brilliant friend. The Wallses and the Raymonds were regularly kind to the Johnson–Dingley connection, entertaining them with Swift and easily accepting his strange relationship with them. In the circle of Swift's ordinary friends this obliging habit was a prerequisite to his goodwill. Some people whom he might

[1] *Ibid.*, p. 230.
[2] *Journal*, 11 Oct. 1710; the point is of course that she was born in England.

otherwise have dropped he cultivated because of their loyalty
to the ladies. John Stoyte, a prosperous merchant and alderman, lived at Donnybrook with his Welsh wife and her unmarried sister. Card parties made up of the Stoytes, the Wallses,
and Swift's ladies were common, especially on winter evenings.
Either on or a bit above Swift's own level in Dublin, he had to
place the Dean of St Patrick's, John Stearne. Though a bachelor,
Stearne liked his food and enjoyed society. The dean's kindness
to the ladies made the prebendary of Dunlavin feel grateful.
Swift was used to nights when the mixture came complete: 'the
dean, and Stoyte, and Walls, and Ppt at play, and Dingley and I
looking on'.[1] As for Stearne's fond patron, Archbishop King,
Swift met him in numberless affairs of business or ceremony, but
not so often at private entertainments. Yet even his grace can be
found at a Saturday's game of ombre when the vicar won over
eleven shillings[2]; and at various times lesser bishops also appeared.[3] For conviviality and dignity combined, however, Swift
liked the Ashes. With a bishopric, a good hereditary estate, and
some excellent church livings to share among them, they could
afford a hospitality which added solid pleasures to the appeal of
their good nature and good sense.

During all these sessions at the card-table the preferred game
remained ombre. At Laracor and Trim, Swift played picquet
with Mr Percival and a Mr Barry; he sometimes played tables (or
backgammon) with another country parishioner, Garret Wesley, or he endured basset with Dr Raymond. But normally the
choice was ombre, then in high enough fashion for Pope to centre
the *Rape of the Lock* upon it. Here is Swift's comic parody of his
own habit of teasing Ppt over a typical evening of ombre:

> Why, the reason you lost four and eight-pence last night but one at
> Manley's, was because you played bad games: I took notice of six
> that you had ten to one against you: Would any but a mad lady go
> out twice upon Manilio, Basto, and two small diamonds? Then in
> that game of spades, you blundered when you had ten-ace; I never
> saw the like of you: and now you are in a huff because I tell you this.
> Well, here's two and eight-pence half-penny towards your loss.[4]

[1] *Journal*, 27 Jun. 1711.   [2] *Accounts 1708–9*, fol. 1ᵛ.
[3] Cf. *Journal*, 5 Oct. 1710.   [4] *Ibid.*

III. HIBERNIAN PATRIOTISM

For all the life he drew from cards and other bagatelles, it was still the crises of church and state that galvanized Swift's energies. What the political weather felt like either at the Castle or in Parliament and Convocation, he knew from his usual reporters; and if the intensity with which he delivered his reactions distinguished him from the bulk of men, yet the creed he professed did not. In the way of constitutional theory there could be even less of a gap between Whig and Tory in Ireland than in England. For all the speciousness of the tinted lights which Swift liked to throw upon party terminology, he was quite sound to insist that Revolution principles and the Hanoverian succession belonged as truly to the high-church Tories as to the low-church Whigs in a kingdom where all the Protestants together formed a small rock in a whirlpool of Roman Catholics. Whatever Addison might report or Sunderland might hallucinate about Jacobite sin facing Junto salvation in Dublin, most of the manœuvres there, whether in Parliament or Convocation, can be accounted for by a few intelligible (if narrow) convictions that Swift shared with fellow clergymen and Anglican laymen but which the Earl of Wharton opposed. As far as principles go, both Parliament and Convocation were searching for conditions that the American colonists were to demand after the Seven Years' War. Although the Irish Protestants felt no magnificent impulse to extend the force of their reasoning to the rights of the native Roman Catholics, they did argue that their own Parliament in Dublin should have the same powers for its kingdom that the Parliament in London exercised there. Upon this general desire, Convocation tried to impose the refined principle that the ecclesiastical assembly in Ireland should further enjoy the same independence of the secular government that the clergy of England demanded.[1] Since the bishops not only sat in the House of Lords (which they attended more responsibly than their lay brethren) but also constituted the Upper House of Convocation, they could blow cold upon the seething priestliness of the clergy with the same breath they used

[1] Cf. Bishop Lindsay's speech, 15 Aug. 1709, as reported in Graham, p. 180.

for warming the Erastianism of the Commons. In both Parliament and Convocation was maintained the attitude of resistance to the growth of Dissent, though the English Lord Lieutenant normally dissipated the discouraging effects.

Not that Lord Wharton possessed nothing at all in the way of a serious, positive policy. Perhaps the venomous report of the scandal-mongering, Jacobitical Thomas Hearne did not stray far from strict truth when he represented the private aims of the Lord Lieutenant as the accumulation of forty-five thousand pounds 'by the most favourable computation', through less than two years of salaries and perquisites, bribery and extortion.[1] This fixed aspiration did not prevent him, however, from formulating grounds for his higher decisions. Primarily, he would of course have liked to extend a legal toleration to the Dissenters and to revoke the now five-year-old Test Act. As early as the day Parliament met, however (eight weeks before Swift returned to Ireland), Addison reported that Wharton was taking particular care to avoid any sign of a hope to repeal the Test, 'which would immediately set all things aflame'.[2] The case of the unauthorized Presbyterian congregation at Drogheda, still under prosecution by Primate Marsh himself, gave continued wrenches to the viceregal withers, but the minister remained in jail. When the eccentric Lord Abercorn, in a motion against his own principles, proposed a toleration for the Dissenters, it was rejected so violently by the House of Lords that it did not re-emerge during the session.[3] Archbishop King, who often gave help to the government, led the attack on toleration.

The rest of Wharton's programme was unsurprising and less explosive: to have supplies voted quickly and freely, and to invent fresh humiliations for the Roman Catholics. Furthermore, if he could not relieve the Dissenters by legislation, he did hope to strengthen their hand by importing some of the Lutheran refugees fleeing from the German Palatinate to England.[4] Yet as a legislative leader Wharton found his strength failing because

---

[1] Hearne, *Remarks and Collections* III (1889), 100. For Swift's charges of corruption, see Davis III. 181–4, 231–40. For Addison's admission of Wharton's corruption, see Graham, p. 197.

[2] Graham, p. 134.   [3] *Ibid.*, p. 137.   [4] Smithers, p. 160.

rumours kept floating across from Westminster that the country had turned against the Junto and that the queen trusted Godolphin less than Harley. Even within the circle of the five great Whig lords, present power was breaking the unity that had cemented them while in opposition. Sunderland found the Lord Lieutenant of Ireland ineffectual, and his excellency quickly balked at the insinuations of Britain's Secretary of State.[1]

Even so, the Lord Lieutenant had ample resources to manage most of his Parliament. Giving up the Test, he proceeded to show off his innocence. In order to deaden distrust, he talked over his aims with men of every colour, assuring them that their sacred shield would be left inviolate. Such mild omens, of course, hardly discharged him of his responsibilities to the Dissenters themselves; and when he opened Parliament, he made the most of the need for a good understanding among 'all the Protestants'.[2] The effect of the gesture was limited because on the Lords' committee to draw up an address of thanks, seven out of eleven members were bishops, among them both Ashe and King.[3] In their draft, consequently, stood a clause which Wharton's supporters disliked but which nevertheless passed; it was a defiant negation of his wish; for it defined the Established Church as the 'best bulwark' of Protestants against Papists, and remarked that:

> all our fellow-subjects are treated with so much tenderness, under her majesty's most gracious government, that we hope they will never have just reason to complain of any uneasiness, but find it their true interest, to join in supporting our happy constitution, in church and state.[4]

The Commons, at the same time, were producing less smoke but more fire. In their address of thanks they showed a happier compliance with his excellency's recommendations; and they dwelt, with a singularity that could not have been better timed or less spontaneous, upon their governor's zeal to unite all Protestants. Coached by the Brodricks and by William Conolly, they gracefully hinted that the high-churchmen were Jacobites; they recalled the happy combination of Anglican with Presbyterian

[1] *Ibid.*, pp. 157, 159.   [2] *J.H.L.I.* II. 243.   [3] *Ibid.*, p. 245.
[4] *Ibid.*, p. 247.

against James II; and they asked for a full liberty of all loyal sects to practise their worship.

The golden fruit of this concord between Wharton and his Commons appeared in a colossal bill to amend the anti-popery act. The original act of 1703 had been so feebly executed and so widely evaded that little of the intended effect had been felt. This triumph of humanity over legality was now to be cancelled. The new bill pursued the old dream of making the Protestant English ascendancy invulnerable; and its South African particularity will be suggested by a provision which allowed Roman Catholics to own no horses worth more than five pounds except stud-mares and stallions intended for breeding![1] The history of the bill touches Swift through the evidence it supplies that he could, at least at this time, easily separate his private friendships from his public views. From the first week to the last day of the session, the bill came almost continually under discussion. A smooth though gradual evolution formed it until it went to the Lords. Here some of the temporal peers and most of the bishops took exception to a clause empowering magistrates to call up any man and require him to renounce the authority of the Pretender. Archbishop King, among other opposers, no doubt saw that such a provision would embarrass a number of Anglicans, especially some parsons, who could not in conscience swear this oath, though they gladly accepted both her majesty's authority and the Hanoverian succession. Rather than throw the invidious light of truth upon a qualm so peculiar to the Established Church and so inapplicable to the Dissenters, the bishops and their allies dragged red-herring scruples across the path of the bill. In the Lords' final vote, though the bill passed, only six bishops supported it, against seven opposed.[2] Swift, like Archbishop King, would have rejected the bill; yet St George Ashe stood behind it. In all Swift's relations with the Ashe family, there is no evidence that he brought this sort of opinion against them any more than he did against Addison.

Meanwhile, Wharton showed his skill at turning traps into ladders by picking up a provision to pay up to five thousand

[1] *Statutes at Large*, Ireland, IV (Dublin, 1786), 213.   [2] Graham, pp. 182-3.

pounds, at the rate of five pounds a family, to converts from Roman Catholicism. The good, pious Lord Lieutenant one day argued that it was a scandal to buy conversions, and persuaded the Privy Council to strike out the clause. Next day, pretending to be inspired by a remark dropped in debate, he urged the Council to petition her majesty that the fund thus saved should go to assist deserving refugee Palatines.[1] Swift, of course, had enough xenophobia to dislike German immigrants even if they conformed to his church, without looking for Lutheran Dissenters. But the Privy Council went along with his excellency.[2]

In another great issue, where the split between Ashe and King gaped again, it is clear that Swift stood not with his old tutor but with his archbishop. The tobacco merchants in Ireland had taken advantage of the expiration of a revenue act to import tobacco at a low duty. But Parliament soon passed a retrospective measure, and the Attorney-General sued successfully to recover the lost revenue. The merchants, however, appealed to the House of Lords and won their suit against the crown. Now Wharton wished Alan Brodrick, the co-operative Attorney-General, to appeal still higher, to the House of Lords in England. This scheme raised the tremendous question of Ireland's independence and the judicature of the Irish peers. In the Privy Council, Ashe backed Wharton on this issue, but King 'violently' opposed him.[3] Swift of course would have given flaming support to King's side. In the form the case finally took, both bishops could vote together, but the difference in their sympathies remained clear.

The same issue reached its crucial turn when the money bill was read to the Commons after coming back from England with serious revisions. Not only did the changes imply that Whitehall did not support Wharton's fiscal policy. They further implied that the power of the purse did not belong to the House of Commons. The members became furious to see their highest prerogative weakened; and they fought back under the guidance of Samuel Dopping, a friend of Swift's, whose father and brother

---

[1] Addison uses delicious language in his account of these somersaults to Sunderland: see Graham, pp. 162–3.

[2] The policy of encouraging foreign Protestants to settle in Ireland was an old one.

[3] Graham, pp. 152–3.

were bishops and who was himself called a Tory. It took all the strength of Will Conolly and the Brodricks to squeeze the bill through, and then the debate lasted eight hours.[1]

In all these proceedings, Swift's position comes nearest to Archbishop King's, or else a bit further along in the direction of high church. King opposed Abercorn and the extremists, but Swift would have stood somewhere between him and them. On the other side, the archbishop repeatedly gave succour to Wharton in opening impasses during administrative crises, but he did not back the government with the consistency of Ashe. The Brodricks of course simply took their orders from Wharton, and Dr Swift would have liked to see their whole family impeached. If the doctor's opinion counted for little, the conduct of Parliament counted for much. Even the Junto were beginning to understand what Irish Whigs knew as well as Tories, and what Addison had the duty of informing Godolphin: that there was a reluctance in 'all sorts' of Irishmen to have it thought that they were a dependent kingdom, or that even acts of the British Parliament might not be superseded in Ireland so far as their own affairs were concerned.[2]

The troubles of Parliament found echoes and re-echoes in the murmuring of Convocation. There the hottest emotions and the smallest effects were derived from a fracas on the usual pattern, setting Lower-House proctors against Upper-House bishops. To begin with, the two houses of Convocation addressed the Lord Lieutenant on the subject of the First Fruits, and he did not discourage them from thinking he might put his weight behind their appeal for the remission. Meanwhile, however, Atterbury's well-wishers resumed their campaign to give the Lower House an authority parallel to that of the House of Commons; and this pressure inevitably set them directly against a Lord Lieutenant whom they already disliked. Yet Wharton felt unwilling to prorogue Convocation because of the resentment he would then face in Parliament. In the Lower House of Convocation, William Percival, Archdeacon of Cashel, played Atterbury's rôle; like his model, he came from Christ Church, Oxford, and Addison (a

[1] Graham, p. 177.   [2] *Ibid.*, p. 161.

Magdalen man) called him the 'principal agent' in Ireland of that high-church institution.[1] On the other side, Wharton's chaplain, Lambert, had published in 1708 *Partiality Detected*, a sharply critical review of the manœuvring which had kept the previous Convocation embroiled. During the new session—well under way before Swift came home—most of the Lower House followed the hot-tempered, high-flying lead of Archdeacon Percival, and tried to get *Partiality Detected* censured by their assembly. As the tug-of-war swayed back and forth, Wharton moved in with an admirably shrewd offer to Archbishop King. Although the reporter of this event is Percival—the last man to underestimate his own mastery of a situation—the essential fact seems reliable.

> My Lord Lieutenant thought fit to interpose, and begged the Archbishop of Dublin to let us know that if we would but let fall this affair about his chaplain he would use his interest with the queen to get a remittal of the First Fruits here as in England; this the archbishop communicated to abundance of our members, and begged of them to put off the farther examination of the affair.[2]

More likely, Wharton said he would not do anything about the First Fruits unless the clergy gave up the attacks on Lambert. But there is no doubt that King tried to quiet the Lower House by 'terrifying some and soothing others'.[3] Yet though King's protégé Stearne was prolocutor and exerted himself to help the archbishop, the skirmishing went on. Just before Swift had sailed from England, the committee which had condemned Lambert's book tried to make their unresponsive chairman present their report. He was Peter Browne, one-time classmate of both Lambert and Swift, and now provost of Trinity College. Preferring the upper to the nether millstone, Browne manufactured excuses while the proctors fumed. Before July there was a stalemate. What Swift made of these twists and turns, he told a year later; for he then said that the Lord Lieutenant's consideration of the First Fruits had ceased when the dispute over Lambert's book was taken by his excellency as an affront to himself and was re-

[1] *Ibid.*, p. 148.
[2] Bodl. MS. Ballard 36, fols. 57ᵛ–8 (spelling etc. normalized). For Percival's detailed account of the sequel, see *ibid.*, fols. 55–6ᵛ.
[3] Graham, p. 143.

ported as such to the court.[1] By August, at any rate, Wharton had
to give up his hope of moderating the language of the Irish clergy.
In spite of his earlier belief that a royal prorogation would not be
needed, he decided to lose face and fall back on this extremity,
even though the altered money bill had not yet passed through
Parliament. Since King and Ashe were both away when the writ
of prerogation arrived, the gnashers of teeth enjoyed some hours
of free expression before accepting the inevitable.[2] Swift must
have shared their exasperation, but he was no great admirer of
Percival.[3] I suspect he felt amused to see both the archdeacon and
the Lord Lieutenant embarrassed.

To Wharton the end of the parliamentary session, which came
(three weeks after the proroguing of Convocation) when the
money bill passed through the House of Lords, meant at least
that he could fulfil his hope of returning to England in September. This also meant that Swift had only two or three weeks left of
Addison's leisure; for the Lord Lieutenant sailed with his chief
secretary about 18 September.[4] It was a mark of prudence for
Wharton to speed to Westminster, because his enemies were collecting evidence which they hoped would serve to impeach him.
While Addison had the pleasanter prospect of helping Steele's
Tatler to become the model specimen of a newly elevated genre,
he also agreed to help prepare Wharton's counter-arguments if
an impeachment should be launched.[5] Addison had a further
project as well. Although the current of peace sentiment and
Tory opinion was running with white-capped violence, he managed to regain his standing as a M.P. after being unseated (on
petition) at Lostwithiel. For at short, sudden notice, when his
health was indifferent and government business was swamping
him, he put himself up for a surprise opening at Malmesbury, a
borough controlled by Wharton, and was duly elected.[6]

[1] *Journal*, p. 679; Williams I. 170.
[2] Ball I. 202–3, n. 1; Graham, pp. 172–3; Landa, p. 60.
[3] Ball III. 141 and n. 4.   [4] Graham, p. 185.
[5] Smithers, pp. 167, 170; Graham, p. 197; Ball I. 227–8 and n. 3. Sir Richard
Levinge was the main person behind the scheme.
[6] 11 Mar. 1710 (Smithers, p. 175).

IV. THE COUNTRY LIFE

With Parliament and Convocation ended, the concentration of society in Dublin broke up, and Swift made his long country visits. Four weeks after Wharton delivered a closing speech to his Commons, brimming with particular praise of the new anti-popery law,[1] Swift was among his willows at Laracor, to live there from late September to mid-November.[2] He slept in a field bed on an earthen floor in a neat cabin built for himself.[3] His gentle, simple, minute congregation[4] required few of his hours here. He could enjoy improving his garden and viewing his river, mending his canal and protecting his fruit trees. He had the willows to trim, hedges to cut, and ditches to make up. If Swift liked to write about the town, he loved to think about the country. 'Oh, that we were at Laracor this fine day!' he wrote, one spring, to Ppt from London. 'The willows begin to peep and the quicks to bud ... And now they begin to catch the pikes, and will shortly the trouts ... and I would fain know whether the floods were ever so high as to get over the holly bank or the river walk; if so, then all my pikes are gone; but I hope not.'[5]

There were bills to clear with his agent, Isaiah Parvisol, or accounts to settle with his man of business, Joe Beaumont. But there were also the hospitable homes of the neighbourhood. Swift fell into his round of dinners with Raymond at Trim, or card parties with punch or wine. He played picquet with Percival or Barry and ombre with them both; or else ombre and 'whisk' with Raymond again, and with his nephew Richard Morgan. He could fret himself freely about Sir Arthur Langford, who subsidized Presbyterianism at nearby Summerhill. But he also had agreeable letters to answer from Addison and Steele, from their common friend Ambrose Philips, and from Sir Andrew Fountaine. Of course, Lady Giffard wrote too, but I do not think she defeated him. And then in November he could move north to Tyrone and the comfort of Bishop Ashe's house at Clogher. For

[1] *J.H.C.I.* II. 635.
[2] 27 Sept. to 19 Nov. 1709: *Accounts 1708–9*, fol. 11 (see under 31 Oct.); *Accounts 1709–10,* fol. 3ᵛ.
[3] Williams I. 373 and n. 1.   [4] *Ibid.,* p. 163.   [5] *Journal,* 19 Mar. 1711.

[365]

four weeks he vacationed here with the bishop and Dilly Ashe.
He won sixteen shillings at cards and tables, and received a letter
from 'Myshessy'. Inspired by the brothers' puns, Swift sent a
paranomasiac epistle to Lord Pembroke, who had just exchanged
his admiral's honours for a pension of three thousand pounds a
year on the post office.

Before Christmas, however, Swift was on his way back to
Laracor. En route, he visited Thomas Parnell, who was then
Archdeacon of Clogher. Swift liked the young poet and thought
his wife an 'excellent good-natured young woman' who lived in
great harmony with her husband.[1] After having Christmas at
Laracor, he moved back to Dublin, Mrs Curry's, and 'Md',
whom he saw constantly for almost the next two months; and
then the end of February sent him back to get Laracor ready for
the spring. This was the period he spent cutting down some of his
willows and planting others, scouring his canal, and riding about
to see what else had to be done.[2] Three weeks later he slipped
back to Dublin, but only to stay through the first week in April.
Then he not only moved himself to Laracor but had the ladies
follow him, to spend seven weeks nearby in Trim, while a frost
destroyed the blossoms on his fruit trees.

In this cheerful circulation of visits and games, Dublin and
country, Swift destroys the myth of the gloomy dean, barred, by
an austere, narrow-eyed scorn of human pleasures, from all sympathy with the condition of his kind. Swift's moral depth lies precisely in the fact that he freely indulged himself in humble pleasures, far more easily than those men of letters today who would
like great ideas and great art to suffice them. Swift welcomed the
common joys of friendship and hospitality. When he composed
his finest work, however, he judged those recreations as less than
the sum of human satisfaction, and he judged men by their
noblest possibilities. If he had not been accustomed to such pleasures, his severe estimate of humanity would have carried less
weight than a hermit's.

[1] Swift was at Clogher from 22 Nov. to 20 Dec. He visited Parnell, 21 Dec. See
Accounts 1709–10, fols. 2, 3^v; *Journal*, 24 Aug. 1710; Williams I. 162–3.
[2] *Journal*, 21 Feb. 1711.

V. DISCONTENT

Content with Ireland Swift was not. Even after leaving Leicester in the summer of 1709, he did not feel well in body. From Laracor in October he wrote that his sickness, 'after a years pursuing', had only begun to leave him.[1] During the autumn and winter which followed, he found relief from the giddiness but was saddened by the long last illness of his mother. She died at the end of April 1710; and Swift, when he received the news, wrote a memorandum which tells all we know of his feeling for her:

> Memorandum. On Wednesday between seven and eight at evening May 10th, 1710, I received a letter in my chamber at Laracor (Mr Percival and Jo: Beaumont being by) from Mrs F: dated May 9th with one included, from Mrs Worrall at Leicester to Mrs F: giving an account, that my dear mother Mrs Abigail Swift dyed that morning, Monday, April 24th, 1710, about ten o'clock, after a long sickness, being ill all winter and lame, and extremely ill a month or six weeks before her death. I have now lost my barrier between me and death; God grant I may live to be as well prepared for it, as I confidently believe her to have been. If the way to Heaven be through piety, truth, justice and charity she is there.[2]

The long series of external details closed by an aphoristic expression of emotion seems characteristic of Swift.[3] By recapturing the circumstances, he revives for himself the movement of feeling. For others he provides the most solemn of occasions with a proper dignity of fact. I suppose his mother was a 'barrier' against death through being his only fundamental, human responsibility; with her gone there was no one left whom he must care for and to whom his death would mean the end of a sacramental tie. The sentence of eulogy is cautiously conditional, but she is praised for the highest virtues, both natural and Christian. It seems just possible that the omission of 'hope' reflects her son's dour view of

---

[1] Williams I. 152. I think Ball misunderstood 'G.' in Swift's accounts to mean 'giddy' rather than 'gave' and therefore supposed him to be suffering when he was not (Ball I. 168, n. 2).

[2] Lyon, preliminaries, fol. 9. 'Mrs F:' is Swift's sister, Jane Fenton. I have normalized the text. Cf. Nichols, 1801, x. 104; Forster, p. 268; Davis v. 196. The memorandum was on a page for May 1710 now missing from Swift's account book. Mrs Swift was buried 27 Apr.; Swift, *Works*, ed. W. Scott (1814), xv. 322n.

[3] Cf. the note on Anne Long (Davis v. 198). The exceptional notes on Stella come many years later, and constitute a character rather than an epitaph.

our fate, for I assume he inherited the view in part from his cheerful mother.

Though the regular expeditions to Leicester were now over, Swift must have felt thankful that he had stayed so long on his final visit to his mother. He had been in regular correspondence with her and had received a letter during the month preceding the end.[1] Immediately, her death made no great disturbance in his routines. I assume that he had been sending her an allowance, and the reversion of this money would now improve his finances. As seasons passed, he would come to rely upon Esther Johnson to shield him, as his mother had done, from exposure to mortality.

By losing his mother, Swift also lost a vital token of his Englishness; for so long as she survived, he had a living parent's ancestral home in the country of his choice.[2] Without depreciating either Swift's attachment to Laracor or his enjoyment of Irish hospitality, or even his concern for the aspirations of Ireland, one must still admit that one of his favourite epistolary games was to compare his own birthplace invidiously with that of his forefathers. If he felt most himself in Ireland, most at ease, most in touch with a nation's essence, he felt positively excited by England, for it represented not what he was but what he wished to become. Nevertheless, there remains one small observation that qualifies though it hardly weakens this truth. Of course, Swift preferred London to Dublin; of course, he felt dissatisfied in Ireland and thought Laracor an absurd scene for his abilities; but a little piece of his complaining seems due to a fear of being forgotten by his great, if not good, friends. Swift wished, I think, to prevent English correspondents from supposing him resigned to living where he belonged; he wished to encourage them to find him a career in their midst. 'Remember me sometimes in your walks up the Park, and wish for me amongst you', Swift wrote from Laracor to Ambrose Philips: 'I reckon no man is thoroughly miserable unless he be condemned to live in Ireland; and yet I have not the spleen; for I was not born to it.'[3]

[1] Forster, p. 268.

[2] I assume that she herself was born in Dublin, though identified by Swift with Leicester through her long residence there and her parents' connection with the city.

[3] Williams I. 154.

These forget-me-not injunctions could take so private and secret a shape as Swift's rash exchanges with Mishessy. They could also become the channel of an appeal which almost shockingly breaks from Swift several times over the decades when famous poets were his friends: *orna me*, as Cicero said: 'When you write any more poetry, do me honor; mention me in it.' If they could not establish him in a post that would bring reputation, they could bestow the boon directly: 'I will contrive it so, that Prince Posterity shall know I was favored by the men of witt in my time.' Gathering the apples on his 'half an acre of Irish bog' at Laracor, Dr Swift could not yet foresee that the Prince would feel better pleased with the *Tale* dedicated to himself than with the productions of Swift's contemporaries, and that his highness would discover the other men of wit through the doctor, not him through them.[1]

The praises of the great only sharpened the irony of Swift's nostalgia. Steele told him of a dinner party at which Addison eulogized their absent friend before Halifax and other Whigs. He sent Swift the great lord's letter promising all promises[2]; and Swift decided to test the offer even while he distrusted it. At the end of an enormous message of compliment, which even Swift cannot keep from cloying, the vicar proposed that Halifax should use his credit to make Dr Swift the Bishop of Cork in case the incumbent should die as he seemed disposed to do.[3] No event could have surprised Swift less than the dénouement of this farce. The Bishop of Cork died, much more obligingly than Dr South, the day Swift wrote to Halifax. But word of his approaching end was not limited to the circle of Swift's well-wishers. Six weeks after the effusion delivered to Halifax, the episcopal nomination went to Peter Browne, the provost who had assisted the government by refusing to transmit his committee's condemnation of Dr Lambert. Thus Swift saw his old and conventional classmate, the author of an inventive attack on deism and the protégé of Primate Marsh, elevated to the eminence that Swift was never to reach.[4]

[1] *Ibid.*, pp. 153–4.　[2] *Ibid.*, p. 150.　[3] *Ibid.*, p. 159.
[4] *Supra*, vol. I, pp. 73–5.

Unlike many of his rivals, Swift persisted in thinking about some preferments that lay outside the church altogether. The same sense of history that pressed him to say *orna me* to Addison and Pope also prodded him to notice the office of Historiographer Royal, carrying only a small stipend but affording high sanction to Swift's vague scheme of writing a grand historical work dealing with his own era. When Addison, in the summer of 1710, asked him what he now had in his thoughts for Addison to tell Somers and Halifax (who had meanwhile written himself to Swift[1]), the vicar not only reminded him of South's prebend but also named the place of historiographer. Neither wish was to be realized, whether through Whigs or through Tories.[2]

VI. THE SHAKING SEASON

Organized as an opposition cabal and held together by plans to carry on a war, the Junto found the responsibilities of office rather disintegrative and the task of designing a peace treaty impossible. Marlborough and Godolphin, so far from entering into their hopes, tended to stand apart, leaving them to their fates. Meanwhile, since no treaty had emerged from the nego-tiations during the spring of 1709, it was essential for Britain to secure the hearty co-operation of the Dutch in the following year's campaign. Unfortunately, while this need was critical, the one notable victory of the summer manœuvres in 1709 became Malplaquet, a battle marked by such frightening carnage on the 'winning' side that it almost counted as a French success; and the cries for peace consequently grew more strident. Yet this was when, in return for a renewed effort, the tired Dutch were includ-ing among their desiderata a great phalanx of Belgian garrison towns to be occupied by them and used as a 'barrier' against the French. Only by sacrificing Austrian and Spanish interests as well as some British commercial advantages, were the Whig

---

[1] Williams I. 167 ('the enclosed').

[2] Halifax, who had been instrumental in the publication of Rymer's *Foedera*, would have been unlikely to propose Swift as Rymer's successor; but the example of Addi-son, who had been trying to buy a similar office in Ireland, may possibly have stimu-lated Swift's desire to become historiographer.

ministers finally able to offer terms that even the disenchanted Dutch could not resist; so in October 1709 the notorious 'Barrier Treaty' was signed, though it was never in fact to be executed and would be eloquently denounced three years later by Swift.

Harley, taking advantage of the ministry's lack of coherence, could begin to draw powerful courtiers into a scheme for an alternative government, responsible not to the Junto or the high Tories but to the crown. He evidently wished to arrange such an equilibrium of party pressures that hopeful men would come to him en route to her majesty. Throughout 1709 the great Duke of Shrewsbury worked more and more closely with the secretive Harley in a direction that he intended to lead toward both a rational peace and the security of the Hanoverian succession. Tired of military emergencies, disgusted by the narrowness of party rule, and sympathizing with their captive monarch, other magnates edged to Harley's side: Argyll, Somerset, Pembroke.

The turn against the Whigs picked up momentum from many sources of energy. One of these was Marlborough's colossal mistake of so far exposing his ambition as to ask Anne to strengthen him, amid the rapidly shifting uncertainties of politics, with the title of captain-general (or commander-in-chief), not during her majesty's pleasure but for the rest of his life. It was bad enough that nobody else supported the Duke's request and that the Queen gave him a furious negative; it was still worse that he persisted to the point where the story became common knowledge, alienating friends as well as enemies. Meanwhile, Anne completely repulsed her old friend the Duchess of Marlborough, who still held high offices in her majesty's household; she treated Mrs Masham with more confidence than ever; and she systematically represented Harley's backstairs advice as her own judgment.

The most dramatic defeat of the Junto–Godolphin combination was inflicted on another part of the domestic battlefield. Dr Henry Sacheverell, who was the English equivalent of Ireland's Francis Higgins, had been preaching violent anti-Whig sermons in important places for several years. On Guy Fawkes Day 1709, he delivered one so nakedly political, so subversive of Revolution principles, and so widely distributed in a printed form that both Godolphin and the other ministers determined to treat the case as constitutional and to impeach Sacheverell before the House of Lords. The Lord Treasurer himself, who had always squirmed under the didactic Toryism of the great bulk of the clergy, felt peculiarly involved inasmuch as Sacheverell had pointedly reproved him under his established nickname of Volpone. However, all the repressed high-church sentiment of the nation broke out in the defence of the preacher. His trial, held with impressive pageantry in Westminster Hall, became a fiasco for the ministry in spite of the prosecution's cogency of logic and the vapidity of the arguments for the defence. After three and a half weeks, the trial ended (23 March 1710) with the old doctrine of passive resistance utterly exploded but also with the priest who had promulgated it set free under a sentence so mild that it counted as acquittal. In speaking on behalf of the accused, Dartmouth gave Sacheverell's doctrine a turn which the parson himself had never intended, though it was commonplace enough for Swift to have applied it in *The Sentiments of a Church-of-England Man*, viz., that passive obedience is indeed due the supreme magistrate but that the supreme magistrate is the tripartite power of King, Commons, and Lords, rather than the King alone.

By this time the great Dukes of Somerset and Argyll were joining Shrewsbury in the plan to replace Godolphin with Harley and to end the war. In the riotously pro-church aftermath of Sacheverell's trial the promise of a general election began to beckon cheerfully to the Tories. Soon the Queen felt strong enough to dismiss her Lord Chamberlain without even consulting Godolphin, and to replace him with the Duke of Shrewsbury. In June the incredible happened, for Anne then took it upon herself to dismiss the egregious Earl of Sunderland as Secretary of State and give the post to Dartmouth, a Tory whose wife was Nottingham's niece. Now Harley's destiny was assured. He had only a matter of months to wait for his golden fruits to mature and drop, while Wharton writhed in Ireland and Marlborough was off at the wars.

VII. THE LORD LIEUTENANT RETURNS

While the Queen was making Shrewsbury her Chamberlain, the time was nearing for Addison's master to revisit Ireland, and the secretary wrote to Swift. In his message the old superlatives re-appear: Addison could not be sorry to leave England when he was going to enjoy the 'satisfaction and honour' of Swift's con-versation; he longed, he said, to 'eat a dish of bacon and beans in the best company in the world'; he begged the vicar to remain a friend to 'one who loves and esteems you, if possible, as much as you deserve'.[1] Addison reached Dublin with Wharton at the beginning of May 1710, while Swift was at Laracor and the ladies were at Trim.[2] After waiting almost a month, the secretary wrote begging Swift to come up to town: 'I long to see you', he said, and 'I love your company and value your conversation more than any man's.'[3] Four days later, Swift was having tea with Addison in Dublin.[4]

The Lord Lieutenant could hardly feel that his footing had grown more secure during his months away in England. The threat of impeachment still hung over his head, and Addison did not sound very persuasive when he tried to belittle the facts of Harley's advance.[5] The wolfish world of political on-lookers knew that both the Queen and the country were slipping out of the ministry's hands, and that the men who abandoned the Junto would be rewarded with more than her majesty's good wishes. The Irish parliamentary session was only half over when Wharton suffered the embarrassment of having to deal not with Sunderland but with Dartmouth, who, as Secretary of State, probably fed the Lord Lieutenant instructions designed to make trouble for him.

---

[1] Williams I. 161–2.

[2] Although the page for May 1710 is missing from the accounts for 1709–10, Swift notes under 3 June that MD were at Trim seven weeks. Under April Swift notes that he went to Laracor about the 8th, and that MD came to stay (*sc.* at Trim) a week later. Swift played ombre with Percival and Barry (*sc.* at Laracor) on 18 and 20 May (*Accounts*, fol. 2). The ladies may have stayed on at Trim without Swift; under July 1 he notes, 'MD come home' (*ibid.*, fol. 8ᵛ).

[3] Williams I. 164.   [4] *Accounts 1709–10*, fol. 8. Possibly they met sooner.

[5] Graham, p. 211.

Nevertheless, the first test of strength in the House of Commons did not cause Wharton to lose face. This was the choice of a Speaker to replace Alan Brodrick, now Lord Chief Justice. The election could fall either on the government's candidate, John Forster, a relative of the Brodricks' who had been made recorder of Dublin,[1] or else on some staunchly Anglican gentleman who would remain independent of Wharton. As a help to the latter side in the contest there was Swift's *Letter concerning the Test*, which had been reprinted in Dublin and was advertised in the autumn of 1709.[2] Now Swift decided to make another contribution in the form of an essay, probably left incomplete[3] and certainly not published, which he called *A Letter to a Member of Parliament in Ireland upon the Chusing a New Speaker There*. Here Swift tries to exalt the defence of the Test into a shibboleth that will separate the righteous from the damned in Irish politics. Instead of reasoned principles he offers only the argument that the Speaker must be a man who supports the Test. Behind this contention lies Swift's obsession with clear, simple solutions, rather than compromises. Just as in the *Argument against Abolishing Christianity*, he implies that to yield the Test is to yield government, morality, and faith. Tendencies are again identified with absolutes; and in a characteristic leap Swift complains that those who feel unconcerned about the choice of a Speaker would 'talk at the same rate if the question were, not onely about abolishing the Sacramental Test, but the sacrament itself'.[4] Yet the support of the Test did have one admirable implication for Ireland which it lacked for England, because it represented a principle of national independence as contrasted with the willingness of its opponents to submit all Irish interests to those of Britain.

Swift's little essay has the structure of a personal letter addressed to an Irish M.P., and might well have been conceived by Swift at Laracor in early May, to be sent to Dublin for printing

[1] Graham, p. 139.
[2] Rothschild, no. 2000. Advertisements in the *Dublin Gazette*, 27 Sept., 8 Oct., 29 Nov.
[3] It sounds unfinished to me, but may simply stop abruptly; Swift opens the penultimate paragraph as if he were approaching a conclusion (Davis IV. 133).
[4] Davis II. 132.

on the eve of the parliamentary session. It would be characteristic of Swift to have a friend handle the publication in town
while he remained unseen in the country. In his opening, Swift
reproaches the Commons for having passed the altered money
bill the summer before, and then urges the members to agree on
a candidate opposed to the court. Next he insists on the power of
the Speaker—whoever he may be—to influence opinion, and he
dwells on the importance of this election. Throughout, he thumps
repeatedly upon the Test drum, on the danger to the constitution
from the Presbyterians, and the wickedness of the Whigs. It is
hard to realize that Swift had not yet made a gesture toward
seeking advancement from Englishmen outside the circle of the
Whigs. And one must remember to Swift's honour that conventionally 'Whig' policies really did run counter to the welfare
of Ireland, whereas 'Tory' policies seemed to foster the kingdom's
prosperity, such as it was.

The moral psychology of this essay, as with most of Swift's
political writing, reminds one of men like Hobbes and La Rochefoucauld. The author derives all actions from motives of self-
interest, and never appeals to his reader's altruism. Yet he implicitly grants himself the privilege of judging his political enemies
by nobler standards, condemning the Brodricks for the same
kind of selfishness that he impartially accepts in his friends. As a
specimen of prose the composition has elegance and vigour,
though falling below the level of Swift's brilliance. One feels that
it came out of a less urgent feeling than the *Letter concerning the
Test*, and that Swift knew Wharton had no chance of achieving a
repeal of the clause. Yet several of Swift's effective rhetorical
devices are here. The most subtle, for a modern reader, is the
reversal of the usual connotations of epithets. 'High-flying', a
conventional description of churchmen or Tories, Swift applies
to Whigs; 'moderate', a euphemistic adjective for Latitudinarians, he applies to the church party. He also has a fine conceit
with an innuendo that alludes to the flourishing of Presbyterianism in the northern regions of Ireland and Britain, for he says the
defenders of the Test think it 'beneath the policy of common
gardners to cutt down the onely hedge that shelters from the

north'.[1] His gift for illustrative anecdote appears at the end in a marvellous fable about a mob of 'thirty thousand' Scottish pedlars who threatened the constitution of Sweden.[2]

Swift's essay remained in manuscript,[3] and Forster easily became Speaker of the House. But no aggressive attempt was made on the Test, and no one dragged the constitutional tangles of Sacheverell's trial into the Irish parliamentary session. One reason for keeping clear of such disputes (as a friend of Swift's said) was that either party in England could crush the whole of Ireland, and both of them had often agreed in voting her ruin.[4] When Wharton opened the new session of the Irish House of Lords, he delivered a prudently mild speech which mingled a tribute to the Queen—as the brightest ornament of her church—with only vague exhortations for a 'union amongst yourselves' and a zeal for the Protestant interest and succession.[5] But in the Lords' address of thanks, while there was a prayer for the Protestant succession, there was only the barest allusion to the Protestant interest.[6] As usual, the bishop-free Commons were less restrained; and in an address prepared by Addison for his excellency, they stated that only 'folly or malice' could insinuate the church was in danger (which was of course what all the English Tories were saying); and they helpfully promised to disappoint those who wished to 'divide' them.[7]

Even in the Commons, however, any air of unanimity was deceptive. The members showed bitter displeasure with the outcome of a vote passed the year before, to build an arsenal, because instead of supplying the rifles from Irish manufacturers, Wharton had arranged for them to be made in England. After struggling for weeks, his excellency at last had to let the House petition the Queen for half the arms to be made in Ireland.[8] The whole graft-feeding arsenal project, which came to be known as 'Wharton's folly', was involved with the all-important money

[1] Davis II. 131.

[2] *Ibid.*, pp. 134–5; presumably, the figure represents the number of Presbyterians in Ireland.

[3] Forster (p. 267) notwithstanding: see Davis II. 285.   [4] Graham, p. 219.

[5] *J.H.L.I.* II. 317, 321.   [6] *Ibid.*, pp. 322–3.   [7] *J.H.C.I.* II. 645–6.

[8] Graham, p. 223.

bill, but that did pass, although little else moved beyond the discussion stage. An awkward strain in communication between his
excellency and the new English Secretary of State dogged the
administration. Wharton found a man appointed to a job that
was not vacant; he was asked to sponsor a bill that would surely
have embroiled him with both the bishops and the parsons; over
his head, clergymen petitioned the Queen against his action in
the case of the Presbyterian minister at Drogheda.[1] Obviously,
the foundations of Whig rule in England were slipping badly.
With a dissolution of the British Parliament generally predicted,
many people who were interested in the new elections drifted
away from Dublin and headed for London. 'We have scarce been
able to get together forty members', Addison reported at the
beginning of August.[2] By the next mails he learned that Godolphin himself was out of office; and Wharton soon let Addison go
home in order to defend his seat at Malmesbury. Meanwhile,
favour-seekers who might have turned to Wharton with their
money decided to wait for the market to change.

In this ambience it is not odd that apart from the supply bills,
Wharton saw no significant legislation enacted. Of course, he
was restive enough to race the others back to England; but the
intriguers at court had no desire to speed his recall. Finally, his
wife, in the last stages of pregnancy, begged the Queen to give
him permission; and Anne yielded.[3] The Irish Parliament was
prorogued 28 August 1710, and three days later Wharton was
gone.

Along with the Lord Lieutenant went Dr Swift. For all his
protests of not mixing with Wharton, Swift not only saw his
excellency from time to time but paid courtesies to him. Except
for a mid-July visit to Laracor, Swift resided in Dublin through
the summer, though making excursions to bibulous Dilly
Ashe's, at Finglas, with Addison, or to the Stoytes' at Donnybrook with MD. In town the ladies and the secretary seem to
have divided his leisure between them. Addison departed in mid-
August, and Swift sent a sympathetic letter to greet him in Lon-

---

[1] L. A. Dralle, 'Kingdom in Reversion', *HLQ*. xv (1952), 422–3.
[2] Graham, p. 229.   [3] Dralle, *op. cit.*

don. 'My Lord Lieutenant askt me yesterday whether I intended for England', he told Addison; 'I said, I had no busyness there now, since I suppose in a little time I should not have one friend left that had any credit and his excellency was of my opinion.'[1] Although Swift's compliments to his friend, in this letter, rose quite as high as Addison's to himself, the tone of his exchange with Addison was not wholly candid; either he meant his correspondent to take the account ironically, or else he was speaking for the record, expecting to be quoted to Wharton and others. At the same time he asked Addison whether he thought that Swift could help himself by coming to England, and this question again seems perhaps devious, because almost two months earlier the author of *A Tale of a Tub* had written to the book's publisher, 'I hope to see you ere it be long; since it is like to be a new world, and since I have the merit of suffering by not complying with the old.'[2] To strengthen this intention, help came from a not unexpected source. Convocation adjourned in Ireland soon after Parliament; but the bishops had decided both to make a fresh plea for the First Fruits and to empower Swift again to serve as agent. Two Irish bishops who happened to be in London already were supposed to be managing the project; and Archbishop King had secured a promise of co-operation from the Archbishop of York.[3] But King still believed that Swift's energy would accomplish more than any casual episcopal meddling; so he encouraged him to take up the scheme once more. Although Swift in the weeks which followed protested repeatedly that the commission was forced upon him, that he only made up his mind to go very suddenly and under pressure, and that he 'neer went to England with so little desire',[4] one cannot help suspecting that he pushed Archbishop King's arrangement of the embassy. Yet the signed commission which he carried with him was dated the same day he sailed; and it is obvious that he had put off his decision, since he was forced to spend as much as two crowns on a special boat to

---

[1] The ease with which he presented Raymond to Wharton does not suggest a lack of contact between the vicar and the Lord Lieutenant (*Journal*, 9 Sept. 1710, pt i); cf. the familiar reference to Lady Wharton (*ibid.*).
[2] Williams I. 166.   [3] *Ibid.*, p. 176.
[4] *Journal*, 2 Sept. 1710; cf. Williams I. 171–2, n. 4; *Journal* I. xx.

carry him to the viceregal yacht. I suppose he was held up by the bishops' delay in granting him the commission. For while King felt eager enough to have Swift carry on the negotiations, the other bishops needed prodding. For one thing they were afraid that a man who had been so *in* with the Whigs might be *out* with the Tories; for another thing, they did not all love Archbishop King or wish to further his projects. If Swift had wanted to soothe them, he might have agreed to accomplish what he could in London without written credentials; but he refused to promise this, and sent Dean Stearne to impress the archbishop with his hesitances.[1] Luckily, in the selection of a 'person fit to be employed', his grace exercised better judgment than some of his episcopal brethren.[2] Convocation held its closing meeting Thursday, 31 August, with only six bishops on hand (since adjournment was the business of the day); but all of them, in their separate, private capacities (i.e., not as the Upper House of Convocation), signed Swift's instrument[3]; and he left with it that evening on his 'sudden and unexpected' journey.[4]

Swift understood as well as other hungry men what was taking place in Westminster. It was about three weeks since some friends of his had come to Swift's lodgings and made him joyful with the sudden news of Godolphin's fall.[5] If he now hesitated to join the eastward migration, it was for fear of reviving the tantalization he had endured for a year and a half together. Of course, he possessed no strong ground for trusting that the incoming ministers would be kinder than those they replaced. Yet he felt the opposite of obligations to the old; and in the proliferating opportunities of so elaborate a crisis, the vicar of Laracor might surely hope to improve his condition. So Jo Beaumont saw him off on Thursday evening, and the yacht sailed at ten at night. Swift's tortuous apprenticeship was indeed done. Before he saw Ireland again, the fame, power, advancement, and exhilaration he craved would all be his, to the point of suffocation. Every good thing but serenity lay in ambush.

---

[1] Williams I. 192.   [2] *Ibid.*, p. 199.   [3] *Journal* I. 2–3, n. 9; 675.
[4] *Ibid.*, 23 Sept. 1710.   [5] Williams II. 91.

Chapter Nineteen

DR SW--T

I. SEASON OF MISTS

There was a dancelike effortlessness about Swift's return to England. Even the numbers of impediments that fell in his path only blocked him a short while, establishing an almost agreeable suspense. He still felt the old, nagging hungers; but this was to be a fruitful autumn.

Because his mother was now dead, he could head straight for Westminster; and since Viscount Mountjoy, who had come over with Wharton's party, desired the doctor's company the rest of the route, Swift's expenses were paid along the way by his lordship. It was a quick thrust of a journey, for Mountjoy was in a hurry. They landed at Parkgate and rode to Chester, with Swift falling off his horse on the road, but no harm done, 'the horse understanding falls very well'.[1] While at Chester, he ran into Dr and Mrs Raymond, who happened to be there on business, and he enjoyed the eccentric satisfaction of introducing the rector of Trim to the Earl of Wharton. As if to make up for the omission of a trip to Leicester, he visited, as usual, the once beautiful but now ageing lady whom he imagined to be a cousin and who was christened with his mother's name, Abigail Swift.[2] Then he and Lord Mountjoy rode the hundred and eighty miles from Chester to London in five days, arriving at noon on Thursday, 7 September. Swift said he had felt weary the first day and almost dead the second, but 'tolerable the third, and well enough the rest'.[3]

He took temporary lodgings in Pall Mall and plunged into

[1] *Journal*, 2 Sept. 1710.
[2] *Ibid*. Her married name was Greenfield; see Williams I. 366, n. 5; III. 186, n.3 ('Walpley' should be 'Welply').
[3] The route was Whitchurch, Newport, Coventry, Towcester, Dunstable; see *Journal*, 9 Sept. 1710, pt 1; *Accounts 1709–10*, fols. 10–10ᵛ.

life at the hub of the world. Even more precisely than the year before, Swift now knew what he wanted and the terms he was willing to offer for it. If he secured a remission of the First Fruits for the clergy of his church, he would have only the outer glow of the success he longed for. Even this small victory, however, he hoped to win through independent work and not by supporting other agents already on the spot. As the peculiar triumph of the vicar of Laracor, it would then make some slender contribution to that long-lasting fame which Swift knew to be the highest of his desiderata. But it could not belong to the category he hoped would supply the main strength of his reputation, since that was to be literary achievement. The fame of authorship, though an old ambition, kept all its appeal for Swift. Yet besides the sweet pleasure of being appreciated for his own work's sake, he also wished to obtain the second-hand renown of being chosen as friend by the true geniuses of his generation. And even under this yearning he still suffered from the more common aspiration to be celebrated as the intimate of the 'great', of those men who turned the wheels of British society and government.

Besides all the exhilarations of fame Swift, in the autumn of 1710, wanted the comfort of some 'small economy' of his own. This meant, above everything, an assured and plentiful income, a regular return of over five hundred pounds annually:

> I often wish'd, that I had clear
> For life six hundred pounds a year.[1]

Along with the income he would expect to hold some post of distinction in the church or the government: a bishopric, a deanery, a really handsome prebend, or a secretaryship. Although the situation might fix him in Ireland, Swift always prayed it would keep him in England.

When the solid opportunities should at last come, Swift assumed they would represent the gift of a great man impressed by his powers, the appreciation of an eminence like Sir William Temple, Archbishop King, Lord Somers, or Lord Halifax, all of whom had already let him down. In other words, Swift, like most

---

[1] *Poems* I. 198 (Horace, *Sat.* II. vi), perhaps echoing *Hudibras* III. i. 1277-8.

ambitious persons of the age, was looking for a fatherly patron who would supply a substitute son with an adequate estate. As each possibility failed him, he found a replacement, but the gratitude he was prepared to feel increased just as the series of disappointments taught him to manage his expectations.

Fortunately, the climate of politics and the complexion of English society had never looked brighter for the promotion of Swift's career than they did in the mellow days of September 1710. No one felt sorry to see him. Everyone suggested agreeable possibilities. As an author he found himself welcomed by editors like Steele and publishers like Tooke. As an agent of the Irish church, he could expect the new ministers to feel peculiarly well disposed toward a class of men that had quarrelled with their enemies. As an office-hunter he could assume that the season of changes would drop some blessing into his extended hand. As an expert conversationalist he knew that many free dinners would be served to him. The first day Swift found time to write from London, he told Archbishop King about his reception, in a tone edged with jubilance: 'I found myself equally caressed by both parties, by one as a sort of bough for drowning men to lay hold of; and by the other as one discontented with the late men in power, for not being thorough[1] in their designs, and therefore ready to approve present things.'[2]

This by no means implies that Swift spent half his time with each side. On the contrary, following his normal routine, he looked up old acquaintances and saw few who would not have called themselves Whigs. If he was fed up with his former patrons, he was not therefore about to fling himself at the directors of a rival enterprise. For all his eagerness to succeed, he needed success on his own terms, among which was the condition that advances must be made to Dr Swift and that he should not have to introduce himself at the risk of being rejected. He felt complacent enough to wait until the right person gestured.

Meanwhile, Swift's letters came franked under cover to his Whig friend Steele, who had not yet lost the post of editor of the *Gazette*. Swift visited Somers and heard that he expected very

---

[1] I.e., wholeheartedly engaged.   [2] Williams I. 173.

shortly to be replaced as Lord President. He dined with Halifax but would not join in a toast to the resurrection of the Whigs: 'I told him he was the only Whig in England I loved.'[1] He went round the coffee-houses meeting people he had known before, and his favourite remained St James's coffee-house. Most of all, he returned to Addison's circle of Whig littérateurs, joining them day after day as a comrade. Addison and Steele sat up with him his first Sunday in town. The next day he dined with Addison. On the Friday he dined with Addison and another friend; on the Monday he dined with Addison and Swift's old school and college friend, Stratford. After a week or so of interruption the intimacy was renewed: a large dinner party including Addison and Steele; dinner with Addison and Jervas, the painter who was now finishing a portrait of Swift. At the end of the month he met the Whig poet and playwright Nicholas Rowe at a dinner party; and soon he was familiar with Dr Samuel Garth, the genial, free-thinking friend of Pope and author of the brilliant mock-epic *The Dispensary*. The collection of names assembled at some of these convivialities begins to sound like the dramatis personæ of a costume play. One late October day Rowe invited Swift to dinner. Going to meet him at his office, Swift found Prior there as well, though Prior did not join the others when they went on together. After dinner Swift and Rowe went to a tavern and met Congreve among a group including the future Lord Cobham, to whom Pope in afteryears was to dedicate his magnificent first Moral Essay.

As a member of these shining circles, Dr Swift inevitably wrote another essay for the *Tatler*, and he also supplied Steele with an excellent poem, a companion piece to the *Description of the Morning*. Like its predecessor this poem dealt with London. After less than a week in the capital, Swift had said he was sorry to be back in it: 'I protest upon my life, I am heartily weary of this town, and wish I had never stirred.'[2] But he scrawled in this mood when his First Fruits affair was at an impasse and he could not tell where to turn next. The energy and brilliant variety of Swift's social projects bear witness to the exuberance released in him by the

[1] *Journal*, 2 Oct. 1710.   [2] *Ibid.*, 12 Sept. 1710.

metropolis. His love of the country life at Laracor did not spoil the pleasure he tasted in Whitehall at election time. There was glorious weather the first weeks of his stay. People said he looked fatter and better than in 1709.[1] His portrait by Jervas, begun on the previous visit to England, was now being completed much to his satisfaction; and it shows large blue eyes under dark eyebrows, with a straight, longish nose, full cheeks, a small, full-lipped mouth, and a well-marked chin over a plump throat.[2] The expression is rather judicious than censorious, proper to the clergyman's gown and neckband. If Swift found London wearisome, Jervas concealed the fact.

II. *THE CITY SHOWER*

The poem, *A Description of a City Shower*, compliments its subject in Swift's usual way, by mock-aspersions. Nearly all the details seem like unpleasant aspects of urbanity. But only an admirer could have gathered together the sharp observations of street life which crowds these lines. It is as though the Irishman were showing off his familiarity with the English scene. Again, as in his *Morning*, Swift looks at London from the opposite of the common point of view, as much as to say the author knows the place so well that he can see through the surface into the essence. So he handles it as a rural landscape. The obvious model for verse descriptions of agricultural prospects was Virgil's *Georgics*, brilliantly translated by Dryden. Swift therefore makes his new poem into a mock-georgic, even as the *Morning* had constituted a mock-pastoral. While the images all come from Swift's direct experience of London—including the foul smells in his lodgings—the form and style are meant to remind us of the great storm in the first *Georgic*, with a hint of the more notorious storm that precedes the seduction of Dido in the *Aeneid*. While there is an element of satire in the poem, it is directed not against Virgil, of course, but against his English imitators, especially Dryden. To

---

[1] *Journal*, 9 Sept. 1710, pt 1.

[2] There are at least three slightly varying copies of this portrait, two in the National Portrait Gallery and one in the Bodleian Library.

draw our attention to this literary ridicule, Swift echoes lines
from Dryden's translations not only of the *Georgics* but also of the
Aeneid. He further imitates the 'turn' or *traductio* which Dryden
affected in many poems, whether translations or originals.[1]

Swift disliked the custom, which he blamed on Dryden, of
varying couplets with triplets and alexandrines, often in combination; and the last three lines of the *Shower* are an obvious
travesty of the custom. Here, for example, is Dryden's tribute to
Oldham:

> Thy gen'rous fruits, though gathered ere their prime,
> Still shewed a quickness; and maturing time
> But mellows what we write to the dull sweets of rhyme.

With this elegant, flexible motion compare the heavy coarseness
of rhythm and image in the closing lines of Swift's poem—each
starting with a trochee or spondee, and each stuffed with accents
and pauses:

> Sweepings from butchers stalls, dung, guts, and blood,
> Drown'd puppies, stinking sprats, all drench'd in mud,
> Dead cats and turnip-tops come tumbling down the flood.

Besides making a savagely bathetic contrast to the seduction
which follows the storm in the *Aeneid*, this ending drags the

---

[1] Beginning the poem before 10 October, Swift had all but the first lines done by
the 12th; a day or two later the whole thing was finished; it was published in the
Tatler, 17 Oct. On the history of composition and publication, see *Poems* I. 136. The
division into omens, preliminaries, and deluge is taken from the tempest in the
Georgics (I. 431–58, 483–538, in Dryden's translation). The *Tatler* reminded his
readers of the Virgilian parallels, particularly of the storm covering the seduction
scene (Dryden's *Aeneid* IV. 231–8). Swift alludes again to the *Aeneid* through an
extended simile centred on Laocoon (II. 52–69 in Dryden). He also employs language recalling that of several passages in Dryden's translation: cf. *Shower*, ll. 13–14,
31, 38, 53, 57 and the following in Dryden's *Aeneid*: IV. 231–8, V. 15–31; also *Shower*,
ll. 17–22 and *Aeneid* VII. 528–33. Swift's l. 39 seems an echo of a line found in the
Aeneid I. 320, 519, and elsewhere. His line 63 seems to echo Dryden's *Georgics* I. 418.
The absurd counterpointing of 'rain' and 'dust' may be a parody of Dryden's use of
the turn, as in *Alexander's Feast*, ll. 56–60. In addition l. 26 of the *Shower* echoes Garth's
Dispensary V. 176, and the influence of the *Dispensary* is generally pervasive. Finally,
in the last three lines of the *Shower* Swift may also, just possibly, be glancing at the
execrable Blackmore, for certain tempest and sea episodes of *Prince Arthur* have lines
very similar: cf. the passage on Judgment Day in *Prince Arthur* (3rd ed., 1696), Bk III,
ca. ll. 73–84 ('Down their scorcht sides . . . tremendous flood'); also Bk IV, p. 98, *ca.*
ll. 207–10 ('Loud, foaming torrents . . . valleys drown'); in *King Arthur* (1697), Bk IV,
p. 102 ('Coursers . . . current fly'); Bk VII, p. 185 (triplet, 'O'er shields . . . dismal
flood').

agricultural countryside up to town. All the life of the farm appears here, decayed to garbage, yet all still in action. (There is a live cat at the beginning of the poem, but it sits still.)

Sewer stenches, aching teeth, drunken vomitings, meet us throughout the *City Shower*; yet they add up not to an indictment but to a cheerful acceptance of the urban scene. It is as if Swift were declaring he all these nuisances exist but he loves the structure of energy, change, potentiality, that underpins them. Here is neither the tenderness of Wordsworth's sonnet nor the fascinated disgust of Baudelaire or Robert Lowell, but rather a humbler sort of humorous comprehension:

> Here various kinds by various fortunes led,
> Commence acquaintance underneath a shed.
> Triumphant Tories, and desponding Whigs,
> Forget their fewds, and join to save their wigs.

But agreeable though it may be, the *Shower* serves to remind us that even the finest of his verse never challenges the supremacy of his prose. The subjects that most excited him he handled best in the 'other harmony'. Even the charm of the lines addressed, in later years, to Mrs Johnson is slight compared with the effect of the notes on her character which Swift composed at the time of her death. The *Shower* is very good for Swift; it is negligible when set beside many of Pope's and several of Gay's pictures of London.

All this did not prevent the *Shower* from being received with delight by enough Englishmen to satisfy Swift. Published in the *Tatler*, it drew the praise of numbers of judges whose opinion he cared for: 'They say 'tis the best thing I ever writ, and I think so too.'[1] Rowe and Prior raved about it. 'They both fell commending my *Shower* beyond any thing that has been written of the kind: there never was such a shower since Danaë's.'[2] But the topical, local, and literary allusions which shone in the poem for Londoners tended to darken it for the Irish. Prior could be trusted to recognize the play on a line from Garth's *Dispensary*, or the correct distinctions made among the various quarters of town. But Dubliners showed less appreciation. Only a few

---

[1] *Journal*, 17 Oct. 1710.   [2] *Ibid.*, 27 Oct.

praised it, and Bishop Ashe liked the *Morning* better.[1] Swift felt annoyed, as he always did, by the difference between the judgment passed on him at home and abroad.

III. IN STAYS

The *Shower* was the last important work of Swift's to be associated with his Whig friends. He had distrusted their party for years, although insisting that political allegiances ought never to weaken social connections. So long as the Junto seemed in the ascendant, his complaints need not have bothered an under-secretary or a Lord President. But now that another set was jostling them for places, and parliamentary elections were running against them, any sober fault-finding became an endorsement of their destroyers. Yet all Swift's experience of the Whigs predisposed him to smile at their despair. He had spent ten years warning them of their sins and asking them for help. He had received promises extended by promises, vows which time had ripened into lies. He had begged for relief for his church and had got a threat in the shape of a whispered bargain. He had proposed advancements, small and medium-sized, for himself, and had been granted large flatteries. As for the casual hospitality and good dinners, he might have considered them overpaid by the pleasures of his company. Years earlier he had felt offended by the arrogance of the high-church prince, Lord Rochester. But he found at last that the pure courtesy of a Halifax or a Somers was no more service to the vicar of Laracor.

Now even the advantage of courtesy began to crumble. In the atmosphere of friendly greetings from both the in's and the out's, Swift went to call upon Godolphin. Elated and inflated by the geniality of his treatment elsewhere, he looked for every courtier to make him compliments. But Godolphin, though he had just inherited four thousand pounds a year by his brother's death, was a tired sixty-five. One month after getting his notice of dismissal, he hardly felt inclined to exercise any tact upon a nagging Irish parson. With moods so clashing, the two men met, and the

[1] *Ibid.*, 30 Nov.

event was disastrous. Instead of coming in to a warm smile, Swift was handled, as he told the ladies, with 'a great deal of cold-ness'.[1] When he complained to Godolphin's supporters, they assured him that the Earl was overrun with the 'spleen and peevishness'[2] natural in so humiliating a crisis. But Swift could not have felt more infuriated. Recoiling in a rage, he turned to the convenient ear of Archbishop King and said Godolphin had insulted him with 'a reception very unexpected, and altogether different from what I ever received from any great man in my life; altogether short, dry, and morose'.[3]

So brief an outburst gave too small a relief to Swift's frustra-tion. In his more direct way of kicking back, he composed a lam-poon on Godolphin which has not the least claim to literary merit, much though its author valued it, but which does suggest that Swift's resentments at this time were still detached from general considerations of political principle. A few years later, Swift would represent the Earl (by then dead) as a Jacobite, a renegade Tory, and a man that had trimmed his opinions to suit whoever wore the crown.[4] In the doggerel attack of 1710, how-ever, Swift makes him only a politician who impartially cor-rupted Parliament, sold public offices for his own enrichment, and sacrificed troops to profits.[5]

Except that to be anti-Whig necessarily marked most levee-attenders as pro-Tory, Swift did not feel committed to support anyone's programme; for the time being, his attitude was not

---

[1] *Journal*, 9 Sept. 1710, pt 1.   [2] Williams I. 173.   [3] *Ibid.*
[4] Davis VII. 8–9.
[5] The poem, *The Virtues of Sid Hamet the Magician's Rod*, was begun 26 September and finished early the next month (*Journal, passim*). It continues, in octosyllabic couplets, the manner of his attacks on Louis XIV, Romney, and Cutts (*Poems* I. 10, 65–7, 82–5). The basic device is once more a parallelism: rods celebrated in scrip-ture, myth, and fiction are compared with Godolphin's white staff of office, which by the Queen's request he had not returned but had broken when he lost his place as Lord Treasurer. The lines were slow work because Swift insisted on packing them with allusions. Most of the rhythms are doggerel; the language is generally clumsy; the tone, erratic. The images are more mean than homely, and the wit is palpably forced. Almost inevitably the end limps and sounds awkward, though Swift tried as usual for a hammerblow. Familiar smells and sights are present—the poisonous reptile, the roué, stinking smoke, genital and excremental details. The poem has a deal of unintentionally phallic imagery, suggesting that Swift was symbolically cas-trating a father figure. It was sent to the printer 4 October and published soon after; see *Poems* I. 131–2 on composition and publication.

ideological. He spoke of 'talking treason heartily against the Whigs', but this was for their 'baseness and ingratitude', and not for specific policies. He rolled resentments in his mind and framed 'schemes for revenge'; he regretted the death of Lord Anglesey, a 'great support of the Tories'; but he also looked upon himself as complacently unattached: 'I laugh to see myself so disengaged.'[1] The direction of his mood is diagrammed in a comment he made to the ladies, revealing how remote he felt from the workings of the new men and how bitter against the old:

> I never remember such bold steps taken by a court: I am almost shocked at it, though I did not care if they were all hanged. We are astonished why the Parliament is not yet dissolved [it was dissolved the next week], and why they keep a matter of that importance to the last. We shall have a strange winter here between the struggles of a cunning discarded party, and the triumphs of one in power; of both which I shall be an indifferent spectator, and return very peaceably to Ireland, when I have done my part in the affair I am entrusted with.[2]

The changes in Swift's heart hesitated in this equilibrium while the ministry suffered further transformations. The Queen had come far since the appointment in June of the Earl of Dartmouth to replace Sunderland as Secretary of State. When Godolphin fell in August, Harley (who was not yet a peer) became not Lord Treasurer but the Chancellor of the Exchequer. Late in September, ten days before Harley at last got Parliament dissolved, the Earl of Rochester supplanted Somers as Lord President of the Privy Council; and on the same day, Harley's young lieutenant, Henry St John, became (with less than his captain's entire support) Secretary of State replacing the Whig Boyle and soon outranking his own confrère Dartmouth. As it was by now publicly established that Harley stood at the head of affairs and was forming the new government, he became a person Swift would in any case have to see about the First Fruits— the sooner the better. But meanwhile a slight flourish came from

---

[1] *Journal*, 10, 19 Sept.; 1 Oct. 1710.
[2] *Ibid.*, 20 Sept. The 'affair' was of course the First Fruits.

the direction of Lord Poulett, who enjoyed some brief show of power as first Lord of the Treasury.

At this stage of his operations Harley had designs of his own on the brilliant Irish priest. He needed popular support for his ministry to survive; he needed a propagandist capable of focusing the sentiments of the country party, the churchmen, and Tories—who together comprised the major political interest of the nation—and rally them behind the new leadership. So many gifted writers were already pledged to Addison's set or in the Kit-Cat Club that Harley was afforded no great range of choice among possible spokesmen. Defoe of course worked for him, but in a covert manner, through productions that could not be openly acknowledged; and anyhow, Defoe had neither the assurance nor the style to write the kind of authoritative pronouncements that Harley needed. Steele was in touch with Harley, but so far from supporting the Queen's changes, he was employing the *Tatler* to condemn them. In two of his June numbers he had taken issue with the presumed new policies; in July he had published a transparent allegory blackening the incoming ministers as leaning toward France, Popery, and the Pretender.

As a counter-attack, a few days before Godolphin fell, the Tories had set up a weekly periodical, the *Examiner*, to be the organ of their ministry. Prior, St John, and Atterbury were among those who wrote the numbers, but all of them had too much other business to manage it regularly. Besides hoping that Swift would undertake the production of the *Examiner* and do so in the secretive style that always appealed to Harley, the new chief minister also felt eager to strengthen his own backing among the profoundly influential leaders of the church. Swift's First Fruits mission offered an obvious occasion for a gesture that would cement the parsons to him, and transform those weekly sermons, which had troubled Godolphin to the point of making Sacheverell an example, into an iterative pledge of fealty to her majesty's government.

If Harley was about to pay court to Swift, the vicar was only waiting to be courted. Writing to Archbishop King immediately after arriving in London, he said Harley had 'formerly made some advances towards me, and unless he be altered, will, I believe, think himself in the right to use me well'.[1] But Harley was less like Sir William Temple than like some of the Restoration intriguers who had given Swift's plain-dealing patron so much discomfort. If he had not already heard enough about Harley's addictions to secretiveness and procrastination, Swift would have learned all he had to know from the minister's arrangements for their first interview. In order to see Lord Treasurer Godolphin in 1708, Swift had needed one or two introductions; but then he had simply gone in. To call on the Chancellor of the Exchequer, Swift had to meet a friend who knew an intermediary who would prepare an appointment which would then be altered.

Soon after settling himself in London, Swift began to meet his old school and college friend, Francis Stratford, now a merchant rumoured to be worth a hundred thousand pounds and known to be lending the government a colossal sum. After calling on him, Swift dined with him, then saw him again and again. One Saturday at the end of the month he was supposed to dine with both Stratford and a government official named Erasmus Lewis, one of the undersecretaries of state in the office of Lord Dartmouth. Lewis had once been secretary to Harley and still remained a kind of confidential agent for him. On this date he was expected to bring Swift to meet the great man. Instead, however, he could not appear at all, because sudden business called him away to Hampton Court. He sent his excuse and with it a promise to introduce Swift to Harley the Wednesday following. Meanwhile, Swift was making sure that the Chancellor of the Exchequer would appreciate his balanced inclinations. For this delicate purpose he had told Erasmus Lewis to describe him confidentially to Harley as a 'discontented person, that was used ill for not being Whig enough'—in other words, as a sufferer for refusing to 'go certain lengths'[2]—and this was a case that Swift considered parallel to Harley's own recent history. Three days

---

[1] Williams I. 173.

[2] *Journal*, 30 Sept. 1710, pt 2; Williams I. 183-4. I assume that 'another hand' must mean Lewis.

after the broken dinner engagement, Dr Swift paid a call on Undersecretary Lewis, evidently to clear the final arrangements. Some hint of the operation may, I think, have leaked out (perhaps by Harley's intent), because late that same evening Swift's landlady brought a servant of Lord Halifax up to his room after he had snuffed his candle; and the vicar was informed that his lordship desired his company at dinner the next afternoon, in the Earl's house near Hampton Court. If this was a stratagem, it had no effect, since, as Swift reported to the ladies, 'I sent him word I had business of great importance that hindered me.'[1]

The morning after this, on 4 October 1710, a Wednesday as promised, while all of Lord Wharton's parliamentary candidates were being defeated in Buckinghamshire, Swift was at last 'brought privately' to the Chancellor of the Exchequer, to confer with him about the First Fruits. After so many omens and out-riders the sight of the important face itself might easily have made an anticlimax. But if Harley was no Temple, neither was he a Godolphin. His informants had told him enough about the proud parson for Harley to understand how to act toward this petitioner. Lewis had assured Swift that he would be entertained with the utmost civility, and the performance immediately surpassed the prediction. Harley did not receive Swift with nonchalance or mere warmed-over politesse but wrapped him in 'the greatest respect and kindness imaginable'. He assured Swift that he had often heard of him and that both he and his associates had 'long expected' Swift's arrival from Ireland. He at once found time for another appointment the following Saturday, when the agent of the Irish church would be afforded more leisure in which to explain his proposals quite fully; and during the days between, Swift was to prepare copies of documents for that purpose.[2]

When Saturday afternoon came, Swift was exposed to a degree of exhilaration that even the first closeting with Harley had not led him to look for. A slight turn of suspense only helped to enrich the bliss that came after. When the black-gowned vicar arrived

[1] *Journal*, 4 Oct. 1710.
[2] *Ibid.*, 4 Oct. 1710; Williams I. 183–4 (dealing with 7 Oct.); Davis VIII. 122. I assume it was Lewis who 'whispered' Swift about Harley's eagerness to see him.

at the door of 14 Buckingham Street,[1] the dignified porter would
not admit him but said his master had just gone in to dinner with
a great many guests and would like Dr Swift to return an hour
later. The porter was—as Swift soon heard—celebrated for his
mendacity, and his sedate good manners did not prevent the
caller from assuming that when he did return, he would be told
that the great man had just gone out. The suspicion was unfair,
however; the liar for once had been honest; and when Swift
reappeared at five o'clock, the Chancellor himself came grandly
forth to meet him in the hall.

Evidently, Harley had sized Swift up at the original interview,
and determined that he was worth charming. On Swift's part,
the domestic setting of the next four hours was probably a deep
reason for the extraordinary pleasure that infused them. Even
more than for most would-be protégés Swift's ambitions took a
filial form. The office and income he hoped to win through a
patron were equivalent to the heritage his own shortlived father
had failed to bequeath him. In yearning to be granted his success
for his own sake, and not for mere services rendered or fees paid,
he was looking for the recognition a parent gives to a child.
Among English political leaders, moreover, Harley was remarkable for an attachment to his private family enjoyments. He
possessed neither Marlborough's greed, nor Godolphin's addiction to the racetrack, nor St John's itch of fornication. He loved
the company of his wife, his children, and his brother. Characteristically, he now brought Swift into a mixed party of family
and friends, presenting the clerical guest to his son, his son-in-
law, and a group that included William Penn. For two hours the
general entertainment continued, steeping Swift in the mood of
intimacy and flattering him by a method superior to any words.
The vicar, who had an Irish palate, did not fail to discern that the
wine they drank all this time was superb.

After the company left, Harley kept him another two hours,
talking about business. The First Fruits made only a part of their
subject matter, for Harley took up the question of the *Examiner*
and also declared that he must introduce Dr Swift to Mr St John.

[1] No longer standing; it had been Pepys's house (*Survey of London*, 1937).

Employing the parson's Christian name and working like a mesmerist on his eager sensibilities, Harley gave him repeated moments of drama and glory. That night, as the happy victim went over his ordeal of euphoria in a letter to the ladies, he observed that the great man had said 'so many things of personal kindness and esteem for me, that I am inclined half to believe what some friends have told me, that he would do everything to bring me over'.[1] Harley asked Swift to come and see him often, but his guest shrewdly replied that he did not like to disturb the head of the state in the midst of all his affairs and preferred, consequently, to see Harley at his ordinary crowded levees; whereupon the great man observed, 'That was not a place for friends to come to.'[2] Swift recognized this retort as a piece of delicate flattery, but his pleasure did not therefore evaporate. Moreover, as if to demonstrate his sincerity, Harley pledged Swift to come to dinner on Tuesday, a mere three days off. Only when the visitor had to depart was the easy openhandedness shut down. Then, as the conversation approached its close and the evening had to be over, the spirit of mystery without imagination descended; for Harley saw Swift off not in his own identifiable carriage but in a hackney coach, and set him down not at Swift's lodgings in Bury Street but at St James's coffee-house.

IV. GATHERING THE FIRST FRUITS

A better token of Harley's sincerity than calling Swift 'Jonathan' or inviting him to dinner was the minister's going to work on the First Fruits with enough speed and effect to put Swift's hopes higher than they had been since Pembroke's act of Indiangiving. As the politic doctor said to the ladies, 'How far we must depend upon new friends, I have learned by long practice, though I think among great ministers, they are just as good as old ones.'[3] Just how much of a friend the Chancellor of the Exchequer was likely to be, Swift would judge from the management of the mission which had ostensibly brought the doctor from Ireland. For in this too Swift wanted his success on his own terms.

[1] *Journal*, 8 Oct.   [2] *Ibid.*   [3] *Ibid.*, 7 Oct.

[394]

It would not satisfy him that the thing should be granted. It would have to be granted in such a manner that Swift's rôle would appear to have been indispensable. His mother, the church, would have to acknowledge that she owed her new comfort to one of the humblest of her sons. Without this necessary condition, Swift's private accomplishment would have none of the value he yearned to add to his public reputation.

Unfortunately for these hopes, Swift could not represent himself as labouring alone on the project. For political reasons any stroke of benevolence that fell from above to assist a public corporation was normally attributed (whatever its true source) to the official power most likely to bestow further favours. With more simplicity than was used in thanking the divine being, the Convocation of the Church of Ireland was accustomed to express gratitude to the Lord Lieutenant for blessings in the command of the government. When a viceroy was not available, a crowned head or Lord Treasurer could usually be fixed upon. Lower agents might be acknowledged for an incidental share in the work. They might be paid off with some sort of advancement or a grant of money. But they were neither likely to find themselves recognized from below, for fear of discommoding some eminence, nor likely to win accolades from above for fear of an apparent slight to others on their own level.

Swift might have thought he was escaping from this danger by applying to Harley during the interregnum between the dismissal of Wharton and the naming of the next Lord Lieutenant. If any credit at all was going to be assigned, it would have to settle itself upon either the Queen, the chief minister, or the vicar of Laracor; and in the absence of other names it would be obvious that Dr Swift, the only active petitioner, must deserve the praise for bringing the project to the attention of the court. What Swift overlooked (among other things) was the opposition within the Irish church to his old patron. It was King who had pushed Swift's claim to this enterprise; and the highest churchmen among the Irish clergy had no reason to regard the archbishop as their ally. The very alteration that had put Harley in power also gave hegemony to the faction of Atterbury and Lindsay. Such

[395]

extremists as Archdeacon Percival or Bishop Pooley would hardly wish to honour the disciple of their enemy. Since Swift for ten years had identified himself with Whigs, the attitude of suspicion was all the darker.

Such forces would have been ready to turn against the vicar of Laracor even if he had been the sole negotiator empowered to remind the government of the First Fruits. But this he was not. Before he even started for London, his mission was supposed to be receiving the attention of two bishops already there: Hartstonge of Ossory and Lindsay of Killaloe. In fact, his commission itself had taken the form of a letter addressed to their graces. It stated that he would work with them and requested that if they could not stay in London long enough to finish the affair, they would hand the necessary papers over to him. Probably the whole arrangement came about because neither of the bishops intended to hang on any further in London. But it did narrow Swift's scope.

Yet when he first arrived, he had the satisfaction of discovering that Hartstonge had been gone for some time and Lindsay was about to clear out, leaving the road open for Dr Swift. Of course, before he could begin to taste the freedom thus allowed him, he underwent the maddening and pointless interview with Godolphin. As it was widely understood that Harley hoped to form a ministry not of extremists but of co-operative Whigs and sane Tories, Swift had no way to be sure who would finally stay in the government and who would be tipped out. The icy interview seemed to make it clear that Godolphin would do nothing whether in or out. Yet Swift let three weeks pass before telling the ladies that he was going to see Harley. It is true he was waiting for the bishops' papers to be delivered to him, and they did not arrive till 26 September[1]; but he had not troubled about these when he rapped on Godolphin's door. Another reason for delay was that Swift thought at first of trying to work through Earl Poulett, a high-churchman who had been made Lord Steward as well as first Lord of the Treasury, and who Swift thought was inclined to help him.[2] But this lead quickly faded out; and the

---

[1] *Accounts 1709–10*, fol. 10^v. Ball erroneously gives 25 Sept. (i. 385).
[2] Williams i. 173.

ultimate cause of delay became the time it necessarily took for
Swift's feelers to communicate with Harley's antennae.

While he hovered, of course, the documents which the bishops
had carried back with them reached him from Archbishop King.
But when Swift transcribed these materials for Harley, he did not
simply copy the original memorial as sent over to him. Instead, he
undertook, a little presumptuously, to expand the conditions of
the favour he was begging for. The remission of the First Fruits
and Twentieth Parts would be worth only a little over a thousand
pounds a year to the Church of Ireland.[1] The scheme already
agreed on was to forgive beneficed clergyman the 'twentieth
parts' altogether and to continue collecting the 'first fruits' fees
but turn them into a common fund for increasing the glebe and
the stipend of poor ecclesiastical livings. What Swift wished to do
was to get exactly the same treatment applied to the crown rents,
which were fees of much higher value than the others. So he drew
up two forms of an abbreviated memorial, one draft suggesting
that her majesty should turn back the crown rents as well as the
lighter fees, and the other draft omitting this appeal. If Swift
could secure the extra benefit, he would not only bring his church
three times the advantage originally hoped for; he would also
possess the entire credit himself, inasmuch as he would be undeniably both the begetter and the executor of the more grand
design. If he could not secure it but could capture the First Fruits
quickly, before her majesty named a Lord Lieutenant to succeed
Wharton, he might still hug some glory to himself. Swift planned
to sound Harley out on the crown rents, and if he seemed encouraging, to give him the draft mentioning them; if not, the
other draft would suffice.

When Swift finished his long evening with Harley, the doctor's
resources of scepticism were nearly exhausted by the minister's
power of insinuation. Swift might tell Archbishop King, 'I never
knew one great minister, who made any scruple to mould the
alphabet into whatever words he pleased'; but he thought he had
at last discovered a statesman whose words matched his intentions. Harley listened attentively to the doctor's exposition; and

[1] Landa, p. 64, n. 3.

when Swift mentioned the blocks put in his way by Lord Lieutenants, the great man cordially sympathized, saying that any
merit for the good deed would belong to the Queen alone and
that he would try to have it done before she named a new Lord
Lieutenant. Swift told him of the crown rents; and since Harley
did not reject the proposal, Swift gave him the longer memorial.
Harley read it at once, put it in his pocket to show the Queen, and
promised Swift to second the motion for the crown rents as well as
the smaller grant of the First Fruits. Reporting to the ladies,
Swift said Harley 'said every thing I could wish'.[1]

This was Saturday, 7 October. Dining with Harley the following Tuesday, Swift was put through a fresh and tantalizing experience of the minister's secretiveness; for he learned not only
that Harley had spoken to the Queen and given her Swift's
memorial but also that her majesty would approve and settle the
remission of the First Fruits in a few days, before naming a Lord
Lieutenant[2]; yet Swift was to keep these hints to himself until
Harley allowed him to pass them on to Archbishop King. The
enforced silence soon led Swift into an impasse so exasperating
that it ought to seem funny if it were not symbolic of all his ambiguous relations with the Irish episcopate. Because Swift had complained of the narrow limits of his original commission, King and
Primate Marsh sent him a letter signed by them both, entrusting
him with the 'full management' of the matter. At the same time,
King was alerting the archbishops of York and Canterbury to
advance the scheme with motions of their own; and he recalled
an old conversation between her majesty and himself in which
she had seemed to hesitate only as to the time when it would be
proper to pass the grant.[3] While these innocent gestures were
emerging, Swift's side of the work was racing ahead. Harley gave
him dinner again in less than a week and said the Queen was
going to announce her remission of the First Fruits at a cabinet
council the next day, but Swift was even yet not to give out the
news. Whether or not she in fact did so, Swift's dinners and
meetings with Harley went on for another three weeks, with
appointments cancelled and talks postponed. On 21 October,

[1] *Journal*, 7 Oct.; Williams I. 196.   [2] *Journal*, 10 Oct., pt 2.   [3] Williams I. 187.

Harley told him her majesty had definitely granted the First
Fruits, although the crown rents could not yet be added. He also
said that the Queen in her formal statement would take notice of
Swift's memorial (she never did). But he still gave no permission
for Swift to inform the archbishop of the grant.[1] Five days later,
alas, the Duke of Ormonde had to be made Lord Lieutenant, and
Swift worried about the stiles and fences his grace's secretaries
might erect. He even went through the pantomime of asking
Ormonde to permit him to apply to Harley. Only so late as Friday, 3 November, was Swift set free to launch his small missile,
and then nobody but King and Marsh were to know; for not
until an official letter reached them from Lord Dartmouth as
Secretary of State would they in turn be privileged to inform
anyone else.

In spite of the hedges and suspense, Swift felt rather dazzled by
his splendid accomplishment. Harley had discussed the grant
with the Queen four times in two weeks and then told Swift she
had passed it 'absolutely, as my memorial desired'.[2] He now promised benignly to present the vicar to her majesty—a consummation that was in fact never to be realized. Sharing his self-
gratulation with the ladies, Swift said, 'I believe never any thing
was compassed so soon, and purely done by my personal credit
with Mr Harley, who is so excessively obliging, that I know not
what to make of it, unless to shew the rascals of the other party
that they used a man unworthily who had deserved better.'[3] Of
course, it is to a politician's advantage to encourage every successful lobbyist to imagine that the finished deed is due to the one
agent's efforts. And Swift deserves praise enough for giving the
strong, decisive, accomplishing lift to a labour that had been
stumbling irregularly toward its goal under a series of feckless
managers. But with the Queen, her new ministry, the church
hierarchy of both kingdoms, and the new Lord Lieutenant all
predisposed to the same end, he might perhaps have moderated
his cockiness. And if he felt disinclined to do so on his own, there
were others at hand who were quite willing to do it for him.

When the Irish bishops heard of Ormonde's appointment, they

[1] *Journal*, 21 Oct. [2] Williams I. 194. [3] *Journal*, 21 Oct.

of course did not yet know of Swift's success. Arguing that to continue employing the vicar of Laracor would mean alienating his excellency, they insisted that Swift should surrender all his papers and that the petition should be channelled through the Duke. Swift's connection with the Whigs, they further argued, would destroy his value as a solicitor with the Tories. Unwillingly, King announced their decision in a message to his protégé which crossed the announcement by Swift that his application had already succeeded. With an irony to be fully tasted only by posterity, Swift told the archbishop, 'I was a little in pain about the Duke of Ormonde, who, I feared might interpose in this matter, and be angry it was done without him: but Mr. Harley has very kindly taken this matter upon himself.' As for credit and gratitude, Swift said, 'The Queen was resolved to have the whole merit of this affair to herself. Mr. Harley advised her to it, and next to her majesty he is the only person to be thanked.'[1] Whether Swift thought he was delivering advice or making an accurate forecast, he was mistaken. In the middle of November the Irish bishops wrote to Edward Southwell, who lived in England but held the title of Secretary of State for Ireland and acted as a kind of resident agent for Irish affairs. They enclosed, in perfect ignorance, an address to Ormonde concerning the First Fruits. About the same time, the Bishop of Kildare told Southwell to expect all the pertinent documents from Swift. Any clarity about who did or did not deserve thanks for the work was destroyed by these blind moves, since the churchman who doubted Swift and King would always remain free to insist that the open proclamation of the remission, whenever it should come, was the consequence of taking responsibility away from the vicar and handing it to the Duke. By the time Swift saw Southwell and heard his directions, he had already got and replied to the archbishop's warning of what was coming. Since all Swift had to do was to point out that the bishops were knocking at an open door, his reply has great dignity; but at one point he brandishes a clenched fist: 'If my lords the bishops doubt whether I have any credit with the present ministry, I will, if they please, undo this matter in as little

[1] Williams I. 190.

time as I have done it.'[1] After seeing Southwell, however, Swift poured off some of the dignity and filled its space with venom. To show the archbishop who was on what terms with the head of the British government or the Lord Lieutenant of Ireland, he threw at him a budget of invidious notes on Dr Swift's court calendar:

> I did not value the slighting manner of the Bishop of Kildare's letter, barely desiring Mr. Southwell to call on me for the papers, without any thing further, as if I had been wholly insignificant; but I was at a loss how to behave myself with the Duke and Mr. Harley. I met the latter yesterday in the Court of Requests, and he whispered me to dine with him. At dinner I told him of the dispatch to Mr. Southwell, and raillied him for putting me under difficulties with his secrets, that I was running my head against a wall; that he reckoned he had done the church and me a favour; that I should disoblige the Duke of Ormond, and that the bishops in Ireland thought I had done nothing, and had therefore taken away my commission. He told me your lordship had taken it away in good time, for the thing was done, and that as for the Duke of Ormond, I need not be uneasy, for he would let his grace know it as soon as he saw him, which would be in a day or two at the Treasury, and then promised again to carry me to the Queen, with the first opportunity.[2]

This explosion relieved Swift's pride more than his spleen; and in order to give the archbishop a true impression of his seething emotions, Swift indulged himself in several expressions bruising enough to make one sympathize with King's uneasy attitude toward him:

> If I had consulted my own interest, I should have employed my credit with the present ministry another way. The bishops are mistaken in me; it is well known here, that I could have made my markets with the last ministry if I had pleased; and the present men in power are very well apprised of it, as your grace may, if I live to see you again; which I certainly never would in Ireland, if I did not flatter myself that I am upon a better foot with your grace, than with some other of their lordships.[3]

Then, as if to flay the skin he had scraped, Swift informed his correspondent of the scheme for the crown rents, claiming that Harley had encouraged him to hope they too might be remitted, but

[1] *Ibid.*, p. 193.   [2] *Ibid.*, p. 195.   [3] *Ibid.*

insinuating that Swift would now feel less impulsion to solicit for them.

King met Swift's outbursts with a warm, even-tempered prudence, sincerely urging him to keep up the pressure and candidly anticipating that Swift would win his recognition when the facts became public. 'If the matter be done, assure yourself it will be known by whom, and what means it was effected.'[1] If the matter be done! For all King's sanguine complexion and Swift's surface of pessimism, it was the archbishop who still waited for an official pronouncement to establish the fact. He had, unfortunately, long enough to wait. On the last day of the year Swift was still pursuing St John with a memorial to get the Queen's letter for the First Fruits. St John promised to supply it 'in a very few days'.[2] And a couple of days later he assured Swift it was all 'granted and done, and past all dispute'.[3] Yet the truth remains that it took two additional months for the warrant to be passed.[4] The comedy of blunders still went on. Swift kept insisting to the archbishop and the ladies that he desired no gratitude, and in the same breath he choked with spite because he had received no gratitude. The ministers kept assuring Swift that the grant was made, with only some negligible forms remaining. Yet no official message went out to establish the deed as accomplished. King applauded Swift and waited for visible proof. The bishops petitioned Ormonde, who said he would in a proper time lay their petition before the Queen. The seasons changed; winter passed, and spring arrived. 'I doubt that matter sleeps', King said drily and not unsympathetically in March 1711, 'and that it will be hard to awaken it.'[5] Nearly two months still later, when Ormonde was getting ready to move to Dublin, Swift, whose steam for this particular engine was now much reduced, said, 'I never mention anything of the First Fruits either to Mr. Harley or the Duke of Ormonde. If it be done before his grace goes over, it is well, and there is an end: if not, I shall have the best opportunity of doing it in his absence.'[6] A month later he said the grant would

[1] Williams, p. 197. But Swift's anger worried him; see King's letter of 30 Nov. 1710 to Jenkins.
[2] Journal, 31 Dec. 1710.   [3] Ibid., 2 Jan. 1711.
[4] Ibid., p. xxii, n. 2; p. 185, n. 24.   [5] Williams I. 217.   [6] Ibid., p. 230.

be included in Ormonde's opening speech to the Irish Parliament.[1] And finally, nine months after Swift was told that everything was settled, Archbishop King wrote that the Duke had indeed mentioned the business as done, and without assuming any merit to himself. At the end of July the letter patent came, dated 17 February 1711, or four months after Ormonde's appointment.

The Lord Lieutenant's modesty could throw no lustre on Swift. Both the Convocation of the Church of Ireland and the House of Lords offered up gratitude for the grant. They thanked her majesty; they thanked Harley, who was now Earl of Oxford and Lord Treasurer of Great Britain; and they thanked their Lord Lieutenant: the peers acknowledged the Duke's 'particular care and mediation'[2]; Convocation described his excellency as 'in a great measure responsible'[3] for the fulfilment of the long hope. From no spokesman at any stage did the least allusion emerge to Dr Swift. The Lord Treasurer told Swift he would write a letter to Ireland, giving the merit of the grant to Swift and the Queen, and letting the bishops know it was all done before Ormonde became their governor. As late as October 1711, Swift still deluded himself with the prospect of this letter's being sent. But of course it never was.[4]

Long after, at a meeting of the Board of First Fruits, several of Swift's friends did go so far as to propose a vote of thanks to the doctor.[5] However, Welbore Ellis, Bishop of Kildare, who in October 1710 had told Southwell to recover the documents from Swift, arose and quashed the motion.[6] It was Ellis, by coincidence, who as Dean of Christ Church Cathedral, Dublin (the office he held *in commendam* as Bishop of Kildare), was carrying on the immense lawsuit of his chapter against the Archbishop of Dublin; so he would hardly have been displeased with the opportunity to stab his grace through a protégé's sides. Yet

---

[1] *Ibid.*, pp. 238–9. [2] *Ibid.*, p. 241, n. 2. [3] Landa, p. 64, n. 3.
[4] Williams I. 260; *Journal*, 20 Oct. 1711.
[5] Bishop Ashe, writing in June 1711, told Swift that Archbishop King had given him much merit for the First Fruits in a full assembly of the clergy, but Swift doubted the account (*Journal*, 3 Jul. 1711).
[6] Landa, p. 65 and n. 2; Williams II. 221, n. 3.

[403]

when the archbishop wrote to Swift about the receipt of the letter patent, even he made no compliment to his own choice of agent. On learning the details of the addresses and proceedings relating to the First Fruits, Swift constructed for the archbishop's benefit a message so eruptive with plain wounded pride that King was forced to echo his correspondent's distress. With a voice that began to scream, Swift said, 'What can be the matter with those people? Do I ask either money or thanks of them? Have I done any hurt to the business?' He went over the ground of the whole affair like a compulsive old man looking for a misplaced jewel, and then returned to his high-pitched tirade: 'I should think the people of Ireland might rather be pleased to see one of their own country able to find some credit at court, and in a capacity to serve them, especially, one who does it without any other prospect than that of serving them. I know not any of the bishops from whom I can expect any favour, and there are not many upon whom a man of any figure could have such designs.'[1]

Although archbishops are usually entered under the rubric of bishops, King was willing to exclude himself from Swift's terms of reference, and honoured him with a paragraph which came as near to providing consolation as any gesture ever would:

> I can't but admire, that you should be at a loss to find what is the matter with those, that would neither allow you, nor any one else, to get any thing for the service of the church, or the public. It is, with submission, the silliest query I ever found made by Dr. Swift. You know there are some, that would assume to themselves to be the only churchmen and managers, and can't endure that any thing should be done but by themselves, and in their own way; and had rather that all good things proposed should miscarry, than be thought to come from other hands than their own, whose business is to lessen every body else, and obstruct whatever is attempted, tho' of the greatest advantage to church and state, if it be not from their own party.[2]

Swift was often more likely to feed than stifle a grudge, and as late as 1716 he was still trying to win himself some credit for the First Fruits. By then a board had been established to administer the fund, and Swift was applying for help in buying additional

---

[1] Williams I. 246 (reading 'who doeth it').   [2] *Ibid.*, p. 253.

glebe for Laracor. He bent so low as to request that a clause be inserted in the deed, mentioning his rôle in securing the remission. Inevitably, he was snubbed and the clause omitted. How often and in what language Swift let himself allude to the affair, one may alas estimate from a sneer which one of his episcopal enemies dropped in 1718: 'If Jonathan Swift is to be believ'd, all this was owing to his zeal and interest among the great ones with you.'[1]

After two hundred and fifty years one can still understand the remorseless grinding in Swift of the brake of pride upon the wheels of vanity. He loathed contemplating the zeal with which he panted for this trifling support to a fame which has come to rest indestructibly upon other foundations. Yet no thoughtful spectator can be surprised that Swift's coevals gave him as little appreciation in Ireland as he gave to Bishop Burnet for the same achievement in England.[2] So far as those outside the highest ministerial circle were concerned, no mote of evidence existed for Swift's claim other than his naked word. He had announced the grant in 1708 and been wrong; he announced it in 1710 and was right. That was as much as a bystander could be sure of. The dates, the names, the official letters were all against him. If Swift had absolutely, naggingly insisted, he might have got the kind of statement he desired. But this would not only have meant an unbearable sacrifice of his self-esteem. It would also have meant risking the loss of the convivial ease on which Swift's intimacy with statesmen depended. What he never could admit to anyone was that the real blame lay on Harley, whose secretiveness and procrastination had snuffed this side light on Swift's glory. By saying a few words to the right listeners, by adding a phrase to a letter, by hurrying what he was going to do anyhow, the Lord Treasurer could have satisfied the anxious parson's small conceit. But he did not. Swift, on the other side, rather than accuse Harley and thus destroy the illusion of perfect sympathy which made their friendship precious to him, transferred his resentments to the bishops, who were remote enough for his image of them to be indefinitely malleable.

---

[1] Landa, p. 65, n. 2. The board meeting that denied Swift's request was the occasion of his friends' motion to thank him (above, p. 403).   [2] Cf. Davis III. 74.

V. THE RHETORIC OF IMPARTIALITY

Harley's initial eagerness to accommodate Swift with the grant of the First Fruits was due to his hope of securing Swift's talent as a propagandist. But for Swift the invitation to become a ministry's mouthpiece easily transformed itself into an opportunity to act as spokesman for the responsible citizens of a nation. In this form Harley's offer was a many-sided satisfaction. It opened a new avenue to literary fame. It gave Swift the chance to help others in the fatherly rôle of public councillor. It conformed to his desire for success on his own terms.

To begin with, Harley made those first advances which Swift looked upon as a token of his own independence. It was Harley who proposed that Swift write for the ministry and not Swift who asked for the work. At their 7 October meeting, Harley probably dropped the earliest suggestions. I think the real understanding was reached a fortnight later, when Swift had dinner with him and stayed till after nine.[1] According to the story Swift told years afterward, Harley (whenever he did open the subject) said that the new ministers needed a good writer who would keep up the spirit already raised in the English people, and would 'assert the principles, and justify the proceedings' of his government. Harley said this province now lay in the hands of persons who were either too busy or else too lazy to manage it. The form their work had taken was of course the anonymous weekly essay on national affairs which had begun to appear several days before the dismissal of Godolphin. In Swift's language the main occupations of the *Examiner* were to make 'just reflections upon former proceed-

---

[1] Swift says that Harley first asked him to write the *Examiner* after the affair of the First Fruits was 'fully dispatched' (Davis VIII. 123). This is impossible because Swift's first number appeared on 2 Nov., long before the affair could be described as 'fully dispatched'. It was, however, during his long visit on 21 Oct. that Harley said the Queen had definitely made the grant (*Journal*, 21 Oct. 1710). Since Swift was with Harley for at least five hours—though other guests came and went—they had plenty of time for delicate subjects. I think it suggestive that apart from the First Fruits, Swift told Stella nothing they discussed. Since the authorship of the *Examiner* was to be kept as dark as possible, Swift never mentioned the paper to Stella until January 1711. Yet on 22 Oct. he told her about Steele's losing his post as Gazetteer for attacking Harley in the *Tatler*, a story which, I take it, Swift had just heard from Harley: it would have been directly pertinent to the plans for the *Examiner*.

ings' and to defend 'the present measures of her majesty', or, as we should say, to damn the Whigs and praise the Tories. With St John, Atterbury, and Prior numbered among the contributors, the standard of writing reached a height sufficient to provoke Addison to edit a short-lived, weak paper on the opposite side, lamely entitled the *Whig-Examiner*. When this expired, its ashes produced the less literate but more lively and durable *Medley*, edited by Addison's friend Arthur Mainwaring, a Whig M.P. and place man who was the Duchess of Marlborough's secretary and also acted as liaison between the politicos and the men of letters. Meanwhile, the *Tatler*, whose first volume was dedicated to Mainwaring, had continued to show no sympathy with the new ministry, although Addison was able to curb Steele's belligerence. Obviously, a man of Swift's calibre was wanted to mount a steady and well-aimed counter-fire to these offensives. With unwitting prescience the number of the pre-Swift *Examiner* for 31 August (the day Swift left Dublin) had twitted the *Tatler* for occupying himself with politics on the Whig side, and had said, 'His friends [i.e., Wharton and Addison], I hear are coming from Ireland. I expect too, some of my friends from the same country.'

Because many of the journalistic arguments back and forth ran *ad hominem*, it was normal for such periodicals to be anonymous. But besides fitting in with Harley's taste for covert manœuvres, this element also appealed peculiarly to Swift. His passion for hoaxes involving various games with his own identity strengthened Swift's instinct for self-protection; for by concealing his name, he of course defended himself against obvious forms of retaliation. But he also lived up to a pseudo-rational principle of his own, viz., that the true genius is too modest to risk the embarrassment of being known before his work has been judged.[1] In Swift I think this principle is the outer aspect of his inner longing to be valued for his own sake. By separating the author from the man, he could insure that the opinions passed on the *Examiner* essays would be untouched by anyone's prejudice toward Dr Swift. If the essays were really excellent, they would be

---

[1] Davis VII. 105. Mainwaring identified Swift as the Examiner almost immediately.

properly esteemed by all men whose taste remained uncorrupted by party loyalties. In turn, he could claim recognition, when it suited him as a person whose accomplishment was unimpugnable, and not dependent on the friendship of his backers.

It appears that Swift laid down some conditions before undertaking the work. Judging from all his comments about the paper, I think he had to feel he was a perfectly free agent. Although in the event he became eager to have Harley's or St John's opinion and to determine his policy by their requirements, I think he insisted that the final say must be his own. In other words, Swift looked on himself as in a sense generously and independently coming to the aid of men whom he approved of, assisting them with his uncoached, honest reasoning. Once more, the success would have to be on his own terms. 'I am of a temper', he said elsewhere, 'to think no man great enough to set me on work.'[1]

I also think that Swift failed to realize how far the effectiveness of political journalism hinges on neither honesty nor intelligence. After all, the greatest asset to such an author's power is timeliness. When a nation is fed up with despotism, any argument for freedom seems irresistible. When a nation is tired of war, whoever praises peace sounds convincing. Another ingredient more important than rhetoric or logic is special information. Neither Swift nor Junius nor Burke could have produced his dazzling effect if he had not been equipped with facts denied to pedestrian hacks. The material may have come from their own experience and study or from the resources of the statesmen they worked with, but it was more persuasive than the finest prose that lacked it. Further, the great pamphleteers share as well a property distinct from this and still not literary, which can also triumph over a great style; and this is an infusion of moral idealism. Only a temporary and narrow political appeal can move men on selfish grounds alone. Even the baldest operation of commercial greed in the War of the Spanish Succession had to be represented as social love. Thus when rhetoric does come into play, whether as logic or as literary contrivance, it strengthens a mechanism which can operate without it, at least in so far as clear, straight-

[1] Davis III. 194.

forward speech is distinguishable from artful rhetoric. But it gains impetus from another dispensable element, which is the personal implication of the author in his work. As a simple fact about human emotions or the psychology of creation, it seems clear that the more a writer feels himself to be part of the cause he is defending, the harder he will search for fresh, strong ways to justify the cause. If he is really fortunate, he will be able to identify his own fate with his party's fate and his party's with his people's.

In writing the *Examiner*, Swift enjoyed all these advantages and felt conscious of several, especially of his unique genius as a writer. The habit of flipping Swift into a drawer labelled 'satire', and then presenting him to the world as nothing but an example of the category, has driven critics to disregard his gifts as a persuasive recommender of courses of action, just as it has blinded them to his excellence as a letter-writer. Yet in his own career it was this positive, persuasive force, infused with his satire and irony, that marked Swift's greatest triumphs. His training as a sermonizer invariably underlies his exercises of mockery; and Swift's mockery is always a preparation for a sermon.

Swift seldom wrote better than in the *Examiner*; for if it is less often read than the *Spectator*, the fault lies not in its style. Each essay was about two thousand words long, and Swift could easily and meticulously compose one within seven days. Somebody took great care that the printing of each number should be correct, because there are almost no typographical errors. Swift himself stopped the press sometimes to make improvements.[1]

Nevertheless, for the effect of the *Examiner*, timeliness meant more than art. The war had lasted so long that both its heroes and their celebrators were growing suspect. The price of corn doubled after the bad harvests of 1709 and 1710. The land tax had no end. Shopkeepers suffered as their customers felt the pinch. Recruiting was slow, and men feared the prospect of a standing army.

[1] Two of the variants in the original issues can be due only to Swift; the insertion of a title before the fable, 1 Mar. 1711; and the complete replacement of one concluding sentence by another, 10 May 1711. Possibly the changes were made for reprints of the separate numbers. (Neither of these variants has been noticed by Swift's editors.)

From the polls in October 1710 the great party of peace, the churchmen, the 'country' faction, and the Tories emerged victorious. Although Swift's assigned message was simple, therefore, it was bound to be popular; blame the Junto for prolonging the war and ruining the nation; praise Harley's ministry for restoring decent government and seeking a just peace.

Swift himself realized his case was intrinsically popular. But he did not always realize how far his authority was deepened by materials that well-placed friends supplied. Recommending the *Examiner* papers to the ladies, he boasts, 'You may count upon all in them to be true.'[1] Even *a priori*, however, Swift's simple awareness of what the politicians wished him to say gave him the immense advantage of not being contradicted by an official source, and of normally seeming corroborated by events. If he foresaw courses of action, they were the ones pursued. In particulars, moreover, he often received expert guidance. When he wrote about a meeting of the convocation of Canterbury Province, Atterbury supplied him with concrete details.[2] When he wrote about an attempt to assassinate Harley, he had accounts from the minister's son and from St John, the most important witness, who also read over the essay before it went to press.[3] The effect of such advantages was sharpened by Swift's anonymity. Mixing with men of all opinions, he could test his theses, estimate his success, and study his enemy close up. Naturally, these advantages were not impregnable. If Swift said in his first *Examiner* that he conversed 'in equal freedom with the deserving men of both parties', he could say so with diminishing accuracy every succeeding week; for as the Whig spokesmen noticed how intimate their friend was with the Tories, they treated him with growing reserve, though some like Halifax still tried to regain him for their side. Receiving his selection of facts through Harley, St John, and their aides, Swift wanted little persuasion to give voice to the same views as those of his informants.

He also enlarged his influence by a degree of moral idealism which, in his writings on England, Swift never surpassed. The

---

[1] *Journal*, 7 Mar. 1711.   [2] Davis III. 50.
[3] Williams I. 213; *Journal*, 8 Mar. 1711; Davis VIII. 128.

constant positive theme of the *Examiner* is the will of the people, the real will, what Rousseau was to call the general will, as distinct from the will of the majority. Swift holds up for his readers' approval the icon of a nation united in worship and in law, the medieval conception of a community with no inner conflicts, of a monarch, her subjects, and their representatives all infused with harmonious impulses. Intuitive reason, the common property of human nature, being free to work, drives them together in the same direction. It is a whole race of men like Martin in *A Tale of a Tub*,[1] men who have recovered their sanity after almost twenty years of being mad like Jack; for 'the people, when left to their own judgment, do seldom mistake their true interests'.[2]

To this constructive, integral community Swift opposes the variety, the inconsistency, the selfishness and destructiveness of the Whigs.[3] He claims that their heterogeneity is the distinct sign of their wickedness and weakness. Whereas the nation is one church, the Whigs are many sects; though the nation acknowledges one supreme legislative power, the Whigs desire rule by a moneyed rabble. The Whigs have a junto of several leaders, each one a self-centred egoist, temporarily united with his fellows in pursuit of common crimes. Continually, therefore, Swift speaks of the depravity of the separate leaders. To make their multiplicity vivid, he must make their individuality concrete. The small gang of dedicated destroyers of England is contrasted with the large, uniform bulk of the Queen, her government, clergy, and people. Ultimately the contest is described therefore as between a faction and the entire country; and by a corollary the Tories appear as setting nation above party, the Whigs as sacrificing the nation to an oligarchy. Thus the *Examiner* re-enforces his own status as that *vox populi* which is *vox dei*. Swift's was of course an Irish method of simplifying English politics. The coherent, viable constitution for which Ireland was starving, England already enjoyed on too solid a basis to be overthrown by political change. It was in Ireland that freedom was impossible without unity, because the most destructive influence upon the kingdom entered from the outside, controlling the whole by dividing the parts. In

[1] Cf. Davis I. 85. [2] *Ibid.*, III. 64. [3] *Ibid.*, p. 122.

England the time had come when liberty depended on variety.

Swift's political morality becomes the deepest spring of his rhetoric. By making the Junto into alien, unsympathetic, rebellious figures, he assigns them to the realm of comedy. We constantly find him characterizing the Whig leaders as of humble origin and mean natures, fit persons for comic rôles. Godolphin, following Sacheverell, even takes his nickname from Ben Jonson's play. Harley's circle, on the contrary, Swift gives to the realm of tragedy. The new ministers are nobly born, magnanimous, risking their lives and their fortunes for the sake of their country. Their deeds are important and dignified. When Swift represents them, his language grows sonorous:

> I confess my self so little a refiner in the politicks, as not to be able to discover what other motive, besides obedience to the Queen, a sense of publick danger, and a true love of their country, joined with invincible courage, could spirit up those great men, who have now under her majesty's authority undertaken the direction of affairs. What can they expect but the utmost efforts of malice from a set of enraged domestick adversaries?[1]

In imputing motives, therefore, Swift again follows an old-fashioned cynical irony like La Rochefoucauld's. When he is dealing with Whigs, he writes as though self-love were the inevitable root of all human behaviour with no exception. Avarice, ambition, lust, revenge are the normal causes of the Junto's deeds. Swift insists that this principle is descriptive and not condemnatory. Nevertheless, he implies relentlessly that self-love is vicious. When he is dealing with Harley's ministers, he reverses the attitude and bathes them in a glow of Christian self-sacrifice, the same standard by which La Rochefoucauld implicitly judges the court of Versailles. In portraying these new ministers, Swift does not suggest that they are curious interruptions of the rule he otherwise adheres to. Rather, he writes as though they constituted another species; the rule suddenly becomes irrelevant and virtue becomes natural, in an anticipation of Gulliver's Houyhnhnms.

Many kinds of formal devices help to communicate these atti-

[1] Davis III. 33.

tudes. But all of them depend upon Swift's usual mingling of self-dramatization with dualism. He divides the situation into two aspects, one praiseworthy and identified with himself, the other blamable and identified with the object attacked. Then he treats each from the point of view of the other, mimicking or impersonating the adherents of each, and pretending himself to belong in between. He is neither Whig nor Tory; only everything he says happens to hurt the Whigs. He is anonymous or a pseudo-Whig or a Whig talking like a Tory; but all his games with selfhood happen to identify the Whigs with knavery.

Simple irony is far from ubiquitous. It pokes through in small ways, from place to place, but full play with it is rare if brilliant[1]; for Swift had to be sure his readers did not misunderstand him. One of his most amusing forms of irony is the old reversal of connotations. In the *Examiner* Swift systematically describes the Whigs by the epithets and principles they applied to the Tories.[2] This trick easily becomes the sort of innuendo by which a vicious charge is taken wholly for granted in the vocabulary of a passage. A shining example is the following compact insinuation both that all Whigs are irreligious and that Dissenters hold their so-called religious views exclusively for political purposes: 'I write this paper for the sake of the Dissenters, whom I take to be the most spreading branch of the Whig party, that professeth Christianity.'[3] In a further refinement of ironic connotation he can attribute to the Whigs those properties which he himself normally attaches to the Tories: unanimity, for instance, can be ironically described as the mark of conspirators in an evil design, and hence characteristic of the Whigs.[4]

A number of remarkable analogies and conceits are to be found working in the same way and wittily associating the Whigs with avarice, rebellion, and atheism. In these mock-conceits, Swift picks up the 'anti-metaphysical' style of *A Tale of a Tub* or his satirical poems, inverting the effects of men like Cowley or Sir Thomas Browne; for the remote but striking parallelism turns out to be figuratively absurd, yet explosive with hostile innuen-

---

[1] E.g., 29 Mar.   [2] E.g., Davis III. 39, second half of page.   [3] *Ibid.*, p. 126.
[4] *Ibid.*, pp. 96–7.

does; here, for instance, are two conceits that add warmongering and madness to the rest of Swift's accusations against the Whigs:

> A dog loves to turn round often; yet after certain *revolutions*, he lies down to *rest*: but heads, under the dominion of the moon, are for perpetual *changes*, and perpetual *revolutions*: besides, the Whigs owe all their wealth to *wars* and *revolutions*; like the girl at Bartholomew-Fair, who gets a penny by turning round a hundred times, with swords in her hands.[1]

Certain commonplace analogies, used by many journalists and also frequent in Swift's other works, will be found repeatedly throughout the *Examiner*. He loves to treat the kingdom as a family and he loves to treat its troubles as diseases.[2] But neither the domestic metaphor nor the medical metaphor is so interesting as the ecclesiastical metaphor. This is the device of describing political events in ecclesiastical terms. It has two effects. One is the obvious reminder that the party divisions have religious aspects, inasmuch as Dissenters in England were more likely to follow the Junto than to support Harley's ministry. The other is the imputation to the Whigs of blasphemous, Papist, or free-thinking sentiments. Their religion, Swift keeps suggesting, is determined by their politics, and their politics become a form of damnable sinfulness. Thus he explicitly attacks the Junto's adopting a spoils system for distributing preferments, but he employs language that implicitly charges them with a love for Dissent: 'these very sons of *moderation* were pleased to *excommunicate* every man who disagreed with them in the smallest *article* of their *political creed*.'[3] The ecclesiastical metaphor seems a narrowed form of the great analogy underlying the alternation of narrative and digression in *A Tale of a Tub*, where first the Dissenters appear as pedantic scholars of false religion, and then the virtuosi appear as heretics or schismatics in learning.

Such conceits and metaphors easily expand themselves into the longer narrative devices with an allegorical tendency, especially

---

[1] Davis, III. 147.

[2] One of Swift's medical metaphors seems drawn from his own immediate experience. Compare the figure in the middle of Davis III. 67 with the description of Fountaine's illness, three weeks earlier, in the *Journal*, 29 Dec. 1710.

[3] Cf. Davis III. 39; also pp. 110–11, 126.

Swift's pseudo-myths and his use of parallel history. In all his examples of these it is the analogies that prompt the narrative rather than the reverse, because he has slight skill with plots.[1] When he employs parallel history in the *Examiner*, however, he shows a characteristic advance beyond his earlier technique, for he now makes his own recourse to it a self-conscious mockery of the Whig pamphleteers' practice. After picking up one of their specimens and deliberately twisting it to suit his immediate arguments, he shows off his superior talent by producing a brilliant example of his own.[2] More flamboyant but also self-conscious are his mythical metaphorical genealogies of terms like 'merit' or 'faction'. These have the peculiar virtue of being as much humorous as satirical: the writer's tone is so comprehending it seems almost tolerant. Thus when Swift describes faction (i.e., Whig factiousness) as the last daughter of liberty, and says that the mother, like many parents, doted on her 'youngest and disagreeablest' child,[3] we seem to have left the style of polemic or invective and to be in the more genial atmosphere of Arbuthnot's John Bull, whose second daughter, Discordia, is a more elaborate form of Swift's idea.

But all these devices are more obvious and less pervasive than the broad movements of Swift's special rhetoric; for his characteristic manners disclose themselves in many forms. The most difficult of his fundamental manœuvres to pin down for study is not his passion for analogizing but his habit of transforming a tendency or leaning into something absolute. In the *Argument against Abolishing Christianity*, when he treats religious toleration as ultimately equivalent to aggressive atheism, he does this. Throughout the *Examiner* he conscientiously confuses the past history of a political movement with its essence; so he traces the Whigs back to the Puritan republicans and then denounces the living leaders of the party for condoning the murder of Charles I. From looking back at the past he can quickly turn to seeing ahead for posterity. So he denounces the money-raising policies of the

---

[1] Cf. the far more eventful or dramatic narrative in which the same sort of allegory is cast in *Tatler* no. 48.

[2] Davis III. 26.   [3] *Ibid.*, p. 103.

Whigs on the grounds that if continued they would bankrupt future generations: contemporary innovations in finance Swift therefore treats as the immediate pauperization of England. Of course, these attitudes disappear when he discusses Harley's ministry, because this government is taken to represent the unchanging essence of English nationhood; the virtues of the regime are the virtues of the constitution. Just as Swift opposes simplicity to heterogeneity, so also he opposes being to change.

Among such prospects of change and fluctuation, Swift must bestow on his private, observing self a degree of stability and authority which makes it the absolute of absolutes. And this is the source of his best-known, most protean device. By attributing an unswervable steadiness to his essential, impalpable being, Swift allows himself the liberty to indulge in all those palpable acts of self-dramatization, mimicry, impersonation, and parody which supply the framework for his irony at the same time as they lend distance to his violence of expression. For behind his whole production sits the 'Examiner', grave and imperturbable. Like the supposed author of the *Argument against Abolishing Christianity*, the Examiner has a poker face. He is what Swift often really thought himself to be: disengaged and public-spirited. Unlike Swift—in truth or fancy—he is ingenuous as well, aiming no insinuations, free from malice. Most of Swift's masks and pseudonyms share this lack of spite or finesse along with an erratic innocence. They often but unpredictably miss the point of an innuendo, or they misinterpret sarcasm as plain talk, or they say they cannot understand an allusion. Finally, they appear to be creatures of common sense: subject to no caprice and owning no special source of knowledge, they merely comment, as any stable, rational person would, on facts liberally available to all.

This assumption that the inner self of the author is steady and unalterable comes nearest to being explicit in those repeated discussions, which Swift enjoys dilating, of the rôle of the *Examiner*. This reflex is altogether different from the autobiographical, self-justifying business of a work like Pope's *Epistle to Dr Arbuthnot*, which perhaps foreshadows Cowper's preparation for the Romantics' great obsession with selfhood. The *Examiner's* preoccupation, on the contrary, is in part the natural result of the periodical essay's being regularly presented as the expression of an idiosyncratic personality. The *Tatler*, the *Spectator*, the *Observator*, the *Review*, and the *Medley*'s authors all habitually write about their own rôles. What Swift does, however, is to pursue his extraordinary impulse to 'mock' any technique as soon as he becomes aware of it. He had written serious conceits in his early odes before he became self-conscious and wrote mock-conceits in *A Tale of a Tub*. He had written serious parallel history in the *Contests and Dissensions* before he wrote mock-parallel history in the *Examiner*. In precisely the same way, he discusses his rôle as a political essayist and then, self-consciously, mimics a political essayist discussing his rôle. Or he mockingly compares his own duties with those of his Whig rivals. Or else he imitates one of them meditating on such duties. Of course, any vocation can be regarded as a kind of identity which is then susceptible to mockery. Just as Bickerstaff one-upped Partridge at his own quack sport, so the Examiner can show up the writer of the *Medley* by taking off the manner of a polemical hack.

All these acts of mockery only strengthen our sense that the essential person behind them is different from the objects of his satire. Besides being stable where they are changeable, he is impartial where they are prejudiced, rational where they are capricious. To give depth to this front of disinterested objectivity, Swift simply talks about it. He claims endlessly that his concern is with moral truths, and not with personalities. He pretends to be steering the middle course between two extremes.[1] He boosts and puffs the *Examiner* for lacking the bias of its rivals.[2] By mere reiteration he compels one to feel that in a writer so consumed with the idea of dispassionate justice there must be a substantial degree of the trait itself. Beyond such deliberate assertions, however, Swift also illustrates the virtue he bestows on himself by constantly going through the motions of a search for basic

[1] Davis III. 85–91.
[2] Since biased propaganda, to be influential, must always present itself as objective truth, claims of impartiality belong to the stock-in-trade of most pamphleteers. For instance, Boyer, in the 'Advertisement' to his *Political State of Great Britain*, explicitly claims the traits emphasized by Swift.

axioms followed by the deductions of logic. Just as in the *Contests and Dissensions* he made a great and earnest show of presenting the elementary propositions of political philosophy and then of rigorously applying these to the impeachment of the four great peers, so in the *Examiner* he keeps seeming to start from universal postulates which he then exemplifies in the events of 1710–11. There are tremendous differences between the two cases, however. Far more than in the *Contests and Dissensions* Swift in the *Examiner* does not really bring established principles to bear on a controversy but rather invents a few specious generalizations that will lead to his chosen conclusions. He obviously has decided in advance exactly which clifftop he means to guide the reader toward, and therefore draws up a map that can direct him nowhere else. Far more characteristically, however, he again turns upon his own device with amazing boldness, and mocks the pose of impartiality; e.g., in comparing the *Examiner* with the papers of those journalists whom he calls 'advocates' of the Whigs' 'faction', Swift writes,

> The advice of some friends, and the threats of many enemies, have put me upon considering what would become of me if *Times should alter*. This I have done very maturely, and the result is, that I am in no manner of pain. I grant, that what I have said upon occasion, concerning the late men in power, may be called satyr by some unthinking people, as long as that faction is down; but if ever they come into play again, I must give them warning beforehand, that I shall expect to be a *favourite*, and that those pretended advocates of theirs will be pilloried for *libellers*. For, I appeal to any man, whether I ever charged that party, or its leaders, with one single action or design, which (if we may judge by their former practices) they will not openly profess, be proud of, and score up for merit, when they come again to the head of affairs.[1]

If we digress from matters of rhetoric to look at questions of biography, it becomes clear that Swift had deeply rooted emotional involvements in the campaigns of the *Examiner*. The pose of disinterested logic, of selfless public spirit, corresponds to the attitude that he consciously believed to be at the bottom of his allegiance to Harley and St John. 'According to the best judg-

[1] Davis III. 117. Cf. par. 2 of no. 26/7, *ibid.*, p. 76.

ment I have', he told the ladies, 'they are pursuing the true interest of the public; and therefore I am glad to contribute whatever is in my power.'[1] In other words, the mask he wore seems to have borne his own features! With an instinctive pleasure in the duties of a father and a long training in the work of a priest, Swift naturally welcomed the *Examiner*'s opportunities to form the opinions of Englishmen. Coming from Ireland, where racial, religious, and political factionalism divided the kingdom among three incompatibilities, Swift naturally regarded government above party—to which so many political theorists paid lip-service —as supremely desirable. As a visitor to England he had less difficulty in simplifying the real complexities of politics into stark, specious patterns than a perceptive native would have had. Finally, to a man whose feelings were so violent and whose intellectual positions were rarely the result of independent analysis, the rhetoric of impartiality must have been a delightful, self-deceiving sport. Now, therefore, Swift's fetish of independence showed its value. His belief that his opinions were unconstrained gave his style a warmth and air of truth which no paid journalist could match. That he still lined up with Harley on issue after issue was due chiefly to his inner assent to the new ministry's professions. In Swift's political writings of the decade before he took up the *Examiner* he had delivered opinions consistent with those of his forthcoming weekly essays.

All things considered, it is hardly surprising that no other publicist could arrive at Swift's style of authority. Steele's outspoken sincerity fails not merely because Steele writes diffusely, repetitiously, and without information, but because he always confuses the gush of spontaneous feeling with the truth of moral insight. 'Believe me, for I am in earnest', seems his motto. Defoe's didactic, knowledgeable glibness fails, for all its vigour, because he cannot smother a tone of intrigue and spite that clashes with his pretence of writing for the public good. Addison can match Swift's elegance and authority but never his power and wit. None of these authors could feel, as Swift truly did, that he was an independent agent, almost an outsider, saying what suited him and

[1] *Journal*, 30 Nov. 1710 (Swift's birthday).

[419]

helping ministers who deserved his support regardless of how they might reward him. If Swift had not been determined to succeed purely on his own terms, the achievement of the *Examiner* would have been impossible.

Through all the numbers, Swift had one obvious, repeated theme—the superiority of the Tories to the Whigs. This often came out in a question: why had the Queen replaced her old government by her new? His standard answer was that the Junto had managed affairs solely to keep themselves on top, and to fill their purses or to indulge their vices, whereas the Tories worked for the nation. Several of the papers are primarily attacks on Whig propagandists. I have suggested how Swift would ridicule them, parody them, scold and preach to them; for he never made the tactical error of replying seriously, point by point, to their assertions. But there is considerable exposition of Tory doctrine (besides one paper in defence of noble families and another defining passive obedience); and Swift took pains to praise the handling of the clergy by the new administration.

The most famous papers—the Art of Political Lying, the Bill of Ingratitude, the Impeachment of Verres, the Examiner Cross-Examined, the Letter to Crassus[1]—come early in the series of thirty-three which he wrote. After the first three months I think Swift found little challenge in the periodical. He must have felt glad that the end of the session meant a halt to these labours. Parliament rose 12 June 1711; Swift's last *Examiner* came out two days later. The best numbers, such as no. 26 (1 February 1711), possess only a few hints of the blemishes that spoil the weak ones. But these are faults vitiating, for most modern readers, the force of the whole series and anticipating the defects of the pamphlets which followed. When Swift does invoke a political ideal in the essays, it turns the reader not toward a promising future but toward a stable past. It is an ideal of saving the best of established things, not of creating the best things possible. It is a judicious conservatism rather than a heroic vitality. In the worst aspects of the *Examiner* these attitudes amount to a snobbery, a xenophobia, a niggling sanctimoniousness that make one wish to

[1] 9, 23, 30 Nov. 1710; 4 Jan., 8 Feb. 1711.

shout at Swift that he should stop trying to divert our attention
from his undistinguished ancestry, his foreignness as an Irishman,
and his associations with rakes; for he often seems to crack down
the hardest on those whose behaviour stimulates the same tendencies in himself.

Swift is most effective when he either sounds perfectly self-
controlled in the face of wickedness or else gets indignant for the
sake of a generous ideal. From time to time in the *Examiner* he
sounds prissy rather than self-controlled and gets angry for the
sake of a selfish passion. When a man curls his lip at a good-
natured blunder, he appears not above the battle but beneath it.
When he falls into a rage over a lost penny, he hardly makes an
impressive figure. Especially in those papers which come after the
start of Harley's invalidism during the middle of March 1711,
Swift tends to rely on an assertiveness and a simulated delicacy of
morals which I find distasteful. When he offers a mealy-mouthed
compliment to Parliament for taking a week's adjournment so the
Speaker might have time to mourn his son's death, the hypocrisy
of the effort corrupts his style, all the more because Swift knew
the gesture was a subterfuge to give the ministry a breathing
space.[1] When he expends a whole shallow essay on the need for a
censorship of his rivals, and remarks in the middle that he has
refused ever to answer a particular one of them because 'it would
have diverted my design', we can only wish the author were less
earnest and more ironical.[2]

The triumph of the *Examiner* is that it achieves a superb appearance of consistency although Swift's programme veers about
from week to week. In one number 'nobody, that I know of, did
ever dispute the Duke of Marlborough's courage, conduct, or
success'[3]; in other numbers his grace is described as a treacherous
would-be Caesar with an 'unmeasurable appetite of power and
wealth'.[4] Swift repeatedly says he will avoid controversy and
repeatedly engages in controversy. He denounces the common
use of the terms 'Whig' and 'Tory', but he continually employs
them himself. That he can succeed in sounding authoritative,

[1] Davis III. 120–1.   [2] *Ibid.*, pp. 152–7.   [3] *Ibid.*, p. 87.
[4] *Ibid.*, pp. 87, 165, and *passim*.

steady, and convincing as he executes so many somersaults is a tribute not to the adventitious aids he had for his work but to the power of his rhetoric.[1]

VI. *MISCELLANIES IN PROSE AND VERSE*

While Dr Swift was spending his best energies on being the un-acknowledged minister of propaganda, his former writings made a new appearance in an imposing form. The event will remind us that nothing Swift produced during his great intimacy with the heads of the government from 1710 to 1714 has the pull of several works belonging to earlier years. *An Argument against Abolishing Christianity* and *Baucis and Philemon* established standards in satire and humour which would be met again only after Swift ended his allegiance to a victorious party. *A Discourse of the Contests and Dissensions* represents a higher level of disinterested political thought than any of the brilliant pamphlets created for Harley's ministry.

The first hint of the *Miscellanies* goes back to the autumn of 1708, when Swift was hoping to get some real preferment out of the Junto upon their rise to new power after the death of Prince George. During this season he drew up a list, headed 'Subjects for a Volume', of almost two dozen pieces in prose and verse.[2] Only three of them had already been published, and several may not yet have been written. Swift thought of making up a collection to be published by Tooke with an introduction by Steele but with-out the author's name on the titlepage. Since Swift was engaged at the time in producing a similar book out of the manuscripts of Sir William Temple, I suppose that he got the idea of such a pro-ject from Temple's example and decided to call it *Miscellanies in Prose and Verse* after the example of his master's *Miscellanea*.

The scheme altered as Swift hesitated. He could hardly have put out a volume including *The Sentiments of a Church-of-England Man* and the *Project for the Advancement of Religion* unless he felt willing to alienate the Whigs. As the months went by and his

[1] On the rôles of Harley and St John in shaping the *Examiner*, see W. A. Speck, 'The Examiner Examined', in C. J. Rawson, ed., *Focus: Swift* (1971), pp. 138–54.
[2] See Appendix B, below.

frustrations deepened, he must have grown increasingly prepared to do just that. But if he did not mind the loss of his interest
with Somers and Halifax, he could hardly accept the sponsorship
of Steele. When Swift was in Ireland, a year after he made up his
list of subjects, he got a reminder from Steele: 'I have not seen
Ben Tooke a great while but long to usher you and yours into the
world.'[1] By this date Swift's *Letter concerning the Test* had been out
for ten months, and he was planning to include it in the volume.
Not only was a Whig editor out of the question, but Swift even
began to think of the book as an act of defiance against the Junto.
It seems reasonable therefore that about the same time as he
determined to add the *Letter* he also decided to drop the *Apology
for A Tale of a Tub*, which would have offended the anti-Junto
churchmen. In June 1710, still in Ireland, Swift wrote to Tooke,
'I would not have you think of Steele for a publisher [i.e., editor]:
he is too busy. I will, one of these days, send you some hints,
which I would have in a preface, and you may get some friend to
dress them up.'[2] In pretending that Steele's busyness would keep
him from carrying out the old plan, Swift was employing a subterfuge which the bookseller must have seen through very easily.
More than four months later, when he was again in London,
Swift wrote to the ladies at home that Tooke was 'going on with
my *Miscellany*'.[3] But just after the book finally appeared at the
end of February 1711,[4] Swift forgot what he had already told the
ladies, and made believe even to them that he had no connection
with the thing:

> Some bookseller [i.e., publisher] has raked up everything I writ,
> and published it t'other day in one volume; but I know nothing of
> it, 'twas without my knowledge or consent: it makes a four-shilling
> book and is called *Miscellanies in Prose and Verse*. Took pretends he
> knows nothing of it, but I doubt he is at the bottom. One must have
> patience with these things; the best of it is, I shall be plagued no
> more. However, I'll bring a couple of them over with me for MD,
> perhaps you may desire to see them. I hear they sell mightily.[5]

Of course, not Tooke but Swift was at the bottom of it; but Tooke

[1] Williams I. 152.   [2] *Ibid.*, p. 166.   [3] *Journal*, 17 Oct. 1710.
[4] 27 Feb. See *Journal* I. 203 and n. 8; also *Tatler* no. 295.
[5] *Journal*, 28 Feb. 1711.

printed the book following Swift's directions, with a preface designed by the author though headed 'The Publisher to the Reader'. Instead of giving it his own imprint, Tooke (again, I assume, obeying Swift, who wished to divert attention from his own link with Tooke) had John Morphew, publisher of the *Examiner* and an associate of Tooke's, appear as responsible on the titlepage. Judging from Swift's lie to the ladies, I suppose that as usual he wished to leave himself free to disown any aspect of the book that might embarrass him.[1]

A few details reinforce one's suspicion that Swift intended the *Miscellanies* in its final form not only to embellish his literary fame but also to demonstrate his political integrity. This I think is one reason that in it he gave 1708 as the time of composition or publication of works that belong to other years; for 1708–9 counted as the peak of the Junto's hegemony. Similarly, he supplied an 'Advertisement' to the *Letter concerning the Test* in which the pretended editor says the author will gain by having the essay reprinted here, 'considering the time when it was writ, the persons then at the helm, and the designs in agitation, against which this paper so boldly appeared'. He asserted here that his authorship of the *Letter* had 'absolutely ruined' him with the Whig ministry.[2] His cancellation of a passage in the *Contests and Dissensions* which put forward an argument in favour of bribery in elections also suggests that Swift did not wish the inconsistencies of his political development to appear too glaring, inasmuch as the passage belongs to an attack on the Tory Parliament of 1701.[3]

The book was printed with unusual care and sold well enough to achieve a second edition in 1713. Admirers of Swift will always value the *Miscellanies* as the form in which two of his best-known works—the *Sentiments* and the *Argument*—first appeared. Many of his readers would cheerfully sacrifice the bulk of the pamphlets he turned out on English affairs, from *The Conduct of the Allies* to *The Publick Spirit of the Whigs*, in order to preserve the contents of the *Miscellanies*.

---

[1] Temple's first volume of *Miscellanea* had a similar preface, in the author's own person, dissociating himself from the book.
[2] Davis II. xxxix.   [3] *Ibid*. III. 301–2.

Chapter Twenty

THE PEACEMAKERS

I. BROKEN CIRCLES

T he true pattern of Swift's social pursuits is less obvious than he often makes it appear. His regrettable need to mix with persons of great dignity and power, his gradual submission to the pulls of partisanship—these strong tendencies easily blend themselves with the general ambitions driving Swift at this time. But through his diaristic talent for dramatizing routines he can give a misleading impression of the rate at which he changed the make-up of his social circles; and scholars sometimes treat the effect of his new political ties on his friendships as simpler and more immediate than it was. While politics did force Swift apart from some good friends, and his success in the drawing-room did incline him to neglect some undistinguished connections, the persistence of many attachments seems remarkable. Few of his Whig acquaintances—especially female—vanish completely during Swift's years as an English political debater, though many Tories emerge. His relatives, his old classmates, his early benefactors and humble clients remain a surprisingly stable part of his life.

Dr Swift, the intimate of statesmen, did not care to be seen in London with scrubby Irish friends who were good enough for Dublin. In fact, he now had little impulse to strengthen any ties with the meaner aspects of his earlier years: 'In my present posture I shall not be fond of renewing old acquaintance', he told the ladies.[1] As for current connections of the lower sort, he was willing enough to lend them assistance of all kinds; he just did not want them to cramp his style. It was a limited but common kind of snobbery. Swift was stingy, and he considered himself to be still

---

[1] *Journal*, 18 Sept. 1711.

on the way up, socially; therefore, while he did not object to receiving humble friends who happened to be passing through London, he did resent any waste of money or extended leisure upon them; and he never wished to be stuck in a place where he might have to introduce them to the objects of his own aspiration. Tractable relatives who could be dismissed summarily, or whom he could charitably aid, he tolerated with more grace; and elegant gentlemen who would make a proper impression or even dignify him by their familiarity, were of course welcome. But to walk in St James's Park with unprepossessing tourists, at the risk of being caught beside them by Prior or even St John, was no prospect for a self-conscious climber to delight in. 'London has nothing so bad in it in winter', he told the ladies, 'as your knots of Irish folks.'[1]

When Archdeacon Walls, the schoolmaster and one of Swift's most intimate confidants, showed up during an empty stretch of summer, he made no trouble. Swift was not much pleased to hear Walls had come, but the meek parson stayed less than a week, imposed himself only once or twice on his grand friend, bought his wife a silk gown, and then rode back to Chester. Ironically, this extravagant degree of self-effacement met with disapproval; and Swift growled, 'He has as much curiosity as a cow.'[2]

In Dr Raymond he found more of a pest. It was one thing for Swift to exert himself with lords and secretaries in order to obtain a small sinecure for the rector of Trim. It was altogether another thing for Raymond to take himself seriously as Dr Swift's friend, looking him up in Bury Street and expecting entertainment. With a little bravado, as if to veil some shamefacedness, Swift told the ladies how he slipped Raymond off on other Irish friends, lending him Swift's own servant, Patrick, to ease the evasion. Swift never dined with Raymond or walked with him or took him along to visit a third person. He forbade Patrick to admit Raymond in the evening; and he only let him call a couple of mornings a week while the Examiner got dressed. But when Swift caught a cold and had to stay in all day, it became obvious that snubbing Raymond was a strenuous occupation:

[1] *Journal*, 15 Nov. 1711.   [2] *Ibid.*, 19–24 Jul. 1711.

Dr. Raymond called often, and I was denied; and at last when I was weary, I let him come up, and asked him, without consequence, How Patrick denied me, and whether he had the art of it? So by this means he shall be used to have me denied to him; otherwise he would be a plaguy trouble and hindrance to me: he has sat with me two hours, and drank a pint of ale cost me five pence, and smoakt his pipe, and 'tis now past eleven that he is just gone.[1]

Irish connections were not always contemptible, and they were seldom fragile. When Dilly Ashe came over, he proved a little more bearable than Raymond but no unmixed felicity. Swift did call on him, and they were sometimes invited for dinner together by common friends like Fountaine. Swift also allowed himself to be visited by Dilly. But prolonged separation, he found, had broken his habit of bearing with his college friend's Hibernian blemishes. 'Just such a puppy as ever', he complained to the ladies: 'and it is so uncouth, after so long an intermission.' Swift saw him as rarely as he could; and when Dilly turned up at Windsor during one of Swift's sojourns there, Swift let him watch the doctor talk to the great, but he presented him to no one. Bibulous Dilly, on the other hand, was glad enough to be freed from two tiresome Irish sisters-in-law; so he cheerfully frequented the theatres and lingered among the unclerical distractions of London. 'He dresses himself like a beau', Swift said, wincing, 'and no doubt makes a fine figure.'[2]

A poor, unlucky cousin like Patty Rolt, 'my favourite from her youth', was different again. She had no pretensions at all, and Swift felt sorry for her—Patty was trying to survive on eighteen pounds a year while neglected by a feckless husband. Swift went to see the poor woman and gave her money repeatedly.[3] His sister Jane Fenton provoked more complicated emotions. Even while accepting a responsibility for her, Swift obviously considered Jenny both weak and misguided; and if he did not lose touch

---

[1] *Ibid.*, 23–26 Nov.; 10, 11, 18 Dec. 1710; 1 Jan. 1711. He was once admitted to have claret and oranges with two Irish gentlemen, Dopping and Ford, and Swift (18 Dec.); but Swift says Raymond was not with him more than four times (1 Jan.).

[2] *Ibid.*, 30 Jun. 1711, pt 2; 1 Jul.; 11 Aug., pt 2; 24, 31 Aug.

[3] *Ibid.*, 4, 27 Jul. 1711; 2 Feb., 10 Apr. 1713. He also saw her 3 Jan. 1713, when he gave her £1 1s. 6d. (*Accounts 1712–13*, fol. 4).

with this nearest of living relatives, the continuity of the tie was more her accomplishment than his own. She remained in Dublin, where Esther Johnson was friendly with her,[1] till the middle of 1711, when she shocked Swift by going to work for Lady Giffard[2]: 'It makes me love England less a good deal', was his irritated response. Their mother had left Jane some money in Swift's trust but in Lady Giffard's hands,[3] an arrangement which required Jane at least to keep track of his whereabouts. But she also turned to him for natural reasons, inviting him to stay at the house for a week when Lady Giffard was away; constantly coming from Sheen to visit him when he was badly sick[4]; and later asking for his assistance on behalf of her son. Once, thinking herself deathly ill, she wrote and begged him to 'think of' the boy.[5] When she seemed to be growing deaf, Swift—I suppose a fellow-sufferer—was immediately sympathetic, but he could not help adding (in a letter to the ladies), 'Her husband is a dunce, and with respect to him she loses little by her deafness.'[6]

However strongly one might wish to hear Swift's remarks through Swift's own ears, one cannot help flinching at some of his caustic reflections on humble persons. Part of the trouble is that many men who would not express such thoughts openly would equally not accept the burden of the creatures involved. If Swift had simply rejected some of his weakling connections, he would not have snarled at them. But the problem is more general than this. For Swift is really, in these eruptions, acting out again the *hypocrite renversé*. Rather than smother and ignore the attitudes that make most of us feel ashamed of ourselves, he dramatizes them as if to ridicule the impulse to hide them. Besides, it is in writing to the ladies that he commonly exposes himself without fear. To somebody who knew and loved him less, he could never have admitted so many of his unpalatable thoughts. It is perhaps

---

[1] *Journal*, 23 Dec. 1710, pt 1.

[2] *Ibid.*, 17 Jul. 1711: I assume this is the reference of Swift's remark, because Lady Giffard noted that Jane Fenton came to work for her at this time (Longe, pp. 352, 357).

[3] *Journal*, 1 Jan. 1711.

[4] Though he would not let her in until he was well, the reason may have been concern for her health (*Journal*, 10 May 1712).

[5] *Journal*, 18 Sept. 1712.   [6] *Ibid.*, 25 Sept. 1711, pt 2.

his misfortune that evidence which the run of men would suppress, he both produced and preserved.

No such qualms have to be stirred by Swift's friendship with the better-bred absentee gentry or peers; he was all too willing to mix with them. His favourite, Charles Ford, went home for the second half of 1711, but Domville returned from his continental travels that autumn, giving Swift frank pleasure. 'I design to present him to all the great men,' Swift said, indicating how he thought one might best prove one's friendship.[1] Domville had supremely the knack of being genteel though Irish. As soon as he could, he spent a day with Swift, going to Pontack's expensive tavern for dinner. Two days later, Swift introduced him to Undersecretary of State Lewis and to Matthew Prior.[2]

With less zest but with equal comfort, Swift enjoyed the company of Mrs John Pratt, whose husband (now Deputy Vice-Treasurer of Ireland) had been at college with him, and who was passing the winter and spring in England. Along with her came two of her relations who seemed rather more interesting—Lord Shelburne and his sister Lady Kerry, both of them children of the famous Sir William Petty, one of the founders of the Dublin Philosophical Society.[3] Though Lord Shelburne was hospitable, he was also sickly, and he argued too much to be wholly amiable.[4] The one person in the family that Swift really loved was Shelburne's sister, who shared Swift's proclivity to dizzy spells. Besides discussing their symptoms and exchanging medicines, Lady Kerry necessarily got on very well with Swift because she was a clever, energetic woman who adapted herself to all his moods. 'Egregiously ugly', he called her, but also 'governable as I please', and perfectly polite.[5] He enjoyed an elaborate expedition with the whole group to see the sights of London; and he spent an agreeable two weeks with them at an estate near High Wycombe, 'in a delicious country'.[6]

Though Swift, like Steele, called himself an Englishman born in Dublin,[7] and liked to appear independent of the kingdom he

[1] *Ibid.*, 26 Nov. 1711.   [2] *Ibid.*, 27, 28 Nov. 1711.
[3] *Supra*, vol. I, pp. 81–2.   [4] *Journal*, 1 Dec. 1710; 14 Dec. 1711.
[5] *Ibid.*, 13 Feb., 4 May 1711.   [6] *Ibid.*, 13 Dec. 1710; 20 June 1711.
[7] Steele, *Englishman*, 19 Jan. 1714.

came from, it is clear that he welcomed Irish society even during the high season in London. Similarly, in the spring of 1711 he drew the ladies' attention to a supposedly radical change in his political flock: 'You hear no more of Addison, Steele, Henley, Lady Lucy, Mrs. Finch, Lord Somers, Lord Halifax, &c.'[1] But he spoke too soon: the transformation of his feathers, though steady, was gradual. If he did not cling to all his familiar comrades, he did not easily abandon them, even when politics and friendship were directly at odds with one another.

Former patrons, like Berkeley and his family, or Lord Pembroke, had become a less regular part of Swift's great world. Pembroke was busy with his new wife and growing household, although Swift did manage to call on him and exchange a few puns from time to time when his lordship came up to town. The old Earl of Berkeley had remained friendly but ailing; as soon as Swift reached England in the autumn of 1710, Berkeley had urged him to visit the Castle in Gloucestershire, but the trip was then out of the question for Swift and the Earl soon died. Eventually, the widow got Swift to provide a Latin epitaph for his old patron's tomb,[2] but he did not take to the new Earl, a young rake who soon acquired an arrogant, adolescent wife.[3] Now it was Lady Betty, five years married, who remained to keep Swift in mind of the days of his chaplaincy. She had him to dinner and invited him to Drayton, her husband's seat. In spite of a miscarriage she was plump and good-looking; but she constantly argued Whig against Tory with Swift, and was obviously too clever for him to beat down.[4] His favourite, Mrs Barton ('I love her better than any body here'), disputed just as hard against him, sometimes with Lady Betty's support; yet she stayed in his best books. If one can put any trust in the couplets that Halifax is said to have written for her on a Kit-Cat glass, Mrs Barton was pretty as well as charming; by the same token she was immovably on the Junto's side. But Swift approved of her careful style of giving him dinner—'just in that genteel manner that MD used when they would treat some better sort of body than usual'. She

---

[1] *Journal*, 29 May 1711.   [2] Williams v. 222–3.   [3] *Journal*, 15 Feb. 1711.
[4] *Ibid.*, 8, 15 Feb.; 17 Oct. 1711.

had good nature, told good stories, and was no hypocrite. Besides being the intimate friend of Lord Halifax, she mixed with Lady Betty Germaine, Sir Andrew Fountaine, Mrs Vanhomrigh, and other people Swift knew. Not surprisingly, he felt quite prepared to put up with her teasing 'Whiggish discourse'.[1]

Only a part of Swift's fondness for English people of fashion was satisfied by such hospitable hostesses. He also kept up with undemanding friends like Sir Andrew Fountaine. Not that Fountaine himself was merely undemanding. It would be hard to exaggerate the extent to which Swift found him easy to get along with. He seems to have been at least as comfortable a fit as Charles Ford. It is unlikely that Swift took him any more seriously than he did Ford, because he almost never saved a letter from Sir Andrew and he never relied on him in a crisis. But to judge from recorded occasions, Swift saw no one oftener than Fountaine. They dined together, played ombre, and collaborated on practical jokes. Fountaine had plenty of money and very little occupation. He was young, learned, and generous. Swift and he called upon each other at all hours, and Fountaine was always admitted by Swift's servant. The first day they met, after Fountaine came up to town, they spent together from early morning (Swift was in bed when Fountaine called) to ten at night, dining, sauntering through booksellers' and china shops, and ending the day over white wine at a tavern.[2] Part of Fountaine's charm must have been his familiarity with other friends of Swift's, especially those connected with Ireland, and above all Mrs Vanhomrigh, to whose lodgings (if we may trust Swift) Fountaine was constantly leading him. They met endlessly as her guests, but they also shared Charles Ford, the Ashes, and others. Fountaine's allegiance to the Whigs never seems to have disturbed this intimacy.

In spite of all this, Swift has hardly left us a single interesting remark on Fountaine's general character, and the nearest thing to a deeply revealing incident between them was the occasion of an illness Fountaine suffered in the winter of 1710–11. The trouble was serious enough to cost the patient ten guineas a day

[1] *Ibid.*, 3, 7, Mar., 4 Apr., 20 Nov. 1711.　　[2] *Ibid.*, 6 Oct. 1710.

for medical attention. His mother and sister came up from the country; his brother (who would have been the heir) sat in the anteroom and cried. Though the doctors despaired, Swift did not think the disease would be fatal; yet he continued day after day either to call himself or to send for information. Twice he assumed his priestly rôle and read prayers to the sick man. The case early reminded Swift of an illness Esther Johnson had once had, and he dreamed a bad dream about a black dungeon. Instead of feeling pleased when the relatives showed up, Swift characteristically and unclerically reversed the usual attitudes, doubting their motives and blaming them for not arriving sooner. 'I fell a scolding when I heard they were coming; and the people about them wondered at me, and said what a mighty content it would be on both sides to die when they were with him.' Of course, Swift was really afraid that the fuss they created would trouble the invalid—'the poor man will relapse among them.'[1] After a slow but complete recovery, Fountaine returned too soon (as Swift thought) to his usual recreations, and had choking spells: ''Tis his own fault', Swift complained to the ladies, 'that will rake and drink, when he is but just crawled out of his grave.'[2]

Being a great convenience to Swift—and no expense—a willing participant in his moods, a sharer of his tastes, and an admirer of his talents, Fountaine must have made a thoroughly agreeable crony; but he does not seem to have touched Swift's deep feelings. The two men were almost like undergraduate chums; and if the parson tended to 'govern' the knight and to sound parental at times, this was his constant manner with friends. I suspect that on the verge of middle age Swift was snatching in fantasy at rosebud hours denied him during appropriate years by a narrow budget. His mock-cynical comment on the possibility of Fountaine's dying suggests the affectionate but manageable quality of the attachment: 'I have lost a legacy by his living; for he told me he had left me a picture and some books, &c.'[3] However welcome Sir Andrew may have been when present, he was not terribly missed when away.

[1] *Journal*, 29–31 Dec. 1710; 1, 3, 5 Jan. 1711.   [2] *Ibid.*, 14 Apr. 1711.
[3] *Ibid.*, 30 Dec. 1711.

During the summer of 1711, while Swift had to spend many uncrowded days in the hot, deserted city, he looked up a number of friends he had been neglecting. Congreve, the most interesting of these, had remained loyal to the Whigs; but so far from securing any new office, he had barely held on to his commissionership of wine licences. Swift called on him in Surrey Street, where Congreve's landlady was the sister of his former mistress (Anne Bracegirdle). The retired playwright still loved good wine, and perhaps in consequence suffered badly from the gout. Though he made reading his chief recreation and was collecting an elegant library, he had to use a magnifying glass while his very myopic eyes were growing cataracts. The autumn before, Swift had found him youthful, fresh-complexioned, and 'cheerful as ever'. Now he found him, with all his afflictions, still a 'very agreeable companion'.[1] But Congreve was certainly no one to envy. Rather, Swift pitied him and decided to persuade the ministry not to disturb him. One day he had seen Congreve in his official capacity at the Treasury with the other commissioners; Congreve told Swift later that after the formal business of that day was finished, the Lord Treasurer (as Harley, now Lord Oxford, had become) had spoken privately to him, 'with great kindness, promising his protection'. At this point Swift's tone becomes rather warm:

> The poor man said, he had been used so ill of late years, that he was quite astonished at my lord's goodness, &c., and desired me to tell my lord so; which I did this evening, and recommended him heartily. My lord assured me he esteemed him very much, and would be always kind to him; that what he said was to make Congreve easy, because he knew people talked as if his lordship designed to turn every body out, and particularly Congreve; which indeed was true, for the poor man told me he apprehended it. As I left my Lord Treasurer, I called on Congreve (knowing where he dined) and told him what had passed between my lord and me: so I have made a worthy man easy, and that is a good day's work.[2]

Swift's feelings here do him credit, but his view of his own function is a bit consequential. Not only he but Halifax was actively

---

[1] Congreve, *Letters and Documents*, ed. J. C. Hodges (New York, 1964), pp. 6–7; *Journal*, 26 Oct. 1710; 2, 8 Jul. 1711; J. C. Hodges, *Library of William Congreve* (New York, 1955), p. 14.

[2] *Journal*, 22 Jun. 1711.

interceding for Congreve. Besides, the Lord Treasurer was on several accounts inclined to retain a non-political Whig of such eminence in a modest office if the man would acknowledge an obligation. Yet for all Swift's sententiousness, his anxiety for an old friend's welfare is transparently affectionate and consciously independent of Congreve's known affiliation. At the same time, since the retired playwright was able to accumulate £1,100 in Bank of England stock within the single year of 1712, one can hardly regard him as destitute[1]; and I'm afraid that his remarks to both the Lord Treasurer and the vicar of Laracor were less ingenuous than Dr Swift supposed.

To say that the strain of politics on Swift's friendships is often exaggerated is not to say that it never existed. Five weeks after his first number of the *Examiner* came out, he was mortified at a coffee-house when Anthony Henley, noticing that a boyish, high Tory peer was playing up to the doctor, suddenly asked Swift in a loud voice whether he intended to keep his promise to visit Lord Somers. (The current number of the *Examiner* carried an attack on Somers in the guise of a bad coachman.[2]) The argumentative Lady Lucy, whom Swift had once regarded as a reliable source of good-natured hospitality, became odious to him when her Whiggish dinner guests ran down *Sid Hamet*, the *City Shower*, and finally one of Swift's own favourite *Examiners*. Besides, she lived so far out in Hampstead that the trip discouraged him from visiting. In the end her constant scolding about politics went too far for him, and he gave her up.[3]

Evidently, it was not necessary that Swift's allegiance to the new ministry should drive him away from any particular old friend unless the person was an unusually bellicose Whig who insisted on badgering him with their differences. But as men like Somers (though not Wharton) realized that Swift was publishing virulent insinuations against their leadership and character, it

---

[1] Congreve, *Letters*, pp. 118, 119, 121. Possibly some of the £1,100 belonged to Congreve's cousin Ralph.

[2] *Journal*, 5 Dec. 1710. Henley may not have known Swift was writing the *Examiner*. 'John' the coachman is sometimes identified as Marlborough, but the italicized *presided* makes the allusion to the Lord President obvious.

[3] *Ibid.*, 10 Nov. 1710; 3 Feb., 4 Nov. 1711.

naturally became awkward for them to meet him convivially. What Swift found hard to accept was that other friends who felt personally attached to the statesmen and policies he denigrated would also draw back from his company. Addison's protégé Ambrose Philips, to whom Swift in recent years had written a series of brilliant letters, was still dear to the doctor at the end of 1710; and when Addison asked him to assist the melancholy poet in a desire to be posted as Queen's Secretary to Geneva (where a charming but impoverished lady was apparently waiting for him), Swift willingly agreed. Addison wrote to Philips, now returned to Copenhagen, and said, 'I have spoken to Dr. Swift (who is much caressed and invited almost every day to dinner by some or other of the new ministry) to recommend the affair either to Mr. Harley or Mr. St John, which I verily believe might be effectual; and he has given me a kind of promise if he finds a favourable opportunity.'[1] At the same time, Swift told the ladies, 'I'll do it if I can, it is poor Pastoral Philips.'[2] Nothing came of his pressure, if only because the post itself was discontinued; and Philips soon appeared in London with no hopeful prospects. The following June, Ford, who knew the doctor's likes and dislikes, had Swift to dinner with Philips and Stratford. Yet the very next week, when Philips sent a message asking Swift to help him secure 'a certain employment', Swift told the ladies, 'I will do nothing for Philips; I find he is more of a puppy than ever.'[3] In the autumn Swift gave Ford a misleadingly benevolent report of the case, saying that he had mentioned Philips to the Lord Treasurer 'as favorably as I could', and that Philips went constantly to his lordship's levee and would probably 'get something'; but I think this report was an evasion meant to soothe Ford as a person specially interested in Philips's welfare.[4] Over a year still later, though at least one friendly meal had intervened, Swift ran into Addison and Philips on the Mall and found them unpleasantly distant. This casual meeting took place during the bitterest season of partisan recriminations over the peace: '[I] took a

---

[1] Graham, p. 249; for the lady in Geneva see Williams I. 91, 100, 154.
[2] *Journal*, 15 Dec. 1710.   [3] *Ibid.*, 15 Dec. 1710; 24 Jun. 1711.
[4] Williams I. 259.

turn with them; but they both looked terrible dry and cold; a curse of party'—so Swift complained to the ladies. But then he went on, as it were, to define 'puppy' and remove any doubts as to his own motivations, because he said he could 'certainly' have got a preferment for Philips if the poet had not 'run party-mad and made me withdraw my recommendation'.[1] Clearly, it was political acrimony that broke up this friendship.

Against these currents Addison stands out with amazing power. More than any of Swift's other literary friends he was deeply involved in affairs of state. But though there were frigid moments between them, Swift could never pretend to dislike him. In the autumn of 1711 Swift was still saying he knew no man 'half so agreeable' as Addison[2]; and a year and a half still later Addison came to a little party in Swift's rooms and they dined privately together after a rehearsal of *Cato*. It was Steele who would not let sleeping dogs lie, and it was Steele about whom Swift had always felt clear reservations. It seemed to him that the soldier-author needed too much to drink before he could act agreeable; and the methodical parson felt annoyed by the captain's habit of ignoring engagements. Once when Steele failed to show up for a punch party with Addison and others, Swift snarled 'Steele was to have been there, but came not, nor never did twice, since I knew him, to any appointment.'[3] Yet Swift enjoyed his company, admired much of his writing, and appreciated both the compliments Steele had paid him and the efforts he had made to serve Swift with the Junto. In addition, Steele had been kind enough to frank Swift's letters. Now that the doctor was in favour, he wished to teach the Whig politicos how they ought to have treated him; and from this impulse as well as out of friendship, he tried repeatedly to intercede with the new ministers on behalf of his old comrades. Steele in particular received the most liberal attention.

What Swift did not realize was that Steele had dealings of his own with Harley. While, as a man explicitly opposed to the government in power, he could hardly stay in the 'sensitive' post

---

[1] *Journal*, 27 Dec. 1712; cf. *ibid.*, 14 Sept. 1711.   [2] *Ibid.*, 14 Sept. 1711.
[3] *Ibid.*, 2 Jan. 1711.

of Gazetteer (or editor of the official newspaper), he did not lose the commissionership in the Stamp Office which paid him £300 a year. It seems that at some time in the autumn of 1710 Harley came to a very quiet agreement with him that if Steele would stop writing the increasingly tendentious *Tatler*, he could keep the commissionership or even hope for something better.[1] That October, Harley had no compunction about asking Steele to see him privately at his own house, although, as it happened, the minister (not Steele, this time) was unable to keep the engagement—possibly because he had meanwhile arranged one for the same hour with Swift![2]

Ignorant of all this, the doctor determined to put his greatest influence to work for Steele's benefit. One morning he spoke at length and forcefully to Harley's agent Erasmus Lewis, urging him to prevent Steele from being dropped from the commissionership. In return, Lewis gave Swift to understand that Harley (when he was Secretary of State) had not only made Steele Gazetteer in the first place but had also raised the salary from sixty pounds to £300; and yet, as Lewis told Swift, Steele had attacked Harley in the *Tatler*. We now know that Lewis's story is most unlikely, and that Sunderland, Addison, and Mainwaring were probably responsible for Steele's preferment; we also know that Steele himself, some time or other, said Mainwaring had much more to do with the favour than Harley.[3] But Swift, so far from questioning Lewis's anecdote, not only retailed it to the ladies but finally put it in print.[4]

In the course of their conversation, Lewis hinted that if Swift could bring Steele around, he might preserve him in the commissionership. On that very evening, therefore, Swift went to see Addison, 'as the discreeter person', and felt him out on the subject. But instead of the grateful co-operation Swift had hoped for, all he got was an evasive doubting of his own motives. Complain-

---

[1] Blanchard, p. 43; Winton, pp. 126–7.   [2] Blanchard, p. 43; *Journal*, 7 Oct. 1710.
[3] Davis VIII. 7; Blanchard, pp. 449–51 and n. 1; Winton, p. 92 and n. 9. In a letter to Steele, Swift represented himself as having spoken directly to Harley (Williams I. 354); this is possible, but I suspect he had in mind only the recorded conversation with Lewis (*Journal*, 22 Oct. 1710).
[4] Davis VIII. 7.

ing as usual to the ladies, Swift said, '*Party* had so possessed him, that he talked as if he suspected me, and would not fall in with any thing I said.' Perhaps what possessed Addison was a supply of information more reliable than his guest's. Anyhow, Swift stopped short in his overture, and their leavetaking was very dry. Rather than risk a yet more distasteful conference with the ebullient, outspoken Steele, Swift chose not to mention the business to him, for fear—he said—of having to report something to his disadvantage.[1]

Eight weeks (and several meals with Addison and Steele) later, Swift was informed of a further development. Lewis now told him that he had reported to his master how kindly Swift would take it if Harley were reconciled to Steele. Purely on Swift's account, said Lewis, Harley had fallen in with the scheme and set aside a time for Steele to come and talk to him. After agreeing to the appointment, however, Steele not only failed to come but did not even bother to send an excuse. To this new episode Swift responded with immediate fury: 'Whether it was blundering, sullenness, insolence, or rancor of party', he said to the ladies, 'I cannot tell; but I shall trouble myself no more about him.' In his rage he stooped so low as to wonder whether Addison had blocked the affair out of jealousy, not wishing his friend to be indebted to Swift for such a kindness![2]

Now Harley took it upon himself to tease Swift with the reproach that to please him the great minister had consented to make things up with Steele and yet that Steele had not troubled to see him about the matter. What peculiarly mortified Swift was that Harley, in front of Secretary St John and Lord Keeper Harcourt, warned him to be more cautious another time and not to engage for more than he could answer for. With these two as witnesses Swift now promised never to speak for or against Steele; but he still argued that unless there should be fresh provocations, his friend ought to remain in the commissionership.[3] Not only did Steele in fact keep his post, but Swift naturally gave himself the credit for preserving him. Yet he could not forgive Steele for

[1] *Journal*, 22 Oct. 1710.   [2] *Ibid.*, 15 Dec. 1710.
[3] Williams I. 348, 354–5; *Journal*, 4 Jan. 1711, 29 Jun. 1711.

his apparent irresponsibility; and months later, when a message came from him requesting Swift to intervene with the Lord Treasurer for a third person, Swift felt most righteously irritated and sent him back a 'biting' reply.[1] If one reflects on the public compliments and private cordiality that had passed between the two men, if one recalls how willing Swift was to put up with eccentricities and political differences in acquaintances whom he found less agreeable and less accommodating than Steele, if one observes how much of the quarrel between them was due to the misrepresentations of others, then I think the coldness that now came to mark their relationship (until it turned into savage enmity) must belong among the most distasteful effects of party warfare upon Swift's circle of friends. After Swift's authorship of the *Examiner* and *The Conduct of the Allies* became known, I suppose it would have been impossible for Addison or Steele to maintain any intimacy with him. But this early, ugly, confused misunderstanding seems only to suggest how ill-equipped Swift was to resist the deceptions that Harley, St John, and their men were prepared to practise on him.

II. THE PRINCE OF DARKNESS

One of the troubles between Swift and his Whig friends was his incapacity to understand that just as he could drown the blemishes of a man he admired in the hero's virtue, so also they might be aware of the defects in their own leaders without consequently mistrusting them. Late in the career of his great friends' ministry Swift was to dine with Addison and some others as guests of St John, who by this time was Viscount Bolingbroke. While the toasts were going around, Swift warned Addison not to offer Lord Wharton's health, because he would not pledge it; and he proceeded to tell Bolingbroke that Addison 'loved Lord Wharton as little as I did'.[2] So far as public responsibility or private morality went, there was absolutely nothing to choose between Wharton and Bolingbroke, as Swift had special reason to be assured; yet he could not see that both Addison, who never

---

[1] *Journal*, 26 Jul. 1711.   [2] *Ibid.*, 3 Apr. 1713.

uttered a recorded word against Wharton, and Steele, who dedicated the fifth volume of the *Spectator* to the noble lord, could respect him, work with him, and admire his politics precisely as Swift accepted St John's vices with his talents.

It would hardly be correct to say that in 1710 Swift broke with Wharton for political reasons, since they never had been friends. Moreover, his lordship, unlike most of the Whigs whom Swift stopped seeing, was perfectly willing to appear amicable long after he knew how vindictively the doctor had exposed his character. Swift once accused him in print of having defecated on the high altar of Gloucester Cathedral—having already described him as 'an ill dissembler and an ill liar, though they are the two talents he most practises'.[1] About a year later, Swift went into White's chocolate-house, to look for a friend:

> Lord Wharton saw me at the door, and I saw him, but took no notice, and was going away; but he came through the crowd, called after me, and asked me how I did, &c. This was pretty; and I believe he wished every word was a halter to hang me.[2]

This was not a man one could 'break' with. But in vilifying his name and utterly dissociating himself from the Earl, Swift made him into an essence of all the faults for which Swift blamed those Whig acquaintances whom he more casually lost or dropped. There was a further reason for Swift's virulence when writing against Wharton. Sir Richard Levinge, the eminent Solicitor-General for Ireland (and in England, M.P. for Derby), who had once hoped to lead an attempt to impeach Wharton, had softened visibly by the end of 1710.[3] Swift, I think, wished to inspirit the backers of the impeachment and to suggest how the evidence available against the Earl might be skilfully employed. Even if a motion for impeachment were never brought, the threat of one could only have a salutary effect upon his excellency.

How high a priority Swift assigned, among all his journalistic schemes, to the denigration of Wharton, we may judge from the fact that the second *Examiner* he wrote was centred brilliantly on

[1] Davis III. 57, 179 (my own reading is from the first edition).
[2] *Journal*, 1 Dec. 1711, pt 2.   [3] Williams I. 202.

his lordship's portrait.[1] This is the paper about the art of 'political lying'. The general method of the essay is to present several apparently unpointed but witty, allegorical anecdotes which connect the dissemination of public lies with the practice of corrupt statesmen. On this level the essay offers a series of very funny conceits ingeniously developed like myths. But the air of generality is only an appearance, and the analogies invoked consistently hint that the Whigs are the supreme artists in misleading their own countrymen. Near the middle of the essay is a paragraph on a 'certain great man' peculiarly celebrated for his lies and easily identifiable as the Earl of Wharton. This personage's lack of religion is dwelt upon, and at the opening of the essay the Earl briefly appears in an allusion to Satan, being the viceroy of a 'western province' who seduced a third of his prince's subjects from their obedience. Since no other individual is alluded to in the essay, Wharton becomes the arch-Whig, and the traits of his tribe are deceitfulness, impiety, and rebelliousness. From other metaphorical clues dropped throughout the essay, and from the explicitly argumentative final paragraph, one learns that if the Whigs have been the dominant political force for two decades, the reason is that their falsehoods and corrupt electioneering prevented the true strength of England from being effective. Of course, the purpose of their operation has not been the good of the country but the enrichment of themselves. Thus Wharton's infamous history is made by Swift into a parable of Whiggery since the Revolution. Wharton's atheism reflects the party's indifference to the Established Church; his contempt for the crown reflects their undermining of the political constitution; his lies reflect their use of dishonest propaganda. Conversely, the best Whigs, like Addison, become indistinguishable from the worst. There are no grounds for doubting that Swift believed the Whigs as a party were exploiting the entire kingdom for their own profit; he really thought the Junto were willing to sacrifice a whole people to the enrichment of their faction; and he really believed that the principles of Harley and St John harmonized with the material, religious, and political prosperity of England. In

[1] 9 Nov. 1710.

choosing Wharton for his target, he easily dramatizes these convictions.

Three weeks later, one of the most famous *Examiner* papers was devoted to Wharton. Ironically, Swift borrowed the main device of this number from an essay that happened to be written by Wharton's secretary, Addison, for the *Whig-Examiner*.[1] The device, not very rare at the time, was to adapt a classical speech to recent occasion, playing up the parallels between the ancient orator or subject and the modern. Swift chose Cicero's denunciations of Verres, which he described as an 'impeachment' brought on account of the proconsul's abominable misgovernment of Sicily. Of course, in this framework Swift could without fear deliver the most vituperative accusations against the former Lord Lieutenant. Besides impeachment the reiterated theme is money. Wharton is represented as having extorted immense sums from the people he ruled and as claiming that this very wealth will exempt him from all punishment. Swift labels him a 'publick robber, an adulterer, a defiler of altars, an enemy of religion . . . [who] sold all employments of judicature, magistracy, and trust, places in the Council, and the priesthood itself, to the highest bidder'. Swift thus implies not only that avarice is the essential motivation of Whig politics but also that the financiers or 'moneyed men', rather than the landed gentry, stand behind this faction. What seems much more ingenious is that he introduces the speech against Verres with a survey of the ministers recently turned out—Somers, Godolphin, Sunderland, and so forth—while the speech itself is concerned with Wharton alone. The effect therefore is again to have him stand out as the arch-Whig, the epitome of all the qualities of his party.

At the beginning of December Swift reported to the ladies that a fresh assault on the Earl had appeared: 'Here's a damned libellous pamphlet come out against Lord Wharton. . . It has been sent by dozens to several gentlemen's lodgings, and I had one or two of them, but nobody knows the author or printer.'[2] When

---

[1] Swift may not have known the authorship of the *Whig-Examiner*.
[2] *Journal*, 8 Dec. 1710. I suspect from Swift's phrasing that the pamphlet was first published this very day. Copies reached Ireland early enough for Bishop Ashe to

Mrs Johnson told him she had seen a copy in Dublin, Swift replied, 'You must not give your mind to believe those things;
people will say any thing.'[1] Of course, the 'people' in this case
were Swift himself; and the pamphlet was his celebrated *Short
Character* of Wharton. Although this may stand among the most
brilliant pieces of vituperation written by Swift, the ultimate purpose remains unchanged from the *Examiner* papers, as one may
infer from the subtitle, 'with an account of some smaller facts,
during his government, which will not be put into the articles of
impeachment'. Nevertheless, the real challenge for Swift now
seems not so much to instigate the impeachment as to find an
adequate expression, through language, of the diabolical nature
incarnated in the sometime governor of Ireland. Following one
of his common styles, Swift introduces the character with some
general principles, the apparent topic of the generalizations being the writing of history. As usual, however, very particular
applications are implied, all of which emphasize the habitual
oppression of Ireland by England. As a result, the analysis of
Wharton becomes merely a specific, if the most outrageous, instance of a long chain of abominations; and the piece achieves the
moral depth typical of Swift's finest prose, through its force as the
agonized shriek of tortured Ireland writhing before her deaf
persecutor. In the character itself the main source of power is the
familiar Swiftian gap between tone and meaning. The Earl's
vices, crimes, and sinister peculiarities are reported in the deliberate manner of an anthropologist describing a cannibal feast.
In order to renew the strength of this familiar tone, Swift, by a
characteristic manœuvre, makes it self-conscious; for he explicitly states that he intends to treat his lordship as a natural phenomenon—like 'a serpent, a wolf, a crocodile, or a fox'—without
involving any private emotions. The consequence of such pronouncements is to suggest that an extraordinary feeling of revulsion is being suppressed by the author in order to achieve the
apparent impartiality of the analysis; and the reader is thus

---

show Mrs Johnson one and for her to tell Swift about it in a letter that reached him
from Dublin by 26 Dec. (*ibid.*, 27 Dec. 1710, 1 Jan. 1711).

[1] *Ibid.*, 1 Jan. 1711.

invited to participate in that feeling. It is normal as well for Swift's accusations to be complex, so that he not only blames a man for two or more crimes in the same phrase but also associates commonly opposed tendencies with one another in the single charge; e.g., Presbyterianism *and* popery are both attributed to Wharton. In the *Short Character*, however, Swift superbly employs a further refinement of vituperation, which might be called multiple innuendo. This is to take one vice for granted and then allude to it as so involved with another vice, also taken for granted, that the man accused could not defend himself from either without admitting to the other and implying that he was really tainted with both. How, for example, could Wharton begin to exculpate himself from the following allegation? 'He is a Presbyterian in politics, and an atheist in religion; but he chuses at present to whore with a Papist.'[1]

Since the move to impeach Wharton came to a permanent halt at the end of the year, Swift's later allusions to the Earl (in print) are less extended and direct. Meanwhile, Archbishop King raised a question that must occur to any thoughtful reader of such anonymous slanders: 'To wound any man thus in the dark', King wrote to Swift, 'to appeal to the mob, that can neither inquire nor judge, is a proceeding I think the common sense of mankind should condemn.'[2] Although the attack on Wharton may hardly trouble our scruples—since there really seemed no proper means of restraining or punishing a shameless person of his wealth in his position, we may feel less indifferent to Swift's unsigned lies about Lord Cowper, whom he accused of bigamy when no slightest grounds could be shown for such a charge. What makes the case more disturbing is that Swift loathed being treated in this manner himself.[3] At the same time, a man like Steele was willing to

[1] The commonplace 'When did you stop beating your wife?' could be similarly refined: e.g., 'If you hadn't hurt your arm breaking open a poor box, you would never have stopped beating your wife.' Cf. Johnson, 'Sir, your wife, under pretence of keeping a bawdy-house, is a receiver of stolen goods' (Boswell's *Johnson*, ed. Hill-Powell, IV. 26). Swift's fullest development of multiple innuendo is his character of Marlborough in the *Four Last Years*.

[2] Williams I. 207.

[3] On Cowper, see Davis III. 57-8. For an instance of Swift's rage over being attacked in print, see *Journal*, 16 Oct. 1711; cf. Boyer, *Political State* for Sept. and Nov. 1711.

put his real name to controversial publications and risk the consequences. I think the great distinction Swift made was between working for pay and writing to serve a cause one believed in. He tended to judge cases of conscience by motivation; and I think he regarded his own motives as above suspicion because he had no money to gain from his publications. By precisely the same logic he could accuse Steele and the Whig journalists generally of being mercenary scribblers who wrote from dictation without considering the truth or falsity, justice or injustice of their accounts and accusations. On a deeper moral level Swift believed that his own friends were underdogs who were not getting a decent chance. He thought that enormously powerful, selfish, destructive forces lay behind the Whig factions; that their control of banking, journalism, dependent peers, bishops, and office-holders, gave them so unfair an advantage over Harley's men that the boldest anonymous libels could not begin to even the balance. As his answer to posterity's complaints I think Swift would have used an analogy like the fire in the palace of Lilliput: when your home is aflame (and he thought the Whigs were rapidly destroying England), you do not quibble about the source of the water used to douse the blaze.

III. NEW ACQUAINTANCE

It is striking how slowly Swift's attachment to the new government brought him comfortable, accessible friends of his own level. Obviously, he was taken up at once by the political leaders, and one recalls the remark Addison made, less than four months after Swift's return to England, about the doctor's being dined almost daily by one or another of the ministers.[1] Swift's journal letters and account books tell us that before the end of 1710 the vicar of Laracor had renewed his earlier acquaintance with the Duke of Ormonde and the Earl of Peterborough; had made friends of Harley and St John; had met Attorney-General Harcourt, who soon became Lord Keeper; the influential Sir Thomas Hanmer, whose wife was the Duchess of Grafton; and Lord Dartmouth, the second Secretary of State. As if to satisfy

[1] Graham, p. 249.

Swift's fondness for seeing the 'great' make advances to him, Lord Rivers, the Constable of the Tower, particularly asked to be introduced to the doctor.[1] Besides these public figures he had also become friendly with Erasmus Lewis, Prior, and John Barber, the printer of the *Examiner*. Dozens of other courtiers or followers joined the number of those whom he often saw at the houses he visited or in Whitehall. Nevertheless, in all this wave of acquisitions he found nobody to match Addison or Ford or Fountaine for easy, casual companionship. The great men might have him to dinner parties, laugh at his puns, quote his verses, and keep him out later than he liked. But he could not feel free to pick them up and put them down to suit his own convenience. As for Erasmus Lewis, he might indeed be manageable, and Swift saw him often and willingly in the way of business; but if Lewis seldom irritated Swift, neither did he charm him: unlike Mr Addison, this undersecretary welcomed the doctor's company rather more than the doctor did his.[2] Barber, however, certainly grew on Swift, turning gradually, during their many hours of necessary co-operation, from a trusted colleague into a close, highly confidential friend; but the process was a slow one.

The one who might really have become an ideal comrade was Prior, now in his late forties but still unfixed. Until the mid-spring of 1711, Prior's time was not so taken up that he had to measure out his leisure with Swift, who enjoyed his gentlemanly wit. Like many brilliant persons of humble background, Prior was more polished than most courtiers to the manner born. The Duchess of Marlborough said, 'The first part of his education was in a tavern, [and] he had a soul as low as his education.'[3] But her grace was not remarkable for tact, charm, or judgment of character. One signal of Harley's rise to power had been the involvement of the Jacobite Earl of Jersey in the profoundly secret first steps taken toward peace negotiations with France. It was at about this point (July 1710) that Jersey's protégé Prior found himself happily reseated at the Board of Trade and once again drawing a comfortable stipend. Soon afterwards, he wrote one of

[1] *Journal*, 12 Dec. 1710.   [2] *Ibid.*, 7 Aug. 1711.
[3] *Private Correspondence* II. 138–40.

the *Examiners*, and he naturally began taking a hand in other projects of the ministry as well. Because of Prior's expert knowledge of the French language, his great experience of diplomacy, and his talent for making himself agreeable, he was soon to be rushed with work as the first official agent handling England's arrangements for a peace with France.

Meanwhile, he and Swift liked to perambulate St James's Park together. 'Mr. Prior walks to make himself fat', said Swift, 'and I to bring myself down.'[1] Prior had the outward gaiety and underlying gloom often shown by pulmonary consumptives. Alongside Swift's well-filled-out face, blue eyes, modest size, and healthy appearance, Prior made a tall, thin, hollow-cheeked figure with a cough he claimed was a cold. They had been introduced, early in the autumn of 1710, at the house of Harley, to whom Prior, like Jersey, was attached. But they also met at St John's, at Harcourt's, and elsewhere; for they were often invited to the same dinner parties. Prior shared Swift's addiction to puns though surpassing him as a lover of wine. Of course, they had poetry in common as well as politics, and took care to praise one another's lines.[2] Prior showed Swift some of his verses in manuscript; he had Swift to dinner at his house in Duke Street and gave him a fine edition of Plautus.[3] From Swift's occasional comments— 'Prior made me go with him to the Smyrna Coffee-house' . . . 'Prior would make me stay' [*sc.* at a Westminster School affair][4] —one gets the impression that in this relationship again the doctor could feel more sought after than seeking, which was a detail likely to sweeten his friendships if he enjoyed his companion. (Of course, it is a kind of humour for Swift to blame another man for causing him to do what he would have wished to do anyhow.) As the summer of 1711 drew near, however, the pace of the negotiations with France began to speed up. Queen Anne had to be won over before she would let the former wine waiter represent her interests at the most splendid court in Europe. 'I always thought it very wrong', she complained, 'to send people

---

[1] *Journal*, 21 Feb. 1711.
[2] *Ibid.*, 15 Oct., 18 Nov., 22 Nov. 1710; 17 Apr. 1711.
[3] *Ibid.*, 16 Jan., 30 Mar., 16 May 1711.   [4] *Ibid.*, 19 Feb., 30 Apr. 1711.

abroad of meane extraction.'[1] But Harley managed to persuade her, and Prior's days became filled with the planning of his secret journey.

By this time Swift had settled himself for a few months in Chelsea, where he discovered at once that the brilliant Dean Atterbury, with his wife and child, occupied the house across the way.[2] At first, Swift's old reservations concerning the high-flying Prolocutor made him unsure that Atterbury's neighbourhood was a blessing: 'Perhaps I shall not like the place the better for that', he told the ladies.[3] But the celebrated mildness and courtesy that the savage controversialist could maintain with those he wished to influence quickly softened the doctor.[4] Atterbury's pleasant appearance reminded Swift of his Irish colleague John Stearne, because both men were short, black-haired, good-looking, and fiftyish; the one had become Dean of Carlisle, the other, Dean of St Patrick's, and each was Prolocutor of his Convocation. But in spite of Atterbury's goutiness, his food and drink were inferior to those of Stearne. In temperament and in ecclesiastical politics Atterbury was remote from Stearne's moderation; for he seemed in some ways the Burnet of the Tories. He had instigated and dominated the vast debate over the revival of Convocation; he had written one of the main speeches for the defence of Sacheverell; he had proved himself almost frantically tenacious of authority. But there was no shortage of topics which Swift and he could discuss amicably. More than a decade earlier, they had borne arms together on the same side in the quarrel between Temple and Bentley, Atterbury having then been the tutor of the young Charles Boyle, ostensible author of the brilliant *Examination* of Bentley. Not surprisingly, Atterbury was an early admirer of the *Tale of a Tub*. The year it was published (in the same volume as the equally congenial *Battle of the Books*) was the year he became Dean of Carlisle, where he owed his security, in the

[1] Churchill vi. 465–6 (quoting H.M.C. *Bath* i. 217).
[2] Swift probably lived on the west side of Danvers Street, at no. 7, now part of Crosby Hall (*Survey of London*, 1913, pp. 13–14).
[3] *Journal*, 26 Apr. 1711.
[4] By 1 May, Swift was unwilling to go into the Westminster School election dinner because neither Harley nor Atterbury was there and he 'cared not for the rest' (*Journal*).

face of the furious Whig Bishop Nicolson, to the patronage of Swift's new hero, Robert Harley. In the *Representation* which Atterbury prepared of the state of religion (published 1711) he rang changes on many of the commonplace censures of the age which Swift had also picked up in his *Project for the Advancement of Religion*; and the new churches for which Swift was willing to take much credit are better traced to Atterbury's initiative than to the remarks of an Irish parson. Atterbury and Prior were old intimates, both products of Westminster School and both belonging to Harley's circle. The dean's powerful backer, Bishop Trelawney, was the same one who had, a few years earlier, offered to make Prior his secretary.

With so much to share, it is not surprising that the temporary neighbours became friends. The Tuesday after Swift moved into his 'one silly room with confounded coarse sheets',[1] Mrs Atterbury offered him the freedom of their library and garden. He sent his compliments; she returned some veal, beer, and ale for his dinner; and he called on her as soon as he could. Obviously, the dean was cultivating the doctor. Within a fortnight, Swift was dining with him and others at Prior's. Visits and dinners in Atterbury's own house followed, and the dean also 'sat with' him one night till eleven o'clock. Though Swift left Chelsea after ten weeks, the friendship remained active till the autumn (when Atterbury received his long-expected promotion to Christ Church, Oxford). Besides visits back and forth, they rambled together on a day's outing in Atterbury's chariot during the lazy summer of 1711.[2] Yet I doubt that Swift ever felt at home with Atterbury's ambitious, cunning temperament. The letter of compliment which he wrote to congratulate him on the appointment to Christ Church sounds too carefully witty; and Swift's insinuation there, that the College felt pleased with the choice, was what he knew to be a lie.[3] After this time the two had few opportunities of meeting, though they obviously remained on excellent terms.[4]

[1] *Ibid.*, 26 Apr. 1711.
[2] *Ibid.*, 1, 2, 3, 16, 18, 19, 28 May; 23 Jun.; 3, 14, 29 Jul.; 21 Aug.
[3] Williams I. 256; cf. *Journal*, 4 Jan. 1711.
[4] Cf. Atterbury's note to Swift, 21 Apr. 1713.

Swift's real immersion in court society was to occur when his trips to Windsor began. Meanwhile, he felt peculiarly close to the secret centre of authority through being admitted to a number of Saturday dinner parties in Harley's house. These affairs had the misleading reputation of including only two or three privileged persons before whom the most confidential facts could be revealed. However, the slightest acquaintance with Harley's methods of doing business would have persuaded an observer that a tête-à-tête was the largest group in which he could talk with any freedom. Swift understood that Harcourt, who had been at Westminster School and Christ Church with Harley, was the only person apart from St John who normally came to the Saturday dinners, and it was not until he had been writing the *Examiner* for nearly four months that he succeeded in cajoling his own way in. Then, alas, though Harcourt and St John did indeed show up, so did Rivers, damping Swift's elation by arriving before him.[1] Swift did not go again for two weeks, but he then felt able to boast that the thing was both customary and exclusive: 'Every Saturday Lord Keeper, Secretary St John, and I dine with him, and sometimes Lord Rivers, and they let in none else.'[2] Swift liked to speak of a 'Saturday Club', but various accidents interrupted any chance of regularity; and the satisfaction he showed in his own admittance faded when the Duke of Shrewsbury suddenly joined the group. As the occasions turned into sporadic but sizeable dinner parties, he lost interest in them. But those few gatherings in the first half of 1711 went far to establish Swift's identification of himself with the ministry. The very process of growing disenchanted with the pretended exclusiveness enabled him to take his own high position for granted in a way that individual relationships with men like Prior or Atterbury could not.

IV. PARTIES IN POWER

The supreme friendships being formed by Swift were of course those with Harley and St John. But although both these bonds were to survive the most extraordinary strains, they were origin-

[1] *Journal*, 16–17 Feb. 1711.　　[2] *Ibid.*, 3 Mar. 1711.

ally built to some extent on Swift's completely false assumptions as to the source of the two ministers' affinity. In those days, when it was not expected that all the leaders of a government should belong to one party, or that they should back the same policies in Parliament or cabinet, it was easy for men of deeply divergent principles to appear together in a ministry. If St John played the rôle of Harley's best-trusted lieutenant, the reason was that he had forced himself upon his 'master' and insisted that the most powerful office available should be delivered to him. When Harley first began assembling his ministry, he had hoped to keep St John in the subordinate place of Secretary at War. It was only under steady pressure from the younger man that he consented to make him one of the Secretaries of State. Even then he assigned him to the Northern Department, traditionally less important than the Southern. But St John quickly overawed his colleague Dartmouth (Queensberry, the Secretary for Scotland, hardly counted at all); and the combination of energy and intellectual brilliance made him rather the rival than the disciple of Harley.

The two leaders represented distinct tendencies in the administration. Harley owed his elementary strength as a figure in Parliament not merely to the votes he could personally command or to the shrewdness of his intrigue with Mrs Masham but to his policy of taking away from the Junto–Godolphin side only as many posts as would allow him to conclude a peace treaty without subjecting himself to Tory extremism in domestic affairs. This balancing of high-church and country party against Whiggism seems in part the consequence of his background. His own family had strong ties with Presbyterianism, and his in-laws' fortune was founded on iron manufacture; so he felt naturally appreciative of social and religious trends that a Seymour (now dead) or a Howe (no longer in the Commons) would have deprecated. Both Robert Harley and his younger brother Edward had married into the immensely wealthy Foley clan, whose industrial wealth had been invested in landed estates in Staffordshire, Herefordshire, and Worcestershire, until they owned enough property to give them a peerage and control over several parliamentary seats. Quite apart from the Foley platoon, not only

[451]

Robert Harley and his brother but also a cousin named Thomas sat in the Commons, supporting Harley's programme; so did Thomas Mansell, who in 1708 had resigned as Comptroller of the Household to follow Harley out of office with Harcourt and St John. Then there were the two valuable friends who had been with Harley at a private school in Shilton, Oxfordshire, and later at Christ Church: Harcourt, who had defended Sacheverell and (in October 1710) became Lord Keeper, and Thomas Trevor, Chief Justice of the Common Pleas, who was sometimes described as a Whig turned Tory. Lord Poulett, a follower of Harley's among the peers, was a high-churchman related by blood to both him and Harcourt. Lord Dartmouth, another high-churchman, was a kinsman of the Earl of Nottingham but had become a close friend of Harley. Further, detailed analysis would only deepen one's impression that the core of Harley support left him free, at first, from any need to serve narrowly 'Tory' claims. It was entirely characteristic of him that his great collaborator in the displacement of the Godolphin ministry should have been not Nottingham or Rochester but Shrewsbury, who had once mortgaged his estates in order to help bring over the Prince of Orange and had identified himself with the Whig party of William III's reign. It was also natural that while foreign affairs belonged to the peculiar province of the secretaries of state, Harley should have excluded St John from any participation in his own subterranean gropings toward a peace until so late a date as the end of April 1711.[1]

To satisfy his private ambitions, St John had to win over the adherents of his master and to secure a following of his own. But in both these operations he was forced temporarily to proceed as the devoted colleague of the Chancellor of the Exchequer, little though Harley himself might be impressed by this appearance. In order to detach a key figure like Mrs Masham, St John appealed quietly to the cynical motives he was one day to describe (in a most un-Harleian rhetoric) as prompting the entire ministry: 'The principal spring of our actions was to have the government of the state in our hands . . . [and] our principal

[1] Churchill VI. 464.

views were the conservation of this power, great employments to ourselves, and great opportunities of rewarding those who had helped to raise us, and of hurting those who stood in opposition to us.'[1] In his efforts to establish a body of supporters in the House of Commons, he could hardly look to those Whigs whom Harley was already cultivating with ineffectual patience but turned instead to the other side, viz., to the inexperienced, rural, Tory backbenchers, many of them young men, who had been elected on the burst of church-and-crown sentiment set off by the trial of Sacheverell. They were called the October Club because a large number of them used to meet at a tavern to drink strong October ale and discuss political questions. It was very tempting for St John to make himself their governor, picking up the rôle that Jack Howe had laid down when his parliamentary career ended in 1705.

For the time being, it was essential, since neither could stand alone, that the Chancellor and the Secretary should appear united. Similarly, they were both forced to proclaim that the changes made during the summer of 1710 were not in policies but in persons; and consequently they had to do all they could to discredit the characters of the late ministry. Until their own administration was secure, therefore, they insisted publicly that the war would be prosecuted as vigorously as ever. It was essential for them to hold on, as best they could, to Marlborough's military prestige while stripping him and his wife of political power. If Marlborough resigned, he would put himself in the wrong, but if they dismissed him, they would be condemned by general opinion. At the same time, in order to control the House of Commons, they were driven to appear sympathetic with the desire of the country members to 'throw the rascals out' and make a quick peace. Still more ticklish was the need to offset the uncompromising hostility of the Junto Whigs by using the crypto-Jacobites in the October Club. For this purpose Harley and St John gave warm, treasonable, covert assurances to the Pretender that they intended to make him the successor to Queen Anne; and his court in turn gave instructions to the Jacobite M.P.s to work with

[1] *Letter to Sir William Windham*, in *Works*, 1754, I. 8–9.

the new ministry. As peace approached, these pressures continued, and the Whigs grew more aggressively suspicious; so it
was inevitable that both Harley and St John should have to lean
more heavily on the ravenous country Tories. A profound issue
of their rivalry thus became the question which of them would
bid the higher for the dangerous backing of the extremists.

In the most furtive way possible, another sign of the rivalry
between the two leaders began revealing itself. Just before the fall
of Godolphin, a small British expedition had succeeded in seizing
from the French what is now Nova Scotia, with the harbour of
Port Royal. St John had hardly known he was to be Secretary of
State when he began organizing a large sequel to this stroke, in
the hope of glorifying himself through the capture of Canada.
Although the scheme meant diverting thousands of troops wanted for the service in Flanders, St John was able to launch it
because he incorporated a mercenary intrigue into the main plan.
He had intended to enrich himself by having the accounts of the
expedition falsified; it was simple to share both the cash and the
kudos with Mrs Masham, thereby estranging her from Harley;
for St John also determined to put Brigadier Hill, her incompetent military brother, in charge of the enterprise, and the
grateful sister was able to persuade the Queen to forward the
secret preparations. Naturally, the Chancellor of the Exchequer
steadily opposed the entire project but avoided showing his hand
openly.

As the parliamentary session went on, Harley's difficulties
swelled. The first return of the French agent for the secret peace
negotiations was disappointing; and the Chancellor's management of the cabinet was indecisive. As a speaker, Harley was
easily outdone by St John, whose oratory and quickness made
him the governor of the House of Commons. Mrs Masham was
edging her way to St John's side even as she put less and less faith
in Harley. Every day, the solid Tories who thought they deserved
government posts embarrassed the Chancellor with their demands. At the same time, public credit was sinking because the
Whig bankers feared the tendencies of the new government.

By March 1711, Harley's reputation and his power were in

need of fresh assistance. Although this arrived, and in miraculously good time, it was by a route that nobody could have foreseen, viz., through an attempt to murder the Chancellor of the Exchequer. This grotesque event was not only to restore him publicly to the height of political power; it was also to demonstrate irrefutably to Dr Swift that the heroic pair whom he had wished to regard as dioscuri felt a mutual distrust as great as their mutual dependence.

V. THE CAPTAIN

If Swift had not passionately admired both St John and Harley, he would have found it easier to tolerate their enmity. In very different ways, however, each became a hero to him. While Harley, though only six years his senior, took on some of the attributes of an idealized father, St John, eleven years Swift's junior, slipped into an essentially filial pattern. His youth dazzled Swift to a remarkable degree. 'A young man with half the business of the nation upon him, and the applause of the whole',[1] is the description Swift once gave of St John at the age of thirty-two. When they first met, Swift exaggerated this side of the Secretary of State: 'Here is a young fellow, hardly thirty, in that employment.'[2] With St John's precocity Swift associated all his other gifts: 'I think Mr. St. John the greatest young man I ever knew; wit, capacity, beauty, quickness of apprehension, good learning, and an excellent taste; the best orator in the House of Commons, admirable conversation, good nature and good manners. . . He is now but thirty-two, and has been Secretary above a year. Is not all this extraordinary?'[3]

It was Swift's universal tendency to boss his friends, whether seriously or ironically. Perhaps his own lack of a father led him to set so high a value on that rôle that he took it whenever he could. Mentor, preacher, counsellor, the various opportunities offered him by the priesthood, all these seem to blend themselves with his essential nature. Consequently, the doctor was accustomed to

[1] Davis VIII. 135.   [2] *Journal*, 11 Nov. 1710, pt 2.
[3] *Ibid.*, 3 Nov. 1711; St John had just turned thirty-three.

scold every sort of acquaintance for the man's own good. Yet there was a radical difference between his warning a man like Harley to take care of his health, or begging him not to risk travelling by coach after dark, and the admonitions Swift was always delivering to St John, against late nights, heavy drinking, and associated recreations. 'I have chid him so severely that I hardly knew whether he would take it well', Swift tells the ladies after one of these sessions[1]; and a few days later, 'I scolded him like a dog, and he promises faithfully more care for the future.'[2] This sounds like the tone of a parent to a boy.

It was part of Swift's worldly good manners, among gentlemen of fashion, not to take censorious account of their immorality unless it impinged directly on him in the way of bawdy conversation or blasphemy, which he always forbade in his presence. A rake like Rivers or a kept mistress like Mrs Manley, so long as propriety was observed before Swift, found it a simple task to keep him well disposed. Yet one cannot help boggling at the parson's willingness to accept St John's warts with his beauties. Here is how a shrewd, unfriendly, Austrian observer sized up the would-be Alcibiades:

> He investigates everything, takes everything in, and can always be relied upon to make a formal statement. Neither his rank, his credit, capacity, or steadiness make one believe him. Moreover, his arrogance and excessive fiery temper are increasing from day to day to such an extent that one cannot penetrate his real ideas. Besides this, he is given to the bottle and debauchery to the point of almost making a virtue out of his open affectation that public affairs are a bagatelle to him, and that his own capacity is on so high a level that he has no need to give up his pleasures in the slightest degree for any cause.[3]

Putting aside the other indulgences, there was St John's notorious and systematic infidelity to his humiliated wife. A frequent visitor to that 'poor disconsolate' woman at Bucklebury (the estate which formed part of the great fortune she had brought St John) reported, 'I met nothing there but sorrow and disorder. That unfortunate gentleman is more irregular if possible in his private

---

[1] *Journal*, 7 Apr. 1711.   [2] *Ibid.*, 12 Apr. 1711.   [3] Churchill vi. 478.

than public capacities.'[1] This was the biased language of a friend of the Harleys, but Swift himself tells of walking in St James's Park with a friend and running into St John: 'Mr. Secretary met us and took a turn or two, and then stole away, and we both believed it was to pick up some wench; and tomorrow he will be at the cabinet with the Queen: so goes the world.'[2] Not everybody Swift knew would have been thus excused by him with a *cosi fan tutte*. I wonder whether St John did not fascinate the author of *A Project for the Advancement of Religion* as a kind of super-id, a person who combined precocity and talents which the late-arriving Swift envied with the vices he never let himself contemplate—rather as a father who had himself been too strictly brought up secretly admires and encourages his son's revolt against authority.

What peculiarly coloured Swift's impression of St John was this new marvel's uncanny similarity to an old one. Out of a total of seven times that Swift mentions Sir William Temple, in his letters (during these years) to Esther Johnson, five are to link or contrast him with Henry St John.[3] The supreme point of resemblance was the post of Secretary of State, which Temple had refused in middle age and which young St John had forced his way into. The handsomeness of both men, their common power of charming through elegant manners and of persuading through oratory, their fondness for classical learning and the country life, their talent as poets and essayists, the high affiliations of their families—such visible features made it natural that the presence of one should call up the image of the other. They also shared several personal attributes which Swift could not approve of, such as a cool attitude toward religious institutions and a youthful reputation for amorous accomplishment. The profoundest difference that excited Swift must have been in their attitudes toward the career of a statesman. Temple accepted public office on his own terms; he used it to advance constitutional and diplomatic policies which he honestly believed in; and his policies tended to moderation, compromise, rationality. St John had

[1] H.M.C. *Portland* VII. 12, 39; cf. *ibid.*, p. 29.   [2] *Journal*, 24 Aug. 1711.
[3] *Ibid.*, 11 Nov. 1710; 3, 4, 15 Apr., 3 Nov. 1711.

Temple's air of candour, but anyone who came to know him even slightly soon doubted his integrity. Where Temple preached steadiness and caution, St John posed as having simple, radical solutions to complex problems. Where Temple stressed tolerance and compromise, St John held out for thoroughgoing, violent action.

To Swift's hopeful Irish mind, St John's reduction of labyrinths to open doors was deeply appealing. Out of touch with the historic convolutions of the English political system, he clung to the vision of an essentially simple government as he did to the vision of a renewable, primitive church. For all his doubts of St John's private character, Swift could not long resist the pull of the Secretary's *simpliste* approach to tedious issues. Under this intellectual sympathy lay the emotional attraction. Writing to St John in later years, Swift once said that the connection between him and Harley made Swift think of 'a youth of sixteen marrying a woman of thirty for love; she decays every year, while he grows up to his prime'.[1] The warm, affectionate, ambivalent admiration provoked in Swift by St John worked more nervously than mere friendship. I think it was as though he had finally met the brilliant figure that he had imagined from the pages of Temple's early letters.

These currents may have run behind the quasi-lovers'-quarrel that Swift provoked with St John in the spring of 1711. On Easter Sunday he dined with St John and felt disturbed by his host's manner—'terribly down and melancholy'. After brooding, the doctor decided that the Secretary had shown him insufficient respect. He therefore seized an early opportunity to reproach him, in a style that must have baffled the object of his complaints:

> I called at Mr. Secretary's, to see what the d - - - - ailed him on Sunday; I made him a very proper speech, told him I observed he was much out of temper; that I did not expect he would tell me the cause, but would be glad to see he was in better; and one thing I warned him of, Never to appear cold to me, for I would not be treated like a school-boy; that I had felt too much of that in my life already (meaning from Sir William Temple); that I expected every great minister, who honoured me with his acquaintance, if he

[1] Williams II. 320.

heard or saw any thing to my disadvantage, would let me know it in plain words, and would not put me in pain to guess by the change or coldness of his countenance or behaviour; for it was what I would hardly bear from a crowned head.

St John agreed that he had not been on his best behaviour but said the reason had nothing to do with Swift; the Secretary had been busy at his office whole nights at a time and then had sat up all one night drinking; hence the gloomy manner. As a peace-making gesture he asked Swift to dine with him but was refused: 'I would not. I don't know, but I would not.' The next day, Swift drew out the comparison of Temple with St John: 'Don't you remember how I used to be in pain when Sir William Temple would look cold and out of humour for three or four days, and I used to suspect a hundred reasons?'[1]

The crisis has the air of a provocation used to test the fidelity of a lover. Swift's reproaches sound disproportionate to their cause; he was responding not to the immediate situation but to his re-capitulation of an ancient distress; he allowed himself to blame St John for Temple's lack of tenderness because he sensed that the younger man was 'safe' and would hold on to him in spite of the provocation. The clinching detail seems his treatment of the invitation to dinner. Honour had already been more than satis-fied; but Swift, having revived the sense of rejection created by Temple, felt dissatisfied until he could even the account by reject-ing Temple's surrogate. Seeing this, one begins to appreciate the deep-seated origins of Swift's long attachment to St John.

Yet over and above these intrinsic reasons for the Doctor's be-ing drawn to the Secretary, a simpler influence was operating. For St John seems to have decided that Swift, even apart from his many *agréments*, was considerable enough to be worth enticing out of Harley's camp and into his own. Apparently, therefore, he set to work to please Swift, to win him over, to turn him subtly against their common leader, and to make him publicize St John's views rather than Harley's.

It later seemed to Harley that any real co-operation between St John and himself ended in February 1711, when an armistice

[1] *Journal*, 1, 3, 4 Apr. 1711.

dinner at the Secretary's house failed to halt St John's efforts to enlist a party under his own direction and to 'set up', as Harley put it, 'for governing the House'.[1] But Swift had strong instincts against recognizing the split. It was not merely a piece of propaganda for him to argue that his own side represented a single essence, as against the Whigs' multifariousness. He truly believed that goodness, unity, and stability were joined against evil, variety, and change. In his mind as well as his heart he assumed that good leadership meant harmonious leadership. Consequently, he made a point of congratulating Harcourt, St John, and Harley on their friendship: 'I told them I had no hopes they could ever keep in [sc. power], but that I saw they loved one another so well, as indeed they seem to do.'[2] If this pretty speech almost coincided with the unsuccessful love feast at St John's house, Swift's irony, I think, was not unconscious. His use of 'seem' in the account to the ladies sounds intentional; and by praising the three ministers for a declining virtue, he probably hoped to restore it.

VI. THE COLONEL

With Harley, too, Swift provoked a test in the form of a quarrel, but the occasion was strikingly different from the affair with St John. One day early in 1711, Swift dined with the Chancellor. Although three o'clock was the normal dinner hour, the party did not sit down till six, and the reverend doctor did not get away till eleven. Swift told the ladies there would be no more such dinners with Harley 'if I can help it' and gave as the reason his dislike of late and irregular hours. The following day, he was invited again and did indeed refuse. But this time he gave the ladies an entirely different reason: 'I fell out with him yesterday, and will not see him again till he makes me amends.' The day after that, Erasmus Lewis showed Swift a letter Harley had written to Lewis, saying he wished to be reconciled to Swift. 'But I was deaf to all intreaties', Swift told the ladies, 'and have desired Lewis to go to him, and let him know I expect further satisfaction.' Then he went on,

[1] Trevelyan III. 118.   [2] *Journal*, 17 Feb. 1711.

If we let these great ministers pretend too much, there will be no governing them. He promises to make me easy, if I will but come and see him; but I won't, and he shall do it by message, or I will cast him off. . . He did something, which he intended for a favour; and I have taken it quite otherwise, disliking both the thing and the manner, and it has heartily vexed me, and all I have said is truth, though it looks like a jest; and I absolutely refused to submit to his intended favour, and expect further satisfaction.

Although an éclaircissement was accomplished by the middle of the month, weeks still passed before Swift revealed the precipitating *casus belli* to the ladies. Then at last it transpired that when Swift had dined with Harley on Monday, 5 February, his host had pressed upon him a bankbill for fifty pounds. Swift had reacted with a furious sense of outrage and had sent the bill back by way of Erasmus Lewis, to whom he also wrote a 'very complaining letter' that was shown to Harley. It does not appear that Harley ever sent Swift the written message that he desired; for though it would certainly have been preserved, none has been found; and Swift himself indicates that he finally visited Harley (on Friday, 16 February) and that as part of the making-up he was admitted to the Saturday dinners: 'He told me he had a quarrel with me; I said I had another with him, and we returned to our friendship, and I should think he loves me as well as a great minister can love a man in so short a time.'[1]

Rather than spell out 'a bank bill for fifty pound', Swift hid the words in a simple code, in order, I presume, to discourage spies; but the fact hardly seems to have been a dangerous secret, and I wonder whether shame was not as much a motive as concealment; for the money offer must have created an especially vibrant shock just because he was so preoccupied with money. If St John had offended Swift by seeming to reject him, Harley did so by accepting him in the wrong way. What Swift wanted was not a boss–worker connection but a familial tie. He did not like to think that his services to the ministry could be reckoned in financial terms, much though he hoped that a striking and permanent improvement in his financial condition would be the outward emblem of their appreciation. The bankbill temporarily

[1] *Ibid.*, 5, 6, 7, 16 Feb.; 7 Mar. 1711.

destroyed the illusion that he and Harley were drawn together by mutual trust and mutual respect. It destroyed the illusion that Swift was helping an older relative who needed him.

Yet Harley's miscalculation was a gesture in the right direction. He must have seen ample evidence of Swift's necessary thrift and have supposed that a simple present (perhaps out of the secret-service funds) would be welcome. It was a protective, fatherly motion. If I am right to infer that Harley never obliged Swift with a letter of apology, his conduct was again that of a senior who does not owe but expects obedience. Swift's final, accommodating resumption of the status quo seems to imply that he recognized the justice of Harley's standing pat and allowed that his own initial complaints had been unduly punctilious. After all, while Swift would have weakened his actual moral position as well as his self-esteem by becoming to any extent Harley's pensioner, a tactful refusal would have seemed a more appropriate response than a burst of indignation drawing on the disappointments Swift's filial hopes had suffered from Archbishop King, Lord Somers, or Sir William Temple.

Harley's character inspired Swift with a very different sort of affection from St John's. In spite of ambivalences, the fundamental feeling was comfortable, with little of the nervous quality attached to Secretary St John. The Chancellor's background reminded the doctor of his own. From the reign of Henry III the Harleys had possessed an important seat in Herefordshire, where Swift's admired grandfather, the reverend Thomas Swift of Goodrich, had established his family. Although Harley's grandfather, Sir Robert, had been an aggressive leader of the Puritans, his son, Sir Edward, had opposed Cromwell and had been favoured by Charles II. This mingling of parliamentary and royalist traditions recalls the similar mixture to be found between the Nonconformist father of Swift's mother and the intensely royalist vicar of Goodrich. Swift may have noticed the coincidence that Harley's mother, Lady Abigail, had borne the same name as his own mother. In Harley's early training there had also been an infusion of pious principles such as were congenial to Swift, who described him to Archbishop King as having 'a true sense of religion' and as being a 'good divine'.[1] Politically, Harley and Swift (under the influence of Sir William Temple) had been on the same side in the 1690s; the Triennial Bill, which Swift had defended before Lord Portland, Harley had defended in Parliament.

In temperament Harley was a reassuring figure, peculiarly mild and affable. He liked to play down apparent crises, and offered goodwill where he could not perform deeds. Swift found his scholarly tastes attractive; the two men shared an interest in English history which Harley demonstrated by his patronage of scholars and by the large-scale acquisition of historical manuscripts as part of the great library he was in the process of assembling. Although Swift blamed him for secretiveness, this trait was probably one aspect of a larger compulsion which the statesman shared with the parson. Harley's drive to collect and withhold books, manuscripts, information, or certain material goods seems oddly parallel to Swift's stinginess, gossipiness, his list-making proclivity, and his lifelong retention of manuscripts or letters written by himself and others. Evidently, Swift felt pleasantly relieved that money, which is one of the commonest objects of a hoarding instinct, seemed excluded from Harley's chief concerns, for the minister's freedom from avarice is a repeated theme of Swift's praise: unlike St John, Harley showed small inclination to carouse at the public trough. As for his habit, endlessly lamented by Swift, of putting off decisions and keeping men dangling in attendance, this seems one more facet of the hoarding impulse.

One virtue better eulogized than imitated by Swift was Harley's bravery. 'A stranger to fear', Swift called him[2]—'the most fearless man alive and the least apt to despond'.[3] Simple physical courage came naturally to Harley. He paid no attention to anonymous threats and walked out alone while he was in danger of being attacked. His composure when seven of his political enemies were straining to find evidence of his treasonable involvement in his own clerk's espionage during the crisis of 1708 had been witnessed by many observers. With so little regard for

[1] Williams I. 249.   [2] *Ibid.*, p. 238.   [3] *Journal*, 4 Mar. 1711.

immediate threats, he naturally felt only contemptuous amusement at the vituperation directed against him by journalists; and thus he dazzled the timorous vicar, who felt infuriated by the same treatment and wanted vengeance.

Similarly, Harley seldom worried about his health. Swift did not always approve the effects of so much intrepidity; and as the spring of 1711 advanced, he fussed again and again over his patron's physical state. I suppose this anxiety was exacerbated by Fountaine's recent illness and slow recovery; but during the early days of March, Swift must also have felt the uneasiness due to the recent quarrel and reconciliation between Harley and himself. Certainly he was distressed by news, one Sunday, that Harley was seriously indisposed: 'Pray God preserve his health', Swift said to the ladies, 'every thing depends upon it.'[1] On Monday he heard that Harley was still unwell, though forced by official business to leave his house. Swift sent and called two or three times during that day, to learn that Harley suffered from a sore throat and had been cupped the night before. On Tuesday the report came of a slight relapse. Two days later, when Swift had so many reasons to feel touched by any danger to his hero, the news broke which horrified the nation and transformed the political scene.

VII. GUISCARD

Early in the afternoon of Thursday, 8 March 1711—the anniversary of Queen Anne's accession—Swift, while walking in the Mall, passed a middle-aged French émigré who called himself the Marquis de Guiscard.[2] Although Swift and he were acquainted, Guiscard surprised him by not speaking. The reason was perhaps that the hard-up refugee was feeling panicky about his own prospects. Swift had recently heard that he was almost penniless, and had even interceded with St John, who had assured him that Guiscard was receiving a pension of four hundred pounds a year.

Though belonging to a distinguished French family, Guiscard had become addicted to riotous amusements and finally left his

[1] *Journal*, 4 Mar. 1711.

[2] Swift called him 'the most tedious, trifling talker, I ever conversed with' (Davis VIII. 127).

country to escape prosecution for some peculiarly violent esca-pades. With the help of several impressive recommendations, he imposed himself on various military leaders and statesmen of the Grand Alliance, as a reliable agent to direct the uprisings which had broken out in the Cévennes mountain region of south-central France. Although a first expedition had proved a failure, Guis-card was able to exist comfortably as a military officer on the salaries and allowances granted him by the Dutch and the Eng-lish while he tried to organize a second attempt. This new project was abortive, however; Guiscard quarrelled with his English superiors, and he soon found himself back in London, living on a much reduced scale. He lost his military commission, and though listed for a pension of five hundred pounds a year (on St John's representation), he found this not only paid most irregularly but lowered soon by Harley's frugality to four hundred. In order to compensate himself for such losses, he began to spy for the French. On the Tuesday when Swift was still worrying about Harley's sore throat, Guiscard discovered that some letters he had left to be delivered by the usual channel were lost before they went out. He did not yet know that his treachery had been exposed, some days before, by the innocent British diplomat whose postbag had been carrying the correspondence and whose wife had turned the ostensibly missing letters over to Harley.

On Thursday, before Swift saw Guiscard, Harley had also noticed the spy in the Mall. At the time, the Chancellor of the Exchequer was on his way to visit the Queen. In keeping with the pomp of her majesty's Accession Day, he had dressed himself in an elaborate, doubly lined waistcoat with metallic embroidery, under a new blue coat, open at the breast.[1] Besides having his audience with her majesty, he secured a warrant for the imme-diate arrest of Guiscard, and he called a cabinet committee meet-ing to examine him.

The messengers located Guiscard still in the park, disarmed him, and took him to the Cockpit. While waiting in one of the Secretary of State's rooms, he was given some food and managed

---

[1] Churchill's account is contradicted by an eye witness of Harley's dressing: H.M.C. *Portland* IV. 669.

to secrete a penknife which he discovered there. Then he was brought in to the committee. It was a daunting group for any culprit to face: not only Harley and St John but also the Queen's aged uncle, Lord Rochester, who was Lord President of the Privy Council; the princely Duke of Ormonde, Lord Lieutenant of Ireland; the Dukes of Buckingham, Newcastle, and Queensberry; and such other officers as Lord Keeper Harcourt and Secretary of State Dartmouth; not to mention St John's two undersecretaries and Lord Poulett, first Commissioner of the Treasury.

By this time Swift had gone for dinner to the house of Lady Morice, a daughter of Lord Pembroke. After the meal, they were quietly playing cards when a young stepson of Pembroke came running in with the announcement that Harley had been stabbed. Stunned and horrified, Swift left Lady Morice's at once and ran to St John's house. However, no one was in. Then he met Mrs St John on her way back, but she could not tell him much. So he took a chair to Buckingham Street and there learned at last that Harley, though wounded, did not appear in danger and was now resting. Edward Harley, the Chancellor's son, was able to supply the frantic inquirer with something like a clear, detailed story which Swift and later historians verified and enlarged.

During the examination of Guiscard by the committee, the evidence produced against the accused man had appeared so strong that though he started by trying to brave things out, he soon realized the case was hopeless. Turning to St John, whose recreations he had sometimes shared, Guiscard asked for a private interview; but the Secretary, seated across a desk from him, inevitably refused. Now messengers were summoned to take the prisoner to Newgate; but just as he was leaving the room, he suddenly leaned over Harley's shoulder and stabbed him in the breast with the hidden penknife. Luckily, Harley's sore throat had caused him to wear some flannel swathing, over which of course lay the embroidered waistcoat. These were enough to impede the small knife, which broke short on the breastbone, so that when Guiscard tried a second blow, it produced only a bruise.

In the mêlée which followed, St John and others ran swords into the criminal while Queensberry called in messengers and footmen, one of whom finally got Guiscard subdued on the floor, where he was tied neck and heels as he bled. Harley showed his normal courage by remaining quite calm; he sent word to his sister not to keep dinner for him, and gave instructions for his attacker's wounds to be looked after. Then he was carried home in a sedan chair, accompanied by the solicitous Lord Poulett. But St John, nervous and impulsive, rushed to St James's Palace, first to tell Mrs Masham what had just taken place and then, accompanied by Dr Arbuthnot, to assure the Queen that Harley was alive.[1]

After hearing the main story, Swift talked it over with Prior and Mansell, whom he met as he returned home. When he reached his own lodgings, one of his first acts was to write a careful, though slightly erroneous, account which he sent to Ireland before nine o'clock that night. I find several aspects of this composition curious. For example, it was addressed not, as one might have expected, to Mrs Johnson, but to Archbishop King. Of course, Swift wanted the correct facts to be circulated in Ireland, since they were much to Harley's credit. But the consternation he emphatically expressed might also imply that the near-loss of a new fatherly patron was driving him to fall back on an earlier one. Some of Swift's anxiety was derived from the hopes he had maintained of preferment to be secured through Harley, and some from the fears he felt of the vengeance he might suffer from Whigs returned to power. But the insistent near-hysteria of his language to the Archbishop suggests that the strongest emotions were unselfish; for he sounds eager to make King appreciate these feelings. Thus, after commenting on the danger to the government if Harley should die, Swift adds remarks like these:

> Neither can I altogether forget myself, who, in him, should lose a person I have more obligations to, than any other in this kingdom; who hath always treated me with the tenderness of a parent, and never refused me any favour I asked for a friend; therefore I hope

[1] I have combined details from Boyer, *Political State* for Mar. 1711; Churchill VI. 385–91; *Journal*, 8 Mar. 1711; Williams I. 213–16; and H.M.C. *Portland* IV. 668–70.

your grace will excuse the disorder of this letter. . . I have read over
what I writ, and find it confused and incorrect, which your grace
must impute to the violent pain of mind I am in, greater than ever
I felt in my life.[1]

It is almost as though Swift meant to reproach King for being a
less satisfactory papa than Harley. To Mrs Johnson he used different though hardly weaker language in a hasty note the same
night: 'Pray pardon my distraction; I now think of all his kindness to me . . . pity me; I want it.'[2] Even if one takes all the circumstances into account, these bold expressions from a man of
Swift's reserve must seem extravagant. By comparison, Harley's
own affectionate daughter sounded cool.[3]

After half a week of brooding and making inquiries about
Harley three or four times a day, after saying that till Harley
should be well, 'I can have no peace', Swift himself finally confessed, 'He is not feverish at all, and I think it is foolish in me to be
so much in pain as I am.'[4] With this remark in mind I cannot help
wondering whether Swift's identification of Harley with his own
parent did not go so far that he felt the guilt of a resentful son over
a father's near-death. This would account for the display Swift
made of his anxiety. After all, granted that no illness could be
counted negligible under the medical practice of that day, still
Harley's wound was absurdly slight.

But as if to show sympathy by imitation, Swift now succeeded
in bruising his shin so badly that he had to stay at home; between
waiting for news of the other invalid and looking after his own
hurt, he could hardly go out for a while. I suppose it pleased him
to feel identified with his hero in immobility; and if he felt any
unconscious guilt, this accident may have taken care of his need
for punishment.[5]

In Swift's capacity as apologist for a unified ministry, he now
faced several embarrassments. The ultimate source of them all
was St John's resentfulness of Harley's glory. Surviving a political assassination meant something more than a period of bed-
rest and light diet. An acclamatory wave of verse and prose

---

[1] Williams I. 215.   [2] *Journal*, 8 Mar. 1711.   [3] H.M.C. *Portland* IV. 667.
[4] *Journal*, 9, 11 Mar. 1711.   [5] *Ibid.*, 14 Mar. 1711.

celebrated the British patriot who had been struck down by a French papist spy. One of the weaker effusions was an impromptu quatrain by Swift.[1] Perhaps the best was a stanzaic apostrophe by Prior.

> The barb'rous rage that durst attempt thy life,
> Harley, great counsellor, extends thy fame:
> And the sharp point of cruel Guiscard's knife,
> In brass and marble carves thy deathless name.[2]

More significant than immortal rhymes or the congratulations of civic bodies, or even the messages of friends and diplomats, was the speed with which crown and Parliament answered the reverberations of popular enthusiasm. If St John had felt any pleasure in the withering of Harley's reputation during the winter, his satisfaction was more than extinguished by the rebirth which followed Guiscard's attack. Harley had never been and was never again to be so popular.

Instead of hastening his recuperation, the Chancellor of the Exchequer prudently extended it. While Guiscard died of his wounds,[3] and his pickled carcass was shown at the jail for a fee (until the scandalized Queen heard and ordered an end to it), Harley stayed home, letting his bruises heal quite perfectly and, incidentally, allowing an address to be delivered, from both houses of Parliament to the Queen, intimating that his fidelity to her majesty and zeal for her service had drawn upon Harley the hatred of 'all the abettors of Popery and faction'. The phrasing was calculated to offend the Whigs, but her majesty echoed it in her reply. When Harley finally let it be known that he felt ready to return to the House of Commons, the members voted that Speaker Bromley should prepare another speech, to congratulate the wounded hero on that occasion. Consequently, at the end of April, a good seven weeks after the catastrophe, the Chancellor of the Exchequer enjoyed the happiness of hearing a public eulogy upon his virtues delivered to his face. The earlier phrasing was reincorporated, with the innuendo strengthened by allusions to the treatment Harley had received from 'some persons',

---

[1] *Poems* i. 140.   [2] 'To Mr. Harley', ll. 13–16.
[3] To screen the noble swordsmen, the coroner brought in a verdict blaming the blows of the messenger.

as well as the 'inveterate malice' of his enemies and the unceasing endeavours made against his 'person and reputation'. In other words, Guiscard's assault was represented as analogous to the supposed attempt that the Whig investigators of Greg's treason, in 1708, had made to ruin Harley. The smell of incense thus mingled with the taste of revenge to give the quasi-martyr some delightful sensations. On top of so many provocations of St John's envy there was further imposed, about this time, the perfectly reliable rumour that her majesty intended shortly to take advantage of the rapid current in her servant's favour by raising him to the peerage and making him Lord Treasurer.

It was hard for St John to deny that Harley had been stabbed, but it was easy to argue that the Secretary of State was the original target of the assassin. Unless this had been Guiscard's intention, he would not, presumably, have tried to secure a private interview with St John. Nevertheless, Harley was unlikely to feel consoled for his near-murder by an assurance that the intended victim was his hated rival. The contention between the friends of the two men as to which of them deserved the larger palm for a martyrdom neither of them had suffered came very early to Swift's notice. He felt he had to devote a number of the *Examiner* to the incident; and although this ineffectual piece was written within a week of the attack, it already embodies lies and evasions revealing a strenuous wish to reconcile mutually contradictory viewpoints. Thus Swift declared that after striking down Harley, Guiscard had tried to murder St John, and that when Guiscard was asked why he had stabbed the Chancellor of the Exchequer, he answered that not being able to reach his first target, St John, he had turned on 'the one person whom he thought Mr St John loved best'! As so often when Swift, without stopping to refine his emotions, works them into a publication, the general effect is strained and unconvincing.

In this *Examiner* Swift did not fail to improve the hints of a parallel between Guiscard and the committee that had questioned Greg; for the best paragraph in the hollow composition is skilfully and poisonously concerned with the theme. The beauty of Swift's treatment is that he can use this analysis in turn to sup-

[470]

port his more general insinuation that the French Papists and the Whig Dissenters, so far from being opposed to each other, are really in cahoots, both of them therefore hating the true patriot, Harley. In several subsequent *Examiners* Swift briefly repeats his charges but hardly varies them.

The Chancellor's friends could not have thanked Swift very warmly for reporting that Guiscard's 'chief design' had been against St John. When, therefore, a fuller account had to be published in the form of a pamphlet,[1] Swift kept prudently out of the way and let Mrs Manley (the hack who also served as mistress to the printer John Barber) cook it up with hints and a first page from Swift. 'I was afraid of disobliging Mr. Harley or Mr. St. John in one critical point about it, and so would not do it myself', he told the ladies—also, I am afraid, assuring them that the circumstances given in the misleading story were 'all true'. Abel Boyer, a Whig journalist whom Swift loathed and who loathed him back, described the *True Narrative* more judiciously as 'confus'd, lame, and, in many places, false'.

The ministerial press gave so much play to the Guiscard–Greg analogy that refutations soon began to appear, among them a diffuse pamphlet, more readable than informative, called *A Letter to the Seven Lords of the Committee*. Here the Tories were reproached for raising such abominable suspicions concerning persons so weighty and exalted as the Whig peers chosen to examine Greg. In August 1711 Swift saw fit to answer this, and published *Some Remarks upon a Pamphlet Entitl'd* etc.,[2] which he determined to write partly because he thought he could turn the controversy into fresh and more productive channels. Like most point-by-point refutations, *Some Remarks* does not lack its sandy stretches. The topics are too particular for the essay to possess enduring interest, and it introduces no aspect of Swift's art which had not been fully exemplified before. Yet it is a fine specimen of how sober irony can redeem moralistic condescension; for the slow fires of this essay have far more strength than the flame of the

[1] *A True Narrative of what Pass'd at the Examination of* . . . *Guiscard*, published 16 Apr. 1711; see Boyer, *Political State*, Apr. 1711; *Journal*, 16 Apr. 1711.

[2] Published 18 Aug. See *Journal* I. 240, n. 27; probably written at Windsor in the summer (July–August) of 1711: see *ibid.*, p. 244, n. 2.

Examiner on Guiscard. Certain phrases and attitudes are further remarkable both for their workmanship and for what they imply about Swift's principles. 'Is this an age of the world to think crimes improbable because they are great?'[1] Swift asks in reply to the charge that he was imputing abominations to very eminent men. Although modern readers have the most solid grounds for echoing the sentiment, it happened, ironically enough, to militate against Swift's whole interpretation of the Greg affair, since he primarily claimed it was absurd to suppose a man of Harley's eminence would have dealings with a person so mean and vicious as poor Greg. 'Is there no difference', he asks, 'between men chosen by the prince, reverenced by the people for their virtue, and others rejected by both for the highest demerits?'[2] According to his own criteria we must infallibly answer, no difference at all. Similarly, in order to exalt his own moral foundation, Swift makes himself an exception to his own rules. 'I am of a temper', he boasts, 'to think no man great enough to set me on work.'[3] Noble words, of course, and in a sense quite true. Swift gained no income from his political writings; he propagated no general views which he did not hold; he stood apart, for independence of conscience, from the mass of journalists. But he could not claim, except by equivocation, to serve no party; neither could he deny that like the rest of his kind, he looked ultimately for a tangible reward. He told deliberate lies, and he was unwittingly the captive of the partial data which his high-placed informants gave him. Even on the level of mere persuasive rhetoric, he could not hope to appear detached from the usual pressure so long as he boasted of having the ministry's confidence.[4]

By associating the seven committee men with the Godolphin ministry, Swift, in *Some Remarks*, makes an easy transition to the broad contrast between the Whig leaders and the Tories. Here he does generalize and enrich the discussion with the help of his common method of escaping from Hobbesian cynicism. For he revives the argument that whatever moral weaknesses the new

---

[1] Davis III. 190.　　[2] *Ibid.*, p. 189.　　[3] *Ibid.*, p. 194.

[4] Contrast the reference to Swift's mastery of secret 'memorials' (*ibid.*, p. 188) with the statement about 'common observation' (p. 195).

government may share with the old, Harley's circle find it their interest as well as their inclination to do what is best for the country, i.e., to end the war. Rhetorically, this analysis is appealing: the author makes himself seem hard-headed and high-minded at once. It depends, of course, on the assumption that author and reader agree as to what is best for the country; and to this extent it suggests Swift is preaching to the converted. However, as a moral basis for national policy it is far stronger than the alternative claim that one set of men are all bad and another all good.

VIII. UNDERPASSES TO PEACE

By the time *Some Remarks upon a Pamphlet* appeared, the split between Harley and St John had reached a new depth of complexity. The main effect of this change was to demonstrate how thoroughly the two rivals had in fact to depend on each other. With the Chancellor disabled and out of action, the Secretary tried to take over the open leadership of the House of Commons, where his main support continued to be the inexperienced, immoderate tribe of the October Club. But lacking Harley to control them, these wild men threw out an essential tax bill in spite of St John's oratory. About the same time, they themselves were in turn sadly disappointed by the Secretary over the affair of James Brydges. In order to blacken the names of the late ministers, Harley's brother Edward, the Auditor, had brought before the House a sensational charge that £35,000,000 of public money had never been accounted for, and he implied that Godolphin was responsible for the negligence. Although this groundless insinuation delighted St John's particular followers, the Secretary himself found it painfully embarrassing. During four of the years when the money was spent, he had been Secretary at War; and James Brydges, Paymaster-General, the man to be blamed above all others if the allegations had any truth in them, was a special friend of his, said to have lent him large quantities of money. Instead, therefore, of heading the assault, St John confounded everyone by defending Brydges and denying that any crime had been committed.

[473]

Behind scenes, he was more effective. Since Harley could not easily block him during the recuperative weeks following Guiscard's attack, St John was able to push his Quebec expedition beyond the point where anyone might turn it back; and at the end of April the fleet sailed with Mrs Masham's brother in charge. Meanwhile, Swift visited the invalid often enough to discover how furious Harley's faction felt about the Secretary's misbehaviour. However, the doctor was still so innocent as to hope the apparent errors of his brilliant young friend were accidental. So in a splendidly ironical episode, worrying that Harley might drop St John from the ministry, he decided to beg the Secretary to 'set himself right'. And sure enough, nine days later, when he was alone with St John, Swift did in fact try to tell him 'my fears of his proceedings', but happened to be interrupted.[1]

If it disgusted St John to see the Chancellor of the Exchequer return to the Commons stronger than ever, it must have infuriated him as much as it did the Whigs to find that Harley had a scheme for further endearing himself to the country gentlemen in Parliament. This was a device to relieve the nation of the allegedly vast war debt which the Tories traditionally regarded as an economic disaster. Harley proposed to establish a South Sea Company which would take over the entire floating debt of £10,000,000 and pay a guaranteed six per cent interest on it. As the main source of its riches, the company would be endowed with a monopoly of the slave trade with Spanish America, which Britain would be guaranteed (to the exclusion of the Dutch) through the treaty of peace; and the company would also be assigned the revenue from certain taxes. Peace, trade, credit, and a Tory government were thus to be magnificently reconciled, and a rival to the Whigs' Bank of England at last erected. This proposal threw a dazzling lustre on Harley's fame; and when the closing week of May saw him created Earl of Oxford and Lord Treasurer, his triumph was complete. Swift exclaimed to the ladies, 'This man has grown by persecutions, turnings out, and stabbing. What waiting, and crowding, and bowing, will be at his levee?'[2]

[1] *Journal*, 27 Apr., 6 May 1711.   [2] *Ibid.*, 22 May 1711.

Still everything from the South Sea Company to the survival of the government hinged on the conclusion of a peace; and if St John had failed to displace Harley in Parliament, it soon appeared that in the *summa rerum* even Lord Treasurer Oxford could not displace the Secretary of State. Yet, paradoxically, by the time the negotiations first became known to St John, hardly a month still remained before the end of the parliamentary session. Fortunately, at this stage the background of the bargaining had been transformed by the death of the Emperor Joseph. Since the younger brother of his imperial majesty was his heir, and since that brother was the very Charles III of Spain for whom England and the Allies were reconquering Flanders, the apparent balance of power had shifted to the political advantage of the Tories. It was one thing to be keeping the French Philip V out so that the crowns of France and Spain should not be united; it was quite another to exhaust England's treasure for the sake of joining the crowns of Spain and Austria. Whatever the realities of Austrian impotence and French energy might be, the slogan of 'No peace without Spain' had been undermined, and a peace on the new Lord Treasurer's terms had been facilitated.

When the French agent Gaultier returned to England with an ostensibly spontaneous offer of peace from Louis XIV, Shrewsbury insisted that the terms be shown to others besides the trio of Jersey, Harley, and himself. At the end of April, therefore, the cabinet, including of course, St John, was informed of this 'paper' and of the South Sea scheme as well. Since the terms offered by Louis were necessarily vague, the ministers decided to send back to Versailles a diplomat who could argue in French and who had expert knowledge of the Sun King's court. It is scarcely surprising that the choice should have fallen upon Harley's and Jersey's common protégé Matthew Prior. Leaving England as unobtrusively as possible, the man of 'meane extraction' reached Versailles on 21 July, N.S. After several conferences with the great foreign minister Torcy, he was admitted to an audience with Louis himself, during which Prior had the opportunity to exhibit his mastery of the French style in compliment.

Though he came back to England secretly and in disguise,

Prior got into trouble when he landed at Dover,[1] because an anxious customs officer imagined he might be a spy and detained him until an express order from London secured his release. Stories spread at once that a British agent had been negotiating a peace with the French. Naturally, the Whig journalists interpreted the concealment of the operation as a sign that the ministry were betraying both Britain and the Allies, although in fact the terms of the preliminaries were such as to sacrifice the interests of the Austrians and Dutch to those of Britain.

IX. A NEW JOURNEY TO PARIS

Swift, who was often entertained at Windsor during the summer of 1711, met Prior there at supper with Oxford, St John, and Mr Masham on 12 August, very shortly after Prior's arrival. But it was almost two weeks before he told the ladies the current gossip, and then he used language that was perhaps intentionally more doubtful than his real opinions:

> Prior has been out of town these two months, nobody know where, and is lately returned. People confidently affirm he has been in France, and I half believe it. It is said, he was sent by the ministry, and for some overtures towards a peace. The Secretary pretends he knows nothing of it.[2]

Since Swift himself believed that the welfare of the nation and the survival of his friends' ministry absolutely required a peace, he disliked the effect that unkind, random murmurs might produce. To confute them quite honestly and openly, however, would weaken the government's freedom of negotiation. Consequently, he decided to employ a more congenial stratagem:

> I am apt to think we shall soon have a peace, by the little words I hear thrown out by the ministry. I have just thought of a project to bite the town. I have told you, that it is now known that Mr Prior has been lately in France. I will make a printer of my own sit by me one day, and I will dictate to him a formal relation of Prior's journey, with several particulars, all pure inventions; and I doubt not but it will take.[3]

---

[1] Swift and Boyer agree on Dover; others name other places.
[2] *Journal*, 12, 24 Aug. 1711; cf. *ibid.*, 25, 27 Aug.   [3] *Ibid.*, 31 Aug. 1711.

A New Journey to Paris was published less than a fortnight after Swift conceived the idea; and though Prior pretended to be annoyed by it, the pamphlet sold two thousand copies in two weeks at the fag-end of the summer.[1] Besides being one of Swift's cleverest inventions, it exemplifies a new development in his use of pseudonyms, but otherwise has little to recommend it. Swift's fundamental purpose was clearly serious: he wished to defend the possibility of a peace that left Spain to a Bourbon, and he wished to defend his ministerial comrades. He hoped the pamphlet would work toward these goals partly by hinting at positive arguments and partly by distracting the malice of scandal-lovers— i.e., 'by way of furnishing fools with something to talk of'.[2]

The *New Journey* purports to be a translation, with preface and footnotes, of a letter composed and originally printed in French. The letter-writer is supposed to be the valet, sometimes doubling as secretary, employed by Prior during his stay in France. This 'Sieur du Baudrier' (or gentleman of the cross-belt!) describes Prior, traces his journey back and forth between England and Versailles, and reports bits of dialogue the valet has heard or overheard between Prior on the one side and Torcy, Mme de Maintenon, or Louis XIV on the other. The gist of his account is that Prior made immense demands and repeatedly threatened to end the negotiation sooner than accept any compromise; that the French were staggered by his terms but were persuaded to yield all of them through his integrity. By one clue, Swift falsely intimates that the terms included the dethroning of Philip V. He

---

[1] *Ibid.*, 11, 12 Sept. 1711. I doubt that 'dictate' means 'compose' (*ibid.*, 4 Sept. 1711). Rather, I suspect that Swift wrote nearly all of the *New Journey* between 31 Aug. (or earlier) and 4 Sept. but made the printer (who was probably John Barber) his amanuensis by dictation in order to ensure his own anonymity. The last page alone he dictated without first writing it down. This is how I understand Swift's remark to the ladies, 'I writ all but about the last page, that I dictated, and the printer writ' (*Journal*, 11 Sept. 1711); see also *ibid.*, 4, 5 Sept. 1711. Swift's use of 'seemed' and 'affecting' in his reports of Prior's reaction suggests to me that he thought Prior was pretending (*ibid.*, 11, 13 Sept. 1711). On the publication see *ibid.*, 1. 357, n. 4; on the sale, see *ibid.*, 12, 24 Sept. 1711. According to Swift the first edition of one thousand was sold out in a day, and the second edition consisted of five hundred copies. There were apparently three editions. See also Rothschild, no. 2021 and Teerink, no. 536. Swift's pamphlet is probably modelled on Martin Lister, *A Journey to Paris*, 1699.
[2] Williams I. 261.

also implicitly contrasts the misery of France under a despot with England's prosperity under a constitutional monarch. For a thrust at Marlborough, Swift has the Frenchman say he has heard that in England 'some subjects had palaces more magnificent than Queen Anne her self.'[1]

The essential form of the pamphlet is that of a hoax, a 'serious' hoax, if the expression is tolerable, as distinguished from the sort of comic hoax that is intended to be seen through by readers of taste. Its superiority in this genre will appear if it is contrasted with a specimen Swift was to publish a few months later, called the *Windsor Prophecy*. I think the distinction is worth making clearer; and therefore I shall digress here and analyse the *Windsor Prophecy* in some detail before coming back to *A New Journey*. The *Prophecy* itself is a piece of doggerel pretended to have turned up as a two-hundred-year-old parchment found by a gravedigger in the cloisters at Windsor. The drift of the meaning is that the forthcoming peace will be a blessing, that the opponents of a peace are enemies of England, and that the Queen (who is apostrophized) should dismiss the belligerent Duchess of Somerset and trust utterly in Mrs Masham.

What Swift hoped to accomplish by the *Windsor Prophecy* remains unclear. If he felt so presumptuous as to hope the Queen herself might see it, he could hardly have believed it would turn her majesty against the Duchess. Probably, he was giving way injudiciously to some misdirected spite. As usual when Swift's feelings are stronger than his deliberate art, the product leaves the modern reader more curious than pleased. If anything, Swift's unrestrained vituperation must have driven well-informed persons to sympathize with a woman blamed for having red hair and falsely accused of helping to kill her first two husbands.

As a 'comic' hoax, the meaning of the *Prophecy* remains dark until its design is understood. Thus one must realize that the work is indeed a deception if one is to make much sense out of it. The real author expected his sympathetic audience to penetrate his disguise and to be entertained by his ingenuity in using 'Thynne', the name of the Duchess's second husband, as an

[1] Davis III. 213.

adverb, or 'Königsmark', the name of Thynne's murderous rival, as a verb and object. If one is so naïve as to be taken in by the framework of the *Prophecy*, one is not likely to grasp the innuendoes.

The *New Journey*, on the contrary, is truly meant to mislead the reader; its dramatic form is far more careful than that of the *Prophecy*. It is not a simple, direct report to the public but a personal letter from the valet to another Frenchman, who, one must assume, was the original publisher. Within this frame, the information we receive comes to us generally as bits of retailed conversation, a technique sharpening the dramatic effect. Outside the letter itself we meet the translator, who also acts as commentator in the footnotes he has added. The francophobia of the British translator sets him dramatically apart from his subject; for he expresses contempt for the French valet, who in turn displays Gallic vanity in pretending to have been Prior's secretary and Gallic servility in his complacent view of the condition of France. All these contrasting points of view, playing against one another, give the piece a remarkably lively verisimilitude.

The form of the *New Journey* is not a free construction but seems derived from the purpose of the real author. Swift wished to be free to omit a great deal of information that he did not possess about Prior's trip or that might undermine his own hope of strengthening the peace party. By making the supposed author a valet, therefore, Swift accounts for his vulgar ignorance. Yet certain facts had to be reported which a mere valet would not have known; so Swift has him pinch-hit as a secretary. The correction of the valet's boastful errors by the translator gives the piece a peculiarly authentic air, as do the plethora of irrelevant but concrete details of Prior's journey .

This little imaginary voyage oddly anticipates the pattern of Gulliver's voyage to Brobdingnag. But it differs from that masterpiece and from most of Swift's pseudonymous works in that the self-characterization of the narrator is consistent. Unlike almost every other pseudonym used by Swift, the Sieur du Baudrier is convincingly coherent in his traits, though false in his French.[1]

[1] See Boyer's attack on Swift and this pamphlet in the *Political State* for Sept. 1711.

It seems wholly natural to me that this sort of coherence, so often mistakenly ascribed to the 'masks' or 'personae' of Swift's important works, should be found perfected in a negligible *jeu d'esprit*.[1]

[1] I have omitted the episode of Archbishop King and the quotation from Tacitus. When the Archbishop heard of Guiscard's attack, he told Swift of a rumour going around Dublin that in stabbing Guiscard, St John had tried to prevent the man from revealing treasonable facts about the ministry. Some persons in Ireland, King said, were quoting a relevant passage from Tacitus *Annales* xv. 66 (Williams i. 216–17). But Swift answered with the report that a letter had come from Ireland to the *Post-Boy*, alleging that the Archbishop of Dublin himself was the first to apply the passage from Tacitus. Swift had assured St John that this story was false, and he had 'stifled the whole letter' with the Secretary's approval; so the libel was never published (Williams i. 219–21). King replied thanking Swift warmly for the intervention and declaring his own innocence at length (Williams i. 223–5). The Archbishop also told Edward Southwell about the incident, saying the story would have appeared in the *Post-Boy* 'if a friend had not accidentally prevented it' (letter of 19 Apr. 1711, to Southwell). Soon, however, Swift was persuaded by several acquaintances that the Archbishop was 'a little guilty' (*Journal*, 28 Apr. 1711); and ten months later, Lord Anglesey still assured Swift that the original charge was true (*ibid.*, 14 Feb. 1712). Studying the evidence carefully, one observes that Swift was reluctant to condemn the Archbishop; and this attitude, I think, is the important feature of the affair.

Chapter Twenty-one

THE CONDUCT OF THE ALLIES

I

St John's indispensability to the new Earl of Oxford became quite obvious during the discussions held in August and September with the French agent Mesnager, who had come over at the same time as Prior. Hammering out the preliminary terms upon which a desirable treaty might be based, St John alone of the British ministers possessed the quickness of thought, the simplicity of purpose, and the command of French needed to handle the clever visitor. Soon, early in October,[1] the diplomats signed a number of all-important secret articles granting immense commercial advantages to England, and also the public articles, which vaguely protected the interests of the Allies and conformed to the specifications of the Grand Alliance. St John evidently foresaw that his policies would, sooner or later, have to be 'sold' to the British public; and I think it was with this requirement in mind that he now particularly cultivated the main propagandist of the ministry, introducing Swift to Mesnager and the French aides at a quiet supper at Windsor the day after the signing of the preliminaries. 'We have already settled all things with France', Swift told the ladies, 'and very much to the honour and advantage of England.'[2]

Less honour than advantage, was to be the judgment of the Whigs and the Allies. To begin with, the articles completely gave up the hopeless task of securing Spain for the Habsburgs; so the greedy Austrians were bound to feel furious. As a corollary, no care was taken of the unfortunate Catalans, who had been most

[1] 27 Sept., O.S.; 8 Oct., N.S.
[2] *Journal*, 28 Sept. 1711.

loyal to Charles III and to England. Similarly, faithful Portugal stood to gain little by a treaty that assigned the Spanish crown to a Bourbon. As for the brave, ruined Dutch, their barrier against France was mentioned in the most general language, and would have to be worked out, in depressing detail, at the conference table. It was well known that the Dutch had misgoverned and alienated the citizens of a number of the Barrier towns in order to make up some of their own losses from the war; and it should have been understood by now that the whole policy of a wall of garrison towns afforded them no protection against an invasion by way of Flanders. Nevertheless, the naked policy of indifference to the desires of this closest of allies would need an elaborate apology. Against all these effectual betrayals of promises which British statesmen had reiterated in agreements from the Grand Alliance to the Barrier Treaty, there lay, hidden and uneasy, the cession of the Asiento, Gibraltar, Newfoundland, and other commercial and territorial gains to Britain.

Before a British audience such policies were defensible enough; and the anger of the Austrians or the Dutch would hardly make a decisive element in the xenophobic House of Commons. But her majesty's ministers could never feel indifferent to the views of the prince whom her ailing body was not long to keep from the British throne. The Elector of Hanover shared none of St John's prejudices. Instead, he backed Marlborough, heartened the Whigs, supported the war, and damned the preliminaries. Inevitably, therefore, those who desired a peace seemed opposed to the rightful Successor, and those who desired war could claim to be fighting the Pretender. Two weeks after the preliminaries were signed, St John gave copies, in confidence, to the representatives of the Allied courts; but almost at once the text appeared, to the ministry's embarrassment, printed in the Whig newspaper, the *Daily Courant*.[1] The British government blamed the Austrian ambassador, Gallas, who probably was in fact responsible and whom, in any case, it would have been convenient at this juncture to hurry out of England. He had already been recalled by the new Emperor, but he was forbidden to come to

[1] 13 Oct. 1711.

Queen Anne's court. Meanwhile, however, the Hanoverian resident, Bothmar, gave open and private help to the Whigs.

A pamphlet campaign now broke out on the largest scale. The Tories' newspaper, the *Post Boy*, published deceptive paragraphs intended to discourage the war party. The *Daily Courant* fired back. Journalists on both sides went over and over the issues without adding to the facts. Parliament was supposed to meet in November, and it was absolutely essential for the ministry's friends to be primed with the right arguments and the right answers. Easily foreseeing and even welcoming the emergency, St John set to work with Swift and the Earl of Oxford on a little volume which would meet every demand.

Possibly the first hints of this polemical defence of St John's peace may be traced as far back as August, when Swift told the ladies, 'There is now but one business the ministry wants me for.'[1] Almost three weeks before the preliminaries were even signed, the indications become quite clear. Swift plans to stay on at Windsor for a week, while St John and Oxford will be in London, because he wants leisure for 'something I am doing'. Beforehand, he spends three hours with St John on 'some business of moment'. When he gets his free week, he tries to devote it to 'some business that . . . will take up a great deal of time', but the tempting social pleasures of Windsor seduce him and slow him down. So he complains, in the midst of his agreeable distractions, 'I have a plaguy deal of business upon my hands, and very little time to do it.'[2] The direction the pamphlet will take suddenly emerges from a comment Swift makes after the supper with Mesnager: regarding the rage he expects the Allies to feel over the preliminaries, he says, 'There will be the devil and all to pay; but we'll make them swallow it with a pox.'[3] It is obvious how completely he had already identified himself with the ministers' case for the peace. But the climax of effort came after the preliminaries were published, and I suppose Swift was taking account of the arguments he had to rebut: 'I am so busy now', he says in mid-October, 'I

---

[1] *Journal*, 25 Aug. 1711. Even the 'business that concerns them', mentioned 6 Aug., may anticipate the *Conduct*.
[2] *Ibid.*, 8, 12, 16, 21 Sept. 1711.   [3] *Ibid.*, 28 Sept.

have hardly time to spare to write to our little MD.'[1] His main source of advice and suggestions was St John.

Now the scene shifts to John Barber's printing house,[2] as Swift begins going into the City for meetings with 'a printer'. During the last fortnight of October and through most of November he has constantly to confer at length with St John or Erasmus Lewis (who transmits Oxford's views), with Prior, or the printer.[3] At moments he releases more specific details about the project, never questioning the logic of his masters:

> The ministers reckon it will do abundance of good, and open the eyes of the nation, who are half bewitched against a peace. Few of this generation can remember any thing but war and taxes, and they think it is as it should be: whereas 'tis certain we are the most undone people in Europe, as I am afraid I shall make appear beyond all contradiction.[4]

With the opening of Parliament approaching, the pace speeded up, and Swift felt rushed and exasperated. He explained why to the ladies: 'Something is to be published of great moment, and three or four great people are to see there are no mistakes in point of fact: and 'tis so troublesome to send it among them, and get their corrections, that I am weary as a dog.'[5] We have notes from St John to Swift covering one of the proof sheets he scrutinized.[6] Swift had steadily to alter and undo, wait and remake. On 21 November he gave the final form of the fifth sheet (there were six altogether) to the printer, and after three more days he was finished with his share of the labour. On the evening of 25 November, advance copies were distributed among the 'great men';

---

[1] *Journal*, 13 Oct.

[2] I'm not sure Barber has been identified before this as the printer of the *Conduct*. But if one combines the evidence in the *Journal* with the notes of visits to Barber in Swift's account books, the fact becomes certain. In the accounts under 18 Dec. 1711 Swift notes that he spent 3s. on coach fare to Barber's; in the *Journal* for that day he says he spent 3s. on coach fare and was with the printer of *The Conduct of the Allies*; there are several corroborating entries. When Swift says 'my printer', he means Barber. Morphew, sometimes named as the printer, is described by Swift as 'bookseller' (i.e., publisher): see *Journal*, 13 Dec. 1711, 15 Jan. 1712. Swift's caution about naming his printer is notable, amidst his comparative indiscretion about many things he wrote to the ladies.

[3] *Journal*, 18, 27, 29, 30 Oct.; 10, 16, 18, 21, 24 Nov. 1711.

[4] *Ibid.*, 30 Oct. 1711.   [5] *Ibid.*, 10 Nov.   [6] Williams I. 272–3.

two days later, *The Conduct of the Allies*[1] was published, at a shilling a copy, predated 1712.[2]

For all the pains he had bestowed on the pamphlet, Swift did not anticipate its record-breaking popularity. The first edition of a thousand copies was gone in two days. When he did not receive a copy of the second edition from the printer, Swift innocently, and with quaint modesty, imagined the book was not selling ('perhaps they are glutted with it already'), but he soon learned that the new printing had been exhausted in five hours. A third edition lasted only until 3 December, or less than a week after the original publication. It was true, as the author of a pamphlet called *Remarks upon Remarks* later claimed, that copies were bought in bulk to be distributed by party leaders, but this took place only after the spontaneous popularity of the work was obvious. In an admirably restrained comment, Swift told the ladies, 'They are now printing the fourth edition, which is reckoned very extraordinary, considering 'tis a dear, twelve-penny book, and not bought up in numbers by the party to give away.' Yet a fifth, outsized edition of four thousand copies went for sixpence apiece; and before the end of January even a sixth was sold out, bringing the total number of copies by this time up to a quite dazzling eleven thousand.[3] The English printer went on; Irish and foreign editions poured forth; but Swift stopped retouching the book after the fourth London edition. The most important change he made was in the second, to amplify in the text, and defend in a postscript, an unfortunate sentence concerning the succession, which Whig journalists had distorted so as to imply Jacobite leanings.[4] But he took immense pains about slighter alterations made in all of the first four editions, and grumbled that the changes took more time than the original composition.[5]

[1] I think the title may come from Temple's *Memoirs* II. 194, where Temple describes the Prince of Orange as complaining 'and with too much reason, of the Conduct of his Allies'. The position of England in 1711 was analogous to that of the Dutch in 1676. [2] *Journal*, 21, 24, 25, 27 Nov. 1711.

[3] *Ibid.*, 29, 30 Nov.; 1, 2, 3, 5 Dec. 1711; 28 Jan. 1712. See Edward Solly in the *Antiquarian Magazine* for March 1885. Swift's success was modest beside that of Defoe with *The True-born Englishman*.

[4] See Davis VI. viii–ix, 205–9.   [5] *Journal,* 4 Dec. 1712.

II

In order to understand *The Conduct of the Allies*, one must regard it not as showing simply the nation's need to end the war but rather as covertly justifying the peculiar articles that the ministry had already settled on. Though the author seems explicitly to be recommending only peace in general, he is really recommending the specific treaty envisaged by St John. Actually, no one had to urge the British to end a struggle that practically the whole country had stopped desiring. The true issue was how to attain this consummation. The Duke of Marlborough and the Elector of Hanover honestly believed that the Habsburg candidate should and could be set solidly on the Spanish throne. Shrewsbury, Oxford, and St John did not. If the Whigs and the Dutch had been given control of the negotiations, they too might soon have agreed to give Spain up to the Bourbon line. But being excluded from the business, they inevitably backed the same policy as the Duke and the Elector.

So the real structure of Swift's argument is traceable to the secret articles of the preliminaries which Mesnager signed. Because the Austrians would implacably resent the loss of Spain, Swift had to expose their fecklessness and cupidity in the whole management of the war. Because the commercial interest of the United Provinces was to be sacrificed to that of Britain, he had to magnify their quite reasonable gains from the war, while belittling their heroic contribution to the ruinous campaigns and lingering vituperatively on the concessions they were to have been granted by the Barrier Treaty. In the face of these accusations he had to account for the continued participation of Britain in a war which her statesmen allegedly knew was destroying her economy. This he did by imputing to Marlborough, Godolphin, and the Junto the most crassly avaricious and power-hungry motives. For Swift's rhetorical programme to be effective, of course, it was essential that the reader should have no sense of being led to a predetermined goal. Consequently, the whole analysis is cast in the form of a general, impartial examination of the facts of the war and the need for a peace.

In Swift's handling of the audience to whom he primarily

addressed himself, a similar ambiguity will be easily observed. It is above all the landed country gentleman with whom he identifies himself. In his endless, insulting contrast of 'upstarts' with 'gentlemen of estates', or of 'usurers' with the 'landed-interest',[1] he shows who he mainly thinks is listening to him. The dichotomy is absurd, of course, since landlords regularly invested in stocks or funds; and merchants, industrialists, and financiers regularly established their families in country seats. However, Swift accepts the vulgar division, aligning himself with property against money. Yet in the language of his pamphlet, he never defines his audience as a class chosen from among the English people. Rather, he explicitly appeals to the whole nation. The happy effect, for his purpose, is to induce the reader to assume that the essential, typical British subject is the English (not Welsh or Scots) country landlord, and that the Whiggish, moneyed clan constitute a negligible, freakish, diseased minority.

This device is all the more brilliant because Swift never defines England as a purely agricultural nation. Instead, he continually invokes the requirements of trade and commerce, harping upon the maritime nature of the people. It is part of his programme to steal the Whigs' thunder by these appeals. Thus he revives the old competition with the Dutch, arguing, for example, that their new towns in the Spanish Netherlands will become centres of industry underselling the British in 'every market of the world'. He warns us that Marlborough's preoccupation with land warfare has let the French enlarge their trade with South America to the point of excluding the British. He foresees that the Barrier Treaty will give Flanders such advantages that Britain will lose her pre-eminence in the trade in woollen goods.[2] Repeatedly, he puts the Tories in the position of giving British merchants advantages which the Whigs would deny them. With these examples in mind, one realizes that Swift, by an audacious paradox, has defined his darling landed gentry as the overwhelmingly dominant class of a maritime, mercantile nation.[3] From this

---

[1] Davis VI. 10, 59. See also Richard Cook, 'The Audience of Swift's Tory Tracts', *MLQ.* XXIV (1963), 31–41.

[2] Davis VI. 21, 22, 28.

[3] It is odd that commentators on Pope have hardly recognized his use of these rhetorical methods in *Windsor Forest*.

point of view he can reproach the Whigs for not only beggaring the gentry but also ruining trade, even while he implies that finance (not trade) and agriculture are mutual rivals. In real life, of course, Swift himself acted the part of a 'moneyed' man, making loans on mortgages, investing in South Sea stock, and owning outright no land to speak of.

A curious advantage of Swift's putting himself in the intellectual (if the word is not strained) position of the country gentlemen is that he relieves himself of the need to be very logical. Most of his theses were propositions long entertained by that class. Such men had always suspected what he wished to tell them, and his frail handkerchief of deductive reasoning was quite sufficient to release the Moorish rage of their jealousy. 'What you feared', he tells them, 'is perfectly true.' He supplies the facts and examples to make their anxieties concrete.

In keeping with these attitudes, Swift effortlessly works into his exposition a number of prejudices dear to his readers. An axiom of Tory military strategy was that Britain should be above all a sea power, and that it was unnatural for her to engage in a large-scale war on land. Such a principle made all Marlborough's victories seem beside the point, and left Swift free to argue not that the nation owed the Duke gratitude for his generalship but that the proper employment of her resources had been disregarded in order for the general to exercise the one skill he possessed. It was also normal for the Tories to lament a national debt supported by interest payments drawn from revenue. Instead of measuring the indebtedness against the colossal growth in national wealth, they only contrasted it with the process they regarded as healthy, of incurring no debt that could not be liquidated within a few years. So Swift could treat the country as bankrupt because at the rate revenue was coming in, the war debts would take decades to pay off. Again the pervasive xenophobia of the Tories proved useful in the tone of contempt Swift directed against the Allies, or William III, or even the miserable refugees.

Contrariwise, the irresistible positive resource of his rhetoric is the appeal to self-interest. It might be all very well for Marlborough or the Elector to preach loyalty to one's allies. But no people will feel instinctively eager to renounce advantages for themselves in order to comfort their neighbours. The treaty St John had in mind was so clearly beneficial to British interests that it might be said finally to have sold itself to the kingdom. Swift was in no condition to make these secret articles public—though accurate rumours of their details were leaking out and spreading daily—but he could clear the way for them. And this he did by putting it all backwards. Instead of revealing what Britain was to win at the expense of her allies, he lingered on what, as he claimed, the Allies had gained at the expense of generous, foolish, victimized Britain. Using once more La Rochefoucauld's method, he openly imputed the motives of the Allies to self-interest, but he connected the motives of Britain with Christian charity; and though the self-interest of the Allies is treated as contemptible, the same impulse of the British is represented as virtuous. The inescapable inference is that if Britain should ditch the Allies in negotiating a separate peace, the event would only be to bury them in the pit they had dug for another.

III

Naturally, Swift does not let the lopsidedness of his case appear openly. Rather, he flatters the intelligence of his readers with a surface of systematic reasoning and a great display of working from objective postulates to particular issues. After an opening section dealing with the general conditions under which wars ought to be undertaken and carried on, he pretends to show that these rules were broken when England first involved herself in the present conflict. In fact, with a boldness derived, I suspect, from St John, he asserts that England ought never to have joined the war; with amazing confidence he describes a struggle which the government had for years been proclaiming essential to England's survival (with his own friends echoing their predecessors months after coming to power) as a blunder from the start.

After this charge he similarly reviews the general management of the campaigns and argues that here, too, England committed error upon error. She ignored her proper powers and her own interests in the strategy of the war, and she let her allies over-reach her in every direction. This last point is the weightiest in the whole book: Swift devotes a quarter of his space to it, distorting documents and producing a skilful selection of facts not otherwise available, in order to make it appear that the Dutch, the Austrians, and the rest of the Allies have treated Britain indecently. By his showing, they have handled her majesty's government with insolence; they have grabbed territorial and economic advantages for themselves while denying them to Britain; and they have shamelessly failed to keep their promises, never coming near to supplying their quotas of men or money.

This polemic naturally leads him to ask why the war leaders of Britain should have connived at such scandalous mismanagement. The answer, insinuated in his third main section, is that the men at the top received immense bribes and other shady perquisites in addition to their legitimate salaries, while the political partisans backing them found their own advantage in financial deals which depended on the continuance of the war. He claims that the whole strategy of Britain's campaigns was so designed as to allow the Whig gang the best possible opportunities for making money.

With these enormous but utterly simple accusations laid down, Swift turns to his final section, a lengthy discourse on the question of Spain. Here his fundamental thesis, which was essentially true to the facts, is that the original signers of the Grand Alliance never contemplated treating the enthronement of a Habsburg in Madrid as a prerequisite to peace: all they desired was to prevent any one man from ruling Spain and France at the same time. For other reasons as well, Swift shows that the slogan of 'no peace without Spain' is wildly impracticable; and thus he closes his essay.

Into this scheme Swift works other materials which suggest that the designers of *The Conduct of the Allies*, like the creators of the peace preliminaries, looked beyond even the great question of ending the war. Not only do Swift's arguments sweep the road clear for the Treaty of Utrecht. They also urge the reader to reject with hatred and contempt all Whiggish tendencies and to trust entirely in the patriotism and sagacity of the peacemakers. The increase in ferocity of *The Conduct of the Allies* over the *Examiner* is obvious today and was pointed out at once by Swift's opponent, Francis Hare. In his periodical essays, Swift had attacked only the Godolphin ministry, the Junto, or the Whig partisans, and even them only at certain points; the war had been touched on with great caution; the Allies had been spared or (sometimes) praised. In the pamphlet, however, no aspect of the ministry or the Whigs is spared; the Allies are thoroughly denigrated; and the entire war effort is denounced. It was evidently St John's hope that if the negotiations moved along his lines, the government would never be able to slip out of the clutching hands of his own sub-party. Unlike his conciliatory master, Oxford, he hoped to entrench his backers so firmly in power that when the Elector of Hanover should succeed to the throne, his majesty would be forced to take directions from the most reactionary churchmen, 'country' partisans, and Tories. I think this is why Swift vilified the memory of William III for allegedly sacrificing the interests of England to those of the Dutch and for supposedly preferring a continental war to a naval war; why he denounces the Treaty of Ryswick; why he sneers at the German princes in general and Hanover in particular; why he insistently divides Britain between a small corrupt moneyed interest and a great, honourable landed interest; why he plays down the danger from the Pretender; why he makes Marlborough the repeated object of the most virulent innuendoes. By widening and deepening the gulf between sides and making neutrality impossible, by deliberately alienating every political element not tied to his own party, St John hoped to isolate and embolden that party, forcing it to rely on those uncompromising extremists who followed himself: ultimately, he hoped, by employing this group, to put through legislation that would ensure their (and consequently his) permanent control of the government.

This ultimate purpose, I think, accounts for the oppressively hostile tone, better suited to an irresponsible journalist than to an authorized spokesman, that Swift uses toward any person who

might threaten the cause. Thus his feline slanders upon Marlborough might perhaps be explained as an essential preamble to
the general's dismissal; but their intensity is such as to imply that
no man of integrity could possibly sympathize with such a
monster of greed, treachery, and ambition. Similarly, the contempt expressed for the Austrians, a tone even more bitter than
Swift's malignity against the Dutch, must be due to the need to
make the Imperial court seem unworthy of the Spanish crown,
which it was to lose by the intended peace. But it was hardly
necessary for Swift to allude to every 'petty prince, whom we half
maintain by subsidies and pensions', or to anticipate that the
Elector of Hanover might suddenly withdraw his quota of troops
if he were himself attacked by the French[1]; such insolence to the
Successor amounts to a declaration that the author's party can
manage without the support of the Electoral Prince. The polarizing effect of these reckless expressions was, I think, precisely what
the Earl of Oxford was trying to avoid; but he could not resist
them openly without losing crucial strength in Parliament.

IV

Any consideration of the literary merits of *The Conduct of the
Allies* must take notice of Johnson's famous complaint that the
power of the essay resides wholly in its facts. 'Swift', said Johnson,
'has told what he had to tell distinctly enough, but that is all. He
had to count ten, and he has counted it right.'[2] Although critics
and scholars often condemn this judgment, it is in several senses
accurate. Perhaps the highest compliment one could pay Swift is
the observation that Johnson accepted the pamphlet as operating
'by the mere weight of facts, with very little assistance from the
hand that produced them'.[3] For much of the *Conduct* is demon-
strably false or misleading. The materials of the essay can be
divided into two sorts: the supposed facts or reasonings that concern the war proper, and the imputation of motives to the Whigs
and their associates. In dealing with the war, Swift relies heavily
on figures, dates, names, events, and simple inferences, many of

[1] Davis VI. 24, 64.   [2] Boswell II. 65.   [3] *Life of Swift.*

which are dishonestly represented but all of them subject to simple proof or disproof. But in tracing the intentions of Marlborough, Godolphin, the Junto, and the Whigs, Swift abandons plain fact and rational inference, relying instead upon innuendo. How could any friend to Marlborough demonstrate, for instance, that the Emperor did not bribe the Duke in order to relieve himself of the necessity of maintaining an army? How could one disprove the imputation that Marlborough hoped to make himself king? How could one show that the co-operation between Godolphin and the Junto was not a revival of the 'Solemn League and Covenant' which had once hastened the eruption of a civil war?[1] It is not merely by assertion and repetition that Swift makes these analyses convincing. It is also through the tone of confidence, the air of self-evident, universal knowledge permeating libels like the following:

> I shall say nothing of those great presents made by several princes, which the soldiers used to call winter foraging, and said it was better than that of the summer; of two and an half *per cent.* subtracted out of all the subsidies we pay in those parts, which amounts to no inconsiderable sum; and lastly, of the grand perquisites in a long successful war, which are so amicably adjusted between him [i.e., Marlborough] and the States [i.e., the Dutch].[2]

But it is even more, I think, through the sandwiching of these greasy allegations between dry slabs of apparently objective data. By interspersing the details of several treaties with the assumption that the ministers responsible for them had accepted bribes, Swift carries over the surface of impartiality from the supposed raw data to the specious insinuation.[3]

Nevertheless, Johnson is right. Without the weight of the genuine evidence, the pamphlet would have been as ineffectual as all Swift's political essays were before he attached himself to the new ministry. The central arguments of the pamphlet were sound. The nation did yearn for peace; the Junto had shown itself incapable of ending the war when peace was easy to make; Marlborough, for all his diplomatic, military, and political genius, shared this incompetence and was indeed both greedy and ambi-

---

[1] Davis VI. 34, 42, 44–5.   [2] *Ibid.*, pp. 41–2.   [3] *Ibid.*, p. 25.

tious; the selfish Austrians had failed to give adequate support to the war; the Barrier Treaty did promise too much to the Dutch; and it was most unlikely that Spain could be secured for the Emperor Charles VI. Although these postulates could easily be documented, the parliamentary spokesmen for the Godolphin ministry had spent years denying them; the government had sponsored resolutions that offered a false appearance of national solidarity behind the war effort even since 1709; and the bulk of journalists, being supporters of Marlborough, had helped to dismiss or suppress evidence conflicting with the official line. Tory journalists might have bellowed many of Swift's generalizations, but their provision of detailed facts was slight, and an opposition press rarely sounds authoritative: consequently, when Swift set forth the main propositions with corroborative details, the effect was explosive.

The effect would have been less explosive if he had not employed resources which his rivals lacked. To the public, many of Swift's facts were new. Aided by the highest officers of state, he had access to information that the former ministry had been careful to hide. It was the novelty of his data that mingled with the familiarity of his generalizations to create the peculiar authoritativeness which thrilled his Tory readers. They found their ancient suspicions at last vindicated against the belittling contempt of Whig parliamentary resolutions and Junto propaganda. Political journalism is never more effective than when revealing crucial but suppressed evidence on a long-debated issue. This power, I suppose, is what Johnson had mainly in mind. Certainly the defenders of Marlborough felt it. Francis Hare, the strongest of them, protested more than once that the author of the *Conduct* had received confidential materials and had employed them treacherously, that he had released what should have been kept back even while withholding details that he knew would weaken his case.[1] Swift himself boasted of the 'several facts' which he had the 'opportunity' to know.[2] A simple example of such official secrets is a paragraph on the financing of the war, in which, as Hare put

[1] Hare, *The Allies and the Late Ministry Defended* (1712), Pt III, p. 8; Pt IV, p. 64.
[2] Davis VI. 53.

it, the author of the *Conduct* exposed the nation's weakness 'at full length, and in such a manner, as would be thought highly criminal in any other country'.[1] The boldest examples are Swift's minute discussions of three treaties which had never been published. In all these passages he writes as though the materials, so far from being confidential, had been available to anyone who wished to discuss them. Yet it would have been dangerous for anyone to publish such a pamphlet, even if the facts had all been fair and accurate, before Harley was in power. As it was, Swift's publisher found himself summoned to appear before the Whig Lord Chief Justice Parker, who questioned him about the authorship and threatened him with prosecution.[2]

A dangerously misleading implication of Johnson's remark is that when Swift does set forth his evidence, he is offering plain facts. Actually, he repeatedly and deliberately errs in both his data and his implications. Among the sharper tricks of the pamphlet is Swift's providing apparently straightforward documentation which is really a falsification of evidence. The boldest of these is perhaps his mistranslation of the eighth article of the Grand Alliance, though his distortion of the treaties with Portugal seems almost as rash. More representative than any of these specimens, however, is an anecdote he tells about the Austrians' fine general, Prince Eugene of Savoy, and King Frederick of Prussia; for the pamphlet is sprinkled with such 'inside' stories. According to Swift, the Prince was so arrogant as to guarantee, on his own authority, that Britain and the United Provinces would raise their share of the payments to Frederick (for Prussian mercenaries) in order to make up for the Emperor's failure to pay his share. Swift says the British ministers did not bother to wait to hear how the Dutch would act, but agreed at once to do as the Imperialist general had promised the King, and that the Dutch then refused to follow suit after all. But actually, Swift here is twisting a perfectly innocuous episode in order to bolster his propaganda. Eugene had gone to see Frederick in order to be assured of a continued supply of Prussian troops, and the King had raised difficulties. Eugene knew his majesty simply wanted more

[1] Hare, Pt IV, p. 64.   [2] *Journal*, 13 Dec. 1711.

R   [495]

money; so he said he would try to help him secure it; and then Eugene naturally went on to present the royal demands to the Dutch and British leaders. It is true that the Dutch could not afford to raise their share of the ante; however, not only was the British government apprised of this fact before agreeing to pay up anyhow, but it was the new Harley ministry, and not the old Godolphin ministry, that made the agreement! If this is not Bickerstaff's kind of hoax, it does demand a histrionic gift like Bickerstaff's.

In making his apparent disclosures, Swift as usual adopts a casual tone which intensifies their sensational effect, because the reader feels shocked by his own ignorance, awed by the author's easy familiarity with the objective facts, and all the readier, therefore, to accept as impartial what are in reality some very biased interpretations. To enhance the effect of impartiality, Swift tries to give distance to his views by moving between the present and the future, continually foreseeing the judgment posterity will make on his contemporaries. Thus he can appear anything but remote himself while conferring the dignity and aloofness of historical wisdom upon his conclusions:

> It will, no doubt, be a mighty comfort to our grandchildren, when they see a few rags hang up in Westminster-Hall, which cost an hundred millions, whereof they are paying the arrears, and boasting, as beggars do, that their grandfathers were rich and great.[1]

This discrepancy between an offhand tone and a sensational meaning is perhaps the only aspect of the rhetoric of *The Conduct of the Allies* that has received the appreciation it deserves. Most modern critics follow Johnson in failing to understand Swift's methods in the pamphlet. The reason is that it seems unique among Swift's masterpieces for lacking several characteristics normally attached to him. Thus there is no self-satire in the *Conduct*; there is no complicated game of identities, mimicries, and pseudonyms; there is little irony of the 'Swiftian' kind; there is almost no coarseness of diction or imagery.

These omissions are due of course to the author's intention of

[1] Davis vi. 55–6.

making his arguments plain and unmistakable; of avoiding any distraction, however entertaining, that might confuse the sympathetic reader or give a handle to an opponent's weapon; of sounding sincerely indignant and at one with his cause. They do not, however, prevent him from employing other methods equally characteristic of Swift.

I have mentioned the 'polarizing' tendency of the *Conduct*, the splitting of the nation between irreconcilable sides. This playing around with opposites is really the nature of Swift's argument in style, structure, and logic; for if he abandons the customary form of his irony, he does not therefore abandon the sources of its power. Abstractly, one may say that power is derived from the use of a large number of paired elements whose conventional relationship is reversed as Swift applies them: e.g., the past history of the war and the present situation. When the campaigns had begun under William III, it seemed unlikely that the Allies could make great advances against the large, victorious forces rallied by Louis XIV. The outlook of the English early became hesitant and uncertain, if not simply apprehensive. Only after the five years of triumphs initiated by Blenheim was this outlook transformed into one of confidence that the British and their allies could be relied on to beat the French. Swift, however, in reviewing the course of the war, looks back at the earliest years as though the invincibility of the Queen's armies had then been an established fact; he therefore ridicules decisions (such as the toleration of Austrian fecklessness) originally based on conditions of anxiety, and assumes that they had been made in the opposite mood. By this brilliant device he turns the very success of the war into a ground for blaming the policies responsible for that success.

Military glory is handled in the same way. The entire country had thrilled to the news of Marlborough's conquests; Tories and Whigs had publicly celebrated them. The service of these miraculous events to the nation's prestige had been questioned only in private conversations or by reckless pamphleteers. But Swift takes the conventional opposition of idealistic glory to selfish prudence and reverses it. He does not dwell in concrete detail on the horrors of war, because his case must not seem emotional or

[497]

unreasoned. Instead, he connects prudence with the rational welfare of Britain and glory with the financial ruin of the kingdom. Incidentally, he gains the advantage of echoing the Christian view of glory, which makes it pagan and cruel in contrast to charity; and he secures at the same time the subtler advantage of converting a Whiggish argument to Tory ends, because considerations of financial gain and mercantile prosperity normally belonged to the programme of the Whigs. Ultimately he opposes military glory to patriotism, by suggesting that loyalty to a military leader means treachery to one's fatherland.

A familiar part of such 'polarizing' rhetoric (and obvious, like the rest of it, in so early a work as *A Tale of a Tub*) is the transformation of an apparent unity into diversity and of diversity into unity. Thus it had been necessary as well as normal for government spokesmen to treat Britain and her allies as bound up together and comprising a single body with united aims. But Swift at every point of his argument sets British welfare against the interests of the Dutch or the Austrians, assuming that whatever profited them must injure Britain. Contrariwise, it had been normal to treat the ambitions of France as incompatible with the prosperity of Britain. But Swift quietly bridges the abyss, writing as though the French had some reason on their side and could be accommodated easily without weakening Britain.

This reversal of connotations can be detected in Swift's vocabulary. He often applies to the Dutch or the Austrians not merely an attitude but a verbal expression that years of polemics had attached to the French. In denouncing the Barrier Treaty, for instance, Swift called the articles allowed to the Dutch 'exorbitant'.[1] Hare, in reply, complained that this word 'has been so long fixed on France, by the sanction of many parliaments, that nobody, but one who is in a French faction, wou'd have taken it from those it belongs to, to apply it to our allies'.[2]

Such a rhetoric, when used on the established associations of war and peace, present and future, money and land, produces an effect much like irony, so long as historical facts, rather than moral principles (the foundation of most literary irony) can be

[1] Davis VI. 38.   [2] *Op. cit.*, Pt II, p. 8.

taken for granted. Since the entire, lengthy essay is permeated by the author's elaborate system of controlled opposites, Swift can touch off simple ironical effects merely by asking questions. I think the extraordinary number of rhetorical questions in *The Conduct of the Allies* is related to the paucity of more 'Swiftian' effects. Again, the questions seem less tricky, less ingenious than the subtleties would be, and so they bear out the impression Swift wishes to give of a plain, indignant citizen. But if he did not, through innuendo, logic, and evidence, make his system effective, he could not dare to rely upon the bold queries to call up their proper answers.

Similarly, the omission of such dazzling satirical portraits as decorate several of the best *Examiner* papers (but which would lower the dignity of *The Conduct of the Allies* and turn readers aside from the arguments) seems compensated for by the quieter multiple innuendoes that stand as a dominating feature of the book. Taking certain unproved faults for granted, Swift repeatedly found others, equally undemonstrable, upon them. For example, he says that in order to augment 'our forces' every year, in the same proportion as the Allies ('those, for whom we fight'!) diminish theirs, the British have had to hire troops from several German princes. But the truth was that the Allies did not diminish their forces, and that the 'English' troops at the very start of the war were mostly hired. A more insidious example is the sort of charge Swift liked to make against the Duke of Marlborough. So long as his grace remained commander-in-chief, Swift rarely lost a chance to impute venality (as distinct from avarice) to him; but in *The Conduct of the Allies* Swift takes for granted the Duke's susceptibility to bribes and goes so far as to assume that the land-tied general refused to let the sea be the main theatre of the war because he could secure more profit from a land campaign. If such slanders cannot be proved, neither can they be disproved, certainly not in the time allowed between the publication of the pamphlet and the voting in Parliament.

V

The popularity and effectiveness of *The Conduct of the Allies* are not to be doubted. 'The book . . . takes, as much as you could wish it', a friend of the Harleys wrote to the family. 'It will put the country gentlemen in the temper you desire.'[1] Not until the fifth London edition were artificial stimulants applied to the book's circulation. But then copies were bought up by the hundreds for Tory leaders to send into the country.[2] In the debates on the peace, speaker after speaker, of both houses, took his arguments from *The Conduct of the Allies*; and in the Commons, heavy majorities passed resolutions which were almost quotations from it. Swift boasted, 'All agree, that it was my book that spirited them to these resolutions', and he said the votes would never have been made without it.[3] 'All agree', he told the ladies, 'that never any thing of that kind was of so great consequence, or made so many converts.'[4]

G. M. Trevelyan once described Swift as having done more 'to settle the immediate fate of parties and of nations than did ever any other literary man in the annals of England'.[5] Swift's political pamphlets are still read though the efforts of his brilliant contemporaries are noticed only by specialists. Yet Addison had more direct experience of politics than Swift, and was as fine a stylist; Steele had almost as much experience as Addison; Defoe knew more about England than all of them. What Swift possessed, I think, was a dramatic immediacy, a force of presence, of personality, a voice addressing us particularly, as contrasted with a show enacted for the general public—or a proclamation, or an oration. Swift seems to be talking directly from his own true self to each separate reader.

It is important to observe that Swift never alludes to his long labours on *The Conduct of the Allies* as eccentric, or as distinct in kind from his normal writing. He seems to have judged the new essay as merely an excellent specimen of his customary work. If one thinks of *A Discourse of the Contests and Dissensions* as peculiarly

---

[1] H.M.C. *Portland.*   [2] *Journal*, 6, 18 Dec. 1711.   [3] *Ibid.*, 4, 8 Feb. 1712.
[4] *Ibid.*, 18 Dec. 1711.   [5] Trevelyan III. 254.

'Swiftian', the author's view seems natural enough. But many critics do not. Instead, they choose certain brilliant aspects of Swift's least occasional satire, make these the essence of his achievement, and try to employ them in the analysis of his masterpiece of polemical rhetoric. It seems to me that the beauties of *The Conduct of the Allies* rarely correspond to those of the 'Digression on Madness' but that they have to be judged equally 'Swiftian'.

Chapter Twenty-two

HIGH LIFE

I. COURTIERS AND BROTHERS

Although Swift crowed over the triumph of his new book, he received the profit of it not in money or preferment but in a double satisfaction of another sort. There were the simple pleasures of an author's success, or a propagandist's control over his audience. There was also the reflection of this primary delight in the confidence with which he could move among the great of the land. To be at ease with dukes and cabinet ministers was an old practice of Dr Swift's. But to find that ease exercised often and variously, with men who thought him a bulwark of their young establishment, was a continuously agreeable novelty.

The gradual, common recognition of the fact that Swift was not only the author of the most effective numbers of the *Examiner* but also the sole begetter of *The Conduct of the Allies* speeded up the process of detaching his old friends from him. By the winter of 1711–12, however, he had acquired more than enough new resources to feel independent of any desertions. If we now move half a year backwards, this development will become clear. As early as the summer of 1711, when Swift was still living in Chelsea, an extraordinary invention of St John's had signalized the happy state of the Irish vicar's social connections in London. When Swift had come back to town, toward the end of June from his long visit to Wycombe, he had discovered that he now belonged to a dining club designed by the Secretary of State so as to mix genius with power, since none but 'men of wit or men of interest' were asked to join. On Swift himself fell the responsibility of systematizing and rounding out the rules laid down in the first meeting he could attend.[1] To him, the most attractive of

[1] *Journal*, 21 Jun. 1711.

these by-laws was probably the convention that members should allude to one another as brothers. Swift was to make an elaborate game of the privilege, not only calling the men themselves 'brother' but referring to their wives as sister and their children as nephew or niece. By reciprocation a daughter of the second Duke of Ormonde could soon address Swift as uncle.

Ostensibly, the purpose of 'The Society', as it was called, differed from that of most social clubs, because the members' cultivation of one another's friendship and conversation was only the first aim. The second and more significant aim was, as Swift said, 'to reward deserving persons with our interest and recommendation'. Evidently, the witty members would help the powerful members to define 'deserving'. A dozen people had joined the Society by 21 June; their eminence will appear from the fact that the principal Secretary of State, the Secretary at War, the Solicitor-General, and the vicar of Laracor were among them. Swift felt exhilarated by the distinction of his fellow members, and said to the ladies, 'If we go on as we begin, no other club in this town will be worth talking of.' But the onset of summer drove so many persons into the country that meetings were suspended for a month.

Already it must have been obvious to Swift that an impartial recognition of merit would hardly be the function of the group. Rather, this club was clearly to act as the Tories' answer to the Kit-Cats. Informally, the Society would (some members dearly hoped) direct patronage toward writers who had served the cause; it would bring together the leaders and their instruments; it would maintain a proper party spirit and supply a centre of discussion for new policies. It is remarkable, therefore, that Swift did not, apparently, draw a further inference from the composition of the Society. The first time he dined with them, he told the ladies, he opposed the admission of Oxford and Harcourt as new members: 'I was against them, and so was Mr. Secretary.'[1] Possibly, the reasoning was that the Lord Treasurer and the Lord Keeper, on account of their towering authority, would exercise a dampening effect on conversation, or else perhaps that

[1] *Ibid.*

R*

[503]

their absorption in public affairs would prevent them from attending regularly. Whatever sort of argument was used, it would have been hard to find a valid distinction between these two and the accepted members of the Society. It is not clear, for example, why other ministers should have seemed less awe-inspiring (Oxford was celebrated for the mildness of his manner, quite different from St John's), and why other conversation-dampeners should have been admitted who were not ministers. Swift's congenital joy in bullying men at the top—or rejecting those who might well have rejected him—partly accounts for his eagerness to exalt the character of the Society by excluding his beloved master. But I suspect the whim would not have taken him so positively if St John had not started it. Ostensibly a non-partisan gathering of the élite, less patently a rallying of the backers of the government, this Society was to be in basic effect (I think) an instrument for consolidating St John's hold on the leadership of his party. So I think St John deliberately encouraged Swift to keep Oxford out. Sir Robert Raymond, one of the first members, was a follower of St John's cousin, General Webb; Granville, another charter member, was an intimate of St John's and had belonged to Lord Rochester's group of Tories. Determined as he was to hold Mrs Masham on his side, St John naturally saw to it that her husband and brother were admitted. But Harcourt, who had been the Lord Treasurer's friend from school-days, was shut out with Oxford.

Meanwhile, Oxford maintained his own irregular and thoroughly informal arrangement of having certain real and supposed intimates come to dinner on Thursdays or Saturdays—a timing which often conflicted with the Society meetings. Swift found himself treated as a member of this 'club of the ministry' as well,[1] and so were a few others of the Society. It amounted to a continuation of the Saturday dinners which the vicar of Laracor had once felt so eager to attend. Sometimes the overlapping of the two groups produced a visible strain, as when Granville one day left the Society in order to accept an invitation from Oxford which Swift and St John refused.[2]

[1] *Journal*, 24 Aug. 1711.　　[2] *Ibid.*, 5 Jul.

If these details suggest that the Secretary and the Lord Treasurer were in competition for the allegiance of Swift (among others), the activities of the summer encourage one to follow that line further; because while Swift hoped he was clearing up the 'misunderstandings' of the two rivals by going between them,[1] it seems more likely that each was trying to separate him from the other. The court moved to Windsor for the hot weather, forcing the chief ministers to commute on weekends between their offices and their monarch. Though Lord Oxford soon invited Dr Swift to Windsor, it was another week before he actually took him there; and then the doctor was put up not by the Treasurer but by the Secretary, who also lent him a shirt to go to court in.[2] The Windsor visit was a 'delicious' experience; Swift's self-esteem bloomed in the warm, close atmosphere. He dined with Mr Masham and got a lift back to town with the Earl of Winchelsea. The following weekend saw the happiness repeated and amplified. St John picked him up (on a day when Swift was to have dined with Oxford) and took him off to Windsor for a week, housing him in his own lodgings. The cosiness of the reduced court, the charms of Windsor's landscape, the amenities of living as a guest of the Secretary—these pleasures were not weakened by a prolonged contact with peers, officials, maids of honour, and the richly various elements of a royal entourage. Swift liked to count the number of people he could exchange bows with in her majesty's drawing-room: 'I am so proud I make all the lords come up to me.'[3] He liked to find the Duke of Hamilton teasing him by pretending to support Swift's train as they walked up the stairs. He liked to have the Lord Treasurer repeat to the courtiers a *bon mot* that Swift had uttered to the Secretary of State. He liked to hear the Duchess of Shrewsbury, an Italian, call him Dr *Presto* because she could not pronounce *Swift*.

But I doubt that even the felicities of the summer court meant so much to Swift as an interruption arranged by St John. A flattering pastoral interlude took place when St John carried him away to his own Berkshire seat of Bucklebury, twenty-five miles west of Windsor. In that beautiful countryside, on the edge of the

[1] *Ibid.*, 15 Aug., 20 Oct. [2] *Ibid.*, 13, 22 Jul. [3] *Ibid.*, 29 Jul.

Downs, he kept Swift for two nights with no other guest, and gave him, I believe, a rare sense of existing on the same absolute level as the most enviable families of England. Swift told the ladies about the seductive informality with which he was entertained: 'Mr. Secretary was a perfect country gentleman at Bucklebury; he smoakt tobacco with one or two neighbours; he enquired after the wheat in such a field; he went to visit his hounds; and knew all their names; he and his lady saw me to my chamber just in the country fashion.'[1] Only a dear friend or loved relative would be paid such personal attentions; and when the Secretary and the doctor returned to Windsor, Swift could extend the charming mood by remaining at court a week, living by himself in a house rented to the Secretary, while St John returned to Whitehall. The doctor could go to the thin mid-week drawing-room and eye the laconic Queen; he could borrow the Vice-Chamberlain's horses to ride about with the Queen's favourite physician and a silly maid of honour; but he missed hearing a song recital by the celebrated Margarita; and a sudden caller prevented him from watching a splendid horse race.[2]

After a few mid-August days in London, Swift found himself shipped back to Windsor with Oxford. It was a Saturday when he already had an engagement with St John, but Swift broke this in order to go. Yet he had hardly arrived in Windsor when he joined half a dozen other Society brothers who happened to be at the court, and had supper with them and the Secretary, who had also come down for the weekend. But the next day, though there was a small dinner meeting of the Society, Swift went to the Lord Treasurer's for supper. Then on the Monday, St John brought him back to London. It looks as if either Swift or the two ministers were making sure he measured out his attentions to them in alternate doses. On three out of the four remaining visits that Swift paid to Windsor this season, he travelled down with the Secretary and up with the Treasurer.

Two of those end-of-summer visits lasted over a week; and the doctor was afforded luxurious opportunities to indulge himself in courtly pleasures or to entrench himself in courtly friendships.

[1] *Journal*, 5 Aug. [2] *Ibid.*, 6–11 Aug.

He loved walking and riding: Windsor supplied delightful resources for both. He enjoyed teasing elegant young ladies: the court provided maids of honour as victims. He found a particular relish in having peeresses seek him out and make advances to him: the Duchess of Hamilton wholeheartedly obliged. Almost daily he was entertained by persons so close to the Queen as her confidante Mrs Masham or her favourite Dr Arbuthnot. He also took a special liking to Mrs Hill, Mrs Masham's sister, who was one of her majesty's dressers. Of the whole range of glittering amenities, a brief, dim glimpse reaches us through Swift's account of a riding party he joined one morning with the Duke and Duchess of Shrewsbury and a group of courtiers; the quantity of names he mentions betokens the satisfaction the occasion gave him:

> It was the finest day in the world, and we got out before eleven, a noble caravan of us. The Duchess of Shrewsbury in her own chaise with one horse, and Miss Touchet with her; Mrs. Masham and Mrs. Scarborow, one of the dressers [sc. of the Queen], in one of the Queen's chaises; Miss Forester and Miss Scarborow, two maids of honour, and Mrs. Hill on horseback. The Duke of Shrewsbury, Mr. Masham, George Fielding, Arbuthnott and I on horseback too. Mrs. Hill's horse was hired for Miss Scarborow, but she took it in civility, her own horse was galled and could not be rid, but kicked and winced: the hired horse was not worth eighteen pence. I borrowed coat, boots, and horse and in short we had all the difficulties, and more than we used to have in making a party from Trim to Longfield's. My coat was light camblet, faced with red velvet, and silver buttons. We rode in the great park and the forest about a dozen miles, and the Duchess and I had much conversation; we got home by two, and Mr. Masham, his lady, Arbuthnott and I dined with Mrs. Hill.[1]

It was at Windsor during this summer that Swift firmly established his friendship with the man who I suspect came closest, during the next few years, to supplying Addison's place in his feelings. John Arbuthnot, immortalized in Pope's masterpiece, was a Scotsman the same age as Swift, who had probably been introduced at court by Mrs Masham. Through his talent as an able but cautious physician and his character as an entertaining

---

[1] *Ibid.*, 4 Oct. 1711.

though highly moral companion, he had recommended himself
to Queen Anne, first to be her majesty's physician extraordinary,
then as physician in ordinary. Swift met him most likely in the
winter of 1710–11, but I do not think they spent many hours together until the summer following. Arbuthnot's combination of
wit, worldliness, and Anglican piety operated with its normal
power on Swift, to a degree that may be gauged by the teasing
eulogy he delivered to Arbuthnot two summers later: 'All your
honour, generosity, good nature, good sense, witt, and every
other praiseworthy quality, will never make me think one jott the
better of you.'[1]

Though Arbuthnot's ironies took a milder form than Swift's,
a fondness for practical jokes was as strong in the physician as in
the parson, and led eventually to his having a rôle in the conception of *Gulliver's Travels*. Thus, while they were still getting to
know each other at Windsor, it was Arbuthnot who suggested a
new hoax to Swift. Queen Anne's maids of honour were hardly
so scandalous as those of her successors, but neither were they
known for good sense or good looks; and their congenital spin-
sterhood was a standard topic for sarcasm. At Windsor they lived
in a Castle tower where crows often perched. Swift once mentioned this fact to St John, who said the reason was that the crows
smelled carrion.[2] Another rake suggested that one of the least
marriageable of the maids might be granted a brevet to act as a
married woman. Arbuthnot's joke was less coarse but implied no
more reverence for the victims. He persuaded Swift to make up a
mock-prospectus for the printing of a biographical index celebrating all the maids of honour at the English royal court since
the reign of the much-married Henry VIII. The expository text
was to show that these ladies made the best wives, and a list was
promised of the two centuries of names. Swift's prospectus called
for subscribers to pay one crown in advance of publication and
another upon receipt of the book. Characteristically, he did not
risk having his own handwriting recognized but got another man
to copy out the manuscript. Then he and Arbuthnot saw to it that
the hoax was circulated among the maids of honour when they

[1] Williams II. 82.   [2] Davis IV. 254.

came in to supper. By one of his peculiar misjudgments of important personages, Swift thought it would be an addition to the fun if Queen Anne heard—as she probably would—of the trick; possibly he imagined this might be a means of drawing her well-inclined attention to himself. Actually, her majesty's sense of humour was minuscule, and she would of course have found the hoax offensive. Meanwhile, the maids of honour were not only drawn in themselves but cajoled other courtiers to lay down their five-shilling subscriptions. Within a few days, Oxford and Harcourt were told of the scheme, but the vestals themselves, when enlightened, shared none of the gaiety of such insiders. Even Swift had to admit they did not 'relish' their humiliation. He tried to squirm out and blame everything on Arbuthnot; but to complete his own part in the plot, Arbuthnot insisted it was all Swift's idea.[1]

A better example of the goodwill early shown to Swift by Arbuthnot was the case of Lieutenant Bernage. Though lacking in drama, this series of episodes will also illustrate Swift's tenacious energy in backing a protégé. There was a young Dubliner named Moses Bernage whom Esther Johnson took an interest in.[2] Having risen to a lieutenancy in the army, Bernage now felt ambitious to get himself promoted again, and Mrs Johnson wanted Swift to help him. In an elaborate campaign to support the anxious applicant, Swift not only wrote out a memorial concerning him but got the Secretary of State to promise that he would present it to Bernage's general, the Duke of Argyll. Swift also spoke directly to Argyll about it in St John's presence. He persuaded Mrs Masham's military husband and brother to back up his own recommendation; and then he drew in Colonel Disney, a friend of St John's. When the Secretary failed after all to give Argyll the memorial, Swift reminded the Duke himself and sent it after him. Now, alas, Bernage blundered on his own part, by offering to pay his colonel for a promotion. Swift managed to correct this mistake and was at last assured that the deed was

---

[1] *Journal*, 19, 21, 23 Sept.; 5 Oct. 1711.
[2] B.A., T.C.D., 1705. Swift had probably helped him secure an ensignship: see *Journal* I. 141, n. 12.

done. While the immediate advance went only to the in-between grade of captain-lieutenant, the rest of the way seemed clear, as soon as a captaincy should be available.[1]

At this critical stage, in the autumn of 1711, Swift discovered that of all people in the world his kind friend Arbuthnot was manœuvring to have a mere Scottish ensign put ahead of the Irish captain-lieutenant, and this was also with the strongest motive, because the new man was Arbuthnot's brother George. So Bernage, who, like Swift, was in London at the time, anxiously imagined he could not beat such a rival; and young Ensign Arbuthnot even wrote to him from Windsor and said he himself had gotten the captaincy. Yet Swift had already appealed directly to Dr Arbuthnot, and he in turn had already promised not to do 'any thing hard' to a friend of Swift's. Indefatigably, Swift now descended on St John and made him write at once to Bernage's colonel while Swift sent a personal message from London to Dr Arbuthnot at Windsor. The next day the Secretary at War informed Swift that fraternity had indeed given way to friendship: 'Dr. Arbuthnot had waved the business, because he would not wrong a friend of mine.' In fact, Arbuthnot had spoken to the Queen, begging her to give Bernage the company, and her majesty had reportedly told the Secretary at War to comply. So young George rose no higher than a lieutenancy, and Bernage definitely became a captain.[2]

It is true that a courtier at Arbuthnot's level of influence could assume that other opportunities would be made available to his brother. The war, however, was not going to last much longer (Swift was sure there would be no more campaigns[3]), and the ministry on which Arbuthnot's influence depended did not seem secure. Neither is it clear that Swift stood in any position to render comparable services. So the favour Arbuthnot performed was undeniably substantial; and its value can be judged by the fact that a whole year passed before George Arbuthnot was actually gazetted captain. Few of Swift's oldest acquaintances would have gone so far in order to please him.

[1] *Journal*, 10, 12, 19, 24 (pt 2) Feb.; 10, 18 Mar. 1711.
[2] *Ibid.*, 26, 27 Sept. 1711. [3] *Ibid.*, 29 Oct.

Even before *The Conduct of the Allies* came out, the vicar of Laracor was so famous that a letter from Ireland addressed simply to 'Dr Swift' reached him in London.[1] He began to be pestered by people claiming they knew him when they did not, or by near-strangers pretending on the slightest introduction to be his friend.[2] He almost never dined in a tavern any more.[3] But during the autumn, when the Queen was at Hampton Court and Parliament (which had not met since June) was repeatedly prorogued, the town remained dull and empty; so Swift, who in any case was straining to finish his great pamphlet, found few occasions for deepening his familiarity with the great world. Once the *Conduct* was off his hands, however, he had leisure to rejoin the hum and buzz as the high season began and Parliament assembled. To his circle of the great he added the Duchess of Hamilton, who had made her advances through Lady Oglethorpe.[4] For steady engagements there were once again the select dinner parties at Oxford's house. The Society also resumed its weekly meetings, and Swift went regularly to court.

From the end of November to the end of March, Swift never missed a Society dinner. He objected to the number of very young men who were taken in, and successfully fought against the admission of the boyish Lord Danby. He gave up the hope that the group would really do anything to encourage promising authors. Above all, he detested the great cost of the dinners, especially when his own turn came to preside and pay. Still, he regularly acted as secretary, reminding the members of the meetings by sending them notes. He helped to amuse them not only by his conversation but by distributing printed copies of some of his squibs before they were published. And he obviously enjoyed himself at most of the meetings.

Among all Swift's occupations in the Society there is one gesture which seems particularly to mark the altitude he had reached in the high life. When the vicar of Laracor introduced his grace the Duke of Ormonde to be a new member, he must, I think, have experienced an unusual pleasure. There was no more

[1] *Ibid.*, 9 Nov. 1711.   [2] *Ibid.*, 22 Nov.   [3] *Ibid.*, 23 Nov.
[4] *Ibid.*, 27 Jan. 1712.

princely lord in Ireland than this grandson of the magnificent Duke who had befriended Swift's family, re-endowed Swift's school (originally founded by the Ormondes), and patronized his university. The second Duke was only a little older than Swift; and in spite of his fine record as a soldier, or his service as Lord Lieutenant of Ireland, he was a modest man, only too willing to be advised. Swift's later praises of him are exaggerated to meet the extraordinary disgrace in which the Duke was to spend the last three decades of his life. But the epithets do suggest how warmly Swift appreciated Ormonde's affability toward the brilliant parson:

> I have not conversed with a more faultless person, of great justice and charity, a true sense of religion without ostentation, of undoubted valor, throwly skilled in his trade of a souldier, a quick and ready apprehension, with a good share of understanding, and a generall knoledge in men and history, though under some disadvantage by an invincible modesty, which however could not but render him yet more amiable to those who had the honor and happyness of being throwly acquainted with him.[1]

If this sounds effusive, it can be approximately matched by Ormonde's tribute to Swift at a time when he had no reason to deceive Swift with flattery: 'We have no new favourite nor never can; you have left so sweet a relish by your conversation upon all our pleasures that we can't bear the thoughts of intimacy with any person.'[2] Swift of course knew the Duke and his family from Dublin, where he had formed the impression that Ormonde genuinely liked him and would help him if possible.[3] In London, Swift paid visits to the two daughters, Lady Betty and Lady Mary, who had made proper 'advances' to him soon after his arrival,[4] and he saw them at Mrs Vanhomrigh's. Lady Mary, who married Lord Ashburnham, he particularly favoured. But Swift's friendship with the Duke, which during two years was to be deepened into a confident intimacy, only began to seem marked in the winter of 1711–12. Before Christmas, Swift was discussing politics quite candidly with his grace. He also dined

---

[1] Swift, *An Enquiry into the Behavior of the Queen's Last Ministry*, para. 5, quoted from the original manuscript in Swift's hand.

[2] Williams II. 166.   [3] *Journal*, 29 Sept. 1710.   [4] *Ibid.*, 19–20 Sept.

with the Duchess, whom he liked, and talked with her at length, tête-à-tête. When Ormonde became a possibility for the Society, Swift was delegated to invite him to join. He now felt so easy with the Duke that he tried to persuade him to help impeach the Duke of Somerset, whom most Tories detested. Before the end of January he was going further and scolding Ormonde 'like a dog' for failing to carry out a promise. By springtime their familiarity had reached the stage where he was pestering Ormonde for favours on behalf of several different acquaintances.[1]

Although Swift hated late hours, mixing with crowds, and meeting strangers, and although he often complained about the effortfulness of fashionable routines, his underlying complacency at being whirled around by it all seems not perfectly decent. 'The court serves me for a coffeehouse'[2] sounds too self-conscious to be amiable. And it is hard to believe that a man in his mid-forties, with Swift's long experience of titled grandeur, could record the following reflection without blushing for it: 'I was at court at noon, and saw fifty acquaintance I had not met this long time: that is the advantage of a court, and I fancy I am better known than any man that goes there.'[3] But it remains a question whether the vanity of such remarks is not cancelled by their ingenuousness. Any man who registers the completeness of his own integration into what he fondly imagines to be a severely limited circle is hardly the insider he boasts of being.

II. CHRISTMAS CRISIS

If Swift's identification of himself with the high life was ambiguous, his identification of himself with the government was not. On the contrary, it became so strong this winter that the effects were to remain visible for ever in Gulliver's voyage to Lilliput. Like the fire in the Lilliputian palace, the War of the Spanish Succession was being extinguished by methods which could not be openly discussed. Although the Tory ministry were no longer able to promise that Spain would go to a Habsburg, or that the

[1] *Ibid.*, 21, 28, 30 Dec. 1711; 7, 14, 15, 21 Jan., 20 Mar. 1712.
[2] *Ibid.*, 23 Mar.   [3] *Ibid.*, 25 Nov. 1711.

Dutch would obtain all their Barrier towns, neither could any-one reveal that by a secret agreement the French had conceded splendid advantages to the British before coming to terms with the other Allies: this was why *The Conduct of the Allies* had to be exclusively destructive in its argument.

As a direct consequence, the Whigs in the House of Lords, where they remained strong, were free to demand peace condi-tions which appeared on the surface to be prudent but which the administration felt compelled to evade. Instead, it was essential now that Parliament should agree to the vague preliminaries which the French had publicly offered; otherwise negotiations between the Allies and the enemy would never reach the point where the British gains from the peace might be made known. But while the House of Commons, with a great Tory majority, showed more than enough eagerness to fall in line, the Lords remained obstinate. No October Clubber appreciated the dilem-ma of the government better than Swift. He believed in the ministry's programme; he had expounded the arguments adopt-ed by their supporters; he was notoriously the propagandist for the cause, and stood to suffer if the cause failed.

To bolster themselves in the House of Lords, the ministers hoped the Queen would give them her unmistakable backing, clearly and forcefully. The Scottish representative peers, who normally took orders from the court, would presumably vote with the peacemakers if they were certain that her majesty wished them to. The ministers also hoped that Marlborough would not rally the opposition by delivering a harangue against the preliminaries. If he kept silent, he would seem, to middle-of-the-roaders, a man resigned to the government's policy; and since he always remained the supreme military authority in the kingdom, his connivance at the negotiations would undermine the logic of those who claimed that Spain was conquerable.

Unfortunately the Junto had found new strength. Both the Duke and the Duchess of Somerset were not only working against the Tories' peace but also openly entertained by the Queen as favourites, making it very awkward for ministerial allies to claim her majesty's undivided loyalty. At the same time, the dour Earl of Nottingham, the high-church leader normally classified as a Tory, was showing dangerous signs of defiance. Nottingham had always believed the purpose of the war was to put the Austrian candidate on the throne of Spain. Accustomed to ministerial posts but shut out of Oxford's government because of a rigid, un-co-operative temperament, Nottingham seemed ready now to run with the Whigs if they could satisfy his churchmanly scruples. What he desired was no less than the passage of the bill to forbid occasional conformity. The Junto leaders no doubt assumed that once they got the Tory clique out of office, it would be easy enough to ditch Nottingham and circumvent the new law; so they promised to back it.

Swift saw disaster coming far ahead but never understood that others did so as well, that they did not require his warnings, and that his simple remedies for the trouble could hardly be applied without turning the Queen against her Lord Treasurer and giving St John the leadership of a crazy party. Swift worried particularly about the vote that the Whig lords were organizing against any peace without Spain. When Nottingham decided positively to close his bargain with the Junto, Swift eagerly followed up a hint of Oxford's and wrote a broadside ballad ridiculing the Earl for pretending to integrity when his only true impulse was fury over his exclusion from high office. This *Excellent New Song*, in raw octosyllabic couplets, takes the form of a speech supposed to be delivered before the Upper House, giving Nottingham's reasons for opposing the peace preliminaries. But instead of presenting his rational grounds, the poem supplies what the Tories alleged to be his inner motives, jealousy and bribery. Though only a day or two passed between Swift's conception and its publication, some of the coarsest couplets have a gutter-song humour that sounds more appealing than daintier efforts by fastidious poets—for example, the lines reporting how the Marlboroughs contributed to Nottingham's delinquency:

> The Duke shew'd me all his fine house; and the Duchess
> From her closet brought out a full purse in her clutches.
> I talk'd of a *peace*, and they both gave a start,
> His grace swore by God, and her grace let a fart:

[515]

My *old-fashion'd pocket* was presently cramm'd;
And sooner than vote for a peace I'll be damnd.

But too much of the hoped-for wit of the thing is derived from a reiterated pun on 'Nottingham' as 'not in game', a weak joke to start with and a tiresome one for a refrain. As a whole the *Song* seems neither bright not effective.

The day after this squib came out, Parliament met and Nottingham made his real speech. He moved that the Lords in their address to the Queen should insert a clause advising her not to make a peace without Spain. Marlborough, who had no intention of keeping still, replied to an attack on himself with a short, dignified defence of his proceedings and a declaration that Europe could not be secure while Spain and the West Indies were ruled by a Bourbon. The motion was carried by a small majority in a committee of the whole house. Swift's precarious hopes plummeted at once; and when the House proper carried the same motion more strongly, he felt so desperate that he decided the Queen must be on the Whig side. Half-seriously, he foresaw consequence after consequence: the defeat of the peace meaning the fall of the ministry, and that in turn meaning the impeachment of Oxford. Identifying himself with the Lord Treasurer, Swift predicted the execution of them both for treason: 'I told Lord Treasurer, I should have the advantage of him; for he would lose his head [i.e., as a peer, entitled to beheading], and I should only be hanged, and so carry my body entire to the grave.'

The near-hysteria of his tone recalls the panic he showed when Harley was stabbed by Guiscard; and once more the contrast of the older man's serenity during a crisis only exacerbated Swift's dismay. A day later, he arrived at the ridiculous point of making arrangements for his own safety when the great defeat should come: he asked Erasmus Lewis to tell Oxford that as soon as the Lord Treasurer was sure the Whigs were going to replace his government, he should send Swift abroad on a minor diplomatic mission to a place where he might remain till the new ministers recalled him, whereupon Swift would pretend to be sick for five or six months until the storm was spent; then, by his plan, he would 'steal over' to Ireland and Laracor.[1]

[1] *Journal*, 8, 9 Dec. 1711.

While Swift's fears were absurdly overwrought, they were not wholly fantastic, as witnessed by a false report, a few weeks later, that he had been arrested for writing the *Examiner*.[1] But when his imagination laboured onward, and he thought of a place where he might hide out in obscurity, communicating with Mrs Johnson through intermediaries, his deep anxiety hardly seemed proportioned to the occasion. He took St John aside confidentially after dinner and told him, in all seriousness, 'how I had served them, and had asked no reward, but thought I might ask security'! Imagining himself in flight, during the days of his anxiety, Swift's conceit carried him so far that he repeated to himself Cardinal Wolsey's lines in *Henry VIII*:

> A weak old man, battered with storms of state,
> Is come to lay his weary bones among you.[2]

This terror at the thought of the perils he would face once the ministry fell seems related to the rage Swift exuded against journalists who had attacked either himself or the government in print. He had begged the Secretary of State to make a lesson of them; but as it happened, neither the policy of the administration nor the practice of the courts of law supplied the opportunities Swift wanted; and those who were arrested could only be threatened and released,[3] while the episodes lingered in Swift's imagination, to become at last one of Gulliver's adventures in Lilliput.[4] I suppose Swift naturally took it for granted that what he felt toward the Whig writers they returned in a concentrated loathing for him; so (he assumed) they would treat him, when their turn came, as he wished to treat them. But more deeply he also felt, I think, a real guilt over the work he had performed and a fear of the punishment he deserved. This is not to say he disbelieved in his friends' avowed principles, or felt his methods of supporting them were incorrect, but merely that he was helping to set immense changes (as he thought them) in motion and that the responsibility for such changes was an immense peril. I think Swift felt one could not dismiss so gigantic a figure as the Duke of Marlborough without suffering a penalty for the deed; one could

[1] *Ibid.*, 22 Jan. 1712.   [2] IV. ii. 21–2, misquoted (*Journal*, 8 Jan. 1712).
[3] *Journal*, 21 Sept., 16 Oct., 24 Oct. 1711.
[4] Ch. ii, par. 3, the 'ringleaders'' punishment.

not terminate wars that had lasted (except for an intermission following the Peace of Ryswick) a quarter-century without some destructive repercussion. Swift hardly looked on himself as a hero; yet he was involved in a heroic enterprise and expected to endure a hero's wounds. Since the pain was necessary to validate the enterprise, Swift was taking no chances: he was, one might say, passing through his ordeal in imagination for fear that it might never come to pass in reality.

In a week, however, the sharpest pangs were soothed, and confidants of Oxford and the Queen were hinting that Swift's martyrdom would have to be deferred. While day followed day, and amused observers saw the Whigs push the Occasional Conformity Bill through the House of Lords, the Treasurer remained cheerful, although he gave out no secrets. Swift stifled his groans but persisted in telling the ladies that the government was ruined. Characteristically, he saw the whole affair not in terms of social pressures or political philosophy but in terms of scheming individuals, their motives and passions: the Queen was capriciously false; the Duchess of Somerset was corrupting the Queen; Lady Oglethorpe might know how to detach the Queen from the Duchess; Mrs Masham must stay close to her majesty. Through this penchant for the psychological analysis of political intrigue, Swift distilled his instinctive fury against persons who, as he saw it, turned their energy to the work of subversion. At this time, as the approach of Christmas made a savagely ironical background to his own despair and suspicion, nobody received more virulent blasts of his hatred than the Duchess of Somerset. He became fixed in the belief that she was the channel by which the Whigs were manipulating the Queen, just as Mrs Masham had served Harley as his intermediary. So long as her grace remained in the royal household—Swift ratiocinated—her majesty would take the Junto's view of the negotiations with France; and consequently, the House of Lords would reject the treaty; the Tory government would fall; and England would be delivered back into the clutching fingers of the Whigs.

I think that now a sudden, pathetic, and shocking piece of news had the effect of deepening Swift's rage against the Duchess even further—though he may not have realized this himself. In all the months since his return to England, Swift had never seen Anne Long, the modest young beauty who had charmed him, years before, at the Vanhomrighs'. Mrs Long had piled up too many debts while waiting for a legacy from a slow-dying grandmother; and finally, in order to hide from her creditors, she had gone to live under a false name, in the dull provincial town of King's Lynn, without giving her friends the address. She did possess a small but sufficient income, and she corresponded with people through some sort of intermediary; but her health broke down, and she showed the symptoms which were then called asthmatic and dropsical. Swift, who exchanged letters with Mrs Long and finally discovered where she was, worried about her condition, praised her courage, and bemoaned her exile.[1]

Her last letter to him, written in mid-November 1711, is full of wit and good humour; among dignified references to many troubles, she sounds warmly, though respectfully, affectionate, and eager for his good opinion. His reply, a week before Christmas, mixes comfort with entertainment, and includes the famous aphorism, 'Health is worth preserving, though life is not.' In his tone he radiates sympathy.[2]

On Christmas Day, just after Barber printed the *Windsor Prophecy*, Swift went to the Vanhomrighs' for dinner; and there his friends showed him a letter from Mrs Long's maid in Lynn, telling of her death. The effect of the news was extraordinary. He reacted with the marks of a grief he found trouble controlling. 'I was never more afflicted at any death', he told the ladies. To the minister of Mrs Long's church at Lynn he sent a description of her true identity and directions for a small memorial in the church; he also included a eulogy which perhaps indicates more about his own feelings than the dead woman's character: 'Neither did I ever know a person of either sex with more virtues, or fewer infirmities.' He begged the parson to reply with some additional details of her last days. Meanwhile, in his private account book Swift placed a memorandum which illustrates yet again the overwrought state of his emotions: 'She was the most

[1] *Journal*, 30 Oct., 12 Nov. 1710.   [2] Williams I. 273–9.

beautiful person of the age, she lived in, of great honor and virtue, infinite sweetness and generosity of temper, and true good sense.'[1]

Yet it was only two days after this affliction that Swift chose to distribute, in the *Windsor Prophecy*, his cold denunciation of what must have seemed Anne Long's antithesis, the Duchess of Somerset. While the hobbling couplets of the poem have as negligible a literary interest as anything Swift wrote, they do illustrate that blindness to fundamental character which so many fascinated analysts of intrigue seem to suffer. As with the joke against the maids of honour, Swift apparently hoped that Queen Anne herself[2] would come across his work, even as he also hoped she would some day approve his appointment to a high post in the church. Yet the scheme of the poem was morally indefensible and practically absurd. From his years at Moor Park Swift knew enough of Lady Giffard's dear friend at Petworth, the young Duchess of Somerset, to be assured that the gossip about the marriages into which she had been forced (as a twelve- and fourteen-year-old) by an avaricious guardian was utterly false. From Mrs Masham, if not from common report, he should have learned enough about Queen Anne to realize that slandering a particular friend of her majesty's was precisely the way both to drive the Queen into the lady's arms and to turn her majesty against the author. If Swift had released this half-sheet libel anonymously, his miscalculation might not have injured himself. But fear and anxiety, which make most people prudent, made him rash; and he handed out the *Windsor Prophecy* to a Society meeting at which he himself was president and host. It was not that he had never been warned. Printed on Christmas Eve, the poem was given to a number of readers during the next day or two. On Boxing Day, Swift visited Mrs Masham, and she particularly asked him not to let the *Prophecy* be published, 'for fear of angering the Queen about the Duchess of Somerset'. Swift made a show of writing to the printer to stop the work; yet it was on the following day that the Society met and the printer (who, Swift assured the ladies, had not

[1] *Journal*, 25 Dec. 1711; Williams I. 280; *Journal*, II. 445, n. 18.
[2] I wonder whether the coincidence of names between the dead girl and the ailing queen may not have influenced Swift.

received his message) brought 'dozens a piece' of the poem to be handed around, carried home, and given to courtiers. We now know the Queen heard about the poem, and it did not endear Swift to her majesty.[1] That Swift came to this conclusion, we may judge from a ferocious pair of couplets he wrote over two years later, slandering the Duchess with the name of the suitor whose friends had murdered her second husband:

> Now Madam Coningsmark her vengeance vows
> On Swift's reproaches for her murdered spouse,
> From her red locks her mouth with venom fills:
> And thence into the royal ear instills.
>
> (*The Author upon Himself*)

It is almost as though in a suicide pact with his supposedly doomed allies, Swift had determined not to survive them. According to the myth at the centre of his philosophy of history, to succeed was to prove oneself corrupt. So the best demonstration of his integrity would have been to court disaster with his leaders. The same, nettle-grasping instinct that produced the most scandalous parts of *A Tale of a Tub* also impelled Swift to write, publish, and in effect acknowledge the *Windsor Prophecy*.

As the new year approached and Parliament remained in its Christmas recess, Swift heard clues of how the Lord Treasurer planned to beat the Whigs in the House of Lords. These rumours, which he did not quite trust, were that the Queen would create enough new peers to adjust the balance in favour of his friends. More and more, now, Swift was feeling personally responsible for the ministry's proceedings and curious to share their secrets. Finally, on 29 December, the revelation came. Swift had finished writing and sealing long letters to the ladies and to Dean Stearne in Dublin. But he at once broke open both seals in order to add jubilant postscripts relaying the miraculous peripety, one of the important events in English constitutional history:

> I have broke open my letter [he told the ladies], and tore it into the bargain; to let you know, that we are all safe; the Queen has made

[1] *Journal*, 24, 26, 27 Dec. 1711.

[2] See Calhoun Winton, 'Steele, Swift ,and the Queen's Physician', in *The Augustan Milieu: Essays Presented to L. A. Landa*, ed. H. K. Miller *et al.* (Oxford, 1970), pp. 147–8.

no less than twelve lords to have a majority; nine new ones, the other three peers sons; and has turned out the Duke of Somerset. She is awaked at last, and so is Lord Treasurer.

It pleased Swift that four of the new peers belonged to the Society and were therefore his brothers. But a more complex cause for rejoicing and a greater honour to a brother transpired at the same time as the peerages. This was the long-awaited change in the public duties of the Duke of Marlborough. Oxford could not possibly have ignored Marlborough's speech in open defiance of the court; and fortunately, with the decisive advance now made toward a vote for the peace in the House of Lords, the government no longer had to retain the Duke at the head of the armies. As expected, the gentlemen of the House of Commons had rejected the motion on Spain by an immense majority, thus supplying the ministers with the broadest support. So the Lord Treasurer felt free and quite strong enough to urge his monarch to turn out at last the greatest subject she possessed. On New Year's Day, therefore, along with the peerages, the *Gazette* announced that her majesty had dismissed the Duke of Marlborough from all his offices and that she had replaced him, as captain-general, by the Duke of Ormonde.

III. *SOME ADVICE TO THE OCTOBER CLUB*

Relief from the pressure on one flank at once exposed Oxford to pressure on the other. With Marlborough gone and the Duke of Somerset soon to be cashiered, the Treasurer found the wilder Members of Parliament even more difficult to control, especially now that he himself sat in the Lords and St John, trying to displace him, remained below. Those meritorious hotheads who had voted dutifully with the government wanted rewards in the form of posts still held by Whigs or waverers. Such slight changes as a recasting of the profitable commission of customs did not come near satisfying the clamorous demands for office. Scores of these malcontent M.P.s used to meet in their loose-knit club of men who drank October ale and discussed politics at a tavern near the House. They argued that the ministry should turn out more Whigs and should also do something drastic to punish the titled criminals who had preceded them in the highest places; and to their taste, St John was distinctly sweeter than Oxford.

In order to assist the Lord Treasurer during such embarrassments, Swift conceived the plan of a little pamphlet that would seem to be by a true insider and would relieve his master of blame for the faults the October Club laid on him. Swift thoroughly distrusted the tyro squires himself, and had prudently refused to dine with them when invited. Finishing his essay in mid-January, he had Ford copy it out so the handwriting would be unrecognizable, and then sent it secretly to John Barber, his own printer friend. While giving Swift dinner three days later, Barber showed him the twopenny pamphlet he had made of the anonymous manuscript and asked for an opinion, apparently not suspecting that the author was his guest. 'I commended it mightily', Swift told the ladies.[1]

But the praise the *Advice* deserves will not recommend it to modern readers. The argument of the pamphlet is that the excellent intentions of the Lord Treasurer have been frustrated by the Duke and Duchess of Somerset, whose machinations keep turning the Queen against his advice. Since Oxford, if dismissed, would be replaced by a Junto Whig (Swift argues), the October Club must continue to trust his lordship, and certainly not encourage the opposition to look for a split between the Treasurer and the church party. Swift's logic of course rejects the possibility that a less cautious politician, with October Club principles, might supersede Oxford; instead of this, he maintains that the danger lies wholly on the other side, the Queen being unwilling to act boldly, and the Somersets inclining her to revert back to the Whigs. As a subtler argument Swift insinuates again and again that the victorious strategy of the Tories has depended on Oxford alone—that he conceived and managed the supreme intrigue with Mrs Masham, and that his indisposition during the autumn of 1711 gave the Junto renewed strength. But Swift also assures his readers that they will soon find the Somersets gone from court.

One suspects that St John would not have thanked Swift for

[1] *Journal*, 22 Jan. 1712; it was advertised the same day in the *Post Boy*.

his own complete elimination from this analysis. At the nadir of the December crisis, however, the best hope he had been able to give Swift was a recommendation to trust in the sagacity of the Lord Treasurer; for, as St John put it, Oxford had deliberately allowed the crisis to grow and had taken careful steps to turn it all to the advantage of their own side.[1] I suppose that when the panic was over, Swift did as he had been told and, in keeping with the advice of Oxford's chief rival, decided that this 'one great person' was the indispensable master of the whole game.[2] Near the beginning of his pamphlet, Swift even goes so far as to blame St John for his unwise haste (as it is now described) in refusing to sit down at the cabinet council with the Duke of Somerset.[3] Swift's effective care in hiding the authorship of the pamphlet not only from his high-placed friends but from the political printer himself was due, I think, to his uneasiness over St John's predictable dislike of the argument; and it might not be misleading to see the pamphlet as directed no less against St John's restiveness than against that of the country Tories. In the same way it could also be considered as one more of Swift's attempts to keep the two great ministers from breaking up their partnership.

To the ladies Swift described *Some Advice to the October Club* as 'finely written, I assure you'.[4] His journalistic enemy, Boyer, praised the essay, suggested Lord Keeper Harcourt as author, and reprinted it in the *Political State of Great Britain*. But its virtues, if striking, are so deeply rooted in a specific occasion that reading it today must be a scholarly exercise. The quality that nevertheless deserves particular admiration is the tone. Without disclosing any confidential fact, Swift wished to give the October Clubbers the sensation of being admitted to the innermost confidence of their leaders, of being trusted as the wise, honest mainstay of the government. To do so, he adopted the rôle of a counsellor placed at the highest level of intimacy with the great men and in effect speaking for them. Not only does he know everything; he will tell everything. To a new recruit no courtesy could appear more flat-

---

[1] *Journal*, 9 Dec. 1711.   [2] Davis VI. 72.   [3] *Ibid.*, VI. 75.
[4] *Journal*, 28 Jan. 1712.

tering than to be handled as an equal by so exalted a being. As in his *New Journey to Paris*, Swift keeps his assumed character steady and consistent, never dropping the mask; for the power of this essay depends on the author's apparent earnestness.

In order, however, to sustain this flattering tone without committing an indiscretion, Swift almost reverses his customary rhetoric, employing the vaguest possible terms for the persons and events he discusses. In the whole production, no individual is given his proper name; even the titles are rare. But expressions like 'power', 'person', and 'great man' are ubiquitous. The style is rich in impersonal or passive constructions and indefinite pronouns; it is almost devoid of irony. Swift darkly touches on transactions which were common knowledge; he ambiguously insinuates motives which had been publicly plumbed. The Duke and Duchess of Somerset are alluded to as 'impediments' or 'instruments'; Oxford becomes 'a certain person'; the vote of no peace without Spain is simply 'an incident'. It is all in the manner of squints, winks, and you-know-what-I-mean. By the time the ale-soaked squire, aided by his nodding cronies, had worked out all the clues, he would be bound to feel in possession of state secrets, no matter how common the references might in fact be. Without conveying a single fresh insight, Swift manages to sound as though he were releasing the uncensored war manual of his leaders.

Yet for all its elements of hoax and mimicry, I doubt that the pamphlet wanders far, in its essential case, from Swift's genuine views: he went over very similar ground in a letter to Archbishop King, and a comparison of the letter with the pamphlet is illuminating.[1] Swift did regard St John as headstrong; he did believe the Tories must sink or swim with Oxford; and he did suspect the Queen of weakness. What we may safely dismiss is his opening compliment to the October Clubbers, as men likely to accomplish 'great things'.

[1] Williams I. 283–5.

IV. MARLBOROUGH

Far more serious, for Oxford, than any mutiny of the October Club, were the consequences of Marlborough's fall. It was simple enough to give the hero's place as Master of the Ordnance to Lord Rivers, and to give the supreme command of the armies to Ormonde. But it became an awkward step for Oxford's administration to justify these decisions—that is, to answer the yelps of ingratitude from the capitals of the Allies, to rebut the more sinister accusations of the Whig party writers, and to appear still prepared for war in case the negotiations for peace should fail. Yet the very man who had devoted himself to the new government, who had served as a primary agent in the overthrow of Marlborough, was curiously hesitant in pursuing the defeated enemy.

Swift never met the Duke or Duchess of Marlborough, just as he never met the Queen. For all his intimacies with the great, therefore, he was denied even an acquaintance with those supreme beings whom his courtier patrons were always eyeing. Just as Swift's impressions of her majesty were deeply tinged by the accounts which reached him through Lady Masham, so his impressions of the Duke depended increasingly on the reports of St John. For pamphleteering purposes this was just as well. With Swift's emotional allegiance fixed on the same persons as his political sympathies, he could hardly distrust the information coming to him through these channels. The brilliantly assured tone of his argument was in part derived from the confidence he therefore felt in what the ministers and their assistants told him.

Nevertheless, the common depiction of Swift as an inveterate, recklessly vituperative libeller of the mighty general seems misleading. The faults for which he mainly censures Marlborough are love of money and love of power, both of which appear amply allowed by careful historians. As for the number of Swift's published attacks, so far from being incessant over an extended period, they seem limited, before Marlborough's fall, to three *Examiners* and *The Conduct of the Allies*, and afterwards to a poem, some brief mentions, and two or three longer references over two and a half years. Later, Swift did bring out additional attacks or allusions, but none of these appeared during Marlborough's lifetime.

Meanwhile, the great Duke, unlike the Lord Treasurer, felt peculiarly troubled by the kind of printed malice that the largest figure in public life necessarily attracts. Shielded as he had been both by his privileged position and by the authority of his political colleagues, and habituated as he had become to cascades of eulogy, year in and year out, the change to the position of victim was not easy for him to digest. When Mrs Manley published *The Duke of M—h's Vindication*, an inelegant but not incompetent blast against his military and political character, the Duke broke out to his wife, 'It is impossible for me to express the real concern I have had on the account of this barbarous libel.' He even allowed himself a lament to his subtlest enemy the Lord Treasurer, with the improbable assertion, 'I doubt not but you will have some feeling of what I suffer', to which Oxford dryly and falsely replied that he knew none of the authors his grace complained about but would willingly take 'any part' in suppressing them.[1]

Swift's earliest and perhaps most dramatic polemic was the celebrated 'bill of ingratitude' in the *Examiner* for 23 November 1710. Marlborough quivered under its whip and was innocent enough to complain to St John, who, with his usual brazen mendacity, first said he had not seen the number and then assured the Duke that the 'Examiner' had received a 'proper hint'.[2] The Duchess, who was forced to writhe along with the Duke, sent the Queen a vindication of herself and his grace accompanied by a copy of the offending paper. Yet if one studies the essay, one must admit that with all its brilliance, it does not blame the Duke for any faults but cupidity and ambition. The power of the essay flows partly from the impregnability of Marlborough's situation before it appeared and partly from the skill with which the author elaborates his charges. Swift's *trouvaille* in this *Examiner* is to represent himself not as an aggressor but as a modest vindicator of the ministry against accusations of ingratitude. He says that many

[1] Churchill VI. 452–3.   [2] *Ibid.*, p. 366; *Journal* I. 208, n. 24.

journalists have censured the Queen and her government for mistreating a man to whom the nation owed an unpayable debt; these writers, says Swift, have drawn many comparisons between the unkindness of the British and similar cases in ancient or modern history. He proposes, therefore, to deal with the arraignment by comparing the rewards given a Roman general with those received by Marlborough. So he draws up a double account, setting side by side the costs of a Roman triumph, estimated at a thousand pounds, and the colossal benefits bestowed on the Duke, which are estimated at half a million.

Simply to publish such a reckoning in print made a sensational impact. Rumours, gossip, even open facts, might have been circulating the same information. But nobody had ever reduced them to the chilling surface of a naked financial account. By disguising his boldness as a simple defence of victims unfairly prosecuted, Swift made it impossible for the Duke's friends to cry shame: they had raised the very issue by which their angel was now damned. The historical parallel was worth any amount of logic, because it would have been hard indeed to discover another military commander who had obtained so much public remuneration.

But within this scheme Swift invented refinements of innuendo that the most talented Whig propagandist could never stifle. Not only was a triumphal procession a negligible expense when compared with the Duke's gains, but it contributed nothing to the personal fortune of the general. Admittedly, the ancient conqueror had found his profit in booty and perquisites; but since Swift limits his own calculations to official grants, he can insinuate that the Duke's unmentioned extras would amount to far more than the Roman's. A further stroke is to dismiss the titles of honour—a dukedom and the Order of the Garter—as inconsiderable by Marlborough's own standard, because the Duke's pride was no less remarkable than his avarice.

On top of the specific imputation, Swift easily piles others, through the beautiful device of explaining what, in the eyes of the Duke's friends, would have constituted proper gratitude; for he easily expounds this as giving a military leader political powers to which he could in decency claim no right; and it is thus that Swift slips in the charge of ambition. Finally, he manages to add the Duchess to the Duke by counting the wife's offices among the husband's profits; and having done so, he can take the last step away from fact into slander with a fable alleging that as Comptroller of the Privy Purse the Duchess had pocketed vast amounts of cash. Her grace later called this fable a 'witty comparison', but the care she devoted to refuting it betokens the emotion she felt on reading it.[1]

Under the particular rhetoric for the unique victim, Swift employs a broad, subtle device found throughout his labours of political satire. This is the implicit alignment of the victim against the nation. By standing beside the fallen Whigs, Marlborough, in Swift's depiction, opposes himself to the irresistible force of the Queen, her Parliament, and the great bulk of her subjects. He appears therefore both wrongheaded and weak. If this connotation is added to the list of his rewards, he comes to seem a shameless mixture of greed and ingratitude, so that the precise charge which the Whigs had brought against the new government rebounds upon their hero's head.

To all these effects an immense aid was the humble element of reality. Whatever the higher motives of the Duke, whatever use he might have made of his instincts and rewards, he did in fact wish to dominate the civil government, to keep his relatives and friends in high office, and to accumulate a princely fortune. Swift gave a poisonous odour to these ingredients, and he lied savagely about the Duchess. Yet essential truth remained, and this is what glued the slime to the hero.

It may sound feeble for me to notice that a week after the 'bill of ingratitude', when the *Examiner* condemned the fallen ministers one by one, he excluded Marlborough from the operation.[2] Yet if he had wished, in Sir Winston Churchill's terms, to stab 'ruthlessly' at the Duke, he would hardly have missed this convenient opportunity.[3] A few numbers later, Swift employed an-

---

[1] *Memoirs* of the Duchess of Marlborough, ed. W. King (1930), pp. 207–9.

[2] 30 November. The attack on 'John', the coachman, often interpreted as Marlborough, is really an allusion to Somers, as I have already pointed out (Davis III. 25).

[3] Churchill VI. 365.

other entire paper upon his grace.[1] The essay is neither brilliant nor barbarous, however. Arguing from ostensibly impartial axioms and pseudo-historical parallels, in the slanting manner of the *Contests and Dissensions*, Swift warns his audience against the usurpation of political authority by military leaders. The whole strength of the analysis depends on the author's tone of moderation: Marlborough's request to be made captain-general for life might, Swift says, have been due to the instigation of his friends 'or perhaps of his *enemies*', and merely for the income and honour, without treacherous designs. Even the common allegation that the general was deliberately prolonging the war is only glanced at. Of course, it was quite enough simply to bring up, in concrete form, the matter of Marlborough's ambition, as a hint of what might be done if he persisted in opposing the new ministers; but this accomplishment remains far from the raging denunciations sometimes attributed to the *Examiner*. When Swift, not yet midway in his career as 'Examiner', told the ladies, 'I think our friends press a little too hard on the Duke of Marlborough', he set himself apart from the extravagance of other Tory propagandists and of St John. At this point, whatever Swift's views of Marlborough's moral character, he believed it was at the least inexpedient to lay him aside before the war was won and the peace was made.[2]

In the *Examiner* for 8 February 1711, appeared the 'letter to Crassus', as the climax to a measured assault on Marlborough's greed. Again, the tone is grave; the argument follows the pattern of a formal analysis of a vice; the prose moves slowly and with dignity. But a colossal degree of insolence underlies the mere journalist's readiness to harangue his exalted grace, and this infuses the essay with a disturbing sort of irony. Otherwise, the paper can hardly be described as violent. Rather, its sharpness is due to Swift's skill at imposing slanderous innuendoes upon general truths. The bitterest of his lies are not detailed but are assumed by the author in brief, casual phrases as he brings his little study to a close. A limited falsehood, like the charge that the army sometimes went without provisions so the general might

[1] 21 Dec. 1710.   [2] *Journal*, 7 Jan. 1711.

enjoy his full perquisites, may occupy a whole sentence. But the outrageous hint that Marlborough preferred Flanders to Spain as a theatre of war because it was a rich territory that supplied him with large profits is tucked into a cadence.

If this seems pretty far for a character assassin to go, one ought to append to it the remark Swift published in the very next *Examiner*: 'Nobody that I know of did ever dispute the Duke of Marlborough's courage, conduct or success, they have been always unquestionable, and will continue to be so, in spight of the malice of his enemies, or, which is yet more, the *weakness of his advocates.*'[1] By itself the remark sounds both insipid and unexceptionable, but not in the mouth of a ministerial spokesman. Lord Rivers, whose undeserved success had hinged on his enmity to his commander-in-chief, and whom Swift later described as 'an arrant knave in common dealings, and very prostitute', found the *Examiner*'s admission inexcusable, and cursed the paper to Swift's face. Three weeks later, Swift had to answer a reproach from the other side, when he told the ladies in Ireland that he disagreed with their censure of his purpose: 'I do not think they [i.e., the *Examiners*] are too severe upon the Duke; they only tax him of avarice, and his avarice has ruined us.'[2]

If a comparatively balanced view of Marlborough distinguished Swift from a group he otherwise felt himself identified with, one need not therefore describe his treatment of the Duke as either objective or generous. While composing the most influential of his published attacks, Swift passed on to the ladies a report, evidently picked up from St John, which could hardly have startled the former Examiner: 'The Duke is not so fond of me. What care I?'[3] Though his grace and the Duchess knew Swift belonged to the band of writers who were denigrating them, they did not, I think, know which items were his particular produce. The Duchess attributed to Prior a larger hand in the *Examiner* than he ever possessed.[4] But Swift was led to believe that Marlborough did single him out; and when *The Conduct of the Allies* appeared, he must have supposed the lack of fondness would find

---

[1] Davis III. 87.   [2] *Ibid.* v. 258; *Journal*, 18 Feb., 7 Mar. 1711.
[3] *Journal*, 19 Nov. 1711.   [4] *Memoirs*, pp. 247–8.

a new depth of revulsion. Here the irrefutable charges of greed and ambition were involved with a network of lying allegations of corruption, some of which Swift believed but some he knew were false. The main scandals enlarged and fattened the slender hints which Swift had planted the previous spring. Now Marlborough also happened to be under investigation by a hostile House of Commons for his alleged acceptance of illicit perquisites and bribes. Quite boldly, therefore, Swift accuses him of fixing the war in Flanders and of prolonging it for the sake of dark profits not obtainable in a time of peace or on Spanish battlefields. The Duke's ambition is now exaggerated into a deliberate hope of making himself king.[1]

Though the slanders of *The Conduct of the Allies* made an essential contribution to the campaign to bring the general down, one should not infer that Swift felt sure his fall was desirable, even during the panic at the end of 1711. Near the beginning of December, Swift, it is true, had wanted the Duke turned out; but on New Year's Day, after a dinner with St John, he said that unless the ministers were certain of the peace, he would himself 'wonder' at the dismissal of Marlborough: 'I shall wonder at this step, and do not approve it at best.' Prudence and expediency, not justice, provoked his qualms. But another element, supplied, perhaps, by the Secretary of State, unexpectedly joined the humbler considerations. This was the improbable tale that not Marlborough's faults but the personal dislike of Queen Anne and the Earl of Oxford had precipitated his dismissal:

> The Queen and Lord Treasurer mortally hate the Duke of Marlborough, and to that he owes his fall, more than to his other faults . . .; however it be, the world abroad will blame us. I confess my belief, that he has not one good quality in the world besides that of a general, and even that I have heard denied by several great soldiers. But we have had constant success in arms while he commanded. Opinion is a mighty matter in war, and I doubt but the French think it impossible to conquer an army that he leads, and our soldiers think the same; and how far even this step may encourage the French to play tricks with us, no man knows. I do not love to see personal resentment mix with public affairs.[2]

[1] Davis VI. 44–5.   [2] *Journal*, 1 Jan. 1712.

Nobody was less likely than Oxford to allow private spite to wreck a careful policy, but Swift's willing belief not only testifies to his psychological interpretation of history. It also suggests how deeply he doubted the wisdom of a wholesale onslaught against the living symbol of England's glory.

After the Duke was down, Swift wrote little against him and published less. What he did publish was mainly restricted to condemnations of the great man's greed. If we trust Swift's own word, we are also to believe that he went out of his way to suppress, in the writings of other ministerial propagandists, slanders which even he considered excessive. 'I have been the cause of preventing five hundred hard things being said against him,' Swift once told Steele.[1] The assumption that a crossfire of personal animosity ran steadily between the vicar and the general was not, however, confined to Swift's fantasy. St John was good enough to inform Dr Swift, a week after the Duke's fall, that a friend of his grace had said, 'There is nothing [the Duke of Marlborough] now desires so much as to contrive some way how to soften Dr. Swift.' Whereupon Swift told the ladies that the Duke was mistaken: 'Those things that were hardest against him were not written by me.' Though I doubt that Marlborough said or intended anything of the sort, Swift's next comment seems the most illuminating expression he ever gave to his sentiments concerning the Duke: 'I'm sure now he is down, I shall not trample on him; although I love him not, I dislike his being out.'[2] If one considers how eagerly the ministers would have welcomed any libellous help in defaming the beaten hero, Swift's position seems oddly independent. He could not prevent the English and Dutch newspapers from reporting that he had been arrested on a charge brought by the Duke of Marlborough,[3] and in the summer of 1712 he included in a pamphlet defending the ministry a few sentences bitterly maligning Marlborough for his opposition to the peace.[4] But the heaviest stone he would cast against him was a stingless, charmless poem comparing Marlborough, not very ingeniously, to Midas, and blaming him for coveting gold and

[1] Williams I. 359.   [2] *Journal*, 8 Jan. 1712.   [3] *Ibid.*, 21 Jan., 17 Feb. 1712.
[4] Davis VI. 133.

accepting bribes.[1] That Swift was sincere in his protests appears undeniable, because he told the ladies his feelings in the clearest language, at a time when every mobile Tory hack was splashing mud on the general:

> I am of your opinion, that Lord Marlborough is used too hardly: I have often scratched out passages from papers and pamphlets sent me before they were printed; because I thought them too severe. But, he is certainly a vile man, and had no sort of merit besides the military. The *Examiners* are good for little: I would fain have hindered the severity of the two or three last, but could not.[2]

A year later, Swift, picking up the old thread, told the ladies that he had sent a message to Marlborough by way of a lady acquainted with both himself and the Duke—'that I had hindred many a bitter thing against him, not for his own sake, but because I thought it looked base; and I desired every thing should be left him except power'.[3] It would be a pleasure to leave this as a final statement of Swift's account. Unfortunately, it cannot be, since about the time he wrote these words, he also composed a character of Marlborough as part of a history of the events leading up to the Treaty of Utrecht. If this history failed to appear in print until forty-five years had passed, Swift was not to blame: he had wished it to come out immediately. And if his wish had been realized, the world would have read, in time for the full flavour to

---

[1] 'The Fable of Midas', published 14 Feb. 1712. In *The Publick Spirit of the Whigs*, Feb. 1714, Swift briefly blames Marlborough for avarice and ambition; but he was compelled to by Steele's remarks in the pamphlet Swift was answering (Davis VIII. 56).

[2] *Journal*, 25 Jan. 1712. I omit from my discussion *A Learned Comment on Dr. Hare's Sermon*, published before Marlborough's fall (about 4 Oct. 1711). This is generally described as written by Mrs Manley under Swift's direction, but I agree with Sir Harold Williams that Swift probably had a larger hand in it than he admitted (*Journal* II. 381, n. 3). Yet the real attack here is against Hare himself; and if there are incidental complaints against Marlborough for prolonging the war, these are not pointed but general, and certainly indispensable to the criticisms of Hare. I also omit *Some Reasons to Prove . . . In a Letter to a Whig-Lord*, published after Marlborough's fall (about 31 May 1712): the paragraph of allusion here is again essential to the main argument; and the malicious thrust, which amounts to no more than a couple of sentences, is comparatively weak, being yet another assertion that Marlborough prolonged the war, combined with the absurd suggestion that he spent more secret service money spying on the new ministry than upon the enemy in Flanders (Davis VI. 133).

[3] *Journal*, 6 Jan. 1713.

be tasted, an aspersion on Marlborough more malevolent, subtle, and misleading than any of Swift's earlier treatments. It is a long paragraph of multiple innuendoes so low-keyed and yet so pervasively insolent that a sentence of quotation may be enough to suggest the difficulties any admirer of Marlborough's would have faced in answering it:

> We are not to take the height of his ambition from his soliciting to be general for life: I am persuaded, his chief motive was the pay and perquisites by continuing the war; and, that he had *then* no intentions of settling the crown in his family; his only son having been dead some years before.[1]

The *Satirical Elegy* which Swift wrote when Marlborough died seems to me far less insidious than this brilliant, terrifying polemical character. However, one can hardly keep from asking, if Swift thought he should not trample on a man who was down, what he supposed he was doing in the final character of Marlborough. The proper explanation seems to be that willy-nilly, receiving his facts from the ministerial circle, and sharing all their imagined anxieties and hopes, this was the nearest Swift could come to impartiality. He would not deliberately help to besmear Marlborough out of office; yet when it was essential to analyse the Duke's character, Swift could only represent him as a monster.

V. *SOME REMARKS ON THE BARRIER TREATY*

While Swift may have stood back from the indiscriminate maligning of Marlborough, his utter loyalty to the men at the top did not therefore dwindle. How far he accepted the guidance of his friends at court and how far he felt himself to be a part of their body, his reactions to public affairs during these months will sufficiently indicate. The most interesting event was a visit of Marlborough's great military colleague, Prince Eugene of Savoy, to England. The desperate mission of the celebrated Austrian soldier was to persuade her majesty's government to continue the war in Spain. Although this goal was now an impossibility, neither Oxford nor St John welcomed the energizing effect

[1] Davis vii. 7.

s*

Eugene seemed bound to have upon Whiggery. Among their own counterblows, they gave out that the visit was connected with an alleged plot to overthrow the government. Ministerial writers had let it be known that a procession on Queen Elizabeth's birthday in mid-November was intended by the Whig organizers to stir up riots leading to attacks on the Tory chiefs, and that the authorities had therefore prohibited it. A coincidental and mysterious series of outrages committed on innocent persons by young rakes calling themselves 'Mohocks', erupted at the end of the winter, and these received a similar interpretation from the same writers. Between the two outbreaks came the extended visit of the Prince, which the ministers saw fit to represent as the vilest scheme of all; for in the committee of Privy Council they produced an ostensibly intercepted letter revealing that the leaders of the opposition hoped to have her majesty's ministers assassinated during the excitement created by the presence of Eugene. In the *Spectator* paper on Sir Roger de Coverley's trip to London for a sight of 'Prince Eugenio', Addison delicately poohpoohs the faked official anxiety over the Queen Elizabeth's Day procession. But he gives the old country gentleman a fine phrase in compliment to 'that extraordinary man, whose presence does so much honour to the British nation'.[1] Swift, alas, writing about the episode the following autumn or winter, elaborately affirms the truth of his friends' melodramatic fantasy: 'As the account was given by more than one person who was at the meeting, so it was confirmed past all contradiction by several intercepted letters and other papers.'[2]

While Eugene still remained in England, the attempts initiated before Christmas to befoul the names of Marlborough and the Whig leaders were rushed forward. In the House of Commons the ministry produced formal charges of peculation against his grace. A thoroughly partisan 'Commission of Accounts' had delivered the indictment on the eve of the adjournment. During the recess, her majesty dismissed the Duke. By mid-January, when the Commons reassembled, their victim had suffered three weeks of malevolently provoked suspicion with no chance to clear himself.

[1] 8 Jan. 1712.   [2] Davis VII. 27.

Hurrying to work at once, the government's agents first dealt with Robert Walpole, the late Secretary at War and now the brilliant, aggressive leader of the opposition in the House. There was evidence of laxity, easy to construe as corruption, in the war office accounts; and after an explosive debate he was, by narrow majorities, expelled from the Commons and committed to the Tower, where he was to remain for nearly five months, no longer a roadblock to the ministerial machine. Meanwhile, the government's spokesman shifted back upon the great Duke, arraigning him furiously for misappropriation of the secret-service money, which was derived from commissions on the army bread contracts and from a two and a half per cent discount on the pay of foreign mercenaries. An immense and noisily climactic debate followed at once (24 January 1712); but the motions of censure were carried, and the friends of Marlborough lost.

In order to back up these manœuvres, Sir Thomas Hanmer, an upright, scholarly Tory who stood closer to Oxford than to St John, undertook to compose a *Representation* for the Commons to present to the Queen on 4 March. It embodied a series of resolutions which the members had passed, carrying out the spirit of *The Conduct of the Allies*. This elaborate polemic proved a more burdensome load than Sir Thomas liked to carry by himself; so he asked Dr Swift for help. The assignment made large demands upon Swift's delicacy and discretion. He had to keep his participation secret, but I think he ended up writing the whole thing under the supervision of Hanmer and St John. Certainly he came to feel so fond of the piece that he went out of his way to commend its 'energy and spirit' when reprinting it in the history he later wrote of the peace negotiations.[1]

The *Representation* is barely readable today, although Swift praised it to the ladies as 'the finest that ever was writt'.[2] What emerges from the troughs of financial statements and the crests of indignation that fill two-thirds of the *Representation* is the simple argument that Britain should refuse to carry on the war unless the Austrians and the Dutch fulfil their treaty quotas—a condition which the ministers knew to be impossible.

---

[1] *Ibid.*, p. 80.　　[2] *Journal*, 8 Mar. 1712.

I think the vicar of Laracor felt proud to be so closely involved in the operations of national government as to draw up a document of fundamental significance for the record of his friends' administration. In this occupation he could suppose himself to be speaking not only for Oxford and Parliament but also for that nation which he preferred to the land of his birth. Though Swift spent many hours during the last week of February in consulting the ministers, reading various papers, and composing the materials for the *Representation*, he never seems to have begrudged the time. Actually, the labour could not have been too arduous, since it went over ground peculiarly familiar to him. The opening two-thirds of the *Representation* are, almost disconcertingly, a carefully rephrased pastiche of passages from *The Conduct of the Allies*. The rest of it seems drawn from a brilliant pamphlet that Swift was just completing when he began preparing the *Representation*, viz., *Some Remarks on the Barrier Treaty*.

It was to justify their insinuations against the Dutch as mercenary, selfish warmongers that the ministry had wanted this new pamphlet. Government spokesmen in the Commons had moved successfully that the text of the Barrier Treaty, already stigmatized in *The Conduct of the Allies* as an act of treachery, should be laid before the House; and this order was obeyed on 29 January. Two weeks later, after a few days of motions and debates, the members passed resolutions condemning both the treaty and those who had advised it. As a primer for the House and the nation, the ministers asked Swift to design a manual of popular sentiment on the issue. Early in February, he went to work.[1] As usual, the Treasurer and the Secretary provided him with confidential documents, and Barber handled the printing. As usual, Swift was at the printer's on the eve of publication, correcting sheets for the press.[2]

If *Some Remarks on the Barrier Treaty* failed to enjoy a particularly wide sale, it was not for lack of eloquence. Again, the Godolphin ministry had cleared Swift's polemical way for him, this

---

[1] If the 'certain reason' mentioned in the *Journal*, 9 Feb. 1712, pt 2, is—as I suspect —*Some Remarks*, Swift began writing about 7 Feb.

[2] *Journal*, 12, 13, 16, 17 ('very busy'), 20 Feb. 1712, all have references to work on the pamphlet. It was published 22 Feb.

time by withholding the details of the agreement from general knowledge. Since the original negotiators had gone embarrassingly far to persuade the exhausted Dutch to remain in the war, the terms would have seemed startling if released even in 1709, when the British government had felt genuinely committed to support the Grand Alliance. But in 1712, when the people yearned for an end of fighting, and the new government depended for its survival upon an early peace, not only the terms but the circumstances in which they were signed could easily be represented as abominable. Although the Duke of Marlborough and Lord Townshend had both gone over as plenipotentiaries to conclude the treaty with the Dutch in 1709, Marlborough had prudently refused to sign the final instrument. Townshend, who alone had put his name to it, was declared by the House of Commons in 1712, when the terms lay before them, to be an enemy to the Queen and her kingdom.

Besides furnishing Swift with the treaty itself, his patrons gave him supplementary documents which seemed to incriminate Townshend and his colleagues still further. One of these was the 'counter-project', or list of alternative terms proposed by the British court in reply to the earliest draft of the treaty drawn up by the Dutch. These inevitably favoured Britain; and since the Dutch had rejected or completely transformed a number of them, it was easy for Swift to make out that the cancelled articles not only were the best part of the whole but had been needlessly sacrificed by Whig negotiators. If this obloquy was not sharp enough, Swift had received for his own use the text of the comments of the Austrian court upon the Barrier as first proposed. Inasmuch as the towns to be included in the Barrier belonged to the Spanish Netherlands, and the Austrian court had cheerfully expected that the Habsburg prince—the so-called Charles III of Spain—would, when peace came, be put in possession of the entire Spanish Netherlands, the Imperialist diplomats naturally wished to limit the jurisdiction of the Dutch as narrowly as possible. The recorded comments of Prince Eugene and Count Sinzendorf were correspondingly critical of Dutch aspiration and sympathetic with the 'counter-project'.

Finally, the new British ministers provided their great defender with a copy of a petition submitted by English merchants
in Flanders, protesting against the Barrier Treaty as harmful to
British trade, because the Dutch were exacting their own duties
above and beyond the Spanish duties on any goods which were
imported from Britain into the Spanish Netherlands and then
offered for sale in Barrier towns. Thus the very commercial class
supposed to benefit from the war appeared to feel oppressed by
the pernicious treaty.

If the government had merely published these supplementary
documents with the text of the treaty, the supporters of the Dutch
would have had to search painfully hard to find answering arguments. But when Swift's insinuating analysis, elaborated under
St John's improving hand, served to introduce the damning
materials, the case seemed clear, distinct, and self-evident. Primarily what Swift does is to reverse the true relationship of the
two maritime powers as they had stood in 1709. It had then been
the Dutch who wished to give up Spain and deliver themselves
from the unbearable load of further war; it was the British who
had then thought one more campaign would compel Louis to
meet their boldest demands. The Junto then had cajoled and in-
veigled the Dutch out of a pacific mood. But Swift turns this fact
around, attributing to the agents of 1709 the attitudes of 1712,
when the Dutch at last did prefer even another year of war to
seeing their little gains evaporate in the secret understanding
between the British and the French.

At the same time, Swift drops the furiously anti-Austrian tone
of *The Conduct of the Allies* and sounds instead as if he respected the
Habsburg cause. By thus splitting the unity of the Grand Alliance
a new way, he can reproach the Dutch for standing arrogantly
alone against the combined interests of Britain and the empire.
The British, he intimates, had imagined themselves to be con-
quering Flanders for a Habsburg prince in Madrid, only to discover that the Dutch, with less generosity, were seizing the hard-
won territories for their own profit.

These fundamental courses of implication Swift cements together with a concoction of lies, ambiguities, and multiple innu-

[540]

endoes. It is not enough for him to possess a valid case built on powerful facts—for the treaty had undeniably granted the Dutch too much, both in territory and in trading privileges. But Swift has to turn the evidence so as to make any compromise with the Whigs seem evil, to remove any qualms of conscience over the handling of the Dutch at the impending peace conference, to let the Elector of Hanover know that his highness will have to meet the terms of the men now in office. Consequently, Swift insinuates that the advisers of the Barrier Treaty in England accepted bribes from the Dutch; he ignores the immense part taken by Dutch forces in the Flanders campaigns, and writes as though the British alone had done all the fighting; he treats the guarantee of the Protestant Succession embodied in the Barrier Treaty as nugatory, twisting its sense into a guarantee of Queen Anne's right to her throne. Above all, he misrepresents the relevant article of the Grand Alliance, making it mean that the Dutch would have their barrier against France when Flanders came once again under the rule of Spain, and not—as in fact the article did intend—that the Dutch would themselves control the fortress towns.

Throughout the pamphlet the great stylistic effect is a tone of indignant contempt, in which I think I hear St John's voice over Swift's hand. It sounds all the more effective because the author explicitly denounces the Dutch for behaving with insolence toward the British. One is reminded of St John's arrogant remark to a British diplomat concerning the fears of the Dutch when Britain claimed the monopoly of the slave trade in Spanish America: 'Does it not make your blood curdle to hear it solemnly contested in Holland whether Britain shall enjoy the Asiento?'[1] This tone of contempt depends itself upon the characteristically assured manner that Swift could adopt thanks to the certainty, as he puts it, that his 'intelligence', or supply of confidential information, was 'at least as good' as that of his opponents.[2] The sting of his complacency and scorn was not lost on the other side; and one of his would-be confuters complained with more bathos than dignity, 'By the air of veracity, which he as-

[1] Trevelyan III. 212, n. *.   [2] Davis VI. 96.

sumes, one would think he had sworn to all his book in *chancery*.'[1]

If the matter of this pamphlet seems remote from the author's private concerns, it may be worth pointing out that Swift had particular reasons for loathing the Dutch. In commerce they remained a rival (some would have said the bitterest rival) to British trade around the globe. Politically, they embodied a form of government that heartened every subversive republican among her majesty's subjects. Above all, in religion they practised a freedom of toleration which Irish and English imitators could hold up as a model to menace the Establishment on which Swift thought the security of his beloved church depended. The moral and social chaos which Swift came to identify with the spirit of Whiggism he always saw brazenly exalted in the United Provinces; and the contemptuous scorn of his pamphlet was to find the loudest echo, years later, in the voice of Lemuel Gulliver.[2]

VI. *A PROPOSAL FOR CORRECTING THE ENGLISH TONGUE*

There seemed no limit to the energy released in Swift by the panic he had felt at the end of 1711, or to the subtlety of those instincts which gave him the anxieties of his patrons. He thought, spoke, and wrote in copious sympathy with the ministers from November to March. Inevitably, the process operated in reverse as well, and Swift attributed to his friends in high office a sympathy with hopes that were largely his own. As early as the summer of 1711 at Windsor, he had begun involving Oxford in a project easier to reconcile with Swift's sanguine complexion than with his reputation for cynicism. Although the essential nature of the thing was drawn from old, deep, steady tendencies in his character, there was, I suspect, an added impulse in the failure of the Society to fulfil its original promise. Among the stated aims of that club at its foundation had been the recognizing and rewarding of men of genius. Yet the members had only trifled with this purpose and accomplished nothing solid. Swift had been thinking of a stronger instrument for achieving larger ends and also casting a perma-

---

[1] *Remarks upon Remarks*, 1711, p. 7.
[2] See E. D. Leyburn, 'Swift's View of the Dutch', *PMLA.* LXVI (1951), 734-45.

nent lustre on his friends' political administration. He wished to establish an academy, in imitation of the French, made up of pensioned men of letters who would take it upon themselves to reform and purify the English language, which Swift feared was sinking only into new and alarming corruptions.

There was nothing essentially novel about Swift's idea.[1] During the seventeenth century in England, the recurrent, uneasy belief that language needed regulation to hold back decay had inspired a series of plans, including one by Defoe. In the *History of the Royal Society*, Sprat had recommended the establishment of an academy to refine and preserve the language. Among the other advocates of such an institution could be counted both Evelyn and Dryden. Swift's own proposal had been long in contemplation; his *Tatler* paper on the decay of speech was a small gesture in this direction.[2] He had subsequently talked the notion over with Addison, who wrote a *Spectator* paper following Swift's recommendation and incidentally describing him as 'one of the greatest genius's this age has produced'.[3]

In the summer of 1711 Swift spoke to Oxford about his project: viz., 'a society or academy for correcting and settling our language, that we may not perpetually be changing as we do'. The Lord Treasurer had seemed at the time to approve 'mightily', and Swift soon found the brilliant Francis Atterbury encouraging him too. Already Swift began planning to publish an essay on the subject in the form of a letter to Oxford.[4] Brimming over with satisfaction, he explained the whole affair to Archbishop King, admitting that even with the collaboration of statesmen the project might eventually come to nothing but nevertheless reporting that the men of wit and learning among his friends were backing him up.[5] I do not know when Swift began to write his essay, but by late February he was making a fair copy for the Lord Treasurer to read. On 21 February he spent six hours writing nineteen

---

[1] See L. A. Landa, introduction to Oldmixon's *Reflections* and Mainwaring's *British Academy* (Los Angeles, Augustan Reprint Soc., 1948); also his introduction to Davis IV; also Hermann M. Flasdieck, *Der Gedanke einer englischen Sprachakademie*, Jena, 1928. Most of my facts concerning the *Proposal* are taken from Landa.
[2] 28 Sept. 1710.   [3] 4 Aug. 1711.   [4] *Journal*, 22 June 1711.
[5] Williams I. 239.

pages; the next day he finished the manuscript and sent it to the dedicatee.[1] As usual, Oxford's entry meant procrastination. Instead of making prompt criticisms of his own, he turned Swift's letter over to Prior, who inevitably delayed handing it back to the eager author.[2] After weeks of angling, Swift did at last manage to retrieve his work. But it was May before Ben Tooke brought it out, with the rare—almost unique—distinction of Swift's own name printed in full at the end.[3]

The common objections brought against Swift's argument by critics and scholars seem oddly tangential. He is accused of misunderstanding the nature of language, in trying to confine a necessarily changing institution within arbitrary rules. He is also accused of misunderstanding human nature in imagining that an academy such as he proposes could possibly be effective. What Swift in fact hoped for was less presumptuous than his discreditors often suggest.

The pamphlet, which falls into three parts, opens with a report on the state of the language. Swift tries to show historically that English has suffered from extraordinary influences tending to make it less refined than the romance languages; he particularly blames military invasions and contamination by French. He admits that all languages are subject to change but observes that endless change and rapid change are not necessary. English, he says, reached its height in the reign of Charles I, and has since been spoiled by neologisms, contractions, shortenings, ephemeral slang, and a general indifference to euphony.

Now he presents his scheme for reforming this confusion. He proposes that a number of persons obviously qualified to judge questions of diction and grammar should be chosen and directed to draw up rules for their labours. They should then set about making grammar more regular and complete; they should condemn improprieties, however familiar; discard some words, correct others, and revive others. Above all, he wishes them to find a method that will keep English from further alteration other than the introduction of useful new words. Once they have

---

[1] The whole manuscript was about thirty pages long (Williams I. 295).
[2] *Journal*, 11 Mar. 1712.   [3] Published 17 May (*Post Boy, London Gazette*).

done their work, the language should be ascertained and fixed. 'It is better a language should not be wholly perfect, than that it should be perpetually changing.'

Lastly, Swift deals with the benefits following from his scheme, especially the preservation of literary works, which—if he had his way—would remain always intelligible. He also points out that his reforms would incite writers to strive harder for perfection, knowing their materials would last. Incidentally, he hints that the best authors of his own day are on his side.

Swift's naïveté and defective learning glare forth from this essay, and his hope of ending linguistic change is of course futile. Nevertheless, the central problem remains serious. To abandon any rational control over language is a degree of irresponsibility as foolish as Swift's rigidity. To avoid any distinction between better and worse speech is to ignore an elementary fact manifest to the untutored. Although continual change is inevitable, there are obvious benefits to be gained from slowing down its rate: Johnson, for example, was to share Swift's hope of restricting new expressions to those which supply deficiencies and fit the genius of the language. If one is to discriminate among levels of usage, one must rely upon examples chosen from a limited number of qualified writers; and Johnson, like Swift, treated the writers before the Restoration as 'the wells of English undefiled'.[1] For all the modern linguist's superior knowledge, once we move from description to judgment, we cannot avoid some remote approximation of Swift's solution. Johnson, who hoped the spirit of English liberty would hinder or destroy the establishment of a linguistic academy,[2] never doubted that stability was preferable to rapid change; he never doubted that many expressions, however widely used, were wrong and others right. No amount of observation can take the place of taste.

I also think it would be unfortunate to connect Swift's view of language with particular developments in English social history; too many writers before and after him have held the same view. Rather it seems not only a natural stage in the history of humanism but also a prejudice of gifted authors generally and a reflec-

[1] *Preface* to the *Dictionary.*   [2] *Ibid.*

tion of Swift's special character. In the *Spectator* Addison had tried to link the supposedly laconic spirit of the English language to the alleged taciturnity of the English people; for he tended to regard the one as an expression of the other. But while this theory might perhaps account for the growth of monosyllables and contractions, it did not seem to excuse them; and Addison deplored the consequent loss of euphony just as he approved the idea of an academy.

About human institutions Swift was far more pessimistic than Addison. His linguistic conservatism is one more outcome of the same anxiety that gave rise to his fears for the stability of Britain's political constitution.[1] It is not simply that Swift connected corruptions of language with corruptions of government, or the highest improvement of English speech with the reigns of admirable monarchs, but rather that he always regarded the achievements of civilization as liable to decay and therefore in need of steady re-enforcement. Just as the Dissenters were menacing the Established Church, just as the Whigs, during the month of December 1711, had almost wrecked the happy constitution designed in 1689, so there were illiterate fops, careless poets, and deaf pedants ceaselessly encroaching on the domain of pure speech; and men of taste had a moral duty to oppose them.

Besides the immense gaps in Swift's scholarship, his pamphlet suffered from the political framework he provocatively gave it. For the opening and close of the epistle he prepared eulogies of the Lord Treasurer so lavishly spiced that the most sympathetic reader cannot hold back a twinge; it is too much like the compliments he had served up to Lord Halifax when Swift was hoping to secure Dr South's prebend. To make the flavour worse, he turned the line of praise invidiously so as to throw his customary aspersions on the Whigs. In an unprecedented gesture he let his own name be printed at the close of the *Proposal*, flaunting the pamphlet as a party document.[2] Swift wished to advertise his intimacy with the Lord Treasurer; so his first sentence touches on

---

[1] Ricardo Quintana, *The Mind and Art of Jonathan Swift* (New York, 1935), p. 216.

[2] See Landa's edition of Oldmixon, p. 2. Swift's name had appeared on the titlepage of the posthumous volumes of Temple's works which he had edited; and he had signed his name to the ode to the Athenian Society.

a conversation they had recently enjoyed, and the style of the essay is pushingly personal.

At the same time, however, he explicitly opens the membership of the academy to those persons who are best qualified, with no regard to profession, rank, or politics. Through a compliment to Steele he plainly associates the scheme with a notoriously Whig propagandist.[1] Writing to Archbishop King, he says that Oxford and himself had drawn up a list of twenty persons 'of both parties' as nominees.[2] I suppose therefore that he did not intend the academy to define itself as a Tory club but did wish the credit for founding so magnificent an institution to belong indisputably to his friends, so that its 'institution and patronage' would remain pure.[3] If Swift could help it, the blunder (as he thought it) committed with the First Fruits, of detaching the heroic deed from the hero, would not be repeated. The absurd side of this calculation is that Oxford, on whose energetic backing the success of the academy depended, would have favoured it more sincerely if it had offered a greater promise of luring Whigs over to his camp. Though Swift claimed, decades later, that his proposal would have taken effect if the Queen had lived longer (twenty years longer?), it surprises nobody that nothing came of it.[4]

Opposition journalists were perfectly willing to seize the gauntlet in the same spirit in which the author had flung it down. The day after its publication, there was a sarcastic reference to Swift's *Proposal* in the Whig *Medley*, which followed this up in the next issue with a long attack on the government, using the *Proposal* as *point d'appui*. Meanwhile, a Whig correspondent got the anti-Tory *Gazette* of Amsterdam to print a report listing the 'brothers' of St John's Society as the suggested charter members of the new corporation. Before the end of May, two polemical pamphlets appeared, denouncing Swift's plan.[5] Yet the author himself, after inviting the onslaught, was so disingenuous as to protest to

---

[1] Davis IV. 16, 'an ingenious gentleman'.   [2] Williams I. 295.

[3] Landa, ed. Oldmixon, p. 3.

[4] Davis IV. 285. In December 1712 Swift still imagined the academy might soon be created (*Journal*, 12 Dec.).

[5] John Oldmixon, *Reflections on Dr. Swift's Letter*, published before 26 May; Arthur Mainwaring *et al.*, *The British Academy*, advertised 30 May.

the ladies in Ireland that his essay was 'no politicks, but a harm-less proposall about the improvement of the English tongue'; and he complained, 'I believe if I writ an essay upon a straw some fool would answer it.'[1]

The attackers had a happy time. Identifying Swift's idea with the French academy—one of his admitted models—they cheer-fully associated the sponsors with French despotism and popery. Even more glibly, they denigrated Swift's character as priest and author, making particular allusions to the scandalous aspects of *A Tale of a Tub*. One of the pamphleteers also dealt seriously with the philological implications.[2] Showing that language is in-separable from thought, he ridiculed Swift's fears that great literary works might be lost through linguistic change; and he argued (quite correctly) that the process is irresistibly forced by the inevitable evolution of any national culture.

Missing a splendid opportunity, the answerers alluded only lightly to a naïve and revealing weak spot in Swift's exposition. This was the fond, implicit judgment that his own works belong among those that deserve preservation. About the much ma-ligned *Tale of a Tub* he had once declared, 'The book seems calculated to live at least as long as our language, and our tast admit no great alterations.'[3] We cannot doubt that he felt a similar fondness for other works by the same author, and that his desire to stifle innovation was nourished by his love of fame. The old humanistic habit of belittling the changeableness of vulgar speech in contrast to the marble permanence of the classical tongues seems only a distant background to Swift's fear. It is not Waller's lament, 'We write in sand', but Chaucer's

> in forme of speche is chaunge
> Withinne a thousand yeer

that vibrates, like Cicero's *orna me*, behind Swift's egoism.

I think the same yearning accounts for the weight of the en-comium of Oxford in the pamphlet. Swift could not suspect that

---

[1] *Journal*, 31 May 1712, contractions expanded and capitals modernized. For all its irrationality, the note of irritation does not seem affected; Swift repeats the com-plaint 17 June.
[2] Oldmixon.   [3] 'Apology' for *Tale*, par. 2.

history would describe the Lord High Treasurer as a friend of the vicar of Laracor. By joining himself openly and intimately to the first minister of Great Britain, and addressing him with conspicuous ease, Swift felt he could guarantee his own immortality; but he only guaranteed Oxford's. The whole of Swift's high life is permeated by this irony. He was repeatedly bored by the great; he found their hospitality exhausting; he missed the summer joys of his country parish. Yet he endured all the strain not merely for the pleasures involved, or the hope of advancing his career, but for the fame such friendships conferred. And now they all crowd like a levee in the footnotes to his letters.

Chapter Twenty-three

LOW LIFE

In mid-autumn 1711, when Swift was perfecting *The Conduct of the Allies*, he returned from the exhilarations of Windsor to face a dull stretch in his London life. There were rainy days, and he saw much of the Vanhomrighs. During this quiet interlude his letters allow us some close glimpses of his ordinary occupations: 'I live a very retired life, pay very few visits, and keep but very little company; I read no newspapers.'[1] A similar break came in the middle of the winter following, because, while Parliament remained in session till early July, and the peace continued to be manufactured behind scenes, there was a sudden lull in Swift's public activities. The new pamphlet that people puzzled or laughed over was not his but Arbuthnot's *Law Is a Bottomless Pit*. For a surprising number of weeks Swift wrote little and felt no pressure on himself from the ministry. He seemed more idle than he had been for a year; he found time to read merely for pleasure; and toward the end of February he spoke of leaving for Ireland within a month.

Although Swift attended the Society with regularity during this break, and did not relax his other intimate connections with the 'great', it is a time when the underplot of the grand action of his career grows unusually visible, when the small routines and unknown people that governed the private hours of his life even in Westminster and even during the months of glory are easy to observe. If we possessed no account of such episodes, our judgment of Swift's intellect and art might remain the same. But the source of his moral energy, the power that drove his genius, would be hidden even more deeply than it is.

One could argue that Swift's typical attitude of *hypocrite ren-*

[1] *Journal*, 2 Nov. 1711.

versé explains the relation between his high life and his low life just as it explains the impersonations that support so much of his best writing. For the anecdotes of his pride or violence we look normally to his friendship with ministers and peers; for peeks at his soft-heartedness we turn to his uncelebrated service to forgotten acquaintances. He deliberately chose to seem arrogant with persons whom most men treated ceremoniously; and he often became gentle or considerate with those whom he could best afford to offend. At court, he once said, he loved to turn, in conversation, from a lord to 'the meanest of my acquaintance'.[1] Thus, in the midst of the flurry following Marlborough's fall, when Swift was producing squibs and pamphlets too fast to be counted, when he was dining with Lord Oxford and supping with Lady Masham, he still found time to look after one of his Laracor parishioners who was staying in London between therapeutic visits to Bath. This was Mrs Garrett Wesley, whose health was so uncertain that she had come up to consult the great Dr Radcliffe. Swift gave her some thoughtful assistance in money matters. On Epiphany Sunday, when she felt dangerously unwell, he read prayers to her instead of going to church himself. A few weeks later, he left a Society dinner early in order to spend an evening with her—she had been suffering convulsions and had undergone a fainting fit that day. On Shrove Tuesday he paid her a long visit, pleased to see her much improved. But in reporting such attentions to the ladies, Swift cannot refrain from undercutting his strongest display of sympathy by complaining of the stench from an assafoetida mixture Mrs Wesley was taking: 'I never smelt it before, 'tis abominable.'[2] Another of Swift's parishioners (Laurence Sterne's grandfather) was having trouble in London persuading a lawyer to pay him a small legacy which he had come over from Ireland to collect. Swift first wrote the lawyer a menacing letter, then met him and vouched for the heir's identity, and the money was paid.[3] Swift went to extraordinary pains to help Mrs Johnson's brother-in-law, a miserable underling in the Salt Office, who wanted a rise in pay. He also

---

[1] *Ibid.*, 12 Dec. 1712.   [2] *Ibid.*, 6, 26 (pt 2) Jan., 4 Mar. 1712.
[3] *Ibid.*, 5 Jan. 1712.

tried to secure some kind of humble post for his cousin Matthew Rooke's grandson.[1] Such attentions to the obscurest people are constantly recorded in his journal letters, and betoken the immense fellow feeling with little, weak beings that underlay his moral indignation.

If the trivia of Swift's private existence were a startling contrast to the elegance or splendour of his connections with the great, nobody appreciated the difference more distinctly than the vicar of Laracor. Supposing he had some inclination to overlook the discomforts of his living arrangements, there was an ironic and unfailing reminder in the shape of Swift's exasperating servant, Patrick. It would hardly have embarrassed the parson for his kindness to Mrs Wesley to become known. But it would only have humiliated him if the *haut monde* had heard of the mock-epic troubles with Patrick.

I suspect it was Patrick's quickness and style that recommended him to Swift. He was evidently good with verbal messages, clever at turning away unwanted callers, and sufficiently well mannered to seem a gentleman's man—though Sir Thomas Mansell swore he had the look of a 'Teaguelander'.[2] If Patrick's sins more than made up for his graces, Swift could not complain of being taken in, since this was the man's second term of office: he had worked earlier for Swift in Ireland, joining him again over half a year before the last departure for England.[3] Although Swift now waited three years before finally sacking him, the delay was due partly to the constantly retreating hope of Swift's early return to Dublin, where it would have been more convenient to drop an Irish servant. 'The minute I come to Ireland', Swift said, 'I will discard him.'[4]

As far as I can judge, Swift supplied Patrick with clothes, a room, and any equipment needed for his work, also paying him five shillings a week in 'board wages', out of which Patrick had to find his own food. There were gifts as well, such as half a crown at Christmas and odd smaller sums at other times, occasionally for particular purposes. When Swift dismissed Patrick, he paid him

---

[1] *Journal*, 13 Dec. 1712.   [2] *Ibid.*, 30 Mar. 1711.
[3] 9 Feb. 1710 (*Accounts 1709–10*, fol. 5ᵛ).   [4] *Journal*, 9 Jan. 1712.

three and a half pounds.[1] His livery cost Swift four or five pounds, and Patrick was vain enough to order himself a laced hat—'the hatter brought [it] by his orders, and he offered to pay for the lace out of his wages.'[2] Swift was an unusually generous master, and his arrangements would represent a high standard for personal servants at the time.

Patrick did not often accompany Swift in town but was mainly useful at home or for errands. When Swift was out, unless Patrick had specific assignments, his time was pretty much his own, except that he had to be on hand when Swift got back. Similarly, he was expected to sleep in his own room and not out of the house, because he might be wanted during the night, for example, when burglars tried to get in through Swift's window.[3]

Swift woke up about six or seven o'clock; but Patrick, who made the fire, had to call him again and again before he would rise. Usually Swift wrote to the ladies before he got out of bed. He would go to town on his various affairs and dine around three. Early evening was for social calls, and by seven he was often home, reading and writing. He might write again to the ladies immediately upon returning or after supper (if he had any), when he was in bed. He retired at eleven ideally, and midnight was the normal deadline for his candle to go out. On Sunday mornings he went to church, attending the eight o'clock service unless he felt too sick to risk it.[4]

Patrick carried messages, answered the door, functioned modestly as footman, valet, and scout, and stood guard when Swift bathed in the Thames. He was essential to Swift's social career. But other people's servants were mainly a nuisance, for they had to receive tips ('vails') for any task that was slightly out of the way. On Boxing Day Swift made the rounds of those grandees whom he regularly visited and from whom he expected favours, in order to give their porters each a half-crown.[5]

Fecklessness and irresponsibility were Patrick's prevailing vices; drunkenness, his main recreation. One day St John was calling for Swift at two o'clock, to take him to Windsor. Swift told

---

[1] *Accounts 1711–12*, fol. 5ᵛ.   [2] *Journal*, 25 May, 30 June (pt 1), 2 July 1711.
[3] *Ibid.*, 9 Jan. 1712.   [4] *Ibid.*, 25 Feb. 1711.   [5] *Ibid.*, 26 Dec. 1710.

Patrick to put up the things his master would need and to be home no later than half-past one. Instead of minding these orders, Patrick stayed out till after two and packed nothing at all. Fortunately, St John was late. But Swift meanwhile became frantic. 'I never was in a greater passion and would certainly have cropped one of his ears, if I had not lookt every moment for the Secretary.'[1]

Patrick bought a tame linnet, intending to take it back to Ireland with him, as a present for Mrs Dingley. Swift let him keep it in a closet, though the bird made a terrible litter. 'I say nothing', said Swift, 'I am as tame as a clout.' The bird grew wilder instead of tamer in captivity. His wings were quilled three times but were soon up again. 'He will be able to fly after us to Ireland', said Swift.[2]

Once Swift went to see Erasmus Lewis and ordered Patrick to follow with his gown and periwig. He waited at Lewis's an hour, but Patrick never showed up.[3] Sometimes one feels that Patrick was a more difficult opponent for Swift than all the Whigs combined. At Windsor one day, Swift came back in the evening to the house he had been lent, and found that Patrick—who was out somewhere—had taken the key with him. Swift spent an hour waiting in the cloisters, then went in to a concert that he did not wish to hear, but soon came out with embarrassing conspicuousness, to spend another term in the cloisters. It was after ten o'clock when Patrick finally came in. 'I went up', Swift reports, 'shut the chamber-door, and gave him two or three swinging cuffs on the ear, and I have strained the thumb of my left hand with pulling him.'[4] Patrick lingered over errands, hid necessities, and wasted coal. His drunkenness was irrepressible: 'I gave Patrick half a crown for his Christmas-box, on condition he would be good, and he came home drunk at midnight.'[5] At Windsor in the summer of 1711 Swift reckoned he saw Patrick drunk three times in five days.[6] Another time, his hand shook so that he could not shave Swift's head.[7] In London Patrick made trouble in the house

---

[1] *Journal*, 28 July 1711.   [2] *Ibid.*, 6 Feb., 7 Mar. 1711.   [3] *Ibid.*, 5 May 1711.
[4] *Ibid.*, 3 Oct. 1711.   [5] *Ibid.*, 24 Dec. 1711.   [6] *Ibid.*, 2 Aug.
[7] *Ibid.*, 29 Mar. 1712.

because he fought with people when he drank too much.[1] Out by himself he was no better:

> We have plays acted in our town [i.e., London], and Patrick was at one of them, oh ho. He was damnably mauled one day when he was drunk; he was at cuffs with a brother footman, who dragged him along the floor upon his face, which lookt for a week after as if he had the leprosy; and I was glad enough to see it. I have been ten times sending him over to you [i.e., to Ireland]; yet now he has new cloaths, and a laced hat.[2]

Meaner and more painful than any involvement with humble people or feckless servants were the discomforts Swift endured for the sake of thrift. 'I love these shabby difficultyes when they are over', he once said; 'but I hate them because they rise from not having a thousand pound a year.'[3] When the cold weather began, he put off lighting a fire in his room. ''Tis very cold, but I will not have a fire till November, that's pozz.'[4] After he finally decided the time for heat had come, he placed some loose bricks at the back of his grate, to catch and husband the warmth; and he sometimes picked off unused coals, to be put back when he wanted another fire.[5] As soon as April came, 'cold or not cold', his fires ended.[6] Yet he loathed dampness and clutter and running noses:

> Last Saturday night I came home, and the drab had just washed my room and my bed-chamber was all wet, and I was forced to go to bed in my own defence, and no fire; I was sick on Sunday, and now have got a swinging cold. I scolded like a dog at Patrick, although he was out with me: I detest washing of rooms: can't they wash them in a morning, and make a fire, and leave open the windows? I slept not a wink last night, for hawking and spitting: and now every body has colds.[7]

There was no end to Swift's economies. Sometimes he would secure writing-paper from the office of the Secretary of State. He hated to provide his own dinner, and would search out well-to-do hosts who might ask him in. Nevertheless, there were visible limits to this practice. Many invitations Swift carefully evaded,

[1] *Ibid.*, 30 Mar. 1711.   [2] *Ibid.*, 30 Jun. 1711, pt I.   [3] *Ibid.*, 17 Jun. 1712.
[4] *Ibid.*, 18 Oct. 1711.   [5] *Ibid.*, 18 Oct., 9 Nov. 1711.   [6] *Ibid.*, 26 Mar. 1712.
[7] *Ibid.*, 13 Nov. 1711.

and sometimes he would eat alone rather than mix with unpre-possessing strangers:

> I left a friend's house to-day where I was invited, just when dinner was setting on, and pretended I was engaged, because I saw some fellows I did not know, and went to Sir Matthew Dudley's, where I had the same inconvenience, but he would not let me go; other-wise I would have gone home, and sent for a slice of mutton and a pot of ale, rather than dine with persons unknown.[1]

As an exception to the general bleakness of Swift's parsimony, book-collecting stands out. He could not resist Bateman's well-stocked bookshop, or the auctions of Charles Bernard's valuable library; and he told Dean Stearne he had spent fifty pounds on buying books by the end of 1711, or roughly double what he normally spent on rent.[2] It was lucky for Swift's purse that he loved exercise and could therefore save chair and coach hire by walking in decent weather. During the autumn of 1711, when the gangs of young toughs ('all Whigs', said Swift) who called them-selves 'Mohocks' roamed the streets and attacked pedestrians, Swift's timorousness had to battle it out with his stinginess:

> My man tells me, that one of the lodgers [viz., in the same house as Swift] heard in a coffee-house publickly, that one design of the Mohocks was upon me, if they could catch me. And though I believe nothing of it, yet I forbear walking late, and they have put me to the charge of some shillings already.[3]

Like many thrifty persons, however, he was not desolated if he had to face large reverses. The most elaborate speculation he made, during this period in England, was the purchase of five hundred pounds of South Sea stock, which in the early stages of the company was no imprudent investment. Swift's rich friend Stratford had once already advanced him money to buy three hundred pounds of Bank of England stock. Now Stratford was similarly engaged to make the new investment possible, using a sum of almost four hundred pounds which Swift could supply

---

[1] *Journal*, 4 Nov. 1711.

[2] Williams I. 282; *Journal*, 6 Jan., 11 Apr. 1711, *et passim*. I calculate the rent as sixty-five weeks at eight shillings a week: see *Journal*, 28 Dec. 1710, 26 Apr. 1711, 9 Oct. 1711.   [3] *Journal*, 12 Mar. 1712.

himself (the result, I assume, of the rise in Bank stock) and adding the remainder as a loan. Swift had a habit (common among writers of the time) of employing his publishers as bankers. Toward the end of November 1711 he made Ben Tooke his agent to accept the shares from Stratford. But in less than two months he discovered that Stratford was on the edge of bankruptcy and sure to topple. Unlike the political crisis which had just terrified Swift, this far more intimate threat left him comparatively tranquil. He was afraid that Stratford had not yet bought the stock and that consequently Swift's fortune was sunk in the general collapse. He told Ford he expected to be undone. Yet he also told Mrs Johnson, 'I called all my philosophy and religion up; and, I thank God, it did not keep me awake beyond my usual time above a quarter of an hour.' The next morning, Tooke told him that the transaction had been completed in time and the stock was Swift's property clear.[1]

There was little conflict between thrift and appetite. If good wine stood high among Swift's carnal pleasures, exquisite eating did not. A 'prodigious fine dinner' was something he hated: 'I have a sad vulgar appetite.'[2] Though he never liked to miss a meal, he preferred simple food, normally having milk porridge for breakfast and limiting himself at dinner to a single main dish. 'I hardly ever eat of above one thing, and that the plainest ordinary meat at table; I love it best and believe it wholesomest.'[3] Especially when he felt dizzy, he avoided heavy dining.[4] Fruit, of course, endlessly tempted and frightened him, since he loved it but thought it a cause of his dizzy spells.

Besides a plain diet and regular hours, Swift continued to regard exercise as the great support of his health. It is true he vastly enjoyed the fast coach rides with Oxford or St John between London and Windsor, but it was not only stinginess that drove him to walk wherever possible. When Mrs Johnson once reminded him that autumn had come and that prudent persons

[1] *Ibid.*, 12 Jan. 1713, pt 2; cf. Ford's letter of 14 Aug. 1725. Orders for Swift's dividend on £500 of South Sea stock (20 Aug. 1712, payable to John Barber) will be found in the H. E. Widener Room of the Widener Library, Harvard University.
[2] *Ibid.*, 12 Mar. 1713.   [3] *Ibid.*, 19 Oct. 1711, 17 Jul. 1712.
[4] *Ibid.*, 26 Oct. 1711.

were in the habit of taking medicine against the change of seasons, Swift replied that exercise, and not a folk remedy, was his prescription:

> I will trust to temperance and exercise: your fall of the leaf; what care I when the leaves fall? I am sorry to see them fall with all my heart; but why should I take physick because leaves fall off from trees? that won't hinder them from falling.[1]

In hot weather at Chelsea he swam in the river, with Patrick watching his clothes. 'I take Patrick down with me, to hold my nightgown [i.e., dressing gown], shirt and slippers, and borrow a napkin of my landlady for a cap.'[2] But walking was always the main resource. He found pleasure in the sights and seasons as well as in his muscular tone: 'Do you know', he writes in May, 'that about our town we are mowing already and making hay, and it smells so sweet as we walk through the flowery meads.'[3] For an alleged anti-pastoralist he took peculiar delight in country landscapes and good weather. In spite of Mohocks, he walked in St James's Park on a 'very fine and frosty' March evening.[4] When business kept him from this simplest pastime, he raised a bitter lament: 'It vexes me to the pluck that I should lose walking this delicious day.'[5] Like most plump men in black cloth, he detested heat: 'Nothing makes me so excessively peevish as hot weather.'[6] He also disliked the shifting character of the early autumn: 'I hate this season, where every thing grows worse and worse. The only good of it is the fruit, and that I dare not eat.'[7] Nevertheless, he disagreed with his master Sir William Temple's theory of the connection between climate and health, leaning rather in Johnson's direction:

> I never impute any illness or health I have to good or ill weather, but to want of exercise, or ill air, or something I have eaten, or hard study, or sitting up; and so I fence against those as well as I can: but who a deuce can help the weather?[8]

In the end it was not bad weather but bad health that terminated this leisurely period; for instead of returning to Ireland

[1] *Journal*, 3 Nov. 1711, pt 1.   [2] *Ibid.*, 5 Jun. 1711.   [3] *Ibid.*, 19 May 1711.
[4] *Ibid.*, 9 Mar. 1712.   [5] *Ibid.*, 16 Mar. 1711.   [6] *Ibid.*, 6 Jun. 1711.
[7] *Ibid.*, 27 Aug. 1711.   [8] *Ibid.*, 7 Jun. 1711.

in the spring of 1712, Swift had suddenly to take to his bed. I think he had got badly run down during all the haste and strain of the winter. The end of the English autumn had struck him with the usual cold in the head, described during November as a 'great' one, likely to last ten days.[1] But it led not to recovery but to a new cold, starting before the old was gone. Then the same misery came again, and still a third cold overlapped the second. 'I never had any thing like it before, three colds successively', Swift reported.[2] Instead of fading as March approached, the thing got worse—'very troublesome'—and was joined by a cough. The days grew 'pure and long' and Swift walked into the suburban fields, but the cold persisted, giving particular trouble in the mornings.[3] Meanwhile, the familiar fits of vertigo did not desert him. There had been unpleasant spasms before his removal to Chelsea in the spring of 1711; a fit struck him in October 1711; and during the following February he was frightened by a return of symptoms.[4]

Then came the catastrophe. While Swift was deciding at last to remain in England till Parliament rose, he began to feel a burning sensation on his left shoulder. The twinges bothered him during an end-of-March meeting of the Society, when Arbuthnot served his term as president. Swift said the company had never been merrier, and he stayed till eleven. But the pains grew worse, and he thought them rheumatic. The weather annoyed him by turning 'abominably cold and wet'; and he suspected he had been aggravating the shoulder pain by drinking wine. He went to bed, rubbed the inflammation with spirits, and put some flannel on it. The next day the pain was in his neck and collar-bone. He could not leave the house except to dine with Mrs Vanhomrigh. The whole first week of April, he hardly went out at all. Red spots broke forth where the pain was. For three days he was almost continuously sleepless and in agony. The spots turned to pimples, but the inflammation and pain did not let up.

Luckily, all this wretchedness was due to a harmless kind of shingles. Swift had a bad case of *herpes zoster*. It was not so humili-

---

[1] *Ibid.*, 16 Nov. 1711.   [2] *Ibid.*, 12 Feb. 1712.   [3] *Ibid.*, 15, 25 Feb.
[4] *Ibid.*, 4, 24 Feb.

ating as his vertigo, but of course any disabling ailment embarrassed him. His sister kept calling, but he preferred not to be seen by her until he felt recovered. The acute torment was replaced by acute itching. Easter came and went. The Duchess of Hamilton paid him a visit and stayed for two hours.

Gaining strength, Swift allowed himself to go out from time to time; but he remained sick, lost weight, and hesitated to indulge himself in walks. It was May before he would go out daily, though the pain, itching, and debility still troubled him. No longer the same 'little fat' man he had been, he took in his breeches by two inches. At last, six weeks after the earliest symptoms had shown themselves, he went, with all his itches, to a Society dinner, and can therefore be said to have rejoined the high life. Still, he said, 'I make bargains with all people that I dine with, to let me scrub my back against a chair.'[1]

[1] *Journal*, 28 Mar. to 10 May 1712; 'little fat', 2 May 1711; 'bargains', 10 May 1712.

Chapter Twenty-four

SUSPENSE

I. THE PEACE

While Swift was recovering from the tortures of shingles, the peace negotiations took their most sensational turn. Once the French had secretly agreed to the demands which St John made for Britain, the Secretary was faced with the immense problem of bringing the Allies and his own countrymen around to accepting the situation as the framework for a general peace conference. At home the ministry's case would have been easy enough if they had been free to reveal the splendid benefits the nation would secure by the articles which Louis XIV had accepted. But to do so would have meant admitting that Britain had already concluded a separate peace, directly contrary to the terms of the Grand Alliance.

In order to justify himself in advance, therefore, St John tried to make the Dutch appear so stubborn and treacherous that no consideration would seem due them. At the same time he collaborated intimately with the French, so as to coerce the Allies into accepting whatever terms the British managed to get for them in the general peace treaties. He hoped that the Dutch and the Austrians would feel so weak, without British support, that they would choose to accept such terms sooner than undertake to fight another campaign. But if they did persist in going it alone, he would do all he covertly could to undermine them.

Yet the appearance of British participation in a fresh campaign had to be kept up until the ministers could, without domestic embarrassment, announce that an honourable peace was imminent. Having replaced Marlborough by Ormonde, therefore, they sent the new captain-general into the field with repeated assurances to the Dutch that the Queen was resolved to push the

war 'with all possible vigour'.[1] In May 1712, however, when
Prince Eugene and Ormonde together were planning a combined, important action against the inferior French army, St
John took the rash and extraordinary step of advising the Duke
not to risk a siege or a battle, because the British and French
courts seemed about to agree on the last great preliminary to a
treaty.

The details of this amazing message have lost little of their
power to shock the reader during the two and a half centuries
since St John conceived them. Not only was Ormonde to refrain
from fighting; he was to conceal from the other generals the fact
that he had received such instructions. And finally, in the most
staggering point of all, he was told, by an incredibly cool postscript, that the French general, Villars himself, knew of the
secret order:

> P.S. I had almost forgot to tell your grace that communication is
> given of this order to the court of France; so that if the Mareschal de
> Villars takes, in any private way, notice of it to you, your grace will
> answer accordingly. If this order is changed on either side, we shall,
> in honour, be obliged to give notice of it to the other.[2]

Unless St John had felt sure that what amounted to a separate
peace was about to be arranged (and that it would solve the
ministry's domestic difficulties), even he would never have dared
to deliver such outrageous commands on his own authority, with
no more backing than the Queen's consent. The reason he could
feel so misguidedly sanguine was that a sudden, colossal obstacle
to peace was indeed removing itself. Although the two British
ministers had openly abandoned the doctrine of 'no peace without Spain', they were not so bold as to welcome a union of the
French and Spanish crowns. By a fantastic series of deaths, however, it suddenly looked as though that union had become inevitable. Philip V, the Bourbon king of Spain, whom the British
government was now eager to recognize, had been at first considered an impossibly remote claimant to the French throne,
because although he was indeed Louis XIV's grandson, there

---

[1] Churchill vi. 538.   [2] Trevelyan iii. 216–17.

were four princely lives between his own and the succession. In 1711 the Dauphin had died without bringing Philip much nearer Versailles and without worrying Europe. In February 1712, however, the new Dauphin—Philip's elder brother—also died, leaving Louis's five-year-old great-grandson as heir apparent; and a few days later this boy died as well. Now only the sickly, two-year-old, second great-grandson of the Sun King remained to separate Philip from the monarchy of France. St John himself found this uncanny procession of dooms an awkward complication of his intrigues. However, by the most ingenious, skilful, and hasty manœuvring, he finally succeeded in by-passing the obstacle. Philip chose to keep his Spanish crown at the price of making as formal a renunciation as was possible of his rights to the French throne. Luckily, it was to the natural self-interest of both the Spanish court and the French royal princes that he should adhere to this promise; and the renunciation was therefore an effective resolution of the supreme issue. Now at last the British ministers could openly bring the peace proposals to the attention of Parliament (6 June 1712).

It was in order to allow time for Philip to make his renunciation that St John had delivered the so-called 'restraining orders' to the Duke of Ormonde in Flanders. But the story of the orders, as far as it had leaked out, arrived in England before the renunciation. The consequence was an immense debate in both houses of Parliament (28 May 1712), with Oxford prevaricating to the Lords and St John lying more boldly to the Commons till the motions against the proceeding were defeated. Swift, though still in pain from his illness, followed all the windings that were revealed to him of his friends' peculiar methods and as usual identified himself with their anxieties and their suspense. Though regretting the dark secretiveness of the negotiations, he assumed it was necessary. He too believed that once the peace was secure, the ministry would be secure; and he thought the terms St John had won for Britain were admirable. Under these influences, therefore, he wrote a pamphlet which unfortunately exposes several of his deepest faults as a rhetorician: *Some Reasons to Prove, that No Person Is Obliged by His Principles as a Whig, to*

Oppose Her Majesty or Her Present Ministry. In a Letter to a Whig Lord.[1]

Although Swift normally poses as a moderate, it is the contrast between his tone and his substance that makes his moderation interesting. If he simply, positively recommends what he takes to be a middle-of-the-road course, he tends to sound weak or dull. When he drew his representation of Martin in *A Tale of a Tub*, he committed this blunder, and the *Project for the Advancement of Religion* is another displeasing instance of the same sort. In conceiving the new *Letter to a Whig Lord*, Swift apparently believed he was being persuasive in advancing a middle course; but he fails doubly, since the reasoning is weak and the course is not in fact moderate. The aim of the pamphlet is to win Whig peers over to the ministerial side. If anybody suggested the aim to Swift, it was more likely Oxford than St John. The foundation of the argument, however, was common to both leaders, viz., that the issues supposed to divide the honest Whigs from the government side were matters belonging wholly to the royal prerogative. Swift takes the line that neither party denies the right of the Queen to choose her own ministers and to make war and peace. Yet, he says, the Whigs object to none of the principles of the ministry but merely to the fact that peace is being made and the Junto are out of power. Since it is her majesty's undoubted prerogative to enforce both these policies, Swift says, there is no reason for an honest Whig lord, who has never held office, to resist the government on either ground.

This argument hardly seems convincing. Although in constitutional theory and political language it was the prerogative of the monarch to appoint ministers and so forth, nobody expected the royal decisions to be made without advice. The doctrine of ministerial responsibility was well established by this time, and the right of Parliament to object to royal appointments was exercised in many ways. For Swift to speak as though the Queen's

[1] Writing to Mrs Johnson on 31 May, Swift describes this as in the press; on 17 June he tells her to read it. Since he refers in the pamphlet to the debate on the restraining orders, it must have been finished after 28 May. There is some evidence that the peer addressed is Lord Ashburnham; see *Journal* II. 536, n. 13. But I think Lord Radnor is a more likely candidate; see *ibid.*, 30 Dec. 1711, 3 Jan. 1712.

personal will properly determined the weightiest issues of government was absurd. Furthermore, he presents his case in an unfortunate, though characteristic, spirit of worldliness, as if personal, material benefits were the normal motive of political agents. Addressing a peer who has never held office, Swift reasons that since the man lost nothing by the change to the present ministry, he should not feel distressed over the ousting of the Whig leaders. Swift does not seem to realize that whether or not a man is impelled by mainly selfish aims, it sounds offensive to argue as though he might be. The tinge of cynicism only hurts Swift's own side, making it appear that there are no profound moral advantages there. Reading the pamphlet, I think one feels the author has lost touch with the people he imagines he is persuading. Swift has identified himself so perfectly with his friends in power that he can no longer appreciate the feelings of their opponents.

A much livelier piece written about the same time shows the value of indirection and dramatic impersonation for Swift's art. William Fleetwood, an ambitious Whig bishop, had brought out a collection of four of his old sermons with a new preface praising William III, defending Marlborough, and warning the nation against the danger that the ministers would bring in the Pretender. Although the *Spectator* was not supposed to dabble in politics, Steele, who had curious ways of making up shortages of copy, decided the bishop's preface deserved a wide circulation and reprinted it as a number of the periodical. But the volatile gentlemen of the House of Commons, whipped on by a furious, arrogant St John, condemned the bishop's book and ordered it burned by the hangman. Swift picked up the affair in a mock-epistle, supposed to be sent to the bishop by the Earl of Wharton: *A Letter of Thanks from My Lord W - - - - - n to the Lord Bishop of S. Asaph, in the Name of the Kit-Cat-Club.*[1] The ebullience of this trifle suggests that Swift felt rather excited by the idea of being inside Wharton's skin; for his tone captures the confident, shallow

---

[1] The preface was published in the *Spectator* of 21 May and condemned by the House of Commons on 10 June. Swift probably wrote and published his pamphlet late in June, certainly after the parliamentary condemnation and before 1 August, when the Stamp Act came into force. See John C. Stephens, 'Steele and the Bishop of St Asaph's Preface', *PMLA.* LXVII (1952), 1011–23.

coarseness of the great electioneer. The permanent appeal of the piece seems less satiric than comic. A modern reader will only grin as he observes in fantasy the discomfiture of a bishop with literary aspirations who finds himself eulogized for his style and doctrine by an illiterate atheist. The pseudo-Wharton inevitably treats the bishop as an admirer of republicanism and Dissent, and, in a triumph of Swift's burlesque manner, praises a display of episcopal regret for the destruction of a Nonconformist meeting-house:

> The generous compassion your lordship has shewn upon this tragical occasion, makes me believe your lordship will not be unaffected with an accident that had like to have befallen a poor whore of my acquaintance about that time, who being big with Whig, was so alarmed at the rising of the mob, that she had like to have miscarried upon it; for the logical jade presently concluded, (and the inference was natural enough) that if they began with pulling down meeting-houses, it might end in demolishing those houses of pleasure, where she constantly paid her devotion; and, indeed, there seems a close connection between extempore prayer and extempore love. I doubt not, if this disaster had reached your lordship before, you would have found some room in that moving parenthesis, to have expressed your concern for it.[1]

If Swift had not felt certain that absolutely no basis existed for the common fears regarding the peace and the Pretender, he would have been incapable of writing with the mocking condescension of this *Letter of Thanks*. Trusting his own friends as far as he did, he had no way to account for the anti-ministerial rumours except as wholesale concoctions disseminated by embittered members of the losing side. To explain their bitterness in turn, he could only use his quasi-cynical analysis of political motivation, and declare therefore that it was not principles but the mere loss of the perquisites of office that inspired the imputations of treason. With the same automatic device Swift conveniently explained the Earl of Nottingham's transfer of allegiance from the church party to the Junto. In a remarkable poem inverting the rhetorical structure of the *Letter of Thanks*, he denounced the high-church Tory for joining the gang of deists

[1] Davis VI. 154.

and republicans. This is *Toland's Invitation to Dismal.*[1] Here Swift treats all the Whig leaders as members of the mysterious Calves-Head Club, which was supposed to meet annually on 29 January to celebrate the execution of Charles I. Swift pretends to be their secretary, whom he identifies as Toland, the famous deist; and in this mask he invites Nottingham to a meeting. Obviously, Swift is basing the whole little dramatic monologue on his labours as secretary to his own Society. So it constitutes a shining example of how much Swift's impersonations retain of his true character and experience. The poem could not be more lively or farcical. Again the satirical element drains away, leaving the comical scene of the Anglican monarchist's embarrassment over being dumped among godless king-killers:

> Wh—n, unless prevented by a whore,
> Will hardly fail, and there is room for more:
> But I love elbow-room whene're I drink,
> And honest Harry is too apt to stink.

To complicate the element of impersonation, Swift composed the verses as a parody of Horace's epistle inviting a friend to a dinner in celebration of the emperor's birthday. The parallels are so happy that one feels Swift was unusually elated by his *donnée*: for instance, the original of the allusion to Wharton, which had seemed uniquely proper to his lordship, is almost the same in Latin:

> Et nisi cena prior potiorque puella Sabinum
> Detinet adsumam . . .

I can't help suspecting that Swift's exhilaration is derived from the ultimate source of his pleasure in impersonations, the fantasied escape from his own severe morality into the saturnalia of a character like Toland's. Here as in the *Letter of Thanks* it must have thrilled the harsh censor to find himself operating in the free, uncontrolled, irresponsible personality of a man he detested; and in using as a second mask the face of Horace, he also succeeds (again unconsciously) in excusing himself for this disgraceful

---

[1] Probably published 26 June; Swift mentions it to Mrs Johnson 1 and 17 July. See *Poems* 1. 161.

licence, inasmuch as he shows that a universally admired figure is the model for his behaviour.

The sequence of public occurrences did nothing to relieve the pressure on Swift's talent for ridiculing the enemies of his friends. In June, St John reluctantly agreed to accept a viscountcy in place of the earldom he passionately yearned for; and the next month he became in due course a peer with the title of Lord Bolingbroke. Meanwhile, he arrived at another bold agreement with the French. All essential points having been settled between the courts of St James's and Versailles, Bolingbroke promised Torcy that if Ormonde were allowed to occupy Dunkirk, Queen Anne would consent to a two-months' armistice, capable of further extension. But because Ormonde felt queasy about marching his troops across the Low Countries amid the watchful forces of his angry allies, it was decided to send a garrison directly from England; and of all the brave soldiers who might possibly be chosen for this notable command, Bolingbroke found that the most proper person was Lady Masham's brother, John Hill, who had bungled the Quebec expedition.

The denunciation of his policies by Whig journalists did not amuse the new viscount; for Bolingbroke's attitude toward the Fourth Estate was much more like Swift's than like Oxford's. He had arrested printers or writers when he could, but the prosecutions had failed.[1] He had driven the House of Commons to condemn Bishop Fleetwood's preface, but the text had circulated freely. As a new repressive measure, therefore, he invented that notorious tax on knowledge, the Stamp Act, assessing newspapers and pamphlets at a penny a sheet and their advertisements at a shilling apiece. Although Swift disapproved of the Stamp Act and said that instead of stifling 'small papers and libels', it would leave nothing else for the press,[2] he disliked still more another parliamentary proposal, viz., that the author's true name and address should be set to every written composition that was printed and published. 'It is most certain', Swift later observed of this scheme, 'that all persons of true genius or know-

---

[1] Laurence Hanson, *Government and the Press 1695–1763* (Oxford, 1936), p. 62.
[2] Williams I. 293.

ledge have an invincible modesty and suspiciousness of themselves upon their first sending their thoughts into the world.'[1] By
good luck this reactionary proposal, which in any case could
never have been enforced, was lost in committee at the very end
of the session.

But the Stamp Act became a direct provocative of Swift's sympathetic eagerness to aid the ministry during their time of
anxiety. In order to beat the impost, which went into effect on
1 August 1712, he produced as many as seven or more 'penny
papers'[2] in verse and prose, on a variety of topics such as the value
of Dunkirk and the hypocrisy of Bishop Fleetwood. Some of
these can no longer be identified, and others are not worth noticing. But one attack on Lord Nottingham deserves attention for
displaying Swift's skill in making a narrow political theme the
occasion for imaginative comedy and for letting us see again how
far his genius can be described as a quintessential playfulness.
The Whigs had of course predicted that Louis XIV would evade
his promise to let the British seize Dunkirk, and Swift himself felt
despondent. 'If the French play us foul', he wrote to Archbishop
King, 'I dread the effects.'[3] It seemed to him that this occupation
would be the clinching guarantee of a peace between France and
Britain, and he continued to suppose, like Bolingbroke, that the
declaration of peace, when it came, would make the ministry
almost invulnerable. 'I wish it were over', he told the ladies; 'If
we have Dunkirk once, all is safe.'[4] So he held his breath until,
on 8 July 1712 (Old Style), Major-General Hill landed and
marched his men into the fortress. To celebrate the great day,
and give expression to his own sense of relief, Swift now composed
a clever squib at the expense of the dour, dark-complexioned
Nottingham. It was published as a half-sheet broadside, *A Hue
and Cry after Dismal*.[5]

The text purports to be an account of how the Earl of Nottingham blackened his skin, tricked himself out as a chimney sweep,
went to Dunkirk with his Negro servant Squash, and there,

---

[1] Davis VII. 105.   [2] *Journal* II. 553–4, n. 10.   [3] Williams I. 300.
[4] *Journal*, 1 Jul. 1712; see pp. 544, 546–7.
[5] Published 17 Jul. 1712; see Davis VI. 210.

'under pretence of sweeping chimnyes cheaper than other people, he endeavored to persuade the townsfolks not to let the English come into the town'. Although the purpose of the rough joke was bitterly satirical, the author's inveterate playfulness produces a detached piece of humour, oddly independent of the occasion. When a file of musketeers discover the pretended chimney sweep, he is hiding out in a tavern kept appropriately by a Dutchman (whom the reader must, I suppose, regard as a natural collaborator with Whig republicans); and their leader can see nothing of his lordship but 'a leg upon each hobb' of the chimney—the rest of the body being hidden above. Surely this scene of ironical farce has little to do with Nottingham or international politics. For all Swift's hatred of his victim, the liberating comic impulse which, more deeply than satire, was involved with his instinct for impersonation, removes the scene from the realm of *utile* to that of *dulce*.

Swift's absolute sympathy with his great friends, even though he knew they had deceived their followers in Parliament, was, I believe, due to his sense of the injustice of the situation. Normally, a ministry occupied with the arrangements to end a great war would not be pressed to communicate each stage of the negotiations to a vast, miscellaneous audience. The Junto, however, though well aware that their own country would receive great benefits from the terms being arranged, blocked the ministers in every way possible and drove them to commit themselves in a manner that would have wrecked conventional diplomacy. What made their tactics still more odious was that the Whigs had wholly failed to conclude a peace when all the power to do so lay in their hands. The objections to 'peace without Spain' Swift considered—with some reason—to be simple hypocrisy. If I am right, he felt that in the circumstances it was essential for evasions to be used with the Commons and the Lords. Even when Oxford misinformed the Upper House that the Allies were 'satisfied with our terms', Swift did not, apparently, think he had committed a breach of trust.[1]

During the summer, the miseries of war brought the Allies, if

[1] *Journal*, 7 Aug. 1712.

hardly to the point of satisfaction with Bolingbroke's terms, at least to a hesitancy about rejecting them. Without the support of those troops which had followed Ormonde off the battlefield and without the genius of Marlborough to lead them, the armies of the Dutch and the Austrians fell steadily back before the re-inspired French. The initial and most dramatic disaster, the sur-prise of Denain, occurred with wretched incongruity a few days after the British had moved into Dunkirk. While the French spread northward through Flanders, pursuing unfamiliar tri-umphs, Swift rejoiced that the Dutch might be cooling off enough to think of a peace, and Bolingbroke prepared to visit France for a few weeks as ambassador extraordinary. 'My lord's business', Swift told the ladies, 'is to hasten the peace before the Dutch are too much mauled.'[1]

At the beginning of August, therefore, Bolingbroke, in the company of Matthew Prior, left England and enjoyed an almost royal progress to Paris, where he was able with his customary speed to conclude several delicate subordinate agreements with Torcy. Then in Fontainebleau the aged king gave him a dignified reception, and Bolingbroke now arranged with Torcy that the armistice between the two nations should continue another four months. Returning next to Paris, the ambassador indulged him-self freely in the social and theatrical refreshments of the capital, where he carried indiscretion so far as to let her Britannic majesty's Secretary of State be seen at the opera at the same time as, and in easy view of, the Pretender to the British throne.[2] Fin-ally, toward the end of the month, he left Prior behind to manage the remaining details and returned himself to England. But here, in an uncharacteristic anticlimax, his lordship was stricken with a fever which compelled him to retire to Bucklebury until his strength came back. He might console himself, during his in-validism, with the assurance that the Dutch would not stand out much longer and that it would then hardly matter what the Austrians chose to do. But he could not foresee that his period of suspense was very far from over.

[1] *Ibid.*   [2] James Macpherson, ed., *Original Papers*, 1775, II. 338.

II. HIGH LIFE

Some time in the autumn of 1712, Swift's life as a courtier may be said to have jelled. His circle of great acquaintance inevitably tightened. He fixed himself on a few choice beings, and they tended to have all the same colour. Whereas he had once been proud to boast that politics could not cramp the freedom with which he chose his friends, he now admitted that conversation with convinced Whigs was hard for him. To Archbishop King he wrote equivocally that in spite of 'resolutions and opinions to the contrary', he found himself compelled to mingle with only 'one side of the world'; and in a quiet irony he confessed that this new habit did impose some prejudice upon him.[1] To Mrs Johnson he reported more simply, 'I avoid all conversation with the other party, it is not to be born, and I am sorry for it.'[2]

Having given up his old regular visits to coffee-houses, he relied, for miscellaneous meetings, on the large, open receptions that were normal at court, and that were now overwhelmingly dominated by people of his own kidney. He shifted his lodgings mainly to follow the court. Thus at the beginning of June he left Westminster and moved, partly for his health's sake, to Kensington, where the Queen had taken up residence.[3] Six weeks later, he moved in her majesty's tracks to Windsor, to remain there (apart from a few days in London) until the end of September.[4] Then he removed to Ryder Street, a minute's walk from the royal palace and just around the corner from the Vanhomrighs in St James's Street.[5]

He had begun to pick and choose among the persons of honour whom he accommodated with his pleasing presence. During the summer days in Kensington he joined the Mashams almost as

---

[1] Williams I. 327.   [2] *Journal*, 7 Mar. 1713.

[3] *Ibid.* I. 143, n. His London landlady's name was Mrs Crane; he moved on 5 June, tipping the maid two shillings. It cost him 3s. 9d. to have his belongings moved (*Accounts 1711–12*, fol. 9).

[4] The London visit lasted from about 4 August to 9 August. He had moved to town when Oxford did and had expected to remain longer; but Oxford soon went back to Windsor, and Swift followed him (*Accounts 1711–12*, fol. 11; *Journal* II. 552 and n. 4).

[5] His landlady was a Mrs Hubbot; his rent, six shillings a week (four less than Mrs Crane's): *Journal* I. 143, n.; II. 561; *Accounts 1711–12*, fol. 10ᵛ.

one of the family. He would go to them for supper or picquet, and Oxford would arrive late and stay later, keeping Swift up after midnight. At Windsor, where he received lodgings that overlooked Eton and the Thames, Swift suffered a troublesome period of giddy spells, and Lady Masham got him some of the Queen's own preserved ginger to try as a medicine in the morning.[1] Late in the autumn, after her ladyship gave birth to a son, Swift was invited to the christening.[2] His gratitude for such attentions must have contributed the graceful element of spontaneity to a panegyric he composed a few years afterward upon her character; for if he had not written under the influence of a warm revival of emotion, he could hardly have expected such superlatives to be credited as other than tokens of his own appreciation:

> My Lady Masham was a person of a plain sound understanding, of great truth and sincerity, without the least mixture of falsehood or disguise; of an honest boldness and courage superior to her sex, firm and disinterested in her friendship, and full of love, duty and veneration for the Queen her mistress. . .[3]

When Lady Masham's brother John was living in Dunkirk as governor of the town, he sent Swift a superb snuffbox of tortoise shell, with a picture at the bottom of a goose driving a snail (on which Swift and Lord Oxford exchanged witticisms) and another picture, inside the box, of Venice and the Rialto in carnival time.[4] In his letter of thanks to the general, Swift tells of taking the box to a great ball given at Windsor by the Duchess of Shrewsbury. But the Duchess did not remain one of his favourites. Back in London that autumn, he began dropping her grace.[5]

Swift's great discovery of the summer was Lady Orkney, who, though ten years his senior and troubled with a bad squint, had the apparent sagacity which a royal mistress with a good memory might produce from years of hindsight. It was her brother, the late Earl of Jersey, who had been King William's favourite, Prior's patron, and Oxford's collaborator in the earliest peace

---

[1] *Journal*, 17 Jun.; 1, 17 Jul.; 15 Sept. 1712.   [2] *Ibid.*, 12 Dec. 1712.
[3] Davis VIII. 163.
[4] D. Swift, pp. 163-4; *Journal*, 18 Sept. 1712; Williams I. 305-7.
[5] *Journal*, 12 Dec. 1712.

feelers. Swift called Lady Orkney 'the wisest woman I ever saw'. She invited him to her fine house at Cliveden, a few miles from Windsor, and treated him—as he said—like a son. She ordered a most elegant writing table to be made for him and sent him letters as remarkable for their orthography as for their kindness. She enjoyed teasing or rallying him in his own manner, keeping him engrossed in long tête-à-têtes elaborately adorned with political anecdote. Addicted as he was to inside stories, Swift soon came to believe that she had exercised a strong influence on ministerial policy. As the final mark of his regard he asked for her portrait; and she gave him an original by Kneller in a fine frame: 'He has favored her squint admirably', Swift told Mrs Johnson, 'and you know I love a cast in the eye.'[1]

With such private amenities at his disposal, Swift took diminishing pleasure in a gathering so promiscuous as the Society. In May he felt delighted with a convivial feast they held under a canopy in Lord Peterborough's arbour while his lordship was abroad: 'I never saw anything so fine and romantick', Swift told the ladies.[2] But the next autumn, when the London meetings were resumed, he decided the club did no good and cost too much; so he proposed that it meet only bi-weekly. This resolution was adopted; yet even so, Swift attended irregularly. When the Duke of Ormonde scolded him for missing a dinner in February and said sixteen members had shown up, Swift retorted, 'I never knew sixteen people good company in my life.'[3] A committee of half a dozen members began to sit every other week, between dinners, in order to discuss worthy projects. Swift persuaded the whole club to tax themselves and raised a fund of sixty guineas for distribution among deserving persons. But the steady flow of money and employments that he had once hoped to channel through the Society was never forthcoming.[4]

The court receptions palled too. Swift boasted of making few formal visits and of avoiding levees. 'My only debauching', he said in the autumn of 1712, 'is sitting late when I dine if I like the company.' Yet he often went to court on Sundays; he still liked to

---

[1] *Journal*, 18 Sept.; 11, 30 Oct. 1712; [?8] Feb. 1713; Williams I. 312–13, 319–22.
[2] *Journal*, 31 May 1712.   [3] *Ibid.*, 26 Feb. 1713.   [4] *Ibid.*, 20, 29 Jan. 1713.

call it his coffee-house where he saw the world; and he kept up his custom there of speaking with the humblest people he liked immediately after a chat with a grandee.[1] Some of his habits which sound like inverted arrogance turn out to be surprisingly rational. During the busy parliamentary season there were immense 'drawing-room' receptions at court every Wednesday, Thursday, and Saturday at one o'clock. The Queen herself did not appear, but 'ministers, foreigners, and persons of quality' crowded in. Swift sometimes went; but if Oxford tried to catch him, Swift would move away at his approach. 'I affect never to take notice of him at church or court', he told the ladies; and once his lordship had to hunt the vicar three times about the room. The reason, however, was nothing mysterious. Swift had simply found that whenever he did exchange words with the Lord Treasurer in a miscellaneous gathering, people immediately closed in on him and pestered him with questions to tease out what had been said.[2]

The ingratiating charm that Swift exerted on the courtiers he wished to encourage is not easily exaggerated. When Lord Peterborough came back from more than a year's travels out of England, he called at Oxford's house, where Swift happened to be sitting after dinner with his host, Lord Bolingbroke, the Duke of Ormonde, and others. Oxford and Bolingbroke went out to the door and escorted the visitor in. But as soon as he saw Swift, Peterborough turned from Ormonde and the rest to run and kiss him before speaking to them; and he reproached Swift bitterly for not having written.[3]

The great Duke of Hamilton, whose hereditary position in Scotland endowed him with a princeliness superior even to that of Ormonde in Ireland, was a more striking case of Swift's powers. This handsome, proud, vacillating orator, immortalized in *Henry Esmond*, was selected to proceed as ambassador extraordinary to France, in order to lend some dignified speed to the last negotiations while Prior accomplished the real work.

[1] *Ibid.*, 12 Dec. 1712.
[2] *Ibid.*, 16 Jan. 1713; cf. Swift's imitation of Horace, *Sat.* II. vi.
[3] *Journal*, 10 Jan. 1713.

Swift had easily won over his Duchess, a beautiful, volatile woman in her mid-thirties, much younger than her husband. She seemed more envied than loved, being bitter-tongued and seldom sparing anyone who even slightly provoked her. The Countess of Orkney, whose husband was younger brother to the Duke, found it virtually impossible to get along with her. But her grace had visited Swift in his lodgings when he was home with the shingles, and she sewed for him a specially designed, pocketed belt to make up for his wearing no waistcoat in the summer.[1] It was the Duke who had jokingly treated Swift's gown as a train on a staircase at Windsor; and he presented Swift with a pound of snuff a couple of months after General Hill gave him the tortoise-shell box. Swift found his grace generous and good-natured though dull. 'I loved him very well', he said after Hamilton's death, 'and I think he loved me better.' Rumour said that the Duke would have liked to take Swift with him to France.

Of course, the Duke never went to France, being killed in the double slaughter of his notorious duel with Lord Mohun. When news of the calamity reached Swift, his extraordinary instinct for associating himself with the troubles of others sent him straight to the frantic Duchess, who had been taken from her house to the seclusion of a nearby lodging. The thoughtful priest was admitted, spent two hours with the miserable widow, and then wrote to the ladies,

> I never saw so melancholy a scene. For indeed all reasons for real grief belong to her, nor is it possible for any one to be a greater loser in all regards. She has moved my very soul. The lodging was inconvenient, and they would have removed her to another; but I would not suffer it; because it [i.e., the other] had no room backwards; and she must have been tortured with the noise of the Grubstreet screamers, mention [sic] her husbands murder to her ears.[2]

He returned several times in the days which followed, but found her hard to be consoled. If the outbursts were less violent, the bitterness seemed 'more formal and settled'. Lady Orkney, though a hated sister-in-law, tried to be kind to the Duchess; and Swift, with his admirable penchant for bringing people together,

[1] *Journal*, 18 Sept. 1712. [2] *Ibid.*, 15 Nov. 1712.

thought that in this time of distress a reconciliation might help the furious woman to digest her grief: 'The Dutchess is now no more an object of envy, and must learn humility from the severest master, affliction', he said. But the project was not a hopeful one.[1]

At the same time, Swift as ministerial propagandist accepted a lie spread by the Tories, to the effect that Hamilton had been stabbed by his opponent's second—the Whig general Maccartney, who had fled after the duel. With this in mind he contributed to the ministerial paper, the *Post Boy*, an account which he himself, with perfect accuracy, called 'as malicious as possible'.[2] Meanwhile, it was compassion, and not natural affinity, that brought Swift so close to the Duchess. As soon as he could gracefully taper off his visits, he did so; and within four weeks of the duel had almost given up calling on her.[3]

The noble house which he did love—besides that of Oxford, Bolingbroke, Masham, and Lady Orkney—was the Ormonde family. The Duke himself, though weaker in every way than his illustrious, short-lived father (sonorously lamented by Dryden), attracted the respectful admiration of an impressive variety of persons and conferred obligations on so many that their gratitude constantly bathed him. Prince Eugene described Ormonde as 'the finest cavalier and most complete gentleman that England bred, being the glory of his nation'.[4] The Whig Steele defended him rashly and affectionately during Ormonde's deepest disgrace.[5] Addison, though on the committee that brought evidence of his treason, refused to vote for the Duke's impeachment.[6] Swift, whose life in Ireland had been passed among memorials of Ormonde beneficence, must have felt a most particular satisfaction in the friendship of his grace.

While the Duke was in Flanders on his mock-campaign, the Duchess entertained the vicar. In October, when Swift was secluding himself from people in London, she tracked him down and made him dine with her. A few days after the Duke came

---

[1] *Ibid.*, 16–17 Nov.   [2] *Ibid.*, 17 Nov.; Davis VI.197–9; cf. *ibid.*, VII. 155.
[3] *Journal*, 12 Dec. 1712.   [4] Churchill VI. 539.
[5] *The Englishman*, 12 Aug. 1715.   [6] Graham, p. 343.

back to England, he made it a point to have a private talk with Swift, at Swift's request. A month later, the Duke sent him a present of some chocolate, supposed to be good for his health. The delicate, warm language of the Ormondes' letters to Swift, and the careful brilliance of a letter from him to the Duchess betoken the strength of this intimacy.[1]

Once more Swift begged the gift of a portrait—he wanted one of all his splendid favourites; and the Duchess supplied him with not one but two, her own and the Duke's—'in fine gilded frames too'. Finding them, with no warning, already delivered to his bedroom, Swift designed a message of gratitude around a conceit that he particularly liked—'You will not so much as let your picture be alone in a room with a man, no not with a clergyman, and a clergyman of five-and-forty, and therefore resolved my Lord Duke should accompany it, and keep me in awe, that I might not presume to look too often upon it.'[2]

The Duke's daughters, whom Swift used to meet at Mrs Vanhomrigh's,[3] were among the young ladies he singled out for praise. When Lady Mary was married to Lord Ashburnham, Swift called it 'the best match now in England'. He liked dining with her—'a very good girl and always a great favourite of mine' —and said she reminded him of Mrs Johnson. On the Queen's birthday (1712), when the courtiers competed with one another for ostentation in dress, Swift thought Lady Ashburnham looked the best of all.[4] He felt shattered and desolate, therefore, a year later when she suddenly died in the middle of a pregnancy: 'She was my greatest favourite'—he told the ladies, in reflections which showed his moral judgment directed (as so often) by his deepest feelings—

> and I am in excessive concern for her loss. I hardly knew a more valuable person on all accounts: you must have heard me tell of her. I am afraid to see the Duke and Duchess; she was naturally very healthy; I am afraid she has been thrown away for want of care. Pray condole with me; tis extreamly moving. . . I hate life,

---

[1] *Journal*, 17 Jun., 30 Oct. 1712; Williams I. 316, 326–7; *Journal*, 12 Dec. 1712.
[2] *Ibid.*, 19 Dec. 1712; Williams I. 326.
[3] I assume this is the 'third place' of *Journal*, 19 Sept. 1710; cf. *ibid.*, 27 Jun. 1711.
[4] *Ibid.*, 20 Oct. 1710; 25 Jun. 1711; 6 Feb. 1712.

when I think it exposed to such accidents, and to see so many thousand wretches burthening the earth while such as her dye, makes me think God did never intend life for a blessing.

One of Swift's gentlest comments on the Duke is the observation he made two days later, having seen the grieving father's reaction to the beloved child's death:

> I was to see the poor Duke and Dutchess of Ormond this morning, the Duke was in his publick room with Mr. Southwell, and two more gentlemen. When Southwell and I was alone with them, he talked something of Lord Ashburnham . . . he bore up as well as he could, but something accidentally falling in discourse, the tears were just falling out of his eyes, and I looked off to give him an opportunity (which he took) of wiping them with his hankerchief. I never saw any thing so moving, nor such a mixture of greatness of mind and tenderness and discretion.[1]

For all Swift's attachment to the chosen few, I doubt that the process of sifting and refining his eminent friendships meant an essential enrichment of his social pleasures. Rather, I think it implies a disillusionment with what Fielding was to call 'much the dullest life'.[2] The shallowness of a work like Swift's *History of the Four Last Years* indicates the desiccating effect of the loyalty he imagined he owed not merely to the ministerial party but to a particular circle of courtiers. And I find it significant that the best work Swift was still to do, before Queen Anne died, would be provoked by a renewed but polemical contact with an old Whig friend, Richard Steele, who, though a Dubliner by birth and a protégé of the Ormondes, could never discipline his amicable instincts with Swift's degree of severity.

III. ELTEE AND LD BOL

When Swift made sure that he might talk tête-à-tête with the Duke of Ormonde on the Duke's return from Flanders, the main topic he planned to discuss was the hatred existing between Oxford and Bolingbroke.[3] But although Swift had long been

---

[1] *Ibid.*, 3, 5 Jan. 1713.   [2] *Tom Jones*, Bk xiv, Ch. i.
[3] 'I design to make him join me in settling all right among our people' (*Journal*, 30 Aug. 1712).

aware of this hatred, he still did not like to recognize its depth. Instead of admitting that his two friends were simply irreconcilable rivals for the same position, he tried to believe that certain accidents and misunderstandings had created and were maintaining the feud. It was St John's jealousy over Harley's heroic rôle in the Guiscard affair that forced the enmity of the ministers inescapably upon Swift's attention. He imagined, however, that this episode was the start of the enmity,[1] rather than an expression of rising tempers.

Bolingbroke himself described another occasion as the moment, not when his hatred started, but when he began to renounce 'in his heart' all his friendship for Oxford.[2] This was the elevation of the Secretary of State to the peerage of England. At the beginning of this parliamentary session, when the Queen had agreed to create the dozen titles, she had deliberately omitted St John because the ministry needed him in the House of Commons until the peace was settled. Therefore, the Secretary had received assurances that when his turn came, he would not lose rank in relation to the earlier creations, but would secure a title giving him precedence over them. St John let it be known that since an earldom of Bolingbroke had lately expired in a remote elder branch of his family, he would be glad to be found worthy of renewing it. There is some evidence that the Lord Treasurer, however, thought it proper to frustrate this hope and encourage her majesty not to raise his rival to his own level. Consequently St John was offered the title of viscount, which, after some undignified manœuvres and futile squirming, he saw fit to accept. To a noble friend who congratulated him, the reluctant peer complained that such a promotion was a 'mortification': 'I own to you that I felt more indignation than ever in my life I had done.'[3]

Bolingbroke understood fairly well that his real strength and superiority to Oxford lay in his power of leading the House of Commons. He knew that by leaving the Commons he would be losing perhaps his chief claim to advancement. An earldom

[1] Davis VIII. 145–6.   [2] *Letter to Sir William Wyndham*, in *Works*, 1754, I. 14.
[3] To Strafford, 23 July 1712.

would perhaps have compensated him for this renunciation; a viscountcy could not. Blaming Oxford for the immense disappointment, Bolingbroke told Swift that he would (in Swift's words) 'never depend upon the Earl's friendship as long as he lived, nor have any further commerce with him than what was necessary for carrying on the public service'. It is a tribute to Swift's genius for balancing between two admirations that he admitted there were 'appearances' to support Bolingbroke's suspicions, and yet that he preferred himself to accept the protestations of Oxford and Lady Masham that the Treasurer was 'wholly innocent' in this matter.[1]

Some hint of the division in Swift's feelings toward the furious partners may be drawn from the way he handled a very personal detail of Bolingbroke's elevation. When Oxford had received his earldom, he had got somebody to compose a gush of panegyric in the form of a preamble to his patent of nobility. From the style of Swift's use elsewhere of certain phrases in this preamble, I suspect that the vicar of Laracor had a hand in its composition.[2] Bolingbroke knew all about Oxford's preamble, which had come out as a pamphlet in Latin and English. He wanted one like it and asked Swift to compose the text. 'I excused my self', Swift told the ladies, 'from a work that might lose me a great deal of reputation, and get me very little.'[3] One recalls Swift's similar hedging in his account of Guiscard's attack. Bolingbroke may have seemed more of a young hero—'If I were a dozen years younger', Swift said, 'I would cultivate his favor and trust my fortune with his'[4]— but Swift's deepest tie was to the older, fatherly Oxford.

Bolingbroke's visit to France only gave a few weeks' intermission to the quarrel; and his rashness while there did not remain a secret from the English court. Swift heard that the Queen felt 'highly and publickly displeased' to discover that her Secretary had gone to the opera the same night as her half-brother. She said, according to Swift's information, that Bolingbroke ought to have withdrawn as soon as the Pretender appeared. Not that Swift agreed. 'To speak with freedom', he said a few years

[1] Davis VIII. 152.   [2] *Journal* I. 265 and n. 25.   [3] *Ibid.*, I Jul. 1712.
[4] *Ibid.*, 23 Feb. 1712, pt 2.

later, 'I think her judgment was a little mistaken.'[1] Even before
Bolingbroke received his title, however, the rumours of his
domestic irregularities had darkened her majesty's picture of
him.[2] Neither was his reputation in the royal household enhanced by reports that while abroad he had reached secret
understandings with French agents on his own behalf. It was
possible, consequently, for Oxford to win the Queen's agreement
to yet a fresh humiliation for his lordship; and when the Secretary returned to Whitehall after the illness that followed the
French expedition, he met startling evidence of the distrust he
had provoked; for her majesty let him know that the correspondence between the courts of Versailles and St James's, which he
had naturally supervised during the peace negotiations, was now
to be taken out of his hands and revert to Lord Dartmouth, the
Secretary of State for the southern department and warm friend
of Lord Oxford. It is no wonder that about this time Swift
should be praying for someone like the Duke of Ormonde to help
him bring Bolingbroke and Oxford together.

Swift's own ability to stay on good terms with the two at once
seems more than natural: 'I had ever been treated with great
kindness by them both', he wrote later in a memoir;

> and I conceived that what I wanted in weight and credit might be
> made up with sincerity and freedom. The former they never
> doubted, and the latter they had constant experience of: I had
> managed between them for almost two years; and their candor was
> so great, that they had not the least jealousy or suspicion of me.[3]

In September 1712 he wrote to Mrs Johnson, 'I am again endeavouring as I was last year to keep people from breaking to
pieces, upon a hundred misunderstandings.'[4]

Meanwhile, Oxford's secretiveness and procrastination never
dimmed his fondness for Swift's company. The doctor became a
member of the family, joining them in small card-games and
entertaining the Lord Treasurer when he was not well enough to
go out: 'I was playing at one and thirty with him and his family
tother night', Swift wrote in October to the ladies. 'He gave us all

---

[1] Davis VIII. 166–7.   [2] *Ibid.*, p. 151.   [3] *Ibid.*, p. 158.
[4] *Journal*, 15 Sept. 1712.

twelve pence apiece to begin with: it put me in mind of Sir William Temple.'[1]

Even if Bolingbroke had not spent most of August in France, he kept much too untidy a schedule to give Swift, in the middle of 1712, the regular, decent domestic setting that nourished the doctor's attachment to the Lord Treasurer. All the thrilling sensations of Guiscard's attack on this older, 'affable and courteous'[2] patron were now, quite unexpectedly, revived in depth and at first hand, during the autumn, when Swift had the extraordinary satisfaction of saving his avuncular friend from another assassin. While the Lord Treasurer was shaving one morning, and Swift was with him, a suspicious-looking box arrived by post. Oxford began opening it but stopped when he caught sight of a pistol inside. His more cautious companion insisted on taking the box to the window for further examination, where, opening it with gingerly circumspection, he found a primitive machine for murder. Two loaded pistols, pointing in opposite directions, were tied with a piece of thread so as to be triggered and therefore shoot anyone who removed the lid of the box brusquely enough.

So sensational an episode could not remain unknown. The story got out quickly and circulated widely, providing agreeable alarms for Tory gossips and emphatic paragraphs for government prints. But alas both the infernal engine and the sacerdotal rescuer were treated with contempt by Whig sceptics. Boyer, who thought the accounts of the alleged plot easily disproved themselves, described Swift's rôle as 'miraculous', in a sneering allusion to the *Examiner*'s sober epithet for the Treasurer's escape.[3] Swift himself felt embarrassed enough to scratch up a sort of apology for Mrs Johnson: 'I wonder how I came to have so much presence of mind, which is usually not my talent; but so it pleased God, and I saved my self and him, for there was a bullet a piece.'[4] Bolingbroke's comment is not preserved.

The way Swift passed New Year's Eve indicates how elabor-

---

[1] *Ibid.*, 9 Oct. It seems worth noting that the reference to Temple is a parallelism, whereas Swift's references to him with Bolingbroke are always contrasts.

[2] Davis VIII. 137.   [3] *History of the Reign of Queen Anne* XI (1713), 294, 296.

[4] *Journal*, 15 Nov. 1712. The 'bandbox plot', as it was called, occurred on 4 Nov. Details vary in different accounts: see below, Appendix D.

ately he was involved with the jealous, ministerial partners. Oxford and he were supposed to dine at Bolingbroke's with the Irish poet Parnell, whom Swift was bringing to their attention. But Oxford caught a cold that made him choose to stay at home. Swift and Parnell still received their dinner from the Secretary. But in the evening Swift went to Buckingham Street and saw the year out with the Harleys. He sat as company to the ailing Lord Treasurer while the younger generation went to supper. Then he joined Oxford's children and their spouses (his daughter Elizabeth had just married the rich son and heir of the Duke of Leeds) while the Countess went upstairs to her husband—'and there were the young folks merry together . . . and the old folks were together above. It looked like what I have formerly done so often, stealing together from the old folks.'[1] No such scenes at Bucklebury.

By this time, Oxford used to make complaints if Swift dined with him less than twice or three times a week.[2] But the late evenings which followed the meals were not to the doctor's taste, and he had other reasons for wishing to avoid his lackadaisical patron. Yet he went regularly enough—as much as six successive times in the middle of March.[3] Meanwhile, in a subplot of his scheme to unite the Treasurer and the Secretary, he was trying to keep a friendship alive between Oxford and Ormonde.[4] As the spring of 1713 went on, however, he grew less and less sanguine about even this prospect. Three of Marlborough's favourite young generals had been forced to sell their commissions in the guards to officers whom the ministers considered politically more reliable. Ormonde, as commander-in-chief, thus lost the profit he might have made if the promotions of the newcomers had passed through his hands. He had understood that the Treasurer would compensate him with a huge lump payment.[5] But when Swift, at Ormonde's desire, pressed Oxford for the money, the Treasurer said he could not spare it. Unfortunately, Oxford's

---

[1] *Journal*, 1 Jan. 1713: probably another parallel with Temple.
[2] *Ibid.*, [?8] Feb. 1713.   [3] *Ibid.*, 18 Mar.   [4] *Ibid.*, 23 Mar.
[5] £10,000, which was, however, no more than the Earl of Portland received when he sold his post of colonel and captain of the first troop of horse guards to Ormonde's son-in-law, Lord Ashburnham (Boyer, *Political State*, 10 Jul. 1713).

secretiveness and growing alcoholism were working on his procrastination to the point where his only policy seemed that of
drifting along while more and more decisive actions were taken
by Bolingbroke.

Swift, I think, made the mistake of confusing sincere affection
with perfect candour. Because he received consistently good-
natured, spontaneous friendship from these great men, he
imagined that they were not misrepresenting their fundamental
principles. 'I never yet knew a minister of state', he said later, 'or
indeed any other man so great a master of secrecy, as to be able
among those he nearly [i.e., closely] conversed with, wholly to
conceal his opinions, however he may cover his designs. This I
say, upon a supposition that they would have held on the mask
always before me, which however I have no reason to believe.'[1]
In a similar style he wrote, about the same time, to Archbishop
King, 'Had there been ever the least overture or intent of bringing in the Pretender during my acquaintance with the ministry,
I think I must have been very stupid not to have pickt out some
discoveryes or suspicions.'[2] Of course, he was wrong. Both Oxford
and Bolingbroke were in touch with the Pretender and assuring
him of their devotion. Few historians now believe that the Treasurer's allegiance was at all genuine, though the Secretary acted
with less ambiguity and more heat than his partner. Yet neither
of them gave Swift a hint of what he was stooping to. No matter
how much they may have liked and trusted Swift, these unsavoury secrets were far too dangerous to be shared. It seems
paradoxical but true, therefore, that the man who practises self-
misrepresentation as an art is often taken in by his own devices.

IV. LIFE AND LETTERS

Apart from the emotional grounds of Swift's absorption in the
ministry's career, his rational approval of their programme always remained steady. To his mind they did seem by motives of

---

[1] Davis VIII. 165–6; I read 'conversed', from the first copy, for 'converseth', from
the fair copy.
[2] Williams II. 238.

self-love to desire what was in the best interests of the whole country. They seemed the party of national unity. They elevated the church and promoted good churchmen. Without their skill and shrewdness, peace would have continued to slip out of reach.

Yet even when he wished to praise them, Swift could not smother an aggrieved feeling that in his own field of journalistic labour they were too easy-going; for he was never one to assume that the truth will prevail of her own unaided strength. He had a Hobbesian distrust of liberty of expression, whether political or religious; and he thought Bolingbroke in particular had worked too coolly to defeat the press-loading enemies of the true church. Nothing, Swift said, would be 'more for the honour of the legislature' than a strong law that might put a stop to the blasphemies published against God and religion; and he blamed Bolingbroke for failing to propose such a law.[1]

A nation could not enjoy a strong established church, Swift thought, without a properly reverenced clergy. Consequently, he denounced those subtle attacks on his own order which emanated from the writings of deists or anti-episcopal sectarians. As a subject of violent argument, the status and spiritual powers of the priesthood had broken into vivid prominence, after years of smoky polemics, when Convocation tried to deal with issue of lay baptism. For if no baptism was valid outside an episcopal communion, no Dissenter could be regarded as Christian, and the House of Hanover must stand in a very dubious position to assume the headship of the Anglican Church. If, on the other hand, a baptism remained valid though performed by ministers who lacked episcopal—or indeed any other—orders, the sacramental status of the priesthood must sink. Nonjurors tended to insist on baptism in an episcopal communion; latitudinarians generally accepted any baptism made with water, in the name of the father, son, and holy ghost; while deists cheerfully magnified the implications of the disagreement.

In the spring of 1713 the House of Bishops asked the Lower House of Convocation to join with them in a declaration allowing

[1] Davis VIII. 103-4.

the validity of irregular baptisms. The Lower House refused to pass the declaration, complaining that the divine authority of the priesthood was already under open assault, and that a favourable vote would only hearten the enemies of episcopacy.[1]

Among the persistent underminers of the priestly order was Locke's beloved disciple, Anthony Collins. The third of Collins's explosive volumes had just appeared, *A Discourse of Free-Thinking*, with a rationalistic, historical argument in the manner of Bayle, demonstrating that the unfettered use of reason made a truer guide to religion and morality than the precepts of ordained clergymen. Naturally, Collins set a peculiar value on those acts of reason which worked against the conventional order; for whereas Swift always joined reason to the institutions hallowed by common acceptance, Collins tried to oppose them each to the other. Hence, that very uniformity in political government and the church, which Swift wished to improve, was what Collins meant to subvert. And although dignified upholders of the church were quick enough to answer the deist's attack—and the mighty Bentley produced a learned refutation of Collins's logic[2]—Swift characteristically felt that a less sober treatment would have more power to undermine the enemy.

In January 1713, therefore, when he was writing little or nothing for the ministry, Swift decided to produce something useful for the church. He called this essay a 'little whim' and handed it to the printer only five days after first conceiving it. The *Examiner* for Saturday 23 January gave advance notice of the pamphlet; and by Monday publication had followed: *Mr. C - - - - ns's Discourse of Free-Thinking, Put into Plain English . . . for the Use of the Poor*.[3] The strong infusion of burlesque compounded with parody has made the rhetoric seem an appealing object for systematic analysis.[4] But Swift's ingenuity here rests on too many suppressed postulates, and becomes, I think, insipid when it is not pretentious. Once again, therefore, he appears less than brilliant in defending things as they are; and even his irony, exemplified

[1] Boyer, *History of the Reign of Queen Anne*, XI (1713), 376-9.
[2] *Remarks upon a Late Discourse of Free-Thinking*, 1713.
[3] *Journal*, 16, 18, 21, 25 Jan. 1713; *Examiner*, 23, 26 Jan.; Davis IV. xvi-xvii.
[4] Bullitt, pp. 97-102; Price, pp. 60-2.

here in zoological variety, sounds hollow and mechanical without the tone of a besieged prophet to give it energy.

Swift's main method of ridiculing Collins is to pretend to give objective summaries of many of his propositions but to twist their sense so as to make them sound heavily irreligious and absurd. The satirist adds examples, explanations, and transitions of his own that coarsen the nonsensical side while underlining the anti-Christian implications of Collins's book. In spite of Swift's energy and unrelenting cleverness (or perhaps because of them), the total effect is drearily repetitious and hard to read. Even if one had the original book by Collins in one's head, so that the affirmations ridiculed by Swift could be recalled, the mockery is too broad, too simple, to hold one's interest. Again, I suppose that Swift did not dare risk the subtleties of *A Tale of a Tub* for fear of sounding blasphemous himself.

The essential scheme of the essay is a burlesque of a logical demonstration, with Swift pretending to prove Collins's doctrines but really making them grotesque. As in the *Argument against Abolishing Christianity*, the crazy examples imply the opposite of the propositions they illustrate, and the conclusions contradict the premises. Swift's positive argument, nevertheless, emerges clearly, through repeated, emphatic sarcasms. He insists that the discursive or speculative reason of the untrained, lay individual is a far more dangerous guide to conscience and faith than an expert priest. Putting the matter of divine ordination aside, he compares the priest to counsellors in other specialized fields—classical scholars, for instance, or lawyers and physicians; and he indicates that it would be as wrongheaded for a man to brush off the one as the other. An allusion to the Convocation dispute makes it quite evident that he means to enhance the 'power and privileges' of the clergy.[1]

Although in both the preface and body of the work Swift draws his usual parallels between church and state, or atheism and the Junto, the effort seems either crude or perfunctory. 'A little pamphlet . . . but not politicks' was his own description of the work.[2] Whigs, including Steele, had also attacked Collins, if only be-

[1] Davis IV. 36.   [2] *Journal*, 21 Jan. 1713.

cause they had no wish to let irreligiosity be a party matter.[1] And in the subordinate articles of his own exposition Swift had nothing to say about Whiggery. He merely reiterates his habitual fear of liberty of expression, claiming that unrestricted freedom will breed endless divisions and consequently put society in a turmoil.

Swift's belief that a proliferation of sects and parties must lead to chaos is too familiar to need any comment. But there is a fascinating polarity here. Swift really believed that intuitive reason could be trusted when appealed to in matters essential to civil order and morality. In fact, his whole refutation of Collins must fail if the reader cannot intuitively recognize the absurdity of the deist's positions. But Swift had no such confidence in the power of the private, speculative (or discursive) reason to handle remoter problems, theological distinctions not necessary for salvation. 'The bulk of mankind', he says, 'is as well qualified for *flying* as *thinking.*' Therefore, it follows that if left to muddle their way through, without the advice of the priest, most laymen would wander into error: 'By *free-thinking,* men will *think* themselves into *atheism.*' Such doubts about human nature, however valid from a Christian point of view, and howsoever rooted in Swift's character, make a shaky foundation for his polemic against Collins's trust in reason. Swift's rhetoric throughout this piece is ironical and negative enough; it requires some ultimate justification that might appear more positive. And the reader who cannot share his fear of schism and heresy will hardly find the essay amusing.

If there are few political references in *Mr. Collins's Discourse,* there is little else in the large defence of the ministry which Swift was (with many interruptions) composing about this time. But apart from that elaborate history, it almost seems that he avoided publishing anything for the service of the government. The approach of peace now dominated all discussion of public affairs, and Swift held his breath with the rest of Europe. Contrary to the hopes of many anxious Tories, the winter of negotiation did not look to be followed by a spring of sunny concord. Spokesmen for the Whigs went on insisting that the treacherous French would never carry out their promises, that Dunkirk, the privateers'

[1] Davis IV. xviii.

sanctuary, would keep her fortifications, and that the Bourbon King of Spain would seize the crown of France as soon as old Louis and the sickly infant heir were dead. The same voices insisted that Oxford and Bolingbroke were plotting with both Versailles and St Germains to break the Act of Succession and bring in the Pretender when the ailing Queen finally died.

Such insinuations against the mightiest officers of state had now become routine; and the friends of the ministers were not likely to be screened from the pellets of dirt flung at their chiefs. Generally, these personal assaults were either returned in kind or else ignored. But one random shot came so dangerously close to Oxford himself that Swift felt it required more expert handling. Erasmus Lewis, who besides working as a kind of special agent for the Lord Treasurer, was undersecretary in Dartmouth's office, had eased the passage of a licence allowing an Englishman who lay under the heaviest suspicion of Jacobitism to return to England after a long residence in France. Because the traveller wished to give his thanks to Lewis directly, he tried to call on him at home. But being misdirected, he visited another Mr Lewis who happened to think the error might be made useful to the Whigs. This person therefore spread the malicious rumour that before discovering his error the caller had given the supposed Erasmus Lewis cordial regards from the Pretender's court. Because the real Erasmus Lewis was so deeply involved with both Oxford and Dartmouth, this makeshift scandal could become an explosive torpedo at a time when opposition journalists regularly described the ministry as Jacobite.

Swift came to his comrade's defence first by slipping a paragraph on the subject into a sympathetic newspaper and then by writing a number of the *Examiner* which told in convincing detail what was supposed to be the true story. Although the *Examiner*'s account is a plain, dull, circumstantial report, the whole feverish episode suggests how twitchy the courtiers were feeling. Inasmuch as Swift devoted an inordinate number of hours to getting the thing right, it also suggests that he found himself under little pressure from other obligations. For he gathered the minute facts from several different sources, composed his report quite methodically, dictated it to the printer, and had Lewis himself correct it. Obviously, these days were not the busiest season for Dr Swift.[1]

On the Continent, meanwhile, the diplomats, like cripples climbing a stairway, were taking their last, shackled steps toward peace. Secretly, in France, the truly effective discussions went on, while the public negotiations at Utrecht remained a dignified dumb show. At the beginning of the new year the Duke of Shrewsbury had arrived in Paris as ambassador to replace the slain Hamilton. He felt properly worried about money, having just completed his great house at Heythrop and being only too familiar with the delays of her majesty's exchequer. His over-sized, handsome Italian wife troubled him with her eccentricities and her social humiliations; his own health was never good. What with the balky gait of the French agents and the fantastic delays of the almost paralysed government in Whitehall, he found what was to have been a ceremonious winding-up turning into an exhausting job of work. In England the ministers had to prorogue Parliament from fortnight to fortnight or day to day as they waited to be assured that the ultimate formality was finally accomplished and they might announce the peace that would end their storms. 'You never saw a town so full of ferment and expectation', said Swift.[2] But it was not until Bolingbroke (into whose nimble hands the correspondence with Versailles had by now returned) menaced the French with a new war that Louis at last consented to Shrewsbury's particulars.

As soon as this gratifying news arrived, the plenipotentiaries at Utrecht were instructed to sign the treaties with France, and the Queen proceeded to meet her loyal Parliament in Westminster. 'Now the great work is in effect done', a much-comforted correspondent told the ladies, 'and I believe it will appear a most excellent peace for Europe, particularly for England.'[3] So he must have felt doubly regaled when Oxford made him a direct participant in this, one of the supreme public events of their lifetime and one which Swift had so passionately hoped to see en-

---

[1] *Journal*, 16, 31 Jan., 1 Feb. 1713. The newspaper was the *Post Boy*, 30 Jan.; *Examiner*, 2 Feb.
[2] *Journal*, 9 Mar. 1713.　　[3] *Ibid.*, 3 Apr.

acted. Weeks before the session was to open, the Lord Treasurer had shown him a draft of the speech her majesty was to deliver to both houses, announcing a general peace in Europe. He asked Swift not only to correct this copy but also to compose the address of thanks which the Lords would return to the Queen.[1] Fulfilling the welcome duties, Swift could not help leaving at least a few traces of his own hand. In one oddly outspoken section of the speech from the throne as Queen Anne finally delivered it, I think I detect the author of the satire on Collins. This is a recommendation that their lordships should prepare a new law for the suppression of seditious and scandalous papers. 'The impunity such practices have met with', her majesty declared on the first day of the session,[2] 'has encourag'd the blaspheming every thing sacred, and the propagating opinions tending to the overthrow of all religion and government.'[3] But it would, I suppose, have been hard to rally the Whiggish Lords to take instant notice of this, and the speech Swift wrote for them is formal and colourless.[4]

Although the proclamation of peace was delayed yet another four weeks, the effects of the event were immediate, in literature as well as politics. So early as the autumn of 1712 the *Spectator* had foreseen the influence that the end of the war would exert upon poetasters aspiring to patronage.[5] And in the ensuing competition of 'eternal rhymers'[6] no versifier seemed more triumphant than Addison's friend Tickell, with his *On the Prospect of Peace*. However, only a single poem on the popular theme is still read, and that of course is Pope's *Windsor Forest*. The young genius had turned a topographical georgic into a celebration of the imminent peace. Even if he still attached himself to the Whig circle of Addison's friends, and even though his poems in Lintot's new *Miscellany* (including the *Rape of the Lock*) had received a sentence of choice praise from the same Spectator who had recommended the *Essay on Criticism*,[7] Pope felt restive. The attention which the

[1] *Journal*, 8, 15, 17 Mar., 7 Apr.   [2] 9 Apr. 1713.   [3] Davis VI. 203.
[4] *Ibid.*, p. 183.
[5] *Spectator*, 30 Oct. 1712, perhaps echoing the opening of Dryden's *Essay of Dramatick Poesy*.
[6] Dryden, *op. cit.*, in *Essays*, ed. W. P. Ker, 1900, I. 30.
[7] *Spectator*, 30 Oct. 1712. 20 Dec. 1711.

'little senate' lavished in print upon the pastorals of Ambrose Philips without even mentioning Pope's superior efforts in the same genre must have galled him; and one assumes that with his ambition and vulnerability he preferred not to appear so thorough a Whig as to sacrifice the patronage of Tory readers.[1] It was one of Swift's brothers in the Society (Lord Lansdowne, the poetical Secretary at War, one of the dozen titles created to pass the Preliminaries) who induced Pope to expand *Windsor Forest*. Swift must have embraced lovingly this tribute from a neutral source to the Tory peace. 'Mr. Pope has published a fine poem called Windsor Forest', he wrote to the ladies; 'read it.'[2] He could easily have met Pope through Lansdowne or else through his own Irish friend Parnell, who, like the poet, was friendly with Steele and agreed to write essays for the new periodical the *Guardian*. Another, more remote acquaintance of Swift's, writing independently to Ireland, reported the appearance of 'a new poem call'd Windsor Forest, written by Mr. Pope who is said to be a most ingenious man, and the poem to be the finest that has yet appear'd in our tongue'![3]

On domestic politics the peace had a polarizing effect quite unforeseen by Swift. With the crisis past, the moment was right for either a new distribution of power, cutting through old barriers, or else an intensification of partisanship, with the ministerial party dropping all Whigs and waverers from office. Oxford, true to type, leaned toward the scheme of realignment; Bolingbroke, no less inevitably, toward partisanship. Now that the government had lost its urgent need of Bolingbroke's talents, Oxford would have been glad to jettison him and his clique if only the opposition would lend the Lord Treasurer the requisite strength in the two houses. Shortly before Parliament met, Oxford had a talk at

---

[1] Sherburn, *Early Career*, pp. 101–23.

[2] *Journal*, 9 Mar. 1713; the poem was published 7 March with a dedication to Lansdowne. Pope uses, perhaps by coincidence, some elements of the rhetoric of *The Conduct of the Allies*. In recommending the peace, he dwells on the importance of agriculture, describes the rural sports of country gentlemen, condemns military violence, and celebrates the British navy. These might be called Tory themes. But he also attacks tyranny and identifies the Tory peace with liberty and commerce. These Whiggish themes Pope (like Swift) treats as naturally derived from the others.

[3] Daniel Dering to Sir John Percival, Bart., 12 Mar. 1713 (B.M. MS. Ad. 47,027, p. 34); I do not mean to imply that Dering was quoting Swift's opinion.

Lord Halifax's house with his lordship and four other Whig chiefs.[1] But few Whigs would trust so evasive a bargainer, and Oxford's shaky health exacerbated his indecisiveness to a point that made real give-and-take impossible. He had meanwhile to offer lip-service to the Secretary's uncompromising programme, so as not to lose the support of the extremists; and Bolingbroke, not to be overreached on his side, made futile gestures toward the Whigs himself. Swift was furious over the rumours that the Lord Treasurer would 'declare for' the Whig interest,[2] but he admitted sadly that Oxford was indeed mingling with his enemies.

At the same time, Swift felt quite ready to help detach from the opposition any useful figures who would stand behind the ministry. The strategy of seduction looks much like the strategy of compromise. It was possible, consequently, for some observers to infer that a coalition government lay in the offing. The Whigs of course could hope to spoil the ministers' reputation for integrity (such as it was) by appearing to receive offers from them, just as the ministers could hope, by their furtive, conditional promises, to soften any attacks the Whigs planned to make on the peace in Parliament. During Christmas week, when Swift had met Addison and Philips on the Mall, they had looked dry and cold in spite of their taking a turn with him.[3] The following spring, however, Addison was preoccupied with the staging of his play *Cato*; and he wanted no political controversy to weaken its chance of success. Steele, meanwhile, planning an exotic series of oratorical-cum-musical entertainments in his new 'Censorium', wished the project to rise above party distinctions, and approached the Lord Treasurer to ask for his co-operation.[4] In February Swift had met Addison and Philips again, at the funeral of a common friend, on a day when Swift had dined with the distinguished Whig author Rowe. With such sensitive and varied antennae extended on both sides, it was not out of the way for Swift to hold a little breakfast 'levee' and invite Addison and

---

[1] *Journal*, 21 Mar. 1713.

[2] *Ibid.*, 22 Mar. 1713; Williams I. 338–9. I take 'some' (p. 339) to include Swift.

[3] *Journal*, 27 Dec. 1712.   [4] Winton, pp. 159–60.

Steele. Among the few other guests entertained was the sweet-tempered idealist, George Berkeley. Hardly two months in London, on his first visit from Dublin, the young fellow of Trinity College had already met and charmed Steele, who soon made him a contributor to the *Guardian* and introduced him to Pope. Berkeley's finest work for the Whig periodical was to be a series of rebuttals of the same 'free thinking' that Swift had caricatured in his parody of Collins. When the unsophisticated philosopher saw Steele enter the room to join the group, he thought the scene augured a rapprochement of parties. Swift himself only complained, 'I had chocolate twice, which I don't like.'[1]

But a few days later, Swift persuaded Bolingbroke to invite Addison and himself to dinner with some others. 'I suppose we shall be mighty mannerly', was his dour prognostication.[2] It looks as if Swift and the increasingly powerful Secretary thought now the peace stood fixed beyond reversal, those who had set their hopes on obstructing it might feel willing to relax their pressure against the ministry, even perhaps joining in some of the government's manœuvres. Berkeley thought the peace had broken the spirit of the Whigs, and Steele admitted to him that he no longer believed Oxford was plotting to bring in the Pretender.[3] The dinner took place on Good Friday, a week before *Cato* was originally supposed to open; and the company felt congenial enough to stay at Bolingbroke's till midnight. 'We were very civil', Swift reported to the ladies,

> but yet when we grew warm, we talkt in a friendly manner of party. Addison raised his objections, and Lord Bolingbroke answered them with great complaisance. Addison began Lord Sommers health, which went about; but I bid him not name Lord Wharton's for I would not pledge it, and I told Lord Bolingbroke frankly that Addison loved Lord Wharton as little as I did. So we laughed—[4]

The sequel to all this was that on Easter Monday Swift went to a rehearsal of *Cato* at Drury Lane. Swift's old tutor and friend, Bishop Ashe, who happened to be visiting England, was also there. So was Berkeley, another protégé of the bishop, who had

---

[1] *Journal*, 28 Mar. 1713; Luce, p. 65.   [2] *Journal*, 1 Apr. 1713.
[3] Luce, p. 61; Winton, p. 165.   [4] *Journal*, 3 Apr. 1713.

ordained the young author of *A New Theory of Vision* in the College chapel.[1] Addison, with most of his guests, stood on the stage, taking advice from them. The whole occasion was reported to the ladies by Swift in a celebrated account:

> I was this morning at ten at the rehearsall of Mr Addisons play called Cato, which is to be acted on Friday, there were not above half a score of us, to see it; we stood on the stage and it was foolish enough to see the actors promptd every moment, and the poet directing them, and the drab that acts Catos daughter out in the midst of a passionate part, and then calling out, What's next? Bishop of Clogher was there too, but he stood privatly in a gallery.

The afternoon of the same day, Swift dined in private with the anxious playwright.[2]

If all this sounds as though an entente cordiale might be emerging between the Junto and the ministry, a more accurate story transpired during the week that followed. At the Privy Council meeting on Tuesday, the Whig Earl of Cholmondeley, who held the office of Treasurer of the Household, spoke against the peace. A month before, Swift had seen him at Lord Pembroke's, where the bibliophile vicar had gone to look at some 'curious books' and had also run into Berkeley; but even then Swift had resented Cholmondeley's politics so furiously (years afterward he wrote him down as 'good for nothing') that he conspicuously refused to talk to his lordship. Now, the day after the Council and before the opening of Parliament, when 'every body's expectations [were] ready to burst', came the word he was indignantly praying for: Cholmondeley was removed from office; Lieutenant-General Temple, another great spokesman against peace, was turned out as well; and other comprehensive changes showed that Bolingbroke's policy had triumphed. The uniformity which Dr Swift found so attractive in politics as in religion seemed happily strengthened. 'This', he imagined, 'is the first fruits of a friendship I have established between two great men.' But it was only the tortoise avoiding the hawk.[3]

---

[1] Luce, p. 43.

[2] *Journal*, 6 Apr. 1713; the opening of the play was postponed to Tuesday, 14 April. The 'drab' was Mrs Oldfield.

[3] Luce, p. 65; *Journal*, 5 Mar., 7 Apr. (pt 2), 8 Apr. 1713; Davis v. 260.

V. *THE HISTORY OF THE LAST FOUR YEARS*

Swift had hoped to make his own splendid contribution to the final effort for peace in the shape of an exact, reliable account, justifying the process by which his great friends had laboriously arrived at the magnificent goal. Like *The Conduct of the Allies*, which he hoped the new and far longer essay would outshine, he planned his revelation to stand ready for distribution when Parliament met again, this time to approve the treaties now ready at Utrecht.[1] Believing that the stealth and apparent treachery of the ministers' operations had been forced on them by Dutch duplicity and Whig malice, he thought the mere facts of his exposition would establish their patriotic honesty.

It was soon after Parliament rose in the summer of 1712 that he began gathering materials for the work. At first, he expected the new session to open in the autumn; so he rushed himself furiously, tracking the Lord Treasurer from Windsor to London and back in order to keep him available for consultation. 'If I study ever so hard', he told the ladies, 'I believe I can not in that time compass what I am upon.'[2] But so far from speeding his quill, Oxford and Bolingbroke were careless and dilatory. Swift had to break off his labours of research and composition, and wait for them to put in his hands the documents he wanted. 'They delay me as if it were a favor I asked of them.'[3] Then spasms of giddiness held him up for a time, and he suspended the practice of poring his eyes out all morning. Or else Bolingbroke went to Bucklebury to get over his own fever, and set Swift back yet again.[4]

But still he could hope to have the book out in time, because the opening of Parliament had to be postponed too, while the last discussions were nudged hesitantly ahead in Paris. As the autumn advanced, he even boasted to Archbishop King of the discoveries

[1] *Journal*, 12 Oct. 1712.
[2] He first mentions it to Mrs Johnson on 7 August; but he had then not written to her since 19 July; and although the undertaking was obviously recent, Swift may have started even before 19 July: see *Journal*, 7 Aug. 1712. In August he allowed himself 'two months' to complete the book (*loc. cit.*). On the composition of the *History* see G. P. Mayhew, 'Swift's Notes for . . . *Four Last Years*, Book IV', in *HLQ.* XXIV (1961), 311–22.
[3] *Journal*, 15 Sept. 1712.   [4] *Ibid.*, 11 Oct. 1712.

he would publish about the effort of the contemptible Dutch to make a separate peace: 'What I tell your grace is infallibly true; and care shall be taken very soon to satisfy the world in this, and many other particulars at large.'[1] His pace let up a little when he learned that Parliament would be unable to meet till after Christmas, but the exercise of composition remained the sort of tedious, derivative fact-stringing that he loathed. 'I toil like a horse, and have hundreds of letters still to read; and squeeze a line perhaps out of each, or at least the seeds of a line.' He lived in obscure lodgings and avoided society in order to gain time. But only at the end of October was the consummation apparently in sight: 'I have about thirty pages more to write (this is to be extracted) which will be sixty in print.' Three weeks later he felt desperate, but the ministers had not reformed and seemed as uncooperative as ever. 'I have a world of writing to finish: and little time; these toads of ministers are so slow in their helps.' Christmas was now near, but still the scope of the book grew and the mirage only floated farther from his grasp: now he estimated six more weeks at the outside—'I have written 130 pages in folio to be printed, and must write 30 more, which will make a large book of 4s.' He spoke to Gaultier, the French agent; he conferred with Benson, the Chancellor of the Exchequer. But at the end of the year the unfinished project clattered to a halt for a new reason.[2]

During months now, in mortifying suspense, the vicar of Laracor had been waiting to hear of his appointment to some post of ecclesiastical eminence, with his private anxiety running oddly parallel to that of Queen Anne's three kingdoms momentarily expecting notification of the peace. On the verge of the new year, therefore, he told Mrs Johnson that he would go no further with the big book until he felt sure of his own promotion. But the impulse was ambivalent; and at almost the same time he indicated a wish for the book to come out with little delay, for in a new letter to Archbishop King he repeated the familiar allegation against the Dutch and in his old tone called it 'a truth that perhaps the world may be soon informed in, with several others

[1] Williams I. 315 (21 Oct. 1712).
[2] *Journal*, 28 Oct., 18 Nov., 12, 13, 24, 29 Dec. 1712.

that are little known'.[1] Similarly, a few days later, he was again groaning because Oxford and Bolingbroke were holding him back by keeping his 'papers' without reading them. At this point it transpires, in an ironical reversal, that Swift was not alone in his reluctance to go to press. But whereas he hesitated through unwillingness to help those who were letting him down, the others hesitated for exactly the opposite reason, i.e., through fear that the book would not help them: 'Some think it too dangerous to publish', Swift told the ladies, 'and would have me print onely what relates to the peace.'[2]

The furious pressure of the summer was now replaced by bathetic deflation. Not only did the tedium of scholarly compilation turn Swift's stomach, but the repeated proroguing of Parliament dissipated his old spirit of urgency. Meanwhile, the ministers completely failed to secure any bishopric or deanery for him, and the consensus against publication grew still louder. Swift gave a big chunk of the manuscript to the cautious Speaker of the House, Sir Thomas Hanmer, for correction and criticism; he also had Oxford look over the elaborate character of the Lord Treasurer which the manuscript included; but he let weeks go by without bringing the work to a conclusion, and he abandoned the hope of publishing it in time for the new session. Yet with all this he never surrendered his faith in the political value of the enterprise. Writing to Archbishop King a little before the opening of Parliament, he grumbled once more, 'And when the whole story of these two last intriguing years comes to be published, the world will have other notions of our proceedings. This perhaps will not be long untold, and might already have been, if other people had been no wiser than I.'[3]

Only in April, when he believed his preferment was secure, did Swift go back with energy to the unpleasant chore and drag it, after so many halts, to some sort of end. Then when the manuscript seemed possibly finished, he turned over to Hanmer those portions which had not yet been examined by him; and late in

---

[1] *Ibid.*, 29 Dec.; Ball II. 3 (3 or 8 Jan. 1713)—I prefer Ball's text to that in Williams I. 329.

[2] *Journal*, 7, 18 Jan. 1713.   [3] *Ibid.*, 3, 27 Feb. 1713; Williams I. 339.

May he received again from Hanmer a packet which left only the last (and longest) of the four 'books' of the *History* in the Speaker's temporary possession. Now of course Swift was more than eager to see the whole work in print; but the ministers responded to this mood by saying definitely no. Although Hanmer found little to blame, the whole summer passed with no step taken to deliver the *History* to the press.[1]

Against all of Swift's confidence that his elaborate, carefully written study would be of positive value to the government, it is easy for modern hindsight to appreciate the reservations of those who sniffed at his proffered service. In the preface which Swift, as an old man, later composed for the *History*, he had the innocence to say, 'I pretend to write with the utmost impartiality.'[2] But if he ever did contrive to be impartial, this was hardly to be that unique occasion. Of the four 'books' into which he divided the work, much the most interesting is the first and shortest, containing as it does some brilliantly polemical characterizations of the government's chief enemies. This book deals with the crisis of December 1711—its background and consequences; for Swift took that episode as the grand peripety of the struggle for peace. In the next and duller book he reviews the steps in the negotiations among France, Britain, and the Allies as far as the opening of the general peace conference at Utrecht in January 1712. A third, lively, and speciously inaccurate book covers the session of Parliament from the dismissal of Marlborough to the summer of 1712, including a long digression on the history of the national debt and a verbatim transcript of the *Representation* composed by Hanmer and Swift. He also found room here for a larger-than-life portrait of the Lord Treasurer. In his final book Swift follows, through a trackless waste of formalities, stipulations, and counterclaims, the path of the remaining advance toward peace: the empty disputes of the public conference, the mock-campaign of Ormonde and the disastrous campaign of the Allies in Flanders, the direct negotiations between England and France, and the signing of the treaties at Utrecht.

The title which Swift finally attached to the work is an obvious

---

[1] *Journal*, 23 Apr. 1713; Williams I. 351–2 and n. 4.   [2] Davis VII. xxxiv.

misnomer. So far from surveying the four last years of Queen Anne's rule, the *History* concentrates on the events of only sixteen months. And while Swift plentifully includes expository flash-backs, or important documents (accurately transcribed), or else his own quasi-philosophical reflections on details of special inter-est to the author, nevertheless the value of the whole work re-mains corrupted by his common reduction of history to the drama of personalities. In his characteristic way, Swift accounts for events by the motives of the chief agents, and he accounts for their motives by the structure of their passions. As in the *Exam-iner*, he founds the driving emotions of those who hinder the peace upon unenlightened self-interest, or the indulgence of animal instincts, whereas the energy of the peacemakers he derives from the sacrifice of egoism to benevolence. Like the characters of a romance, the sides line up in easily distinguishable dark or bright helmets. As if to enhance this fabulous element, Swift opposes only a single full-scale portrait on the side of virtue to the many on the side of vice. Oxford consequently stands forth in heroic isolation against the crew of vipers whom he miraculously de-feats.[1] Similarly, as if Homer, rather than Thucydides, were his model, he starts his narrative in the midst of a highly dramatic episode and then works backward into the preparatory events, focusing the history on a single brief sequence of actions within the large frame of the whole long war.

If the work fails as history, it hardly succeeds as polemic. The denigration is too assertive; the facts seem neither fresh nor shocking; the several reflections on constitutional issues lie de-tached from the main argument of the whole. If one contrasts the *History* with *The Conduct of the Allies*, the reasons for Swift's ineffec-tuality will appear. In the earlier masterpiece the striking truths were facts which the old ministers, enemies of Oxford's govern-ment, had suppressed. In delivering the simple data, therefore, Swift was exposing the errors of his friends' predecessors. No restraint was needed because any benevolent deeds of Godolphin and his backers had of course been sufficiently celebrated by their own propagandists; so it was most unlikely that new prob-

---

[1] Cf. the imagery of stanza viii of Swift's *Ode to Sir William Temple*.

ing and research would produce fresh information to refurbish their characters. In the *History*, however, he was going over the record of his own patrons. Great tact was essential to cover up their nakedness. He could by no means afford to publish all the shocking story that had unfolded itself behind-scenes. Besides, his own eulogistic matter was far from new. Ministerial journalists had already made the most of it. The Historian could scarcely hope to improve on the Examiner.

If the facts failed Swift in his representation of the domestic scene, his worldly morality weakened him in his treatment of foreign affairs. As Swift repeatedly told Archbishop King, he hoped to defend the ministry against the charge of making a separate peace behind the back of the Dutch, mainly by demonstrating that the Dutch would have liked nothing so well as to make a separate peace behind the back of their ally. Similarly, any complaint against the greed displayed by the British negotiators at the expense of the Allies, Swift hoped to refute by showing that the Dutch and Austrians had tried to make the French grant them advantages at the expense of the British. Unfortunately, an historian cannot effectively condemn a sin in one nation at the precise moment when he is condoning it in another. If the British were therefore to be exonerated for going the way of the world, the author could hardly expect the reader to flame with indignation because the Dutch had set them the example. One ostensibly moral principle Swift does invoke to justify the generous size of Britain's portion: this is the doctrine that those who have done the most for the common cause deserve the largest reward: it was Britain that had won the war for the Grand Alliance; so it was Britain that ought to benefit most from the peace. But unluckily for this logic, Swift implies throughout his *History*, as throughout *The Conduct of the Allies*, that the immense rôle of the British had been their supreme blunder, that the victorious general had been a villain, that the whole war was, from the viewpoint of self-interest, a criminal mistake. In effect, therefore, he suggests that the new ministers have a right to claim the rewards for the apostasies of the old. As fuel for moral indignation, the argument is scarcely combustible.

Whether Swift envisaged his long book as propaganda or as objective history, it was equally essential for the facts to seem reliable. In this department too, however, he could not claim any triumph. We may set aside the accurate texts of speeches and documents, since those which were not easily available elsewhere added no strength to his side. But when he defended the lost bill for resuming royal grants (a scheme directed against those Whigs who had profited from King William's gifts of forfeited lands to his favourites), by claiming that the grantees would have received an advantage, inasmuch as Parliament would only have taxed them three times the annual income of their property and then have established their title in perpetuity, I wonder whom he expected to convince.[1] Or when he said Oxford had probably foreseen and desired that opportunity to create new peers which had resulted from Nottingham's motion against any peace 'without Spain'![2] Today, when details are familiar which neither Swift nor his imagined audience could have known, the texture of his materials looks even thinner. For example, there is the remarkable insinuation against Prince Eugene of Savoy, that his highness had proposed assassination as a means of removing the Earl of Oxford from the leadership of the peace party—

> since it was impossible for him [i.e., Eugene] and his friends to compass their designs while that minister continued at the head of affairs, he proposed an expedient, often practised by those of his country, that the Treasurer (to use his expression) should be taken off *à la negligence*.[3]

In general, Swift's error was his old one of relying on 'inside' information, of trusting what in his preface he called 'the confidence reposed in me ... by the chief persons in power'.[4] Perhaps the best instance of this fallacy of confidential sources will appear in Swift's version of the furtive opening episode of the peace drama. The truth is that Harley in the first instance let Torcy know by way of Gaultier that Britain was inclined to make peace. However, Swift had been told that Torcy was the one who

---

[1] Davis VII. 101. In a letter to Archbishop King, Swift makes the projected tax six times the annual income (Williams I. 301).
[2] Davis VII. 19–20.   [3] *Ibid.*, p. 26.   [4] *Ibid.*, p. xxxiv.

initiated proceedings, by sending a message to London through Gaultier; and this is the fiction Swift offers in his *Four Last Years*. When Archbishop King, corresponding with him, argued against the ministry's treatment of the Dutch during the mock-campaign of 1712, Swift replied, with his own composition of the *Four Last Years* in mind,

> Some accidents and occasions have put it in my way to know every step of this treaty better, I think, than any man in England; and I do assert to your grace that if France had been closely pushed this campaign, they would, upon our refusal, have made offers to Holland, which the Republic would certainly have accepted; and in that case the interests of England would have been wholly laid aside. . . [Two] of the French plenipotentiaries, were wholly inclined to have begun by the Dutch; but the third, Abbé de Polignac, who has most credit with Monsieur Torcy, was for beginning by England . . . it was a mere personal resentment, in the French King and Monsieur Torcy, against the States, which hindered them from sending the first overtures there.[1]

Actually, Swift is here combining two of his characteristic prejudices, one in favour of confidential sources, the other in favour of a psychological analysis of events; for he assumes that Louis XIV would sacrifice immense advantages to his kingdom merely in order to satisfy a quite capricious pique. Inasmuch as the French were responding to English advances, and not vice versa, Swift's whole argument falls to the ground.

Yet there are beauties in the *History*. It contains a number of passages revealing Swift's peculiar views on topics close to him, sometimes contradicting or even censuring the judgment of his ministerial friends. His old fascination with constitutional principles comes out in the discussion of the twelve new creations, the hesitant apology for tacking, and the argument against freedom of expression and religion. His preoccupation with thrift appears in the long account of the national debt. His views on population, anticipating *A Modest Proposal*, are illustrated in an attack on the naturalization law.

Yet the most successful literary ingredients of the whole book are the characters. The meticulous study of Oxford is by no means

[1] Ball ii. 2; I prefer his text of this letter to that of Williams.

a blanket panegyric. Against the radiant setting of elegant praise Swift produces a careful analysis of the Lord Treasurer's public faults, though ignoring such blemishes as his dependence on wine and absolving him from other sins which were really chronic. For the height of Swift's style, of course, one must return to the polemical portraits, handily situated at the beginning of the book. Several of these, such as the Duchess of Marlborough and Willem Buys, lack the refinement of implication that one expects from Swift's best work. But most of them possess inimitable touches. On Sunderland: 'It seems to have been this gentleman's fortune to have learned his divinity from his father, and his politicks from his tutor.' On Wharton: 'He hath imbibed his father's principles in government, but dropt his religion, and took up no other in its stead: excepting that circumstance, he is a firm Presbyterian.' The character of Marlborough I have already singled out as an unexceptionable masterpiece of multiple innuendo and venomous irony. The Duke is accused of avarice and cowardice, megalomania and hypocrisy, treachery and barbarism, in a tone that might be listing the trees in an orchard.

As a supposed aid to easing the treaties through Parliament the defects of the *History* are palpable. It was indeed too 'dangerous' but Swift refused to castrate it.[1] His account of the peace proceedings, though dull enough, would have stirred up inquiries and answers that could only have embarrassed Oxford if they did not disgrace him. The portraits of the Whigs and the abominations attributed to them are openly provocative and would not have smoothed but blocked the way of the treaties in Parliament. Scattered hints in the book and elsewhere suggest that Swift's incendiary passages may reflect the judgment of those who thought the government should open the session with a bitter attack on the opponents of the peace, while the more impersonal, justificatory sections represent the cautious approach of avoiding offence. One almost surely hears Bolingbroke's whisper behind a sentence like the following:

> It will have an odd sound in history, and appear hardly credible
> that in the several petty republicks of single towns which make up

---

[1] Cf. his comment to Arbuthnot, 'they shall never have it again' (Williams II. 47).

the States General, it should be formally debated whether the Queen of Great Britain, who preserved the commonwealth at the charge of so many millions, should be suffered to enjoy after a peace the liberty granted her by Spain of selling African slaves in the Spanish dominions of America.[1]

With the two ministers trying to destroy one another, their disagreement over the value of Swift's *History* would have been enough to keep it from reaching a printer.

[1] Davis VII. 123–4.

Chapter Twenty-five

THE LIFE OF A SPIDER

I. PATRON WITHOUT PREFERMENT

While Swift was joining in the universal suspense over the peace treaties and was writhing in private ignominy over his lack of advancement, he also suffered the normal fate of men known to be close to the rulers of a nation, and found himself petitioned relentlessly to help others wring favours out of patrons. In no aspect of his conduct does Swift's rôle of *hypocrite renversé* make him less amiable than in some uses of the power bestowed on him by his proximity to the chief ministers. One day in the summer of 1711 he was visiting the office of the Secretary of State when Undersecretary Hare recommended to Secretary St John that a man who was to be hanged for rape should be pardoned: Swift's response is hard for even a tolerant reader to allow: 'I told the Secretary', he wrote to the ladies,

> he could not pardon him without a favourable report from the judge; besides, he was a fiddler, and consequently a rogue, and deserved hanging for something else; and so he shall swing. What; I must stand up for the honour of the fair sex? 'Tis true, the fellow had lain with her a hundred times before; but what care I for that? What! must a woman be ravished because she is a whore?[1]

It would be hard to decide which gives more offence, the priest's unasked-for intervention to doom a man about to receive mercy, or the priest's adoption of a rakish tone for reporting the fact. But I still suspect the original incident was less grim than Swift lets it appear in this private, sarcastic report to his most trusted friend. In order to tease and shock Mrs Johnson, he poses as what some readers might call a thick-skinned sadist, perhaps in half-

---

[1] *Journal*, 25 Jul. 1711.

conscious reaction to the manner and the scabrous reputation of
a man like St John.

Almost two and a half years later, White Kennett, a Whig
clergyman who disliked Dr Swift and had been feuding with
Atterbury over the rights of Convocation, gave the following distasteful account of Swift at Windsor with the court:

> Dr. Swift came into the coffeehouse, and had a bow from every
> body but me. When I came to the antechamber to wait before
> prayers, Dr. Swift was the principal man of talk and business, and
> acted as a master of requests. He was soliciting the Earl of Arran to
> speak to his brother the Duke of Ormond, to get a chaplain's place
> established in the garrison of Hull for Mr. Fiddes, a clergyman in
> that neighbourhood, who had lately been in gaol, and published
> sermons to pay fees. He was promising Mr. Thorold to undertake
> with my Lord Treasurer, that, according to his petition, he should
> obtain a salary of 200 per annum, as minister of the English church
> at Rotterdam. He stopped F[rancis] Gwynne, Esq., going in with
> his red bag to the Queen, and told him aloud that he had something
> to say to him from my Lord Treasurer. He talked with the son of
> Dr. Davenant to be sent abroad, and took out his pocket book and
> wrote down several things, as *memoranda*, to do for him. He turned
> to the fire, and took out his gold watch, and, telling him the time of
> the day, complained it was very late. A gentleman said 'he was too
> fast'. 'How can I help it', says the doctor, 'if the courtiers give me a
> watch that won't go right?' Then he instructed a young nobleman,
> that the best poet in England was Mr. Pope (a papist), who had
> begun a translation of Homer into English verse, for which he must
> have them all subscribe; 'for', says he, 'the author *shall not* begin to
> print till *I have* a thousand guineas for him'. Lord Treasurer, after
> leaving the Queen, came through the room beckoning Dr. Swift to
> follow him: both went off just before prayers.[1]

Even allowing for the malicious distortions of an enemy, one cannot offhand, I think, respect the person described here—unless
one considers him to be deliberately overplaying the part of an
insider before an audience generally sympathetic but including
at least one observer proud to be an outsider. Where it is possible
to look on from another point of view, the meaning of a detail
changes dramatically. Thus if Swift seems arrogant in listing
commissions for Henry Davenant to carry out, we should remem-

---

[1] Williams v. 228–9.

ber that the young man was a relation of Swift's (his cousin's nephew) and that Swift was interceding on his behalf with the Lord Treasurer.[1] A more interesting case is Kennett's quotation of Swift's speech about Pope: in this I hear a sneer at the superlative 'best poet', an innuendo against Swift on account of that poet's religion, and incredulous contempt for Swift's boast about the money he would collect. But the young Pope, who had not yet detached himself from Addison's coterie of Whigs, was just launching his Homer: the first proposals had begun to circulate less than a month before Kennett made his notes. Swift had dined with Pope at least twice during those weeks, and I suppose the subscription was the main topic they discussed (with Swift as usual offering abundant advice). A modern witness would probably admire Swift for ignoring the difference in religion between himself and his new friend, and nobody would disagree with his judgment as to the poet's pre-eminence. As for the boastfulness about the Homer, Swift early became the most active promoter of the subscription to Pope's *Iliad*, and his success laid the foundation of a lifelong friendship.[2]

That Swift appreciated and enjoyed his recommendatory powers is endlessly obvious. 'I can serve every body but my self', he said wryly.[3] But like most patrons he tended to exaggerate his influence. For all his obsessional repetitions, there is small evidence that he was any real use to the Whig authors he prided himself on helping. It is also a question who at court genuinely deserved the credit for many of the benefits conferred through his channel. It was normal for a man who performed any favour to tell as many persons as possible that he had done it for their sake. Similarly, a good courtier thanked as many agents as he could for any blessing he received. Yet even if one counts no more than near-certainties, one must feel agreeably impressed by the items of Swift's benevolence on record, especially considering that many more were never mentioned. The vicar of Laracor had, I suspect, known so much humiliation through the failure of great

[1] *Ibid.*, I. 399–400.
[2] Sherburn, *Early Career*, pp. 72, 123. I base my allusion to the two dinners upon imperfectly legible entries in Swift's *Accounts 1712–13*, fol. 13: 20 and 27 Oct. 1713.
[3] *Journal*, 8 Mar. 1712.

men to fulfil their promises that he drove himself to establish a violent contrast in his own performances. It would be hard to say which seems most remarkable, the variety of his efforts, his persistence in getting the desiderata, or the lack of any substantial return to himself for securing them. Surprisingly few of his schemes were merely to serve friends or other men to whom he owed a solid obligation; surprisingly many were on behalf of simple creatures connected with some person he trusted. But the prime objects of his solicitude were literary men, and the main fields in which he planted them were government offices or church livings. When such dignified benefits were not to be had, he tried to provide gifts of money.

Swift showed immense competence in wheedling plain jobs out of his powerful friends, especially Bolingbroke, whom he got to accept the Tory versifier, Joseph Trapp, for his chaplain.[1] Swift had early persuaded the Secretary to appoint Ben Tooke and John Barber as printers of the *Gazette*.[2] Barber had also become printer of the *Examiner* during these years, and normally took care of any odd works by Swift, including *The Conduct of the Allies*. When Lord Rivers succeeded Marlborough as Master of the Ordnance, Swift at once cajoled him into naming Tooke and Barber stationers to the Ordnance:

> He immediately granted it me; but, like an old courtier, told me it was wholly on my account, but that he heard I had intended to engage Mr. Secretary to speak to him, and desired I would engage him to do so; but that however he did it only for my sake.[3]

If Tooke and Barber also requested the privilege of supplying the Ordnance with oil, tallow, etc., Swift merely said, 'I will then grease fat sows', and talked Rivers into allowing them this job as well.[4]

The same kind of person-to-person preferment worked well on behalf of young Berkeley. Of course, with the backing of Bishop

---

[1] *Journal*, 17 Jul. 1712.
[2] *Ibid.*, 26 Jul. 1711; but Steele said Arthur Moore had won the *Gazette* for Barber (Blanchard, p. 48 and n. 1).
[3] *Ibid.*, 5, 15 Jan. 1712. I assume his lordship was also paid off by the grantees.
[4] *Ibid.*, 16, 18 Jan. 1712.

Ashe and the Earl of Pembroke, and the acquaintance of Addison, Steele, Pope, and Parnell, the agreeable author of three important philosophical treatises hardly required a push from Dr Swift to launch him upon London society. But it was the doctor after all who introduced him at court, only two weeks after including him in the select breakfast party. Swift reported the occasion to the ladies:

> I went to court to day on purpose to present Mr. Berkeley one of your fellows of Dublin Colledge, to Lord Berkeley of Stratton. That Mr. Berkeley is a very ingenious man, and great philosopher: and I have mentioned him to all the ministers, and given them some of his writings, and I will favor him as much as I can. This I think I am bound to in honor and conscience, to use all my little credit towards helping forward men of worth in the world.[1]

In the few weeks that remained before Swift went back to summer in Ireland, he dined at least twice with Berkeley and presented him to Arbuthnot.[2] But the greatest kindness he did him was to arrange for the travel-hungry don to enjoy a ten-month tour of France and Italy at negligible expense, because Swift induced the Earl of Peterborough, newly made ambassador to the King of Sicily, to take Berkeley along as his chaplain.[3]

The degree of Swift's persistence in no way depended on the status of the applicant. 'It is my delight', he said, 'to do good offices for people who want and deserve them';[4] and apart from its insipidity the sentiment is not misleading. Esther Johnson's sister Anne had married an incompetent named Filby, a baker who had done badly in his own line and now held a humble post in a salt tax office, at forty pounds a year. Mrs Johnson asked Swift whether he couldn't manage to improve her brother-in-law's income. It was a couple of months before Swift decided which doorbell to ring. Then, while he was in a flurry over Hamilton's duel, he heard from an influential lady that one of the Commissioners of Salt would be the proper person to accomplish what Swift wanted—viz., to raise Filby's salary by fifty per cent. She put him in touch with the commissioner, a former acquain-

---

[1] *Ibid.*, 12 Apr. 1713.   [2] *Ibid.*, 16, 21 Apr.
[3] Luce, p. 66; Williams III. 31.   [4] *Journal*, 11 Oct. 1712.

tance of Swift's named Humphrey Griffith. But when they met at
the lady's residence, Griffith gave him discouraging news about
Filby: 'He said frankly, he had formerly examined the man and
found he understood very little of his business.' If Filby improved,
Griffith promised to supply the increase asked for. Swift told
Griffith he would hold him to the promise, and advised Mrs
Johnson to warn Filby that he must be diligent. Three months
later Swift had stopped thinking about the level of Filby's
efficiency and said he would ask Griffith to produce the rise
'whether he deserves or no'. Seeing the commissioner the next
day, he extracted a new promise, simply to get Filby a better-
paying job. Not knowing where the object of his benevolence
lived, Swift asked Mrs Johnson to write to him: 'Bid him make
no mention of you; but only let Mr. Griffin [Swift's name for
Griffith] know, that he had the honour to be recommended by
Dr. S---- etc., that he will endeavour to deserve etc.; and if you
dictated a whole letter for him it would be better; I hope he can
write and spell well.' It was only a week before Griffith reported
cheerfully that Filby was now to be examined and would receive
a higher post if he seemed capable—'some employment a good
deal better than his own'. But the upshot could not be called
satisfactory; for when the elaborate negotiation was over and
Filby found himself installed in a new job, his salary came to
merely ten pounds a year more than before: 'I wish I could have
done better', Swift said to Mrs Johnson.[1]

This was by no means the most delicate or prolonged of Swift's
negotiations. His projects to help the mournful, bibulous Thomas
Parnell involved Bolingbroke, Oxford, and Archbishop King.
As one turn he contrived to make the Lord Treasurer come up to
Swift at court and ask whether his companion was Dr Parnell.
'[He] spoke to him with great kindness, and invited him to his
house.'[2] Poor William Diaper, the starveling author of some 'sea
eclogues', who was an ill-paid country curate in deacon's orders,
with pretensions to being a gentleman in town, received a pains-

---

[1] *Journal*, p. 563, n. 14; 11 Oct. 1712; 18 Nov. 1712; 20, 21, 28 Feb., 21 Mar.
1713.
[2] *Ibid.*, 31 Jan. 1713.

taking series of attentions from Swift. Though I find no evidence that any great personage was sponsoring Diaper, he became the repeated focus of the doctor's busy solicitations. Money for him was extracted from the Society; and Swift had him confirmed in priest's orders as a preliminary to fixing him in a decent living to be secured from among those in the gift of Lord Keeper Harcourt. When Diaper lay sick in a nasty garret, Swift paid him a visit, bearing a provision of twenty guineas from Bolingbroke. 'Tis a poor little short wretch, but will do best in a gown [i.e., a parson's]', said Swift. And when immediate efforts seemed unfruitful, Swift wrote a gently sympathetic letter of reassurance to Diaper: 'I will move heaven and earth that something may be done for you.'[1]

Of all the ironies in Swift's unconventional career, few seem sharper than the fact that while the bulk of these philanthropies were in progress, he remained himself miserably unsure of his fate. I assume that consciously or not he read his own struggles and despair into the lives of his protégés. In no case did the identification sink deeper than in his fatherly care of William Harrison.[2] Like so many of Swift's clients, Harrison had other backing besides the doctor's. His father was Master of St Cross's Hospital, and Harrison went to nearby Winchester School before continuing the Wykhamist route to New College, where he did well enough to be made a fellow at the age of twenty-one. That same year, 1706, he attracted praise and attention with the appearance of his most important work *Woodstock Park*, a celebration of Marlborough's Oxfordshire seat, in the manner of *Cooper's Hill*. For a while, Harrison was tutor to a son of the Duke of Queensberry, who was then Secretary of State for Scotland; and when he began finding his way in London, he had the advantage of knowing Tickell, a good friend of his at Oxford and an early protégé of Addison. Harrison also knew Edward Young, another ambitious contemporary at Oxford; and perhaps most important of all, he was a kinsman of Henry St John. With these

[1] *Ibid.*, 12, 21 Mar., 23 Dec. 1712; 13 Feb. 1713; Williams I. 345–6.

[2] My account of Harrison is based on R. C. Elliott, 'Swift's "Little" Harrison, Poet and continuator of the *Tatler*', *SP*. XLIV (1949), 544–59; see also Smithers, p. 200.

connections and the usual hopes of a young poet, Harrison easily
drifted into the circle of Addison, whom he had eulogized in *Woodstock Park* and who recommended him to Swift.[1] Short, clever,
and gifted at making himself agreeable, Harrison charmed Swift
when they met in the autumn of 1710; and his Swiftian combination of little income, high social expenses, and slow advancement
easily excited his avuncular friend's indignation:

> There's a young fellow here in town we are all fond of, and about a
> year or two come from the university, one Harrison, a little pretty
> fellow, with a great deal of wit, good sense, and good nature; has
> written some mighty pretty things; that in your 6th *Miscellanea*,
> about the *Sprig of an Orange*, is his: he has nothing to live on but
> being governor to one of the Duke of Queensbury's sons for forty
> pounds a year. The fine fellows are always inviting him to the
> tavern, and make him pay his club. Henley is a great crony of his:
> they are often at the tavern at six or seven shillings reckoning, and
> always makes the poor lad pay his full share. A colonel and a lord
> were at him and me the same way to-night: I absolutely refused,
> and made Harrison lag behind, and persuaded him not to go to
> them. I tell you this, because I find all rich fellows have that
> humour of using all people without any consideration of their
> fortunes; but I'll see them rot before they shall serve me so.[2]

The fact that Harrison was a Whig only spurred Swift on: 'Is not
this a plaguy silly story? But I am vext at the heart; for I love the
young fellow, and am resolved to stir up people to do something
for him.'[3]

Almost three months later, on the very day when Steele suddenly ended the life of his *Tatler*, Swift was supposed to pass an
evening drinking punch with him, Addison, and Harrison, whom
he could now describe as 'a young poet whose fortune I am making'. Steele never showed up, but Swift's proposed road to
Harrison's fortune was probably marked out that evening as the
company discussed the demise of the paper; for the concrete
scheme that Swift offered him during the week that followed was
to write and edit a continuation of the *Tatler*. Other friends had
already delivered the same advice; and Harrison's relation, Secretary St John, joined with Dr Swift in encouraging him and

[1] *Journal*, 4 Feb. 1711. [2] *Ibid.*, 13 Oct. 1710. [3] *Loc. cit.*

elaborating the plan. Yet even while Swift was busy recommending him to the printer—his own cousin Dryden Leach—and helping the two settle their terms, he already felt queasy about Harrison's literary and editorial powers. After going over the first essay in manuscript, he did not gain confidence but groaned, 'I am tired with correcting his trash'; and when the piece came out, he sighed, 'I am afraid the little toad has not the true vein for it.' In a couple of weeks, Harrison broke up with Leach; and by transferring his business to Morphew (publisher of the *Examiner*), he merged another continuation of the *Tatler* with his own. But the project was moribund from the start; and only a month after the merger, when the *Spectator* began to appear, Harrison's doom became fixed. Although Swift revised his protégé's work, contributed essays of his own, and saw his direct efforts supplemented by those of Congreve and Edward Young, there was no remedy for Harrison's ineptitude.[1]

At the same time, though, Swift and St John were negotiating a more promising benefit for their dependent. At one point in the peace talks the illiterate but arrogant Lord Raby was chosen to establish himself at the Hague as ambassador extraordinary; and Harrison was now found worthy to be his secretary. (Perhaps it is more than a coincidence that Harley was staying home at the time, recuperating from Guiscard's attack.) Mr St John, said Swift to the ladies, 'has given me for young Harrison, the Tatler, the prettiest employment in Europe'.[2] It was late April when Harrison sailed, taking fifty guineas with him as a present from the Secretary of State; and a month later his *Tatler*, to nobody's distress, expired.

Swift crowed to the ladies over his new success as a patron: 'An't I a good friend?' he asked. But Harrison met the common afflictions of diplomatic subordinates in all days. Henry Watkins, an old hand at the Hague, was much his senior as Queen's Secretary; and though the newcomer became the ambassador's favourite, he needed all his tact and prudence to stay clear of the difficulties that developed between his two elders, especially since Bolingbroke took a particular interest in the career of Wat-

[1] *Journal*, 2, 11, 13, 15 Jan.; 3, 4, 11, 13 Feb. 1711.   [2] *Ibid.*, 15 Mar. 1711.

kins. But when Harrison superseded his rival in his more valuable
post (March 1712), and Watkins had to leave, it was inevitable
that jealousy and suspicion should break out. An immediately
painful consequence was that the Treasury would issue no funds
on Harrison's account so long as that of Watkins remained out-
standing, and Watkins refused to settle his own. Toward the end
of December 1712 the young secretary's seething frustrations
found expression in a long letter sent to Swift with some Holland
shirts dispatched at his patron's order. Harrison closed his plaint
with a *cri de cœur* which must have dissolved Swift:

> I beg, Dear Sir, the continuance of your kind care and inspection
> over me, and that you would in all respects, command, reprove, or
> instruct me, as a father, for I protest to you, Sir, I do, and ever shall,
> honour and regard you with the affection of a son.[1]

By this time the public centre of the general peace negotiations
had shifted to Utrecht, and a new Barrier Treaty had been drawn
up between the Dutch and the British. It was a token of the goodwill felt by the Secretary of State toward Harrison that he should
be designated to carry the text of this treaty from the United
Provinces to London. But meanwhile, even though Swift had
'teazed their hearts' out of the ministers, they had never paid a
groat of the young man's salary. 'I long to see the little brat', said
Swift—and added, 'my own creature.' Overnight, the wish was
granted; for Harrison had arrived a month after his letter,
utterly penniless, ill, and miserably in debt:

> We talked three hours, and then I carryed him to court. When we
> went down to the door of my lodging; I found a coach waited for
> him, I chid him for it, but he whispered me, it was impossible to do
> otherwise; and in the coach he told me [he] had not one farthing in
> his pocket to pay it; and therefore took the coach for the whole day,
> and intended to borrow money somewhere or other, So there was
> the Queens minister, entrusted in affairs of greatest importance,
> without a shilling in his pocket to pay a coach. I payd him while he
> was with me seven guinneas, in part of a dozen of shirts he bought
> me in Holland. I presented him to the Duke of Ormond, and
> severall lords at court.[2]

[1] *Journal*, 19 Apr. 1711; 12 Mar. 1712; Williams I. 323–6.
[2] *Journal*, 30, 31 Jan. 1713.

It was February in damp, drafty England; Harrison's illness became an inflammation of the lungs, and he turned feverish. His mother and sister looked after him, but he sent a letter asking Swift to come. By the time Swift got there, on a Thursday morning, Harrison was in a decline. Action followed at once. Swift had him moved to Knightsbridge for the air, wrung thirty guineas out of Bolingbroke, and procured a Treasury order for a hundred pounds more, to be paid the next day. But when Swift's man came back from calling at the invalid's lodging, he brought frightening news. 'He is extreamly ill', Swift told the ladies, 'and I very much afflicted for him, for he is my own creature, and in a very honorable post, and very worthy of it. I dined in the City. I am in much concern for this poor lad.'

On Saturday morning, taking Parnell for a companion and carrying a hundred pounds to give Harrison, Swift went to call; he ended a letter to the ladies with an account of what he found:

> I told Parnel I was afraid to knock [at] the door; my mind misgave me. I knockt, and his man in tears told me his master was dead an hour before. Think what grief [this is] to me; I went to his mother, and have been ordering things for his funerall with as little cost as possible, to morrow at ten at night. Lord Treasurer was much concerned when I told him. I could not dine with Lord Treasurer nor any where, but got a bit of meat towards evening. no loss ever grieved me so much. poor creature.—Pray God almighty bless poor Md—adieu—
>
> I send this away to night and am sorry it must go while I am in so much grief.

The funeral was Sunday night at ten o'clock, and dismally in a rain. Harrison's mother and sister rode in the single coach with Swift and his man. But at the funeral, Addison and Philips also appeared. On the way back afterwards, to blacken the darkness, the braces of the coach broke; and Swift and the women had to wait in it at eleven o'clock with the rain streaming down. His man went out and brought back sedan chairs for them. Swift got home 'very melancholy', paid his chairman a shilling, and went to bed. The next day he tried to chase away grief by dining out in company; yet he had to leave early and at home turned to a book in

[617]

the hope of diversion. But at last (with little prescience) he wrote to the ladies, 'I shall never have courage again for making any body's fortune.' Meanwhile, Bolingbroke had discovered the right person to replace Harrison as Queen's Secretary at Utrecht, viz., his own half-brother, George St John.[1]

II. DEAN SWIFT

In his letter to Swift from Utrecht, poor Harrison had said that no news would please him so much as word of Swift's advancement: 'It grieves me to the soul that a person, who has been so instrumental to the raising of me from obscurity and distress, should not be yet set above the power of fortune.'[2] Although Swift's gloom over the same fact was profound, he could not have expressed it so simply. Even to himself, Swift had trouble admitting how bitterly he yearned for visible success in his career as a priest. Once a man has identified virtue with failure, he is condemned to moral discomfort unless promotion is thrust upon him. With his sceptical analysis of motivation, Swift could hardly shove a hand out for rewards if he did not wish to throw withering suspicion upon his record of service. Quite apart from the issue of virtue stood the needs of his dignity. To vindicate his confidence in the ministers, he had to believe they would not require him to wriggle and crawl as ambition usually did. The new leaders might leave him as naked as the old; but they would never, he hoped, insist on his acting the ignominious, self-advancing rôle that Somers and Halifax had been content to observe. They would never, he hoped, abandon him to the doubled sneer of his enemies—that he had finally shoved and grabbed like the rest, and that his friends had handled him like the rest.

From the start of his long stay in England, Swift was set upon conserving his outward dignity, no matter what disappointment he might finally face. I don't think he ever reckoned with the

---

[1] *Journal*, 12–16 Feb. 1713. I assume that Mrs and Miss Harrison were in the coach with Swift and his man because Swift says that 'four of us' were in it (15 Feb.). For the presence of Addison and Philips see the *Wentworth Papers*, p. 319. The shilling for the chair is recorded in Swift's *Accounts 1712–13*.

[2] Williams I. 325.

chance that despair might make the proudest man struggle openly for a post he could not regard as enviable. It took him two and a half humbling years to discover that so far from coming on one's own terms, success of the sort he desired rarely meets a man except in a form mingled with self-contempt. An inner conflict between Swift's acute ambition and his ideal of integrity, an outer conflict between dignity and despair, operated to narrow the course of his approach to preferment.

We are hardly surprised therefore to hear inconsistent statements overtake one another as Swift gives voice to opposing moods. For months, caution and self-denial had been in the ascendant, with bitterness breaking through. 'Every body asks me, how I came to be so long in Ireland', he wrote in his very first letter from London, 'as naturally as if here were my *being*; but no soul offers to make it so.' Even before meeting Harley, he had expected 'good usage' from him, and reported that some Tories said Swift could now make his fortune if he pleased—upon which he commented, 'But I do not understand them, or rather, I do understand them.' During this short interlude he could still say he felt disengaged; and still after writing five *Examiners*, he remained cautious, trying to keep public service before personal gain. The new ministers might be no more 'grateful' than the others, he said; but 'according to the best judgment I have, they are pursuing the best interest of the public; and therefore I am glad to contribute what is in my power.'[1]

Midway in his career as Examiner, when he could appreciate the difficulties of the ministry and the ambiguity of his own hopes, Swift's underside showed itself. He suddenly admitted that his motives were oddly mixed, and promised Mrs Johnson that if this stay in England failed, he would not try again:

[Poor Pdfr] has not had one happy day since he left you, as hope saved.—It is the last sally I will ever make, but I hope it will turn to some account. I have done more for these [*sc.* ministers], and I think they are more honest than the last; however, I will not be disappointed. I would make MD and me easy; and I never desired more.

[1] *Journal*, 9, 30 Sept., 1 Oct., 30 Nov. 1710.

Gradually and unevenly, his tone shifted. As the first winter turned to spring, he changed from the suppression of all expectancy to the bracing of his character against the dashing of radical hope; from saying he did not count upon his new friends' promises to feeling that so much cordiality could not be without consequence. He could still rise to a pitch of noble scepticism:

> They call me nothing but Jonathan; and I said, I believed they would leave me Jonathan as they found me; and that I never knew a ministry do any thing for those whom they make companions of their pleasures.

But cheerfulness would break through, and he had to watch the spontaneous growth of visions he must be always prepared to destroy:

> I have been used barbarously by the late ministry; I am a little piqued in honour to let people see I am not to be despised. The assurances they [i.e., Harley and his colleagues] give me, without any scruple or provocation, are such as are usually believed in the world; they may come to nothing, but the first opportunity that offers, and is neglected, I shall depend no more, but come away.[1]

Swift's insistence on independence became his most vulnerable feature. Johnson only exaggerated a genuine insight when he said, 'No man ... can pay a more servile tribute to the great, than by suffering his liberty in their presence to aggrandize him in his own esteem.'[2] Swift failed to see that men with four- and five-figure incomes could never be as open with him as they were in their own society. By not demanding a payment, Swift imagined he would win a man-to-man respect that could not exist between patron and client. I believe he hoped that integrity and charm would produce a stronger tie than services yet unrendered; and I think he was wrong. Too many petitioners were flinging themselves upon Harley, I think, for him to feel anything but relief at Swift's not insisting on an immediate plum. The example of Addison, who kept the highest reputation for probity without once faltering in a career of place-seeking and time-serving, should have taught Swift how to behave. His elemental fear of hypocrisy failed him when it was most needed. He never liked to

[1] *Journal*, 16, 24 Jan., 17 Feb., 5 Apr. 1711.   [2] *Life of Swift*.

believe that he shared, in quite its full strength, the essential need of common humanity to be paid for work done. But in mid-spring 1711, with the end of his term as Examiner in sight, he exposed his feelings more freely; and when the Earl of Peterborough pressed him, Swift was willing to estimate the fee he thought he deserved, in the knowledge (I suppose) that others would receive the bill from his lordship: 'My ambition', he told Peterborough, 'is to live in England, and with a competency to support me with honour. The ministry know by this time whether I am worth keeping; and it is easier to provide for ten men in the church, than one in a civil employment.'[1]

A few weeks later, impatience superseded resignation as the tone of his remarks on the subject to Mrs Johnson. In the bitterness of his outburst he of course implies a compliment to the lady whom he misses. But he is also venting an emotion which the delay of profound desires had steadily poisoned. 'To return without some mark of distinction would look extremely little', he said three weeks before Parliament was due to rise; 'and I would likewise gladly be somewhat richer than I am.' He admitted feeling gloomy and declared that all the pleasures of London were soured by his ordeal of suspense: 'Every thing here is tasteless to me for want of being as I would be.'

Once the ministers began dealing directly with his hints, a tantalizing era opened of contradictory rumours about his preferment. If Swift had imagined that his heightened pressure would shame them into freeing him from anxiety, he was soon enlightened. Harcourt had declared he would present Swift to a living in the gift of the Lord Keeper; but Swift refused—I assume, because he was looking for something better than Harcourt could ever offer. St John, without even asking Swift, turned down a possibility in his name. Already it was full summer 1711, and work on *The Conduct of the Allies* was about to begin. Meanwhile, bitterness, suspense, and frustration were creating a mixture very hard for pride to digest; and when Mrs Johnson asked her usual question about Swift's prospects, he replied,

I had no offers of any living. Lord Keeper told me some months

[1] Williams I. 227 (4 May 1711).

ago, he would give me one when I pleased; but I told him, I would not take any from him: and the Secretary told me t'other day, he had refused a very good one for me; but it was a place he did not like, and I know nothing of getting anything here, and, if they would give me leave, I would come over just now.

As the significance of Oxford's quarrel with St John sank in, Swift wondered still more grimly what might lie ahead for himself; and he told Ford that though everybody else expected something handsome to come from his closeness to the ministers, he did not. Having launched the *Conduct*, however, he decided to make that the terminus of his plans. Whatever the great men might offer him would surely be visible by the time that had done its work. When the officious Archbishop King, meanwhile, with sublime insensitivity, urged him to get himself some post good enough to 'make a man easy', Swift with less candour than panache said he was indifferent to his fortune: he would leave the ministers to act as they pleased, he wrote, and would never solicit for himself. And he assured Mrs Johnson he was quite prepared to retire to his 'old circumstances'.[1]

Only after the publication and unparalleled success of the *Conduct* does the final, longest, and most brutal period of Swift's trial start. The fifteen months of European suspense over the peace negotiations were to be almost coterminous with Swift's suffocating humiliation over his preferment. Just as the official Congress of Powers was lodging itself in Utrecht, the Dean of Wells died and left an excellent English preferment vacant. Immediately, Swift sent a note to the Lord Treasurer, informing him of the event and adding, 'I entirely submit my good fortune to your lordship.'[2] For a man who would not solicit for himself, this was going pretty far. But it was not far enough. What Bolingbroke was to call the 'ultimate end' of Oxford's administration was being carefully perfected at this time, viz., the marriage of the Lord Treasurer's son to the daughter of the late Duke of Newcastle; and his late grace's chaplain, Matthew Brailsford, was among the several clergymen who made themselves conspicu-

---

[1] *Journal*, 23 May, 17 Jul., 25 Aug., 29 Sept. 1711; Williams I. 254, 259, 262; *Journal*, 22 Oct. 1711.
[2] Williams I. 288.

ously available for the deanery of Wells. There were also objections to Swift at court. If we may trust the evidence, both the Archbishop of York and the Duchess of Somerset had warned her majesty against the character of Dr Swift.[1] Others were not wanting to discredit a man who had discredited so many. 'I have many friends and many enemies', Swift said; 'and the last are more constant in their nature.'[2]

From the talk of the ministers themselves, Swift could distill no definite information about the deanery of Wells though weeks and months went by. But to his agonized embarrassment, other men steadily heard and carelessly repeated the probable rumour that the government's brilliant chief propagandist had already received this decent recognition. Even in Ireland Mrs Johnson heard it, and inevitably questioned Swift, who snapped with exasperation, 'No—if you will have it, I am not Dean of Wells, nor know any thing of being so.' In March the deanery of Ely also became vacant by death; and Swift must have added reflections on this event to his fading hopes of Wells. He began serious preparations to visit Ireland but was struck down by the grotesque attack of shingles; and when he recovered, he said he could not leave England 'in prudence or honour' so long as 'a business' remained undetermined. He would get out the moment he felt himself 'used ill'; but he had to stay through the suspense. Now, in the spring of 1712, he innocently imagined that peace would be made soon: 'and then there will be no further occasion for me, nor have I anything to trust but court gratitude'. A few weeks later he poohpoohed the idea that he might linger in London through the summer; and by now a third deanery, that of Lichfield was vacant, again through death. But a month still later, in midsummer, Swift repeated the forlorn cry that had risen to his lips so often since he left Ireland: 'I wish I had never come here ... what had I to do here?'[3]

The rumour about Swift and Wells had persisted in Dublin, and Swift underwent the ignominy of receiving Archbishop King's tentative congratulations on a promotion that had never

---

[1] A. T. Hart, *Life and Times of John Sharp*, 1949, p. 103. Cf. Winton (cited above, p. 521, n. 1).

[2] *Journal*, 22 Oct. 1711.   [3] *Ibid.*, 21 Mar., 31 May, 17 Jun., 17 Jul. 1712.

been granted. Hugging his dignity, Swift waited an ample period before answering, but then had to admit that nothing yet had come his way. In a series of balanced statements whose cumulative ambiguity should, I suppose, have guarded him against any turn of events, Swift indicated that he expected nothing but knew no reason to be fearful: 'I am not very warm in my expectations, and know courts too well to be surprised at disappointments.'[1] The true violence of his smothered emotions broke loose when Mrs Johnson innocently supposed he was (as so often) teasing her, and took the rumour as fact, telling him so in a letter which happened to arrive while Bolingbroke was visiting France and Swift was beginning to compose his *History of the Four Last Years*. After saying he had received the letter, Swift let himself explode:

> I just read it, and immediately sealed it up again, and shall read it no more this twelvemonth at least. the reason of my resentment at it is, because you talk as glibly of a thing as if it were done, which for ought I know, is further from being done than ever, since I hear not a word of it; though the town is full of it, and the court always giving me joy and vexation. You might be sure I would have let you know as soon as it was done; but I believe you fancyed I would affect not to tell it you, but let you learn it from news papers, and reports.

Soon it was the edge of autumn, and Swift endured several frightening fits of vertigo. He found himself sick three or four days in a row—'ready to totter as I walked'. He took dozens of pills, swallowed bitter drinks, and lasted out another maddening term of impotent suspense.[2] Now he fixed the date of his departure for Ireland at the moment when he should discover that any one of the vacant deaneries had been given to somebody else. What survived of his macerated pride dropped so low that he groaned to Mrs Johnson,

> I have expected from one week to another, that something would be done in my own affairs, but nothing at all is nor I dont know when any thing will, or whether ever at all . . .

Swift always hated to admit that he felt downcast or unhappy, and insisted that he was cheerful by nature. So in his sociable, amusing, scolding manner he met the Lord Treasurer as usual

---

[1] Williams 1. 308, 316.   [2] *Journal*, 7 Aug.; 15, 18 Sept. 1712.

but avoided requesting favours for anybody.[1]

Now at last a streak of light glimmered through a new door-way. Early in the autumn the eccentric Bishop Pooley of Raphoe in Ireland had died. From Marmaduke Coghill, an Irish judge and a friend of Swift's (who had seen him in London when the rumour about Wells was first spreading), came a suggestion that seemed practicable. Coghill pointed out that if Swift could per-suade the government to make Dean Stearne the new Bishop of Raphoe, he would leave the deanery of St Patrick's Cathedral vacant for himself. Hearing this proposal, Swift would have real-ized that it contained several hopeful factors. Though he dearly desired to live out his years in England, an Irish preferment was easier to secure than an English one; and while a bishopric would have required the unlikely consent of the crown, the deanery was in the gift of Swift's 'brother' and Lord Lieutenant, the Duke of Ormonde. Besides, Archbishop King, as the affectionate friend and patron of Stearne, would be glad to see his ally seated on the episcopal bench. Finally, if the deanery of St Patrick's should be made vacant through a promotion, the government would have the right to present the new dean, and the chapter's desires would be without force. Swift held too many grudges against Stearne to thrill with pleasure at the idea of helping him. But he told Mrs Johnson at once that if he were asked who would make a good bishop, he would name Stearne; and in actual deeds he went much further to press the claims of his erstwhile friend.[2]

As autumn darkened into winter, Swift still turned easily from brooding over his doom to playing the convivial courtier. He could even joke with Lady Orkney (whom he must have told about his worries) over the staggering length of his wait; for when she gave him an elaborate and hardly portable writing table, he said, 'You have more contributed towards fixing me, than all the ministry together.' But as if to tinge the whole scene with the colours of farce, this was the interval when the egregious Arch-bishop of Dublin suddenly chose to urge Swift to lay aside his modesty and push hard for a preferment that would make him

[1] *Ibid.*, 15 Sept.. 11 Oct.

[2] For Queen Anne's view; see Winton (cited above, p. 521, n. 1), pp. 148-9.

comfortable! In a letter that sounds callous even for an Irish bishop, King warned Swift to 'make hay whilst the sun shines'. Naturally, his grace was happy to relieve himself of any responsibility for the vicar of Laracor, and certainly did not relish Swift's coming home with a revived claim on the Archbishop's distribution of benefices.[1]

Meanwhile, once Ireland had become a possibility for Swift, not only the Lord Lieutenant but the Queen was involved, because it was her majesty's duty to approve the choice of Stearne as a bishop. Luckily for Swift, the Duke of Ormonde was in reality his own warm and sincere friend; but unluckily for the great negotiation, the Duke liked neither Stearne nor King. By a curious definition of 'solicit', Swift could tell Coghill that he was soliciting nothing anywhere, though at the same time he carefully named Stearne to Oxford, Bolingbroke, and Ormonde as a good man for a bishopric; and he told Mrs Johnson, 'I did it heartily.' By now the deanery of Wells had stood vacant for a year, and Swift's shyness had thinned to transparency. He had lost most of his pride about advertising his desires and—rather pathetically —threatened the ministers with a refusal to publish his *History* unless the government that was to benefit from it found him a place: 'I will contract no more enemyes, at least I will not imbitter worse those I have already, till I have got under shelter.' Through the winter of 1712–13, Oxford only irritated him by demanding to see him more often. 'Mighty kind with a p[ox]', Swift snarled to Mrs Johnson, '—less of civility and more of his interest.'

The death of another Irish bishop, Pullein of Dromore, gave Swift further room for his elaborate manœuvres; for if they refused to give Raphoe to Stearne, they might grant him Dromore. Then, like an adverse omen, came the fate of Swift's beloved young Harrison. He could hardly have escaped linking such a disaster to the failure of his own hopes. But even after this bleak, late event, the suspense went on. Still at the end of February nothing was decided; and when the Treasurer scolded Swift because he had not dined with him for three days running, Swift

[1] *Journal*, 28 Oct. 1712 and n. 4; Williams I. 320, 318.

growled to Mrs Johnson, 'What will this come to—nothing.'[1]

False reports continued to multiply and circulate while Swift denied them. 'Talk not to me of deanry's', he told Mrs Johnson, 'I know less of that than ever by much.' Among the Irish visitors whom he often saw, in the spring of 1713 was his old friend the bon vivant Benjamin Pratt, who had been an undergraduate with him. Now an unpopular Provost of Trinity College, Dublin, Pratt fanned the winds of gossip by aspiring to one of the vacant Irish bishoprics. Immediately, speculators went to work canvassing the list of possible successors, and Swift had to assure Mrs Johnson that he was not on the road to becoming the new provost. Then people said Swift was to be Master of the Savoy, and he had to discourage yet another file of well-wishers.[2]

Hardly any aspect of this purgatorial affair seems more impressive than Swift's resistance to despair. His congenital power of mixing playfulness with gloom did not desert him. 'I have not the spleen', he had told Mrs Johnson in the autumn of 1712; 'for that they can never give me though I have as much provocation to it as any man alive.'[3] It was in the midst of one of the worst trials of his patience that he struck George Berkeley as 'one of the best natured and agreeable men in the world'.[4] One of the funniest letters Swift ever wrote belongs to this period. Sir Andrew Fountaine had asked Swift to join him in accepting an invitation to dinner at Mrs Vanhomrigh's; and Swift, in what reads like a parody of Justice Shallow, accepted; as the letter-writer, he plays the rôle of a moronically naïve, timorous bumpkin who takes compliments seriously and cannot understand irony—

> Now as to what you say of hoping I will excuse your boldness and the trouble: I do not take it in good part that you should please to think that anything that you think to command me in is any boldness or trouble. I hope I am better bred than so, and that I know how to behave myself to my betters as well as another.[5]

As All Fools' Day approached, Swift felt sufficiently disengaged to join in another epistolary joke. Bishop Ashe, visiting London

---

[1] *Journal*, 4 Feb. 1713; 29, 26 Dec. 1712; 25 Feb. 1713. The Bishop of Dromore died 22 January 1713.

[2] *Ibid.*, 1, 5, 20 Mar. 1713.   [3] *Ibid.*, 18 Sept. 1712.   [4] Luce, p. 65.

[5] Williams I. 336.

with the rest of Ireland, had told Fountaine and Swift a riddle that he was proud of inventing: 'If there was a hackney coach at Mr. Pooley's door, what town in Egypt would it be?' The answer, I'm afraid, is *Hecatompolis*. The bishop liked his invention so much that he decided to send it to his brother Tom Ashe in Dublin. But Swift and Lord Pembroke made Fountaine trick him by writing ahead of time to Tom and asking him to send the pun to the bishop as his own. The plot succeeded; and soon the bishop told Pembroke that he wondered how he and his brother Tom could have hit on the same odd thing at the same time.[1] Swift's own exercise on 1 April was less successful. He persuaded Arbuthnot and Lady Masham to join the game with him, and they were all to send their servants out, asking various friends whether it was true that Richard Noble, hanged the week before, had in fact been rescued by his friends. Even though Swift had his own man go to several houses (without knowing the secret himself), the story never caught on, and nobody was 'bit'.[2]

In less than two weeks, however, Swift touched his nadir of frustration. He wrote a highly confidential letter to Stearne, making quite sure the candidate for a bishopric understood what was under way. But almost a week later, on the day after Swift presented Berkeley at court, he received the worst possible news from Erasmus Lewis. In spite of all his hints, in spite of all his fencing, the insult he most feared had arrived. Not only were the three English deaneries given to others—Wells went to Brailsford —but Oxford, for whom he had just finished the Lords' address of thanks, had failed to warn him beforehand. Lewis, who was an undersecretary of state in Lord Dartmouth's office, came to see Swift at ten o'clock in the morning of Monday, 13 April, and showed him Dartmouth's order for a warrant for the deaneries. 'This is what I always foresaw', Swift wrote to Mrs Johnson. Still, a vestige of dignity survived: he asked Lewis to tell Oxford that he blamed him only for not giving Swift timely notice.

At noon on the same day an undignified peripety began. Hearing that Swift was in Lewis's office, Oxford came around, and said 'many things too long to repeat'. But Swift clung to his plan:

[1] *Journal*, 19 Mar., 4 Apr. 1713.   [2] *Ibid.*, 31 Mar., 1 Apr.

'I told him I had nothing to do but go to Ireland immediately, for I could not with any reputation stay longer here, unless I had something honorable immediately given to me.' Later in the day they both dined with the Duke of Ormonde, and Oxford announced that he had stopped the warrants, because he wished to settle Swift's preferment at the same time as the others; and he hoped to manage everything by that very night—on which Swift commented, 'But I believe him not.' Swift told Ormonde his plan for Stearne to be a bishop so he himself might have the deanery of St Patrick's, and the Duke agreed. 'But I believe nothing will come of it', Swift added.[1]

The next day, Tuesday, Swift began arranging to depart. As soon as he heard the warrants were released, he said, he would move from the court end of town to the City, where condolers could not annoy him; and then he would set out for Ireland. Again Oxford told Lewis that Swift's appointment would be fixed that night. Swift commented, 'So he will for a hundred nights.' On Wednesday Swift dined with Bolingbroke, making himself 'as good company as ever'. Now, he was informed by the Secretary, the delay was about whether he should be Dean of St Patrick's or a prebendary of Windsor. On Thursday he saw Lady Masham, who was already distraught over the illness of her eldest son. Telling Swift how she had spoken of him both to the Lord Treasurer and to the Queen, she broke into tears. Swift reported, 'She could not bear to think of my having St. Patrick's.' Lewis saw him again and corroborated Bolingbroke's story, saying the Duke of Ormonde had seen the Queen that day, and she had agreed to let Stearne be made Bishop of Dromore (not Raphoe) and Swift Dean of St Patrick's, but that Oxford had insisted on Swift's having a prebend of Windsor. 'I expect neither', said Swift: 'but I confess, as much as I love England, I am so angry at this treatment, that if I had my choice I would rather have St. Patrick's.'[2] Meanwhile, not Stearne but another man was named to be Bishop of Raphoe.

Not until Saturday was he summoned to the Lord Treasurer's lodgings in St James's Palace and told that her majesty had made

[1] *Ibid.*, 13 Apr.   [2] *Ibid.*, 14-16 Apr.

up her mind to give Stearne his bishopric and Swift his deanery. But that evening, he wrote to Mrs Johnson, 'I do not know whether it will yet be done, some unlucky accident may yet come; neither can I feel joy at passing my days in Ireland: and I confess I thought the ministry would not let me go; but perhaps they can't help it.'

Then Sunday brought a formidable reversal that could hardly have been looked for at this stage. The Queen said she could not definitely approve of Stearne's elevation till she knew Ormonde consented. Swift therefore went to see his grace in Whitehall and asked him to tell the Queen he did approve of Stearne. But now of all times Ormonde demurred. 'He made objections, desired I would name any other deanery, for he did not like Stearne, that Stearne never went to see him, that he was influenced by the Archbishop of Dublin etc.; so all is now broken again.' Swift at once told this latest story to Oxford, who made reassuring remarks which did not reassure Swift.

The ultimate reversal took place on Monday, a week after Lewis had shown Dartmouth's order to Swift. Going to see Ormonde at the Cockpit, Swift found him still ready to offer himself any deanery except Stearne's. Finally, Swift altered his tactics and triumphed: 'I desired, he would put me out of the case, and do as he pleased; then with great kindness he said he would consent, but would do it for no man alive but me.' Keeping his promise the next day, Ormonde gave the Queen the message, and she effectively consented to let Swift be a dean. Too uncomfortable to sit among ministers, Swift refused to dine with Lord Dartmouth although (or perhaps because) Oxford was to be there. 'I said I would if I were out of suspense.' Instead, he spent two shillings at an alehouse with Berkeley and Parnell. But already the news was spreading. Bolingbroke had told Dean Atterbury on Monday, and before noon on Tuesday Swift received a note assuring him that no man in England felt more pleased than Atterbury.[1]

If the immense nightmare was over, a number of palpitations lingered. After sixty-odd weeks of hovering, Swift felt in no con-

[1] *Journal*, 18–21 Apr.; *Accounts 1712–13*, fol. 8; Williams I. 344.

dition to trust solid ground. The Queen might change; the Duchess of Somerset might step in. He could not begin to feel secure until his formal warrant was signed and sent; he could not finally relax until his actual installation was over. Yet now he heard that the Queen would sign no single warrant until all five —for the deaneries in England and the two bishoprics in Ireland —were brought to her together, after which Ormonde could sign the particular warrant for Swift. This decision caused a new tremor and further delay. But by the time all the signing was over and Swift could say, 'I think tis now past', his anxiety had only given way to a characteristic depreciation of his victory. Unable to let himself simply enjoy contemplating the fulfilment of his hopes, Swift began to reckon up the distasteful expenses and fees that his promotion involved—buying the dean's house, for example, and paying the First Fruits. He imagined it would take three years for him to pay off the debt, for he vastly underestimated the value of the deanery. Writing to Coghill at once, Swift asked him to take care of the passing of Swift's patent in Ireland, so that no obstruction might arise there. Though he also begged Mrs Johnson to comfort him with a 'good humored letter', he let some feeling of triumph slip through by quoting his friends' remark that Swift had made a bishop in spite of all the world, to get the best deanery in Ireland. In his account book, at the top of the page for April, he had written, 'ubi nunc?' After this he wrote, '–23d Warrant signd, sent 25th'.

Yet even so incredibly late as 25 April there had been a small crisis. Thomas Lindsay, who was being translated to the bishopric of Raphoe, did not wish to lose the income accruing there since the death of his predecessor. As he happened now to be in London, he told the clerk responsible for posting the warrants to stop them until Lindsay could secure an order for that money. Swift heard about this delay from Lewis and went himself to make inquiries. But meanwhile the order came from Lewis to the clerk to disregard Lindsay; and so the warrants were put in the post. Now Swift fretted because it was too late for his own letter to reach Mrs Johnson before the news of the warrant would. That afternoon, however, he dined again with Oxford and his Saturday guests, and had the satisfaction of hearing everyone call him 'Dean'. And the next day, at St James's, the congratulations were so profuse that they overcame him: 'I was at court to day; and a thousand people gave me joy, so I ran out.'[1]

I think it was not until 16 May that Swift heard his patent had been passed in Ireland[2]—after which no further step could be taken before he went over to be installed. But in his account book, at the top of the page for May, he wrote a cryptic note which I read as a sign of the anxiety he felt on 6 May because of what he called *red thing*: 'ubi nunc? –6. ibid sed dubi ne. ob Red Sing.' I conjecture that the red-headed Duchess of Somerset was the red thing, and that Swift suddenly heard of some new move she had made to block his promotion, a move which was of course ineffectual. If this is so, it turns us at once to the question of who did advise the Queen against giving him an English deanery. Swift blamed the Duchess and Archbishop Sharp, and I take these to be the only serious candidates for the agency.[3] The day the Queen signed the warrants, Swift told Mrs Johnson that the Archbishop of York wished to meet him: 'A. Bp York, my mortall enemy, has sent by a third hand that he would be glad to see me; Shall I see him or not?' They never did meet,[4] but on Sunday, after telling Mrs Johnson that he had dined with the Saturday club the day before, Swift added, 'A.B. York says he will never more speak against me.' In a poem he composed a year later, Swift wrote,

> York is from Lambeth sent, to shew the Queen
> A dang'rous treatise writ against the spleen;
> Which by the style, the matter, and the drift,
> 'Tis thought could be the work of none but S[wift]
> Poor York! the harmless tool of others hate;
> He sues for pardon, and repents too late.[5]

---

[1] *Journal*, 22–26 Apr. 1713.

[2] I read a note at the top of the page for May in the account book for 1712–13 (fol. 9ᵛ) as '–16. heard Patent past'.

[3] See *Poems* I. 191–6. Bolingbroke's statement to William King of St Mary Hall, blaming the Lord Treasurer alone, I take to express only his old hatred of Oxford.

[4] *Journal*, 23 Apr. 1713. My inference that they never met is drawn from Swift's note to line 52 of *The Author upon Himself*; this note, which Swift wrote long after the event, sounds like one of the gross exaggerations of his old age.

[5] *Journal*, 23, 26 Apr. 1713; *Poems* I. 195.

Whether or not Archbishop Sharp actually showed Queen Anne *A Tale of a Tub*, it was general gossip that he opposed Swift's advancement[1]; and as early as 1714 Abel Boyer put the story into print, asserting that Sharp had

> strenuously opposed the promotion of Dr. Swift, one of [the Tory ministers'] *prostituted tools* to a deanry in England: Having, with becoming firmness, represented above [i.e., to the Queen], what a scandal it would be, both to church and state, to bestow such a distinguish'd preferment upon a *clergy-man*, who was hardly suspected of being a Christian?[2]

I see no reason to contradict the received story, though I intuitively doubt that Sharp either regretted giving his advice or strove to justify himself to Swift.

The case against the Duchess seems weaker. She had no reason to love the author of the *Windsor Prophecy*, and Swift's natural fear of those he maligned made it easy for him to swallow the rumours of her vengefulness. But even apart from his suspicions and inferences, some evidence appears that her word counted: more than a year after Swift became Dean, his friend John Barber, who was intimate with Bolingbroke, wrote to him, 'L[ord] B[olingbroke] told me . . . he would reconcile you to Lady S[omerset] and then it would be easy to set you right with the Q[ueen] and that you should be made easy here [i.e., in England], and not go over [i.e., to Ireland].'[3] Unless there was a conspiracy to create evidence against her grace, a remark like Barber's can only mean that the courtiers, including Lady Masham, agreed with Swift's view.

If Swift felt his defeat of these enemies meant a victory, he did not much enjoy it. In return for twelve years of deferred hope followed by fourteen months of grinding doubt, what recognition could possibly seem adequate? Certainly not a post delivering a

---

[1] Hart, *Life of Sharp*, p. 103 and n. 2.

[2] *Political State*, 2nd ed., 1719, VII. 183; in the 1714 text Boyer omits Swift's name; see also Firth, pp. 12–13.

[3] Williams II. 100. In the summer of 1711 Oxford and St John told Swift they had been talking about him to the Queen, and she said she had never heard of him. Unless their story was fiction, it implies that Sharp had not yet spoken against Swift. Possibly the ministers were recommending him for a preferment, and possibly it was after this that her majesty consulted Sharp. (*Journal*, 6 Aug. 1711.)

man back to a country he had been trying to avoid. 'I am condemned to live again in Ireland', Swift wrote to his protégé Diaper, 'and all that the court and ministry did for me, was to let me chuse my station in the country where I am banished.'[1]

---

[1] Williams I. 345–6. Some Tory churchmen considered Swift to be Whiggish, and were unhappy with his rise. The Whig Robert Molesworth said Swift's promotion 'vexes the godly party' (28 Apr. 1713; H.M.C. *Var. Coll.* VIII [1913], 262). One of the 'godly' told a friend that the clergy of Ireland detested Swift for being an enemy to episcopacy: 'When he lived among them, he was a vehement Whig; even in bad times a Whig clergyman was there thought to be a monstrous composition, and abhorred by the rest of the body' (Landa, p. 73). Archbishop King was delighted to see his protege made a bishop. But he had been going through the motions of recommending a young Lord Ikerrin for the deanship, and certainly did not want Swift in the place. He told Southwell, 'The Dean has taken a turn I could not foresee.' (See King's letters of 18 Dec. 1712 and 16 May 1713 to Southwell.)

Chapter Twenty-six

VANESSA AND PPT

I. SWIFT AND HESSY

In order to make perfectly sure of his deanery, Swift thought it only prudent to go to Dublin as soon as possible and see himself definitely installed. He delayed just long enough to complete the manuscript of his *History*. Then, for the convenience of an early getaway, he followed his plan of staying with John Barber in the City immediately before taking off. At this point we suddenly get a detailed view of an affair that had been rubbing hesitantly along all the time he was in England—the untidy relation between himself and the young Esther Vanhomrigh. Late the night before he was due to leave Barber's, Swift took time out, while people were waiting to say goodbye to him, and wrote a message, undated, with no salutation or signature, but fulfilling a promise he had made to send the girl a letter before he went away. The tone is both intimate and cautious, the usual tone of his correspondence with her; for he always combined conscious avuncularity with unconscious blandishment. Swift now expected to return to England in the autumn but could not be certain of this; and his language reflects the distasteful possibility that he might have to be gone for a very long time. 'It is impossible for any body to have more acknowledgements at heart for all your kindness and generosity', he says discreetly, near the beginning. 'Pray be merry and eat and walk; and be good', he says didactically in the middle. 'Pray God preserve you and make you happy and easy.—and so adieu bratt—' he says affectionately, near the end.

The next morning he started out, planning to ride the hundred and eighty miles to Chester in only six days. As far as St Albans he had Barber for company; and there Swift gave him another

[635]

letter for Hessy. Then he rode to Dunstable, where he sent a letter to 'Moll', or Mary, Hessy's younger sister, but posting it under cover to Erasmus Lewis. The day Swift reached Chester, Hessy wrote a letter to him that hardly wavers in pitch from start to finish. She opens, 'Now you are good beyond measure in sending me that dear voluntary from St. Albans.' She goes on to worry about his health and scold him for not writing to her from Dunstable. She ends with a proprietary declaration, 'I am very impatient to hear from you at Chester.'[1]

But from Chester, Swift wrote not to the daughter but to the mother, in a charming, chatty, witty style. He was obviously trying to support the fiction that his attentions were addressed impartially to all three women, and so he said his absence made the daughters into widows like the mother. It was the same device he used when he addressed letters for Mrs Johnson to Mrs Dingley. But here the teasing touches Hessy much more than the others, and he writes, 'I desire you will let me know what fellows Hessy has got to come to her bed-side in a morning.'

For all his speed, Swift only reached Chester the day after the ships sailed for Ireland in a 'rare wind'. Tired with so much riding, after almost three years of urban stagnation, he nevertheless decided to rest only two nights and then ride to Holyhead (probably another three days), because he had to take the oaths before 25 June if he did not wish to wait till the next quarter sessions. Swift's dizziness had returned and persisted for weeks now, and he was to carry it with him to Ireland. In Chester he visited as usual his supposed cousin Abigail Greenfield, finding her still good-natured but, with advancing age, no longer beautiful. 'I wonder how it comes about', he said in mock-surprise to Mrs Van.

He got himself to Holyhead according to plan, caught a boat for Ireland the morning he arrived, and landed that evening, Wednesday, 10 June, at nine o'clock, in Dublin. Three days later, still feeling sick, he was able to have the installation ceremony.[2]

---

[1] Williams I. 360–1, 364–5. The heading for Swift's letter of 6 June should read 'Mrs.' and not 'Miss' (p. 365).
[2] Ibid., pp. 365–7, 372–4; Accounts 1712–13, fol. 10.

Meanwhile, Vanessa, on the edge of St James's Park, longed for her inaccessible father-lover and copied out epistolary appeals from drafts which she carefully preserved beside the letters Swift sent to her. 'Here is now three long weeks passed since you wrote to me . . . confess, have you once thought of me since you wrote to my mother att Chester?' She was reading a book I suppose Swift had recommended, Fontenelle's *Dialogues des morts*: 'I am so charmed with them that I am resolved to quit my poste, let the consequence be what it will, except you will talke to me; for I find no conversation upon earth comparable but yours; so if you care I should stay, do but talke, and youl keepe me with pleasure.'[1]

Swift did not choose to reply to this letter; but while she was left in suspense, Hessy wrote again. Now she felt in a filial panic over his health, having heard from Erasmus Lewis that the vertigo remained serious and persistent. 'Oh what would I give to know how you doe at this instant. My fortune is to hard; your absence was enough without this cruill addition. . . I have done all that was possible to hinder my self from writing to you till I heard you were better. . . I hope I shall soon have you here.'

As if to give the girl a taste of the suspense he had endured, Swift still did not answer; but Hessy wrote yet again. She had heard from Lewis (who was forwarding her letters with his own) that Swift was now well: 'If you think I write to often your only way is to tell me so, or at least to write to me again that I may know you don't quite forgett me, for I very much fear that I never imploy a thought of yours now except when you are reading my letters.' In the midst of her lament occurs a suspicion that he has found the normal consolation for her absence: 'If you are very happy, it is ill-natured of you not to tell me so except tis what is inconsistent with mine.'

Now Swift did reply, but hardly as she had hoped. With a few scraps about himself and some mock-gossip about Laracor and Trim, he included a Swiftian reference to her sighs:

> I had your last spleenatick letter: I told you when I left England,
> I would endeavor to forget every thing there, and would write as

[1] Williams I. 367–9. Here and below I have modernized the capitalization and added italics and punctuation in Vanessa's letters.

seldom as I could ... neither will I leave the kingdom [sc. of Ireland] till I am sent for, and if they have no further service for me, I will never see England again.[1]

An impasse so dramatic is not constructed within a few weeks, even by persons so given to rash self-assertion as Vanessa and Swift. Her fearful ardour, his eager reluctance, took years to establish their shaky equilibrium. Swift had never lost touch with the Vanhomrighs since the family's first arrival in England, more than five years before he was made a dean. While he lived again in Ireland during Wharton's lord lieutenancy, he had exchanged letters not only with the elder Mrs Vanhomrigh but with 'Mishessy' as well.[2] During the earliest weeks after Swift returned to London in the autumn of 1710, Mrs Vanhomrigh had suffered the death of Ginkel, her adolescent son and youngest child, who was buried in St James's church the day after Dr Swift's long introductory conference with Robert Harley.[3] Meanwhile, Sir Andrew Fountaine, who had just come up to town, was (in the autumn of 1710) much too intimate with the Vanhomrighs for Swift to put off seeing them very long. If Ginkel was confined by serious illness for any time leading up to his death, the two bachelors may have waited to call until the funeral was past. But before the end of October 1710 Swift was dining with the mother and daughters, while the elder son was in Oxford, at Christ Church.[4]

Because Swift lodged near the Vanhomrighs, it was easy for dinner to succeed dinner through the autumn and winter. In February 1711, Swift and Ford opened the Lenten season by going to Vanessa's birthday party—she was already twenty-three, though Swift probably did not know this—which meant dinner and an evening of drinking punch.[5] When Mrs Johnson, in a letter, showed some puzzlement at Swift's addiction to the Vanhomrighs, he shot back, 'You say they are of no consequence: why, they keep as good female company as I do male; I see all the drabs of quality at this end of town with them; I saw two Lady

---

[1] Williams I. 369–74.   [2] Ibid., v. 218.   [3] Buried 8 Oct. 1710.
[4] Journal, 20, 30 Oct. I assume that Bartholomew was in Oxford during term. He was entered in Christ Church, 15 April 1708, aged 15.
[5] Ibid., 14 Feb. 1711: I assume the unnamed daughter is Vanessa.

Bettys [i.e., the daughters of the Duke of Ormonde and the Earl of Berkeley] there this afternoon, the beauty of one, the good breeding and nature of t'other, and the wit of neither, would have made a fine woman.'[1] Three days later, as if to demonstrate what he had declared, Swift reported that he had dined at Mrs Vanhomrigh's and that Ormonde's daughter, knowing it, had invited him to visit her the same evening, after she had already asked the 'Vans' beforehand. During the spring of 1711 when Swift hurt his shin, he avoided walking and dined with Mrs Vanhomrigh three times in four days. When it rained and he had no better invitation, he often went to her house for dinner. On at least one day he had both breakfast and supper there—and that was a fast day, Good Friday![2]

While he lodged in salubrious Chelsea during the spring and summer of 1711, Swift left a chest of wine and some other things with Mrs Van. Walking into town from Chelsea, he used to start out wearing an old gown and wig but would stop off at her house and there change into his best, which she kept for him. Over these weeks she also set a little room aside for him, where he could read and write. And in hot, lazy weather, when the town was empty, it was nothing for him to share his wine and dine with her three times a week, whether or not Fountaine came too: 'An ugly rainy day; I was to visit Mrs. Barton, then called at Mrs. Vanhomrigh's, where Sir Andrew Fountain and the rain kept me to dinner; and there did I loiter all the afternoon, out of perfect laziness, and the weather not permitting me to walk; but I'll do so no more.' But the very next day he repeated the performance without the excuse of Sir Andrew's company or encouragement.[3]

Although Mr Vanhomrigh had been dead for almost eight years, his highly complicated estate remained unsettled, still managed in Ireland by one of his executors, a slow, money-loving lawyer named Peter Partington, who thought the entire family a gang of irresponsible spendthrifts. While Swift was out of town on one of his visits to Windsor, Mrs Vanhomrigh quarrelled with her landlord and decided to move. I suspect that she could not afford

---

[1] *Ibid.*, 26 Feb. 1711.   [2] *Ibid.*, I, 13–16, 27, 30 Mar. 1711.
[3] *Ibid.*, 26 Apr.; 7, 21, 30 May; 6, 7 Jul. 1711.

the rent and chose to live farther from court and reduce her expenses. She also told Swift that Hessy had come of age and was going to Ireland in order to get her fortune into her own hands: the one statement was a lie, and the other was a mistaken prediction. Swift thought the new landlady had the eyebrows of a bawd. Soon Mrs Vanhomrigh came to agree with him, and moved again, after six or eight weeks, to lodgings more conveniently located for Swift, who had just shifted to St Martin's Street at ten shillings a week. The Vanhomrigh establishment was now, I think, distinctly narrower than before, and the new landlady undertook to provide meals; so the family had sunk to the level of boarders. But once Swift's trips to Windsor were over, he took up with the friendly household again, as busily as ever— he described himself as 'always there in a very rainy day'.[1]

What reflections Mrs Vanhomrigh allowed herself on the motives of the clergyman who treated her family as his own, one cannot be sure. But unless she was a most eccentric widow, she could hardly have refrained from wondering at times whether he might not eventually marry either Hessy or Moll, or indeed herself. I assume that Swift assiduously hinted he had no such intentions. I also assume that a moderately shrewd woman would judge him rather by his conduct than his hints. Other bachelors hung about and enjoyed her hospitality. Merely among Swift's friends there were Fountaine, Ford, and Lewis. But no one else came so near to boarding with her. Even supposing that Swift explicitly dismissed matrimony from the prospects of the three ladies, he knew enough of the world to realize that other onlookers would be quick to impute familiar motives to familiar manners. With his interest in propriety, he must have considered the danger of scandal.

One should, I think, assume that his deep ambivalence between discretion and a contempt for vulgar rules was strengthening Swift's peculiar talent for self-deceit. Years later, Vanessa was to remind him, 'You once had a maxime, which was to act what was right and not mind what the world said.'[2] This echo of his

[1] *Journal*, 14 Aug., 14 Sept., 12 Oct., 2 Nov. 1711; *Accounts 1711–12*, fol. 2ᵛ.
[2] Williams II. 148 (punctuation changed and slip of pen corrected).

early advice to the reluctant Varina suggests the manœuvre by which Swift justified a dubious line of conduct. I suspect it was a confidence in the technical purity of his intentions that allowed him to expose a girl half his age to a dangerous notoriety. And even if Hessy did have a mother to guard her, this scarcely excused Swift from his duty as a conscious moralist. The moody, impetuous young woman excited him by her combination of superficial docility and underlying passion. What was in fact self-indulgence he preferred to describe as indifference to common malice.

These speculations get some bolstering from a few direct glimpses of the unsavoury affair in the year which followed the success of *The Conduct of the Allies*. One incriminating symptom is the disappearance of Mrs Vanhomrigh's name from Swift's letters to Mrs Johnson. Time and again, when his account book tells us he visited the easy-going family, a letter to Ireland mentions either nothing or simply 'a friend'. On a Tuesday in mid-November he writes, 'I dined privately with a friend to-day in the neighbourhood'; but his accounts read, 'Wine. Van's 1s. 6d.'[1] On the next Friday he writes openly that he and Fountaine dined with the Vans, 'and my cold made me loiter all the evening'. But on the Monday his letter reports dinner with 'a friend in St. James's-street', though the accounts reveal that he played piquet at Mrs Van's, where he had almost certainly dined as well.[2] A week later he reports dining with 'a friend' of Erasmus Lewis's, and the accounts again list piquet at Mrs Van's.[3] When he does mention Mrs Vanhomrigh now, it tends to be a dinner including at least one other guest, particularly Fountaine. One would be hard put to it to clear Swift from the appearance of using fellow bachelors as a screen not only from the mother's speculations but from those of miscellaneous friends. Certainly he employed the mother as an instrument to screen himself from appearing preoccupied with the daughter.

The reason for Swift's caution becomes obvious in the middle

---

[1] *Journal*, 13 Nov. 1711; *Accounts 1711–12*, fol. 3^v.

[2] *Journal*, 16, 19 Nov. 1711; *Accounts 1711–12*, fol. 1^v.

[3] *Journal*, 26 Nov.; *Accounts 1711–12*, fol. 1^v. Similarly *Journal*, 1 Dec., pt 2, and 14 Dec.; cf. *Accounts* for these days.

of his Christmas 1711 panic over the Lords' vote against peace without Spain. Having written to Anne Long, the beautiful, self-exiled friend of the Vanhomrighs and himself, he asks Hessy to forward the letter but to read it first. He makes this unorthodox request in a note with which he encloses not only the message to Mrs Long but also a third, fraudulent epistle which Hessy is to show to others as the real letter to herself: 'See what art people must use', he says, writing to her early in the morning, 'though they mean ever so well. Now are you and Puppy lying at your ease, without dreaming anything of all this. Adieu till we meet over a pott of coffee, or an orange and sugar in the sluttery, which I have so often found to be the most agreeable chamber in the world.' In the message to Mrs Long, who had already left London because of her money troubles, Swift included an analysis of Hessy's character which was clearly the reason he wished Hessy to read this letter:

> She poor girl, between sickness, domestic affairs and state speculations, has lost a good deal of her mirth. But I think there is not a better girl upon earth. I have a mighty friendship for her. She had good principles, and I have corrected all her faults; but I cannot persuade her to read, though she has an understanding, memory and taste that would bear great improvement. But she is incorrigibly idle and lazy—thinks the world made for nothing but perpetual pleasure; and the deity she most adores is Morpheus. Her greatest favourites at present are Lady Ashburnham, her dog and myself. She makes me of so little consequence that it almost distracts me. She will bid her sister go downstairs before my face, for she has 'some private business with the Doctor'. In short, there would never be an end of telling you the hardships she puts on me, only because I have lived a dozen or fifteen years too much.[1]

The doctor appears worried about Hessy's melancholy, about her imprudence, and about the nature of her attachment to himself. I presume that he hoped to maintain a delicious intimacy without paying the normal price. Judging from Swift's habits over many years, I believe he made no improper advances to Hessy and never remotely intimated that he might be drawn into matrimony. I am also afraid he felt these precautions excused

[1] Williams I. 275–8. Lady Ashburnham was of course Ormonde's daughter.

him from any profound regard for the consequences of his behaviour.

Soon he was able to substitute another kind of attention for the sort that women usually seek from a man they passionately love. Instead of going to Ireland, Vanessa decided to co-operate with the rest of the family in submitting to Parliament a private bill that would allow them to transfer their property to England. In mid-January, when Swift spent an evening with Sir William Robinson, the old partner of Hessy's father, his purpose was probably to discuss the petition for the liquidation of the estate.[1] On 22 January the petition was referred by the House of Lords to two judges, one of whom was an old friend and neighbour of Lord Oxford's[2]; and in due course they recommended that the bill be passed. In March the bill began its slow progress through Parliament; and at least twice that month Swift went to the House of Lords or the Court of Requests in order to secure favourable votes.[3]

Besides financial guidance I think Swift soon offered Hessy even rasher intimacies than before. During his bout of shingles, the only dinners he had out were apparently at Mrs Van's.[4] But in addition, scattered through the year, one finds hints of secret meetings between himself and 'Mishessy'. On 27 February, for example, he summarized for Mrs Johnson a day so crowded that he could hardly have gone to a place not mentioned, and he does not mention the Vanhomrighs; yet his accounts show that he gave Hessy fourpence that day. Since he also dined in the City with Barber, it is probable that she turned up there, for he could not possibly have met her at the other places. Although Swift often visited Barber, dined with him, and employed him as a financial agent, he usually suppresses his name, and calls him 'a friend in the City', because it would have been ruinous for them both if anyone could prove that Swift wrote the libellous pam-

---

[1] *Journal*, 15 Jan. 1712. This ingenious suggestion I take from Sybil Le Brocquy's *Cadenus*, p. 11 (Dublin, 1962).

[2] Robert Price.   [3] *Journal*, 7 Mar. and n. 45; 24 Mar.

[4] *Ibid.*, 30 Mar. 1712, he says he dined with her; 22 Apr. he dined with a 'neighbour'; 9 May his accounts list 'coach &c. Vans 3s. 6d.'. During this period no other dinners or visits are recorded.

phlets ιnat Barber printed. Their friendship and mutual trust grew, I think, far deeper than anyone has realized; and Swift extended this trust to include Barber's mistress, the scandal-writer, Mary de la Rivière Manley, who, in her editorship of the *Examiner* and other propaganda for the ministry, would often take her orders from Swift himself. Near the beginning of January, Swift tells Mrs Johnson he has dined with 'an authoress and a printer'. Near the end of the month Mrs Manley—then very ill —dined with Swift at Mrs Vanhomrigh's. 'She is about forty, very homely and very fat', Swift reported to Dublin; but he gave her Pickwickian praise, as having 'very generous principles for one of her sort'.[1]

Early in June 1712 Swift notes in his accounts the one-shilling fare for a boat to and from Barber's, immediately beside the cost the same day of two shillings 'to Miss hess for Coach'. The simplest interpretation is that Hessy went to the printer's house by coach while Swift went separately by boat. Later the same month he again notes two shillings to Hessy for a coach. Still later he notes sixpence spent on a boat for himself the same day as sixpence lost to 'M—y' (Mishessy) playing hazard.[2] On Monday, 30 June, he notes spending the large sum of eight shillings at Pontack's famous eating-house, sixpence on a boat, and two shillings on a coach; but in the course of a long letter to Mrs Johnson the next day, though he tells of visits paid and received on the Sunday before, he has nothing to tell about Monday except to hint that in the evening he saw Oxford.[3]

It is in the summer of 1712, while Swift was at Windsor, that we get another close-up of the affair. Just as he was about to follow Oxford back to town in order to have the minister's assistance with the *History*, he sent a letter to Hessy ('Misheskinage'), who had been urging him to write: here, after apologizing for the delay, he said he would be seeing her soon and sent his respects to her mother: 'I will come as early on Monday as I can find opportunity; and will take a little Grubstreet lodging; pretty near where I did before; and dine with you thrice a week; and will tell

---

[1] *Journal*, 4, 28 Jan. 1712.   [2] *Accounts 1711–12*, fols. 9, 1ᵛ (7, 12 Jun.).
[3] *Ibid.*, fols. 5ᵛ, 9.

you a thousand secrets provided you will have no quarrells to me.'[1]

After this London interval, Swift returned to Windsor, earlier than he had expected; but he seems to have taken Bartholomew, Hessy's brother (on vacation, I suppose, from Christ Church), with him for a few days' visit. Shortly after Bartholomew left, Swift wrote to Hessy again, a chatty, advice-giving letter, saying he longed 'to drink a dish of coffee in the sluttery'. The most surprising turn of the message is an impulsive suggestion that the whole family should now visit Windsor. In one of his characteristic modes of humour, Swift pretends that they have already organized such an expedition: 'How came you to make it a secret to me, that you all design to come for three or four days.' Now it looks as though Hessy seized and developed the suggestion in a way that did not at first suit him. He teased her about it, refusing to write and sending word through Erasmus Lewis that if Hessy's scheme were pursued, Swift would leave Windsor before they arrived. When Moll got sick, the trip was cancelled overnight. Swift sent them some venison, thanks to Lady Masham; and in response to a bill Hessy had submitted, he said he had ordered Barber to give her some money. I am afraid the particular facts remain dark, but Swift does seem to be helping Hessy out of a money shortage that her mother knew nothing about. He now expected the family still to visit Windsor when Moll got well.[2] But in the next of the letters which have been preserved—over three weeks later—he says, 'Why then you should not have come; and I knew that as well as you', which sounds as though he disappointed her. She certainly came to Windsor, because in letters a decade later Swift was to remind her of the visit; but then he also mentions 'the indisposition at Windsor'. I suspect she finally made the trip either alone or improperly chaperoned, and that Swift felt either too embarrassed or not well enough to look after her in the style she had hoped for.[3]

---

[1] Williams I. 304–5.

[2] *Ibid.*, pp. 304–5, 308–11. I assume the 'overplus sealed up' and to be sent by Barber means money. Swift certainly sent money to Hessy through Barber's hands at other times—e.g., *ibid.* II. 56–7.

[3] *Ibid.* I. 313–14; II. 427, 433.

After this point (the end of September 1712) only a few clues survive to outline their relationship before Swift went to Ireland in order to claim his deanery. In letters years afterwards, he mentions to her, 'Madam going to Kensington', 'the sick lady at Kensington', and 'the colonells going to France'.[1] I assume that Hessy visited Kensington (and perhaps secured a view of the sick Queen at court) during the weeks Swift lived there in June and July 1712; this is the period when his accounts twice list payments of two shillings to her for a coach.[2] The other reference is to her brother's visit to France in the spring and summer of 1713: Prior mentions him when writing to Swift from Paris. The boy suffered the family vice, for Prior describes him as having 'run terribly here into debt'.[3]

By February 1713 Swift seems to have reached the point where he was willing to sacrifice the kind of Society dinner he had once found so alluring, in order to secure a few hours with Hessy. On 26 February Swift tells Mrs Johnson, 'Our Society met at the [Duke of Ormonde's] but I had business that called me another way, so I sent my excuses, and dined privately with a friend.' His accounts show he played hazard that day at Mrs Van's. A week later he tells Mrs Johnson he refused an invitation to Lord Oxford's in order to 'dine with Lord Masham; and played at ombre . . . and I was once a great loser, but came off for 3s-6d.' His accounts show it was at Mrs Vanhomrigh's that he lost three shillings and sixpence playing ombre that day; in fact, this was the invitation he had accepted in his parody letter (which I have already quoted) to Sir Andrew Fountaine.[4]

It seems likely that if Swift had not essentially performed a father's part, the fatherless Hessy would not have preferred him to younger, more accessible men. Obvious, immediate duties bored her; like the rest of the Vanhomrighs she yearned to live above her station; and she enjoyed having her fantasies excited by Swift's news of the great world. I suspect that she envied her brother's opportunities and longed to possess the scope of a man's

---

[1] Williams II. 356, 427, 433.   [2] *Accounts 1711–12*, fol. 9.

[3] Williams I. 341, 381.

[4] *Journal*, 7 Mar. 1713; *Accounts 1712–13*, fol. 2; Williams I. 336–7; see above, p. 627.

career. Swift enjoyed playing his usual games with a widow and her firstborn daughter. Many childhood patterns of travel, separation, and reunion were repeated in his links with the Vanhomrighs. Hessy's sobriety, her bad health, her name, and her studiousness were direct copies of Hetty Johnson's traits. Just as Mishessy could identify her vague aspirations with Swift's eminence in national politics, so he could satisfy the frustrated emotions of an orphan childhood by caring for the melancholy girl. And there was always the simple bliss of being adored by a highly eligible woman many years his junior. Each provoked the other by going beyond the limits of the main rôle. Hessy's violations of decorum alarmed and thrilled a man obsessed with discretion. Swift's alternation between cheering invitations and cautious evasions teased Hessy's passion.

II. *CADENUS AND VANESSA*

During the autumn of 1713 Swift composed a fictitious account of his affair with Mishessy in the form of a poem which he called *Cadenus and Vanessa.*[1] Here he produces a comic version of the device used by many embarrassed lovers when their conquest is too complete. It is not the solution Swift had hit upon when he chose to dismiss Varina. Then he had relied on the less tender but invariably effective method of ignoring the victim's sensibilities and telling her in unmistakable language that he no longer found her amiable. With Mishessy he falls back on the alternative and generally useless method of saying she is deeply seductive but he lacks the amative faculty. This must reflect Swift's real attitude. He did not wish to end the exciting friendship, but

[1] The date of composition is uncertain. I believe, since he calls himself *Cadenus*, an anagram of *Decanus*, throughout the poem, that it was written after he became dean. Because of its comic tone, I do not believe Swift would have written it after the death of Vanessa's mother, which occurred at the beginning of February 1714. In 1726 Swift said the poem was written at Windsor in 1712; but he was also at Windsor in the autumn of 1713, and his memory is usually unreliable. It was natural for Swift to give the poem too early a date because the scandal consequent on its unauthorized publication made him eager to separate it from his older self as written 'many years ago' (Williams III. 130). Generally I agree with Sir Harold Williams's reasons for giving the autumn of 1713 as the most probable date (*Poems* II. 684–5).

neither was he willing to let it follow the normal, sexual path. His poem, therefore, was meant to reconcile Hessy to an equilibrium already established.

This is why there are two, paradoxically related arguments in the poem: first, that Vanessa has every decent charm and secondly, that she has failed to attract a man worthy of her. The central action of Swift's poem, therefore, deals with a beautiful girl who possesses too much intelligence and virtue to love or be loved by the empty-headed men or to be appreciated by the frivolous women she meets in conventional society. After a long term of bored dissatisfaction she finally discovers Cadenus, a literary and political genius twice her age—'grown old in politics and wit'—who enjoys performing the duties of teacher and moral guide. On him she soon fixes her heart. If Cadenus could respond sexually to any woman in the world, Vanessa would enthrall him. But he cannot:

> Cadenus, common forms apart,
> In every scene had kept his heart;
> Had sigh'd and languish'd, vow'd, and writ,
> For pastime, or to shew his wit;
> But time, and books, and state affairs
> Had spoil'd his fashionable airs;
> He now cou'd praise, esteem, approve,
> But understood not what was love.   (ll.540–7)

Now, in a series of well-matched speeches, the couple proceed to explore the possibilities of the situation, with each one trying to reason the other out of his stubborn conviction. But apart from arguing, they make little headway. Cadenus still offers only friendship for passion:

> But friendship in its greatest height,
> A constant, rational delight,
> On virtue's basis fix'd to last,
> When love's allurements long are past;
> Which gently warms, but cannot burn;
> He gladly offers in return:
> His want of passion will redeem,
> With gratitude, respect, esteem:
> With that devotion we bestow,
> When goddesses appear below.   (ll.780–9)

[648]

Vanessa still prefers being treated like a woman to being respected like a goddess. And with the resulting impasse the central
action ends:

> But what success Vanessa met,
> Is to the world a secret yet:
> Whether the nymph, to please her swain,
> Talks in a high romantick strain;
> Or whether he at last descends
> To like with less seraphic ends;
> Or, to compound the business, whether
> They temper love and books together;
> Must never to mankind be told,
> Nor shall the conscious[1] muse disclose.   (ll. 818–27)

Although the Freudian implications of the deadlock—a female
agent and a male patient provoking one another to childish ex-
citements—appear too commonplace to need inspection, some
biographical connections may be less obvious. The view of love as
destructive and shortlived, of friendship as rational and enduring, is hardly strange in a man whose father died just after the
son's conception. The view of desirable women as goddesses who
seldom walk here below would be strengthened by the memories
of a boyhood in which Swift's mother and sister had lived not only
apart from him but in another kingdom. And I think the incon-
clusiveness of the central episode of the poem suggests the ambiguous motives of a man who had never been able to live either
with women or without them.

In the structure of the poem, art serves to flatter the woman
who is in fact rejected and to punish the man who is nevertheless
loved. Thus the main episode and the speeches drawn from it
endow Vanessa with an easy superiority. She is described in far
more detail than her partner and from a consistently eulogistic
point of view. Cadenus receives fewer lines, many of them
amounting to ridicule. By such distributions the bored lover-poet
scarifies himself in order to placate the cast-off mistress. In a
subtler way the ambiguity of Cadenus's attitude seems reflected
by the attributes conferred on Vanessa. She lacks the woman's
absorption in personal appearance, the woman's love of idle

[1] I.e., knowing.

[649]

conversation, the woman's addiction to frivolous pastimes. She has a man's virtues: honour and thrift; 'knowledge, judgment, wit'; 'justice, truth, and fortitude' (ll. 205–17). But Cadenus is an impaired man, lacking health, youth, and passion—

> Interpreting her complaisance,
> Just as a man *sans consequence*.   (ll. 658–9)

Thus by desexualizing both partners, the panicky poet removes the element that threatens him.

Furthermore, the central action is embedded in an elaborate mythological setting which directly involves rewards and punishments. For the whole career of Vanessa appears as part of an experiment designed by Venus to resolve a lawsuit in the court of love. At the opening of the poem the entire masculine sex must stand defendants before Venus as presiding judge assisted by the muses and the graces. The accusers are of course the women, charging that men no longer marry for love. In reply, the men's counsel declares that women themselves are to blame, because they have substituted gross passion for rational love. Rather than determine between the two sides on the basis of law and precedent, Venus chooses to set up her critical experiment. She blesses one infant with beauty and virtue, and exposes mankind to the girl when she has reached sixteen. As we know, the experiment fails, with the fops finding Vanessa dull and Cadenus seeming beyond love. In the final section of the poem, therefore, Venus gives judgment:

> She was at Lord knows what expence,
> To form a nymph of wit and sense;
> A model for her sex design'd,
> Who never cou'd one lover find.
> She saw her favour was misplac'd;
> The fellows had a wretched taste;
> She needs must tell them to their face,
> They were a senseless stupid race.   (ll. 864–71)

With these most explicit words Swift blames his own kind and says Vanessa is too good for our world. The appeasement of the injured lady could hardly seem nearer perfection. Yet that he does not really mean this one may infer from the full terms of his story. Thus except for Vanessa, all the women in the poem are vain, scandal-mongering, and vicious. At the same time, Vanessa herself is defined as a miracle and not a normal woman. Venus and Athene, the graces and the muses, have had to collaborate in order to manufacture her. Cadenus, on the contrary, though a rare specimen, is quite natural, and superior to all but Vanessa. Ultimately, therefore, it is man's and not woman's nature that triumphs.

The poem is loose-knit, and the couplets are not meticulous. It is comic verve, rather than poetic art, that gives the poem life. Swift's rhythms are neither awkward nor elegant; but if they lack music, they are often expressive. His rhymes have less of farce than humour, and his ear for idiom is unfailing. Several passages combine these ingredients in a genial movement quite appropriate to the voice of a fatherly admirer trying to cheer up a solitary spinster:

> Vanessa, not in years a score,
> Dreams of a gown of forty-four;
> Imaginary charms can find,
> In eyes with reading almost blind;
> Cadenus now no more appears
> Declin'd in health, advanc'd in years.
> She fancies musick in his tongue,
> Nor further looks, but thinks him young. (ll. 524–31)

III. PDFR AND PPT

As a tribute to a lady, *Cadenus and Vanessa* makes a pathetically weak contrast to Swift's brilliant series of letters now called the *Journal to Stella*.[1] To the common reader ranging among them for the first time, these letters present the difficulties of all diaries, in the number and variety of persons named and the casual allusions to places or events no longer familiar. But a magisterial editor has levelled these obstacles, and the rewards of passing beyond them remain almost as various as Swift's materials. It

---

[1] Unless otherwise stated, all the facts about the *Journal* are taken from the edition by Sir Harold Williams. The misleading title *Journal to Stella* was attached to the letters by John Nichols in 1779 (*Journal* i. l, n. 2).

can hardly sound exciting to say the so-called *Journal* consists of sixty-five diary letters addressed by Swift to Mrs Johnson and Mrs Dingley from September 1710 to June 1713. Perhaps a descriptive account would be more provocative. They are, then, letters by the finest prose stylist of his time to the woman he trusted supremely, recording the most dramatic years of his life and involving the main historical figures and public events of those years. It has been standard practice for scholars to search the *Journal* for information about Swift's life or the reign of Queen Anne. Other appeals of the letters have received less appreciation.[1]

Apart from this 'journal' and one or two other letters, all the extensive correspondence between Swift and Esther Johnson has been destroyed—I assume, by Swift himself. If he saved the *Journal*, the reason was not his admittedly profound devotion to Stella but the value of the contents as historical data. The whole idea of keeping an epistolary diary, sent by instalments to his darling friend, was a new one for Swift[2]; and he gave it ingenious turns which made him feel constantly in touch with her. He tried to write every day, often just after waking up and just before going to sleep; it was common for him to write in bed. When both sides of a leaf were filled, he would send it to her and then start a new letter the same day. 'I shall always be in conversation with MD, and MD with Pdfr.'[3] The scheme broke down during Swift's attack of shingles in the spring of 1712, and he never perfectly restored it, though he became very regular after the middle of December. Among the two dozen of the letters for which addresses are preserved, only three carry Mrs Johnson's name; all the rest are to Mrs Dingley. But if many of Swift's remarks and greetings are also delivered to Mrs Dingley, no one doubts that the reader Swift had normally in mind was her companion. The purpose of the misleading address was of course discretion; and

---

[1] But see Virginia Woolf's essay in the *Second Common Reader*.
[2] *Journal*, 9, 16, 21, 30 (pt 2) Sept. 1710.
[3] *Ibid.*, 9 Sept. 1710. I use the original 'Pdfr' for Deane Swift's 'Presto'; although the manuscripts of letters 2–40 and 54 are lost, it is certain that he never wrote 'Presto' and Deane Swift says his own 'Presto' is a euphonic substitute for 'Pdfr': see *ibid.* i. lviii.

for the same reason Swift indulged his love of codes and word-games by calling himself Pdfr, pronounced 'Podefar' (?poor dear foolish rogue). Similarly, Mrs Johnson is Ppt (?poppet); Mrs Dingley, Dd (?Dear Dingley); both ladies together are MD (?my dears); all three friends, PMD.

Swift also used to interrupt or end the ordinary flow of comment in order to convey particularly tender messages, especially at bedtime, by additional abbreviations and by an affectionate babble of slurred or distorted words that look like the seventeenth-century baby talk recorded by the Duchess of Newcastle.[1] Here, 'fw', often repeated, seems to mean 'farewell'; 'me' may mean 'remember me'; 'lele' may mean 'dear'. Other words in the 'little language' are distorted by childish mispronunciations, so that *l* and *r* become interchangeable; *d* becomes *g*; *c* becomes *t*; some final sounds are omitted; other sounds are repeated or reversed; etc. *Sirrah* is *sollah*; *little* is *richar*; *fiddlesticks* becomes *figgarkick*.[2] It was by slightly systematizing such habits that Swift created what he called his 'little language', in which sentences take bizarre forms that need translation to be understood: thus, 'O rold hot a cruttle' is only 'O Lord, what a clutter'[3]; 'spreene-kick ferrow' is 'splenetic fellow'.[4]

In the extant manuscript somebody has lightly scratched a pen over most of the 'little language'. I think the person was Swift, going over the whole collection and eliminating material that would not contribute to the history or memoirs for which he planned to use these letters as sources. Having once embarked on the scheme of an epistolary journal in 1710, he soon recognized its historical value and wished the letters preserved. By the time

[1] 'When nurses teach children to go, instead of saying go, they say do, do, and instead of saying come to me, they say tum to me, and when they newly come out of a sleep, and cannot well open their eyes, they do not say My child cannot well open his, or her eyes, but my chid tant open its nies, and when they should bid them speak, they bid them peak, and when they should ask them if they will or would drink, they ask them if they will dinck. . . Likewise they learn them the rudest language first, as to bid them say such a one lies, or to call them rogues and the like names, and then laugh as if it were a witty jest.' (Margaret Cavendish, Duchess of Newcastle, *The World's Olio*, 1655, pp. 60–1.)

[2] Not previously understood: see *Journal*, 3 Jun. 1711 and n. 18.

[3] *Ibid.*, 21 Mar. 1712; see also my *Personality of Jonathan Swift*, 1958, pp. 50–8.

[4] *Journal*, 31 May 1712.

he explicitly looked forward to reviewing such memorabilia in later years, he must also have begun more or less consciously to dwell, in the journal, on facts that would remain interesting: he became a recorder of his own times. 'This will be a memorable letter', he says near the end of 1711, 'and I shall sigh to see it some years hence.'[1]

Because Swift's accounts sound fresh and immediate, the reader often forgets that they need not be first-hand. Sometimes Swift is retailing what Bolingbroke has said to him; sometimes he gives a précis of several common reports; and generally he chronicles an event without indicating whether his story is hearsay or direct knowledge. One is ill-advised to treat Swift by himself as a reliable source for an anecdote except when one knows the basis of his information. Even if he gives the ladies his confidential report of an episode in which he has participated, Swift may distort the truth. In a newsletter to Archbishop King he once assured his grace that the chief ministers 'never tell any thing' and that 'it is only by picking out and comparing, that one can ever be the wiser for them.'[2] This is *de la poudre aux yeux*. But it suggests a practice I think Swift often followed, of hiding information from the ladies unless he knew that a number of courtiers already had it, and it was therefore no true secret. Consequently, he often sounds imprudent when he isn't.

There are many instances of Swift's withholding from his beloved correspondent fascinating details of public events. About his own political and literary life he was also circumspect, concealing his authorship of many works and his connections with many persons when the facts might have been dangerous to himself or to others. The really exceptionable omissions are those by which he deliberately misled Ppt about aspects of his private life which especially interested her, such as his rash conduct in the Vanhomrigh household. But elementary prudence was always at work: 'My letters would be good memoirs if I durst venture to say a thousand things that pass; but I hear so much of letters opening at your post office, that I am fearfull.'

From the masses of information supplied by Swift, certain bits

---

[1] *Journal*, 15 Dec. 1711; cf. *ibid.*, 8, 23 Oct. 1710.   [2] Williams I. 201.

have become famous; the best of his court anecdotes are often
quoted, such as the story of the Mohun–Hamilton duel; so are his
immediate responses to public phenomena like the Mohocks or
the October Club; and some of his other opinions, aphoristically
expressed, are well known—'I will not meddle with the Spectator, let him fair-sex it to the world's end'; 'I hate Lent, I hate
different diets, and furmity and butter, and herb porrige, and
sour devout faces of people who onely put on religion for seven
weeks.'[1]

What has been generally neglected is not the detachable fact,
phrase or anecdote—i.e., the characteristic beauties of any good
letter or good diary—but the unique expression of Swift's instinct
for mimicry, parody, and self-dramatization. Continually in the
Journal one can observe his art springing from its deepest source,
his games with identity, and with human speech as the most precise register of personality. A simple example is the story Swift
tells of happening to be stopped in Pall Mall by a madman who
said he had an army of 200,000 men for the Queen's service and
that the Queen owed him £200,000; the poor lunatic had been
turned away from the palace and now wondered whether to go
back immediately or the next day. This is the way Swift dealt
with his client:

> [I] begged him of all love to go and wait on her immediately; for
> that, to my knowledge, the Queen would admit him; that this was
> an affair of great importance, and required dispatch: and I in-
> structed him to let me know the success of his business, and come to
> the Smyrna Coffee-house, where I would wait for him till mid-
> night.[2]

This little act, almost a complete music hall turn, indicates how
spontaneous Swift's passion for hoaxing was, how intimately
linked to his skill in mimicry, and how thoroughly embodied in
spoken language. Though delivering quite unpremeditated lies
to a stranger, he talks naturally and normally.

In a more demanding situation, he will not speak normally but
will ape a manner which could be natural to him at other times.
For instance, when Swift was just consolidating his position with

---

[1] *Journal*, 14 Mar. 1713; 8 Feb., 5 Mar. 1712.   [2] *Ibid.*, 18 Nov. 1710.

the new ministry and had his mind fixed on improving his place among the great, he happened to dine with a printer cousin in order to see his favourite relative, Patty Rolt. Among the printer's colleagues was an inglorious hack responsible for producing the *Post Man*—a person whose acquaintance Swift would have taken peculiar pains to escape. Reporting the incident to Mrs Johnson, Swift deliciously modulates his comic tone so as to match his remembered changes of attitude as boredom gave way to mock-horror:

> I dined to-day with Patty Rolt at my cousin Leach's, with a pox, in the City: he is a printer, and prints the *Postman*, oh, ho, and is my cousin, God knows how, and he married Mrs. Baby Aires of Leicester; and my cousin Thomson was with us: and my cousin Leach offers to bring me acquainted with the author of the *Postman*; and says, he does not doubt but the gentleman will be glad of my acquaintance, and that he is a very ingenious man, and a great scholar, and has been beyond [the] sea. But I was modest, and said, May be the gentleman was shy, and not fond of new acquaintance; and so put it off: and I wish you could hear me repeating all I have said of this in its proper tone, just as I am writing it. 'Tis all with the same cadence with oh hoo, or as when little girls say, I have got an apple, miss, and I won't give you some.[1]

To see how closely this instinctive style of expression can come to Swift's literary excellence, one must watch him turning it full upon Mrs Johnson, exactly as, in his masterpieces, he turns it upon the reader. In the following passage he replies to a mistaken piece of news: his friend had evidently written that while she was at the Irish spa of Wexford, taking the waters, she had heard that the Bishop of London was dead:

> Did the Bishop of London die in Wexford? poor gentleman! Did he drink the waters? Were you at his burial? Was it a great funeral? So far from his friends? But he was very old: we shall all follow. And yet it was a pity, if God pleased. He was a good man; not very learned: I believe he died but poor. Did he leave any charity legacies? Who held up his pall? Was there a great sight of clergy? Do they design a tomb for him? Are you sure it was the Bishop of London? because there is an elderly gentleman here that we give the same title to: or did you fancy all this in your water, as other do

[1] *Journal*, 26 Oct. 1710.

strange things in their wine? They say, these waters trouble the head, and make people imagine what never came to pass. Do you make no more of killing a bishop? Are these your Whiggish tricks? —Yes, yes, I see you are in a fret. Oh faith, says you, saucy Pdfr, I'll break your head; what, can't one report what one hears, without being made a jest and a laughing stock? Are these your English tricks, with a murrain?[1]

Swift starts with self-parody, speaking as he might if the news were true. Then he mimics a conventional person mouthing platitudes over the allegedly dead bishop. Then he reverts to his true manner, ridiculing the ladies (unfairly) for retailing a false rumour. Finally, he imitates them, speaking as they would in response to his teasing. The speed with which he plays, taking all the various rôles unto himself, suggests a preference for speaking through a mask, as if to shield his fragile *propria persona*.

Apart from the literary or historical significance of the *Journal*, and its immense value as a general source of information about Swift's years among the rulers of Britain, it constitutes a monument to his love for Esther Johnson. To nobody else did he ever reveal himself so intimately and so fully as to her. In fact, the fullness of the revelation goes beyond most modern notions of eighteenth-century decorum. The freedom with which Swift details to Mrs Johnson the progress of his illnesses hardly accords with the common associations of periwigs and minuets: 'The spots encreased every day and had little pimples which are now grown white and full of corruption', he writes about his shingles.[2] Here and elsewhere both the coarseness and the severity of Swift's language can be misleading. He often pays little respect to his friend's femininity, but his very freedom proves he could not trust her more: 'Mrs. Tisdal is very big, ready to ly down. Her husband is a puppy. Do his feet stink still.'[3] (This about a man who had once tried to marry Mrs Johnson!) When Mrs Johnson writes a whimsical remark that pleases him, he tells her he said out loud, 'Agreeable bitch.'[4] Swift often blurts out violent expressions which he knows Mrs Johnson will either soften or else treat as irony. If he calls his protégé Harrison a 'little toad' or 'jacka-

---

[1] *Ibid.*, 24 Aug. 1711.   [2] *Ibid.*, 8 Apr. 1712.   [3] *Ibid.*, 6 Jun. 1713.   [4] *Ibid.*

napes', he doesn't have to warn her not to take him seriously.[1]
Often Swift's ambivalence toward filth and obscenity appears in
his both producing and concealing an unsavoury word; for in
this way he indulges both his impulse and his shame. He tells her
he hates the word 'bowels'; yet he can't let the word alone in front
of her. Obscene or bawdy humour is handled with a similarly ex-
hibitionistic modesty: mentioning the London visit of an amorous Irish lady, Swift says, 'It may cost her a clap'; but he
smudges the letters of *clap* and adds parenthetically, 'I don't care
to write that word plain.'[2] All this does not prevent him from
scolding Ppt when she sounds indelicate,[3] or from growling about
poor, beautiful Anne Long: 'I had a letter from Mrs. Long, that
has quite turned my stomach against her: no less than two nasty
jests in it with dashes to suppose them.'[4] Yet he does precisely this
sort of thing with Mrs Johnson. For instance, speaking of an
appointment with Harley, he says, 'He has appointed me an hour
on Saturday . . . when I will open my business to him; which
expression I would not use if I were a woman. I know you
smoakt [i.e., understood] it; but I did not till I writ it.'[5] Neither
does he always apologize: thus he quotes some lines about St
John's dissipations, supposed to be spoken by the statesman
during his years out of office:

> From business and the noisy world retir'd,
> Nor vex'd by love, nor by ambition fir'd;
> Gently I wait the call of Charon's boat,
> Still drinking like a fish, and —— like a stoat.

—so far from seeming embarrassed, Swift only points out the
effectiveness of the three-line build-up.[6] It is common enough for
a man with deep resentments against women to allow himself
indecencies in the presence of his beloved while requiring her to
remain pure. But Swift varies the pattern with his other methods
of evading sexuality: acting, through his 'little language', as an
innocent child with Mrs Johnson as a tolerant mother; or treating
her as an erring child with himself as a fatherly mentor; or else

---

[1] *Journal*, 13, 15 Jan. 1711.   [2] *Ibid.*, 21 Mar. 1712.   [3] *Ibid.*, 30 Nov. 1710.
[4] *Ibid.*, 11 Dec. 1710: cf. Mrs Long's reference to his complaint, Williams 1. 273.
[5] *Journal*, 4 Oct. 1710.   [6] *Ibid.*, 13 Jan. 1711.

endowing her with masculine qualities so no acknowledgement need be made of the difference between them. His games played with identity are a valuable aid in such evasions. With his facility at shifting rôles, Swift can manage to keep himself always on the 'other' side of the line between the sexes.

It was essential for Swift's comfort that he should keep his partner dependent while he remained free. In opening and closing the geographical gaps between himself and Mrs Johnson (a process which seems to recall the treatment he underwent as a child), he exercised endless ingenuity so as to retain control of any decision. I suspect that he felt guiltily anxious about her not visiting England while he was there; like some of his other friends from Ireland, she could hardly have avoided cramping his style. Yet her chronic illness seemed the kind that a stay at Bath might relieve. Swift, in the midst of apologizing for not returning to Ireland as he had promised, suddenly proposes that both ladies should visit Bath. The backing and filling that immediately break out at this point in his letter imply, I think, his underlying distaste for the idea, especially if the expedition should bring her to London; and his phrasing seems calculated to convey his true opinion to her in such a way that she would spontaneously reject the scheme and leave him free, if necessary, to blame her for rejecting it: 'You may be good housewives', he says, 'and live cheap there [i.e., at Bath] some months, and return in autumn, or visit London, as you please; pray think of it.' He will pay their expenses, and he encloses an order on his man of business:

> If the frolick should take you of going to the Bath, I here send you a note on Parvisol; if not, you may tear it, and there's an end. Farewel.
> If you have an imagination that the Bath will do you good, I say again, I would have you go; if not, or it be inconvenient, burn this note. Or, if you would go, and not take so much money, take thirty pounds, and I will return you twenty from hence. Do as you please, sirrahs. I suppose it will not be too late for the first season; if it be, I would have you resolve however to go the second season, if the doctors say it will do you good, and you fancy so.[1]

Almost four weeks later he urges Mrs Johnson to spend at least

[1] *Ibid.*, 5 Apr. 1711.

part of the spring in the country for the sake of her health. After naming five places in Ireland as possibilities, he says, 'Go to the Bath: I hope you are now at the Bath, if you had a mind to go; or go to Wexford.'[1] Of course, they went to Wexford, and Swift gave them twenty pounds toward their expenses.[2]

In the same way, from the moment Swift arrived in England, he confidently and mistakenly predicted his early departure for Ireland. In September 1710 he said he'd be home by Christmas.[3] In November he ridiculed the notion that he might remain till spring—though offering no earlier date.[4] In January he said he would wait for 'spring and good weather' before coming over.[5] In March he said he would come as soon as Parliament rose.[6] A month later, when Mrs Johnson had said she did not see how he could get away in such a hurry, he replied, 'I know you repine inwardly at Pdfr's absence; you think he has broken his word of coming in three months, and that is always his trick', and he now indicated that he meant to stay until he received preferment or else till it was obvious he would not.[7] In November 1711 he hoped to see the ladies in Ireland soon after Christmas.[8] But at Christmas he told Dean Stearne he would see him in the spring.[9] The plan of going to Ireland for at least a spring-and-summer visit in 1712 seems to have been serious: Swift began packing his books and making purchases to carry with him, looking forward to his willows and quicksets in Laracor.[10] But the attack of shingles destroyed this plan. Yet as late as June he scolded Mrs Johnson for thinking he would remain in England through the summer; and in November 1712 he again said he would be over the following spring.[11] When he finally did take off, at the end of May 1713, it was because he wished to be installed as dean as soon as he could.

Clearly, Swift was unconscious of any systematic plan to mislead the lonely friend who had originally moved to Ireland at his request. That he missed her painfully is undeniable: there are too many spontaneous messages like this: 'Farewel, dearest beloved

---

[1] *Journal*, 1 May 1711. [2] *Ibid.*, 23 Aug. 1711. [3] *Ibid.*, 9 Sept. 1710.
[4] *Ibid.*, 30 Nov. 1710.   [5] *Ibid.*, 30 Jan. 1711.   [6] *Ibid.*, 4 Mar. 1711.
[7] *Ibid.*, 5 Apr. 1711. [8] *Ibid.*, 15 Nov. 1711. [9] Williams I. 282.
[10] *Journal*, 7, 9, 27, 28 Feb., 21 Mar. 1712. [11] *Ibid.*, 17 Jun., 18 Nov. 1712.

MD, and love poor, poor Pdfr, who has not had one happy day since he left you.'[1] He worried incessantly about her health, her eyesight, her melancholy. He urged her to walk and ride, to amuse herself with visits, card-games, books. He worried about her expenses but implored her to use his money for country holidays. He performed commissions for her, assisted her friends, bought her presents. To all this solicitude there is a distasteful side. By attaching himself to an invalid, a man can relieve himself of angry impulses without openly admitting them, because the beloved is always suffering a punishment that he has not administered. Without feeling guilty, therefore, he can indulge a kind of sadism, even prolonging the existence of the woman in order to prolong his participation in her suffering.

A comparison with Vanessa is futile. The younger woman was a peripheral pastime, a quasi-mistress. One of her great charms for Swift must have been that he would not be seeing her long: the visit to England would end, this playmate would be left behind when the game was over. Ppt was for all hours and all moods. As Swift became increasingly disillusioned with the ministers, as Vanessa became more disturbing and less comforting, Swift turned warmly toward Ppt. She was the refuge against the rest of the world's desertion.

IV. IRELAND

If Swift felt the deanery of St Patrick's was not good enough for him, others thought it far in excess of his merits. At Oxford, one gossipy high-church extremist denounced the appointment to another: 'The clergy of [Ireland] detest Dr. Swift because they think him an enemy to the order, when he liv'd among them he was a vehement Whig, even in bad times a Whig clergyman was there thought a monstrous composition, and abhorred by the rest of the body, and even the station Dr. Swift is now preferr'd to, will gain him very little respect from them.'[2] At the same time, Archbishop King, who was a strong churchman but no Tory, derived only one agreeable sensation from Swift's advancement,

---

[1] *Ibid.*, 16 Jan. 1711, pt 1.   [2] Landa, p. 73.

and that was relief that it had gone no further—'a dean could do less mischief than a bishop.' Molesworth, the fine Whig statesman who loved tolerance more than episcopacy, was tickled to observe the frowns of the highest flyers, and reported to Ireland that Swift's promotion had annoyed 'the godly party beyond expression'.[1] Meanwhile, the subject of these derogations, underestimating the income of his deanery even while hurrying to secure it, had insisted on retaining his old benefice of Laracor and had surrendered only the tiny prebend of Dunlavin. At the same time he had warned the ministers that they owed him a sum sufficient to balance the fees and debts which his preferment would impose on him. Though he must have realized that the thousand-pound bonus which Oxford now let him hope for was the cloudiest remote prospect, Swift never shut his eyes to it but rather made this dim possibility one of his reasons for returning to England before winter. Yet when he had originally started on his ride from London to Chester, Swift had meant to pass at least three months in Ireland, and not to see London again till October. He had looked forward to a long summer in the country, at Laracor, and to many evenings with Mrs Johnson and their friends.

Besides brooding over worries like the fate of Vanessa and the remoteness of his thousand pounds, Swift did not forget the duties of a patron. Among the blessings diffused by Stearne's translation was the release of a small benefice called Moymet which Stearne had held when rector of Trim and which he had kept during his tenure of St Patrick's. Because the government had promoted Stearne, this rectory, worth no more than forty pounds a year, was now in the gift of the Lord Lieutenant. Almost as soon as Swift became dean, he determined to secure Moymet for his old friend Raymond, who was now rector of Trim. While Swift had avoided being seen with Raymond in London, he did not therefore shrug off his responsibilities to a loyal ally whose hospitality gave continual comfort to Mrs Johnson. I suspect that Swift also felt guilty toward Raymond, because he had once said that if he himself should secure a preferment he wanted, he would ask Ormonde to make Raymond

---

[1] Landa, pp. xiv, xv.

vicar of Laracor.[1] At the same time, since Moymet was only two miles from Trim and not worth much, it did seem right for the same minister who had the one to hold the other. But alas, no article of profit is so minute or so inconveniently placed that men will refuse to reach for it. A whole parade of aspirants, some with influential patrons, offered themselves for Moymet. Less than a fortnight after he knew his own warrant was posted, Swift wrote a memorial to be signed by himself and Pratt, provost of Trinity College, who was still in London. This brief statement recommending Raymond Swift left with the permanent chief secretary for Ireland, Edward Southwell.[2] Then Swift spoke to the Duke of Ormonde about the case. Meanwhile, however, Ormonde had heard so much in support of a blind clergyman named Dunbar— supposed to have no other means of livelihood—that he decided to present him to the living. Luckily, Raymond heard about this soon enough, and sent over a certificate showing that Dunbar was already provided for. So many other conflicting opinions reached Ormonde at the same time that Southwell wrote to the Lords Justices of Ireland, 'Some inform his grace that Moymet is a sinecure, others say not. Some tell his grace that Dr Raymond has above £200 a year without this, and others say he cannot live if he has it not.'[3] Ormonde wished the Lords Justices to make inquiries and to keep the living vacant till he gave further orders.

Swift had momentarily given up before this stage, and he wrote to Mrs Johnson, 'Tell Raymond I cannot succeed for him to get that living of Moymed; it is represented here as a great sine-cure, severall chaplains have sollicited for it.' Mrs Johnson responded with a mock-project of hanging Dunbar, which at least amused her correspondent. But Swift tried yet again, even though the crisis of his own affairs was not quite over. Toward the end of May he spoke to Ormonde and presented a memorial from the Bishop of Meath showing how hard it would be on the church of Trim if Moymet went elsewhere. 'I laid it strongly to the Duke', Swift said; and, as often happened with Ormonde, he did at last succeed. Now, however, the two Lords Justices chose to cling to the hesitancies planted by his grace, and would not sign Ray-

---

[1] *Journal*, 18 Sept. 1712.   [2] Williams I. 346–7.   [3] *Ibid.* I. 371, n. I.

mond's warrant. At the end of June, therefore, Swift interceded at least one more time. He wrote a forceful letter to the permanent undersecretary at Dublin Castle, insisting that the Lord Lieutenant had indeed named Raymond and, 'if any difficulty yet remained', referring the issue to Lord Chancellor Phipps, the stronger of the Lords Justices. When the case was finally closed, Raymond, like his predecessor Stearne, did hold Moymet.[1]

Other matters of preferment also troubled Swift's mind during his journey to Ireland. He felt deeply responsible for poor Thomas Parnell, who lingered in London with flickering hopes; and Swift wished as well to find something for Thomas Warburton, his own conscientious curate at Laracor. For both these men his first plans involved Archbishop King; but just as the new dean was starting out for Dublin, the archbishop went to Bath for the sake of his health. I think that Swift believed King owed him some gratitude as well as some little degree of deference. When Harley was attacked by Guiscard, a malicious story about the archbishop got into circulation; according to this, his grace had publicly referred to an episode in Tacitus so as to imply that the true reason for prosecuting Guiscard was to stop him from revealing Harley's intrigues with the French. The scandal almost got published in the *Post Boy*, but Swift saw the text in time and was able to suppress it. When he deliberately reported to King what he had done, he received the archbishop's warm appreciation.[2] But in spite of this spasm of fellowship, the political differences between the two men gaped more and more widely as the peace negotiations advanced, until by the spring of 1713 there was practically a feud between them. King disliked the secretiveness of the ministry; he disapproved of the bill to resume royal grants; he had no faith in Philip V's renunciation of the French crown; he believed England should go on fighting up to the formal conclusion of peace; he worried about the Pretender; and on all these points he repeatedly turned aside Swift's assurances.[3] Still, even an archbishop could not accomplish much if he alienated

---

[1] *Journal*, 18 Sept. 1712; 16 May 1713, 6 Jun. (assuming the 'blind parson' is Dunbar); Williams I. 346–7, 370–1 and n. 6.

[2] *Journal*, 8 Apr. 1711 and *passim*; Williams I. 219–21, 223–5.

[3] Williams I. 298–9, 301, 303, 331–4, 338–9, 342–3.

the government in power; and I think Swift believed that his grace was at least slightly intimidated by his own friendship with the men in power. There were, after all, services the dean might perform for the Metropolitan; and when King saw his great lawsuit with Christ Church about to come at last before the English House of Lords, he did not hesitate to enlist Swift's help in securing favourable votes.[1]

For Parnell Swift wanted the prebend of Dunlavin, which he himself would vacate in becoming dean. Since King had been a guardian of Parnell during the poet's minority, and had helped to make him Archdeacon of Clogher, Swift might have supposed the archbishop would feel naturally disposed to co-operate. But two letters from Swift to his grace had no effect at all: King had already disposed of the prebend.[2] For Warburton Swift wanted some livings vacated in July through the death of the vicar of Rathcoole. While King was still at Bath, Swift wrote recommending his curate as 'a gentleman of very good learning and sense'. But King, about to leave now for Ireland, replied that over a dozen letters concerning these livings had already reached him, and he would not make the final decision until he had spoken to Swift in Dublin. The archbishop arrived home in the latter part of August, and Swift was able to see him within a matter of days. But the interview proved unsuccessful, and Warburton never received what his patron had asked for.[3] Such frustrations were not wholly unilateral. At that time St Patrick's Cathedral lacked the spire which now deforms it; and the archbishop keenly desired one built. His obliging friend Stearne had put aside two hundred pounds for the purpose during his deanship; so King urged Swift to carry out the scheme. Swift, with less than his utmost tact, put off a definite judgment, though indicating that he found the idea unalluring. King, with characteristic obstinacy, clung to his proposal.[4] But no spire rose in the lifetime of either contestant.

I cannot believe that these failures of reciprocity amazed Swift. He had told Ford long before that he expected no sincerity

---

[1] *Ibid.*, pp. 343, 353.   [2] *Ibid.*, pp. 344–5, 353, 356–7.
[3] *Ibid.*, pp. 377, 382, 411.   [4] *Ibid.*, pp. 350, 354, 357.

from the archbishop[1]; and he had several reasons to wonder whether a recommendation from himself might not hurt a man's chances with his grace. Even before leaving London, Swift had discovered that two livings in the gift of the dean and chapter of St Patrick's, which he had anxiously hoped to dispose of with his own hand, had been settled by Stearne in defiance of his explicit wishes; and almost certainly Stearne had taken King's advice in these decisions.[2] I suspect that part of Swift's strategy was to accumulate a number of disobligations from King precisely so that when a request travelled from the archbishop to the dean, he would be comfortably placed to deny it.

With so many disappointments hovering about him, Swift must have turned his feelings wistfully toward the pacifying sympathy of Mrs Johnson. He had so often missed her attentions when he was ill in London; he had so often wanted her conversation when public events astonished him. Over the years he had pictured her in imagination—'O Madam Ppt, welcome home; was it pleasant riding? did your horse stumble?'—'Ppt will be peeping out of her room at Mrs. de Caudres' down upon the folks as they come from church'—'Ppt is naturally a stout walker, and carries herself firm, methinks I see her strut, and step clever over a kennel.'[3]

But the let-down after the immensely prolonged strain was too much for any agency to relieve quickly. Exhausted from travelling, sick with vertigo, and burdened by his worries, Swift arrived in Dublin only to face a stream of new chores. Straight from the boat he had to fix himself in the fortnight's lodgings he hired for twelve shillings. Then came the oaths and the preparations for his installation, which followed the landing by only three days. Swift's return home filled him with the usual aching discontent of the traveller who discovers that home has shrunk and lost colour while the world has been gloriously expanding. After the colossal anxieties of thirty-three months, even a Roman triumph would have seemed bathetic. Finding the same old

[1] Williams, pp. 257–8.   [2] *Journal*, 16 May 1713.
[3] *Ibid.*, 30 Jun. 1711, pt 1; 25 Mar. 1711; 10 Nov. 1711. I read 'Ppt' for 'Stella', and I suspect my last quotation is irony.

routines and the same small obsessions in the lives of his acquaintances, Swift must have drifted as near to spleen as he ever let himself go.[1] Through the summer, Ford and Lewis kept him minutely informed of events in Whitehall; and memories of England kept chilling his bleakness. When he thought of the great life from which he felt excluded, he grew doubly bitter.

Official callers competed with his old friends for any leisure he had to spare. He allowed them a single day and returned no visits—they were, he said, 'all to the Dean, and none to the Doctor'. After four weeks in Ireland he told Vanessa, 'At my first coming I thought I should have dyed with discontent, and was horribly melancholy while they were installing me, but it begins to wear off, and change to dullness.'[2] Later, Archbishop King reported what must have been the common impression, that Swift 'behaved himself with an appearance of contempt to everybody here'.[3]

After two weeks of formalities and visitors, he fled from Dublin to Laracor—with a very unsteady head and some bitter infusions prescribed by the best doctors. Here in the country was another sort of spectacle that had haunted his memory while he lived in England: 'Don't you begin to see the flowers and blossoms of the field?' he had written one spring—'How busy should I be now at Laracor.' Thinking of his rural parish had made him sigh: 'All the days I have passed here, have been dirt to those.' And now the reality did not betray him. He lived in the little earth-floored cabin he had built, sleeping on a field bed and riding all he could. His river walk looked pretty, and he could watch the trout playing in his canal. He passed hour upon hour cultivating the garden, supervising improvements, pruning willows, making up a ditch, cutting hedges. To keep him company, the ladies moved to Trim, where he could easily see them with the Raymonds. He conferred with his curate Warburton and with his eccentric man of business, Jo Beaumont. He went shooting with Mr Wesley, whose wife he had so generously befriended in London. He rode

[1] Williams I. 365–7, 372–4; *Accounts 1712–13*, fol. 10.
[2] Williams I. 372–3, 375.
[3] Ball II. 81, n. 2.

out to meet the judges when they came to hold assizes at Trim.[1]

Meanwhile, in England, the course of affairs looked less and less auspicious for his friends. Lewis and Ford kept Swift in touch with the calamities as they fell—Lewis reflecting Oxford's judgments and Ford, as Gazetteer, closer to Bolingbroke. Lewis begged him to come back at once, for the Lord Treasurer's sake. Ford wanted help getting a post in the office of Bromley, the incoming Secretary of State.[2] In general, the great peace which so many people had thought would solve the ministry's old problems was only breeding new ones, and the murderous rivalry of Oxford and Bolingbroke was almost halting the processes of government. Even while Swift was first starting on his journey from London, a tumultuous vote on the Union had shaken the whole constitution. The Scots, furious over English economic policy, brought in a bill to dissolve the Union. The violent country gentlemen who supported Bolingbroke would have liked nothing better. But Oxford's statesmanship made one of its extraordinary efforts, and the bill was defeated. A few weeks later, Bolingbroke's darling measure, the commercial articles of the treaty with France, came up; and on this fundamental issue the government met its worst defeat since 1710. From the drift of the evidence it appears that Oxford was not inclined to exert himself for his detested colleague's brainchild; he may even have encouraged Sir Thomas Hanmer to withdraw his support. Certainly Oxford told Swift he did not care whether or not the commercial treaty was passed in this session; the Whigs organized frantic opposition to it; Hanmer's followers voted with the Whigs; and Bolingbroke could soon claim a fresh grudge against Oxford.[3] Less than a fortnight later, the Whigs threw the most sinister reflections on the ministry by forcing a vote—necessarily

---

[1] Williams I. 373-4; *Accounts 1712-13*, fols. 10ᵛ, 12. I infer the shooting from the purchase of powder and shot and the gift of a shilling to Wesley's groom (fol. 12).

[2] I assume this is the reference of Swift's letter (Williams I. 377-8), because Lewis, who remained undersecretary under Bromley, is mentioned as able to help Ford if he gets the post; because Bolingbroke, who was of course the principal Secretary of State and also Bromley's backer, received a letter from Swift on the subject; and because Bromley was just in process of becoming Secretary in place of Dartmouth, so that other changes, within the office, would be natural.

[3] Williams I. 375; Trevelyan III. 254-9.

favourable—on a motion that the Duke of Lorraine should be asked to expel the Pretender from his dominions. About the same time, Convocation was growing unpleasantly fractious, and on 1 July the Lower House accepted a report savagely attacking the bishops. Harcourt, who took his stand with Bolingbroke against Oxford, had put immense pressure on the Queen, and she had finally agreed to elevate Atterbury, the contentious leader of the Lower House, to be Bishop of Rochester; and Swift, in congratulating him, predicted an early promotion to the bishopric of London.[1] As one more bold sign of the strength behind the cabal of Bolingbroke, Harcourt, and Lady Masham, the Lord Treasurer, in mid-August, had to allow his friend Dartmouth to give up the office of Secretary of State for the Southern Department and see it go to the highflying Speaker Bromley, while Dartmouth was made a harmless Lord Privy Seal. It was when so many quakes and tremors were already dividing their leaders that the Tories now found themselves yet further troubled by the need, in accordance with the Triennial Act, to hold a new parliamentary election.

By the time the polling began, Lewis had persuaded Swift to move the date of his departure forward. Oxford, he said, had confided in Swift more than any other man, and wished him to come over without any further delay.[2] After still demurring a few times, Swift indulged his own desire to give in at last. With his health far improved, he ended his rural holiday and returned to Dublin in time to act as godfather at the christening of Archdeacon Walls's new child (a daughter who had been planned as a son). The festivity cost Swift a present of £2 2s. 5d. to Mrs Walls; and a week later he had to lay out a pound more on a treat for his cathedral chapter.[3] The sociable Irish circle he had been used to meeting as an informal little club was broken up, now that Stearne lived in Dromore and he himself was to be yet again in England. Even the ladies decided to withdraw from Dublin and live in Trim until Swift came home.[4] I suspect he thought the change would be good for Mrs Johnson's health as well as her

---

[1] Williams I. 379.　　[2] *Ibid.*, pp. 378, 383.　　[3] *Accounts 1712–13*, fols. 12, 18.
[4] Williams I. 387.

finances, but he also thought his friends would miss the society of Dublin and hoped they would spend Christmas in town.

Before setting off for England, Swift managed to have his talk with the newly returned archbishop; but by the end of August he was waiting for the earliest ship. Sailing from Dublin on Saturday, 29 August, he reached Parkgate on Monday. Sir Gilbert Dolben, a wealthy Irish judge and a friend of Lord Oxford's, had invited the dean to visit his seat at Finedon in Northants. So Swift turned aside to pass four days there. Otherwise his trip was not remarkable. He spent two and a half pounds for the hire of horses, and on some days he covered nearly fifty miles. He arrived at Finedon on Friday, 4 September, left the following Tuesday, and was in London the next evening, 9 September.[1]

[1] Williams I. 411, n. 4; p. 420, n. 1. Swift's route was Dublin, Parkgate (overnight), Chester (overnight), Whitchurch, Newport in Shropshire (overnight), Coventry (overnight), Dunchurch, Northampton, Finedon (four nights), Market Street (overnight), Barnet, London: see *Accounts 1712–13*, fol. 12ᵛ.

Chapter Twenty-seven

BOLINGBROKE'S RISE

————————————

I. SWIFT AND OXFORD

In Swift's lifelong yoking of preacher with jester, few periods
called for more elaborate operations than the year that began in September 1713. It was the preacher and senior partner who spoke when Swift told Arbuthnot, 'I would never let
people run mad without telling and warning them sufficiently.'[1]
But the return to London gave him so many reasons to draw on
his conciliatory powers that he soon felt depleted; and all his
talent for self-mockery could not stop him from groaning with
disgust over 'courts, and ministers, and politics'.[2] As he saw the
prospect, it was frantically exasperating. The Queen, her ministers, a small majority of the Lords, and a great majority of the
Commons had the appearance of being all united as to fundamental policy; yet the two chiefs remained so eager to ruin each
other that they were sacrificing the government and their country to a passion for mutual slaughter. The irony providing the
whole crazy structure with its essential support was that Bolingbroke could not possibly be at the head of the administration because too few people trusted him and because his principles were
too unsteady. Yet Oxford had grown so immobile, uncommuni-
cative, and incoherent that hardly any of the decisions on which
efficient government depends were being made at all. More and
more when the Lord Treasurer did choose a course, it was based
on little besides spiteful opposition to something he knew Bolingbroke wanted.

What Swift underestimated was the extent to which his
mighty friends and their various associates stood for irreconcilable ideologies. Oxford simply could not believe in the radical

[1] Williams II. 75.   [2] *Ibid.*, I. 389.

Toryism of Bolingbroke's gang. He did not believe in flinging out of office or refusing to promote all those who co-operated with the Dissenters or the Junto. In spite of his secret dealings with the Pretender, Oxford took no positive steps to ensure James III's succession. As much as he could, he held out hope to low-church partisans, refusing to dismiss people like Steele or the Duchess of Somerset, and opposing the more radical enactments of the furious country gentlemen.

Yet Oxford could not make these attitudes explicit without losing the support he needed in Parliament and consequently the façade of power essential to his kind of politics. So his natural vagueness and secrecy were aggravated by the need to hide his thoughts even from a friend he trusted so deeply as Swift. Instead of speaking out, he took to blocking appointments he disliked, or silently arranging compensating promotions when he could not prevent a disagreeable one. In the summer of 1713, for example, while the elections for a new Parliament were in progress, he had to let Bromley displace Dartmouth as Secretary of State. But in managing the elections themselves, Oxford held his hand, refusing to eliminate Whiggish or low-church office-holders who might impede an overwhelming victory for the Tories. The outcome was a slightly weakened majority for the government in the House of Commons, making the administration more dependent on moderates like Hanmer, who succeeded Bromley as Speaker. When the elections were over, Oxford showed his power by undermining whatever strength Bolingbroke had gained through making Bromley his colleague; for at the end of September it transpired that the Queen had revived the offices of Secretary of State for Scotland and Lord Chancellor of Scotland, filling them both with Oxford's sympathizers. Such announcements doubly humiliated Bolingbroke: not only did his authority shrink as responsibilities were transferred to the new appointees, but the Queen's distrust of him was clearly displayed both by the event and by his own lack of forewarning. 'These things make Lord Bolingbroke stare', said Erasmus Lewis.[1] In Irish affairs the pat-

---

[1] Trevelyan III. 260. The Earl of Mar was made Secretary of State for Scotland 30 Sept. 1713; the Earl of Seafield was reappointed Lord Chancellor of Scotland 14 Sept. 1713; Bromley was appointed 17 Aug.

tern was reversed. Oxford saw to it that the Duke of Shrewsbury was made Lord Lieutenant, and Shrewsbury insisted, against the express desire of Bolingbroke, on taking the Whiggish Sir John Stanley with him as secretary[1]; but Sir Constantine Phipps, who had come in under Ormonde, remained as Lord Chancellor and Lord Justice—and Phipps belonged to Bolingbroke.[2]

As if to console the Lord Treasurer for the tribulations deriving from his office, Oxford now enjoyed the most splendid domestic triumph of his life, one of his two great achievements as marriage broker. At the end of August 1713 his studious son was at last married to the handsome, red-headed heiress of the late Duke of Newcastle. The colossal amount of property involved fascinated many observers, including Swift, who once guessed that the girl would come into about ten thousand pounds a year.[3] Nine days after this ceremony, Swift reached London; and the next day, though the court was still at Windsor, he saw Lord Oxford in town.[4] I assume the main subjects of their talk were political; but some words must have passed about the wedding, and I suspect that the Lord Treasurer complimented the dean on a poem Swift had written for that occasion, entitled *To Lord Harley*. This prothalamion is a eulogy of bride and groom, congratulating them on a range of moral and intellectual virtues which include the power to appreciate one another. It was never published in Swift's lifetime, and it is too conventionally mythologized to be interesting in its own right. The themes, conceits, and language are so reminiscent of *Cadenus and Vanessa* that both poems must have been composed about the same time.[5] But apart from this aspect the neat tetrameter couplets seem important only as a token of Swift's intense loyalty to a feckless patron.[6]

By this time the paradox of his alliance with both Oxford and Bolingbroke appears understandable. Certainly the programme

---

[1] Somerville, p. 311. But cf. Simms, pp. 84–5.

[2] Shrewsbury was appointed 22 Sept.; Stanley's term began at the same time.

[3] *Journal*, 8 Nov. 1711; cf. Williams II. 68.   [4] *Accounts 1712–13*, fol. 12ᵛ.

[5] This is Professor Herbert Davis's suggestion (*Poems* II. 684–5); cf. *Poems* II. 703, n. to l. 539, and 'To Lord Harley', l. 66.

[6] There is no proof that a copy of the poem ever reached Oxford or his son, though I do assume one did: no transcript seems to have survived among the Harley papers, and the poem was only published twenty years after Swift's death. It may be incomplete, or Swift may possibly have judged it unworthy of the occasion.

the dean recommended was close to the Secretary's, although he would have executed it less belligerently than Bolingbroke wished. Yet, like everyone else, he could not attach himself whole-heartedly to Bolingbroke's leadership; he admired the young man's talent while distrusting his ambition. Oxford, on the other hand, provoked continual complaints against his blunders as a politician, but Swift clung to him beyond the point of ruin.

I assume that certain obscure notes which Swift wrote in the autumn of 1713 are detailed evidence of his impatience with the Lord Treasurer.[1] These jottings look like an *aide-mémoire* for a conversation he planned to have with Oxford, or else, perhaps, notes for a memorial to be left with him. Swift complains here against the chronic delays, presumably of the Lord Treasurer, in reaching essential decisions: 'No orders of any kind whatsoever, given till the last extremity'. These delays, he says, are making efficient administrative processes quite impossible. They need-lessly inflate the cost of government and they stifle what feeble impulse toward co-operation still survives among public officers. Among the dozen particulars that Swift denounces is the govern-ment's failure to carry out its promise of asking friendly princes to keep the Pretender out of their dominions—this failure, says Swift, will make 'us' be called Jacobites. He says the appointment of a Secretary of State and a Lord Chancellor for Scotland must cause dissension among all the secretaries. He complains that Sir George Byng, a Junto associate who was naturally distasteful to the Tories, is permitted to remain on the Admiralty commission.

Obviously it was Oxford's character but Bolingbroke's pro-gramme that held Swift. He later came near saying as much when he told the Lord Treasurer, 'In your publick capacity you have often angred me to the heart, but, as a private man, never once.'[2] There seems more than a touch here of Swift's old relationship with Sir William Temple, another feckless patron whom he in-variably eulogized in print. The way the powerful Treasurer reached out and drew the humble parson into the freedom of his household left Swift continually grateful. 'His personall kindness to me was excessive', he wrote to Vanessa; 'he distinguished and

[1] See Appendix E, below.   [2] Williams II. 44.

chose me above all other men while he was great.' Swift never addressed a poem to Bolingbroke. And as evidence that Oxford's tenderness for Swift was genuine, we have a remarkable passage in one of the very few letters he ever wrote to him: asking Swift to visit him in his retirement, Oxford says, 'If I have not tir'd you tête-à-tête fling away so much time upon one who loves you, and I believe in the mass of souls ours were plac'd neer each other.'[1]

Several of these relationships are hinted at in a fine poem which Swift published during the last week of October—an imitation of an epistle by Horace, 'Address'd to a Noble Peer'.[2] Possibly Swift wished to enhance the Lord Treasurer's reputation in a season when it had sunk dangerously low. Certainly he wished to celebrate his own intimacy with the chief minister of Great Britain. The poem, a very free version of Horace's, purports to tell how Dr Swift met Lord Oxford, how they became friends, and how his lordship only made the doctor wretched by giving him a deanery. Except for the names and characterizations, little of the story pretends to be factual. Oxford notices an interesting-looking parson in the street and sends Erasmus Lewis to find out who the man is. When he discovers it's the witty Dr Swift, he has Lewis ask him to dinner with the Lord Treasurer. Swift assumes the invitation is a joke, and refuses. A few days later, Oxford sees him again and beckons him over to the coach. Realizing his earlier mistake, Swift now apologizes and accepts a new invitation. The two men fall at once into an easy camaraderie, and Oxford soon makes his new friend the dean of a cathedral in Ireland. Swift takes up the promising post only to discover it is a compound of vexations and expenses. He hurries back to London, deep in debt, and appears, dirty and exhausted, before Oxford. When the Treasurer scolds him for looking so shabby, Swift begs him to restore the dean to his original state; and so the poem closes.

The emphasis, in the last third of the poem, on money troubles suggests that the writer hoped the politician would respond to an implicit plea for the thousand pounds Swift thought he had been

[1] *Ibid.* II. 85.
[2] *Part of the Seventh Epistle of the First Book of Horace Imitated*, published 23 Oct. 1713.

promised by Oxford.[1] But the motif is not oppressive, and the general zest and lightness of the lines tend to astonish one by the ease with which the comic poet was able to smile at himself during another grim epoch of his life. All through the story, the jester mocks the preacher. Instead of representing the deanery as a serious preferment, Swift treats the apparent elevation as in fact a practical joke played on him by an oddly Swiftian Lord Oxford, who 'loves mischief better than his meat'. The poet is thus the victim rather than perpetrator of a hoax. It was commonplace for expectant protégés to flatter their patrons by calling them Maecenas, but Swift's reversal of the usual relation between his witty self and a naïve butt seems a more delicate compliment.[2]

Like Horace, Swift was proud of his knack of working real bits of conversation into a regular meter; unlike Horace, of course, he sacrifices music and expressive sound to rhyme or idiom. He never attempts the allusive subtleties that Dryden and Pope could produce when imitating Latin classics. The broad application of an ancient tale to a modern instance seemed enough for him. But the effect of lifelike, characteristic speech remains brilliant. In the following extract it is combined with a clever matching of rhythm to tone, for the line disintegrates into short, quick units as the tone changes from comfortable to wretched:

> Suppose him, now, a *Dean* compleat
> The silver virge, with decent pride,
> Stuck underneath his cushion-side:
> Suppose him gone through all vexations,
> Patents, instalments, abjurations,
> First-fruits and tenths, and chapter-treats,
> Dues, payments, fees, demands and cheats,
> (The wicked laity's contriving,
> To hinder clergymen from thriving) . . .

The not inconsiderable measure of *hubris* in Swift's nature seems revealed by the impudence of many details. It was hardly discreet for Swift to describe himself as 'a clergyman of special note, / for shunning those of his own coat', or to publish his hope of dis-

---

[1] Swift's enemy Boyer makes this the sole purpose of the poem: *Political State*, Nov. 1713, p. 349.

[2] Actually, Swift speaks as Mena, in Horace's poem, addressing Philippus.

training a thousand pounds from the public till. The Whigs were glad to turn such phrases against him, and Boyer asked, 'Who else should be so *hardy* as to offer such balderdash to a *prime minister*?'[1]

Four weeks after the poem appeared, Oxford found himself stricken by just the sort of catastrophe he had always managed to escape in his private life. Lady Betty, his beloved elder child, had married the son of the immensely rich Duke of Leeds. Swift deeply admired the young lady, often praised her, and once said she was 'adorned with all possible good qualityes'.[2] Early in November 1713 she bore her first child, a son and the cause of the usual rejoicing. But during the lying-in she seems to have been infected with puerperal fever, because two weeks after the birth, at the age of twenty-eight, she died.[3] Swift, acting both as priestly guide and condoling friend, immediately sent Oxford a beautifully composed message of sympathy. The sentiments are conventional, and the praise of the dead woman sounds excessive (a common fault in Swift's condolences); but the grave, dignified tone is perfectly correct, and the writer's attachment to the Lord Treasurer could not be more sincere: 'God almighty, who would not disappoint your endeavours for the public, thought fit to punish you with a domestic loss, where he knew your heart was most exposed.'[4]

Swift saw the Lord Treasurer twice during the week after this calamity. The court was still at Windsor, and the dean used to go out for many visits, spending more than a week there around 1 October, and two or more days on most of the weekends which followed until the Queen moved to St James's for the opening of Parliament. He often sent his new servant Tom by stage coach (3s. 6d. each way) and usually travelled himself with Oxford.[5]

---

[1] *Political State*, Nov. 1713, p. 349.   [2] Williams I. 411; see also pp. 404–6, 409.

[3] Boyer, *Political State*, p. 383; Williams I. 411, n. 2.

[4] Williams I. 405; the text is probably that of a draft.

[5] Much of this is inferential: see *Accounts 1712–13*, fols. 12^v, 1 3; *Enquiry*, pp. 54–5 and n., 131–3; Williams I. 386; 410, n. 1; 411; V. 228. In his imitation of Horace, *Sat.* II. vi. 77–8, speaking of Oxford and himself, Swift writes, 'As once a week we travel down / To Windsor, and again to town.' The accounts indicate that Swift was at Windsor 26 Sept. to 5 Oct. (two weekends and the days between), and Saturday–Sunday, 10–11, 17–18, 24–25 Oct.; but then they end. Kennett's portrait of Swift at

About the time of Lady Betty's fatal illness, a startling rumour spread, that the Lord Treasurer would soon resign from office. The new intrigue to oust him had begun, ironically enough, while Oxford was staying in Cambridgeshire for his son's wedding. Lady Masham had joined with Bolingbroke to wheedle the Queen into removing him.[1] Their attacks on Oxford became so insistent that he soon appeared ready to step down. In the middle of November the *Examiner* published a weird essay, all cryptic hints and misty anticipation, which sounded like a reproach, inspired by Oxford, to schemers plotting the Treasurer's fall. The nearest the writer came to an intelligible argument was to warn radical Tories that by overthrowing Oxford they would only expose themselves to the triumph and vengeance of the Whigs: 'The tryal at this time is extremely dangerous, and may serve to open an unhappy breach, whereat all our inveterate foes may enter and devour us.'[2] Boyer, in a blast of contempt, reported the rumour as a 'current whisper, that the person who *Atlas-like*, has for above three years sustain'd the weight of public affairs, entertain'd thoughts of laying down his great burthen'.[3] But Dartmouth and some others were able to stiffen Oxford's resistance to his rivals; and there is evidence that Swift was among those urging the Treasurer to stay on.[4] By the last week of November the crisis had passed without the effect intended by the conspirators. Oxford swallowed down his many mortifications and wrote to Dartmouth, 'I will hasten, according to your admoni-

Windsor is dated 2 Nov., a Monday. On 2 Feb. Swift says he 'came yesterday [i.e., Sunday] from Windsor with Lord Treasurer' (Williams II. 9). None of Swift's surviving letters during this period (9 Sept. to 16 Feb.) bear the date of a Saturday or Sunday, although there is one for Saturday, 6 Mar., from London. When he did spend weekends at Windsor, I think he would have put off correspondence till a weekday. He endorsed a letter which reached him 4 Mar. with the note, 'I was then in London', which seems to imply that he had been spending much time out of town (Williams II. 12). Steele's *Englishman* of 15 Feb. 1714, addressed to 'Mr. —— at Windsor', is supposed to be addressed to Swift (Winton, p. 194).

[1] Trevelyan III. 260.   [2] *Examiner*, 16 Nov. 1713.

[3] *Political State*, Nov. 1713 (VI. 397). '*Atlas-like*' may be an allusion to Swift's poem *Atlas*, circulating in manuscript.

[4] In July 1714 Arbuthnot told Swift that Lady Masham had blamed Arbuthnot, Lewis, and Swift for keeping Oxford in when he offered to resign. I assume, unlike Williams and Swift, that this refers to the events of Nov. 1713 (Williams II. 81 and n. 4; 109).

tion, to return to my duty.'[1] Swift must have felt relieved. He was still scheming to reunite the Secretary and the Treasurer. Decades later he told the story of his supreme effort as he then remembered it:

> When I returned to England, I found their quarrells and coldness increased; I laboured to reconcile them as much as I was able; I contrived to bring them to my Lord Masham's, at St. James's. My Lord and Lady Masham left us together. I expostulated with them both, but could not find any good consequences. I was to go to Windsor next day with my Lord Treasurer; I pretended business that prevented me . . . and so I sent them to Windsor next day, which was Saturday, in the same coach: expecting they would come to some éclaircissement, but I followed them to Windsor; where my Lord Bolingbroke told me . . . that my scheme had come to nothing.[2]

A priest gets used to nagging people into reformation. One may blame Swift for naïveté in supposing that mere reason could prevail against mercenary, power-hungry hate. But he was at least acting consistently with his own view that private character is the best clue to public events; and he was sticking to the rule he recommended to Arbuthnot, of not letting people run mad without warning them.

II. SWIFT AND STEELE

Shortly before the earliest of Swift's autumn visits to Windsor, Steele published a bitter attack on the government with his own name printed on the title page. I suppose it was a relief for Swift to suspend the frustrations of internecine hatred and pounce openly on an enemy to his whole faction. At the end of September, when the pamphlet had just come out, he bought a copy for a shilling[3]; but his reasons for wishing to administer a public flogging to his old comrade go back much further, to the spring of the year. By April 1713, Steele had come to feel chronically indignant over what he regarded as the indecent allegations of

---

[1] Trevelyan III. 260.

[2] Williams v. 45–6; cf. *Enquiry*, p. 54. I now doubt my own earlier belief that this incident occurred in September or October.

[3] *Accounts 1712–13*, fol. 12v.

Tory journalists against the patriotic band of Whigs and their allies. In particular Steele blamed the *Examiner* for spreading its venom over his hero, the Duke of Marlborough. Like most impulsive, passionate men, Steele habitually identified his private self-interest with motives of noble altruism. Since the same pamphleteers who slandered the great Duke also slandered the great Duke's defenders, it was easy for Steele to sound recklessly loyal when defending his own rhetoric against the unkind analyses of ministerial writers.

Toward the end of April the *Examiner* had published an attack on the Earl of Nottingham and his daughter. Steele found the details unforgivably offensive and replied immediately in a number of his six-week-old periodical the *Guardian*—which had pretensions to neutrality and received contributions from Tories as well as Whigs. In a mock-letter to 'Nestor Ironside', the pseudonym he himself used as editor of the *Guardian*, Steele described the Examiner as a 'miscreant' who would 'trample on the ashes of the dead' and was 'worse than an assassin'. He also alluded furiously to the *Examiner*'s vilification of Marlborough.[1] When the *Examiner* nevertheless went ahead, in an early issue, to attack Marlborough again, Steele shot back with another letter to the *Guardian*, printed this time over his own name.[2] While the true editor of the *Examiner* was now a genial hack named William Oldisworth, it was universally known that both Dr Swift and Mrs Manley had written many of the papers; and though Oldisworth explicitly announced that Swift had no share in his present work, few people believed him.[3] We know from Swift's letters to Mrs Johnson that he had in fact given orders and aid to the authors of the *Examiner* on occasions since the summer of 1711, when his full responsibility had stopped. (He certainly wrote the *Examiner* of 2 February 1713; and I suspect he wrote one as late as 31 May 1714.) We also know that long before John Barber installed the plump Mary Manley as his mistress, she had obliged Captain Steele with her choicest favours. In the course of his fresh explosion Steele saw fit to guess at the authorship of the paper he was

---

[1] *Examiner*, 24 Apr. 1713; *Guardian*, 28 Apr. 1713.
[2] *Examiner*, 11 May; *Guardian*, 12 May.   [3] *Examiner*, 23 Mar., 22 May 1713.

denouncing, and said, 'I am heartily sorry I called him a miscreant, that word I think signifies an unbeliever.' Then with a characteristic lapse of taste he indulged in a quite gratuitous indiscretion. Remarking that some friends claimed they had seen him talking to the Examiner and that others reported he had 'formerly lain with' the Examiner, Steele went on to declare, 'It is nothing to me whether the *Examiner* writes against me in the character of an estranged friend or an exasperated mistress.'

The day after this number of the *Guardian* appeared, Swift heard of it, secured a copy, and read it.[1] Charges of irreligion had been tossed at him so often that he had grown not callous but feverishly sensitive to them, for he reacted to printed malice with just the opposite emotions from a man like Oxford. To hear anybody call the new Dean of St Patrick's an 'unbeliever' would have enraged Swift; to receive the label from Steele, for whose sake he thought he had performed several utterly disinterested favours, must have staggered him; to find that Steele grounded his insult on a paper which his victim never wrote, made the gesture appear so unforgivably vile that even Swift looked for conclusive evidence before dealing with the offence.

When he began taking action, his first step suggests that he was determined to put Steele 'as much in the wrong as we can'—a policy Swift recommended as the best procedure in controversy.[2] Rather than march directly up to the calumniator, therefore, he addressed a letter to Addison.[3] I suppose Swift expected the more sober of the pair of friends to manage the more reckless one. But Steele was not the only man who would regard such an approach as unflattering. Anyhow, there was no indirection in the content of Swift's message. He said Steele had insinuated 'with the utmost malice' that Swift wrote the *Examiner*. He said Steele had abused him in 'the grossest manner he could possibly invent'. He reproached Steele for signing his own name to the paper (as, I suppose, giving the libel the authority of Steele's known acquain-

---

[1] Williams I. 347.   [2] Davis VIII. 96.

[3] Williams I. 347–8 (13 May 1713). Since the published text of this letter goes back to a copy found in Swift's own papers, it is probably a draft of what was actually sent to Addison; and we cannot therefore be sure that any particular detail was finally preserved in the message which Addison saw.

tance with Swift) and for disregarding Oldisworth's statement that Swift did not write the *Examiner*. He accused Steele of 'the highest degree of baseness, ingratitude, and injustice'. He said Steele should have expostulated with him as a friend before maligning him in public. He ended with the claim that Oxford had kept Steele in his post of stamp commissioner upon Swift's pleading. Thus with an appearance of roundabout tactfulness Swift let himself employ the most provocative language.

Of course, Steele had his own private connections with Lord Oxford, which Swift knew nothing about; and one did not have to be born in Ireland to feel aggressively insulted by Swift's tone. So far from stirring himself toward any effort to soothe Steele, or to bring the old acquaintances together, Addison merely turned Swift's inflammatory letter over to him; and the result was an admirably candid and only moderately provocative letter in reply.[1] It seems a token of the mixed guilt and resentment which both parties to the quarrel were feeling that barely a month after the staging of *Cato*, when the political fires had appeared to burn so low, they should have chosen the medium of epistolary correspondence for an exchange of their views, rather than the more natural and healing way of conversation. Steele declared it was not Swift's interposition that had kept him in his office: the ministers 'laughed' at Swift if they said so. He very properly insisted that Swift's remarks on the authorship of the *Examiner* were equivocal, and said he still thought Swift was an accomplice of the real author. He closed with a generous congratulation to Swift upon his deanship.

Swift's riposte was a bit less inflammatory than his opening missile but much longer.[2] When he wrote it, he was obviously shaking with rage though driven by the need to justify himself. He had once laid down a rule with Lord Oxford that when any complaint was brought against him, Oxford should take it to Swift, if an explanation was wanted, and not sulk or hold a secret grudge.[3] He had recently quarrelled with the Duke of Argyll for

---

[1] Williams I. 351.

[2] *Ibid.*, pp. 354–6 (23 May 1713). Again the published text seems taken from a draft which Swift had preserved and not from the actual copy which Steele read.

[3] *Ibid.*, p. 330.

ignoring this rule.[1] So he bitterly resented Steele's bursting into print before making inquiries of Swift. The humiliating suggestion that Oxford had kept his tongue in his cheek when he told Swift of Steele's missing the appointment arranged at Swift's request, also seemed insufferable. After a detailed précis of that awkward affair, Swift commented, 'Suppose they did laugh at me, I ask whether my inclinations to serve you merit to be rewarded by the vilest treatment, whether they succeeded or no? If your interpretation were true I was laughed at only for your sake; which, I think, is going pretty far to serve a friend.' He denied having 'the least hand' in writing the *Examiner* and announced that he had often prevented ministerial writers from publishing reflections upon Steele. He also blamed Steele for saying the 'vilest things' of him and for inflicting 'the most savage injuries in the world'.

Meanwhile, as if to supply a main plot for these low episodes, Steele had decided to stand for Parliament in the elections that were to begin during Swift's summer in Ireland. Since he could not be eligible to do so while remaining a Commissioner of the Stamp Office, he determined to resign that post, and began composing a message to Oxford on this subject the same day he received this new letter from Swift. In addition, because the *Examiner* had just attacked Marlborough again,[2] Steele also found the time to draft yet another epistle from 'Richard Steele' to 'Nestor Ironside' which appeared punctually in a *Guardian*.[3] Here he not only rebuffed the *Examiner* and denounced the ministry, but also undercut his own original insinuation against an 'estranged friend or an exasperated mistress' by remarking that the names sometimes given for the author of the *Examiner* included 'one for whom I have a value, and another whom I cannot but neglect'. I suppose Swift's reproaches had encouraged him to offer this public quasi-apology, but Steele was not prepared to shift any closer to a recantation. In replying privately to Swift's fresh and elaborate challenge, therefore, Steele indulged his usual instincts. Rather than confine himself to merely the issues between Dean Swift and Captain Steele, he hoisted in the repu-

[1] *Ibid.*, pp. 330–1.   [2] 22 May.   [3] 23 May.

tation of Marlborough and the altruism of Marlborough's eager defender. At the same time he showed his fury over the allegations made in Swift's letter to Addison, and rejected for himself the label of 'the vilest of mankind'.[1] Jumbling these topics together, Steele emerged with the sublimely irrelevant vow that he would sacrifice his career sooner than halt his praise of the great Duke. By hinting at his resignation of the commissionership but not at the motive that made it necessary, he bathed his head in a fine halo of disinterested virtue. But in one sentence Steele's native, independent generosity peals out above the theatrical sentiments: 'I do not speak this calmly, after the ill usage in your letter to Addison, out of terror of your wit or my Lord Treasurer's power, but pure kindness to the agreeable qualities I once so passionately delighted in, in you.'[2]

But Swift had the last word and managed to make it superb.[3] Steele had described the language which first precipitated the quarrel as an 'allusion' to Swift, whereupon the retort came, 'This allusion was only calling a clergyman of some little distinction an infidel. A clergyman who was your friend, who always loved you, who had endeavoured at least to serve you; and who, whenever he did write any thing, made it sacred to himself never to fling out the least hint against you.' Swift now utterly denied writing or speaking to the author of the *Examiner* and repeated that he had often recommended Steele to the ministers. He also picked up the theme of Marlborough and declared that he had prevented many 'hard things' from being said against the Duke. Finally, in a postscript, he reminded Steele of the compliment paid to him in Swift's *Proposal for Correcting the English Tongue*. The spectacle of the two anglicized Irishmen shaking their dignities at one another in a contest of mutual recrimination is hardly edifying. But it must have been a relief to them both to jettison the load of decayed friendship which impeded the push they both felt to sail into battle as the chief propagandists of their respective sides. So much belligerence could not exhaust itself without fur-

---

[1] This expression does not appear in the preserved text of Swift's letter but may have existed in the copy Steele received.
[2] 26 May (Williams I. 358).   [3] 27 May (*ibid.*, pp. 359–60).

ther release; and if Swift had not been on his way to Ireland when he closed the correspondence, a public display might have come sooner than it did. I find it significant that their approaches to the quarrel differed so sharply. Steele, the latitudinarian, Whiggish spokesman for the future, claims that his high-minded impulse, his sincerity, vindicate his possibly rough manners. Swift, the rationalist defender of a supposedly precarious order, will not allow benevolent intentions to excuse a personal insult. Steele says he cannot help it if in running to save his country he treads on a friend's toe. Swift says Steele is adding hypocrisy to insolence by using patriotism as a cloak for malicious ingratitude. Two generations earlier, the roundhead and the cavalier had fought under similar slogans.

During the summer, while Swift remained in Ireland, Steele made his parliamentary campaign. He first gave up not merely his stamp commissionership but also his old pension as gentleman-usher to the late Prince George; and thus he freed himself from immediate obligations to the government. For all of July and portions of August he left the *Guardian* to the composition of Addison, who set it back in the path of non-political belles-lettres while Steele was putting himself forward to be Member for the borough of Stockbridge. Early in August, when he took up the *Guardian* again, Steele (or his Junto patrons) chose the question of Dunkirk as a handy cause for denouncing the government. Although the French had promised to dismantle the privateers' great harbour, the mole and the dykes were still standing, intact. The magistrates of Dunkirk begged Queen Anne to spare their port, and less public efforts were made to soften her majesty through applications to Lady Masham. When a second memorial was published in French and English by Tugghe, the magistrates' deputy, Steele decided it was time to take alarm. In the *Guardian*,[1] therefore, he made public yet a new letter to his obliging *alter ego*, Ironside, but signed this one 'English Tory'. With more repetition than elegance Steele points out that the time stipulated for the demolition is long past and that it is essential to England's security for the work to be done soon. 'The British nation', he

[1] 7 August.

says more than once in the short but disjointed essay, 'expect the demolition of Dunkirk.' And he gave this number of his paper the motto, *Delenda est Carthago*.

It was customary for government supporters to represent any attack on the ministers as an attack on Queen Anne, and Steele now suffered the most absurd inflictions of this technique. Within a week Defoe replied to the *Guardian* with a characteristically diffuse tract[1] accusing Steele of both thanklessness and arrogance. He gratuitously involved Steele's insolvency and his West Indian estate by declaring that the essayist treated the Queen with the imperiousness of a Barbados planter giving orders to a slave. 'See how the villain treats the best of sovereigns, the best mistress to him, whose bread he has eaten, and who has kept him from a gaol!' The *Examiner*[2] followed suit, using a slightly different recipe with the same ingredients: charges of ingratitude and insolence with abuse *ad hominem*:

> I believe I may challenge all the nations of the world, and all the histories of this nation, for a thousand years past, to show us an instance so flagrant as what we now have before us, viz. whenever a *subject*, nay a *servant* under a *salary*, and favoured, *in spite of ill behaviour past*, with a considerable employment in the government, treated his sovereign in such a manner . . . *and went unpunished*.

All this denigration did not keep Steele from being returned to Parliament for Stockbridge by a five-to-two majority. But as reports were circulated in newspapers—coming from Antwerp or Dunkirk—that the notorious mole and harbour remained untouched, the Whigs' *Flying Post* broke into a rhythmic cry by printing this baying refrain at the end of every number during late August and September: 'Dunkirk is not yet demolish'd. The Pretender is not yet remov'd from Lorraine.'[3] Among the new pamphlets which kept appearing on both sides of the issue were several imitations of Steele's banal epistolary form, such as one ministerial scribbler's *Second Whigg-Letter, from William Prynne to Nestor Ironside*. The climax but not the end of the campaign was

---

[1] *The Honour and Prerogative of the Queen's Majesty Vindicated.*   [2] 21 August.
[3] Davis VIII. xi.

reached when Steele himself produced a lengthy tract rehearsing much of the material already in print and heavily justifying himself against his multiplied accusers. It was this shapeless work, *The Importance of Dunkirk Consider'd*,[1] that gave Swift his pretext for teaching the new M.P. just what it meant to feel the 'terror' of the angry dean's wit.

Steele's book takes the most tedious form used in polemical writing, a point-by-point reply to an unsystematic list of other men's arguments. In the desert stretches which open the little volume, he reprints Tugghe's memorial and his own letter to the *Guardian*, not to mention long extracts from Defoe's and Oldisworth's refutations of Steele. Then he proceeds to expound, in a clear if pedestrian style, the danger of Dunkirk to English trade. At last he arrives at the core of his work; but this, alas, is designed as a series of comments on the separate articles offered by Tugghe. In spite of the elegant variation Steele adopts when starting each of Tugghe's topics, he deals with them so insipidly as to defy the hardy reader to struggle through the lot. Still we are far from our repose. Steele now discusses, again *seriatim*, the aspersions thrown on his character by Tory essayists and pamphleteers writing about Dunkirk. He repudiates the charge of ingratitude, mentioning his resignation of the government appointments before standing for Parliament. Unluckily, his bombast does not add strength to his analysis: 'These writers', says Steele, 'shall treat me as they think fit, as I am their brother scribler, but I shall not be so unconcern'd when they attack me as an honest man.' He very soundly insists that an attack on a ministry is not an attack on the crown, but he embodies this truth in a putty of impertinent though standard complaints against the peace negotiations, with a eulogy of Marlborough and Godolphin and similar stuff worked in. There are patches of simple irony and bursts of Shaftesburyan cant on the bliss of serving one's fellow men. There are *obiter dicta* on brand new pamphlets brought to Steele's attention while he was writing. Near the close there is an unknowingly prescient reference to the ministerial writers, doomed to labour without Steele's delicious sense of

---

[1] Announced in the *Guardian*, 8 Sept., published 22 Sept.

abandoning honour and riches for the 'satisfaction of an enlarged and publick spirit':

> The prostitute pens which are employed in a quite contrary service, will be very ready to entertain a pretender to such reformations, with a recital of his own faults and infirmities; but I am very well prepared for such usage, and give my self up to all nameless authors, to be treated just as their mirth or their malice directs them.

He might almost have been daring the dean to do his worst. If so, Swift felt willing to oblige him. Nearly seven weeks later, after the work of demolition had at last begun, there appeared one of Swift's most amusing, though least influential, political essays, *The Importance of the Guardian Consider'd*.[1] The framework of national events and constitutional arguments underlying most of the compositions dealing with Dunkirk have only a secondary significance for Swift's pamphlet. His intention seems far less public than private. One feels he is taking advantage of a general mêlée to land some hard brass knuckles on a particular enemy's face. Not Dunkirk or the Pretender but the character of Richard Steele is the main theme of *The Importance of the Guardian*.

Although Swift's pamphlet is loose-jointed, it does not blindly follow the structure of his victim's. By eliminating the bulk of Steele's reprinted matter as well as the sober new data or arguments concerning Dunkirk, Swift immensely narrows the circle of his topics. Most of his retorts also echo the work of earlier writers on his side, but he transforms their rough commonplaces into polished ironies. Taking advantage of Steele's expressed willingness to be attacked as a 'brother scribler', Swift concentrates not only on the character of the man but on those aspects of his character which are most deeply exposed in his life as an author.

The first part of the essay is a sarcastic outline of Steele's biography, ending with the events leading up to the writing of *The Importance of Dunkirk*. Next, Swift analyses a number of offensive passages in the work, ridiculing the style as well as the logic, and dwelling on Steele's ingratitude and arrogance. Two-thirds of the

[1] Advertised in the *Examiner*, 31 Oct., 2 Nov. 1713.

way through, Swift produces an imaginary exchange of letters between Steele and the Queen, to illustrate his victim's impertinence. In the following and last part, he turns to Steele's vindication of himself, supplying what Swift considers the true motives of his conduct. Then Swift ridicules Steele's representation of the Queen as a monarch who might possibly profit from his advice. To end the pamphlet, he provides a savage reinterpretation for a story which Steele had employed as illustrating the dependence of rulers upon advisers but which Swift turns against the Godolphin ministry.

By sharply focusing on Steele as a literary figure, Swift gains the advantage of appearing to stick to the point at issue when he is merely ridiculing Steele's language. It must have made Swift struggle between fury and contempt to read the diffuse eloquence of the new M.P. Steele's rhetoric, especially in passages of apologia or of patriotic zeal, is careless as well as hollow. Swift's satire on his varying of the introductory phrases in the refutation of Tugghe's ten arguments is wholly convincing, and the final sarcasm seems no worse than the victim deserves: 'I could heartily wish Monsieur Tugghe had been able to find ten arguments more, and therefore given Mr. Steele an opportunity of shewing the utmost variations our language would bear in so momentous a trial.'[1] The contempt, surprisingly enough, becomes not that of a professional writer for an incompetent craftsman but a civilized gentleman for a mercenary hack.

This supposed amateur who writes better than a professional must sound effortless in order for the satire to be effective. An air of ease therefore pervades the essay, and all of Swift's finest sentences come out as though he hardly realized their deadliness: 'I would only have his friends be cautious, not to reward him too liberally: for, as it was said of Cranmer, *Do the Archbishop an ill turn, and he is your friend for ever*: so I affirm of your member, *Do Mr. Steele a good turn, and he is your enemy for ever.*'[2] To so gentlemanly a wit, Swift's old-fashioned, cynical analysis of motives seems perfectly appropriate. When he deals with the moral implications of Steele's mantle of public benevolence and self-sacrifice, one

---

[1] Davis VIII. 11.   [2] *Ibid.*, p. 16.

[689]

hears a blasé aristocrat confronting a sentimental arriviste. Replying to Steele's absurd claim that he gave up his public offices to make himself eligible for election to Parliament so he might then exercise his charity by 'serving his prince and country in a more eminent manner', Swift offers a number of less sublime reasons (such as escaping arrest for debt) and then alludes to Steele's unfortunate but notorious dabbling in alchemy:

> But it may be still demanded, Why he affects those exalted strains of piety and resignation? To this I answer, with great probability, That he hath resumed his old pursuits after the *Philosopher's Stone*, towards which it is held by all *adepts* for a most essential ingredient, that a man must seek it meerly for the glory of God, and without the least desire of being rich.[1]

Comic irony is the inevitable accompaniment of such attitudes. The joy of the essay is that Swift lets Steele act the preacher while he himself is the clown. To give his work coherence of tone, he employs an ingenious kind of impersonation. Addressing himself to the Bailiff of Stockbridge, he pretends that Steele's *Importance of Dunkirk* is obscure and that Swift will interpret and clarify Steele's meaning for the benefit of simple country readers. Thanks to this schema, he can play the games he loves best with the pose of naïveté, and yet leave himself free to be as subtle and worldly as he pleases. By turning alternatively naïve and knowing, he uses the single point of view as a device for exposing every absurdity in Steele's manner of logic. Vengeance is disguised as helpfulness, sophistication as innocence. The result is uniformly happy: 'What bailiff would venture to arrest Mr. Steele, now that he has the honour to be your representative? and what bailiff ever scrupled it before?'[2]

But the most exquisite passages of the essay are based on another sort of irony, the multiple innuendo which Swift had used so brilliantly in his character of Marlborough. Almost detachable from the rest of the piece, these passages fit directly into reality, because in them Swift takes certain unflattering details of Steele's life (some of them not generally known), mentions these as obvious truths, and then with an air of innocence discovers their most

[1] Davis VIII. 21–2. [2] *Ibid.*, p. 14.

malicious implications. As usual the victim could not begin to refute the innuendoes without incriminating himself:

> Mr. Steele is author of two tolerable plays, (or at least of the greatest part of them) which, added to the company he kept, and to the continual conversation and friendship of Mr. Addison, hath given him the character of a wit. To take the height of his learning, you are to suppose a lad just fit for the university, and sent early from thence into the wide world, where he followed every way of life that might least improve or preserve the rudiments he had got. He hath no invention, nor is master of a tolerable style; his chief talent is humour, which he sometimes discovers both in writing and discourse; for after the first bottle he is no disagreeable companion. I never knew him taxed with ill-nature, which hath made me wonder how ingratitude came to be his prevailing vice; and I am apt to think it proceeds more from some unaccountable sort of instinct, than premeditation.[1]

In spite of all these powerful and witty elements, *The Importance of the Guardian* is no success. Swift may have it all over Steele as a rhetorician or a moralist, but when he does interrupt his witty performance to examine political principles, his case collapses. The fuss over Dunkirk had a coercive side which the Whigs fully appreciated: if the demolition did not proceed, they could argue that they had expected the true course of events; and if the demolition did proceed, they could argue that the happy outcome had resulted from their pressure. Swift tries to defuse this bomb by exposing the manœuvre; but since a serious delay had undeniably occurred, and the stipulated date had already passed, he visibly squirms while he works. The deeper constitutional principles also remained entirely opposed to Swift's reasoning. In fact, his appearance of reasoning directly contradicted his own genuine views. Steele very rightly claimed that every citizen had the privilege and duty of voicing his opinions on public affairs. Swift merely produces obfuscation when he answers that the Queen has excellent ministers to guide her and wants no assistance from the ill-informed Member for Stockbridge. Steele also claimed that in attacking her majesty's ministers he was not attacking her prerogative. This of course is undeniable as well

[1] *Ibid.*, pp. 5–6.

as being fundamental to constitutional government. Yet Swift, abandoning his normal adherence to precisely this rule, declares that Steele is acting rebelliously and associates him with the revolutionary Puritans. It is not odd that *The Importance of the Guardian* never reached a second edition, but it is unlucky that so many of Swift's superb effects are buried in it.

III. SWIFT AND BURNET

Fear of the Pretender comprised only half the vulgar slogan which Junto rhetoricians invariably shouted against the government. The other half was fear of popery. Just as the wrangling about Dunkirk was all meant to insinuate that the ministers were joining with the King of France to alter the succession, so the furor over popery was meant to counteract the lower clergy's distaste for the Whigs. No organ of information had so direct an influence on common Englishmen as the Sunday sermon. As if to supply an ecclesiastical drive to parallel Steele's campaign, therefore, the septuagenarian Bishop Burnet now chose to disburden himself of his nightmare anxieties concerning the Church of Rome.[1]

The much-deferred publication of the final volume of Burnet's great *History of the Reformation* was now imminent. But Swift, who had read the earlier volumes as well as his grace's less scholarly productions, had long felt that Burnet was a turncoat hypocrite. He detested Burnet's many expressions of contempt for parsons; he disbelieved Burnet's patriotic zeal; he condemned Burnet's sympathy with Dissent; and he regarded the bishop's terror of popery as either a pose or an hallucination. The fracas over the rights of the Lower House of Convocation had not died down; and Swift stood much closer to Atterbury than to Burnet in that division.

In the autumn of 1713 Swift also was convinced that Burnet was giving Steele advice as a polemicist. I think the sympathy between the captain and the bishop did in fact lie deeper than

---

[1] Much of what follows is drawn from Professor Louis Landa's erudite introduction to Davis IV.

politics. They shared not merely a latitudinarian view of Dissent but an emotional view of morality. Unlike Swift, they assumed that warmth of sincerity was a nobler guide to conduct than reasoned principles. In their language they both rely upon a breast-beating, sanctimonious self-righteousness which in Swift's nose stank of Puritanism, though in ours it seems a whiff of the sentimentality to come. It must have appeared more than a coincidence that while Swift was writing his reply to Steele, the bishop decided to anticipate the appearance of his own new folio by issuing ahead of time what purported to be an introduction, although it was more like a tract for the times. This pamphlet *Introduction to the Third Volume of the History of the Reformation*[1] is a grotesque farrago: after an absurdly sensational review of the horrors of Roman Catholicism, Burnet officiously pleads with an apostrophized Parliament to resist popery; and he frantically admonishes the clergy to warn parishioners against this deadliest of evils. Incidentally he drops brief insinuations against Convocation for tending to make the church less dependent on the state and for displaying a more than papist terror of irregular baptisms. Age had not made the bishop less wordy or more cautious. He really did seem to imagine that within the Church of England, few besides the Whig bishops would offer a strong resistance to any new imposition of Roman superstition upon the kingdom.

It is not Swift the wit but Swift the priest who answers Burnet in *A Preface to the Bishop of Sarum's Introduction*.[2] But the political journalist Steele had also been discussing ecclesiastical matters in the *Englishman*; the *Examiner* had attacked both Burnet's *History* and his *Introduction*; and since Lord Oxford had opened his great library to nonjurors searching for historical arguments, the Whigs made that into a political issue. In marching forth against Burnet, therefore, Swift was not leaving the arena of general controversy. Actually, the habit of re-issuing old works with new, tendentious prefaces was a device the publicity-loving bishop had often found convenient for turning the problems of the church into secular, political debate.

[1] Published about mid-October 1713 (Boyer, Oct. 1713, VI. 284).
[2] Published 7 Dec. 1713.

[693]

Swift's strategy in the circumstances is wholly commendable. Instead of yielding to the temptation either to handle the business as a joke or to concentrate his essay on the livelier political topics, he makes the church his real theme. By implication, this approach appears to rebuke the bishop for secularism at the same time as it lifts the author of *A Tale of a Tub* above the charge of impiety. More than Swift's satire on Collins, far more than his *Project for the Advancement of Religion*, the new pamphlet suggests the devotion he felt to real Christianity. In keeping with this tone, Swift again makes the question of style itself a proper part of the main argument. His own seems almost ideal for his purpose. He abandons impersonation; and if there are some playful fantasies and much sarcasm among his provisions, they are kept subordinate to the dignity of the main essay. Swift writes here with a grave, self-conscious intensity which can rise to indignation or fall to plain reasoning.

His case seems as strong as his rhetoric. Burnet had excluded very few besides bishops of his own sort from a general censure of the Anglican clergy. He said or implied that the lower clergy had no right to hold opinions on matters of state; he doubted the value of Convocation, arguing sometimes as though parish priests were no more than mute instruments of Parliament and the bishops; he broadcast slanderous insinuations against saintly nonjurors and kind remarks about Presbyterians. Generally, he refused to view the church as in any valuable sense a self-directing community devoted to things of this world. Instead of considering his church as the sanction of worldly morality, he made the state the sanction of religious doctrine. Swift in return asserts that the clergy should enjoy the civil rights of other men, that they deserve respect for their function and pity for their condition, that the visible church must strive by its own lights to redeem sinful humanity. His attitude recalls the earliest, most direct expression of his deep faith, the ode to Sancroft, with its lament that 'the church is still led blindfold by the state.'[1]

For a modern reader the essay is too long and specialized to seem fascinating. But the excellence of the prose and the impor-

[1] *Poems* I. 40, l. 177.

tance of the themes remain obvious. Swift is most entertaining in his ridicule of Burnet's style and most impressive in his defence of his fellow priests. The two motifs are not distinct from one another. Burnet's groaning accumulation of Biblical texts and diffuse anxieties suggests the manner of a Nonconformist pastor; his tolerance of Nonconformity inclines him to bear down hard on the Tory vicars. Because Steele in the *Englishman* was devoting his exclamatory periods to similar events, Swift yokes him equally with the bishop in a characteristic remark:

> I cannot but observe, that his fellow-labourer, the author of the paper, called *The English Man*, seems, in some of his late performances, to have almost transcribed the notions of the bishop: These notions, I take to have been dictated by the same masters, leaving to each writer that peculiar manner of expressing himself, which the poverty of our language forces me to call their stile.[1]

Dealing with Burnet's character, Swift employs more decorous language but no less severe judgments than he had used in maligning Steele. Burnet's lack of charity toward humbler churchmen infuriated Swift, who ripostes by boldly praising the goodwill of several notorious nonjurors. Burnet's arrogance and complacency, his passion for self-advertisement, are brilliantly satirized in Swift's opening pages. Although there are strong passages in defence of the government, it is improbable that any minister had much to do with the writing of the essay, which reads like the independent outburst of a spontaneously indignant man. When Swift contrasts the low income of most parish priests with the wealth of a bishop who scolds the clergy for coveting lost temporalities, he achieves a plain, frank eloquence suiting the anger he always felt against chronic injustice:

> I take his lordship's bishoprick to be worth near 2500*l.* annual income; and I will engage, at half a year's warning, to find him above 100 beneficed clergy-men who have not so much among them all to support themselves and their families; most of them orthodox, of good life and conversation; as loath to see the fires kindled in Smithfield, as his lordship; and, at least, as ready to face them under a *Popish* persecution. But nothing is so hard for those, who

---

[1] Davis IV. 57; I prefer 'forces', the reading of the first edition, to 'forceth', Swift's revision.

abound in riches, as to conceive how others can be in want. How can the neighbouring vicar feel cold or hunger, while my lord is seated by a good fire in the warmest room of his palace, with a dozen dishes before him?[1]

IV. *THE PUBLICK SPIRIT OF THE WHIGS*

Swift's next attack was on Steele; and unlike *The Importance of the Guardian*, the new pamphlet ran through several editions in a short time. During this fresh collision, the forces on both sides quickly transcended details of personality, but the dramatic balance of the literary antagonists still seems prodigious. At one of the signal crises in English history, both great parties chose to be represented by advocates who shared an Irish origin, whose families had been neighbours, and whose acquaintance with one another had begun in mutual assistance. For Steele, like Swift, was 'an Englishman born in the City of Dublin'.[2] His grandfather, a merchant adventurer, courtier, and soldier, had settled in Ireland before the Civil War; his father became a lawyer belonging to the King's Inns, Dublin, where Swift's father and uncles were among his colleagues. Like them, Steele's father had lived in a house between St Patrick's Cathedral and Dublin Castle, and like them Steele's family had enjoyed the benevolent patronage of the Duke of Ormonde. Though the elder Richard Steele lived long enough for his son to remember him, he left the boy a half-orphan at about the age of five; and though the boy was sent to school in England before he was twelve, it was much longer before he became independent of the Ormonde family and his other Irish benefactors.

So many similarities in their beginnings would have made Swift peculiarly sensitive to Steele's defects, quick to understand his character, quick to flinch at his faults, quick to regret the fundamental likeness which must have led others to classify them together and which led Steele, at the crest of their quarrel, to say, 'The English would laugh at us, should we argue in so Irish a manner.'[3]

[1] Davis IV. 65.   [2] *The Englishman*, 19 Jan. 1714.   [3] Williams I. 351.

A week after publishing *The Importance of Dunkirk*, Steele had brought the *Guardian* to a close.[1] By this time the death of Mainwaring and the flight of Ridpath (editor of the *Flying Post*) had left the Whigs with a shortage of spokesmen to confront the ministerial press. Toland the deist, and Robert Walpole might write an occasional powerful essay, but they had too many responsibilities to do more; and the run of Whig journalists brought a very moderate supply of talent to their enterprise. Meanwhile, Swift, Defoe, and humbler allies were turning out a flow of good or excellent articles for the ministry. It was essential for the Whigs to secure a propaganda chief of a level high enough to be admitted to inner councils, one they could trust to put their case before the nation without minute supervision. For immediate effect they particularly wanted a book that would expound with impassioned but dignified authority the panic they felt concerning the peace and the succession. I suppose they looked for the sort of miracle Swift had wrought when he published *The Conduct of the Allies*. Steele was asked to assume this duty, and one imagines that the terms of payment were liberal. Addison, who tried to dissuade him, said, 'I am in a thousand troubles for poor Dick, and wish that his zeal for the public may not be ruinous to him'; but Steele rejected his old friend's advice and, as he told Mrs Steele, 'settled all things to great satisfaction'. He would for the time being devote himself altogether to party journalism.[2]

Immediately, Steele launched a new periodical. He named it the *Englishman* and filled it with disquisitions on public affairs. But he also began planning the large work to be called *The Crisis*. For the purpose of publicizing and financing this scheme, he received support from the belligerent young Hanover Club, a political association founded by the Whigs shortly before the peace with France had been signed. Bothmar, the Hanoverian envoy, also advised the Elector to support *The Crisis*. The projected book was, pretty absurdly, offered for subscription at a shilling a copy, obviously with less intention of raising money than of assembling a tremendous list of names. While Steele's publisher advertised the approaching parturition in the *English-*

[1] 1 Oct. 1713.   [2] Graham, p. 280; Blanchard, p. 291; Winton, p. 178.

man and elsewhere, the essayist himself secured the collaboration of lawyers and statesmen in the labours of gestation. Not only Walpole but Walpole's best friend Stanhope lent an obstetric hand. Beginning in late October, successive advertisements continued to inform the world that the controversial analysis of the succession problem was in the press. As delay followed delay and announcement pursued announcement, a well-founded rumour spread that in spite of assistance from Addison, Bishop Hoadly, and others, Steele was working against time and had not completed his book. At Christmas, while he was suffering from the gout, Steele let it be known through the *Englishman*[1] that publication of *The Crisis* would be postponed again, to afford the ladies a fresh opportunity of joining the list of subscribers! One cause of this gallantry may have been a sudden change in the Queen's health a few days before. A violent ague[2] brought her so low that rumours of her death became common. Although she recovered in a few days, the effect was an inevitable heightening of the general preoccupation with the succession, as Tories panicked over the prospect and Whigs cheered. For Steele's pamphlet the moment could not have been better chosen.

Meanwhile, Swift, who was wavering between rage and scorn over the pompous exhibition of Steele's advance notices, wrote a rough but lively poem to ridicule the parade.[3] Again his form was an imitation of Horace, in the usual octosyllabic couplets and in a burlesque style recalling the coarser parts of *Hudibras*. If the verses have little to recommend them, Swift's instinct for aphorism and idiom still gives special force to some of the couplets—

> . . . madmen, children, wits and fools
> Shou'd never meddle with edg'd tools—

and—

> Thou must no longer deal in *farce*,
> Nor pump to cobble wicked verse.

Swift pretends to be a low acquaintance of Steele's, who urges him to stop posing as a political philosopher and return to living

---

[1] 26 Dec.   [2] It began the night of 23 Dec. (HMC. *Somerset, Ailesbury*, p. 223).

[3] *The First Ode of the Second Book of Horace Paraphras'd*, published around 6 Jan. 1714: see *Poems* I. 180.

as a tavern wit. Incidentally, the poet manages to review most of the scandalous charges vulgarly brought against Steele by his Tory opponents; and as often happens, Swift's assumed personality draws heavily on the true relation between himself and his victim.

Less than two weeks later, *The Crisis* at last dropped from the teeming press. As a controversialist Steele was chronically addicted to padding and was undersupplied with thought. Declamation, not analysis, was his strength. So one is not surprised that the new work amounted essentially to a compilation of long extracts from the laws dealing with the succession of the crown since the Glorious Revolution. On the pages before this anthology Steele placed an address to the clergy and a preface attacking the doctrine of hereditary right. Following the legal texts, he had an essay on the reasons one should still feel insecure about the succession. In the whole book this essay is the nearest Steele comes to an original exposition. He starts it by recalling the marvellous period from 1704 to 1710 when, as he claims, the succession was secure and England glorious. With dubious relevance he praises Marlborough at length, recalling the Duke's great battles. Then lachrymosely contemplating the different world today, he finds France as strong as ever; he complains that Dunkirk still has its mole and harbour; and he weeps over the fate of the Catalonians: 'I mention the Catalonians, but who can name the Catalonians without a tear? Brave unhappy people.' And so forth. Next Steele dwells on the likelihood of a Popish successor if Hanover should be rejected; and he warns the evidently insensate reader of the miseries and persecutions that must come with Roman Catholicism. The close is meant to be a rousing recommendation of the Hanoverian succession as both lawful and providential.

The whole epilogual essay hardly bears out Boyer's judgment that Steele's own writing in *The Crisis* is 'every way, *so excellent,* that there can be no *abridging* of the *least part,* without *maiming* the *Whole*'.[1] Nothing would mend Steele's verbosity so well as abridgement. His ruling vice is even more oppressive in the open-

---

[1] Jan. 1714 (2nd ed., 1719, VII. 2).

ing dedication of the book to the clergy of the Church of England. With the same officiousness that pervaded Burnet's *Introduction*, Steele advises the lower clergy to support the Hanoverian succession in their preaching. The writing here is repetitious and dense with epithets. The argument insinuates that the clergy are all eager to commit treason. Superficial unction and implicit insolence alternate in the humourless appeal. Steele even urges the university tutors, most of whom were in fact as Tory as the parsons, to alter the instruction they give their pupils: if, he says, the legal texts in *The Crisis*

> had been from time to time put in a fair and clear light, and had been carefully recommended to the perusal of young gentlemen in colleges, with a preference to all other civil institutions whatsoever: this kingdom had not been in its present condition.

From the 'Preface' which reposes between the dedication and the large collection of laws, one may infer some of the historical antecedents of Steele's book. The subject here is a denunciation of the doctrine of hereditary right, ostensibly meant to explode one argument for the Pretender but really implying that most enemies of the Whigs are Jacobites. Higden's great *View and Defence* had been recently answered by an elaborate, scholarly treatise called *The Hereditary Right of the Crown of England Asserted*, supposed to be written by the eminent nonjuring Jacobite savants Charles Leslie and Robert Nelson—both of whom Swift deeply respected as writers on church doctrine though repudiating their political views. While the bookseller and a confessed author were prosecuted by Bolingbroke as Secretary of State, the book itself was unfortunately known to be based in part on unpublished manuscripts in the Earl of Oxford's collection; and the book had been rashly advertised in the government newspaper the *Gazette*.[1] The more furiously it was attacked, therefore, the more culpable the ministry would seem for conniving at its production and distribution. In November 1713, a flimsy pamphlet called *Treason Unmask'd* had appeared, clumsily refuting *The Hereditary Right*. But in *The Crisis*, Steele's 'Preface' (almost half of which

[1] 17 Oct. 1713; also *Post Boy*, 10, 13 Oct.

consists of long quotations) was meant to keep the issue still alive and thus to throw further suspicion on the government.

Immediately before his collection of laws, Steele had inserted yet another prolegomenon, this one being devoted to the praise of political liberty. Since 'liberty', as a watchword of the Whigs, had gradually become opposed, in the quarrels of parties, to the Tories' stress on obedience, Steele's praise of the principle does more than magnify a desideratum which the Pretender would destroy. Steele's exposition, however, is painfully fatuous, offering neither brilliance of example nor freshness of thought. When he is not praising the recent past and lamenting the immediate prospect, he indulges in such boneless propositions as, 'Liberty is essential to happiness.'

One does not have to be an eighteenth-century Tory to feel maddened by Steele's rhetoric or by his hasty logic. It's still hard to believe that many persons voluntarily read all or even most of *The Crisis*, packed as it is with desiccated texts interlined by pointless minutiae (e.g., 'the articles of union were agreed on, the 22d day of July, in the fifth year of her majesty's reign, by the commissioners nominated on behalf of the kingdom of England, under the great seal of England, dated the 10th day of April, then past') and obscured by jejune comments. Yet quantities were bought up and disseminated by those who thought it would have good effects.[1]

Swift must have quivered as he read. One passage not directly bearing on the general topic was calculated for special reasons to provoke him. This was a remark on the Act of Union, which had included clauses committing the united nation to the Hanoverian succession. After condemning (on curiously weak grounds) any notion of dissolving the Union, Steele tried to show that the Scots enjoyed only a moderate participation in the Lords and Commons of Great Britain:

> For the late kingdom of Scotland had as numerous a nobility as England, and the representatives of their Commons were also very numerous: They have by the articles of Union consented to send only sixteen peers and forty-five Commons, to the Parliament of

[1] Winton, p. 196.

Great Britain, which hath the same number of Lords and Commons
for England that were before the Union.

With his loathing of the Presbyterian, regicide Scots, his fury
over their failure to support the ministry in Parliament, and his
disapproval of a union denied to Ireland, Swift found this line of
thought disgusting. A peculiar vexation was that the Duke of
Argyll had recently abandoned Swift's friends, reconciled himself to the Duke of Marlborough, and joined the councils of the
Whigs.

The sitting of the new Parliament had been put off almost as
often as the publication of *The Crisis*, and Swift's friends badly
wanted an authoritative reply to the Whigs' masterstroke before
the debates began. Swift must have set to work very quickly, for
the desired pamphlet went on sale only five weeks after the other.[1]

Swift called it *The Publick Spirit of the Whigs: Set Forth in Their
Generous Encouragement of the Author of the Crisis*. It deserves on
several grounds to be described as one of his finest works. Swift's
central and brilliantly effective line of attack is to exploit a crippling self-contradiction in Steele's case. Underlying the redundant
polemics of *The Crisis* there was a consistent political philosophy
which Swift agreed with. According to this, a good government
rests upon a representative legislature and an executive who en-
forces the laws impartially. In England's tripartite constitution
and in the laws governing the succession, Steele admittedly found
all these essentials. He praised the good people of England for
supporting, vigorously and by an immense majority, both the
constitution and the laws. Yet he insisted that the nation was in
extreme danger, from domestic intrigues and foreign aggression.

Swift's reply is that Steele cannot be right on both counts. If all
the machinery of government is correctly organized and the
people are loyal, the lawful successor has no right to feel anxious.
In a country like England in 1714, it is certainly not foreign
powers that can name a new king. As for domestic intrigues for
the same evil end—if no visible sign is produced, only a cheat will
assume they exist. Thus, to Steele's leading question, 'What are
the marks of a lasting security?' Swift replies by confounding

[1] 23 Feb. 1714.

him with his own legalism.[1] A related weakness in Steele's exposition was the assumption that any remote claimant to the English throne, descended from a daughter of the early Stuarts,
might be elevated into a Popish pretender and constitute an imminent threat. Swift replies that this, like several other bugbears
of Steele and his friends, is absurd: Steele's *ad hoc* criteria of
security are thus exposed as deliberately and maliciously impracticable. For the government can hardly exterminate all the royal
cousins of Europe; and if a loyal people are no guarantee of the
succession, nothing is:

> Well; by this author's own confession, a number of infinitely
> superior, and the best circumstantiated imaginable, are for the
> *succession* in the House of *Hanover.* This *succession* is established, con-
> firmed, and secured by several laws; her majesty's repeated declar-
> ations, and the oaths of all her subjects, engage both her and them
> to preserve what those laws have settled. This is a *security* indeed, a
> *security* adequate at least to the importance of the thing; and yet,
> according to the Whig-scheme, as delivered to us by Mr. Steele, and
> his coadjutors, is altogether insufficient; and the succession will be
> defeated, the *Pretender* brought in, and *Popery* established among us,
> without the farther assistance of this writer and his faction.[2]

Beneath these explicit refutations there always runs Swift's
usual obsession with motivation. What finally destroys the Whigs'
arguments, according to him, is their purpose. He will grant them
no genuine fears for the national welfare. Endlessly he repeats
that they desire only to fling the present, honest government out
and to seize again the profits and power of administration. By
strenuous implication he accuses them of creating a colossal to-
do about the succession purely to capture the confidence of the
House of Hanover, so that when the Queen dies, it will be impossible for the Tories to keep any stitch of power.

There was of course much truth in this sceptical analysis of
Junto self-interest. Most Englishmen were not Whigs; the Queen
and the House of Commons were clearly dominated by Tory
principles; and the House of Lords, thanks to the twelve creations
and the Scottish peers, tended to vote the same way. The laws
declaring the succession were strong, lucid, and mutually re-

[1] Cf. Winton, p. 197.   [2] Davis VIII. 66.

inforcing. Inasmuch as James II had been able to ascend the throne in peace amid all the uproar of his brother's last years, it might easily appear (I should say) that Sophia and her son had a very slight foundation for their qualms. Finally, no one will deny that the Whigs looked forward with joy to the monopoly they presciently hoped to obtain under the new ruler.

Although Swift's essential argument follows this pattern, the order of his pamphlet does not. Rather, he retraces the sequence of Steele's book, taking up in turn the dedication, the preface, the introductory pages to the legal texts, and the questions raised in the terminal essay. After a devastating burlesque of Steele's advertising techniques, Swift considers the dedication to the clergy. Quite predictably he switches here from motley to cassock in a superb modulation of tone. With priestly gravity he denounces Steele for arrogance in treating the church as implicitly the least loyal sector of the people, and for malice in pretending to honour the clergy at the precise moment he insults them. The politico-philosophizing rôle that Steele assumes in the preface, Swift treats with a *reductio ad absurdum*, ridiculing the implicit fallacies and self-contradictions. When Swift reaches the panegyric of liberty that introduces the legal texts, he carries the same reductive method still further, sharpening it with parody and concentrating upon Steele's false logic and loose definitions.

It is at the next position, two-fifths of the way through *The Publick Spirit of the Whigs*, that Swift lets his heart get the better of his head. Coming to Steele's praise of the Union with Scotland, Swift starts burning too brightly for his own good; and in a quite unnecessary digression he sees fit to defend the Tory extremists' recent effort to break up the Union. Relying on the arguments of his old *Story of the Injured Lady* and his old poem 'On the Union', he allows himself the most savage invective against the Scots, as a 'poor, fierce, Northern people', a drain on England's wealth and a menace to her constitution. The climactic passage rises to a sarcastic denunciation of the representative peers, who had helped the ministry far less steadily than Swift thought was their duty:

> Their nobility is indeed so numerous, that the whole revenues of their country would be hardly able to maintain them according to

the dignity of their titles; and what is infinitely worse, they are never likely to be extinct till the last period of all things; because the greatest part of them descend to heirs general. I imagine, a person of quality prevailed on to marry a woman much his inferior, and without a groat to her fortune, and her friends arguing, she was as good as her husband, because she brought him as numerous a family of relations and servants, as she found in his house. Scotland in the taxes is obliged to contribute one penny for every forty pence laid upon England; and the representatives they send to Parliament are about a thirteenth: Every other Scotch peer has all the privileges of an English one, except that of sitting in Parliament, and even precedence before all of the same title that shall be created for the time to come. The pensions and employments possessed by the natives of that country now among us, do amount to more than the whole body of their nobility ever spent at home; and all the money they raise upon the publick is hardly sufficient to defray their civil and military lists. I could point out some with great titles,[1] who affected to appear very vigorous for dissolving the Union, though their whole revenues before that period would have ill maintained a Welch justice of the peace; and have since gathered more money than ever any Scotchman, who had not travelled, could form an idea of.[2]

But after this invidious vituperation almost half Swift's pamphlet deals, as it ought to, with the arguments of Steele's closing essay. Here, though he necessarily goes over many different articles, his weight falls most heavily on the distortions and malicious innuendoes (as he judges them to be) of Steele's exposition. To Steele's ostensibly plain, impartial survey of the affairs of Europe, Swift returns a boiling denunciation of Marlborough and the Junto, and an impressive defence of the government's war policy.

The glory of *The Publick Spirit*, however, is neither its structure nor its reasoning but its magnificently polemical style. In this final defence of the Oxford ministry, Swift seems determined to show what he can accomplish with none of the secondary aids one usually designates as 'Swiftian'. There are no hoaxes here, no impersonation, no self-ridicule, no elaborate, satirical fantasies.

---

[1] Apparently an allusion to Argyll: see Boyer, *Political State*, Mar. 1714 (edition of 1719, p. 233).
[2] Davis VIII. 50–1. I have taken the readings 'till' for 'until', 'has' for 'hath', and 'though' for 'although' from the first edition.

The voice throughout is the true author's. He may bathe the whole essay in transparent irony through a thin pretence of thanking the Whigs for encouraging Steele. He may conceal or shade awkward facts; he may resort to consciously fallacious arguments. But he does not assume a character or recommend opinions which he does not hold. So far from playing clever games with Steele's propositions or wilfully misunderstanding them, Swift's regular (though not invariable) procedure is to cut down the implications and innuendoes to simple language and then refute them as squarely and openly as he can. His manner therefore seems less reminiscent of *The Importance of the Guardian* than of the *Remarks on Tindall* or the *Preface* to Burnet[1]; and I think this is significant; for in defending the ministry at this last barricade, Swift is also defending his tenderly beloved church and his precious art: the wit and the priest join to rescue the nation from Steele's supposed irreligion and barbarism. There are almost no arguments *ad hominem*. I find so little evidence of special information or secret intelligence that I am inclined to believe the ministers had no significant part in the composition. Swift is writing as a truly independent citizen whose sense of justice has been outraged.

The tone of the *Publick Spirit* sounds deeply compelling. It is that of bored disgust. Swift untiringly sneers at Steele for being a copyist, a hack, who apes the egregious Burnet and takes orders from the Junto. By a marvel of language Swift expresses this boredom through an abundance of fresh effects, suggesting his own energy and life in contrast to Steele's lack of both. He continually picks up Steele's images and rhetorical figures in order to burlesque them. He invents a number of ingeniously belittling, compact analogies and conceits, most of them operating with shining precision. The incessant irony is raw and sarcastic but never careless. Swift's sudden but easy modulations of his tone, from calm rationality to wild invective, from logic and arithmetic to moral fervor, give his style a characteristic pressure of authority; for it is the grip of a wise man driven mad by oppression.

To control his gush of negative emotions, Swift imposes on the

[1] Cf. the discussion of 'obtuseness' in Price, pp. 58–60.

whole of his essay a scheme beautifully mortifying to his victim. This is the pretence that Swift is commending the Whigs for their charity in sponsoring so menial a pen as Steele's. All through the pamphlet Swift is thus free to exhibit his enemy's faults in a dramatic context. Particularly he is once more able to comment liberally upon Steele's literary blemishes without appearing irrelevant. The following passage, in which Swift compares Steele with the paid hack Ridpath, editor of the *Flying Post*, and with Dunton, the sometime travelling bookseller and scribbler of crude Whiggish pamphlets, shows what the possibilities of Swift's method are:

> Among the present writers on that side, I can recollect but three of any distinction, which are the *Flying-Post*, Mr. Dunton, and the author of the *Crisis*: The first of these seems to have been much sunk in reputation since the sudden retreat of the *only true genuine original author*, Mr. Ridpath, who is celebrated by the Dutch Gazeteer, as *one of the best pens in England*. Mr. Dunton hath been longer and more conversant in books than any of the three, as well as more voluminous in his productions: However, having employed his studies in so great a variety of other subjects, he hath, I think, but lately turned his genius to politicks. His famous tract, entitled, *Neck or Nothing*, must be allowed to be the shrewdest piece, and written with the most spirit of any which hath appeared from that side since the change of ministry: It is indeed a most cutting satire upon the Lord Treasurer and Lord Bollingbroke, and I wonder none of our friends ever undertook to answer it. I confess, I was at first of the same opinion with several good judges, who, from the style and manner, supposed it to have issued from the sharp pen of the Earl of Nottingham; and I am still apt to think it might receive his lordship's last hand. The third and principal of this triumvirate is the author of the *Crisis*; who, although he must yield to the *Flying-Post* in knowledge of the world, and skill in politicks, and to Mr. Dunton in keenness of satire, and variety of reading; hath yet other qualities enough to denominate him a writer of a superior class to either; provided he would a little regard the propriety and disposition of his words, consult the grammatical part, and get some information in the subject he intends to handle.[1]

It is only necessary to add that of course Swift was both unfair and mistaken. Steele was no hypocrite, but certainly believed in

[1] Davis VIII. 31–2.

his heart that some high ministers wished to alter the succession; and he was right. Swift knew nothing of the profoundly secret messages Oxford and Bolingbroke were sending the Pretender, pleading with him to turn Protestant. Swift blamed on the Queen a number of policies that in fact were due to his friends. He never gave Steele the immense credit he deserved for daring to put his real name to his work. In political controversy, however, fairness is seldom offered or expected, and the rhetorical virtues of *The Publick Spirit* easily overwhelm the practical and moral faults.

At least three authorized editions of the pamphlet appeared in England during the early months of 1714, all printed by Barber. But before all of the first edition had gone on sale, a striking change was made in the text, because the entire discussion of the Union with Scotland was cancelled in many copies. Apparently, Barber had already begun a second edition, and some copies of this too got abroad with the passage on Scotland included. However, the rest were cancelled, as was the whole third edition.[1] The reason for this sudden change was a scandal that Swift might have had the prudence to expect, for the authorship of the pamphlet was widely recognized. Reprinting Swift's discussion of the Union in his monthly survey of public events and controversial literature, Boyer remarked that in view of the usefulness of the Scottish peers to the government, the cancelled paragraphs had seemed '*impolitick* and *illtimed*'. He sneered at 'Jonathan, who was shrewdly suspected of being the author of this *doughty lampoon*', and declared that the cancellation was made in haste before the authorities took notice of the pamphlet.[2] Argyll, the most eminent object of Swift's Scotophobic mockery, had been infuriated; and on 2 March, Wharton complained against the original publication in the House of Lords.

With exquisite malice—and more appropriately than he may have realized—Wharton alluded to the Queen's complaints (polished, as I suppose, in 1713 by Swift and echoed in her speech

---

[1] Davis VIII. xxi–xxii, 201–2. My analysis is not authoritative; the printing of this pamphlet deserves more study; but I do not trust Boyer's statement that the printer merely gave the cancelled copies of the first edition a titlepage marked 'Second Edition' (*Political State*, Mar. 1714; edition of 1719, VII. 233).

[2] Boyer, *loc. cit.*

a year later) against seditious and scandalous libels. He said he knew a pamphlet of this description and held up a copy of the *Publick Spirit*, claiming he had read it only after somebody thrust it into his hands. But his solemn little act was transformed into farce when he tried to read the offensive passages aloud, because in the copy he actually held, they were cancelled, and he was forced to call to some lords who had brought the first edition with them.[1] During the discussion which followed, Oxford announced —no doubt, to the edification of the whole body of peers—that he knew nothing of the pamphlet; and he exclaimed in horror against the malicious insinuations carried in it. The House passed a resolution condemning *The Publick Spirit of the Whigs* as a 'false, malicious and factious libel'.

It became a worrying period to a man so timorously daring as Swift. For years he had looked unquietly forward to the vengeance the Whigs would wreak on him, and now the moment of accomplishment seemed close. He thought of flight if his friends should appear unable to stifle the Whig firebrands. Less than two weeks before the *Publick Spirit* came out, he had asked Joshua Dawson (in Ireland) to make sure his licence of absence from the deanery was renewed for another half-year with no specification as to residence: 'I would not be limited in point of place'—and his unexpressed reason had been just such a contingency as this.[2] Two days after Wharton opened the proceedings in the House of Lords, Swift received a bankbill of a hundred pounds from Oxford, sent with the kind of gratuitously cryptic message that his lordship favoured, and written inevitably in a disguised hand:

> I have heard that some honest men who are very innocent, are under troble touching a printed pamphlet. a friend of mine, an obscure person, but charitable, puts the enclosed bill in your hands to answer such exigencys as their case may immediately require. and i find he wil do more, this being only for the present.
> If this comes safe to your hands it is enough.[3]

---

[1] *Manuscripts of the House of Lords* x. 266; *J.H.L.* xix. 628; *Wentworth Papers*, p. 359. I am indebted for these details to a forthcoming essay by Professor Maurice Quinlan, who very generously allowed me to draw upon it before publication.

[2] Williams ii. 11; cf. p. 91.   [3] *Ibid.*, p. 12.

In a staged pretence of judicial inquiry, the Lords brought Barber and Morphew the publisher before a committee to be examined; but as everybody must have expected, they secured no useful information. Meanwhile, Swift still felt so anxious that he wrote to his friend Archdeacon Walls in Dublin and asked him to make quite certain that nothing went wrong with the licence of absence. 'I am now under a great deal of uneasy business', he said, 'which I hope to get over.'[1] Before the dumb show could get out of hand, however, the Earl of Mar, as Secretary of State for Scotland, instituted a mock-prosecution of Barber, whereupon further parliamentary inquiries were stopped; and on 9 March Barber and Morphew were released from custody.

But instead of conceding defeat, the Whigs at once moved that the Lords should address the Queen, asking her majesty to ease their pain by promising a reward for a discovery of the author of the pamphlet. This motion succeeded, and a large committee was named to draft the required address. Nottingham, Wharton, and Argyll were all on it, as well as the Earl of Mar. When their text reached the floor of the House of Lords, Nottingham's brother, Winchelsea, moved an amendment declaring that a particular cause of the peers' request to the Queen was the unknown writer's pretensions to 'know the secrets of your majesty's administration'. The source of this extraordinary motion probably appears in some notes still preserved among the papers of the Earl of Nottingham. Here the Earl has copied out, in his own hand, a number of sentences from the *Publick Spirit* which sound as though their author had received confidential information from members of the government. Below, the Earl has written a short but aggressive statement arguing that if the quotations are lies, the pamphleteer is guilty of the greatest insolence to the government; but if they are facts, then he must indeed have been trusted with secrets of state, and the Queen ought to be warned —besides, the Earl points out, the establishment of their truth would help concentrate the search for the author. Obviously, the backers of this threat were aiming beyond Swift at Oxford and Bolingbroke, whom they hoped to expose as criminally indis-

[1] Williams II. 15.

creet. But Nottingham's understandable zeal to ruin a man who had slandered him remains visible. Although the motion for the amendment was lost at last after a long debate, Swift character-istically resented the Earl's vengefulness without blaming him-self for provoking it. In a poem written (but not published) two or three months later, therefore, he dropped new ridicule on Nottingham:

> Now Finch alarms the Lords; he hears for certain,
> This dang'rous priest is got behind the curtain:
> Finch, famed for tedious elocution, proves .
> That S - - - - oils many a spring which Harley moves.

Meanwhile, all the Tories in the House of Lords could not pre-vent the address, as finally adopted (11 March), from including a well-directed stab at the government for retaining Barber, printer of the 'seditious libel', as printer of the *Gazette*.[1]

On the other side, within a few days her gracious majesty obliged the troubled peers with a proclamation offering three hundred pounds to whoever would make the welcome revela-tion.[2] Swift at last enjoyed the distinction of having a price put on his head. 'So well protected are those who scribble for the govern-ment', he said when he reported the affair to Peterborough, weeks afterward.[3] Nevertheless, as the indefatigable Boyer said, 'Jonathan . . . being under the wings of some great men, escaped discovery and punishment.'[4] No informant appeared; the hunt-ers gave up the chase; and Swift was secure for a decade. Not till 1724 would another price be put on his head.

Probably, one of the main blocks to the Whig lords' pursuit of Swift was a business already on their hands of defending their own man from similar embarrassment. As soon as Steele's candi-dacy for the Stockbridge seat was known, the ministry had begun plotting to fling him out of Parliament; and hints of that prospect

---

[1] *J.H.L.* XIX. 634–5; *Wentworth Papers*, p. 360; *Poems* I. 194. The details of Notting-ham's notes will appear in the essay already mentioned, by Professor Quinlan, to whose kindness and learning I am again indebted for the facts in this paragraph.

[2] Davis VIII. xxi–xxii and facing p.; also pp. 198–9; and Boyer, 2nd ed., 1719, VII. pp. 233–6.

[3] Williams II. 22. He may have thought the littleness of the reward was discredit-able to him, because he evidently felt called on to account for it: see Davis VIII. 30.

[4] Boyer, *loc. cit.*

kept dropping throughout the autumn and winter, 1713–14. After considering various other types of unpleasantness, they decided to bring him up on charges of seditious libel, precisely the method the Whigs used against Swift. Again the fates of the two men seem uncannily parallel, but the moral implications seem opposed. For Swift had taken his usual minute pains to be sure that no link might be established between himself and his writing, whereas Steele had advertised his responsibility for his own work. Swift found the heads of the government secretly on his side; Steele had the ministers and the Commons openly against him. Swift thought of running from danger; Steele stood and faced it.

By mid-February the Queen had got well enough again to leave Windsor; and on 16 February Parliament met to choose a Speaker. As if to make himself worthy of the coming noontide of wrath, Steele had closed his periodical the *Englishman*, the day before, with a paper even more inflammatory than Swift's abuse of the Scots; and at the end of this effusion Steele placed a letter to 'Mr.— at Windsor', which may have been aimed at Swift. In the contest for Speaker, the next day, Hanmer, who had led the so-called 'whimsical' branch of the Tories against the commercial clauses of the French treaty, was chosen—an outcome which naturally weakened Bolingbroke's forces. And as soon as this choice was made, Steele rose from his brand-new seat to address the House—probably instigated by the Whig leaders, who were said to have conceived a project of printing and publishing the bold speeches they intended him to deliver regularly. Congratulating Hanmer, Steele adopted a polite old idiom derived from the Latin, and said he wished to 'do him honour'. The reason he gave was that Hanmer had been instrumental in throwing out the 'pernicious' bill of commerce.[1] Within a few days, the ministerial writers, through either ignorance or perversity, were making fun of Steele's little phrase, pretending it was a blunder; and one is sorry to find that Swift, who certainly knew better, saw fit to join them.[2]

When Parliament met again, two weeks later, the Queen's Speech included the request that measures be taken to suppress

---

[1] Winton, p. 200; Boyer VII (1719), 169–70 (Feb. 1714).   [2] Davis VIII. 52.

'seditious papers'. Although the Whig lords cleverly turned this upon Swift, it was of course aimed at Steele. Consequently, on the second day after the Lords addressed the Queen for a proclamation against the author of *The Publick Spirit of the Whigs*, a Tory member arose in the Commons and requested action against Steele. A cousin of the Lord Treasurer's seconded the motion immediately; but Steele, by a series of manœuvres, got the case postponed until 18 March, while his friends helped him prepare a defence. Then, with Stanhope and Walpole (the new, post-Junto generation of Whig leaders) beside him, and with Addison prompting him from notes, Steele talked for over three hours. When he withdrew, Walpole took the floor, making a notable speech which the sympathetic Prussian envoy described as 'worthy of Augustan times'.[1]

Since the ministry still held a strong majority in the Commons, and since the project for the moment was one on which even Oxford might co-operate with Bolingbroke, no force of reasoning could save the Member for Stockbridge. The noisy session prolonged itself into the night, but when the fury of debate at last stopped, the vote went five to three to expel Steele from the House. After little more than a month, his parliamentary career was over during this reign.

V. IRELAND

If the frustrations and fears of the autumn and winter ever made Swift picture Ireland to himself as a cosy retreat, no news from Dublin encouraged this idea. He pretended, as always, to be contemptuous of Irish affairs, but they filled many of his reflections and added to his despondency. On every level of private, political, and church affairs, what he heard made him angry. The finances of his deanery displeased him at once. I don't suppose Oxford for a moment thought seriously of finding Swift the thousand pounds the new dean considered his due. Yet Swift's agent Parvisol, whom he hesitantly retained even while distrusting his accounts, seemed incapable of collecting as much as the

[1] Winton, pp. 200–2 and n. 26.

worried absentee expected in tithes and rents. 'I look upon him as a knave', said Swift. Debts and fees connected with the deanery still remained unpaid, and Swift had to support himself in London on odd money he had brought over or was receiving from other sources.[1]

But Swift's inveterate obsession with his own income did not keep him from seizing on the privileges and duties of his new post. The vicars choral of St Patrick's Cathedral had presumed so far as to renew the lease of a valuable tract of Dublin land, near St Stephen's Green, already granted to Swift's friend and sometime host, Lord Abercorn. On hearing of their decision, the dean reacted with spontaneous fury, partly because he always worried about the need to raise rents for church lands as the value of money sank, but also because he believed the vicars choral were infringing upon a decanal prerogative when they renewed a lease without the consent of the dean and the chapter. He threatened to deprive every person involved in the business, and said the church would be 'well rid of such men who to gratify their unreasonable avarice would starve their successors'.[2]

Yet at the same time Swift also showed his determination to maintain the cathedral and its functions in the handsomest style possible. If he refused to allow improper liberties to a clique of 'singing men', he did not therefore intend to weaken the quality of cathedral music. On the contrary, Swift went to immense pains to ensure that anybody appointed to his choir had the best voice that could be secured. Under earlier deans the standard of singing had, according to expert advisers, declined; and though Swift might accuse himself of comprehending music 'like a Muscovite', he made strenuous efforts to regain the lost ground. Once when an old friend urged him to give a musical employment to a protégé of the friend, Swift made minute inquiries, explaining,

> If you had recommended a person to me for a church-living in my gift, I would be less curious; because an indifferent parson may do well enough, if he be honest, but singers like their brothers the poets must be very good, or they are good for nothing.[3]

[1] Williams I. 389, 392; II. 9, 30, 48 (quoted)–49, 90.
[2] Mason, pp. 97–8, n. 1; Williams I. 427; II. 7, 133, 177.
[3] Williams II. 339; Mason, p. 420, n. x.

So one is not surprised that in the autumn of 1713 Swift should have hesitated before promoting a 'half vicar' in the choir to a full vicarship. 'If we want a singer', he told Archdeacon Walls, 'and I can get a better, that better one shall be preferred, although my father were competitor.' Since Christ Church Cathedral shared the same choir as St Patrick's, Swift had to clear certain appointments with Bishop Ellis, who held the deanship of Christ Church *in commendam*. But even Ellis, normally an enemy of Dr Swift's, had to thank him for his extraordinary pains in choosing a new singer.[1]

Promotion to a deanery did not, moreover, weaken either Swift's loyalty to the lower clergy of the Church of Ireland or his distrust of the bishops. It was probably to indulge both these leanings that he broke with ancient tradition and refused to keep up any longer the custom of having the canons of St Patrick's take turns in preaching at Christ Church. Swift had always resented the obligation and had been fined at least once for skipping his own turn. Anyhow, a certain jealousy was habitual between the two chapters, so that not only Swift but his colleagues felt this special duty to be an unfair type of subservience. In the autumn of 1713 it must have been with a cheerful complacency that Swift failed either to provide a substitute for himself or to schedule the other canons of St Patrick's in continuance of the tradition. Ellis, already deeply embroiled with Archbishop King, sent a dignified, peculiarly mild reproof to Dean Swift but also complained to a more sympathetic correspondent that the new dean was bringing a 'new broil' upon the two cathedrals. Of course, Swift's fellow canons willingly backed up their chief; and in due course the dean and chapter of St Patrick's formally announced to Bishop Ellis that they proposed to make the old rule 'null and void'.[2]

It was one thing for Swift to assert the prerogatives of an achieved office. It was quite another for him to act as a leader in his own right. The same fear of being rejected that made him require first advances from ladies or noble lords also prevented him from taking the emotional risks that must be accepted by a

[1] Landa, pp. 65, 70–3, 184; Williams II. 392–3. [2] Landa, pp. 72–3 and n. 4.

public manager of men. A profoundly illustrative episode took place in the autumn of 1713. The Convocation of the Church of Ireland was due to assemble soon after the Irish Parliament; and the Lower House of Convocation would then have to choose a Prolocutor, or presiding officer. In 1711 the Dean of St Patrick's had served in the office; and several important churchmen hoped to see Swift follow Stearne's example. Yet when Archdeacon Walls sounded Swift out ahead of time, he received a disconcerting reply. If things could be so organized that he was assured of election, Swift said he would come over and act as Prolocutor. But if he had to campaign for the office, he would have nothing to do with it. 'But I should make the foolishest figure in nature, to come over hawking for an employment I no wise seek or desire, and then fail of it.'[1] Archbishop King probably used his considerable influence against Swift, but in any event it was hardly reasonable to desire to be 'chosen freely by a vast majority' while remaining in another kingdom.[2] I suppose Swift felt far too deeply absorbed in English affairs to leave London except for a sure thing; and I also suppose he liked to feel he had been treated unjustly and to reproach others for not making the job available to him. But he obviously would have welcomed the recognition for which he dared not struggle.

Yet the welfare of the Irish church remained among his constant preoccupations. For all his many declarations of indifference to his country's troubles, Swift at this time was almost eaten up with a desire to place the bishoprics of the kingdom in hands that would administer them along lines he approved of. Because of the bishops' hegemony in the Irish House of Lords, the project had large political implications. The united diocese of Kilmore and Ardagh Swift wished to see split up again (after the death of Bishop Wetenhall), and thus provide two opportunities for the right sort of men. Both Raphoe and Derry also became vacant while Swift was living in England. Out of the four possibilities thus created, however, only a single one was filled in the winter of 1713–14, and the choice did not please Swift.[3]

---

[1] Williams I. 389, 391–2, 395 (quoted).   [2] *Ibid.*, p. 410.
[3] *Ibid.*, p. 419; II. 46; Davis VIII. 159. Among the State Papers of this period in the

But the supreme episcopal appointment in the Church of Ireland did happen to fall within his tenuous area of influence. Eight weeks after Dean Swift, fully installed, returned to England, the long-awaited death occurred of Narcissus Marsh, Archbishop of Armagh and Primate of all Ireland. Swift, who disliked him, had once said, 'No man will be either glad or sorry at his death, except his successor'[1]; and the prophecy was fulfilled, if only because the old man suffered a long deterioration and illness during his final years, while Archbishop King took up most of his duties. If Marsh had died a few years earlier, King would have been his natural successor. And once when the decrepit Primate had seemed so near his end that he could not sign a document, Swift had told King, not without condescension, that he would 'drop in a word' to back his grace of Dublin for the appointment.[2] Now, however, the dean and the archbishop belonged to opposite camps; and so far from sending any encouragement to King, Swift let him know, through their common friend Stearne, that another selection had already been made. 'I should be thought a very vile man', he said, 'if I presumed to recommend to a [minister] my own brother if he were the least disinclined to the present measures of her m—y and ministry here.'[3] It was an exquisite but not unforeseen irony, and one about which Swift felt deeply conflicting emotions, that after years of seeking preferment from a really great man who would grant him nothing, he could at last take some responsibility for denying that person the highest ambition of his life; for if King was now excluded from the primacy for seeming too mild a Tory, he was, a decade later, to be again excluded for seeming too weak a Whig.

Thomas Lindsay, whom Swift and the ministers pushed instead of King, belonged to a plainly inferior race, and is chiefly remembered for the splendour of his funeral. Even a consistent

---

Public Record Office is a list of persons recommended to fill the bishoprics of Killaloe and Dromore in case Bishop Lindsay of Killaloe should be removed to the bishopric of Raphoe. They are Thomas Vesey (who was finally preferred); William Jephson, Dean of Lismore; Benjamin Pratt, Provost of Trinity College, Dublin; John Travers, vicar of St Andrews, Dublin; and Jeremiah Marsh, Dean of Kilmore (S.P. 63/369).

[1] Davis v. 212.   [2] Williams I. 200.   [3] *Ibid.*, p. 419.

apologist for the Established Church in Ireland had to admit that few men who occupied Lindsay's 'station of pre-eminence' left so little to be recorded in commemoration of their service.[1] The singular virtue of his weak character, in the eyes of those who promoted him, was his unimpugnable devotion to the policies of the government. It does not appear to have occurred to Swift that there was a connection between this loyalty and Lindsay's incompetence, just as he failed to see King's independence as a sign of his superiority. Swift had no great liking for Lindsay, whom he considered unfriendly to himself and a former obstacle to the First Fruits mission.[2] Yet he did wish the primacy to go to a man of Irish sympathies and Tory convictions. So he gave in favour of Lindsay the 'word' he had once promised to drop in support of King. It seems hardly probable that Swift's push did more than speed a decision already on the way. But he was enough of a courtier to desire the credit of his beneficence, and made sure that Lindsay heard of it. As go-between for this communication he employed a new friend, Richard Nutley, an Irish judge who had some notion of making Swift a bishop in the course of all the translations that seemed about to be realized. Lindsay's gratitude took the conventional form of offering to serve Swift in turn; and Swift immediately put him to work as a collaborator in his own grand scheme of filling the Irish episcopal bench with party stalwarts.[3] Amid so much pulling and prodding, it was surely a wit and not a preacher who spoke when Swift disingenuously said, 'We do not care to be troubled with the affairs of Ireland.'[4]

It also seems ironical to reflect that when Swift delivered that remark, he had in mind not church affairs but politics—because the English government was in fact not simply troubled but maddeningly bedevilled by the goings-on of the Irish Parliament. In the eyes of a Protestant minority governing a Roman Catholic nation, no threat to the Established Church could seem a more terrible prospect than the invasion of a Roman Catholic Pretender. The volcanic violence of the 1641 uprisings and the miseries of 1688–90 remained far too vivid in their collective

---

[1] Mant II. 407–8.   [2] Williams I. 406; *Journal*, 28 Mar. 1713.
[3] Williams I. 401–2, 406, 407–8, 422–4; II. 1–2.   [4] *Ibid.*, I. 425.

memory. They foresaw immense confiscations reversing the pain-fully achieved settlement of Irish land tenure. They foresaw monetary inflation, destitution, exile.[1] With such bogeys looming around them, the leaders of Whiggery in Ireland found it easy to work on the panic-ripe instincts of the Anglican landlord and Dissenting merchant. At the same time, however, the high-church spokesmen continued to reckon their own strength in conventional terms, disregarding the effect of the succession crisis and the struggle of Bolingbroke against Oxford. By their reckoning, the Irish House of Lords, the English House of Com-mons, the Queen, and her majesty's government stood united behind them, and in the recent history of Ireland such a team had appeared unbeatable.

For three years the loud, belligerent leader of the Irish Tories had been Sir Constantine Phipps, Lord Chancellor of Ireland. Phipps was a bigoted English lawyer whose most eminent service to his countrymen had been to manage the ambiguous defence of Sacheverell. As soon as he took the oaths in Dublin to be a Lord Justice of the kingdom, he began trying to enforce the sort of poli-cies which Bolingbroke advocated, and by the winter of 1713–14 he held the confidence of Bolingbroke's faction. He seemed pos-sessed with the anachronistic ambition of playing a second Went-worth to Charles I's grand-daughter.

I suspect it was as a counterstroke that Oxford got the tem-perate Duke of Shrewsbury put in as Lord Lieutenant.[2] Arriving home from his nerve-racking French mission at the end of August, Shrewsbury accepted the Irish appointment early the next month.[3] The move had been long anticipated, and Swift had been predicting it. 'He is the finest gentleman we have', Swift told Archbishop King, 'and of an excellent understanding, and capacity for business.'[4] The tone of the commendation sounds equivocal; and Swift did not see fit to point out that Shrewsbury had offended Bolingbroke by rejecting the Secretary of State's choice for the Lord Lieutenant's chief secretary and taking in-stead Sir John Stanley, a man of Whiggish associations.[5] Yet

[1] *Supra*, vol. I, pp. 12–17.   [2] Cf. Simms, p. 91.   [3] Somerville, p. 316.
[4] Williams I. 397.   [5] Somerville, pp. 311, 316–18.

Stanley himself was on good terms with Swift, who liked his wife and his hospitality.[1] Soon after the viceregal party was settled in Dublin, Stanley wrote to him, describing the impression Ireland now made: 'We are got here in the most eating, drinking, wrangling, quarrelsome country that ever I saw. There is no keeping the peace among them.'[2]

At least, nobody could quarrel with this analysis. The arrival of the Lord Lieutenant precipitated new and frightful crises in a long-drawn-out, merciless contest among the stubborn Irish factions.[3] Since the time of Wharton, the Whigs had dominated the City of Dublin corporation; but Phipps had been striving to install a Tory mayor over them. It was the mayor's responsibility to nominate sheriffs, and the sheriffs in turn had such fundamental duties as jail deliveries, the selection of juries, and so forth. Even though the Tory Privy Council backed Phipps, the Whig alderman refused to budge; and in the deadlock which followed, all municipal business gradually slowed to a chaotic halt. In this thunderous atmosphere, elections were held for a new Parliament, summoned before Shrewsbury arrived. During the Duke's first fortnight in Dublin, a riot broke out; for the polling had been shifted from a customary place on the north side of the Liffey to the Tholsel in the centre of town. Here the belligerent John Forster, one of the chief Whig candidates and a powerful ally of the Brodricks, kept his office as Recorder of Dublin. Whig partisans speedily occupied most of the building, leaving no space for the Tories, who reacted by storming the Tholsel and pulling down the platform to make room for themselves. One of Phipps's own servants helped to inflame the mob. When soldiers arrived and tried to halt the pandemonium, the maddened Tories beat them back with planks from the dismantled platform. The troops fired; a man died; and Shrewsbury finally had to step in, restoring order by dividing the poll between the old site and the new.[4] But

[1] *Journal*, 9 Oct. 1710; Williams IV. 537.
[2] Williams I. 404. Shrewsbury had arrived in Dublin 27 Oct. 1713.
[3] See the important article by J. G. Simms, 'The Irish Parliament of 1713', in *Historical Studies* IV, edited for the Irish Conference of Historians by G. A. Hayes—McCoy, Cambridge, 1963.
[4] I take the details of the riot from Simms and Somerville.

Phipps and his cronies felt a really hubristic confidence about the elections. 'We shall have a majority of three to two', he told Swift, 'and there is a great spirit of loyalty even among the mob.'[1] He was grotesquely wrong. When Parliament met, Shrewsbury named a Whig moderate as the member whom the government would like to see made Speaker. But the Whigs held the majority in the House of Commons, and the aggressive Alan Brodrick, whom Swift detested, was chosen by a vote of 131 to 127.[2]

Nothing went right after this. Neither the Privy Council nor the aldermen would compromise with the Duke's moderation. Working through the very secretary that Shrewsbury had chosen for himself, the Whigs inevitably discovered opportunities for conferring with the Lord Lieutenant which were denied to the outraged Tories. Phipps, however, made it standard procedure to appeal over his grace's head directly to Bolingbroke, and it soon manifestly appeared that the ministry in Whitehall would not stand behind the Duke in Dublin. When Primate Marsh died, Shrewsbury hoped the successor would remain unannounced till the end of the parliamentary session; and he named three Englishmen as his candidates. But the court acted at once, choosing the Tory Lindsay, who Phipps had predicted would become Primate.[3] When the Whigs realized that Shrewsbury was not coming over to their side, they in turn opposed his requests; and instead of the customary two years' supplies, the House of Commons voted only three months' worth. Meanwhile, Convocation met,[4] with William Percival, a contentious Tory, as Prolocutor; in the Upper House, not Archbishop King but Archbishop Vesey of Tuam presided. Under this undisciplined leadership, the members noisily expressed their satisfaction with Phipps, picked a quarrel with the House of Commons, and condemned Robert Molesworth—one of Brodrick's main collaborators—for a harmless witticism directed against their own body.

By the beginning of December, the Commons, after requesting the dismissal of Phipps as a Jacobite, had got so far out of hand that some members proposed changes in the legislative proce-

---

[1] Williams I. 403.   [2] Somerville, p. 312.   [3] *Ibid.*, p. 319 and n.
[4] 30 Nov. 1713.

dures, allowing themselves new freedom to initiate legislation. Then the Tory House of Lords battled with the Commons over the complaints brought against the Chancellor. Shrewsbury found himself powerless. His correspondence was tampered with; his chronically bad health declined. He took advantage of the Christmas recess to adjourn the houses and soon received permission to prorogue them altogether.[1]

Swift received excellent, detailed accounts of the hubbub from the archbishop, whose advice was thoroughly rational. But Swift could hardly believe there was no skulduggery in such a train of disasters. Instead of simply accepting King's very probable arguments, he indulged his usual suspicions of hidden intrigue and imagined that people like the archbishop and the Lord Lieutenant were leading good Tories astray through secret dealings with the Whigs. A couple of years later, he said that Shrewsbury had hated Lord Oxford and that in Ireland he had acted a part 'directly opposite to the court' in order to recommend himself to the Elector of Hanover after the Queen should die.[2] But I think Shrewsbury enjoyed the tacit encouragement of Oxford, and followed a policy not very different from the Treasurer's.[3] At the same time, for all Swift's commitment to the 'thorough' tradition of Laud and Strafford, there are hints that he admired neither Phipps nor his proceedings.[4] With Swift's prejudice in favour of uniformity it seemed unnatural to him that Ireland should march on a different 'foot' from England. If only to strengthen the ministers' position in London, he thought the Whigs in Dublin would have to be reduced.[5] The Chancellor's ostentatious violence was not, however, the way to do this. Even when pressing for radical measures, Swift believed an air of moderation should be maintained.

VI. SCRIBLERUS

While frustrations nagged the preacher, the wit had a refreshing success. Swift's old ambition to form a club joining power to

---

[1] Prorogued 14 Jan. 1714; see Williams II. 3–6; Somerville, pp. 318–23.
[2] Williams I. 424–6; Davis VIII. 156.   [3] H.M.C. *Bath* I. 245.
[4] Williams II. 120.   [5] *Ibid.* I. 425.

genius and throwing a permanent lustre on his friends' regime was at last fleetingly fulfilled in an association of brilliant writers and one powerful statesman.[1] Bolingbroke's Society had never connected patronage and talent as Swift thought it should; and the scheme of an honorific, non-partisan linguistic academy had hopelessly evaporated. It was only when Swift gave up the plan of rivalling the Kit-Cats and accepted instead something like Addison's informal cluster at Button's that he approached the ideal so often envisaged in the European imagination of a *convivium* of equal, creative minds.

The germ of the brief enterprise was due less to Swift than to his clever young friend Pope. With the plans for translating Homer employing most of his literary energy, Pope still found time to entertain the very different scheme of a satire on useless learning. It was as though the comic elements that must be excluded from an epic style had to be drained off another way.

Having contributed some essays to the *Spectator* and the *Guardian*, he thought for a while of a mock-periodical pretending to report on valuable scientific or scholarly research but really describing the new absurdities of pedants and quacks. During the autumn of 1713, after Steele had shut down the *Guardian*, the opportunities for non-political, periodical essays looked unusually promising.

Pope's slightly older friend Gay had got some experience of this sort of journalism through the columns of the *British Apollo*, a question-and-answer, poem-and-essay paper which he had helped to manufacture.[2] Now, of course, Gay was known in his own right as a poet, essayist, and playwright. Yet he had originally received no more than a grammar-school education at Barnstaple, his native town. After a few years' work in London as a tradesman's apprentice, the boy had gone back to Barnstaple, staying there until, in his early twenties, he once more came up to the capital, this time to pursue the literary life. Working as a hack writer, Gay managed to make friends with Pope and other men in

[1] My discussion of Scriblerus is drawn from the edition of the *Memoirs of Scriblerus* by C. Kerby-Miller, New Haven, 1950; see also Sherburn, *Early Career*, pp. 69–82.
[2] Irving, pp. 40–56.

Addison's coterie. He also secured a comfortable post as steward to the Duchess of Monmouth, with secretarial duties which left him free to compose poetry and mingle with her grace's courtly guests. A clever essay on contemporary authors, some verse in one of Lintot's miscellanies, and an unsuccessful farce were among his recent efforts.

In the autumn and winter of 1713–14, if Swift was busy turning out denunciations of Steele and Burnet, or manipulating the preferments of the Irish church, he did not therefore abandon more congenial society. Between trips to Windsor he had the pleasure of improving his acquaintance with Pope and of getting to know Pope's overweight, sweet-tempered comrade, Gay, who came up to town in November, after a term at his Duchess's country seat. The scheme of a satirical periodical to be called *The Works of the Unlearned* must have appealed at once to the Bickerstaff in the dean; and along with Swift now went his sad compatriot Parnell, already a friend of Pope's. Dr Arbuthnot had to remain at Windsor with the court until the opening of Parliament; but as soon as he heard of Pope's project, he began playing with the idea, elaborating and altering it.

In the early months of 1714 it was peculiarly convenient for the five wits to spend cheerful hours together. Dean Swift was often at court; Dr Arbuthnot had lodgings in St James's Palace; Parnell and Gay hovered in hopes of securing some post from the government; and several Tory ministers considered the author of *Windsor Forest* to be worth cultivating. Although they sometimes met in a coffee-house, Arbuthnot's chamber at the palace supplied a pleasanter setting. And, because this room was easy for the Earl of Oxford to visit from his own apartment below, they found their circle at times magnificently enlarged by the company of the Lord High Treasurer.[1]

If Oxford, however, had the knack of roughing out a few stanzas in rhyme, he was hardly up to the standard of the rest. Rather he became their honoured guest and chief audience. Versified invitations were sent to him, and he tried modestly to respond in kind. Considering the miseries and humiliations Oxford

[1] Some of these details are conjectural; see Sherburn, *Early Career*, p. 78.

suffered from his daughter's death, his tug-of-war with Bolingbroke, the decay of his health, and the disasters in Parliament, I
wonder whether Swift might not have drawn him into the little
club in order to distract and console him:

> The Doctor and Dean, Pope, Parnell and Gay
> In manner submissive most humbly do pray,
> That your lordship would once let your cares all alone
> And climb the dark stairs to your friends who have none:
> To your friends who at least have no cares but to please you
> To a good honest Junta that never will teaze you.[1]

After one's initial surprise that men so heavily burdened as
Oxford, Swift, and Arbuthnot could throw off their deep anxieties and pursue *la bagatelle*, one realizes the naturalness of the
impulse. Simpler troubles send humbler men to relief in frivolity;
and affairs of state provide no sharper pain than other preoccupations. Yet there remains a special drama in the sight of Swift
with a price on his head, Arbuthnot with his secret knowledge of
the Queen's desperate health, and Oxford with the catastrophe
of his long career in view, all playing literary games with Parnell,
Gay, and Pope.

As the games went on, Pope's scheme of a collaborative periodical was distilled into a more demanding enterprise. The club
was to busy itself with the life and works of an imaginary pedant
to be named Martin Scriblerus, the given name being derived
(one assumes) from Dryden's blunderer, Sir Martin Mar-all.
This hero was to be a dabbler in all sciences and master of none.
Like Panurge in Rabelais's *Third Book*, he was to search for truth
through every field of systematic knowledge but never meet it.
The club was to produce pseudo-treatises supposed to be by
Scriblerus, and to attribute to him the real work of real men. Like
the Stultitia of Erasmus, he was to take credit for all abuses of
learning.

Performed in a spirit of sympathetic humour, the biography of
such a figure could have made a profound commentary on the
limits of reason or the dangers of the imagination. But from the
evidence that has survived, the conception seems closer to *Hudi-*

[1] *Poems* I. 185.

[725]

bras than to *Don Quixote*. Swift must have been an ebullient talker on the subject. Whether he was recalling Jack in *A Tale of a Tub* or germinating Captain Gulliver, he had similar ingredients in his finest work. But neither he nor anyone else in the group possessed the staying power and the narrative skill requisite to making the story coherent and compelling; and indeed the biographical form deprived the work of the rhetorical unity which Erasmus gave to his *Praise of Folly*. Anyhow, the Scriblerian mode appears more valuable than the Scriblerus Club, which in itself amounted to a diminished embodiment of Lucianic tradition. For a moment in London these kindred talents signalized their harmony in sketches and trifles. But only years later did the true power of their mode display itself in *Gulliver*, the *Beggar's Opera*, and the *Dunciad*.

It seems more than an accident of politics that neither Addison nor Steele belonged to this little circle. Swift and his friends shared a distrust of human nature, an ironical pessimism, on which their characteristic work depends. In their morality, man's intuitive reason is a marker of boundaries, a warning that our essential condition is hardly open to fundamental improvement. On the contrary, Addison and Steele assumed that the systematic application of reason to physical and moral nature would indeed ameliorate the human lot. Therefore, the same occupations which Scriblerians ridiculed as frauds or delusions were sometimes recommended in the *Tatler* or *Spectator* as worthy and serious pursuits. William Whiston, the eccentric theologian and mathematician, was an object of jeering contempt to Swift and Arbuthnot; and Gay wrote a ditty ridiculing him. But Addison and Steele sponsored his mathematical lectures at Button's coffeehouse, and the *Guardian* announced his crackpot scheme for determining the longitude of ships at sea.[1]

As usual, Swift could not divorce conviviality from patronage. The presence of Oxford lured him into yet new devices for making his friends' fortunes. He had been straining to find something for Parnell; now he added Gay to the number of his wards. In the spring of 1714, as a rather Scriblerian resource for ingratiating

---

[1] Kerby-Miller, *op. cit.*, pp. 334–5; Winton, pp. 157–8.

himself with the Elector, Oxford was arranging to send a new, confidential envoy to Hanover. Swift turned this little plan to profit by suggesting Gay as secretary to the embassy and Parnell as chaplain.[1] But of course weeks crept by before any decision was reached.

Meanwhile, the amenities of the 'club' were not due merely to the *bagatelle* of Scriblerus or the retreat supplied from the pressures of ugly politics. Among themselves the half-dozen men clearly enjoyed a satisfaction in pleasing one another and a sympathy of inner temperament. There was no rivalry or enmity to disturb their ease: so long as the Treasurer joined them, the Secretary could not; and Scriblerus missed Bolingbroke as the Society had lacked Oxford. The spread of ages, from Pope at twenty-six to Oxford at fifty-three, made for a variety of youthful and avuncular relationships. Above all, there was the excitement of fresh acquaintance. Half the group were delightfully out of touch with the cares of the others; and Pope and Gay brought novel associations into the familiar talk. The excitement of getting to know people with complex and interesting minds was a pleasure felt by them all.

[1] Williams II. 27, 29, 34–5.

Chapter Twenty-eight

OXFORD'S FALL

I. LETCOMBE

As the spring advanced, the bleakness of reality overwhelmed the fascinations of literature and society. After a period of hopefulness, from Christmas to Easter, Swift sank into gloom until he found the strain intolerable. The Queen's terrifying illness in December had restored some trace of rationality to the duelling ministers. Swift was told she felt so offended with the open rejoicing of the Whigs at her near-death that she gave up the old hesitancies and, instead of trying to reconcile the two great parties, determined to go along with the highest Tory policy. Since Swift had imagined that her majesty's balkiness was the main block to the execution of this policy, he now assumed that Oxford, Ormonde, Harcourt, and Bolingbroke could at last join in hearty unanimity. Of course he did not know that Oxford and Bolingbroke were at this very time demanding that the Pretender should become a convert to the Established Church and were offering him the British crown if he would do so. Nor that the young prince, at the end of February, told the Queen and the two ministers, in separate and intelligent letters, that he could not renounce his faith.

At this point, instead of rushing together into ardently Hanoverian measures, the ministers renewed their old, murderous feud. Anyhow, the failing Queen was in no mood to make a great show of confidence in the Elector; and the French court had enough evidence to destroy both the Secretary and the Treasurer if they dared to abandon a Francophile policy.[1] As common suspicion of the government's tactics became deeper and wider, the resistance to them grew more general. In the House of Lords, of course, not

[1] Trevelyan III. 266–9.

only the bishops and Lord Nottingham but the Duke of Argyll had already joined the Whigs in worrying the ministers about the succession. In the House of Commons, Hanmer's Tories had stopped co-operating with the government.

Swift continued to see this breakdown of leadership in terms of the personalities involved. He put great weight on the quarrel between Oxford and Ormonde over the ten thousand pounds the Duke wanted in return for commissions forfeited by officers cashiered for alleged sedition. And Swift felt that a burst of frankness between Oxford and Bolingbroke would, with the intervention of helpful friends, have gone far to close the abyss between them. He thought the Queen was displeased with Oxford not merely because of his irresponsible torpor but also because he was not seconding her new resolution to have done with all Whigs and Whiggism. This was the period when Swift made the experiment already described, of tricking the Secretary and the Treasurer into occupying the same coach on a trip to Windsor, with no other company. This was when he innocently hoped that during the four hours thus imposed upon them they might arrive at a 'good understanding'—although, as we have seen, nothing of the sort took place.

Testy and miserable, Swift still hung on at court because he hoped to influence the choice of the four bishops for Ireland. But though he understood that candidates had been named to the Queen and approved by her majesty, the mandatory letters were nevertheless held back. Swift pestered Oxford on this matter but received only the characteristic delays and excuses. At last, he erupted with rage, demanding that the Treasurer settle this crucial business at once; and then Oxford said he had been 'earnest' with the Queen to determine the bishoprics about ten times in the preceding fortnight, but to no effect—'He found his credit wholly at an end.' Telling the story years later, Swift goes on,

and two nights after sitting with him and Lord Bolingbroke in Lady Masham's lodgings at St. James's for some hours; I told the Treasurer, that having despaired of any reconciliation between them, I had only stayd some time longer to forward the disposall of those bishopricks in Ireland, which since his lordship told me was out of his power; I now resolved to retire immediatly, as from an evil I could neither help to redress nor endure the sight of; That before I left them, I desired they would answer me two questions: first whether these mischiefs might not be remedied in two minutes; and secondly, whether upon the present foot the ministry would not be infallibly ruined in two months; Lord Bolingbroke answered to each question in the affirmative; and approved of my resolution to retire; but the Treasurer after his manner evaded both, and only desired me to dine with him next day.[1]

His scheme of withdrawal was probably one he had pondered while contemplating flight in February—if not years before. As early as the crisis of December 1711, Swift had spoken of retiring for some months if the ministry should be turned out, and then said he had 'pitched upon the place already'.[2] An old friend of Swift's from Moor Park days was living in rural Berkshire, among the downs near Wantage. He was a parson named John Geree, for whom Swift had secured the promise of a living from Lord Chancellor Harcourt. Geree's college at Oxford had presented him to the rectory of Letcombe Bassett, a small village in an immensely beautiful countryside, where the young parson also kept a tiny school. Swift thought him a 'very worthy creature', but Geree had got married in 1712, after consulting Swift ('when it was too late to break off'), and could now use a better preferment. He had long since invited Swift to come for an extended visit, and now at last the famous dean would accept. The change from an unmanageable gang of courtiers to a quiet parsonage and the country life among attentive inferiors must have seemed delicious in anticipation. Swift could plan to sort out his accumulated papers, write a few things he had in mind, keep clear of exasperations, and finally proceed to Ireland rested and in good health. As he wrote to Peterborough, 'What has a man without employment to do among ministers, when he can neither serve himself, his friends, or the public.'[3]

Geree's connection with Farnham and Sir William Temple was no irrelevance at this time. Swift's old patron, Sir William, had withdrawn from ministerial chaos in the same manner as the new dean was planning; and he had acted *Hoc erat in votis* in Moor

[1] Davis VIII. 159.   [2] *Journal*, 15 Dec. 1711.   [3] Williams I. 22.

Park just as Swift hoped to do in Letcombe and Laracor. (It seems ironical that this was the precise moment chosen by Swift's hated pursuer Boyer to publish a life of Temple which drew incriminating parallels between the government of Sir William's enemies and that of Swift's friends.[1]) Being a sober, taciturn character, Geree would leave Swift to his writing and his country walks. It would all cost—at Swift's insistence—only a guinea a week for the dean and his man together.[2]

I think there was a punitive element in Swift's impulse to leave London without returning at once to Ireland. Of course, Dublin could not have seemed very enticing at this time. Although the Parliament there remained prorogued, and Convocation had risen, the Lord Lieutenant was just managing to keep the streets quiet, and the City corporation was still returning as mayor and sheriff persons whom the Privy Council refused to approve. While itching to get home, Shrewsbury had to linger in Ireland, dousing spontaneous combustions and worrying about Queen Anne's disappearing health. He had apparently come to regard Phipps as so dangerous that he disliked leaving the government of Ireland to him as a Lord Justice. Furthermore, in order to repair the shortage of revenues caused by the three months' limit on parliamentary supplies, the government had decided to disband some regiments in Ireland, a most unfortunate proceeding when fears of a Jacobite invasion were chronic and the French were actively recruiting Irish soldiers for the Pretender—promising the men they would be back home again within a year.[3] In these monstrous conditions, Shrewsbury's fair dealing had a soothing effect. Archbishop King told Swift's friend Bishop Ashe about the Duke's success:

> Our city still continues in confusion. The jails are crammed full and there can be no jail delivery for want of sheriffs. . . No debts can be recovered, no malefactors tried, no regulation of markets, the streets unpaved, the poor undone. . . My Lord Lieutenant keeps himself very close and quiet, and I cannot tell how, but he keeps

[1] *Political State*, VII (1719), 492–3 (May 1714).
[2] *Journal*, 10 May 1712, 22 Dec.; *Architects' Journal* (London), 31 Mar. 1949; Williams II. 25–6, 35.
[3] Simms, p. 90.

everybody, in spite of their . . . party quarrels very quiet also, in so much that though we have had no government these last seven months, yet the city is as peaceable and quiet as if there had been the best magistrates.[1]

To exchange the bedlam of Westminster for siege warfare in Dublin could not have tickled Swift's desires; and we need hardly wonder why he had hovered over a crisis that made him unhappy. He pretended his retirement was due to bad health.[2] But I also think he was giving his great friends a kind of imaginary birching by walking out on them. It is as if he were declaring, If you won't take my advice, you can't have my company. Certainly, he wished his departure to be heralded far in advance. For six weeks the court heard that Dean Swift was going away, and the effect of that rumour was pleasant for neither the Secretary nor the Treasurer. I am sure John Barber knew it would please the dean when he wrote, after Swift's final remove, 'Every body is in the greatest consternation at your retirement, and wonder at the cause.'[3] Swift himself boasted, 'I sett abundance of people at a gaze by my going away.'[4]

The great men's poisonous hatred of each other was meanwhile tumbling them both into the prophesied ruin. By the most ingenious manipulations within the South Sea Company, Oxford's agents made it obvious that a scandalous fraction of the revenues of the company had been mysteriously reserved for unnamed persons who were of course surmised to be Lady Masham and Lord Bolingbroke; once the arrangement was exposed, however, it was easily, if all too publicly, cancelled.[5] In Parliament the affairs of Steele and Swift had overlapped with motions by the Whig peers against the Pretender, the Peace of Utrecht, and the treaties of commerce. The Whigs knew how deeply the ministry was split; and they were anxiously waiting for the Queen's early demise. Steele, whose suspicions of the Treasurer had been cooling a year before, was more fidgety than ever after his own expulsion from the Commons; and he told his wife, 'According to the

[1] Somerville, pp. 323–5, letter dated 8 June: I have altered capitals and punctuation and supplied 'can' where it seemed wanting.
[2] Williams II. 49. [3] *Ibid.*, p. 29; cf. Thomas Harley, *ibid.*, p. 39.
[4] *Ibid.*, p. 49. [5] Boyer VII (1719), 171–7.

situation of affairs nothing but divine providence [i.e., Anne's death] can prevent a civil war within a few years.'[1] The dismissals of the Duke of Argyll and the Earl of Stair, the steady transformation of the army from Whig to Tory, the changes in the county lord lieutenancies, all aggravated the fulminous tension; for it was very hard to find enough officers and magistrates who were utterly loyal to the government in power without accepting real or crypto-Jacobites.

In order to escape from involvement in such mortifications, Swift began moving by the middle of April, when he sent Geree a shipment of Bolingbroke's wine. As substitutes for St James's Palace and Hessy Vanhomrigh, he could expect the humbler amenities which the parson promised to supply: 'a horse, and garden, and pretty good study of books, and the master and mistress entirely at your service'.[2] He decided to travel to Letcombe not directly but by way of Oxford. After shipping six cases of his own books to Dublin, and dispatching a housemaid to Hessy with a bandbox full of her legal papers, he left London by coach on Monday, 31 May 1714, accompanied by his servant Will. (Twelve years were to pass before he saw the capital again.) They arrived in Oxford the same day, to stay three nights. While there, Swift saw Lord Bolingbroke's protégé Dr Trapp but not Lord Oxford's protégé Dr Stratford, although he did slip into Christ Church. On Thursday morning he left the city, with a huge burden of books and clothes trailing him, and went straight to Geree's.[3]

II. PROSE AND VERSE

If seclusion was what Swift thought he wanted, he found isolation. Three miles from Letcombe was the small market town of Wantage with its ancient associations with King Alfred. All around were fields, downs, and thatched cottages, a little twelfth-century church which had no steeple, and Parson Geree's rectory. The dean's host was a laconic contrast to his chatty friends in London, and provincial life ran on an unfamiliar timetable.

[1] Blanchard, p. 299 (30 Mar. 1714).   [2] Williams II. 19.
[3] *Ibid.*, pp. 25–6, n. 7; 27, 31–2.

They rose at six and went to bed at ten.[1] Instead of sitting down to a formal dinner in mid- or late-afternoon, Swift dined by choice at Geree's normal hour, between noon and one. For supper they had bread and butter with ale at eight o'clock. 'Wine is a stranger, except a little I sent him, of which one evening in two, we have a pint between us.' Swift spent the day reading, writing, and walking.[2]

After a week of such unruffled solitude, Ireland looked tempting, and Swift thought of shortening his healthful visit. He quickly found that serenity was not the invariable consequence of rusticity. News kept blowing in from London, to roil and vex him, because he kept writing to his friends and they replied all too punctually. In Parliament, he heard, Bolingbroke was trying to smash Oxford and to distract the world's attention from the succession crisis by introducing the monstrous Schism Bill, which forbade Dissenters to maintain their own schools. The appeal of this measure to the Queen and to the high-church party was vast; it represented a darling policy which the Lower House of Convocation had been recommending for years; and Bolingbroke knew that the very opposition of the low-church men would discredit them with her majesty. But the Treasurer throughout his career had tried to bring Dissenters over to his own side; and he saw the bill as destroying one of his fundamental principles. Therefore, Oxford had his own brother vote against the bill in the House of Commons; but he dared not oppose it himself, and only sat dumbly seething with visible discontent while Bolingbroke cheerfully harangued his fellow peers. When there was a vote on a petition of the Presbyterians to be heard against the bill, Oxford left the House to avoid committing himself; but his allies, Poulett, Foley, and Mansel, voted in favour of the motion and thus against Bolingbroke.

Although the Schism Bill did not finally become law till the last week of June, the crucial debates took place just after Swift left London.[3] One of the widely reported contributions to the debates was a furious allusion which the Earl of Nottingham made to

---

[1] Williams II. 35.   [2] *Ibid.*, p. 26.
[3] Crucial debates, 1 and 4 June; final passage, 23 June.

[734]

Swift. Though a far more devout churchman than Bolingbroke's cronies, Nottingham thought parents had a natural right to educate their own children, and he denounced the bill. Seizing on the provision that any schoolmaster must hold a licence from the appropriate bishop, Nottingham told the Lords, 'I tremble when I think that a certain divine, who is hardly suspected of being a Christian is in a fair way of being a bishop, and may one day give licences to those, who shall be entrusted with the instruction of youth.'[1] It is always ironical and sometimes pathetic to find Swift's religious faith doubted by a man of his own persuasion. This time there was the further irony that the dean was no stronger supporter of the Schism Bill than the Earl of Oxford.[2]

Swift's chronic resentment of this reputation for infidelity, I think, aggravated his instinct to hide the strength of his religious faith. By a natural reaction, the more he was doubted, the less he would stoop to defend himself. But the trembling fury of his indignation is palpable during the quarrel with Steele, and it appears again as one of the chief elements in a poem he wrote at Letcombe. Too reckless to be published in Swift's lifetime, this poem contains some of his most impressive lines.

Swift's poems about himself may be divided into two classes: a larger group which are built on self-mockery and a smaller group which are free from literary pose and lean toward self-justification. Although Swift commonly seems more interesting when he indulges his love of mimicry, some of his strongest effects depend on precisely the opposite style. In *The Author upon Himself* it is the bitter, frank lack of reserve that gives the couplets their force. Unlike the imitations of Horace this poem has the sound of a man speaking without a screen. It is not the wit but the priest who harangues us.

Rhetorically, the poem suffers from a tone of self-admiration or complacency which undermines the *saeva indignatio* of the finest passages. The theme of the whole is the conflict between integrity and malice. Reviewing the series of events that have brought him to Letcombe, Swift blames his enemies for gulli-

[1] Boyer VII (1719), 516 (June 1714). Cf. *Wentworth Papers*, pp. 385–6.
[2] Williams II. 83.

bility, vanity, or opportunism, and sets himself up as inspiring
jealousy through his talents and virtues. The implication is that
if he had been more selfish and less gifted, he would have met no
blocks in his upward path. It's a token of the potency of human
self-deception that a satirist like Swift, who expressly described
himself as a libeller, could picture himself as so innocent, and feel
baffled because his victims paid more attention to their gaping
wounds than to his exalted motives.

The positive source of the poem's intensity is the concentration
of simple meaning in the vituperative lines, where without seeming cluttered or awkward each sentence holds a surprising number
of thunderous expressions which are nevertheless not repetitious:

> By an old, redhair'd, murd'ring hag pursued,
> A crazy prelate, and a royal prude . . .

One does not ordinarily think of bishops and old women as either
murderers or pursuers; nor does one associate royalty with pru-
dishness, at least in the eighteenth century. The epithets have no
conventional link to the substantives or to one another—red hair,
craziness, and royalty do not suggest one another. Yet the phrases
hold themselves together with an aphoristic strength. As usual
with Swift, the rhythms add little beside the hammering note of
their accents. But the profoundly idiomatic combinations of the
words appear to endow the poet's accusations with objective
validity. Elsewhere, satanic touches are added to the hints of bedlam:

> Now Madam Coningsmark her vengeance vows
> On Swift's reproaches for her murdered spouse.
> From her red locks her mouth with venom fills:
> And thence into the royal ear instills.

At the other pole from this serpent, Swift portrays himself, but
again with a deliberately objective tone, enhanced by his device
of attributing these remarks to other voices than his own:

> Swift had the sin of wit, no venial crime;
> Nay, 'twas affirm'd, he sometimes dealt in rhime:
> Humour, and mirth, had place in all he writ:
> He reconcil'd divinity and wit.[1]

[1] I have altered the use of capitals and punctuation in these quotations.

The fullness, neatness, and colloquial directness of the couplets make them sound as honest and reliable as a proverb. The light oxymoron and ironical bathos suggest the rationality and restraint of the speaker.

If self-justification was the main direction of this poem, the important prose essay that Swift was writing at the same time had just the opposite tendency.[1] Again the startling fact is that with few of the marks of the 'Swiftian' style, this discourse—*Some Free Thoughts upon the Present State of Affairs*—remains a shining monument of Swift's dignified prose. In general structure the essay follows no formal rhetorical pattern; but a few carefully expounded generalizations are first elaborated and then applied. After examining the characters of the chief ministers in the light of these principles, Swift similarly analyses some recent crises and then presents his own, plain recommendations.

As a consequence of the informal, though obviously thoughtful, structure, one does not feel that the author is stuffing his data into a pre-shaping mould but rather that he is fairly taking up the real issues in terms of real principles. Conceits, striking ironies, innuendo, and impersonation would only jar on Swift's pervasive, almost homiletic earnestness; so those 'characteristics' and witty elements hardly appear. Instead, the sentences employ generic subjects and impersonal constructions more often than in most of his work; and if his allusions are plain enough, they are neither sharp nor abundant.

Instead of violence and sarcasm, the mode of the writing is deliberation; the movement of the argument is solemn; the author writes rather in philosophical pity than in polemical anger. Swift could afford to be so moderate because, like *Some Advice to the October Club*, this essay is aimed at the Tories alone, and not at the general public or the Whigs. The author assumes, therefore, that the reader shares his political views; he wishes less to convert than to enlighten us.

Yet there is nothing lifeless about the style. Where a weaker writer would use a substantive or a pronoun, Swift finds a verb or a verbal phrase to act as the pivot of his sentence. He changes the

---

[1] Cf. J. Béranger, 'Swift en 1714', *Etudes Anglaises* xv (1962), 233–47.

grammatical point of view often but comfortably, so that the object of the discourse seems held up from a number of different angles. I do not think critics have noticed how cleverly Swift invents a dramatic or personified subject for a statement where most writers would be content with a flat 'one' or 'person': e.g., 'An illnatured or inquisitive man may still perhaps desire to press the question further . . .'[1]

Of course, Tacitus and not Cicero is Swift's ancestor; but within the apparently free pinning of clause upon clause he still runs a thread of irony or dialectic that gives an elegant shape to his spontaneity. Thus *Some Free Thoughts* contains some of his best aphorisms:

> God has given the bulk of mankind a capacity to understand reason when it is fairly offered; and by reason they would easily be governed, if it were left to their choice.
>
> I suppose if a man thinks it necessary to play with a serpent, he will chuse one of a kind that is least mischievous; otherwise although it appear to be crushed, it may have life enough to sting him to death.[2]

The casualness of the syntax draws us one way; the concentrated purposiveness of the meaning draws us another; and between them both we are subjected to a remarkable pressure.

And yet, for all its stylistic achievements the essay has radical flaws as argument, mainly because the attitude of the speaker keeps shifting from praise to blame. One might almost say he mixes Bolingbroke's doctrines with Oxford's manner. Swift's first impulse seems to complain against the Treasurer's secretiveness, presumably in the hope of persuading him to be more open. (Why a printed pamphlet should seem more likely to move him than the repeated exhortation of a trusted intimate, I do not know.) Swift's unvarying contempt for 'the secrets of court' reminds one of Sir William Temple's reliance upon candour. The intrigues of Charles II's court were a last, faint ripple of Renaissance absolutism operating through the devious manipulations of human instruments. But Swift, in spite of an ideology reminiscent

---

[1] Davis VIII. 96.
[2] *Ibid.*, pp. 77, 89. I have omitted some words and altered the capitalization.

of Laud, is paradoxically in revolt against the system that Laud defended, and wants intrigue replaced by plain dealing. At the same time, the minister he was censuring stood further from Restoration statecraft than Swift did himself, inasmuch as Oxford felt enough confidence in England's constitution not to fear the coexistence of rival Christian sects.

As a balance to the elaborate complaint against Oxford for not delegating authority, Swift more briefly blames the Secretary for demanding more power than he could handle, and as usual attributes the troubles of the government to the competition of the two chiefs: 'I am confident . . . that a much inferiour degree of wisdom and experience, joined with more unanimity and less refinement, might have born us through all our difficulties without any suspicion of magick.'[1] This complaint is lighter and shorter than the detailed case against Oxford. Like that, however, it sounds candid enough.

The apologies for the regime do not. When Swift suspends his fault-finding in order to clear himself of any intention to 'condemn the councils or actions of the present ministry',[2] one can only translate his words into the slogan, Better a bad Tory than a good Whig. Although this weakness appears only once or twice in the long essay, it is serious, and must keep an unprejudiced reader from trusting the writer's impartiality.

A worse mistake is Swift's confident representation of Bolingbroke's programme as expressing the general will of the English people. It is one thing to say a majority of the House of Commons will eagerly enforce certain policies if their leaders recommend them. It is another thing to claim that 'a very great majority of the kingdom appear perfectly hearty and unanimous' in desiring a specific course of action. The sagacious reader of Swift's essay would have known that the author was canting here, and that the unanimity of the nation years earlier behind Marlborough's campaigns would have counted as nothing to him in this same analysis. To fling the Whigs and low-churchmen out of office, to install none but Tories in the commissions of the army, to demand immense concessions from the Elector in return for establishing

---

[1] *Ibid.*, p. 88. [2] *Ibid.*, p. 85.

his grandchild as a royal prince living in England—such policies are obviously enough the author's own; but if there were no considerable opposition to them throughout the country, they would hardly require all the eloquence he devotes to promoting them.

The ultimate cause of these weaknesses was probably the ambiguity of Swift's intentions, because he wished to scold as well as instruct the audience of two that he had most in mind, and yet he did not wish to weaken their reputation vis-à-vis the Whigs. 'I have a mind to be very angry', he told Arbuthnot, 'and to let my anger break out in some manner that will not please them, at the end of a pen.'[1] But one cannot scold a friend in a public street and expect bystanders to revere him. When Ford said he thought *Some Free Thoughts* would 'do great service', Swift replied, 'As for service it will do, a fiddlestick. It will vex them, and that's enough.'[2]

The fascinating history of the essay's *non*-publication was a product of this impasse. Keyed up by the quick and unpredictable turns in his friends' irreversible course, Swift saved so much of his correspondence, during these weeks, that we can trace in unique detail the route of his manuscript from the hand of the chastising dean to the desk of his reprimanded parishioner, and thence to obscurity. In order for *Some Free Thoughts* to achieve its proper effect, Swift thought the printed pamphlet must seem to have no connection with himself; so he employed all his favourite methods of concealment. The talent for impersonation which he did not apply within the essay, he devoted to arranging its debut.

He had begun writing the essay before he left London.[3] By the end of June he had finished it and somehow contrived to get a copy made by another person. This second copy he sent to Charles Ford in London on 1 July. But Swift wished to suppress Ford's connection with the piece as well. So he coolly asked him to send the manuscript to Barber by a porter who in turn should be hired for the purpose off the street, and not when Ford was at home! Swift even wished the manuscript to be delivered on a Saturday night or a Sunday (when the Wantage carrier did not

[1] Williams II. 36 (16 June).   [2] *Ibid.*, p. 60.   [3] *Ibid.*, p. 32.

travel up), so it could not appear to come from Swift in the country. With the manuscript Swift enclosed a note which he inevitably asked Ford to have copied out by some obliging acquaintance who would also address and seal the packet. The note, signed 'Samuel Bridges', directed Barber to return the manuscript to St Dunstan's coffee-house in Fleet Street if he decided against printing it within a stated time. Ford meanwhile was to watch for the publication; and if the pamphlet did not come out soon, he was to send a man to ask for it at Dunstan's.

A remarkable detail suggests the willingness of the greatest of prose satirists to submit his work to correction; for Swift gave Ford a free hand in emending his tautologies: 'Spend an hour in reading it, and if the same word be too soon repeated, vary it as you please, but alter your hand.'[1] But Ford admired the essay too much to make many alterations. He wished Swift had not at one point blamed the Queen for her timidity; he did modernize Swift's spelling, changing 'onely' to 'only' and 'scheame' to 'scheme'; and in one paragraph he made the tenses of the verbs consistent, changing present to past, four times. Yet he regretted going even so far. Then, having done his chore as editor, he sent the manuscript to Barber, as instructed, on Sunday, 4 July, expecting to see it printed immediately.[2]

Alas, Barber was too subtle to be content with the rôle assigned him in this pantomime. Instead of handing the manuscript to his compositor, he turned it over to Bolingbroke, of all people, and desired his lordship's advice—intending, of course, to ingratiate himself yet further with a powerful patron. Bolingbroke declared himself charmed with the piece but naturally could not resist an inclination to make a few 'small alterations and additions' (turning the argument, as we now know, wholly to his own advantage). Barber asked his unknown correspondent to grant him this permission but did not yet reveal who the emender was to be. This farcical midnight scene of four intimate acquaintances blindly negotiating with one another by way of footmen and coffee-houses, like characters out of *The Country Wife*, was what Swift's passion for mystery had accomplished. Her majesty's chief Secre-

[1] *Ibid.*, pp. 43–4.　[2] *Ibid.*, pp. 50–1.

tary of State was bargaining with a nameless scribbler for the privilege of refinishing his composition.

When Ford demurred at Bolingbroke's proposal, the printer in a new message went so far as to name his lordship to 'Samuel Bridges'; and Ford then felt compelled to let him keep the manuscript, only insisting that Mr Bridges see the alterations before the printing. However, Barber neither published nor returned Swift's essay. I assume that Bolingbroke was too busy to find time for the last editorial labours, and that Barber dared not go ahead on his own. And there the whole affair stuck. Some of the cuts the Secretary had in mind, we can infer from the condition in which the essay first appeared, a quarter-century later; and two or three of those cuts do small credit to the great man's honour; for though he removed a number of passages that merely seemed indiscreet, he also deleted praises of Oxford and censures of himself.[1]

Meanwhile, Swift gave Ford permission ahead of time to accept changes of non-essentials, including the expunging of a complaint against Bolingbroke which his lordship had independently marked for deletion. But Swift refused to let the blame of Oxford be sharpened. When nothing emanated from Barber but fresh delays, Swift took Ford's indignant advice and sent another copy to London. But by the time Ford got hold of this, the political situation had deteriorated to the point where any such pamphlet had to be stifled.[2]

Instead of brooding passively over the fate of *Some Free Thoughts*, Swift proceeded with a completely different sort of composition. Reverting to his mode of Horatian self-satire, he wrote a good-humoured imitation of *Hoc erat in votis*, completed about 1 August.[3] The contrast between the humorous tone of the poem and

[1] Williams II. 58–60, 64–6; Davis VIII. 205–9.

[2] Williams II. 71–3, 77, 83–4, 99.

[3] *Poems* I. 197–202. I do not accept Sir Harold Williams's attribution to Swift of the twenty lines added after line 9 in the 1738 edition, which also included Pope's continuation of the poem. I find it significant that in these twenty lines, as in the continuation by Pope, there are feminine endings, though there are none in the text transcribed by Stella. I believe that Pope planted the twenty lines in this poem to back up his allusion to Swift in his own imitation of Horace, *Sat.* II. ii. 161–4, an allusion which Swift had explicitly resented (Williams IV. 249 and n. 1). Although lines 105–12 are also attributed to Pope by some scholars, the external evidence is so strongly on Swift's side that I do not question them. I do not think it has been noticed

the poet's exacerbated feelings at the time is almost Mozartian. It is as though Swift had divided his parsonical and his jesting selves between this poem and *The Author upon Himself*. I suspect he felt proud of being able to sound so dégagé when he had so much to annoy him; for he was the same man who had boasted of being 'as good company as ever' when he felt frantic over his deanship.[1]

The poem is also an oddly appropriate termination for Swift's literary history under Queen Anne. The theme is the contrast between his superficial consequence at court and his real detachment from power. The opening and closing lines describe the retired but comfortable existence the speaker loves. The rest of the poem comprises a few scenes with dialogue, illustrating the fruitless pressures of the court. Swift's recall from Ireland (the previous autumn) is followed by his appearance at Oxford's levee, where a crowd of petitioners ask him to assist them. The central scene is a reminiscence of coach rides with the Lord Treasurer, between London and Windsor—where the only conversation is trifling small talk. Finally we return to a scene of Swift with miscellaneous outsiders trying to extract from him secret information that he actually does not possess.

What charm the poem has, depends on the symmetrical tonal pattern. For at the centre of all is the scene of Swift and Oxford relishing each other's company without ever touching on the politics that meaner people imagine them to be discussing. This intimate, innocent friendship is therefore set against the preceding and following episodes of false friends seeking to make use of a dean who has not himself made any 'use' of the statesman. The idyllic, framing passages which open and close the poem are a further contrast of a more traditional sort; and they present the circumstances in which true friendship can best flower.

---

that the opening couplet is an echo of a famous passage in *Hudibras* iii. i. 1277–8:
> What makes all doctrines plain and clear?
> About two hundred pounds a year.

The text published in 1727 was probably the result of Swift's polishing the version completed in the summer of 1714, though I myself write above as if there were no difference between the two.
[1] *Journal*, 15 Apr. 1713.

It is not a very fine achievement, even for Swift. But it does sum up the futility of his last months in London. Of course, the speaker's remoteness from influence and from the secrets of the court are not Swift's own; for the dean possessed some genuine power over his great friends, and he knew many details of high policy which were denied to outsiders. Nevertheless, the utter failure of his most serious advice and his exclusion from the darkest truths amounted to a comparable futility.

The speaker is of course a created person, though his elements are drawn from the facts of Swift's life. Yet the theme of true friendship indicates what the poet most deeply treasured in his relations with Oxford, Bolingbroke, and Ormonde. Perhaps the depth of this sentiment gave him the nostalgic energy for the composition of the poem. In technique it displays several peculiarly Swiftian traits besides impersonation. The rhymed dialogue, in which stichomythia harmonizes with the syntax of easy speech, is one of his hallmarks; and the quietly ingenious rhymes are another. Yet the most appealing couplets seem to me those which bear no special token apart from the fluency with which meter and meaning collaborate:

> I often wish'd, that I had clear
> For life, six hundred pounds a year,
> A handsome house to lodge a friend,
> A river at my garden's end,
> A terras walk, and half a rood
> Of land set out to plant a wood.

III. HISTORIOGRAPHER

There is a recapitulatory quality to many of Swift's gestures during the summer of 1714—a sense of winding-up. This would seem less poignant if he had, at the time, envisaged himself as about to leave England for ever. But we know he did not. Rather, he was waiting for the catastrophe which his friends at court were momentarily expecting, the fall of Lord Oxford. The idealized portrait of the Treasurer, in *Hoc erat in votis*, as a man too strong to show his strength, is a kind of farewell to Oxford's greatness.

The Author upon Himself is explicitly Swift's own farewell to his patron's ministry, but it can now be read as a valediction to the court of Queen Anne. *Some Free Thoughts* becomes, in retrospect, the last sermon Dr Swift preached before his favourite congregation.

If the main source of this mood was Swift's inborn habit of stepping aside and viewing himself *sub specie historiae*, that habit was intensified by his gnawing impression of a great, tragic drama enacted as he watched, with the remoteness of Letcombe happily providing the esthetic distance which his sympathy with the falling hero would otherwise have denied him. 'Your letters will make good memoirs',[1] he told Ford, who was volleying bulletins to him from Whitehall; and the composition of memoirs filled his prospective thoughts.

In such a temper it nettled Swift that his large *History* should still remain unpublished. His early ambition to produce something memorable in the noblest of prose genres had never faded. Unable to foresee that his greatest contribution to historical writing was to be his letters to Esther Johnson, he brooded constantly over a hope of delivering to posterity a true account of Queen Anne's last ministry, to vindicate his friends and refute the miserable Burnets and Steeles. He pestered Lady Masham, Lord Oxford, Dr Arbuthnot, and others for materials to fill out his design[2]; and I think he regarded the history already composed as no more than the framework of his masterpiece.

With so deep an attachment to a work that might or might not be in progress, Swift could hardly keep from dropping hints that it would soon appear in print. As early as March 1713 a correspondent of Sir William Trumbull wrote, 'Dr. Swift is coming out with another new book, giving an account of the history of the negotiations at Utrecht.'[3] The following January, the *Examiner* foreshadowed the same coming event.[4] And in *The Publick Spirit of the Whigs* Swift once more hinted that 'an impartial historian'

---

[1] Williams II. 60.   [2] *Ibid.*, pp. 36, 46.

[3] Ralph Bridges, 6 Mar. 1713, ms. in Berks. Co. Record Office, Reading. I am indebted to the late George Sherburn for this reference. I have normalized the spelling and capitalization of the quotation.

[4] 29 Jan. 1714.

might return the annihilating answer to the Whigs' falsities.[1]

With these instincts and aspirations, Swift had reacted sharply to the news of the death of Thomas Rymer, about the same time as Queen Anne's nearly fatal illness (December 1713). Rymer had held the office of Historiographer Royal and had compiled one of the greatest works of English history, the *Foedera*, incomplete in fifteen monumental, rare, expensive folio volumes, which Swift had made it his business to secure for the library of Trinity College, Dublin.[2] Swift had been hankering for the office of historiographer at least since 1710,[3] and he now set his heart upon finally securing it. The money must have been an attraction, though Swift sniffed at its slight value[4]; and he also welcomed the excuse an English preferment would give him of visiting London from time to time. Primarily, however, he seems to have felt (however irrationally) that the dignity of the title would bestow a special validity upon his account of his own era. This belief is incongruous if not grotesque, because Swift would have been the first to agree with Rymer's declaration, 'You are not to expect truth from an historiographer royal.'[5]

The office happened to be in the gift of the Lord Chamberlain, who was still the Duke of Shrewsbury. His grace, however, had left for Dublin (as Lord Lieutenant) two months before Rymer died. Swift therefore applied to Bolingbroke, who sincerely assured him of his heartiest backing: 'Non tua res agitur, dear Jonathan. 'Tis the Treasurer's cause, 'tis my cause, 'tis every man's cause who is embark'd in our bottom.'[6] Acting with commendable integrity, Bolingbroke wrote to both Oxford and Shrewsbury in support of Swift's separate requests to them,[7] and he reported that the Duke, though under 'some engagement', had

---

[1] Davis VIII. 56. In an attack on 'that modest man and good Christian, Dr. Swift', the author of a Whig pamphlet, *A Letter to the Examiner, Suggesting Proper Heads for Vindicating His Masters* (ca. April 1714), called for the publication of Swift's 'great work'.

[2] *Journal*, 16 May 1711 and n. 11; 22, 25 Feb., 31 May 1712. The 'book' mentioned 6 Mar. 1713 is probably a volume of Rymer.

[3] Williams I. 170.   [4] *Ibid*. II. 62.

[5] Quoted in *Encyclopaedia Britannica*, 11th ed., s.v. 'Rymer'.

[6] Williams II. 2 (7 Jan).

[7] I assume Bolingbroke wrote to Oxford because he says he has already done so; for the letter to Shrewsbury see Bolingbroke's *Letters* II. 574, 579–81.

come through with a promise to give the post to the dean.[1] But alas, Bolingbroke's dark fame as a pledge-breaker was too strong for his good deeds to bleach. As whole months passed with no further word, Swift decided the irresponsible Secretary had behaved with his usual carelessness and had failed to lend him any backing.[2] During the summer of 1714 Swift also directly reproached Oxford for ignoring his petition.[3] By then Arbuthnot understood what Swift wanted and sounded out Lady Masham. But she judged that this was not a 'fit season' to speak about it.[4] Swift had already decided that her ladyship no longer favoured him; and now, in mid-July, he sent to Arbuthnot a copy of a memorial for Bolingbroke to give the Queen. Swift's smothered hesitancies and oscillating demurrals, in his covering message, painfully suggest his embarrassment over the strength of his desire for the post:

> I thought Lord Bol— would have done such a trifle, but I shall not concern my self, and I should be sorry the Qu— should be asked for it, otherwise than as what would be for her honor and reputation with posterity etc. Pray how long, do you think I should be suffered to hold that post in the next reign. I have inclosed you the originall memoriall as I intended it; and if Lord Bol— thinks it of any moment, let him do it; but do not give him the memoriall, unless he be perfectly willing: For I insist again upon it, that I am not asking a favor; and there is an end of that matter, only one word more, that I would not accept it if offered, onely that it would give me an opportunity of seeing those I esteem and love, the little time they will be in power.[5]

As soon as the memorial came to him, Arbuthnot handed it over to Bolingbroke, and then informed the dean that the Secretary said it would be scandalous for ministers who owed so much to Swift to let him suffer 'the least uneasy thought about such things'. As he accepted the memorial, Bolingbroke said he would claim Shrewsbury's promise.[6]

But the Secretary might have spared himself his generous indignation, and Swift might have spared himself his delicate em-

---

[1] Williams II. 62 and n. 4. [2] *Ibid.*, p. 96. [3] *Ibid.*, p. 45. [4] *Ibid.*, p. 57.
[5] *Ibid.*, p. 62. I have expanded contractions and altered the capitalization.
[6] *Ibid.*, p. 69.

barrassments. For the coveted post had found a tenant ten days before Swift sent Arbuthnot the memorial. 'I thought you had heard the historiographer's place had been dispos'd of this fortnight', Ford suddenly wrote to Swift late in July. Once more the amateur patron had failed to help himself. I suspect that both Shrewsbury and Oxford possessed too sound a judgment in historical scholarship to believe that the author of *The Publick Spirit of the Whigs* was a proper person for the title Swift desired. Certainly Oxford's wide experience as a collector of historical manuscripts, his familiarity with researchers and antiquaries like Hickes and the Elstobs, would not have inclined him to set Swift in a class with Thomas Madox, the meticulous scholar who did succeed Rymer.

Although students of literary history have naturally sympathized with the Duke of Shrewsbury's decision to elevate a man of their tribe, Swift had other feelings. He appreciated the irony of Arbuthnot's and Bolingbroke's acting out their ritual for a blessing that did not exist.[1] But he dismissed Madox as a 'worthless rogue that no body knows'[2]; and years later he was still to denounce Shrewsbury for lacking the 'smallest share of steddiness or sincerity'.[3]

IV. VANESSA

The very first letter Swift wrote from Letcombe was addressed to Miss Hessy. Her mother had died in January after a prolonged illness, and had left Hessy, who enjoyed dealing with legal duties, to be sole executrix.[4] I think the young woman made her bereavement and her immediate need of financial and legal guidance a new pretext for animating the avuncular tenderness of Dr Swift. At a later time she was to remind him of how, as an 'indulgent friend', he had been willing to see her 'some times' during that gloomy spring, and to approve or alter her decisions.[5] For all his airs of worldliness Swift could be oddly susceptible to certain forms of emotional blackmail. I have already indicated that one

---

[1] Williams II. 83.   [2] *Ibid.*, p. 96.

[3] *Ibid.*, p. 367. It seems notable that by this time (i.e., January 1721) Swift had convinced himself that he had 'disdained to accept' the office of historiographer.

[4] Le Brocquy, pp. 36, 140–3.   [5] Williams II. 148–9.

I will add one thing more, which is the highest compliment I can make, that I never was afraid of offending you, nor am now in any pain for the manner I write to you in. I have said enough, and like one at your levee having made my bow, I shrink back into the crowd.[1]

Swift did not tell Oxford what he later (and perhaps misleadingly) told Bolingbroke, viz., that he had determined to have nothing to do with whoever emerged as victor in the contest between the Secretary and the Lord Treasurer.[2]

Contrary to Swift's expectations, this letter pleased Oxford.[3] But by mid-July so many whispers were afloat that Swift could hardly be sure exactly what was happening. With the acrid fumes of their hatred blowing about them, Oxford and Bolingbroke still met continually for intimate social occasions. 'The Dragon and his antagonist meet every day at the cabinet', Ford told Swift: 'they often eat, and drink, and walk together as if there was no sort of disagreement, and when they part, I hear they give one another such names, as no body but ministers of state could bear without cutting throats.'[4] For all his sympathy with Bolingbroke's avowed principles, and his conviction that the Treasurer should at once resign, Swift still regretted the Schism Act, and he frowned on the 'dispositions' of the Secretary and those who would probably come in with him.[5]

But the forces concentrated against Oxford could no longer be resisted. Ormonde, who was in with the Jacobites deeper than Bolingbroke, had advised the Queen to dismiss Oxford; and a sudden conference among Harcourt, Bolingbroke and her majesty led many courtiers to suppose that the act was complete. But the consummation still took another week. Swift heard that the Queen had been due to leave for Windsor on 27 July; and the change would have been announced after this remove. Her departure had to be put off, however; and so a cabinet council was held that same day. Queen Anne, weak, sick, and in pain, declared her decision to part with Oxford. The Lord Treasurer openly accused his enemy of financial corruption and kindred

---

[1] *Ibid.*, p. 45.　　[2] *Ibid.*, p. 110.　　[3] *Ibid.*, pp. 57, 83.　　[4] *Ibid.*, p. 77.
[5] *Ibid.*, p. 83. For further information, see below, p. 763, n. 1.

vices. And before the meeting broke up, the cheerless, suffering Queen had to sit through a squalid interlude of noisy vituperation between the old favourite and the new.[1]

While Swift, in the narrow routines and anxious suspense of his days at Letcombe, was listening to the reverberations of these sinister events, and awaiting the resolution of what he called the *summa rerum*, he also met a series of light distractions timed as if to counterpoint the steady sounds of doom. At the beginning of July, Pope came over from Binfield with their friend Parnell, who had been visiting him; and together they stayed in Letcombe for several days.[2] Swift made them coffee of his own roasting and confessed to whiling away time by trying experiments with a burning-glass on paper. Diverting letters also arrived, either from Gay, who had indeed become Lord Clarendon's secretary on the Hanover trip, or from Arbuthnot and Pope. With these came entertaining news of Scriblerus and his projects. From Lord Harley, the Treasurer's bookish son, came word that he and his recent bride were going to visit the city of Oxford, and he invited the dean to join them there late in the month. So Swift took a vacation from Letcombe and went over to stay three days with Stratford in Christ Church, where he talked sadly with the young couple about Lord Oxford's loss of allies and the certainty of his fall. Drinking toasts to absent friends, they found the number so diminished that they arrived at Arbuthnot's name 'six glasses before the usuall time'—as Swift reported to the doctor. Stratford and Lord Harley denounced Lady Masham as bitterly as they denounced Bolingbroke. Lord Harley said later that Swift had seemed 'horridly in the dumps'.[3]

It became almost an obsession of Swift's that he must pass a considerable period with Oxford after the Treasurer was dismissed from office. Besides wishing to cheer up a discarded statesman, Swift hoped to extract from him further details of certain episodes to be included in the great history of the regime. A subtler appeal of the prospect hung, I think, on the forfeits it would

---

[1] Trevelyan III. 293–4.
[2] 4 July and following: see Williams II. 59 and n. 3; 69; Sherburn I. 234–5.
[3] Williams II. 68, 75, 80, 82–3.

entail. By displaying a loyal attachment to his disgraced bene-
factor, Swift thought he would sacrifice the goodwill of Lady
Masham and of Bolingbroke's circle. If so, he would then have no
power under the new Tory government. Yet he thought Oxford
had immense faults and ought to give up his office. If I am right,
Swift consequently felt charmed by the purity of his own moral
gesture. He would be renouncing an alliance with greatness in
order to comfort a powerless, cashiered courtier whom he no
longer respected. While the martyrdom he thus anticipated may
have been illusory, I think it pulled him strongly; he would stick
by whoever was *not* kept in office: 'I shall lose all favour with
those now in power by following Lord Oxford in his retreat.'[1]
From Swift's tone at this crisis one may perhaps infer the sort of
conduct he expected of men whom he judged to be heroic.

Two days before the council at which the Queen finally
dropped her pilot, Swift wrote to him again, renewing the offer to
stay with him in the country: 'If you resign in a few days, as I am
told you design to do, you may possibly retire to Herefordshire,
where I shall readily attend you.' To this Oxford returned the
affectionate message from which I quoted earlier: 'If I have not
tir'd you tête-à-tête fling away so much time upon one who loves
you . . .'[2] Patron and client would be joined in decrepit isolation.
Swift's attitude eerily suggests that perhaps the posthumous son
had at last found a way to be united with his vanished father.

VI. WEARY TRAVELLERS

After the council meeting of Tuesday, 27 July 1714, the Queen's
feeble body gave way; her chronic illness became acute; and for
several days she lay with her faculties failing while throughout
the court, the government, and the kingdom there was a vast
holding of breath until, on Sunday morning, 1 August, the sad,
lonely, dutiful woman died. 'I believe sleep was never more welcome to a weary traveller than death was to her', Arbuthnot told
Swift.[3] Like everyone else at court, Swift had been waiting as

[1] *Ibid.*, p. 90.   [2] *Ibid.*, p. 85. Swift's letter is probably printed from a draft.
[3] *Ibid.*, p. 121.

much for this pathetic act as for the fall of Oxford; and to this degree it was more than coincidence that his own plans tallied with the extraordinary public events.

Although he was not caught out by his double disaster, Swift had never imagined it would imprison the Dean of St Patrick's in Ireland. I suppose his mind now went back to the death of William III, which had produced a change of regime as radical as what Swift—with his speculations narrowed by his memories— now expected. At that earlier epoch, of course, he had made the transition into a new reign more gracefully than he could hope to do again. Yet a man who had lived through 1685 and 1688 would not feel inclined to tremble at the approach of a Duke of Brunswick.

The brilliance of the fresh illumination which broke upon him in the first days of King George is poignantly reflected in the shifts, suspensions, and reversals of his plans before as well as after the accession. Almost like a tourist, Swift wished to avail himself of the resources of England on the slow way he would take to Dublin. He might visit a county that had always interested him. He might spend time with various friends. He might cheer up the Earl of Oxford. But above all, he covertly wished to loiter somehow till the political realignment was definitely accomplished and he knew whether or not he might be useful.

On originally heading for Letcombe, Swift had vaguely supposed that when he was done with his writings and papers, he would spend the late summer and autumn in Ireland, returning to London toward the winter, when he would have a less troublesome rôle to play. Nevertheless, either to guard himself against the vengeance of the incoming reign or to avoid the financial slump that the Whigs kept foreseeing from the chaos of Tory leadership, Swift decided to transfer his capital to Ireland: 'As times are like to be', he told Walls, 'I should be glad to have my money in another place'—i.e., not in England. He proposed that Walls join with him in buying land to the value of a thousand or £1,500, taking a mortgage as their common investment.[1] Otherwise, he seems to have planned no fundamental change in the rhythm of his life.

[1] Williams II. 31.

The first shift in his immediate plans had followed his boredom with the monotony of Geree's household. We have seen that by the time he wrote to Hessy, he was thinking of slipping away to Ireland ahead of his original schedule. Then he told Walls to expect him in Dublin no later than the end of the summer.[1] But Swift had soon accommodated himself to a simple diet and the company of rustics. Absorbed in the plot of the scandals at court, he hung on from week to week, commenting on the episodes like a Sophoclean chorus. Bolingbroke tried to lure Swift back as an aide in his own political adventures; but by the beginning of July the dean had abandoned any idea of even a visit to London, and spoke of touring Herefordshire on his way home.[2] It was his revered grandfather's county, and of course there was Swift's scheme of getting materials for his contemporary history from the Harley family seat at Brampton. Simultaneously, he hoped Oxford would go to Brampton and entertain him there as soon as the débâcle was over.

Later in July, but before he felt quite sure that Oxford's resignation was really imminent, Swift still expected to start for Ireland about Michaelmas, after some sort of 'ramble' and with the summer definitely behind him. One cannot help feeling he hoped something would turn up to delay even this arrangement, and that as he had done year after year, he would once more fail to wrench himself free from his English attachments as quickly as he promised. I suppose one more reason for the Herefordshire trip was that it would simply keep him on 'this side Trent', for he also toyed with the idea of visiting Erasmus Lewis in Wales.[3] But whether or not he went straight to Ireland, he had made up his mind not to linger in Berkshire beyond the first week of August.[4]

After he heard that the Treasurer would certainly be out in a day or two, Swift altered his leisurely timetable and told Ford he would leave for Ireland on Monday, 2 August. With all his rational forebodings, it still seems a little uncanny that he should have settled on the day following the Queen's death. But his licence of absence was running out, and he preferred not to ask for a renewal. Suddenly, however, along came the Earl of

[1] *Ibid.*, pp. 26, 30.   [2] *Ibid.*, p. 49.   [3] *Ibid.*, p. 88.   [4] *Ibid.*, pp. 72, 75.

Oxford's acceptance of the offer to visit him; and so, as usual, the departure for Ireland had to be put off and his licence renewed after all. At this point Swift spoke of being home by the end of the autumn.[1]

Lady Masham added a peculiar relish to the changing mixture when she begged Swift to return to London.[2] By choosing Herefordshire, he could (I think) feel he was spiting the two main enemies of his helpless patron.[3] Any suspicions he had of Bolingbroke's conduct must have been quickly aggravated when he heard that the Secretary had entertained Walpole and other younger Whig leaders (though none of the Junto).[4] In a few days he was to learn that the dying Queen had made not Bolingbroke but Shrewsbury the new Lord Treasurer. But he would also discover that Bolingbroke had intended to reconcile Swift to the Duchess of Somerset and secure him a preferment in England.[5]

Then at last came the supreme reversal. On Sunday at noon, word of the royal death was brought to Wantage, and Swift's correspondents soon assured him the information was correct. I suppose he had been so long expecting it, and brooding on the consequences to England, that he could not at first appreciate the significance of the event for himself. Or perhaps he had so many observations to make on Oxford's fall that he could not immediately see how irrelevant they had all become. With Shrewsbury as Lord Treasurer and Oxford in the clear (through being dismissed), it may briefly have appeared to Swift that the new world would not after all be so very far from the old.

Certainly, his first reaction was a sharpened determination to stay put in England.[6] I wonder whether he did not feel relieved to have so unimpeachable an excuse for doing so. Bolingbroke, through Barber, pleaded with him to come up to London at once, and further sent a remarkable message of his own, almost commanding Swift's presence: 'I have lost all by the death of the Queen but my spirit, and I protest to you I feel that encrease upon me. "The Whigs are a pack of Jacobites." That shall be the cry in

---

[1] Williams II. 85, 89–92. [2] *Ibid.*, pp. 87–8.

[3] Cf. *ibid.*, p. 96, where I assume 'some body' is Lady Masham, and Swift feels gleeful about refusing her.

[4] *Ibid.*, p. 89. [5] *Ibid.*, p. 100. [6] *Ibid.*, p. 99.

a month if you please.'[1] I don't think Swift was inclined to be moved by such infatuation. He seemed rather to think of harbouring himself in Letcombe till he could be sure of Oxford's new course and the most proper behaviour for himself.[2]

But now for Swift a very small, new peripety utterly transformed the moment from climax into bathos. He had forgotten how the mere mechanics of a new reign affected men of his level; and it was his confidant Ford who had to remind him that he was required to take the oaths to the King in Ireland within three months.[3] This practical detail blew up all Swift's half-formed designs. He could hardly risk putting off the ceremony in the face of a hostile government; so he abandoned at once any scheme of a diversion at Brampton. Meanwhile, the one-sided list of regents appointed to govern the nation till King George came over, made it unpleasantly clear to Swift that his new monarch had no grain of an intention to compromise with the Tories.[4] Though Swift still clung to some idea of an early visit to England after a season at home, the hope was cautious. He told Bolingbroke he would be with him 'by the beginning of winter' if Bolingbroke thought he might prove useful.[5] But his settled mood became more elegiac and renunciatory as he felt his old fears at last materializing and understood that the environment to which he had so well accommodated himself was to disintegrate while he remained cut off in Ireland.

Once he decided to leave, Swift also determined to avoid the great rush of travellers like himself. So he arranged to start for home in the middle of August. As if to signalize his departure, he fired off a few missives to the great persons in London.[6] He took a dignified leave of Lady Masham, supplying her with some priestly comfort on the immense catastrophe she had suffered by the Queen's death.[7] He withdrew his acceptance of Oxford's invita-

---

[1] *Ibid.*, pp. 100–2.

[2] He was going to wait for Ford to send him the *Gazette* of 9 August, which would probably reach Wantage on 11 August (*ibid.*, p. 100).

[3] *Ibid.*, p. 102.   [4] *Ibid.*, pp. 111, 113–14.

[5] *Ibid.*, pp. 112, 113, 126. I suspect that when Swift assured Hessy that he would probably be in England again at the beginning of winter, he was partly motivated by the desire to discourage her from following him to Ireland (*ibid.*, p. 123).

[6] I think all three texts are from drafts.   [7] Williams II. 108–9.

tion and gave his lordship (who was remaining in London with the visible hope of remaining in politics) a wise admonition about the reefs and bars before him. But Swift's main effort was a long epistle to Bolingbroke. In the edited draft of this which has survived, he answers the message he had just received from the Secretary and provides us with a last, recapitulatory glance at his years at court:

> All I pretended was, to speak my thoughts freely, to represent persons and things without any mingle of my interest or passions, and, sometimes, to make use of an evil instrument, which was like to cost me dear, even from those for whose service it was employed.[1]

It appears that Swift was on horseback 16 August, as he planned, and that he rode from Letcombe to Chester and then to Holyhead, where he embarked in time to reach Dublin on 24 August.[2] While he journeyed mournfully across England and Wales, the friends he had made and lost since the fall of Godolphin were assuming their first positions under King George. I don't think Swift should have felt unfortunate by comparison with them. Dr Arbuthnot never received the legacy intended for him by the Queen, because she died without signing her will. As Arbuthnot entered on a quite private life, he watched the venal writhings of hopeful courtiers and confirmed himself in that dark picture of human nature which he shared with Swift: 'I have an opportunity calmly and philosophically to consider that treasure of vileness and baseness that I allways beleived to be in the heart of man, and to behold them exert their insolence and baseness, every new instance instead of surprising and greiving me really diverts me and in a manner improves my theory.'[3]

Poor Gay was returning from Hanover with no money and no prospects, since his Duchess had dismissed him when he joined Lord Clarendon's embassy. But his faithful friend Pope was hardly touched by the royal death, being occupied in polishing the first volume of his Homer. The worst sufferer of all was unhappy Prior. He had been living suspended in Paris for over a year and a

---

[1] Williams II. 110. From a hint in Bolingbroke's reply to this letter, I infer that Barber delivered it in person to Swift in Letcombe (*ibid.*, p. 117).

[2] *Ibid.*, pp. 123 ('horseback'), 126-7 (arrived 24 Aug.), 131 and n. 2.

[3] *Ibid.*, p. 122.

half, ever since Shrewsbury left. For Oxford and Bolingbroke had never managed to agree on his successor, and therefore he could not be ordered home. But neither was he supplied with the funds needed by her Britannic majesty's sole representative at the splendid French court. Living too high, on over-extended credit, he had gradually foreseen the judgment that lay ahead. When the Queen died, he was still unprovided for, though spectacularly in debt, and on terms with his new Whig rulers that ranged from ambiguous to desperate. Yet the full depth of his wretchedness was to be revealed only when he returned to England; for he would then see himself handled like a criminal, abandoned by both parties, and allowed almost no visible means of support.

Addison, who had expected everything from the great revolution, got no more than he had held years before. Appointed Secretary to the Regents as soon as the Queen died, he worked hard and efficiently, enjoying unrivalled prestige. After the King arrived, however, his only reward was a 'great fall' to being secretary to the Lord Lieutenant of Ireland—the post he had held in his far less meritorious days under the Earl of Wharton. Addison had briefly revived the *Spectator*, but at the end of the summer he turned the few remaining numbers over to an essayist friend while he himself wriggled for a profitable place on the Board of Trade.[1]

It was Swift's fellow Dubliner Steele who looked like a happy man. His great wager had suddenly paid off. He was returned to King George's first Parliament, knighted, made Governor of Drury Lane and Surveyor of Hampton Court stables. Beyond the stipends attached to these posts, he also secured a royal new year's gift of five hundred pounds and formed a profitable political connection with the Earl of Clare. His friends were at the top, and Steele was in.

Yet for the moment Swift could feel personally jealous only of the privilege his old friends kept of living in England. As Dean of St Patrick's and vicar of Laracor, he had more than would have contented him in England. And his hopes of a bishopric had been extinguished before the Queen died. Besides the gloom over his

[1] Graham, pp. 301-3.

exile he of course felt, as always, worried about his finances; and he found leisure to share the griefs of various unhappy friends. But his serious emotions were reserved for public, not selfish concerns. Through all his complaints after the death of the Queen, what he bemoaned was the consequence to the nation; he barely alluded to his own disappointments.

The pathos evoked by Swift's lonely ride from Berkshire to Holyhead does not have to remain unresolved. There is some meaning in his apparent punishment. Vast though the gulf may have been that separated the life of his countrymen from that of the English, it was not the infinitude that Swift tried to make it. There is a vulgar myth of English aristocracy, according to which a brilliant intellectual glow and a high moral vision illuminated those few splendid families who exercised decisive political power in their great country mansions. Swift knew too much about the Irish to imagine this myth might be realized in the families of county Dublin. When he was a young stranger in England, he found one of the rare, true instances of the ideal in Moor Park. For almost fifteen years he tried to discover it elsewhere and, I think, could not admit he had failed. In Ormonde, Oxford, and Bolingbroke he persuaded himself that he had found the real thing. In *The Conduct of the Allies* he made that discovery the positive aspect of a deeply destructive book. If he had been right, however, they would not have exiled him.

So it is difficult wholly to forgive Swift for remembering the ministry of Oxford as the golden years of his entire existence. He was too often spiteful, pusillanimous, or credulous. Outside the rooms of scholars and historians the world was to know him only for what he created after this era. It was the years ahead, in the Ireland he pretended to despise, that would afford public expression to his own nobility. One of Swift's first remarks in Dublin was 'I hope I shall keep my resolution of never medling with Irish politicks.'[1] It is our good fortune that he was incapable of such restraint.

As one reviews Swift's career from the death of Sir William Temple to the death of Queen Anne, it would be simple enough

[1] Williams II. 127.

to censure his character if one chose certain of his contemporaries as a standard. Archbishop King on one side, George Berkeley on the other, showed a level of courage and integrity that Swift could not match. But Swift was also endowed with an imagination which they lacked and which perhaps undermines innocent courage. Swift faced elements in human nature that neither Burnet nor Addison liked to think about. If he misjudged scores of individual men, it was not by supposing them incapable of acts that other men committed hourly. Swift's peculiar gift was for seeing as much as he did without deserting the ideals that are normally destroyed by such a vision. His deepest humour depends on his appreciation of this paradox; for he was the first to confess that experience gave him no ground for hope. [1]

[1] (Add above, p. 753, n. 5, on Swift's relations with Oxford and Bolingbroke in the spring of 1714:) Onlookers received some curious impressions. Sir John Percival reported, ' 'Tis generally expected the Treasurer will give way to his Antagonist very Soon, to whom the other Friends fall frequently off; I was told that of late Swift is not so frequent at the Treasurer's Levy as he us'd to be, insomuch that the other [i.e., Bolingbroke] twitted him with the Comparison of a Rat which leaves a falling House' (letter of 22 Jun. 1714, to Daniel Dering; B.L. Add. MS. 47087, fols. 76ᵛ–7).

Appendices

APPENDIX A

The Date of Swift's *Sentiments*, 1704

Swift himself gave *The Sentiments of a Church-of-England Man* the date of 1708. For my main arguments in favour of 1704, see *RES.*, n.s., III (July 1952), 272–4. I have heard doubts that Swift's memory could have been so unreliable. Yet he assigned *A Letter to a Member of Parliament in Ireland* to 1708 although it was written in 1710 (Davis II. xxxii); and writing in 1714, he made the amazing error of mentioning Godolphin's fall as an event of 1712, though it was a sensational event of 1710 (Williams II. 91). To supplement my other arguments, I offer the following notes. (1) The opening of Section Two of the *Sentiments* echoes the first of Swift's *Thoughts on Various Subjects*, which was probably written before October 1706 (Davis I. 241; cf. p. xxxv). (2) The whole piece repeatedly echoes his *Discourse of the Contests and Dissensions* of 1701. (3) The sneer against those who consider every schism to be of a 'damnable nature' is probably an allusion to the pamphlets of Charles Leslie which Swift mentions in a letter of February 1704 (Williams I. 43). (4) The paragraph on 'moderation' (Davis II. 13) echoes James Owen, *Moderation a Virtue*, 1703, and related pamphlets (see above, p. 127, n. 1) so directly that Swift seems to have them freshly in mind after a recent reading. (5) Swift in 1714 attributed to the period 1702–5 in his life a set of opinions which we find put in similar language in the *Sentiments* (Davis VIII. 120). Even if the essential validity of my dating be granted, one might argue that Swift could have worked on the essay right up to the eve of publication in 1711, and that therefore no deductions can fairly be made from it as to his opinions in 1704. I should be inclined to bow to this logic if the state of Swift's manuscripts generally did not show that while he often fiddled with details or added amplifications, he seldom made fundamental changes in the arguments of things which he kept long by him. The texture of the *Sentiments* is consistent; the implications I dwell upon emerge repeatedly from various points in the work. Moreover, I am influenced by Swift's use of the *Sentiments* as evidence to vindicate himself from the charge of having altered his views after 1708 (Davis VIII. 122); for unless he had left it essentially in its primitive state, this evidence would have been false; and it was not like him to manufacture an alibi in this way.

[767]

Swift's List of Subjects for a Volume, 1708

[This list is preserved in a transcript made by John Lyon and inserted between pages 36 and 37 of his copy of Hawkesworth's life of Swift. Nichols printed the list in his *Supplement*, 1779, among the prefatory 'Biographical Anecdotes' (1. xx) and also as a note to Sheridan's life of Swift (1784, p. 75). Sir Walter Scott reprinted it in his *Memoirs* of Swift (1814, p. 112), as did John Forster in his life of Swift (1875, p. 257). Ball refers to it with unfortunate vagueness (1. 111, 183).

I give Lyon's transcript below, not indicating insertions or raised letters. The reading of 'Oct' is not certain; 'K—' stands for Killaloe; the 'Apology' is for *A Tale of a Tub*.]

What he was about publishing in Oct 1708, appears from these words in his own hand on ye back of a Letter directed to him at that time at Lord *Pembroke*'s in *Leicester Fields*.

> *Subjects for a Volume*—
> Discourse of *Athens* & Rome,—
> Bickerstaff's Predictions
> Elegy on *Partridge*
> Letter to Bishop of *K*—*
> H'— Petition
> Baucis & Philemon
> Vanbrug's House—
> The Salamander
> Epigram on Mrs *Floyd*
> Meditation on a Broomstick
> Sentiments of a Church of *England* Man
> Reasons agt Abolishing Christianity—
> Essay on Conversation—
> Conjectures on ye thoughts of Posterity about me
> On the present Taste of Reading**
> Apology for the &c
> Part of an Answer to Tindal
> History of Van's House
> *Apollo* Outwitted. To Ardelia

[768]

Project for Reformation of Manners
A Lady's Table Book
Tritical Essay

Percival's Sketch of Swift

[Sir John Percival (or Perceval), an important Irish political figure who became the first Earl of Egmont, amassed a huge collection of papers—now in the British Museum—relating to his family and acquaintances. Among these is a long series of biographical notices of his contemporaries, with a page devoted to Swift, who knew and visited him. Although Percival himself headed this '1732', the reference to the death of Stella (28 January 1728) as happening 'a year or two ago' may indicate an earlier date of composition. In the *Journal to Stella*, 23 March 1711, Swift mentions the visit described in Percival's third paragraph. I transcribe the manuscript (B.M. MS. Ad. 47,119, p. 100) without indicating abbreviations, insertions, deletions, or raised letters. I completed the word 'himself' as indicated.]

Swift (Jonathan) Dean of St. Patricks. living 1732

This Wit of uncommon and peculiar Genius, was born in the Kingdom of Ireland of English Parents and educated in Trinity Colledge near Dublin. He left Ireland as soon as he had taken Orders, and coming into England was some time entertain'd by the famous Sir William Temple. He was next received into the family of the late Earl of Berkeley in the quality of Chaplain, and attended his Lordship when he was Lord Justice in Ireland. After this he was intimate with the Lord Hallifax; but upon the change of Ministry, My Lord Oxford drew him into his Interest, and he was concern'd in writing the famous State paper call'd the Examiner, levell'd against the administration of the Old Ministers. Before the Queens death, he had the good fortune to be made Dean of St. Patricks in the City of Dublin, which he now holds with one of the best livings in that Kingdom.

Numberless are the pieces he has wrote in verse and prose, and he is every now and then entertaining the World with some new thing. His Wit is inexhaustible, all he writes is agreable but some times he descends too low, and is even too ludicrous. These shew he does not make his proper function his chief application. It was by his stirring, and writing, that the Nation of Ireland peremptorily refused to admit the new coin'd halfpence of One Wood, who by the favour of some Germans about the Court had obtained a Patent (in which they shared) for supplying that Kingdom with the value of 100,000 £ but the mony was so bad, and the cheat so gross that with all Sir Robert Walpole could do, who strenuously supported Wood, his Majesty withdrew his Patent. This for the time got the Dean immortal honour, but he gradually lost it again by the roughness of his behaviour, and the satyricalness of his Wit, for friend nor foe can escape his jest.

I remember that dining with me at the time when my Wife sat up to receive company on her first ly-ing in, he abruptly went up into her room, and regardless of the Ladys that were present threw him[self] all four upon the bed to salute her, as flat as the Prophet in Scripture when he rose the dead child to life, which surprised every one, wondering what drunken bear had broke in, but it was his humour, nor is drunkenness his failing. Perhapps women is more so, and therefore it may be, he took to him Mrs. Johnson, (who lived several years with him and died only a year or two ago) hoping the World would esteem her his wife, though not own'd by him as such. He thought his humour being confessedly odd, they would pass over this part of his conduct what ever they imagined, but marry'd he was not, for when a little before her Sickness he proposed it to her, she declined it, telling her acquaintance that she perceived him every year to grow more bizarre, and she did not know how he might use her when so much in his power.

I once knew a great many Storys of him very diverting, but they have now slipt my memory, but I recollect this One. King George deceased, having made several odd and illiterate English Clergymen Bishops in Ireland, when they came over, the Kingdom were surprised at his choice, and were very free to condemn it. Upon which Swift said with a grave face, ye are in the wrong to blame his Majesty before you know the truth: He sent us over very good and great Men, but they were murder'd by a parcell of highway Men between Chester and London, who slipping on their gowns and Cassocks here pretend to pass for those Bishops.

An Account of the Bandbox Plot

[B.M. MS. Ad. 47,026, pp. 272–3: from a letter dated 11 November 1712 from William Wogan in London to Sir John Percival, Bart., transcribed into a letterbook of Percival's. I have not kept abbreviations, raised letters, or 'ye' for 'the'.]

On Friday last the Peny post brought a band Box directed to one of Lord Treasurers family. within it was a woden box directed to his Lordship, out of which came Strings through the sides. when it was brought up to my Lord, the oddness made him I suppose suspect Some mischief, and Doctor Swift being present he bid the Doctor take it— with these words—here is a present Doctor but have a Care I believe there is some mischief in it. the Doctor could perceive through the holes where the Strings came out, the Shining of Iron, and cutting first the strings very gently, when the lid was taken off, they found an Engine made with four Barrells crosswise, and charged with powder and Ball, and the Strings fastned to the Trickers, which upon the pulling of the Strings would have gone off, and could not fail of doing execution, and there was powder and combustible matter in the box which was to make the blow the more effectuall.

This Gunpowder plot being so happily prevented, people judge of the authors of it according to their severall humours and partys. I hope and doubt not but they will be discovered. In the mean time I cannot but observe that such instances of Diabolical malice, as it shows my Lord Treasurers Enemies to be the worst of men, so it ought to indear him to all those that are good.

Swift's Notes on Oxford's Ministry in the Autumn of 1713

[Rylands English MS. 659, no. 13. For a transcription that preserves the forms of the manuscript, together with a commentary, see the *Bulletin of the John Rylands Library*, xxxvii (March 1955), 382–4. In the text given below I expand abbreviations, give words for numerals, and ignore deletions. The reading of 'yo' in the penultimate sentence is uncertain.]

Speedy and pressing Instances

Two Addresses from House of Commons last Session. First to desire that all Princes in amity with Queen not to suffer Pretender to be in their Dominions. Second to give particular Orders to prevent Exportation of Wooll. Answer to first that it should be done. to second that Her Majesty had given Orders alredy. Yet neither yet done—Danger of the first it will make us be called Jacobites; it must be known, in all Gazettes; so it will be known it has not been yet done: second by Proclamation so all will know it. The Secretarys do it unmistakably, yet to be done in Council and he to direct Secretarys how to be done—

The great Exceedings in every Article of the publick Expence, for want of timely Orders to break the Forces both by Sea and Land

The want of concerting matters last Parliament, occasioned the sitting of it longer, had like to have broken all in pieces etc. the same apprehended for next Year

No estimate made of Queens expence, nor Receits, to proportion one to tother.

No Orders of any kind whatsoever, given till the last Extremity, which puts us under the necessity of passing many great Seals by immediate Warrant, which should not be etc.—

The Commission for three Commissioners of Trade passt after two Commissioners were elected; and the third saved it only by one day.

Not communication in things absolutely necessary to the Service.

Appointing Lord Mar Secretary of Scotland without agreeing with him or Secretarys on what foot it was to be the like with the Chancellor of Scotland without consulting Lord Chancellor both supposed to be against Law, as making the Union less an Union. Mar upon the Foot

[773]

of an English Secretary yet not to decide . . this will cause Dissention.
between the Secretarys. This will raise the Scotch Demands—
    Oeconomy the Secret of our Government no Oeconomy etc.
    Insolence of a Commissioner of Hackny-Coaches, affronting him to
his Face
    The Fleets the Admiralty though Toryes governed by Bing:
besides severall things they cannot do without yo
    Touch his Honor and Ambition as concerned etc.

Abbreviated References

Accounts 1702–3; etc.

Swift's mānuscript account books, each one detailing his finances for a year beginning 1 November. All the account books I refer to are now in the Forster Collection of the Victoria and Albert Museum (48. D. 34/ 1–5) except that for 1703–4, In Lord Rothschild's collection. (See Williams v. 222.)

Autob.

Swift's unfinished autobiographical essay, headed 'Family of Swift'. I refer either to the manuscript, now in the library of Trinity College, Dublin, or to the text in Davis v. 187–95. (See Davis v. 352–6.)

B.L.

The British Library.

B.M.

The British Museum.

Ball

The Correspondence of Jonathan Swift, ed. F. Elrington Ball. 6 vols. 1910–14.

Ball's *Dublin*

F. Elrington Ball, *A History of the County Dublin.* 6 pts. Dublin 1902–20.

Beckett

James Camlin Beckett, *Protestant Dissent in Ireland.* 1948.

Blanchard

The Correspondence of Richard Steele, ed. Rae Blanchard. Oxford 1941.

Bodl.

The Bodleian Library, Oxford.

Boswell

James Boswell, *Life of Johnson,* ed. G. B. Hill, rev. L. F. Powell. 6 vols. Oxford 1934–50.

Boyer

Abel Boyer, *The History of the Reign of Queen Anne, Digested into Annals.* 11 vols. 1703–13. *The Political State of Great Britain.* 8 vols. 1711–15. (Where no title is given, the reference is to *The Political State.*)

Bullitt
John Marshall Bullitt, *Jonathan Swift and the Anatomy of Satire*. Cambridge, Massachusetts, 1953.

Burnet
Gilbert Burnet, *History of His Own Time*. 6 vols. Oxford 1823.

Burtschaell
G. D. Burtschaell and T. U. Sadleir, comps. *Alumni Dublinenses*, new ed. Dublin 1935.

Butler, *Hudibras*
Samuel Butler, *Hudibras*, ed. Zachary Grey. 2 vols. 1726.

Cal. Tr. P.
Calendar of Treasury Papers.

Churchill
Sir Winston Churchill, *Marlborough, His Life and Times*. 6 vols. 1933–8.

Clark
Sir George N. Clark, *The Later Stuarts*, 2nd ed. Oxford 1961.

Complete Peerage
The Complete Peerage, ed. G. E. Cokayne, rev. V. Gibbs. 13 vols. in 14. 1910–59.

Coxe, *Walpole*
William Coxe, *Memoirs of . . . Robert Walpole*. 3 vols. 1798.

D.N.B.
Dictionary of National Biography.

D.U.M.
The Dublin University Magazine, vol. XVIII, 1841.

Davenant
Charles Davenant, *Essays upon . . . The Balance of Power . . .* 1701.

Davis
The Prose Works of Jonathan Swift, ed. Herbert Davis. 13 (of 14) vols. published. Oxford 1939– .

Delany
Patrick Delany, *Observations upon Lord Orrery's Remarks*. 1754.

Enquiry
Jonathan Swift, *An Enquiry into the Behavior of the Queen's Last Ministry*, ed. I. Ehrenpreis. Bloomington, Indiana 1956.

Every
George Every, *The High Church Party*. 1956.

Eves
Charles Kenneth Eves, *Matthew Prior*. New York 1939.

Ferguson
  Oliver Watkins Ferguson, *Jonathan Swift and Ireland*. Urbana,
  Illinois 1962.

Ford
  The Letters of Jonathan Swift to Charles Ford, ed. D. Nichol Smith.
  Oxford 1935.

Forster
  John Forster, *The Life of Jonathan Swift*, Volume One. 1875.

Foxcroft
  T. E. S. Clarke and H. C. Foxcroft, *A Life of Gilbert Burnet*. Cambridge, England 1907.

Freeman
  Vanessa and Her Correspondence with Jonathan Swift, ed. A. Martin
  Freeman, 1921.

Froude
  James Anthony Froude, *The English in Ireland in the Eighteenth
  Century*. 3 vols. 1872–4.

Graham
  The Letters of Joseph Addison, ed. W. Graham. Oxford 1941.

HLQ.
  Huntington Library Quarterly.

H.M.C. *Ormonde*; etc.
  Historical Manuscripts Commission. *Calendar of the Manuscripts of
  the Marquess of Ormonde*; etc.

Harth
  Phillip Harth, *Swift and Anglican Rationalism*. Chicago 1961.

Hodges
  John C. Hodges, *William Congreve, the Man*. New York 1941.

Irving
  William H. Irving, *John Gay*. Durham, North Carolina 1940.

JEGP.
  The Journal of English and Germanic Philology.

J.H.C.I.
  The Journals of the House of Commons of Ireland.

J.H.L.
  The Journals of the House of Lords.

J.H.L.I.
  The Journals of the House of Lords of Ireland.

Jack
  Ian Jack, *Augustan Satire*. Oxford 1952.

Jesse
  John Heneage Jesse, *Memoirs of the Court of England During the Reign of the Stuarts*. 4 vols. 1840.

Journal
  Jonathan Swift, *Journal to Stella*, ed. Sir Harold Williams. 2 vols. Oxford 1948.

Landa
  Louis A. Landa, *Swift and the Church of Ireland*. Oxford 1954.

Lawlor
  H. J. Lawlor, *The Fasti of St. Patrick's, Dublin*. Dundalk 1930.

Le Brocquy
  Sybil Le Brocquy, *Cadenus*. Dublin 1962.

Lecky
  W. E. H. Lecky, *A History of Ireland in the Eighteenth Century*, new ed. 5 vols. 1892.

Liber munerum
  Liber munerum publicorum Hiberniae, ed. Rowley Lascelles. 1852.

Longe
  Julia G. Longe, *Martha, Lady Giffard*. 1911.

Luce
  Arthur A. Luce, *The Life of George Berkeley*. 1949.

Luttrell
  Narcissus Luttrell, *A Brief Historical Relation of State Affairs*. 6 vols. Oxford 1857.

Lyon
  John Lyon, Manuscript notes in a copy of J. Hawkesworth, *The Life of Jonathan Swift*, 1755, now in the Forster Collection of the Victoria and Albert Museum (48. D. 39). Many of the important notes in the first quarter of this volume were printed among the 'Biographical Anecdotes' in Nichols's *Supplement*, 1779, vol. 1.

MLQ.
  Modern Language Quarterly.

MP.
  Modern Philology.

Mant
  Richard Mant, *History of the Church of Ireland*. 2 vols. 1840–1.

Mason
  William Monck Mason, *The History . . . of the . . . Cathedral Church of St. Patrick*. Dublin 1820.

Murry
  J. Middleton Murry, *Jonathan Swift*. 1954.

N. & Q.
 Notes and Queries.

Nichols, *Supplement*
 A Supplement to Dr. Swift's Works, ed. John Nichols. 3 vols. 1779.

Ogg II
 David Ogg, *England in the Reigns of James II and William III.*
 Oxford 1955.

Orrery
 John Boyle, Earl of Cork and Orrery, *Remarks on the Life and Writings of Dr. Jonathan Swift.* 1752.

PMLA.
 Publications of the Modern Language Association of America.

P.R.I.A.
 Publications of the Royal Irish Academy.

Phillips
 Walter Alison Phillips, ed., *A History of the Church of Ireland.* 3 vols.
 1933–4.

Pilkington
 Memoirs of Mrs Laetitia Pilkington, ed. Iris Barry. 1928.

Poems
 The Poems of Jonathan Swift, ed. Sir Harold Williams, 2nd ed. 3 vols.
 Oxford 1958.

Price
 Martin Price, *Swift's Rhetorical Art.* New Haven 1953.

RES.
 The Review of English Studies.

Reid
 James Seaton Reid, *History of the Presbyterian Church in Ireland.* 3 vols.
 1853.

Rothschild
 The Rothschild Library. 2 vols. Cambridge, England 1954.

SEL.
 Studies in English Literature. Rice University.

SP.
 Studies in Philology.

SPD.
 Calendar of State Papers, Domestic.

Scott, *Memoirs*
 Sir Walter Scott, *Memoirs of Jonathan Swift.* 1814.

T. Scott
The Prose Works of Jonathan Swift, ed. Temple Scott. 12 vols. 1897–1908.

Segar
The Poems of Ambrose Philips, ed. M. G. Segar. Oxford 1937.

Sherburn
The Correspondence of Alexander Pope, ed. George Sherburn. 5 vols. Oxford 1956.

Sherburn, *Early Career*
George Sherburn, *The Early Career of Alexander Pope*. Oxford 1934.

Sheridan
Thomas Sheridan, *The Life of Dr. Swift*. 1784.

Simms
J. G. Simms, 'The Irish Parliament of 1713', in *Historical Studies* IV, ed. G. A. Hayes-McCoy (for the Irish Conference of Historians). Cambridge, England 1963.

Smithers
Peter Smithers, *The Life of Joseph Addison*. Oxford 1954.

Somerville
Dorothy H. Somerville, *The King of Hearts*. 1962.

Spectator
The Spectator, ed. Donald F. Bond. 5 vols. Oxford 1965.

Spence
Joseph Spence, *Anecdotes, Observations, and Characters*, ed. S. W. Singer. 1820.

D. Swift
Deane Swift, *An Essay upon . . . Jonathan Swift*. 1755.

T.C.D.
Trinity College, Dublin.

Tale
Jonathan Swift, *A Tale of a Tub*, ed. A. C. Guthkelch and D. Nichol Smith, 2nd ed. Oxford 1958.

Teerink
H. Teerink, *A Bibliography of the Writings of Jonathan Swift*, 2nd ed., ed. A. H. Scouten. Philadelphia 1963.

Temple, *Introduction*
Sir William Temple, *An Introduction to the History of England*. 1695.

——, *Letters* I
Letters Written by Sir W. Temple . . . In Two Volumes. 1700.